Welcome to
Mac
for Beginners™

Welcome to **Mac for Beginners**. If you are new to the wonderful world of Mac, then this is the place for you. We'll take you through everything your shiny new machine has to offer, from sending emails and creating calendar events to an introduction to iLife and creating documents in iWork. As well as covering all the basics of Lion's fantastic new features and iCloud, there are also guides to iTunes and the Mac App Store. Covering everything you need to get up and running, you'll be a master of your Mac in no time at all... so let's get started!

Mac
for Beginners™

Imagine Publishing Ltd
Richmond House
33 Richmond Hill
Bournemouth
Dorset BH2 6EZ
☎ +44 (0) 1202 586200
Website: www.imagine-publishing.co.uk

Editor in Chief
Dave Harfield

Production Editor
Amy Squibb

Senior Art Editor
Danielle Dixon

Design
Charlie Crooks

Printed by
William Gibbons, 26 Planetary Road, Willenhall, West Midlands, WV13 3XT

Distributed in the UK & Eire by
Imagine Publishing Ltd, www.imagineshop.co.uk. Tel 01202 586200

Distributed in Australia by
Gordon & Gotch, Equinox Centre, 18 Rodborough Road, Frenchs Forest,
NSW 2086. Tel + 61 2 9972 8800

Distributed in the Rest of the World by
Marketforce, Blue Fin Building, 110 Southwark Street, London, SE1 0SU.

IMAGINE
PUBLISHING

Contents

Feature
8 The ultimate guide to your Mac

Getting Started

Learning Apple Apps

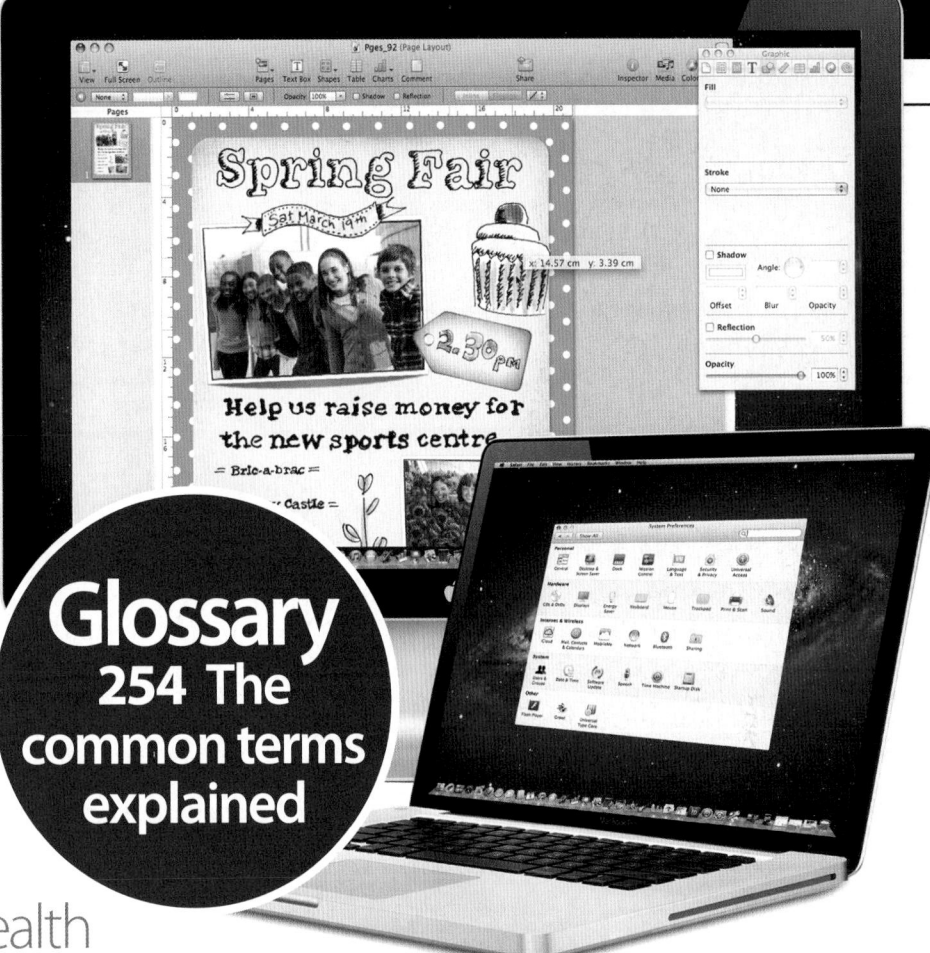

Introducing iLife

Glossary 254 The common terms explained

"Your Mac offers you a wealth of opportunities, and they're all covered in this complete guide"

Introducing iWork

Essential Apps

Ultimate Guide

Finder File Edit View Go Window Help

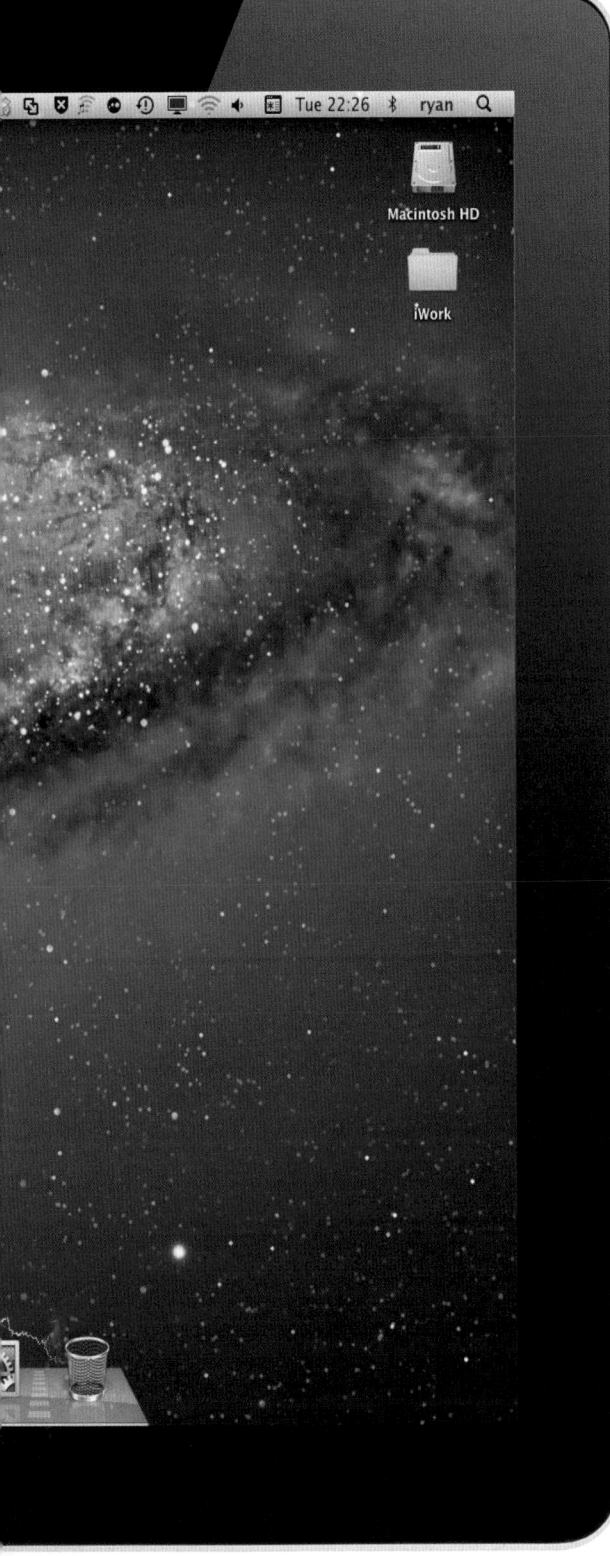

The ultimate guide to your Mac

Taking you through everything you need to know to get started on your Mac

Welcome to the Mac, and welcome to the Mac community. If this is the first time you've owned a Mac, trust us: you're in for a real treat. The Mac is a multi-talented computing phenomenon: part entertainment device, part office workhorse, part creative tool, part media hub. But among all its talents, there's one constant: you'll enjoy using it. If you're used to fighting to get a PC to do the simplest thing, you'll find your new Mac a breath of fresh air. It doesn't get in the way. But many of the joys of discovering the Mac's benefits lie ahead.

"Among its talents, there's one constant: you'll enjoy using it"

However easy the Mac is to use – its reputation in this regard is well earned – it's also true that starting out on a new computer or on a new platform can seem daunting at first. Parts of it will inevitably seem unfamiliar at first. And that's where this book comes in. Over these pages we'll take you through everything you need to get going and start enjoying your iMac and MacBook. Soon you'll be taking off with the Mac. It won't be long before you find yourself offering tips you've discovered to other Mac users – and gently extolling the benefits of the Mac to others.

Ultimate Guide

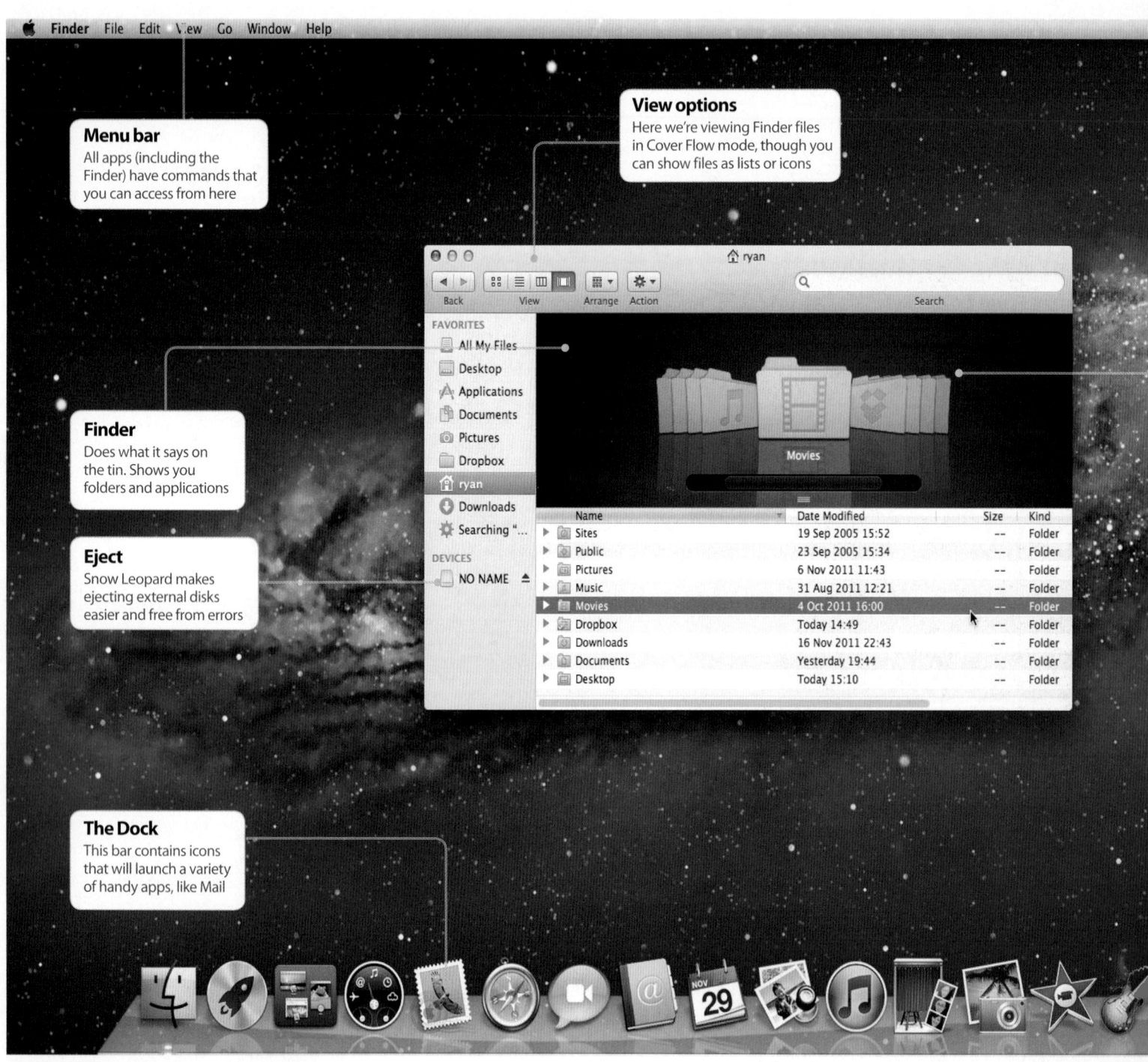

Menu bar
All apps (including the Finder) have commands that you can access from here

View options
Here we're viewing Finder files in Cover Flow mode, though you can show files as lists or icons

Finder
Does what it says on the tin. Shows you folders and applications

Eject
Snow Leopard makes ejecting external disks easier and free from errors

The Dock
This bar contains icons that will launch a variety of handy apps, like Mail

Finder File Edit View Go Window Help

OS X

The advantages of the sophisticated Mac operating system

OS X is the operating system that all Macs use to run their software. Each incarnation of the OS is named after a member of the cat family (that's big powerful cats like Cheetah, Puma, Tiger, Snow Leopard and so on – we're unlikely to see OS Kitten any time soon). The latest OS (version 10.7) is called Lion and we await to see which cat is going to pounce in the next update.

OS X Lion is designed to make it quicker and easier for you to interact with your Mac. For example, if you open multiple documents using different applications, you could take a while to find a specific file, as all the open windows will overlap each other. OS X's new Mission Control feature enables you to tap a single icon and view all of the open documents as tiled thumbnails, so you can find what you're after in an instant.

Lion also takes up a smaller amount of disk space than older Mac operating systems. This smaller footprint enables you to fill your hard drive with more apps, videos and photos. Like its predecessors, Lion is a very stable and versatile OS, so crashes are the exception rather than the rule.

10 Mac for Beginners

Date & Time
You can view the time as an analogue or digital clock by clicking and holding the mouse button here

Cover Flow
You can view folders and their contents as scrollable thumbnails in Cover Flow mode

Background
The desktop wallpaper is set to Aurora by default, though you can change this in the System Preferences' Desktop & Screen Saver menu

Searching for a particular file can be a challenge on a PC, but with the powerful Spotlight OS X search engine you can find files with ease. Spotlight works so quickly because it automatically indexes the files on your Mac.

Entertainment

The Mac has made a name for itself as a creative device, but if you're just looking to relax, it will happily fill that role too. In the mood to watch a movie? iTunes has expanded from its original role as a music player and organiser, and now it can handle your video collection just as easily as it does your audio library. At the same time, the iTunes Store also holds a growing video collection that you can either rent or buy and watch on your Mac. Both current and classic films are available, and there's a good choice of television episodes too, particularly when it comes to comedy. Don't forget podcasts either. Some of the video podcasts in the iTunes Store – all free, remember – offer excellent quality.

But what's the best way to watch this downloaded content? You can play video

Browsing

If we were to make the bold claim that the Mac offers the best way to browse the web, you would probably ask for evidence.

So here's exhibit one: Safari, the Mac's built-in web browser. It's not only one of the fastest and best-looking browsers around, but it also complies with modern web standards, which means that the latest cutting-edge websites should appear exactly as they were intended. Safari also comes with clever features such as private browsing, which hides your browsing history from prying eyes, and a neat 'Top Sites' view that presents small previews of your most-visited sites on one page and lets you visit them with a single click. Very convenient. In Top Sites view, Safari even lets you know when new content has been added to these sites.

"On a Mac, the web really isn't something you worry about. It's something to enjoy"

full-screen from within iTunes, although some users – particularly those who own big-screen Macs and an Apple Remote remote control device – enjoy sitting right back and watching their movies through Front Row. This is the Mac's built-in media software that allows you to easily navigate your iTunes music and video content or iPhoto pictures.

And, of course, AirPlay – Apple's wireless streaming technology – lets you stream video as well as audio from your Mac over a Wi-Fi network to your Apple TV. So even if you download your videos to a MacBook, you can still enjoy them on a really big screen.

Don't forget that you can also watch live or archived television footage on your Mac through a web browser. The BBC's iPlayer (**www.bbc. co.uk/iplayer**) has earned a fine reputation, but several other channels also offer either a live view or an on-demand service archive of previous television shows.

If your entertainment interests are more cerebral, what about reading a book? Your Mac might not be the first choice for reading, but if your iPad or Kindle device is out of reach, you can still browse books on your Mac. Amazon's free Kindle application for Mac lets you read books you've downloaded from the Kindle store – it will also synchronise bookmarks and annotations with other Kindle devices. There's so much on offer from your Mac to keep you entertained.

Another great feature, for those of us who hate the ads that clutter webpages, is Safari's Reader mode. With a single click, webpages are transformed to show the important text in a simple scrolling, image-free window. Safari also comes with many other features, from full screen mode to a reading list that allows you to save pages to read later.

Exhibit two: choice. It might surprise many, but Macs come with a far bigger range of web browsers than PCs do. You may not find Microsoft Explorer here, but on top of other big browsing names (Chrome, Firefox and Opera), there are delightful niche alternatives such as Omnigroup's OmniWeb (**www.omnigroup.com**) and Camino (**caminobrowser.org**) for you to try.

Exhibit three: security. You'll be more comfortable browsing the web on a Mac because you're far less susceptible to viruses or other malware than you would be on a PC. That's not necessarily because the Mac is immune, but because malicious software tends to target Windows PCs, you don't have to worry nearly as much about the risk of malware infecting your Mac. And if it's the kids you're worried about, you can rest assured that Mac OS X comes with parental controls – found in System Preferences – that can be configured to block websites unsuitable for younger eyes before they are displayed. On a Mac, the web isn't something you worry about. It's something to enjoy.

Ultimate Guide

Music

As the creator of the iPod, the most successful music player in history, Apple has long had a special relationship with music. "Why music?" asked then Apple CEO Steve Jobs rhetorically in 2001, the year iTunes was launched. "We love music. It's part of everyone's life." Nowhere is this view more apparent than with iTunes, the hub of all music operations on your new Mac. It's a fantastically versatile program. Some will use it as a simple music player, either with music you have imported (stick a CD into your Mac and it will convert its tracks and add them to your iTunes library automatically), by importing digital music from another source (iTunes can automatically convert music held in Windows Media format), or by buying it from the iTunes Store, which you can reach through iTunes. Here you can browse and preview short samples of tracks, buy them with a single click, and be listening to them on your Mac seconds later.

But others will use their Mac as an audio hub. iTunes can sync your music library to iPods, iPhones and iPads wirelessly using your own personal iCloud, so you can take your tracks wherever you are. iTunes also comes with a cool feature called AirPlay. If you have a compatible device, such as AirPlay-enabled speakers, an AirPort Express wireless device or an Apple TV, you can stream your music straight from your Mac to them. Another feature, Home Sharing, allows you to share your music with other iTunes users (Mac or PC) over your home network.

The Mac isn't just great for listening to music. You can create it too, thanks to GarageBand. GarageBand is part of the Mac's bundled iLife suite and allows you to create your own music, either using the built-in instruments, or by recording a real instrument by plugging it into your Mac. Even if you're an absolute beginner, GarageBand can be fun. You can drag pre-built 'loops' of audio onto tracks to build up a song, and even begin to learn how to play an instrument by downloading free basic music lessons from within the program.

Top 10 tips

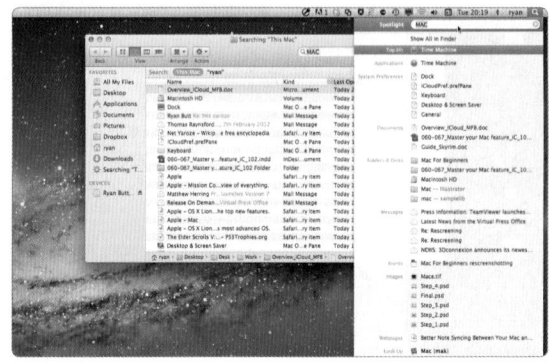

01: Using Spotlight

Spotlight enables you to find text, image or movie files anywhere on your Mac (even if they're buried deep in an old email). Click on the Spotlight Icon at the top right of the screen and type a phrase into the search field. Click Show All to see search results from a variety of sources.

02: Changing brightness/volume

We all like to work in different ways, especially in relation to sound volume and image brightness. You can control sound volume using sliders within an app like iTunes, or drag the master volume slider up or down from the top right of the main menu bar. To change Brightness, simply use the slider in the System Preferences>Displays option.

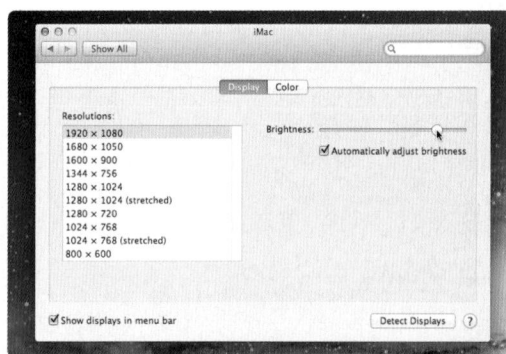

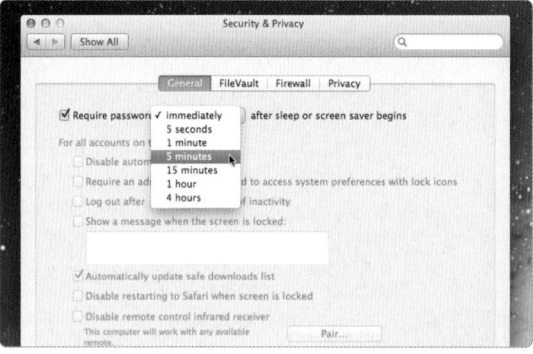

03: Setting up passwords

If you pop out of the office and leave your Mac unattended, you can get it to lock when the screensaver activates. Go to Apple>System Preferences and click on the View drop-down menu. Choose Security. In General, tick 'Require password after sleep or screensaver begins'. Choose a time for this password protection to kick in.

04: Minimising/maximising windows

The desktop can soon get cluttered with multiple open Finder or app windows. You can use Mission Control to tile them, then click on the one you want to view full size. Alternatively, click on the yellow Minimize icon at the top left of any window and it'll shrink to the Dock. The green Maximize icon will make the window expand to full size.

Mac OS X is a joy to use compared to Windows, with many user-friendly and powerful features to make your life easier. Here are some top tips to get started with OS X, from changing the desktop appearance to creating multiple user accounts and securing your system

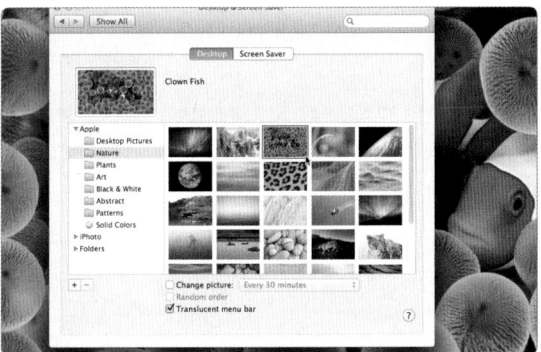

05: Change the background

To make yourself feel more at home you can change the default desktop background. Go to Apple>System Preferences>Desktop & Screensaver. Browse through a variety of themed folders for an eye-catching image (or rummage through your iPhoto Library for something more personal). Click to select a new background.

06: Set up multiple user accounts

To stop others tinkering with your files or settings, give them their own user account. Go to Apple>System Preferences>Accounts. Click the padlock and enter your Admin password. Click '+' to add a new account. This user can choose their own password. Changes they make to things like the desktop background will be unique to their account.

07: Create and rename folders

To create a new folder, click the Gear icon at the top of an existing folder and choose New Folder from the drop-down menu. Alternatively, on the menu bar, go to File>New Folder. By default, each folder is labelled as 'untitled'. Click on the label and type something more informative.

08: Add applications to your Dock

Docking a favourite application makes it easier to access. Browse to the Applications folder to see a specific application's icon and then drag it to the Dock. You can then launch it by clicking on its docked icon. Remove unwanted docked applications by dragging them from the Dock. They'll vanish in an animated puff of smoke!

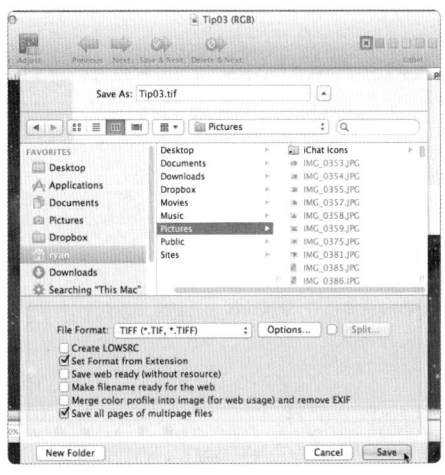

09: Save edited files under another name

Let's say you've adjusted the colour of an image using Preview. Go to File>Save As and give the file a name. Click on your house-shaped Home directory and browse to the Pictures folder. Click Save. The edited version of the shot can be found and reopened by going to the Pictures folder.

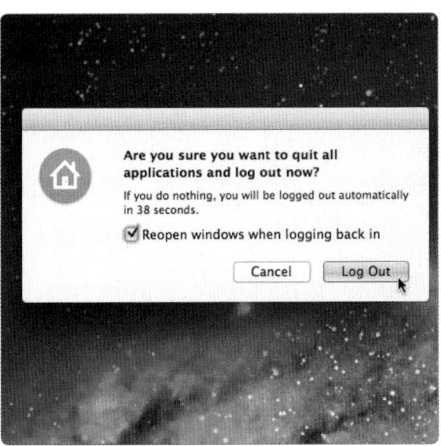

10: Log off and shut down

To log off after a hard day's work (or a fun gaming session) go to Apple>Log Out. Click the Log Out button. This will take you to the Mac OS X screen, where you can click Shut Down (or let someone else log in to use their account). Alternatively, press your Mac's power button and choose the Shut Down option.

The Dock

The Dock at the bottom of the screen enables you to access commonly used applications with ease

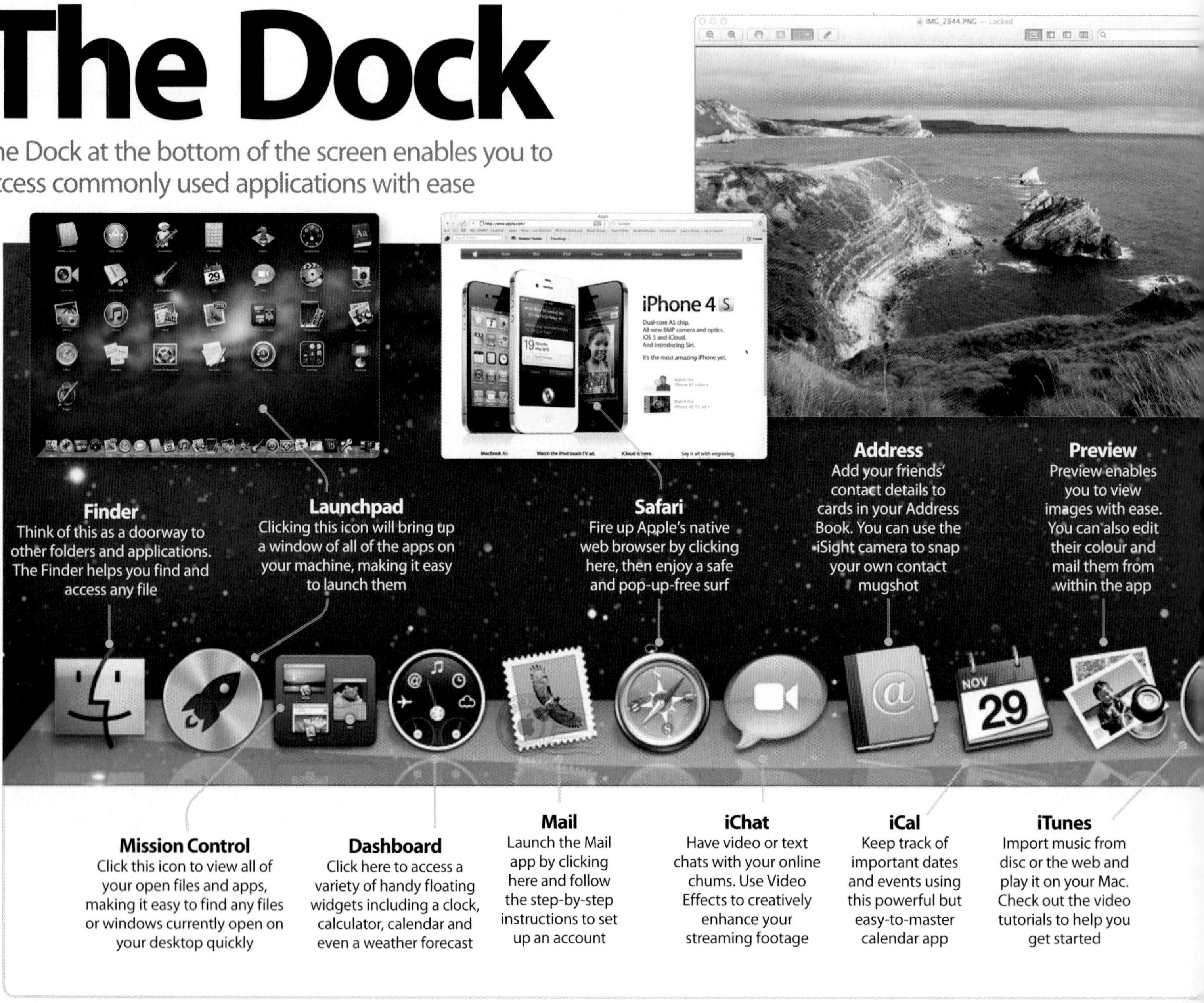

Finder
Think of this as a doorway to other folders and applications. The Finder helps you find and access any file

Launchpad
Clicking this icon will bring up a window of all of the apps on your machine, making it easy to launch them

Safari
Fire up Apple's native web browser by clicking here, then enjoy a safe and pop-up-free surf

Address
Add your friends' contact details to cards in your Address Book. You can use the iSight camera to snap your own contact mugshot

Preview
Preview enables you to view images with ease. You can also edit their colour and mail them from within the app

Mission Control
Click this icon to view all of your open files and apps, making it easy to find any files or windows currently open on your desktop quickly

Dashboard
Click here to access a variety of handy floating widgets including a clock, calculator, calendar and even a weather forecast

Mail
Launch the Mail app by clicking here and follow the step-by-step instructions to set up an account

iChat
Have video or text chats with your online chums. Use Video Effects to creatively enhance your streaming footage

iCal
Keep track of important dates and events using this powerful but easy-to-master calendar app

iTunes
Import music from disc or the web and play it on your Mac. Check out the video tutorials to help you get started

Photos

If the extent of your photo organisation in the past has been to loosely organise them in folders on your PC, or even just to shove prints in a shoebox, you'll be stunned by the organisational prowess of your Mac's iPhoto application.

iPhoto gives you a whole new way to easily sort and group your photos. For example, its Faces feature automatically recognises faces in images and lets you add names to them. iPhoto learns from your choices and can suggest other photos that might include that person after a while, this automatic recognition gets very good. You can then browse your photos in a special Faces view which gathers all photos of one person together.

In the same way, iPhoto's Places view uses location information often embedded in a digital image to display their location on a map, while an Events view groups photos by the date they were taken. And if that's not enough flexibility, how about iPhoto's Smart Folders, whose contents automatically update to hold images depending criteria you set.

If there's a downside to digital photography, it's the tendency for shots to be kept on your computer rather than shared. But iPhoto encourages you to post images to Facebook or online photo sharing site Flickr. And if you're after permanent keepsakes or gifts, it can design letterpress cards, books and calendars which can be ordered from within the program.

Storing photos in iPhoto also makes them available in other iLife and iWork programs, making it easy to put your slideshows to DVD using iDVD, or home movies using iMovie. iPhoto isn't an all-singing, all-dancing photo editor, but it will happily handle basics very well. You can crop, straighten and correct odd colours in a photograph easily and its tool to correct red-eye is almost foolproof.

Perhaps the best feature of all though is that through your own personal iCloud, you can activate Photo Stream, which automatically pushes photos taken on your iPhone or iPad 2 to all of your devices, including your Mac, without the need to plug anything in or manually transfer files. Magic!

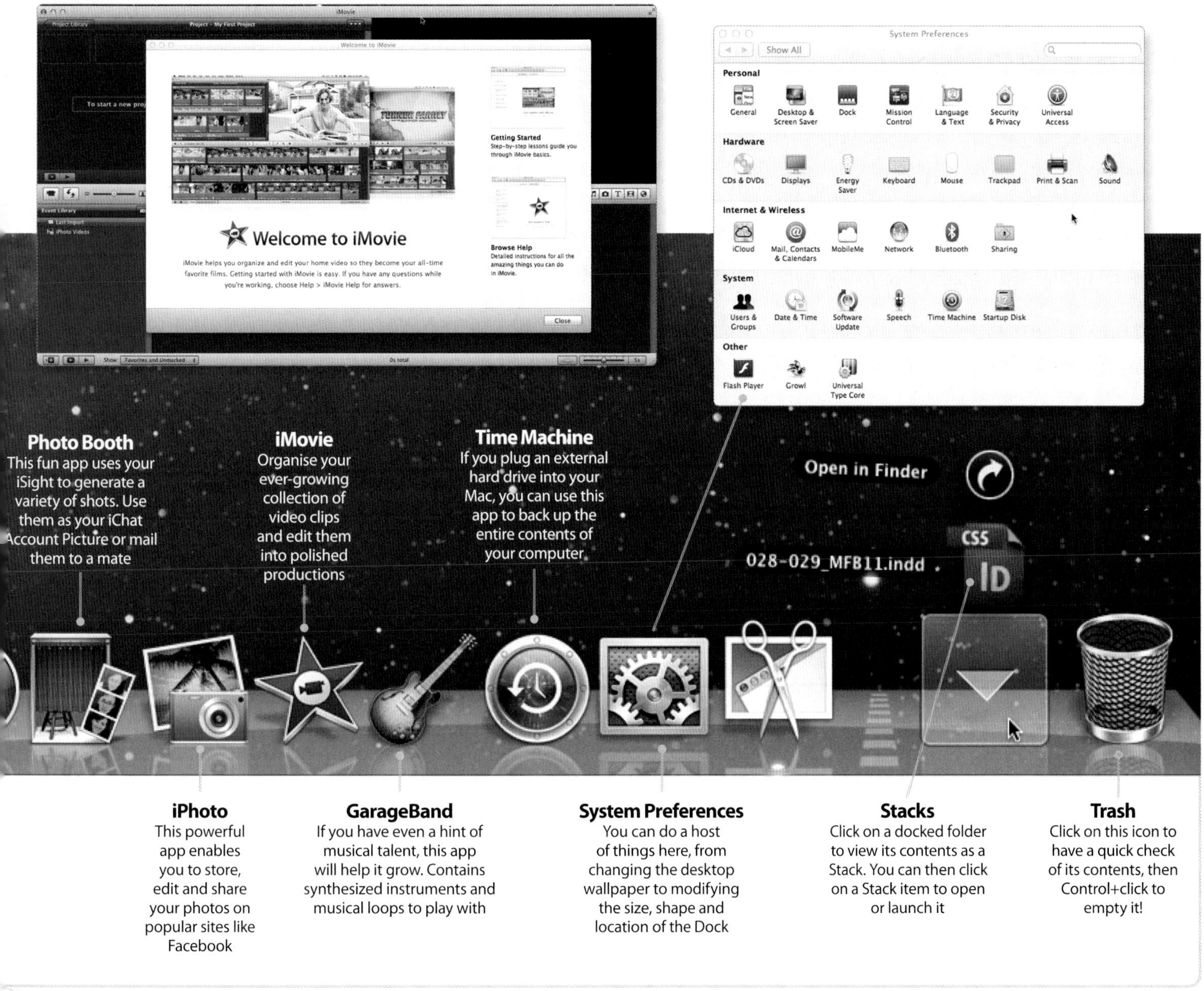

Welcome to iMovie
System Preferences
Personal
General
Desktop & Screen Saver
Dock
Mission Control
Language & Text
Security & Privacy
Universal Access
Hardware
CDs & DVDs
Displays
Energy Saver
Keyboard
Mouse
Trackpad
Print & Scan
Sound
Internet & Wireless
iCloud
Mail, Contacts & Calendars
MobileMe
Network
Bluetooth
Sharing
System
Users & Groups
Date & Time
Software Update
Speech
Time Machine
Startup Disk
Other
Flash Player
Growl
Universal Type Core
Open in Finder
028-029_MFB11.indd
Photo Booth
This fun app uses your iSight to generate a variety of shots. Use them as your iChat Account Picture or mail them to a mate
iMovie
Organise your ever-growing collection of video clips and edit them into polished productions
Time Machine
If you plug an external hard drive into your Mac, you can use this app to back up the entire contents of your computer
iPhoto
This powerful app enables you to store, edit and share your photos on popular sites like Facebook
GarageBand
If you have even a hint of musical talent, this app will help it grow. Contains synthesized instruments and musical loops to play with
System Preferences
You can do a host of things here, from changing the desktop wallpaper to modifying the size, shape and location of the Dock
Stacks
Click on a docked folder to view its contents as a Stack. You can then click on a Stack item to open or launch it
Trash
Click on this icon to have a quick check of its contents, then Control+click to empty it!

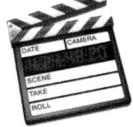

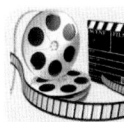

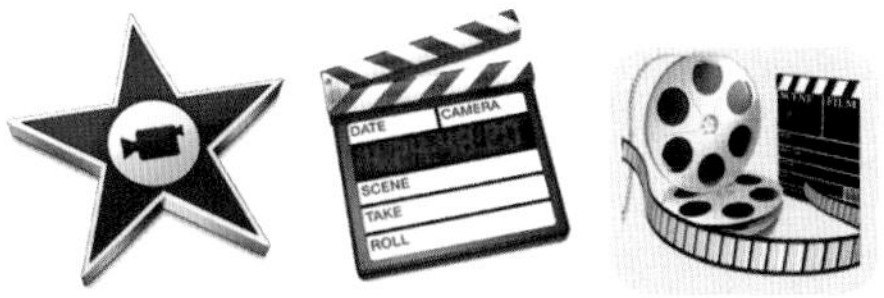

Video

What do *True Grit* and *The Social Network* have in common? Apart from being two box-office blockbusters, both movies were edited on a Mac using Mac-only software. It's a growing trend, and one that's becoming accessible to more people – not just professional film-makers. Ten years ago you would need to have sold your house and car to be able to afford that sort of editing functionality, but now you can do it using equipment costing a few hundred pounds.

If you've got a video camera and a Mac, you already have all the hardware you need. If your camera is a relatively recent model, it's a decent bet that you'll be able to start working with it without even having to install drivers or tweak settings.

While many top-of-the-range movies are edited using the high-end Final Cut Pro and the Mac, iLife's own bundled iMovie is the gold standard of home video editing. Editing in iMovie is as simple as importing your footage and then dragging it into a project area. Simply drag and drop to add transitions between scenes or titles – and there's a full array of sound effects that you can use to enhance audio. Even if your original footage isn't top quality, iMovie can improve it. It has a stabilisation tool to correct shaky video, and individual clips can be colour-corrected. The professional look is enhanced through iMovie 11's templates that help you to quickly create short and memorable trailers for your work.

The real beauty of iLife applications is the way they work together. With the iLife media browser, you can add a soundtrack from iTunes or images from iPhoto or export your video to iDVD to create permanent keepsakes on disc. That's not the only export option either: you can also share directly to popular video-sharing sites such as YouTube or Vimeo.

And naturally, there's an easy transition to even more powerful tools. Final Cut Express isn't an expensive purchase, yet is only a slightly cut-down version of the high-end studio application. It imports existing iMovie projects while allowing you to work with multiple audio and video tracks.

Gaming

It used to be said that the Mac lagged behind Windows when it came to games, but that's far less true now. There are plenty of reasons for this change. The attention of games developers has been grabbed by the Mac's ever-increasing market share. And the Mac's transition to run on Intel processors a few years ago resulted in both performance improvements and easier porting of games from the PC platform.

The arrival of the Mac App Store has also proved critical. It has given exposure to Mac games developers who would otherwise struggle for the limelight. That has benefited the developers of games like *Call Of Duty* and *Batman: Arkham Asylum*, which have been some of the App Store's biggest sellers since it launched in January 2011.

The arrival of the Mac App Store has also encouraged existing iPhone and iPod games developers, already familiar with the App Store format and Apple's development tools, to try their hand with Mac games.

The conversion process is comparatively simple and as a result, titles that originally grabbed attention on the iPod, such as *Angry Birds*, *Flight Control* and *Plants vs Zombies,* have been ported successfully to the Mac. Crucially, in many cases, this transfer has come ahead of their arrival on PC or console systems.

And Mac users don't just have a better choice of games now. The Mac App Store means no more hunting around the recessed corners of computer shops to find a compatible game. Like the iTunes Store, gratification is instant: purchase, download and run games within seconds of buying them.

There's another reason for the Mac's growth: the arrival on the Mac platform of Steam, a digital distribution platform that boasted 25 million user accounts before it arrived on the Mac. But now Mac gamers have feature parity: Steam games release simultaneously on Windows, Mac and the Xbox 360. And if you're a Windows Steam user, there's great news: if you already own the PC version a game on Steam, you get Mac versions at no extra charge.

Shortcut tips

The brilliant thing about OS X Lion is the way it lets you control the way your Mac behaves with a few taps on the keyboard. These keyboard shortcuts can speed up the way you interact with your Mac, so you can clear away clutter, find files fast or jump between open applications in a click. By knowing the keyboard shortcut for a command, you no longer have to drag the mouse up to the main menu and rummage around in submenus! We'll cover shortcuts that work with OS X, plus show you some generic key combinations that will work in most applications (like copying and pasting). Many shortcuts use the key with the Apple logo on it – we'll refer to this as the Command key in our tips (since some wireless keyboards don't feature the Apple logo on the Command key). The key with Alt on it is the Option key.

Command+Z
This is the Undo function in most applications.

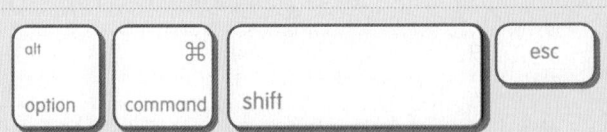

Option+Shift+Command+Escape
If you hold these keys down for three seconds, you'll Force Quit the currently open app. Only do this if an app freezes up.

Command+C
Copies selected text, documents or even images.

Command+Shift+3
Takes a screenshot of your display and saves it as an image file to the desktop.

Command+V
Pastes anything you copied with the Cmd+C shortcut.

Command+S
This shortcut saves the current document, using the same name.

Command+N
This will give you a new document in any application you're using.

Command+Tab
This activates a handy mini-Dock. Keep pressing tab to switch between currently open applications.

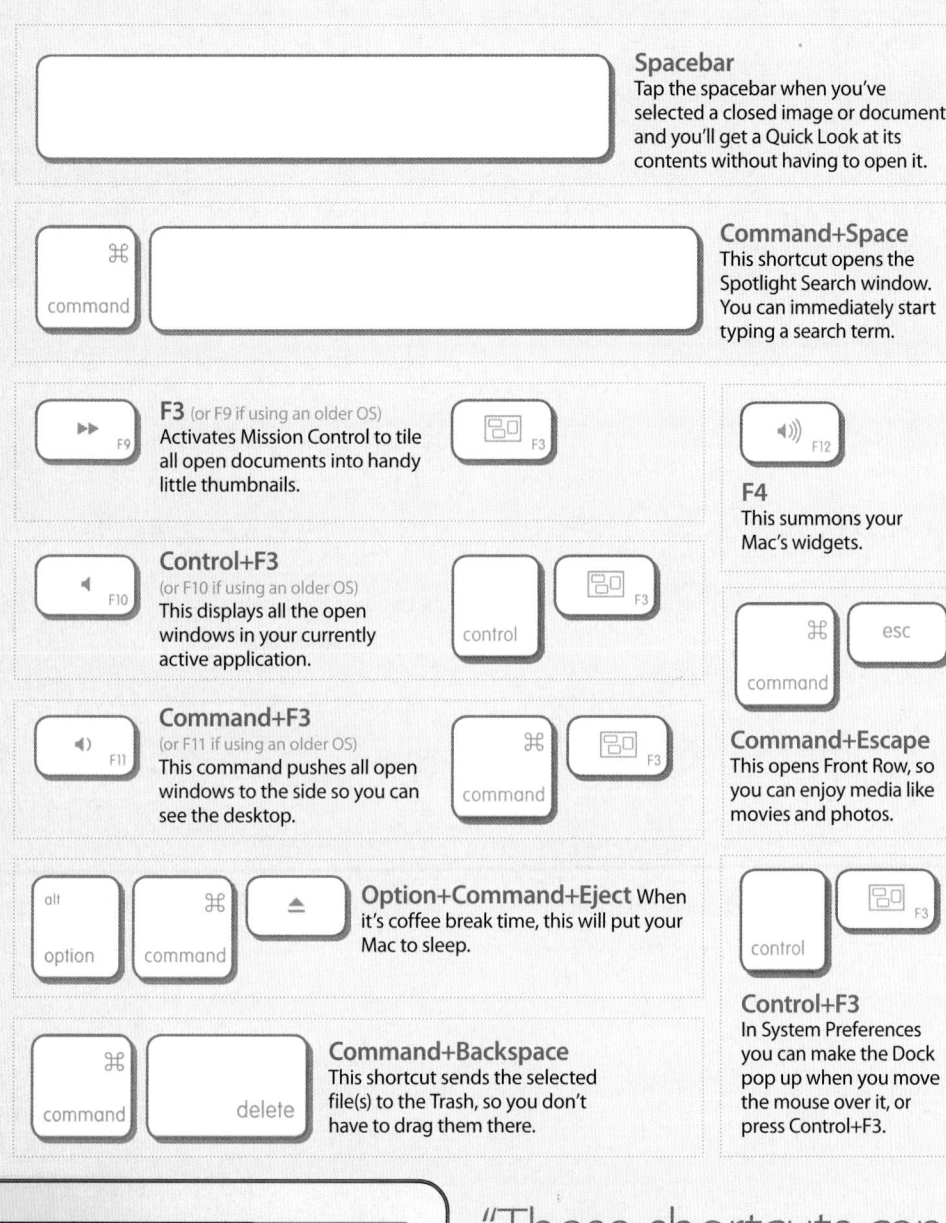

Spacebar
Tap the spacebar when you've selected a closed image or document and you'll get a Quick Look at its contents without having to open it.

Command+Space
This shortcut opens the Spotlight Search window. You can immediately start typing a search term.

F3 (or F9 if using an older OS)
Activates Mission Control to tile all open documents into handy little thumbnails.

F4
This summons your Mac's widgets.

Control+F3
(or F10 if using an older OS)
This displays all the open windows in your currently active application.

Command+F3
(or F11 if using an older OS)
This command pushes all open windows to the side so you can see the desktop.

Command+Escape
This opens Front Row, so you can enjoy media like movies and photos.

Option+Command+Eject When it's coffee break time, this will put your Mac to sleep.

Control+F3
In System Preferences you can make the Dock pop up when you move the mouse over it, or press Control+F3.

Command+Backspace
This shortcut sends the selected file(s) to the Trash, so you don't have to drag them there.

"These shortcuts can speed up the way you work"

MacBook Air

MAGIC MOUSE

Right click
If you do this while selecting a word in Safari, you can choose 'Look Up in Dictionary' from the context-sensitive pop-up menu.

Scroll button
By default this activates Spaces, though you can use System Preferences to change its behaviour.

Control+Scroll
This combo enables you to zoom in to get a magnified view of what's on the screen.

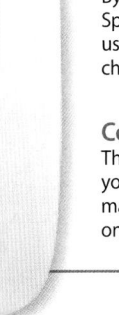

Office

If you didn't think of the Mac as an office workhorse, think again. Easy to use, supremely resistant to viruses and coming with a reputation for reliability, Apple desktops and laptops tick plenty of hard-nosed business boxes.

But what about the software? The good news is that the dominant office software is available on the Mac – and it's just as good as the one on Windows. Microsoft Office 11 for Mac has virtually the same functionality as its PC sibling, but looks better. You can swap Word and Excel files with PC users and even share Outlook calendars on a connected server. And recent Macs come with built-in support for Microsoft Exchange Server 2007, so if you use Exchange at work, chances are you can access all your emails and calendars at home too.

But Apple has been making its own steps in the office space. Its Mac-only iWork suite, which comes in a fair bit less expensive than Microsoft's offering, also features word processing, spreadsheet and presentation capabilities. If its word processing and spreadsheet tools lack the complete range of functions of Microsoft's equivalent tools, they are at least arguably easier to use. iWork's Keynote presentation software is generally accepted to be better than PowerPoint, with more polished templates and more impressive transitions.

iWork files are also Office compatible: files saved in Office on the PC can be opened in Pages, Numbers and Keynote, while you can export them from iWork in PC format too. What's more, you can sync documents to your iCloud and access them from any computer in the world to continue working on them. The only thing missing in both Microsoft Office and iWork suites is a decent database. But even here you're spoiled for quality Mac choice: pick between the excellent Filemaker (**www.filemaker.com**) or its budget equivalent, Bento (**www.bento.com**).

Office work isn't all about spreadsheets, letters and slideshows, though. What about managing your accounts? There's plenty of choice here. AccountEdge (**www.mamut.com/uk/mac/accountedge**) and Business Accountz (**www.accountz.com**) are both capable desktop applications – but the Mac is also open to the growing number of excellent web-based alternatives, such as Xero (**www.xero.com**) and FreeAgent (**www.freeagentcentral.com**).

Productivity

Keeping yourself organised has never been more demanding. But your Mac, and its built-in iCal calendar application, can help you to keep on top of things. iCal supports multiple calendars – so you can track work and family commitments separately – and you can view calendars in several ways: by day, week or month. You can invite others to events you create, and set an alarm to remind you before it starts.

iCal also lets you sync appointments with iPhone, iPod touch or iPad calendar apps using iTunes as a handy go-between (if you use Apple's new iCloud service, you will also have the ability to sync your calendar without an actual physical connection, and you will also be able to share calendars between multiple Macs too).

Beyond iCal, the Mac has been built to take control of the chores while you do what you want to do. For example, every computer user knows they ought to back up regularly, but the organising of backup discs and choosing what to copy invariably gets in the way. Not on a Mac. Here, backing up is as simple as attaching an external drive. Apple's Time Machine backup utility takes care of the rest.

To be truly productive, you need to get as much done while avoiding those repetitive tasks that can use up a lot of your time and become quite frustrating. Automator is a drag-and-drop tool for automating common chores. You build a workflow by piecing together actions and the saved result automates the task in the future. With some applications you can just record your mouse and keyboard movements and save the result to an Automator workflow, where they can be stored and replayed. It's like programming without the hard work.

Another often overlooked productivity treat for many Mac users is Services, small pieces of functionality that can be shared between different applications. Accessed from the application menu (if you are in iTunes, for example, Services can be found under the iTunes menu), services suitable for the current application automatically appear – so if you're working in a word processor, you might see a service to send the currently selected text in an email. And if you don't find a service you would like to see, you can easily build one of your own, using Automator of course. There are plenty of option on your Mac to make you more productive.

iTunes top tips

Organise your entire music collection with iTunes, rediscover favourite tracks from yesteryear and sync songs with mobile devices

The way that we manage music has changed dramatically since iTunes and mobile devices like the iPod and iPhone came along. Once you've copied your CDs into your iTunes app, you'll rediscover music you haven't listened to for years. Think of iTunes as your personal digital jukebox! You can use it to store and organise your music collection, as well as discover and buy new music (or movies) via the iTunes Store. Your digital tracks can be turned into Playlists (like cassette mixtapes of old!) and transferred to your iPod or iPhone to be enjoyed on the move. Here's how to transfer (or sync) music from your iTunes library to your mobile device, such as an iPod, iPhone or iPad.

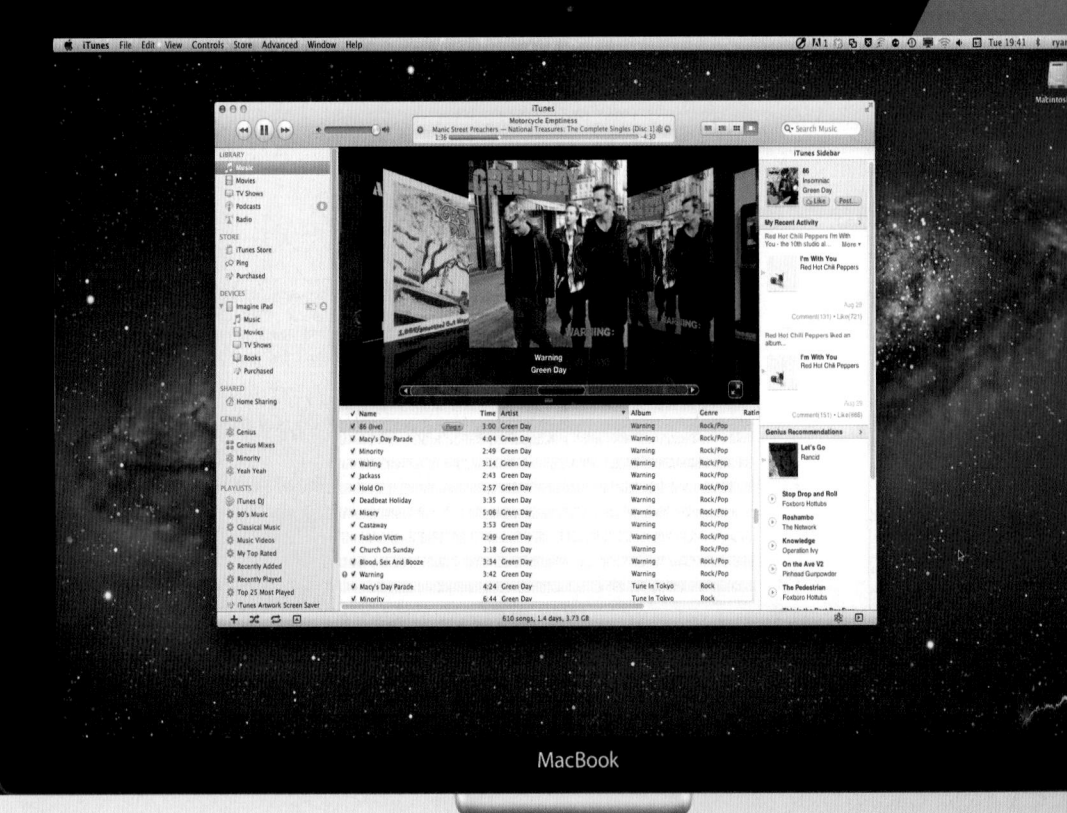

MacBook

New software

Like other apps, iTunes is always evolving to include improved performance and extra features. You may be informed that newer versions of iTunes are available when you open the app, but you can also check out any updates by going to the Apple menu and choosing Software Update. You can then download and install the latest version of iTunes.

Mini Player

To reduce the size of the iTunes interface, simply click the small green circle at the top-left of the interface. This turns iTunes into a small floating mini player that enables you to perform useful commands like playing, pausing or jumping forward to the next song. You can adjust volume too.

Create a Playlist

It can be daunting deciding what songs to listen to in a huge music library. Thankfully, you can create Playlists of your favourite songs. Click the '+' icon at the bottom left of the iTunes window. Label your Playlist. Click on Music in the Library section. Drag tracks from the Library into the Playlist. When you click on the Playlist, only these selected songs will play.

> "Once you've copied your CDs into your iTunes app, you'll rediscover music you haven't listened to for years"

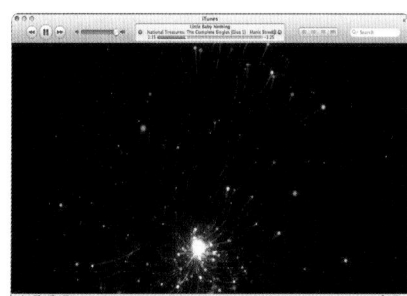

Visualizer

By pressing Command+T you can activate the Visualizer and enjoy real-time animated graphics that react to the track you're currently playing. To see different types of graphics, go to View>Visualizer and choose an option like Jelly. By pressing Command+F you can expand the Visualizer to full screen and create a psychedelic light show to accompany your music.

Get Album Artwork

An Album gets some of its character from the accompanying cover artwork. To enjoy this important aspect of any album in your collection, go to Advanced>Get Album Artwork. iTunes will then trawl an online database for appropriate covers. You can display and browse through downloaded album covers using Cover Flow.

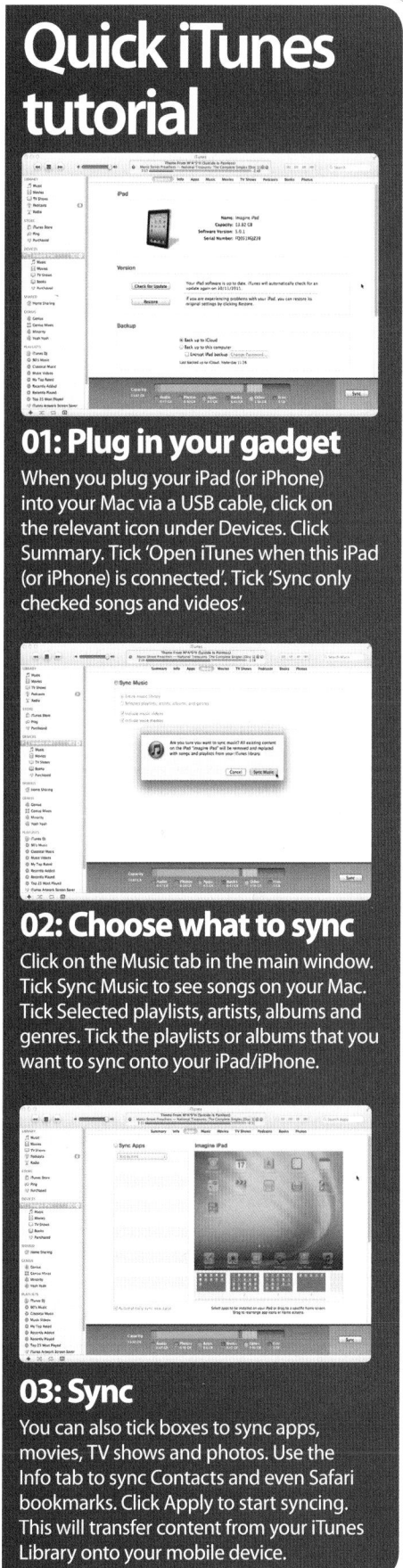

Quick iTunes tutorial

01: Plug in your gadget

When you plug your iPad (or iPhone) into your Mac via a USB cable, click on the relevant icon under Devices. Click Summary. Tick 'Open iTunes when this iPad (or iPhone) is connected'. Tick 'Sync only checked songs and videos'.

02: Choose what to sync

Click on the Music tab in the main window. Tick Sync Music to see songs on your Mac. Tick Selected playlists, artists, albums and genres. Tick the playlists or albums that you want to sync onto your iPad/iPhone.

03: Sync

You can also tick boxes to sync apps, movies, TV shows and photos. Use the Info tab to sync Contacts and even Safari bookmarks. Click Apply to start syncing. This will transfer content from your iTunes Library onto your mobile device.

Mac App Store

Browse thousands of Mac applications, all located in one convenient App Store

Launched back in July 2008, Apple's original App Store was initially accessible via an app on the iPhone – and subsequently the iPod touch and iPad – enabling users of those devices to peruse thousands of downloadable apps designed for iOS devices. Apps span a wide range of categories (from Photography to Education) and let you extend your iPhone's functionality in many exciting ways. The iPhone-centric App Store has proven incredibly successful, so there was little surprise when a Mac OS X App Store appeared early in 2011. On its first day, the new Mac App Store sold a million apps.

The Mac App Store enables you to find useful software for your iMac or MacBook in one convenient place, without having to trawl the internet. To browse it, you'll need the Mac App Store app, which is available as standard with Lion (you can use your Apple>Software Update menu command to install the latest version of older operating systems). Once you've updated Mac OS X, the Mac App Store will appear in your Dock. Double-click on the app's icon to fire it up.

As there are thousands of Mac apps to explore, it can be a daunting task finding what you need, so it's worth starting with a rummage through one of the 21 categories. As on the iOS App Store, these Mac app categories cover a wide range topics, including Games and Social Networking. Once you've found a category that you're interested in, you can refine your hunt by looking at the Top Paid or Top Free Apps to see what is popular. Alternatively, you can search the App Store with a relevant keyword. Once you've clicked on an app that catches your eye, you can find out more about it by viewing screenshots of its interface. More importantly, you can read the reviews of people who've already downloaded the app to see whether it's worth your time (and money!).

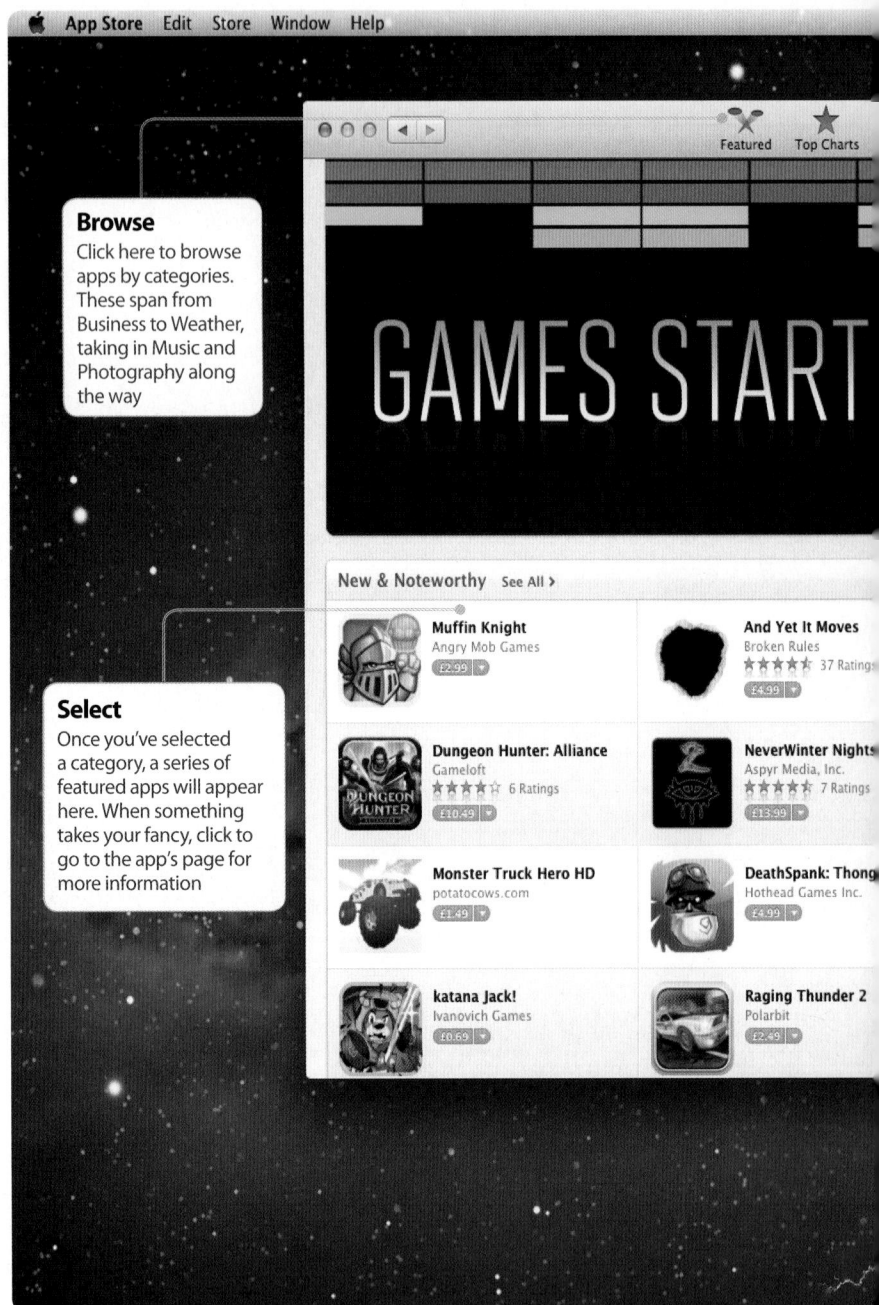

Browse Click here to browse apps by categories. These span from Business to Weather, taking in Music and Photography along the way

Select Once you've selected a category, a series of featured apps will appear here. When something takes your fancy, click to go to the app's page for more information

Quick tutorial

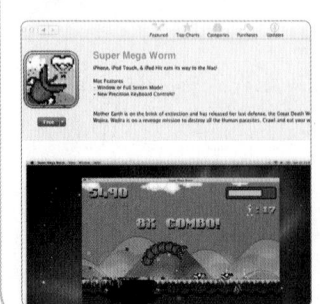

Locate an app
Use the Categories list to home in on the type of app you fancy, then check out other users' ratings and reviews to see if it's worth downloading.

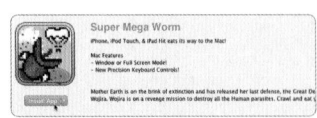

Download it
Click on the app's price and sign in using your Apple ID. The icon will change to 'Installing' and the app will download in your Dock.

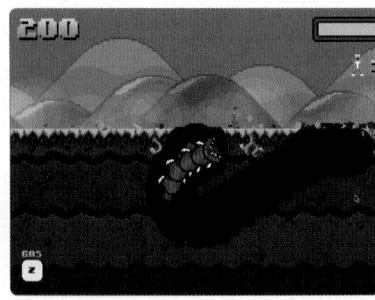

Launch it
Once the app's download progress bar disappears, it's ready for action. Click on the app's icon in the Dock to launch and explore it!

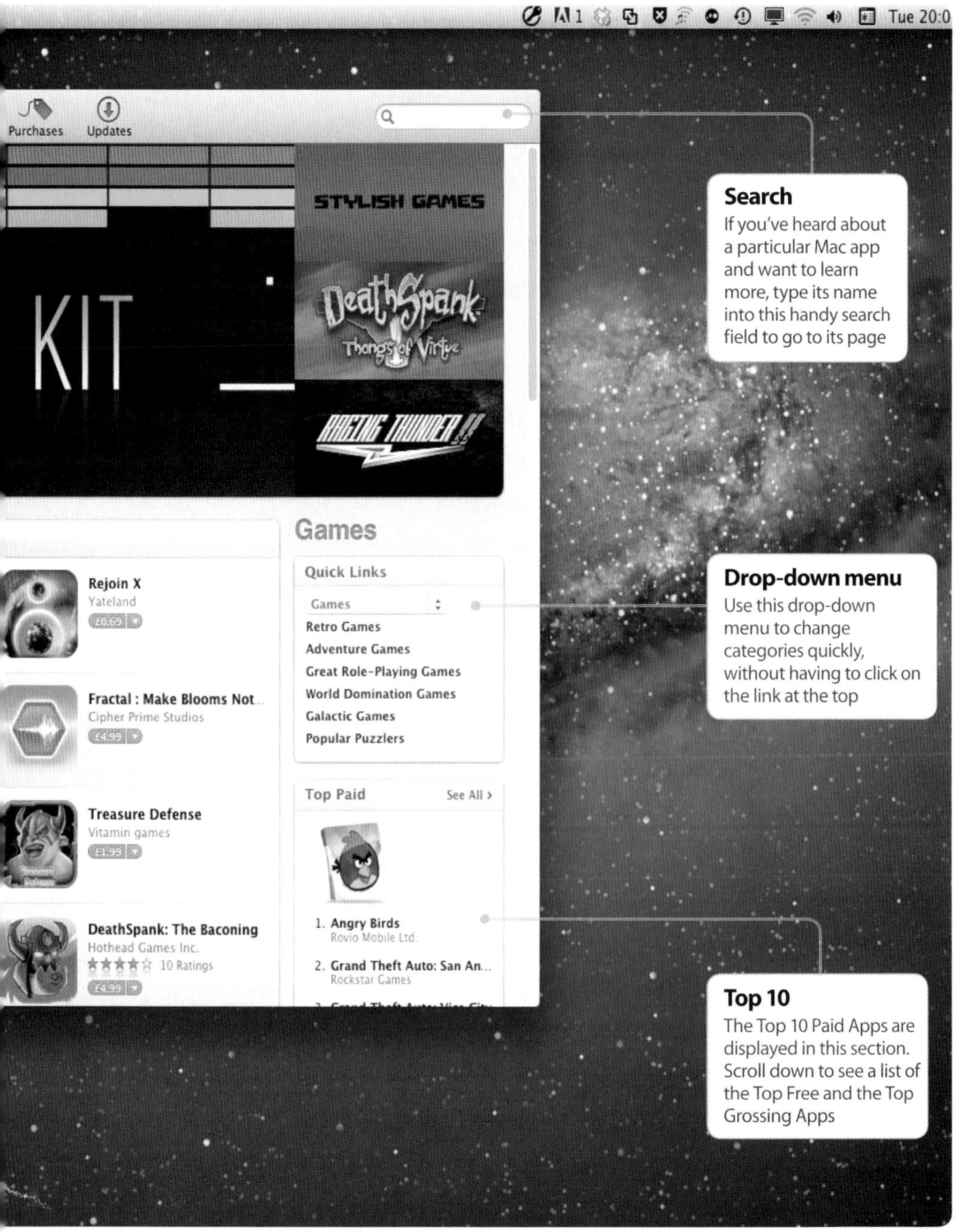

Search
If you've heard about a particular Mac app and want to learn more, type its name into this handy search field to go to its page

Drop-down menu
Use this drop-down menu to change categories quickly, without having to click on the link at the top

Top 10
The Top 10 Paid Apps are displayed in this section. Scroll down to see a list of the Top Free and the Top Grossing Apps

STYLISH GAMES

KIT

DeathSpank
Thongs of Virtue

RAGING THUNDER II

Games

Rejoin X
Yateland
£0.69

Fractal : Make Blooms Not...
Cipher Prime Studios
£4.99

Treasure Defense
Vitamin games
£1.99

DeathSpank: The Baconing
Hothead Games Inc.
★★★★☆ 10 Ratings
£4.99

Quick Links

Games
Retro Games
Adventure Games
Great Role-Playing Games
World Domination Games
Galactic Games
Popular Puzzlers

Top Paid   See All >

1. Angry Birds
   Rovio Mobile Ltd.
2. Grand Theft Auto: San An...
   Rockstar Games

Creativity

The Mac, at its heart, is a creative tool. It seems to have always been that way. The desktop publishing industry began on the Mac back in the Eighties and 30 years later, today's web design industry still favours the platform. How can that be? Perhaps the Mac's ease of use has something to do with it, or the fact that creative peripherals, such as drawing tablets, are designed to work seamlessly on it.

It's as likely, though, that the quality of Apple's hardware strikes a note with creatives. And that applies from a practical, as much as an aesthetic, point of view. Those Mac screens – particularly the larger iMac displays – not only look great, but offer great colour reproduction. And the Mac's built-in Colorsync technology ensures that what's great-looking on screen will look just as good (and colour-accurate) when it prints out.

Above all, it's the software that appeals. A quick scan of the Mac App Store will reveal dozens of cool budget drawing and illustration tools – not forgetting Pages' superb layout tools – while the industry-standard design applications all work well on the Mac, from QuarkXPress to Adobe's Creative Suite, which comprises popular applications such as image editor Photoshop, drawing tool Illustrator and page layout application InDesign.

The web is the catalyst for much creative work nowadays. For those who want to put a creative site together without having to get their hands dirty with code, iWeb, which comes as part of the iLife suite, is a great start. You can base your website on pre-built templates and customise it by dragging other iLife components – video from iMovie, images from iPhoto or audio from iTunes – into it. Instead of having to hand-code functionality to add features such as embedded YouTube video, you can just drag a widget to your page. Publishing to the web is a single click away.

If iWeb whets your appetite to get more serious about web development, there are plenty of more powerful tools available to help. Another Mac-only tool, Coda (www.panic.com), offers a single window coding environment that's popular with Mac web coders and developers.

> "There are dozens of cool budget drawing and illustration tools in the Mac App Store"

Apps to download right now!

Comic Life 2
This app provides comic-book-style graphics and fonts that enable you to turn your photos into panels from a graphic novel.
PRICE: **£20.99/$29.99**

Twitter
Keep tabs on the latest tweets on this popular social network, or send out tweets of your own to inform your Followers.
PRICE: **FREE**

Pixelmator
Edit and enhance your images with this pixel-pushing app (and it's much cheaper than the popular Photoshop Elements!).
PRICE: **£20.99/$29.99**

FAQs

Common OS X questions answered for you...

How do I set up iCloud?

A *Simple, ensure you are running Lion (Mac OS X 10.7.2) and then go to System Preferences and click on iCloud under 'Internet & Wireless'. Now log in with your Apple ID (the same login details as iTunes) and start enjoying the many free services it offers.*

Can I reposition the Dock?

A *Yes. Just go to the Apple menu and choose Dock. You can then tick an option to position the Dock left or right. If you click on Dock Preferences, you can change the size of the Dock so that it can display more icons, and turn on Magnification.*

How can I change the Dock's contents?

A *Simply drag an application's icon to the Dock to add it. You can then launch that application from the Dock. Drag unwanted applications from the Dock and they'll vanish (though they'll still be accessible in the Applications folder).*

How can I make certain apps open automatically upon startup?

A *If you always check your mail after starting up your Mac then go to Apple>System Preferences>Accounts. Click Login Items and tick the + icon, then browse to choose Mail from the Applications folder.*

How can I stop pop-ups when browsing the web?

A *Open Safari. Go to the Safari menu at the top left and choose Block Pop-Up Windows (or press Shift+Command+K). This will keep those pesky adverts out of your hair!*

How can I save battery power on a MacBook?

A *Go to Apple>System Preferences and click Energy Saver. Click on Battery. Tick the boxes that make the hard disk sleep whenever possible and set the display to dim a little when being powered by the Mac's battery.*

Accessories

Expand your Mac with a variety of add-ons

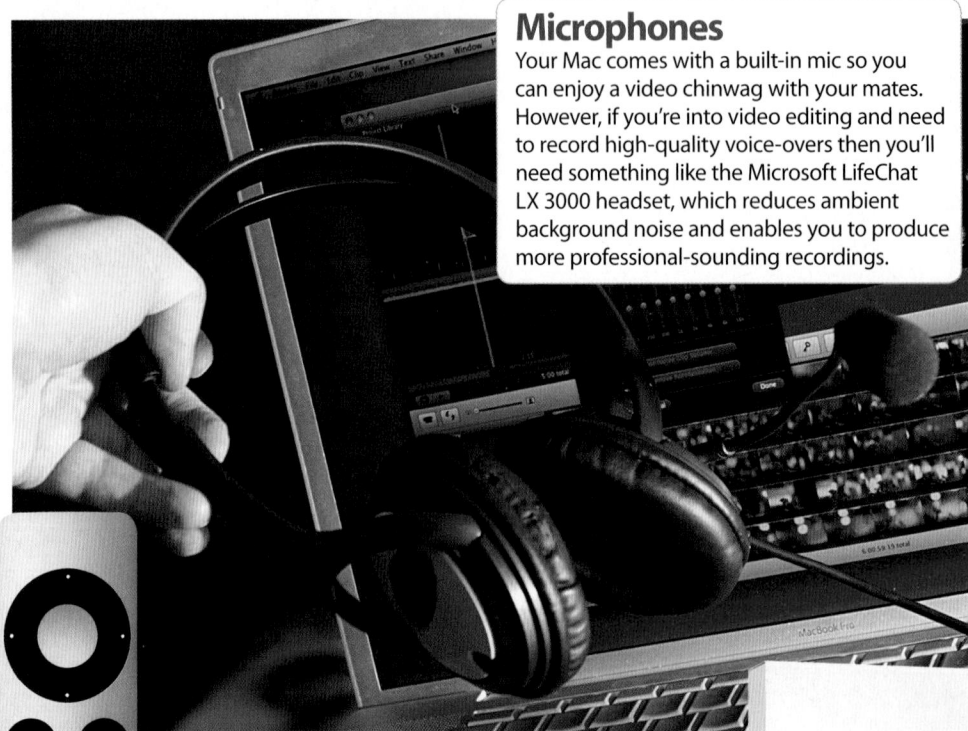

Microphones

Your Mac comes with a built-in mic so you can enjoy a video chinwag with your mates. However, if you're into video editing and need to record high-quality voice-overs then you'll need something like the Microsoft LifeChat LX 3000 headset, which reduces ambient background noise and enables you to produce more professional-sounding recordings.

Remotes

If you're enjoying music via iTunes, or have your MacBook plugged into your HD TV to watch a video clip then a remote control device will let you control the content while keeping your feet up. The Apple Remote interacts with Front Row, so you can enjoy all your Mac's media (or download rentals from iTunes).

Protection plans

You may be very dependent on your Mac, especially if it helps you earn a wage. You get complimentary technical support up to 90 days after purchasing your Mac and a one-year limited warranty. The Apple Care Protection Plan enables you to extend this support to three years. See the Apple Store for more details.

AppleCare
Protection Plan

Communication

The Mac is all about communication, whether by email, text message or video. Apple Mail, the email program that sits in the Dock of every Mac, is a superb way to keep in touch with friends, family and colleagues. It can handle multiple email accounts and, thanks to the Mac's

External speakers

Your MacBook or iMac provides many ways for you to enjoy music, like playing MP3s in iTunes or streaming songs via Spotify. For a richer range of sounds, get hold of a speaker system like the Harman Kardon Soundsticks. This gives you a wider stereo field and a deeper bass thanks to its subwoofer.

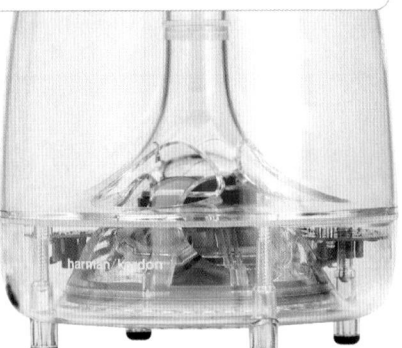

Printers

It's all very well sharing photos via Facebook or Flickr, but nothing beats a hard copy print that you can frame. You may also need to print a boarding pass before you can fly. The all-in-one, Mac-compatible Epson Stylus SX525WD consumer inkjet printer is one of the best available on the market.

External drives

No matter how large your Mac's hard drive is, you're going to fill it! An external drive (like the Seagate GoFlex for Mac) will give your Mac's OS space to breathe. You can set up new iPhoto libraries on an external drive too, and tell Time Machine to back up the contents of your Mac onto an external drive.

Memory sticks

If you have a MacBook and a desktop computer, you may want to transfer files between machines. One way to do this is to plug a memory stick into a Mac's USB port, then copy files onto it. Once you eject the stick, you can pop it into your other machine and then transfer files to its hard drive.

Bags and cases

When you're out and about, you'll need to carry your MacBook in a bag or case to keep it safe. A shoulder bag like the Small Alley will enable you to carry and protect a 13" MacBook plus other bits and bobs like cables, mouse and iPhone.

Spotlight search engine, all its messages can be searched in an instant. Want to add files or photos to your email? Just drag them over your message window or use Mail's photo browser to grab snaps from your iPhoto collection. In Mail, email doesn't need to be drab: you can style it using beautifully designed templates.

Mail is clever too, analysing the contents of incoming messages, not just to check whether they contain spam – in which case they will be neatly removed from view – but also to interpret the contents. So if you get an email asking you to meet someone tomorrow at one, you can click on this

invitation to add it to your iCal calendar. And Mail works neatly with the Mac's own application for storing contacts – Address Book - which syncs with your iPhone or iPad via iCloud, so your contacts are with you all the time.

Facebook is becoming an ever more popular way to communicate and while most people are happy using the Facebook website, there are plenty of Mac applications that integrate with it. Even iPhoto offers a way to upload your images directly to your Facebook account – and comments about the photo made by Facebook friends can be seen within iPhoto.

You can also use the web to keep up with your Twitter contacts – although it's easier to use one of the Mac's own applications: the Twitter application itself is a free download from the Mac App Store.

FaceTime is another cool feature that allows you to have a video chat with other FaceTime users, whether on the Mac, iPhone, iPad or iPod touch. Then there's iChat, which offers similar features, but also supports text messaging. And if you want to keep up with friends using other text messaging services, such as Microsoft Messenger, look no further than the excellent Adium (**www.adium.im**). The possibilities are endless.

Gestures with your Magic Trackpad

Lion has introduced new gestures to make it easier for you to interact with your machine. We look at what each is, and how they work…

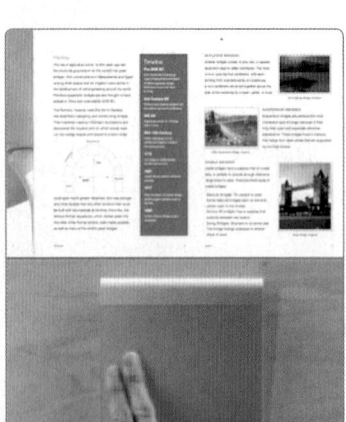

Swipe between pages

Hold down two fingers, and swipe either to the left or right in order to navigate through pages of your history in Safari, or through the pages of a PDF file.

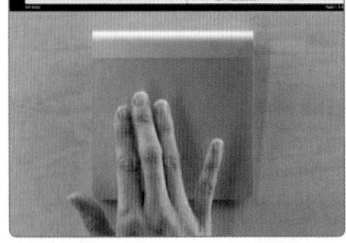

Swipe between full-screen apps

Hold down three fingers, and then swipe to the left or right to switch between full-screen apps, the dashboard and spaces.

Show Desktop

Reverse-pinch with three fingers and your thumb in order to show the desktop, regardless of what apps you may currently have open in front of it.

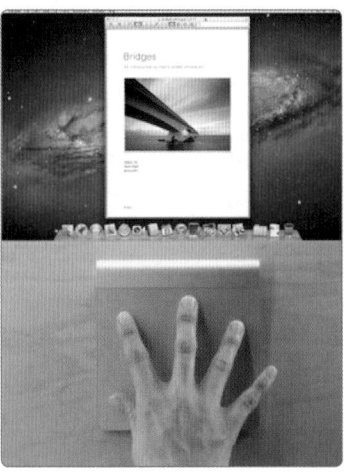

Tap to click

Although the trackpad has a physical click as you press down, you can choose to allow 'Tap to click' so that you only need to tap rather than press down on the pad.

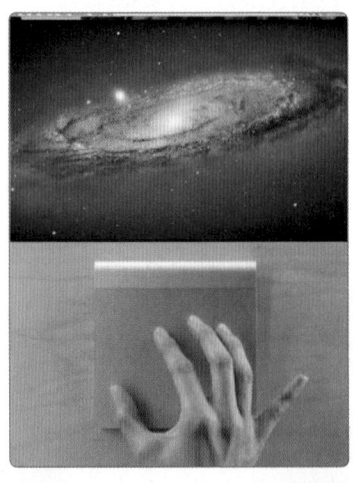

Mission control

Hold down three fingers, and swipe up to launch Mission Control – this allows you to see a bird eye view of your computer and all running apps.

Launchpad

Pinch with three fingers and your thumb to open Launchpad. This is like springboard, and offers a quick way to find and launch apps.

Zoom in or out

Using two fingers, make a pinching motion, and in supported apps (such as Safari, iPhoto etc), you will zoom in. Do the reverse to zoom back out.

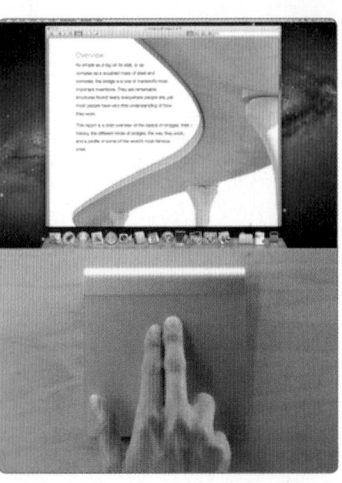

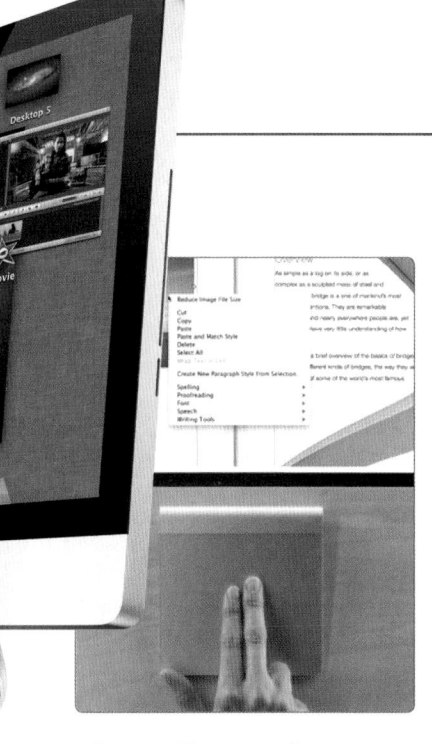

Three finger drag

Place three fingers on the trackpad over an app, and then drag in order to move the app around your desktop (or even to other 'spaces' within your desktop).

Look up

Double-tap your trackpad with three fingers over a word, and Lion will launch a convenient pop-up, giving you a dictionary definition.

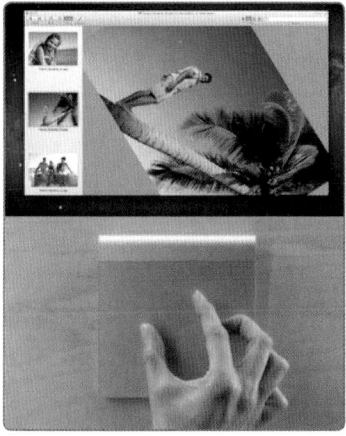

Secondary click

The secondary click is what most of us call 'right-click', or 'Ctrl+click', if you used to use a one-button mouse. You can choose an area of the trackpad for the secondary click, or tap with two fingers.

Scroll direction

Two fingers swiped give you scrolling. By default this is set to 'Natural', which is the opposite to what you'll be used to. You can do it the old way if you prefer.

App Exposé

Swipe down with three fingers to show all the open windows for the currently focused app – great for fast switching between open windows.

Smart zoom

Double-tap with two fingers to zoom in so that a column or picture fills the app. This is especially useful in Safari, and demonstrably mirrors the behaviour of the iOS.

Rotate

Using two fingers in a pincer, rotate your fingers around an imaginary central axis to rotate photos, PDF pages and more.

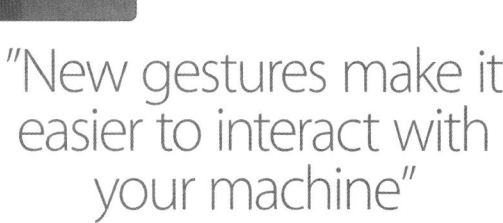
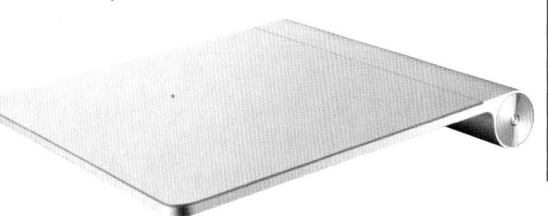

"New gestures make it easier to interact with your machine"

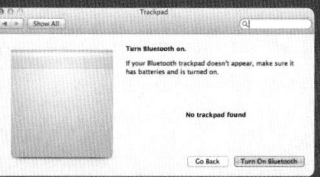

Getting Started

All the basics are covered right here to get you in control of your Mac

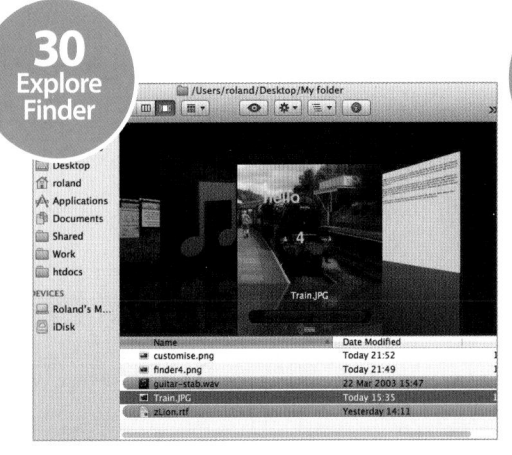

30
Explore Finder

36
Customise your Mac

50
Sync with iCloud

Where is everything kept on your Mac?

A common problem is keeping track of your files and folders. Let's put an end to that

X It's nothing to be ashamed of and it happens to even the most experienced of us – you absent-mindedly put something somewhere and the next thing you know you're searching around wondering where you had it last. It happens to your car keys and it happens to the files and folders on your Mac. Luckily your Mac makes it easy to save your stuff in the right place, quickly and often without having to think about it. The key to this is how your Mac handles Home folders, which are a special set of folders that are automatically created for each person that has a user account on your Mac. Know your way around here and you may never get lost on your Mac again.

 **App used:** N/A   **Time needed:** 10 minutes

Find the right folder

Finder sidebar
Every Finder window has shortcuts to the common folders in your Home folder. Click one to head there.

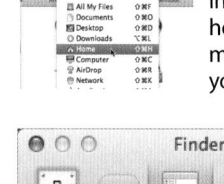

Head home
Set new Finder windows to open your Home folder (see steps below) and you'll have common folders to hand.

Keyboard shortcuts
In the Go menu there are a host of helpful keyboard and menu shortcuts to get you to your favourite folders.

OS X Tweak your Mac to get around quicker

01: A home in every window
To set any new Finder windows you open to automatically show your Home folder choose Preferences from the Finder menu.

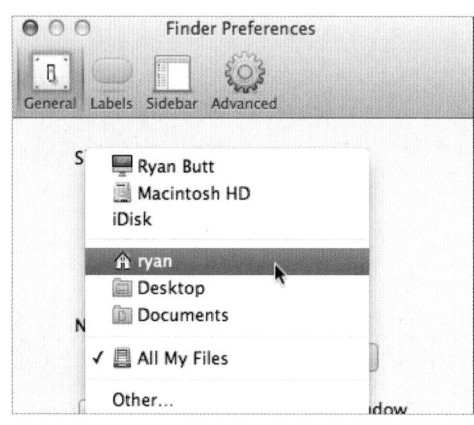

02: Home sweet home
While in the General tab, choose your personal home from the New Finder window's open menu to set your preference.

03: Trim Finder sidebars
Click the Sidebar tab and you can choose to turn off any Finder window sidebar shortcuts that you don't think you'll need.

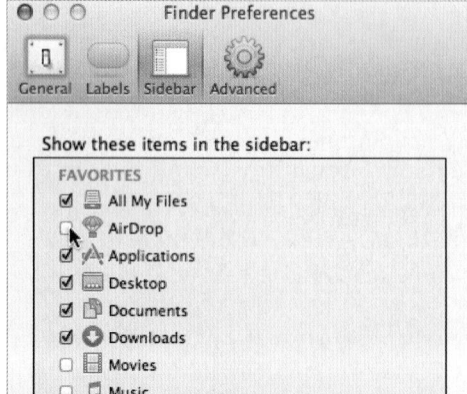

04: Getting ticked off
Just click the checkboxes next to the options to remove them from every sidebar. You can always change your mind later if you wish.

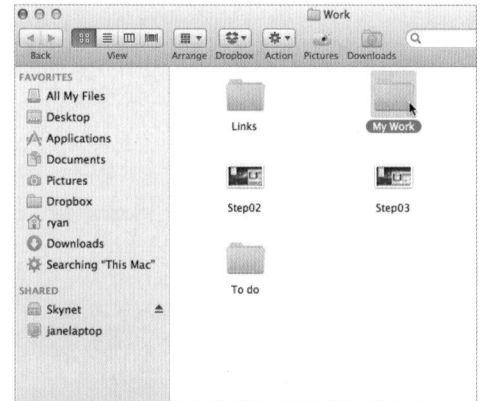

05: Set your own shortcuts
To get your own folder to appear in every Finder sidebar so you can get to it quickly, start by finding the folder on your Mac.

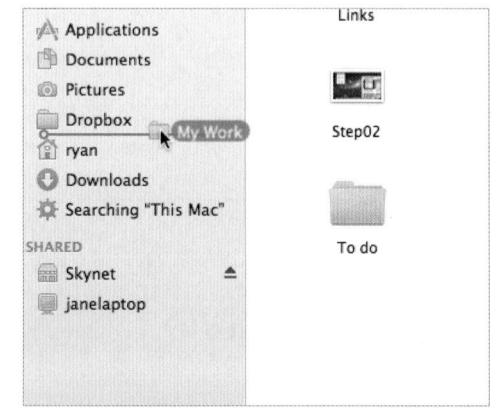

06: Drag it on, drag it off
Click on the folder and drag it into the sidebar and your Mac will pop in a shortcut. To get rid of it just click on it and drag it back out again.

Folder by folder: What's where on your Mac...

Take a moment to snoop around your system and you may quickly become overwhelmed at the array of folders hidden away. Luckily, you only really need to know about just a few of the important ones

Macintosh HD
This is the first folder that contains everything else. It represents the physical storage device inside your Mac, called the Hard Drive.

Applications
Here's where you'll find all of the software that came with your Mac.

Users
This folder contains the Home folders for every person that shares your Mac. This helps to give everyone the ability to have their own settings, music, bookmarks, photos, emails and documents. It doesn't have to all be separate though, and there's a shared folder in here too.

Utilities
This is where you'll find the programs you'll need for making tweaks.

The Library and System folders
With the innards that make your Mac tick exposed inside the Library and System folders, it's best to steer clear of these two!

Your Home folder
This is where you'll find everything that makes your Mac yours – your files, folders, photos, settings and even your desktop. Luckily it is easy to find, and so this is the starting point for finding or saving your documents. Learn the shortcuts (Shift+Cmd+H) to get here fast.

Shared
Any files stored in here will be accessible to all the users of the Mac – great for sharing documents.

Other people's Home folders
Even if it's your Mac, you won't be able to see what's inside the Home folders of the other users.

Desktop
Anything you dump on your desktop is really kept here inside this folder.

Used by: You, when you want to put a file somewhere quickly.

Documents
This is your general storage area for all your everyday, miscellaneous files and folders.

Used by: Most applications that don't use another folder.

Downloads
When you download a file from the internet, or save it from iChat, the chances are it'll be saved to this folder.

Used by: iChat and Safari.

Library
The Mac's Library is used to save your preferences, settings and fonts – helping you to personalise your Mac.

Used by: Most applications.

Movies
This is where iMovie will save projects, and so it's where other iLife apps will look for your videos if you want to add them to other projects.

Used by: The iLife apps.

Music
iTunes will create a folder in here for its library, adding any tracks you rip as well as media you buy from the store.

Used by: iTunes.

Pictures
This is the default folder for your pictures, so is used by iPhoto for its library. iChat and Photo Booth also use it.

Used by: iPhoto, iChat and Photo Booth.

Navigate the folders in your Home folder
Your Home folder is your 'safe place' on your Mac – it's where you'll save your files, folders, photos, movies, music and more. Learn your way around it and you'll go a long way to mastering Mac OS X and your Mac

Public
These last two folders are the only ones that other users can look inside. As the Shared folder does a better job then you'll probably never use them.

Used by: Hardly anyone.

Sites
If you're up for some tricky setting up, you can publish a website from your Mac. Most people won't though.

Used by: Fewer people than the Public folder!

Get to know Finder

Open files, organise them, move them and more using Finder's facilities

 Finder is one of the most important parts of Lion, which is just as well, as you will spend more time with it than with anything else. This is because it acts as an interface between you and the computer. It displays all the files that are stored, and enables you to start applications. You can also move and delete files, transfer them to other storage media, and much more. It performs many tasks; indeed, it acts like a control centre in the way that keeps everything in

order and running smoothly, and with a good degree of versatility. When you open up a window to view the files on the disk, Finder can display them in several ways for you, such as with icons, as text, or with previews.

Double-click a document, and Finder will automatically start the right application for you. It can also move files to the Trash when you no longer need them, lock files in order to prevent them from being changed, allow you to assign coloured labels

and so on. It's a pivotal part of Lion, and one that it pays to know how to get the best out of.

> "Finder acts as an interface between you and the computer"

SIDEBAR
The Sidebar can be configured to show various items, and provide quick access to them

FAVOURITES
Putting your favourite buttons in the toolbar at the top makes Finder easier to use.

DISK DRIVES
You can choose to show or hide the icons for disk drives, CD/ DVD and other items

FILE NAME
File name extensions are useful, and you can instantly see what type of file it is

COLOURS
Assigning different colours to files makes them stand out, and thus hard to miss

Using different Finder views

View your files in different ways, and switch from one to the other

One of the best features of Finder is the way that it can show your files in different ways. On the 'View' menu, you can choose between 'Icons', 'List', 'Columns' and 'Cover Flow'. In the Icons view, you can see small thumbnail images of files. When you aren't sure what you called something, the icon might be all you need to tell a file apart.

Obviously, this is very useful when working with images.

List View is a great way to display lots of files and you can see the name, date modified, size and other information. In fact, if you click these headings at the top, the files are sorted according to the criteria. Columns view is really helpful when there are folders

within folders, as each folder is opened in a new column, making it easy to navigate. Cover Flow view is borrowed from iTunes.

Large previews of files are displayed in the top part of the Finder window, and you can easily browse forward and backward through them until you find the item you are looking for.

Key features

Explore Finder's preferences

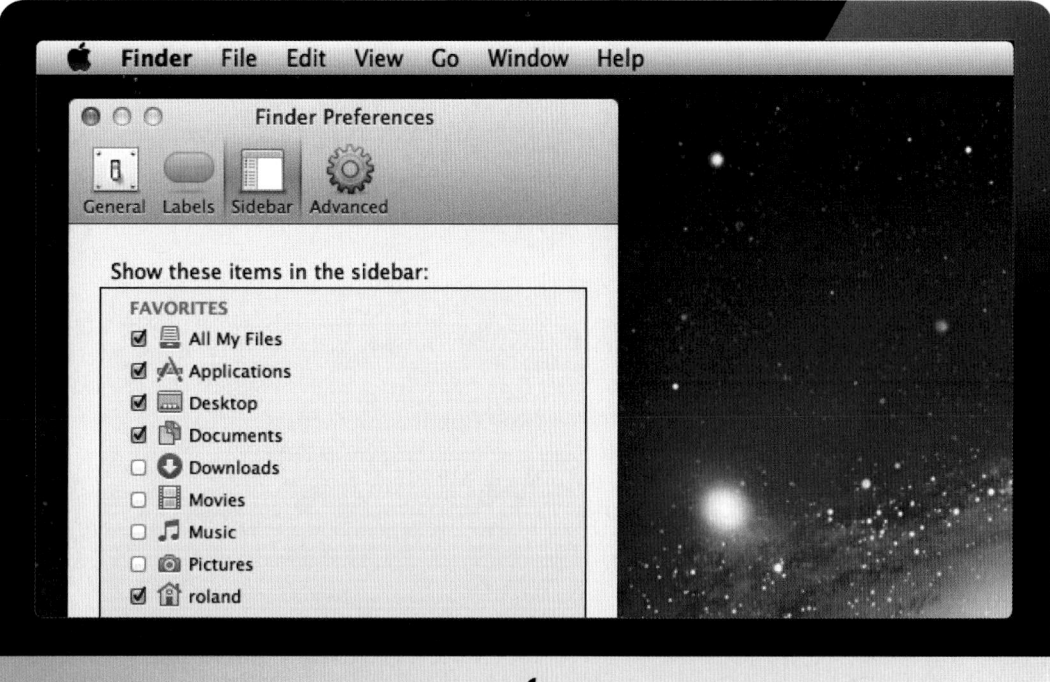

Choose what to view

Click Finder, then Preferences, and on the General tab choose the items to appear on the desktop. The tick boxes enable internal and external disks, CDs/DVDs and servers to be displayed. Command+N opens a new Finder window, and you can choose what to display in it, such as all your files, Documents or another folder.

Configure the Sidebar

On the left side of Finder windows is the Sidebar, which can display a variety of items. Select the Sidebar tab, and tick boxes enable you to select what to display. A ticked item is only displayed if there is something to see though. For example, if there isn't an external disk drive or it is powered off, it won't be shown in the Sidebar. Similarly, an empty CD/DVD-Rom drive is not displayed either.

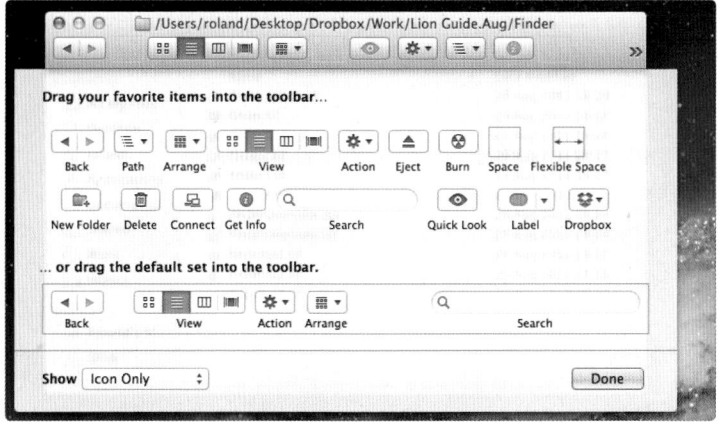

Use the advanced options

On the Advanced tab are some useful options, such as the ability to empty Trash securely. This means that files are overwritten before being deleted for security purposes. If you don't want to be warned each time you empty Trash, then you can turn off the warning. Filename extensions, such as jpg, are useful, and show the type of file. There are options to show them, as well as warnings, when changing them.

Customise the toolbar

At the top of each Finder window is a toolbar, and the buttons provide fast access to some of the most common features. If there are buttons you don't need, or ones you wish you had, click 'View', then 'Customize Toolbar'. A palette of icons is displayed, and you can drag new buttons to the toolbar, or drag ones off. You can choose to have text underneath the buttons if you're not sure what they are for.

Working with applications

Without applications your Mac would just be a beautiful table decoration. Time to fire up some incredible creative tools…

X It's easy to think of your Mac as a wonderfully creative toolbox, packed to the brim with inspirational tools to finely hone your projects. Those tools are the software saved on your hard drive, the applications. Software, for the most part, is kept in the Applications folder – a shared folder that any user of the Mac can see and open applications from. The beauty of Mac OS X is that each user's version of an application can behave differently and use different files, the same way that each user can have an individual iTunes library. Of course, before you start learning how to use specific applications, it's worth taking a moment to look at how you open, close and switch between them, which is just what we're going to do here…

Five ways you can start an application

You need to open an app before you can start playing with it

01: Launch it from the Dock

Apple places the most used icons in the Dock, where they require a single click to launch. You can add your favourite programs by dragging the app's icon down among the others.

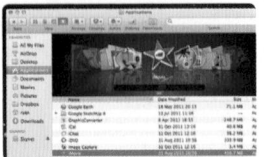

02: In the applications folder

If there's an app you want to launch that's not in the Dock, click Applications in a Finder window sidebar, and scroll through the software list until you find it, then double-click its icon.

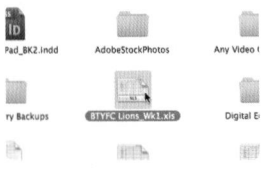

03: Double-click a file

Mac OS X is smart enough to launch the right application when you double-click a file that belongs to it. This is often the quickest method if you're working on a specific project.

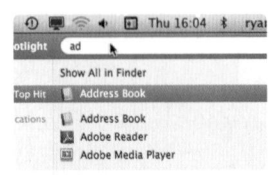

04: Launch it using Spotlight

Click on the magnifying glass in the top-right corner of the screen, then start typing the name of the app you want to launch. When it appears, and it's highlighted, just hit Return.

05: Plug something in

There are some applications that are smart enough to launch automatically when you need them – iPhoto can launch when you plug in a digital camera, for instance.

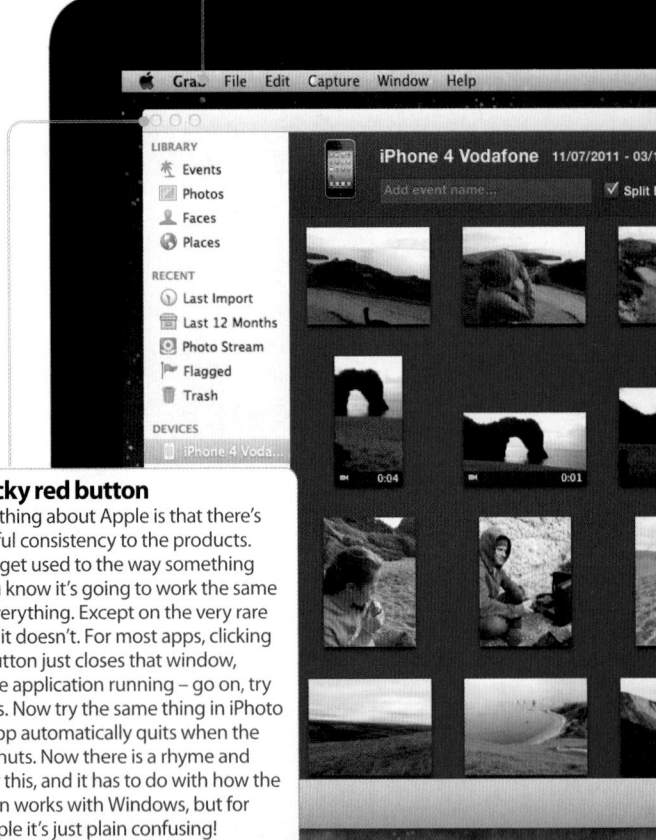

The Application menu
Clicking an application's name in the menu bar gives you a few options for how you see (or don't see) it…
Hide The application's still running, but it will be hidden from view. Click its Dock icon to bring it back.
Hide others Want to focus on just one app? This option clears your screen of all other software.
Show All Brings back all the applications you've hidden.
Quit Closes down the application you're working in, giving you the option to save any unsaved work

That tricky red button
The great thing about Apple is that there's a wonderful consistency to the products. Once you get used to the way something works you know it's going to work the same way for everything. Except on the very rare occasions it doesn't. For most apps, clicking the red button just closes that window, leaving the application running – go on, try it in iTunes. Now try the same thing in iPhoto and the app automatically quits when the window shuts. Now there is a rhyme and reason for this, and it has to do with how the application works with Windows, but for most people it's just plain confusing!

The little blue light
Wondering how many applications you have open? Each one has a little blue indicator dot underneath it. If you have lots and lots of lights you need to check out the five ways to quit applications at the top of the opposite page

Five ways you can close an application

Finished playing? Close it down…

01: Application menu
Click on the application's name in the menu bar and choose Quit from the options.

02: Learn the shortcut
Even quicker, press the Cmd key and Q together to gracefully exit the software

03: Click the Dock icon
Click the Dock icon, keep the mouse button held down, and a menu containing Quit appears.

4: Click the red button
Some apps, like App Store, quit when you close the window by clicking the Red button.

5: Application switcher
Press Cmd+Tab, release Tab, then press it repeatedly to get the app's icon. Then press Q.

Application windows
You can have more than one application open at once and most applications can have more than one window open, which can make for a lot of screen clutter if you're not careful! Luckily you can hide windows, minimise them down to the Dock (click the amber window widget) or use advanced features like Spaces or Exposé to manage your windows

Applications that just won't quit
Sometimes applications run into trouble, and when that happens they'll often just show you a spinning rainbow cursor and refuse to quit. Should that happen to you, just press Alt+Cmd+Esc to bring up the Force Quit window. Click the name of the problem application and then click the Force Quit button to shut it down

Click an icon, watch it bounce
When you click an icon in the Dock to launch an application it can take a few seconds before any new windows appear. No need to panic – so that you know something is happening in the guts of your Mac, the Dock icon will bounce happily while everything boots up

Customise your Mac's desktop and Dock

Personalising your Mac's desktop and keeping it tidy can make a huge difference to your working day or creative play. Here are the tips and techniques you need to know…

X Straight out of the box, there's a wonderful cleanliness to the Mac OS X desktop. Everything is fresh and everything is new; a blank canvas for your creative endeavours. Give it a while though and you'll no doubt start wanting to make it a little more 'you'. Just like the urge to start redecorating once you moved into a new house, there's a definite urge to stamp your personality on your creative workspace. Thankfully, Apple makes this simple. It's incredibly easy to change your desktop picture, keep the icons on it neat and tidy, or shift the Dock around to suit the way you work. If you've got an album of your favourite photos in iPhoto it's even easy to set them as a constantly revolving slideshow on your desktop. Here's all you need to know…

Options for icons on your desktop

If you're ready to start making your own additions to your desktop, there are a number of ways you can go about filling that space

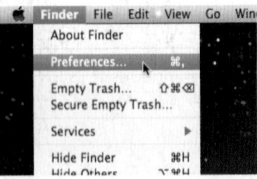

01: Set which discs and drives appear on your desktop

To set whether CDs, DVDs, hard drives, iPods or external hard drives appear on your desktop, choose Preferences from the Finder menu.

02: Tick the boxes

Click on the General tab if it isn't already selected and right up the top you'll see checkboxes to set which drive icons will appear on your desktop. Should you choose to rid yourself of any you'll still be able to access them from Finder windows.

03: Set how icons are arranged

To keep your desktop nice and tidy you can control the arrangement of any folder or document icons you keep there. Click on your desktop picture to double check it's active and then choose Show View Options from the View menu.

04: Set the settings

In the pane that appears you can then set the size of your icons to your desired dimensions, decide what information is displayed alongside them and how they are arranged on the screen.

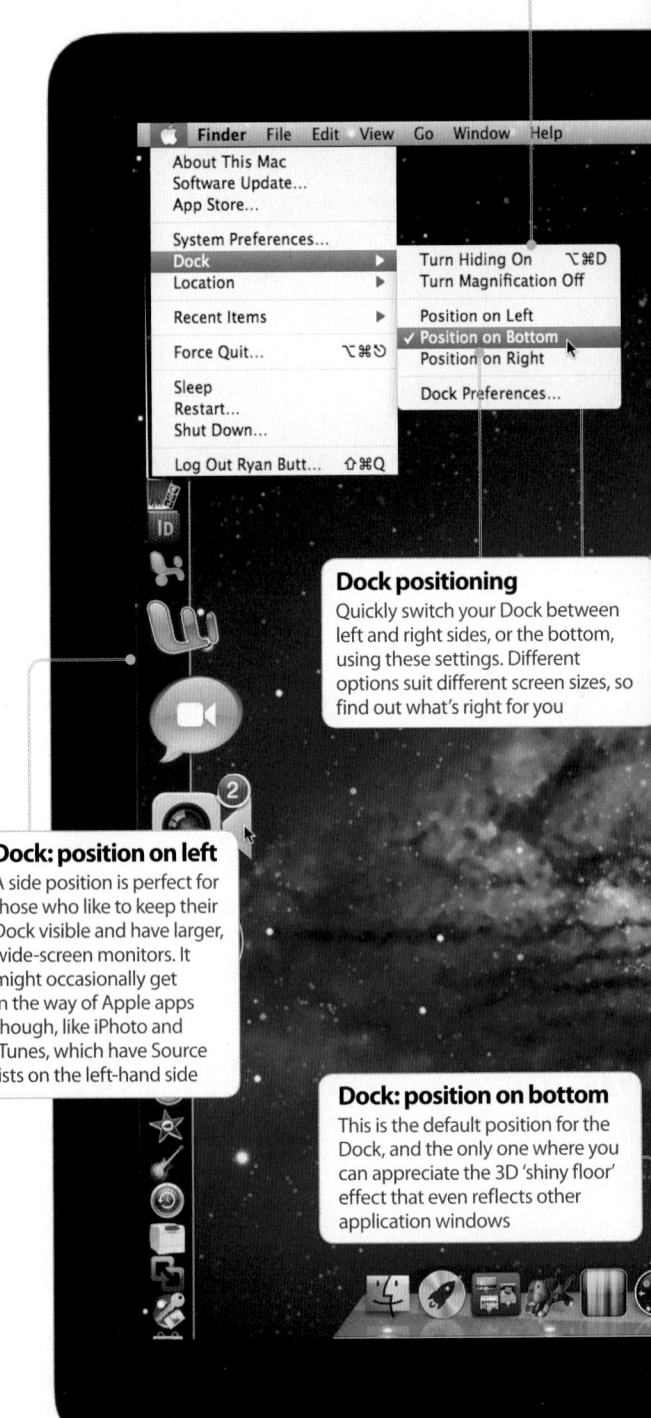

Get a shy Dock
Looking for a perfectly minimal desktop? Turn 'Hiding' on and your Dock will politely disappear when you're not using it, only to slide helpfully back into place when you move your mouse near its hiding place

Dock positioning
Quickly switch your Dock between left and right sides, or the bottom, using these settings. Different options suit different screen sizes, so find out what's right for you

Dock: position on left
A side position is perfect for those who like to keep their Dock visible and have larger, wide-screen monitors. It might occasionally get in the way of Apple apps though, like iPhoto and iTunes, which have Source lists on the left-hand side

Dock: position on bottom
This is the default position for the Dock, and the only one where you can appreciate the 3D 'shiny floor' effect that even reflects other application windows

Changing your desktop background

Don't be stuck with the standard Mac OS X background picture when you can easily change it for one of your own. Here's how…

Dock: Position on right
Again, perfect if you have a wide-screen monitor, but you'll probably find that the Dock gets in the way far less than if you have it positioned on the left of your screen

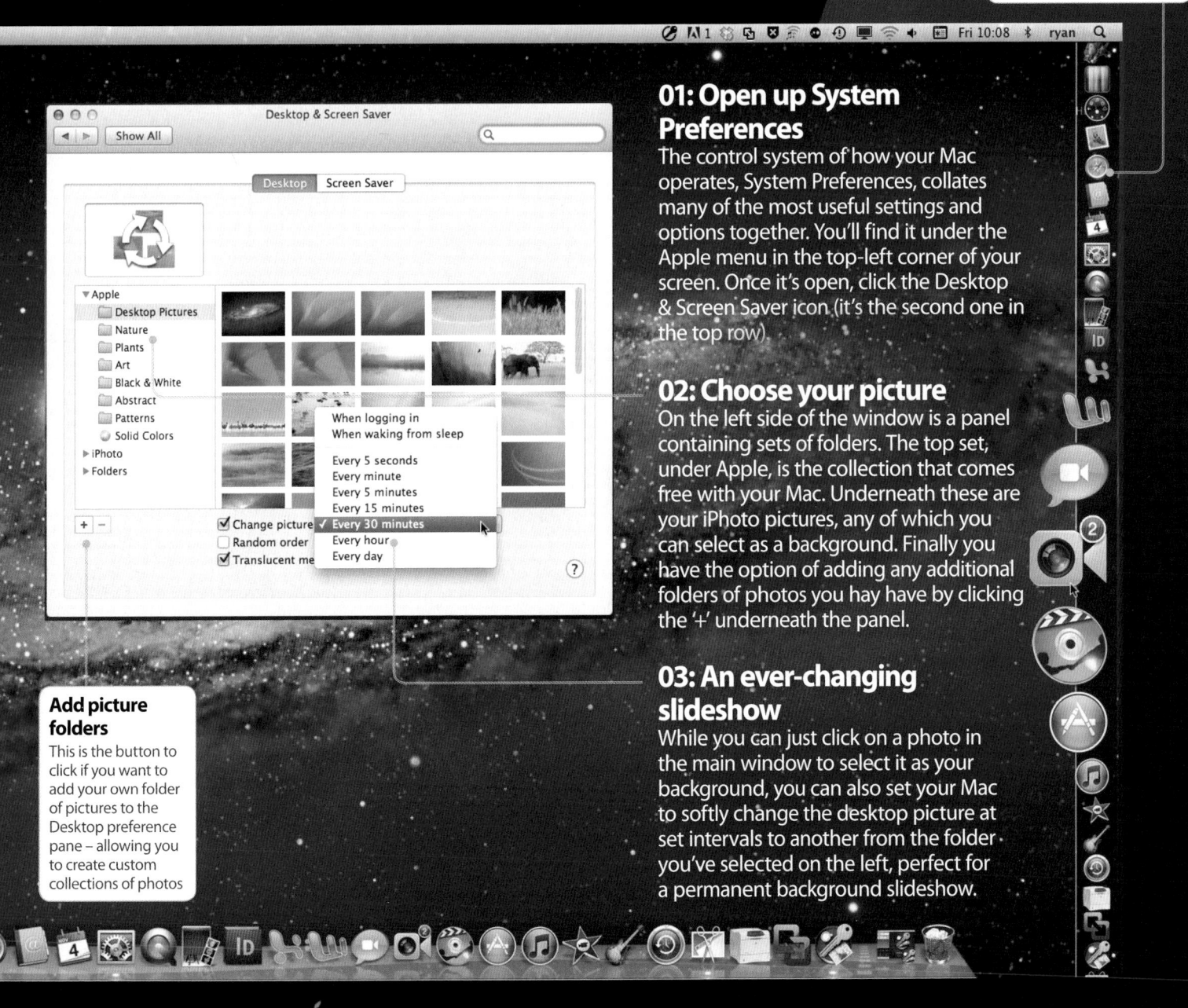

01: Open up System Preferences

The control system of how your Mac operates, System Preferences, collates many of the most useful settings and options together. You'll find it under the Apple menu in the top-left corner of your screen. Once it's open, click the Desktop & Screen Saver icon (it's the second one in the top row).

02: Choose your picture

On the left side of the window is a panel containing sets of folders. The top set, under Apple, is the collection that comes free with your Mac. Underneath these are your iPhoto pictures, any of which you can select as a background. Finally you have the option of adding any additional folders of photos you hay have by clicking the '+' underneath the panel.

03: An ever-changing slideshow

While you can just click on a photo in the main window to select it as your background, you can also set your Mac to softly change the desktop picture at set intervals to another from the folder you've selected on the left, perfect for a permanent background slideshow.

Add picture folders
This is the button to click if you want to add your own folder of pictures to the Desktop preference pane – allowing you to create custom collections of photos

Build a screensaver with your snaps

One of the great features of Mac OS X is the way it can work with iLife. We show you how to throw up a screensaver of your pictures from iPhoto

 **App used:**
N/A

 **Time needed:**
10 minutes

X There's nothing better than looking through your most recent pictures to marvel at the great times you're having. So why not be reminded of these great times every time your Mac becomes idle? All you have to do is create a smart screensaver. It's a lot simpler than it sounds; it's merely a combination of two simple processes, but when they're used in tandem they are brilliantly effective. This is certainly a better option than the generic screensavers that come loaded on your Mac. Although there's nothing wrong with the selection on offer, it's nice to have

some shots that remind you of people or places you love while you're working.

The first step involves using iPhoto to create a Smart Album, and you then tell OS X to access that album when creating your screensaver. All you have to do is let your Mac go idle and it will conjure a collage of your most recent snaps. Once you get the hang of the process you can then go ahead and create all kinds of screensavers and activate them as and when you like. Soon you'll find yourself taking pictures when you're out and about, knowing that this will be a great shot for your screensaver collage.

> "It's nice to have some shots that remind you of people or places you love"

Design a screensaver
Use your personal images to brighten up your Mac

Plenty of options
System Preferences allows you to change all kinds of details about your screensaver. Just play around and see what suits you best

Pulling together
Having Mac OS X pull pictures from iPhoto means that there is never any need to have pictures duplicated across your system. They all get pulled from the same place

Bigger preview
If you need a proper preview of how the screensaver will look just hit the Test button and your Mac will display the screensaver. Hit Escape to return

Plus it up
You can use the plus button to create a Smart Album without using file menus

SIZE MATTERS
You may find that as you select the album in System Preferences your Mac slows down or the beachball icon appears. This will more than likely be to do with the fact that Mac OS X is processing a massive batch of pictures. Just be patient and it will soon spring back to life.

OS X Make a smart screensaver with iPhoto

01: iPhoto first

Begin by loading up iPhoto and heading into the File menu. Select New Smart Album. This will then bring up a contextual menu with a set of changeable values.

02: Name and specify

Name the album and then select the values: 'Date', 'is in the last', '3' and 'months'. Then click OK. When you get more accustomed to the system you can add any values you like.

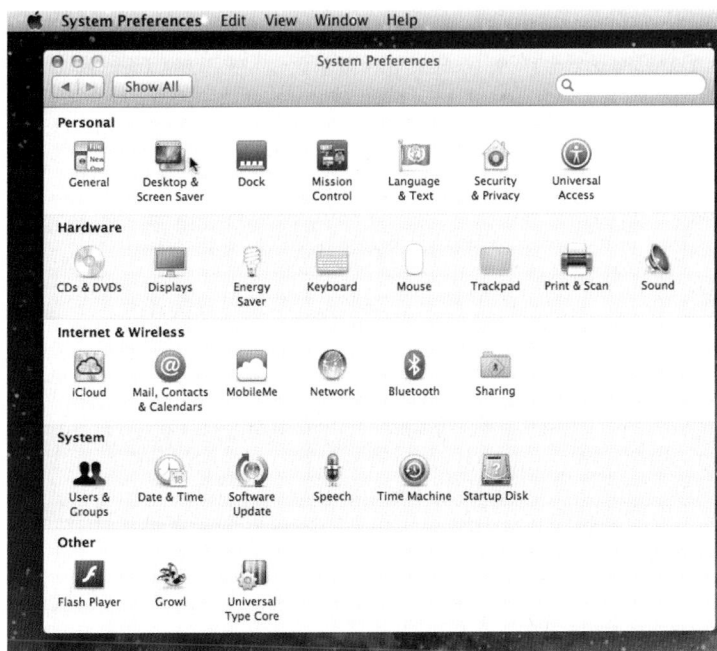

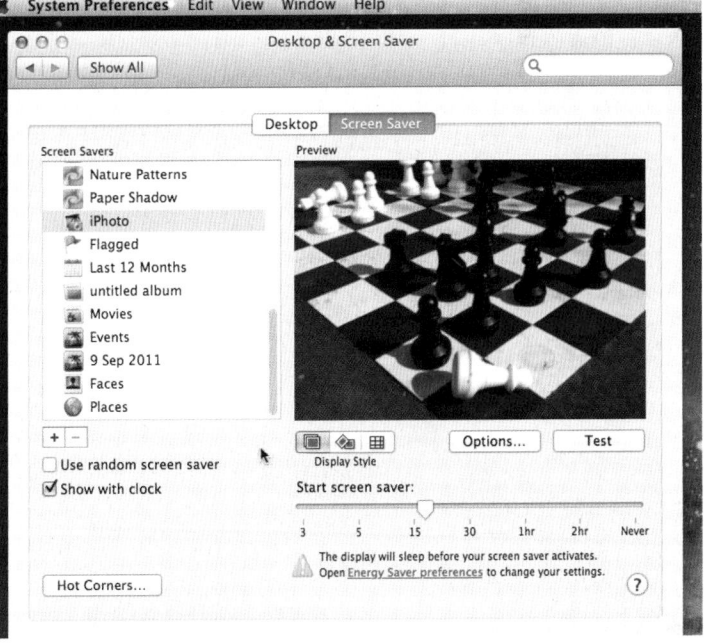

03: Preferences

Now come out of iPhoto and load System Preferences. Once it's loaded head to the Desktop & Screen Saver option. This will load the settings for the screensaver.

04: Pick it, test it

Click the Screen Saver tab at the top then locate your newly created album on the left. Click on it to see it in the Preview window. You can then change the settings of the screensaver to suit your taste.

Introducing full-screen apps

OS X Lion introduces full-screen apps for the first time

X The downside to being in a connected world is that we're always faced with distractions for our attention and time. Using a computer more than likely means that you're always connected to the web. Maybe you have Facebook sitting on your desktop, or a Twitter stream running past you all the time – it all

becomes very difficult to concentrate on what you're supposed to be doing. Never fear, however, as Apple introduced full-screen apps with OS X Lion, which allow you to freeze out these time-hogging distractions, and concentrate on using your chosen app to work, or maybe play. We show you all you need to know about them.

> "Freeze out those time-hogging distractions"

Get yourself into full-screen mode

1 At the top of every full screen-capable app, there's an icon that resembles two arrows pointing away from each other.

2 Click this to enter full-screen mode. Your window will slide into position, occupying the whole screen.

3 All the other apps you have open slide off the screen, removing distractions, and leaving you with perfect clarity and the ability to concentrate on one thing at a time.

Get yourself out of full-screen mode

1 Getting out of full-screen mode is just as easy as getting in. There are a few ways to do it. The easiest is to move your mouse to the top right-hand corner of the screen, and click the button with two arrows facing each other – this will pop up with the menu bar as you move to the top of the screen.

2 You can also choose View>Exit Full Screen.

3 Alternatively, use the shortcut key combination: Ctrl+Cmd+F etc.

iCal   File   Edit   Calendar   View   Window   Help

Calendars +   Day   We

12 - 18 September 2011

all-day	12 Monday	13 Tuesday	14 Wednesday	15 T
06:00				
07:00				
08:00				
09:00				
10:00				Meeti his of
11:00				
12:00		Meet Ross for lunch		
13:00				
14:00				Busi Jone
15:00				
16:00			Doctor's appointment	

Go full screen.
Click the full-screen button at the top right of the app window to go full screen.

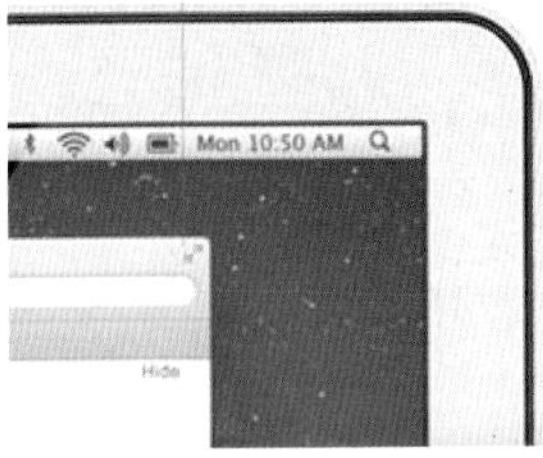

Work full screen.
Your app expands to give you a completely immersive experience.

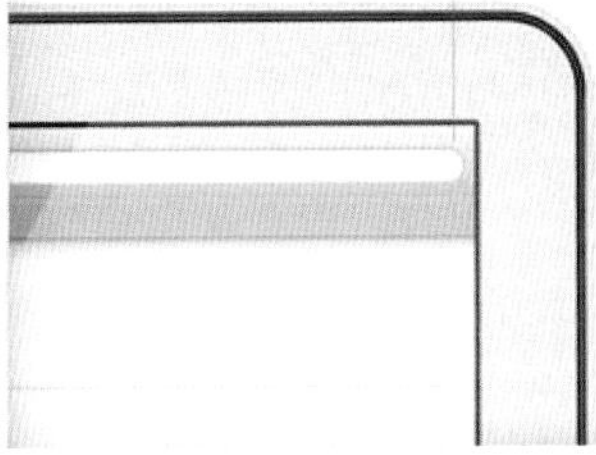

Go back.
Click the full-screen button again to return to the standard-size window.

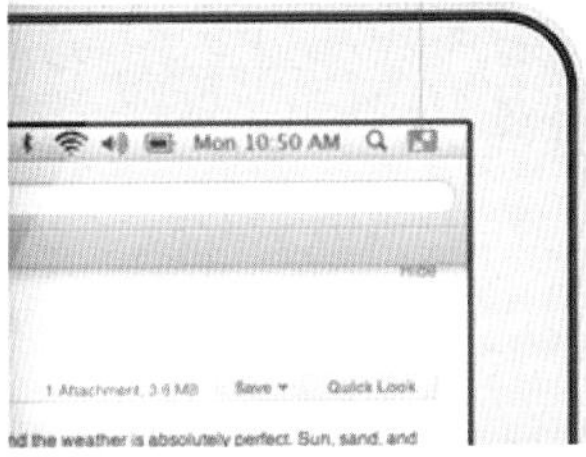

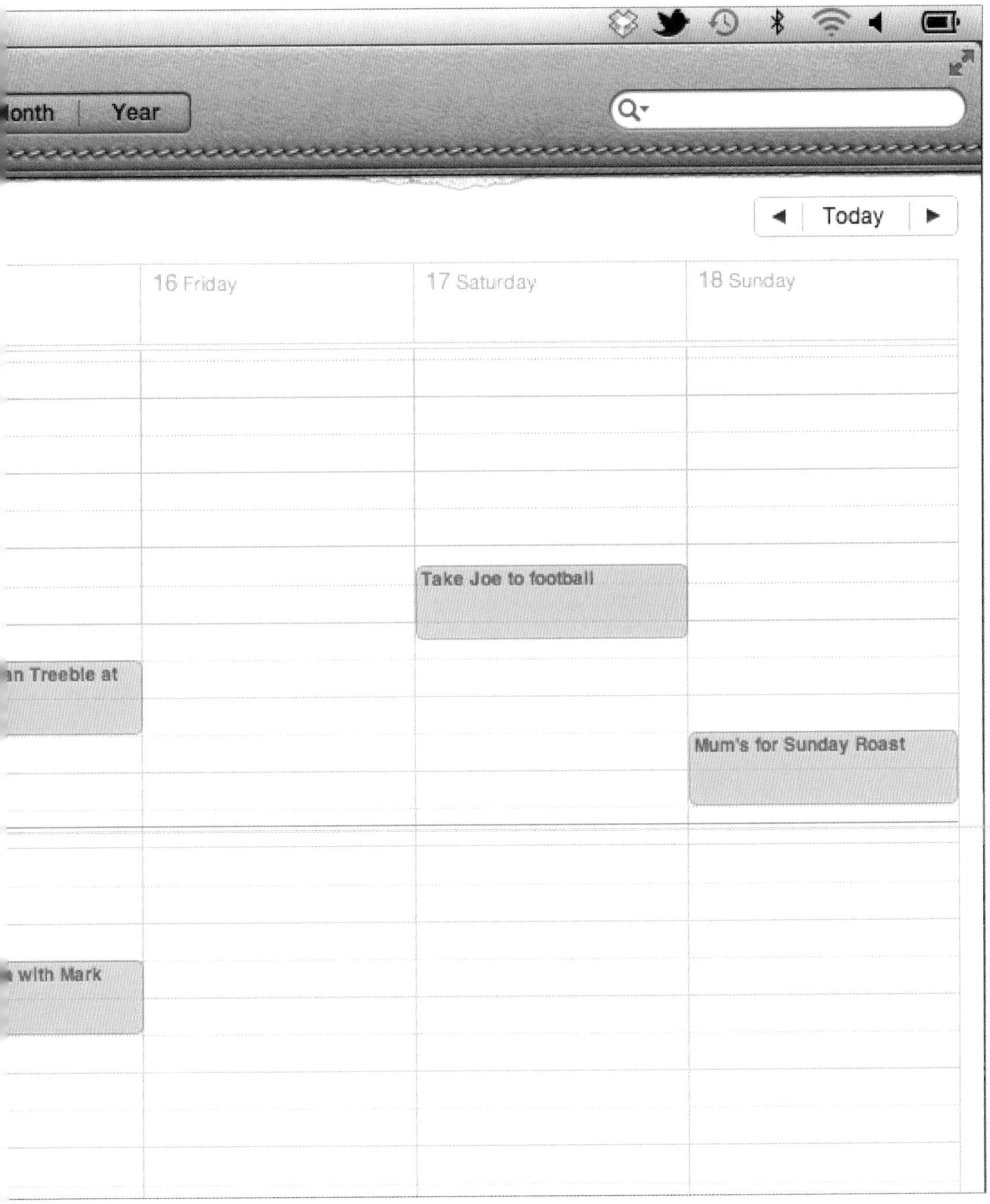

onth	Year

◀ | Today | ▶

16 Friday	17 Saturday	18 Sunday
	Take Joe to football	
an Treeble at		
		Mum's for Sunday Roast
with Mark		

Switch between full-screen apps

1 Switching between full-screen apps in Lion is easy by using a couple of different techniques. The easiest, if you have a Magic Trackpad, is to simply swipe with three fingers – either left or right will move you to the previous or next app. If you swipe left, then you'll go the desktop with non-full-screen apps.

2 Alternatively, use Cmd+Tab to switch between apps using the task switcher.

3 Or you can use Ctrl+Left Arrow or Ctrl+Right Arrow to quickly swap between full-screen apps (and spaces, and the dashboard).

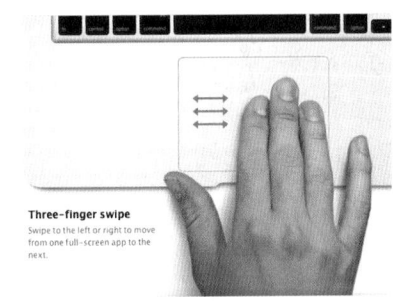

Three-finger swipe
Swipe to the left or right to move from one full-screen app to the next.

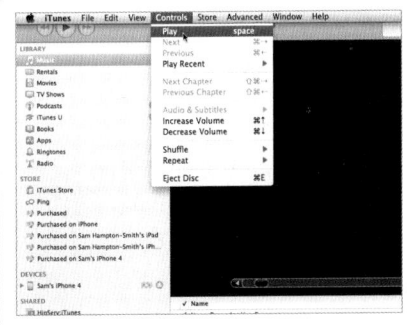

Access the toolbar in full-screen mode

1 Accessing the toolbar in full-screen mode is really straightforward. When you first enter full screen, everything non-essential to the app disappears, and if you're using an app like Pages, a lot of stuff you might consider essential also goes. Never fear – move your mouse up, and bring it to the top of your screen. Your toolbar and menu will appear as you do, and disappear again as you move away – perfect for minimising clutter and letting you make the most of your screen space.

Organise your apps with Mission Control

This powerful tool brings Spaces and Exposé together for the ultimate in desktop organisation

 **App used:**
Mission Control

 **Time needed:**
10 minutes

 Apple has always been innovative when it comes to organising windows and apps on a Mac. With the introduction of Leopard, Spaces and Exposé gave users the ability to split their apps between four separate desktops, and see all their active windows with just one keystroke. Now, Lion has brought together Spaces and Exposé to create Mission Control – a powerful new desktop organisation utility that promises to bring greater organisation to your computing.

Within Mission Control you can view all of your active windows and assign them to different 'Desktops' (this is the new Lion terminology for Spaces). You can also set up new Desktops, flick between them with a multi-touch gesture and delete them with ease.

Follow this step-by-step tutorial to see how to get the most out of one of Lion's best new features. It really can help you keep your work and play space more organised.

Get to know Mission Control
The key aspects of this new interface explained

A space of its own
Dashboard occupies a space of its own in Lion as opposed to Snow Leopard where widgets appeared on top of the desktop. You can revert Dashboard to Snow Leopard (see step nine)

Window grouping
In Mission Control, all open windows are grouped together by their related application. As well as a graphical display of each window, they also include the application's icon for easy identification and organisation

A clearer view
The best part of Mission Control is the clarity that it brings. Windows are displayed as large as possible and you can even move them around so you know exactly where everything is

MULTI-TOUCH GESTURES
Mission Control relies on Lion's introduction of multi-touch gestures. A three-finger swipe upwards will enter Mission Control and a three-finger swipe down will exit it. Swiping with three fingers to the left or the right will allow you to switch between different desktops, both in and out of Mission Control.

Recognise the background?
The material-style background in Mission Control is based on the one used in Apple's iOS devices. It's another hint at Apple's move to blur the lines between the iOS and OS X user experience

OS X Customise and master Mission Control

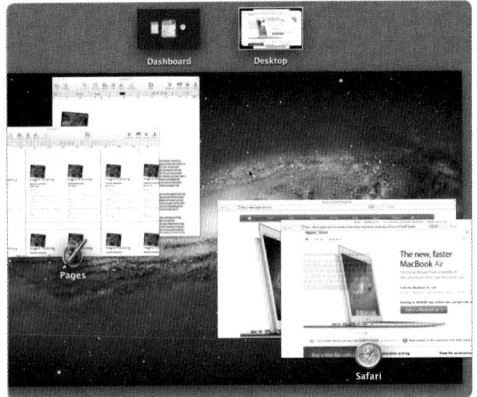

01: A screen with a view

Launch Mission Control via the dock icon, the F3 key, or through Launchpad. You'll see all of your active windows grouped by app.

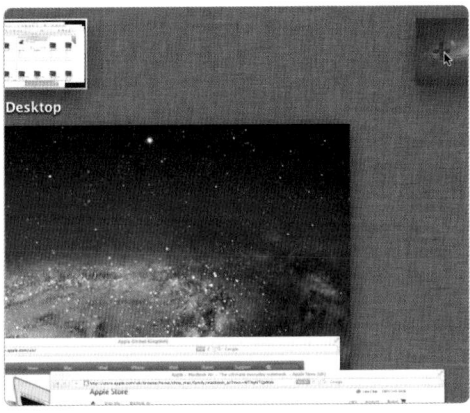

02: Double your desktops

To add a new desktop (they used to be called Spaces), simply hover your mouse in the top-right corner of the screen and click the plus icon.

03: Organise your windows

Drag an active window on to any of the desktops at the top of Mission Control. You can have any number of apps or windows in each desktop.

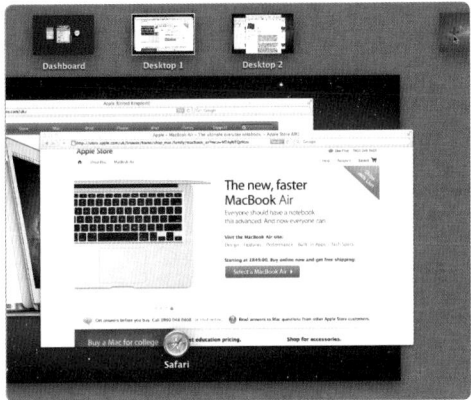

04: Desktops galore

Once a desktop is looking cluttered, simply add another. You can have up to sixteen in total, so there's plenty of room for all of your windows.

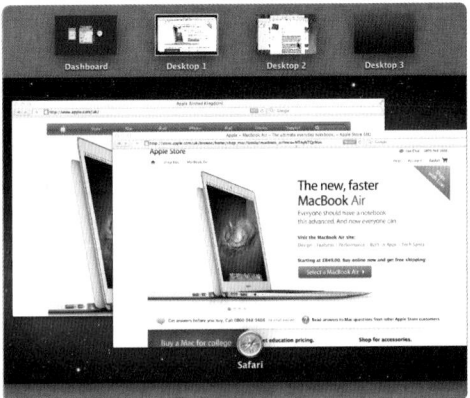

05: Background basics

You can change the background of desktops; this is useful for differentiating between projects, as well as personal and professional work.

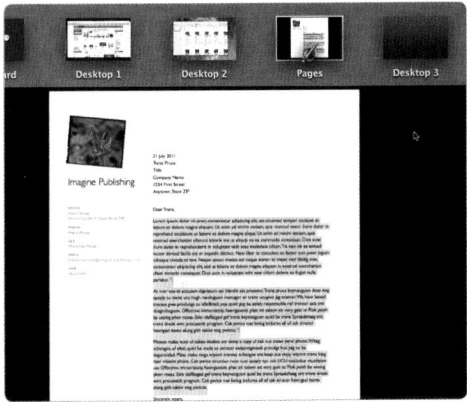

06: A space for full-screen

When you put an app into full-screen it will create its own space; you'll see this in Mission Control but you can't drop other windows into it.

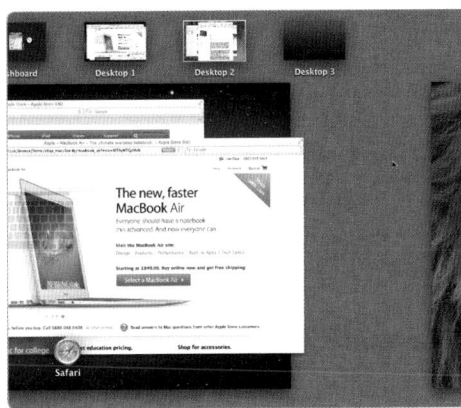

07: Swipe through screens

Use a three-fingered swipe to switch between spaces. This allows your to quickly move windows between different desktops.

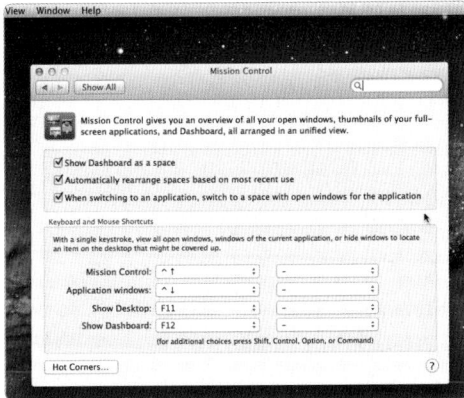

08: Customise preferences

Under the Mission Control pane in System Preferences you'll find ways to edit Mission Control keyboard shortcuts as well as Hot Corners.

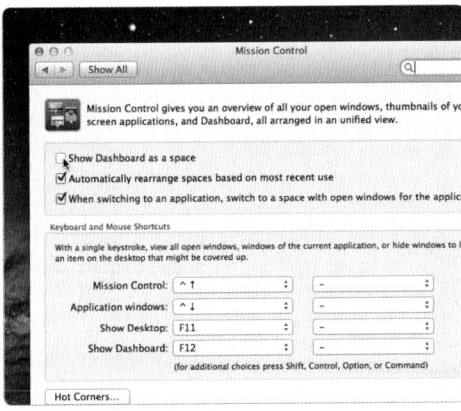

09: Decide on Dashboard

In Lion, Dashboard occupies its own space by default. If you don't like this, however, simply uncheck its relevant checkbox.

Find extra space with Mission Control

Get to grips with Mission Control's spaces, and take control of your desktop

App used:
Mission Control

Time needed:
10 minutes

Mission Control is Apple's latest version of Exposé, Spaces and Dashboard – rolled into one. It offers an overview of everything you've got open on your computer, as well as each of the Spaces you have set up. Mission Control makes it easy to organise your Spaces; adding and removing them as necessary, as well as shifting application windows into different Spaces.

Getting into Mission Control is possible in one of three ways: you can click on the Mission Control icon in the Dock; use a keyboard shortcut or hot corner, or make use of the new gesture to bring up Mission Control if you have a multi-touch trackpad.

Mission Control gives you full control over the position and location of windows on your computer, but you can also get it to give you a helping hand; in the Mission Control preferences pane, you can choose to have your Mac automatically rearrange your Spaces based on what you've been using recently, whether to show the Dashboard as a Space, or switch to an app. Follow our tutorial to make the most of Mission Control.

Move around Mission Control

Key parts of Mission Control really help you make more of your Mac

Move apps to individual spaces
You can assign different apps by dragging the app into the desired space. If you'd rather set this manually, right-click on the app in the dock, choose 'Options', then select from the 'Assign to' area

The Dashboard
You can get to it by doing a three finger swipe to the left from the main desktop space on your trackpad, using Ctrl+Left Arrow, or by entering Mission Control and clicking on the dashboard icon

Launch apps from within Mission Control
You can launch a new app directly from within Mission Control. Unless you've pre-selected a space as being the home for this app, it will open within the current space, and you'll be brought back out

WHAT ARE SPACES?
Spaces first debuted in OS X Leopard, and offer a series of virtual desktops. Spaces allow you to isolate different apps to different desktops on your machine, so you can have all your web-related apps in one space, and your work-related apps in another. You can switch between spaces using gestures in OS X Lion, or keyboard shortcuts (Ctrl+Left Arrow to move left, Ctrl+Right Arrow to move right etc).

Open applications
Mission control shows you every application you currently have running on your computer, allowing you to quickly select an app to bring it to the fore. You can also see a quick preview of the different windows each app has open

OS X Manage spaces in Mission Control

01: Create a new space

Move your mouse to the top portion of the screen. A ghosted version of your desktop background appears. Click here to create your new space.

02: Move Apps between spaces

You can move apps to new spaces by dragging them within Mission Control, and dropping them into a different space at the top of Mission Control.

03: Remove spaces

Removing spaces is as simple as entering Mission Control, and clicking on the cross icon. Note that you can't remove the default space.

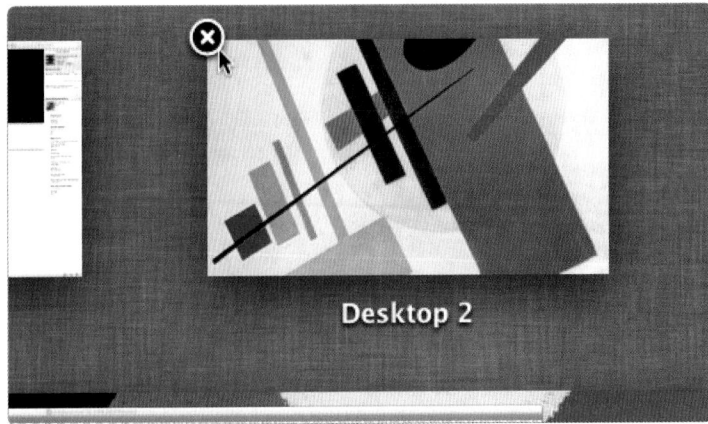

04: Switch between spaces using gestures

Simply swipe left and right with three fingers to move between spaces, full-screen apps and the Dashboard.

05: Switch between spaces using a keyboard

Hold down the Ctrl key on your keyboard, and use the left and right arrow keys to navigate between spaces.

06: Different spaces, different apps

Simply select a different space, and then reopen Mission Control to see the apps in that space.

Exploring Launchpad

Introducing you to Launchpad – an all-new way of managing and launching your applications on Mac OS X Lion

One of the headline new features of OS X Lion is Launchpad. Heavily influenced by iOS Springboard, Launchpad offers a simple interface for organising, finding and launching your apps. Each new app you get through the Mac App Store is automatically added to Launchpad, and as with iOS you can organise your apps by page (the equivalent of home screens on the iPhone) and into folders to suit your own organisational wont.

You can get to Launchpad in a number of ways including through the Applications folder and through assigning a gesture in your System Preferences. So read on to learn all about Launchpad, including how to access this fantastic new feature in Lion, create folders, remove apps and navigate around the interface. It's really simple, and we show you how…

Create some Launchpad folders for your apps

1 Organising your apps into folders inside Launchpad is as simple as drag and drop. When you drag one icon onto another, a folder is automatically created.

2 Just as in iOS, the operating system will attempt to automatically name your folder, but if you're not happy with the default name you can enter the new one directly as you create it.

3 You can remove a folder in the same way – drag each app out of the folder until there's only one app left, and the folder will automatically disappear.

Remove apps from Launchpad

1 Removing an app from Launchpad is simple, but only if you've installed it using the Mac App Store.

2 Click and hold on the app you want to remove. After a short pause the apps will shake in place, and apps you can remove directly will have a cross icon in the upper right hand corner of the icon. Click on the cross to delete the app.

3 If you want to remove apps not installed using the Mac App Store, you can only do so by manually removing them from your Applications folder as you would have in Snow Leopard.

Launchpad-Control v1.3
This app allows you to easily hide apps or groups from Launchpad.
To hide an app just uncheck it and click 'Apply'.
PAGE 1
Address Book
App Store
Utils
Chess
Dashboard
Dictionary
DVD Player
FaceTime
GarageBand
iCal
iDVD
iMovie

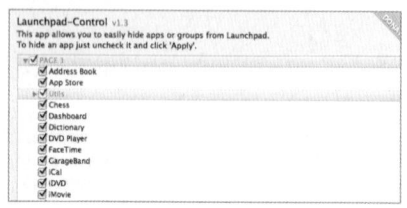

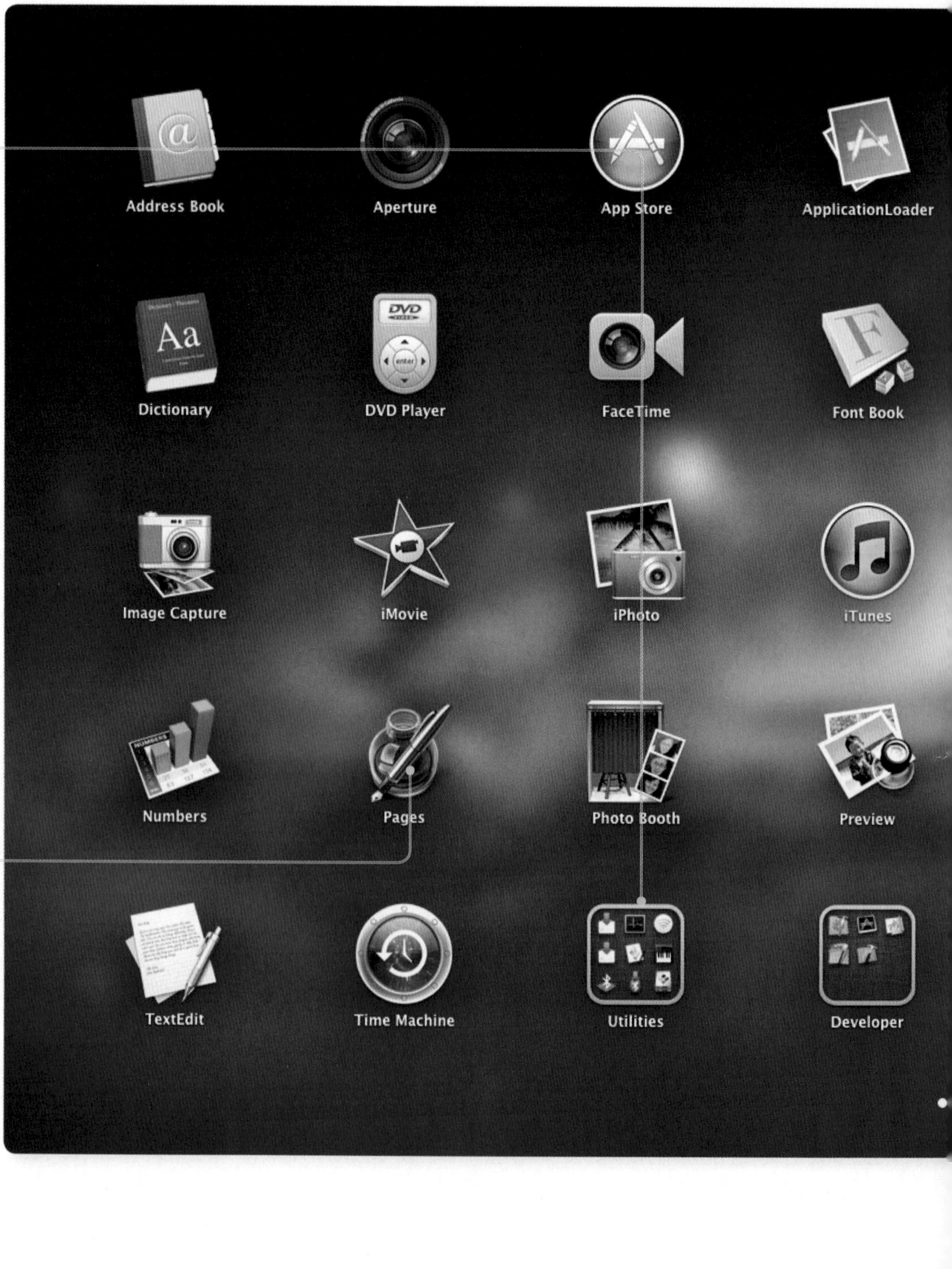

Address Book
Aperture
App Store
ApplicationLoader
Dictionary
DVD Player
FaceTime
Font Book
Image Capture
iMovie
iPhoto
iTunes
Numbers
Pages
Photo Booth
Preview
TextEdit
Time Machine
Utilities
Developer

"Launchpad is a simple interface for organising, finding and launching your apps"

Get into Launchpad

1 The quickest way to get into Launchpad is to use the new Trackpad gesture. Place three fingers on your Trackpad, as well as your thumb. Pinch the three fingers towards your thumb, and Launchpad should take over. This might take a bit of practice, so if you don't get it to work first time – try again!

2 If you don't have access to a Trackpad, you can access Launchpad directly from the Dock at the bottom of your screen. The Launchpad icon is a brushed steel disc with a rocket punched in to it.

3 If you're a keyboard junky, or fancy making life difficult for yourself, you can also access Launchpad by using Spotlight to type the name of the app, "Launchpad", or for the ultimate irony why not launch directly from the Applications folder on your Mac?

Trackpad
Show All
Point & Click
Scroll & Zoom
More Gestures
Swipe between pages
Swipe between full-screen apps
Mission Control
App Exposé
Launchpad
Show Desktop

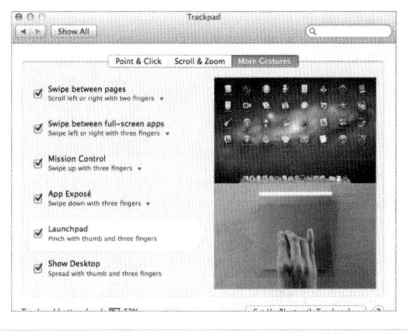

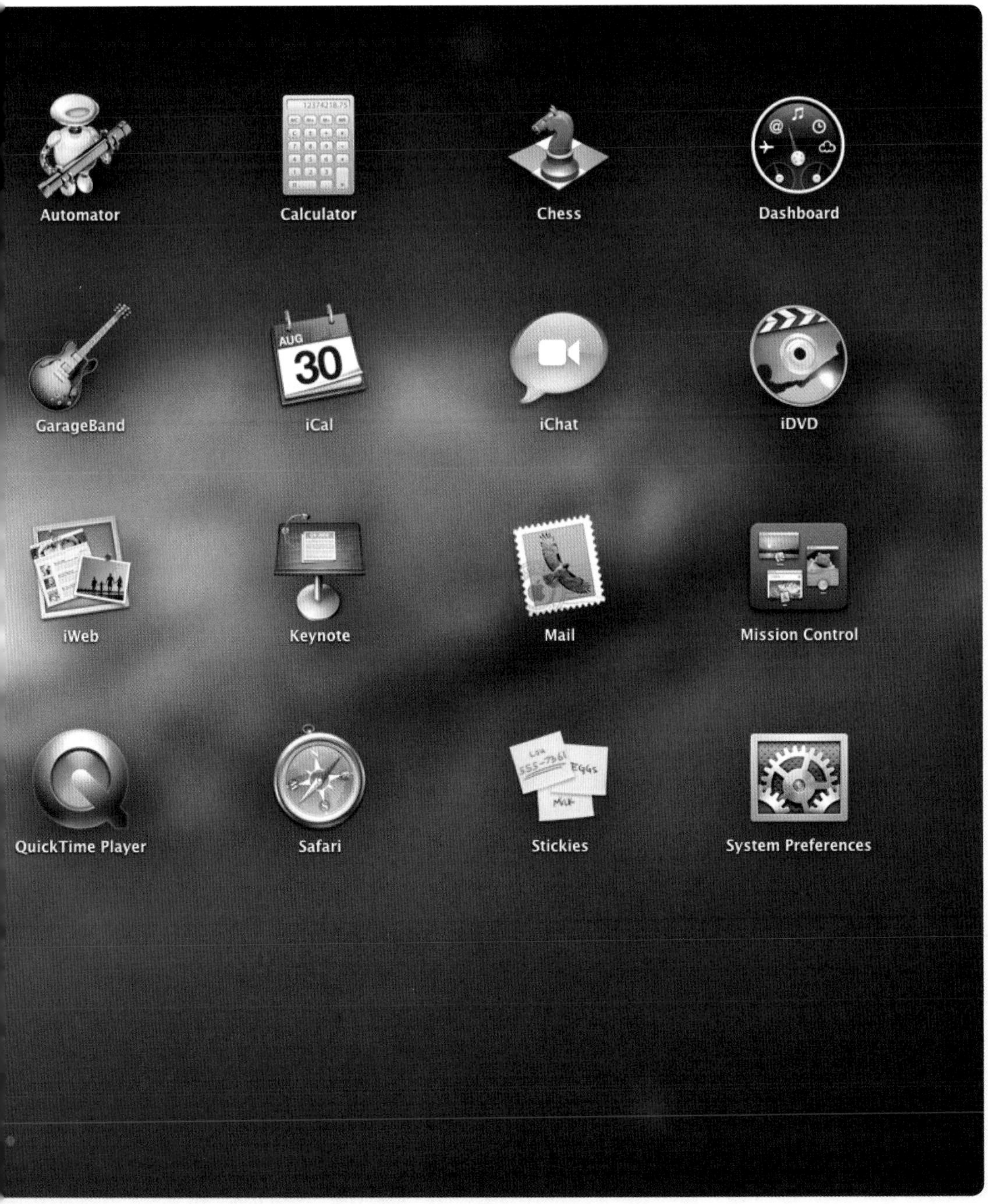

Automator
Calculator
Chess
Dashboard
GarageBand
iCal
iChat
iDVD
iWeb
Keynote
Mail
Mission Control
QuickTime Player
Safari
Stickies
System Preferences

Navigate around Launchpad

1 Finding your way around inside Launchpad is really easy. To move between different screens/pages of apps, swipe with two fingers left or right as appropriate. Notice how each screen/page is indicated by a single dot at the bottom of Launchpad.

2 To open an app, just single click on it. You can open a folder by single clicking on it, and close an open folder by clicking outside the expanded folder area.

3 A sneaky little shortcut to get to a particular screen/page is to click on the screen/page dots at the bottom of Launchpad – this allows you to jump directly to a particular screen.

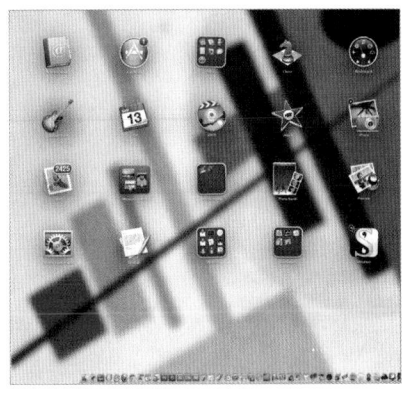

Organise Launchpad

Make Launchpad work for you with folders and home screens

Launchpad is one of the headline new features of Mac OS X Lion, and it mirrors the functionality of Springboard on iOS. Springboard is the app launcher that you'll find on your iPhone or iPad, and allows you to arrange icons for each of your apps across many home screens and, if desired, nested into folders.

Every app you install appears automatically on your home screen, and the same applies for apps installed on your Mac, with each finding its way onto your Launchpad. But unlike the iPhone, the Mac App Store isn't the only means of getting apps onto your Mac, so how do you add, remove and control these non-App Store apps?

We've collected together a series of hints and tips to help you get the most out of Launchpad, including taking control of those apps you don't want to appear. We'll also show you how to spice up the appearance with custom icons, organise your apps, and navigate around Launchpad quickly. Read on to find out how to tame Lion's Launchpad into submission.

 **App used:**
Launchpad

 **Time needed:**
10 minutes

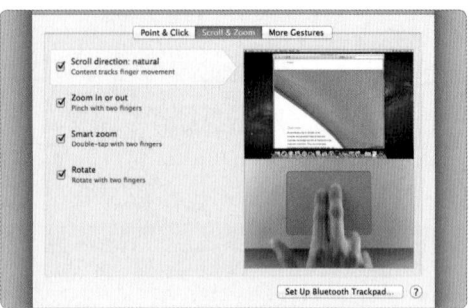

Organise your apps

Control Launchpad to keep things in their rightful place

Hide apps
Hide unwanted apps by installing the free System Preferences add-on, which is available from **http://chaosspace.de/launchpad-control**

Folders
Arrange your apps into folders by clicking and dragging one app onto another. This will create a folder that is automatically named for you. Rename the folder by clicking on its title and typing over the highlighted text

Gestures
Swipe with two fingers to slide between pages of apps, hold down Opt/Alt to automatically enter the organisation mode (where the apps quiver and allow you to move them around). Do a four-finger reverse pinch to exit Launchpad quickly, or tap escape on your keyboard

REMOVING NON-APP STORE APPS

One of the limitations of Launchpad is its reluctance to let you remove apps that didn't originate in the Mac App Store. Unless you're brand new to the Mac platform, it's very likely that you've got a reasonable collection of apps that didn't come from here, but when you enter quiver mode, these apps don't have a remove option, so how do you get rid of them? There are a couple of solutions: the easiest is to simply drag all your undesired apps into one folder and hide it on a screen all of its own at the end of the screens. The second is to install the preferences pane found at **http://chaosspace.de/launchpad-control**. This lets you untick apps you don't want to appear, removing the link from Launchpad, but not the app from your computer.

Pages
Each dot represents a different page of apps inside Launchpad. You can navigate between pages by swiping with two fingers, or quickly jump to a page by clicking on the relevant dot to save time

Launchpad Make Launchpad your own

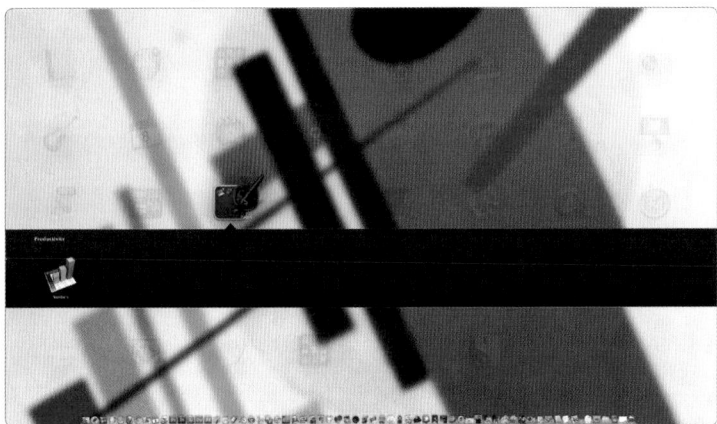

01: Create folders

Drag one app icon onto another. As you release your mouse, the two apps will form a folder, which will be named automatically for you.

02: Move your apps

Click and hold on an app icon until all the icons quiver. Once they're moving, drag and drop to reorder your apps.

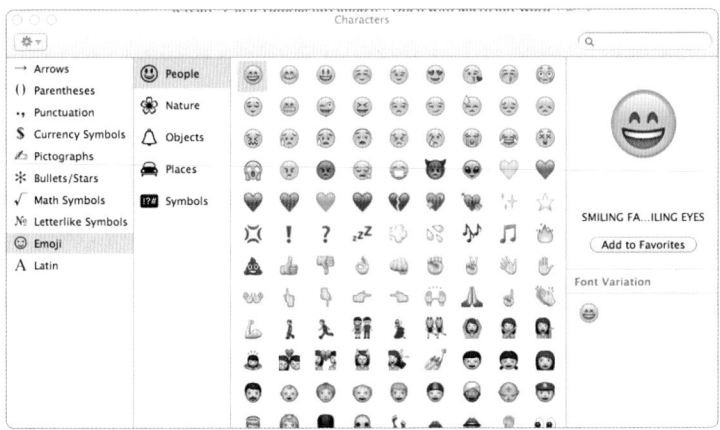

03: Liven it up

Use Emoji icons in your folder names by opening a new TextEdit document, choosing Edit > Special characters, and copying/pasting to the Launchpad.

04: Hide unwanted apps

Hide unwanted apps by installing the System Preferences add-on, which is available from http://chaosspace.de/launchpad-control.

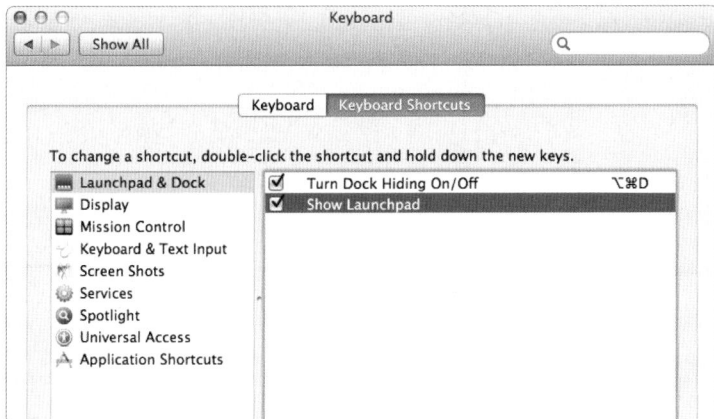

05: Set up a shortcut key

Choose System Preferences > Keyboard, and add a shortcut key into the Keyboard Shortcuts tab.

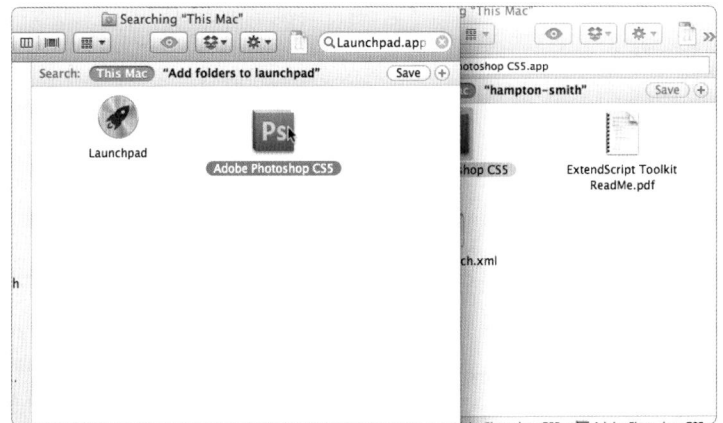

06: Manually add apps

Drag and drop an app onto the Launchpad icon. You can also drag them onto Launchpad in the Applications folder, where there's also an icon for it.

Get started with Dashboard

Learn everything you need to know about how
Dashboard can make your life easier

The one thing that has always niggled us about the iPhone is that there isn't really an opportunity to personalise the interface without jailbreaking it. The same is true of the iPad – with one little difference. Apple has allowed users the ability to change the background of the home screen as well as the lock screen. This may seem like a trivial addition to the software set but for Apple it's pretty big. It is a company that deals in absolutes and who employs a closed system to prevent people making the environment look bad. So we're glad that we get to add a little

individuality to the home screen and we're also pretty pleased when we discovered you can also

"At its most basic, the Dashboard is a place in which you can put widgets"

have two different images for the lock screen and home screen.

Making changes to the system is very simple and this is a perfect first venture into the settings system of the iPad. It works in a very similar way to the iPhone, only you can see much more of the action path that you take to get to a change in settings. This makes the system clearer, more memorable and much easier to use. Proficiency at this simple task should give you the courage to explore the settings to get even more use from your iPad and make improvements to the way it works for you.

Which widgets are which?

Discover exactly what each
standard widget is for in Lion

World Clock
Displaying the time from anywhere in the world, adding a few of these lets you keep track of as many time zones as you want

Unit Converter
Whatever you need to convert, the Unit Converter widget will do it for you. Weight, time, pressure and energy are just a few of the options for this powerful little widget

Dictionary
The Dictionary widget allows you to search any word quickly, getting you a definition or synonym quickly

Safari Webclip
You can add a snapshot of your favourite blog or video by opening the page in Safari and choosing 'Open' in Dashboard

Weather
This weather app will tell you what it's like anywhere in the world. If you click it once, you can get a weekly forecast of your choice

Calendar
The calendar app features three columns – today's date, a month view, and a column that displays your iCal events for today

Translator
The translator widget lets you choose from a wide range of languages, translating text quickly and easily

Stickies
If you're always forgetting things, use Stickies to keep notes. Fonts and colours are changeable, making sure your notes will stand out

Tile Game
A simple game widget, the Tile Game is just the tip of the iceberg when it comes to widget-based games. Check out the Apple website for more

Ski Report
If you're off on holiday to the mountains, and want to check the Ski Report, you can type a resort name in here, and view the conditions of the snow

Address Book
This widget allows you to quickly search your computer's contacts to find the person you need, without the need to open the Address Book app

ESPN
If you're an American Sports junkie, the ESPN widget is made for you. Get news and scores for hockey, football, baseball and more

Calculator
Small, neat, and much quicker than Lion's app. Typing numbers and symbols is supported to increase productivity

Flight Tracker
Choose an Airline, departure city and arrival city to view the status of flights. Incredibly useful if you travel with your Mac

Movies
If you live in the US, you can quickly check the latest times in your area, as well as buying tickets once you know what you want to see

Stocks
If you're financially minded and like to keep an eye on stocks, this will help do just that. Input your companies, and away you go

Key Features
Starting the Dashboard

Two ways to access Dashboard

Lion makes it even easier to access your Dashboard. In the new version of OS X, the Dashboard is a space to the left of your main desktop and it is there whenever you need it. Getting to it is very easy. You can simply swipe your fingers quickly to the right on your Trackpad or Magic Mouse, and watch the Dashboard slide onto your screen, ready for you to put to use. Alternatively, if you open up Mission Control, you can then just click on the Dashboard thumbnail to open it up and start using it.

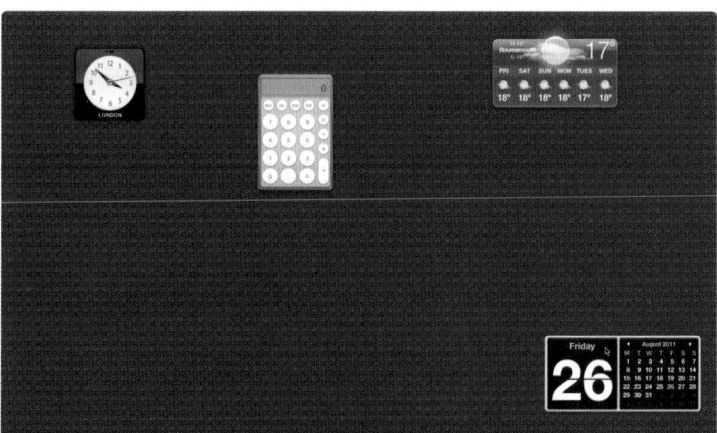

Arrange your widgets

When you first see your Dashboard, there should be four widgets in the middle of the screen; the Weather, World Clock, Calculator and Calendar. They certainly aren't stuck in those positions; if you want to move them around, you can click and drag them to a different area of the Dashboard. Unlike normal windows, there isn't a bar you have to click to move each widget – clicking and dragging from anywhere will work.

Adding new widgets

While there are only four widgets on the screen when you first open the Dashboard, there are a lot more available. Click the '+' symbol in the bottom left corner of the screen, and a bar will scroll into view with all the available widgets. You can scroll though the pages and when you see one you like; just drag and drop the icon into Dashboard. It will instantly be added to your display.

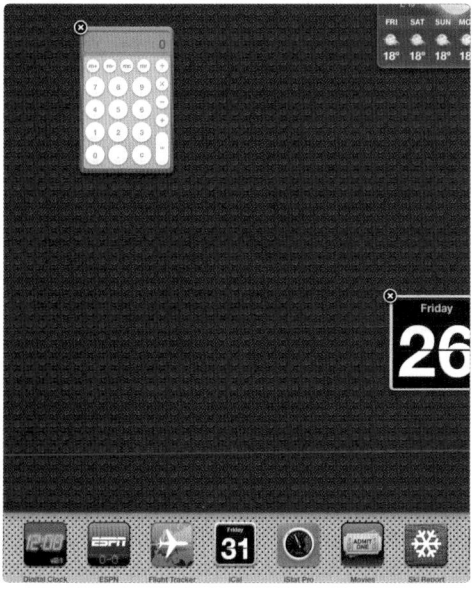
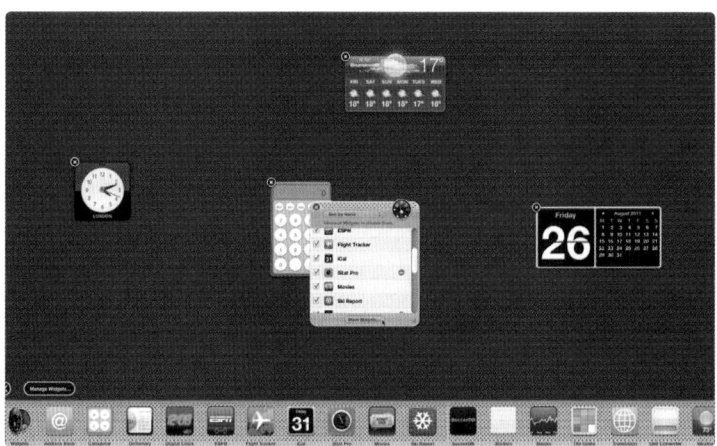

Manage your widgets

To organise your widgets, click the 'Manage Widgets' button, which is displayed after clicking the '+' symbol in the lower left corner. You will see this window, which lists all the widgets you currently have. You can quickly deactivate a widget by unchecking the box by its name, and to download new widgets, click the 'More Widgets' button at the bottom of the window, and choose from the hundreds of free choices on the Apple website.

Introducing iCloud

Store your music, photos and files in your own virtual storage space that you can access from all your devices

 Out with the old, in with the new – Apple's internet service, MobileMe is no more, replaced by a more organic and accessible service called iCloud. One of the best new additions to the OS X Lion/iOS universe, this service is free to all Mac and iOS users and it is essentially 5GB of cloud storage space. However there is no manual transferring of files or data to

worry about, your personal cloud simply hovers over you at all times, soaking up and absorbing data, such as back-ups, photos, music files, documents, apps and so on, ensuring that everything you need is close at hand.

By extension, there are many great services that become available thanks to this system, such as photos you take on your iPhone, or music files you

download on your iPad being automatically pushed to all of your OS X Lion/iOS devices without you having to lift a finger. To enjoy the features of iCloud on you Mac, click on Software Update that can be found in your Apple Menu and download the latest version of Lion (10.7.2). Once installed, a quick visit to your System Preferences will allow you to start using it straight away.

YOUR ACCOUNT
You have to enter your mac address and password to log in and start using your iCloud

MANAGING YOUR ACCOUNT
You can manage your backups and purchase more storage space by clicking on the 'Manage…' button

APP COMPATIBILITY
You can determine which of your apps take advantage of iCloud

STORAGE SPACE
You get 5GB of free iCloud storage space and can pay for additional space if you come to require it

Log on from anywhere

Like Apple's MobileMe service before it, iCloud isn't reserved entirely for Macs

There are still loads of cool iCloud features that we haven't even talked about yet – such as the way any bookmarks you make on your iPhone or iPad will be saved on your Mac and any ideas that you jot down in your iOS version of Notes will magically appear under the Reminders section of your Mac's Mail window. But perhaps the best thing about iCloud

is the way in which you can access it from any computer.

As iCloud is replacing Apple's soon-to-be defunct MobileMe internet service (Apple has ceased taking subscribers for the service and is encouraging existing customers to migrate to iCloud), many of the features have been carried across, such as the ability to access your mail,

contacts, calendar and documents from any computer, even a PC. All you have to do is get to icloud.com and you'll be able to log into your personal iCloud account and access any of the your files. So if you happen to be away from home without your computer or one of your iOS devices then you can still access a host of essential services to stay in the loop.

Key features
What your iCloud can do for you

In sync

iCloud makes it quick and effortless to access just about everything on any of your Mac or iOS devices. The service will automatically store your content (including your music, photos, files, calendars, contacts, etc) so that you can access it anywhere – everything is backed up quickly and efficiently. Not only does this provide sound piece of mind that your files will always be safe, but anything that is updated on one device will instantly be updated across all devices.

iTunes in the Cloud

Long gone are the days when you have to drag all music and videos purchased from iTunes to your various devices to copy it across. With iCloud you can have iTunes automatically download new music and purchases to all of your devices the moment you tap 'Buy'. With the iTunes app you can also browse your purchase history and choose songs, albums or shows to download again at no additional cost.

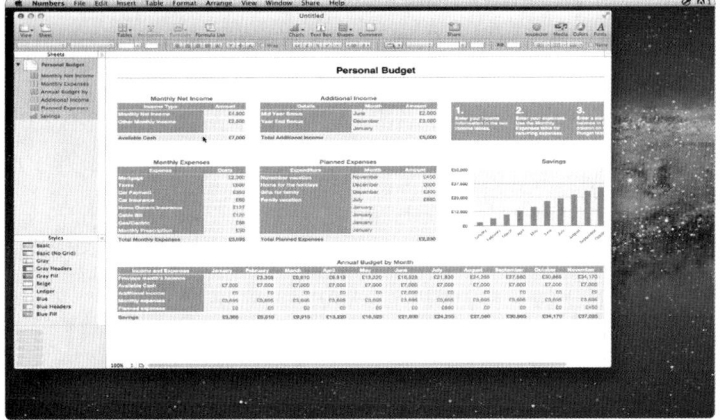

Photo Stream

With Photo Stream, you can take a photo on one device and it will automatically appear in the albums on all of your other devices, including your Mac or PC. What's more, if you import pictures to your computer from a digital camera, iCloud will send copies of them to your iPad or other device over Wi-Fi and you can also view your images on your TV via Apple TV without the need to sync or manually transfer the files

Documents in the Cloud

Who needs to 'save' work any more? Thanks to the wonders of iCloud you can keep your work up to date across all of your devices. If you are working on a Keynote presentation on your iPad, or you've designed some documents in Pages, or if you are updating some spreadsheets in Numbers, any changes you make will automatically appear on your Mac or other iOS devices, completely eradicating the need to save or transfer any files.

Set up an iCloud account

Start taking advantage of Apple's cloud storage service and make your life easier

 **App used:** iCloud

 **Time needed:** 10 minutes

Now that we have highlighted the main services and cool features that iCloud provides, you'll no doubt be chomping at the bit to start exploring them for yourself – and it's easy, all you need to do is download and install the latest system update and then login using an Apple ID.

If you are already running OS X Lion then you'll be able to get the latest update for free by clicking on the 'Software Update' option in the Apple Menu. Once it has installed, you will be able to access iCloud from System Preferences – click on the icon and then enter your Apple ID (the same email address and password that you use to make purchases from iTunes or the App Store). If you are new to Macs and don't yet have an Apple ID then you can create one from within iCloud and then use it to access anything Apple-related, including the option to log on to your own personal iCloud from any computer, even PCs.

Once set up, your iCloud can then be used to back up data, store all of your important files, update details across all of your devices and push music and pictures from one device or Mac to another without having to manually transfer items. Here's how to set it up on your Mac.

"iCloud can be used to backup data and files across devices"

Get to know iCloud

Discover how using iCloud can make your life simpler

Image streaming
Take a photo on one device and it automatically appears on all your other devices, including your Mac or PC. It'll even push images imported from a digital camera

Access your documents
If you are working on a Keynote presentation on your iPad, for example, any changes you make will automatically appear on your Mac or other iOS devices

Your personal iCloud
Enter your email address and password to log into iCloud. Using these details, you can also log into iCloud from any computer or device simply by logging onto icloud.com

Storage capacity
You get 5GB of free iCloud storage space free and can pay for additional space. If you wish to purchase more, click on 'Manage', followed by the 'Buy More Storage' button

WHAT IS AN APPLE ID?
An Apple ID is a user name that you can use for everything you do with Apple – such as at iTunes and App Stores. You may already have an Apple ID, but you can create a new one when logging into iCloud, if you need to.

iCloud Set up a new account

01: Get updated

To start enjoying the numerous features of iCloud, you must ensure that you have the latest software. Click on your Apple menu and then choose the 'Software Update' option to scan for the latest updates. The iCloud feature comes with OS X Lion 10.7.2, so ensure you have it installed on your Mac.

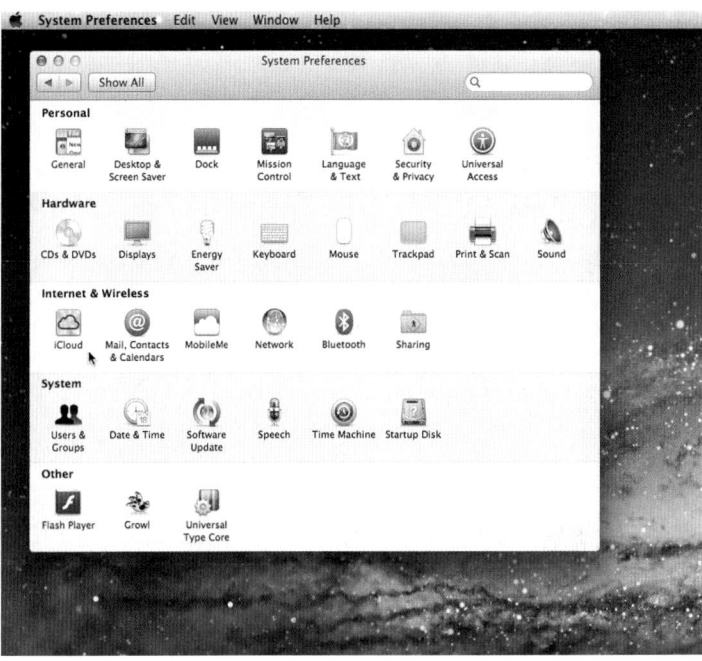

02: Open System Preferences

When your Mac has been updated to at least OS X Lion 10.7.2, open your System Preferences app and, in the 'Internet & Wireless' section, you will see a new option called 'iCloud'. Click on this to open it and you can go about creating a new account or logging in with an existing one.

03: Enter details

Now enter your Apple ID (email address) and password into the required fields to access an existing account or click on the 'Create an Apple ID' option underneath the first text entry field to start a new, free account. You can also retrieve forgotten passwords from this page.

04: Select your apps

Once your account is up and running you can tick which apps you wish to sync to your iCloud, manage your account (check how much space you are using, for example) and, if necessary, increase the storage capacity of your personal iCloud in System Preferences.

Search your Mac's hard drive

It's so frustrating when you lose a file or folder on your hard drive. Luckily the search features built in to Mac OS X make it easy to find wayward documents

X If you've been using the internet for any time it probably feels quite natural to head over to the top-right corner of your browser window to search on Google (or another search engine). Mac or PC, there's a search field up there on almost every browser and it's how most people find what they're looking for. The good news is that it's exactly the same if you want to search the hard drive inside your Mac. There's a search field in the same place on every Finder window and there's even one, called Spotlight, in the top-right corner of your desktop, just at the end of the menu bar. Learn how to use these to search the contents of your Mac's hard drive and you need never be stuck looking for a file, folder or application again.

Searching a specific folder

If you've misplaced a document or are suffering from a bad case of amnesia, Apple has made it easy to search for and track down those missing files…

01: Open up the folder

Open up the folder so you can see all the contents listed. Your search will include all these items – including the contents of any folders.

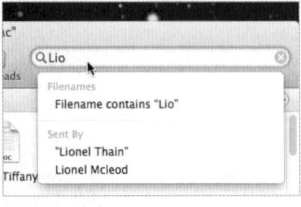

02: Type in your search

Click by the magnifying glass in the top-right of your window and start typing your search. The results will automatically start appearing in the menu below.

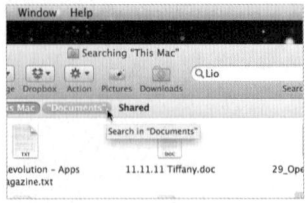

03: Narrow it down

These results will be from everywhere on your hard drive. To narrow it down, click the name of the folder you started in (it's located at the top in quote marks).

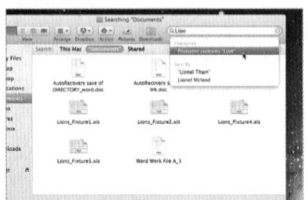

04: Filter and find

Now the results will be filtered to only include the ones that are inside this folder. Find the one that you're looking for and double-click it.

Narrow down the search

If you're searching from the search field in the top-right corner of a Finder window, you can easily narrow down where you want to search by clicking these headers. The 'This Mac' tab will search your entire computer, while the tab named with your account name (in this case John) will search only your files and folders. You'll also get the option to search only the folder you started from – useful for when you know you're in the right place but just can't find that file (see the step-by-step bottom left)

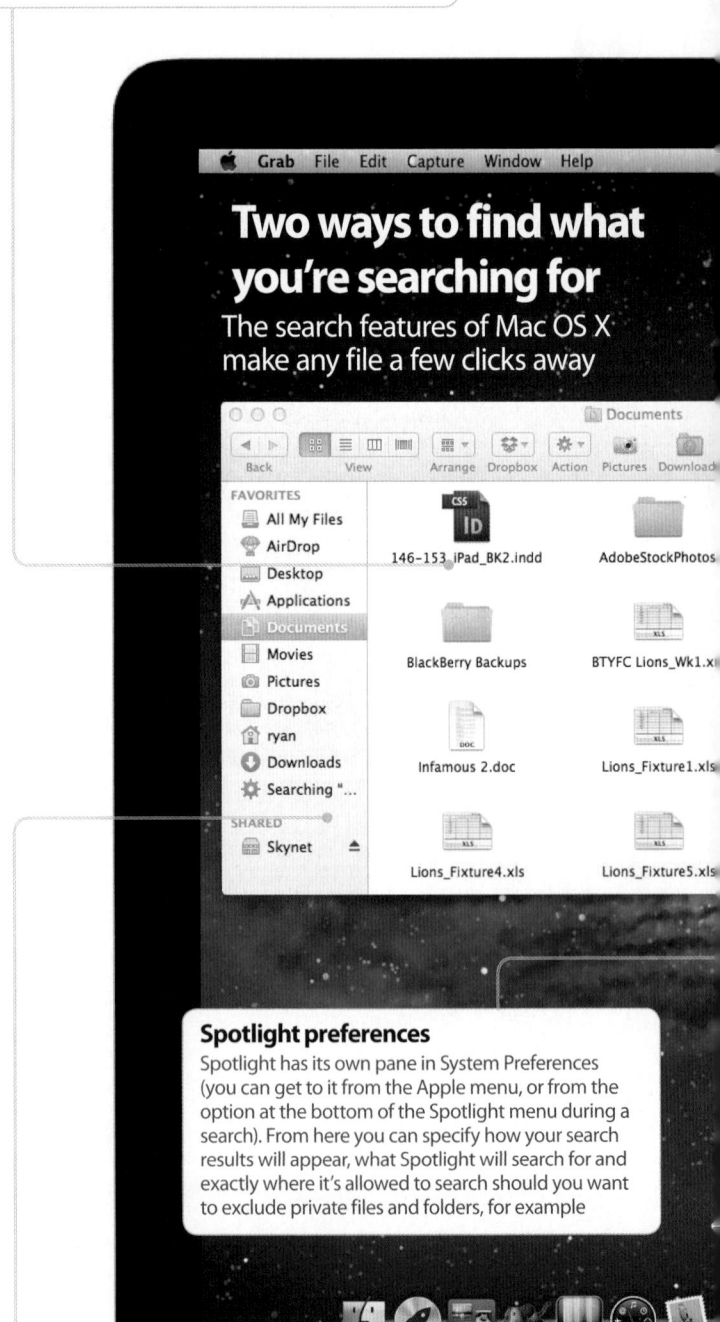

Two ways to find what you're searching for

The search features of Mac OS X make any file a few clicks away

Spotlight preferences

Spotlight has its own pane in System Preferences (you can get to it from the Apple menu, or from the option at the bottom of the Spotlight menu during a search). From here you can specify how your search results will appear, what Spotlight will search for and exactly where it's allowed to search should you want to exclude private files and folders, for example

Saved searches

Every Finder window comes with a preset list of Searches in the sidebar. Click one to search for files created recently, or of a specific type

Search by more than just name

Can't remember what a file was called? No matter, you could still find it…

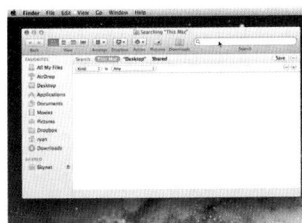

01: Start a search
Press the Cmd+F keyboard shortcut to open a new Finder window with a blank search.

02: Chose your criteria
Use the pop-up menus to choose what you want to search by, including date created.

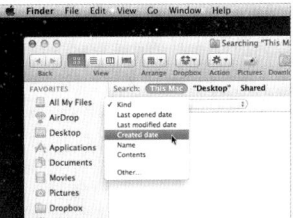

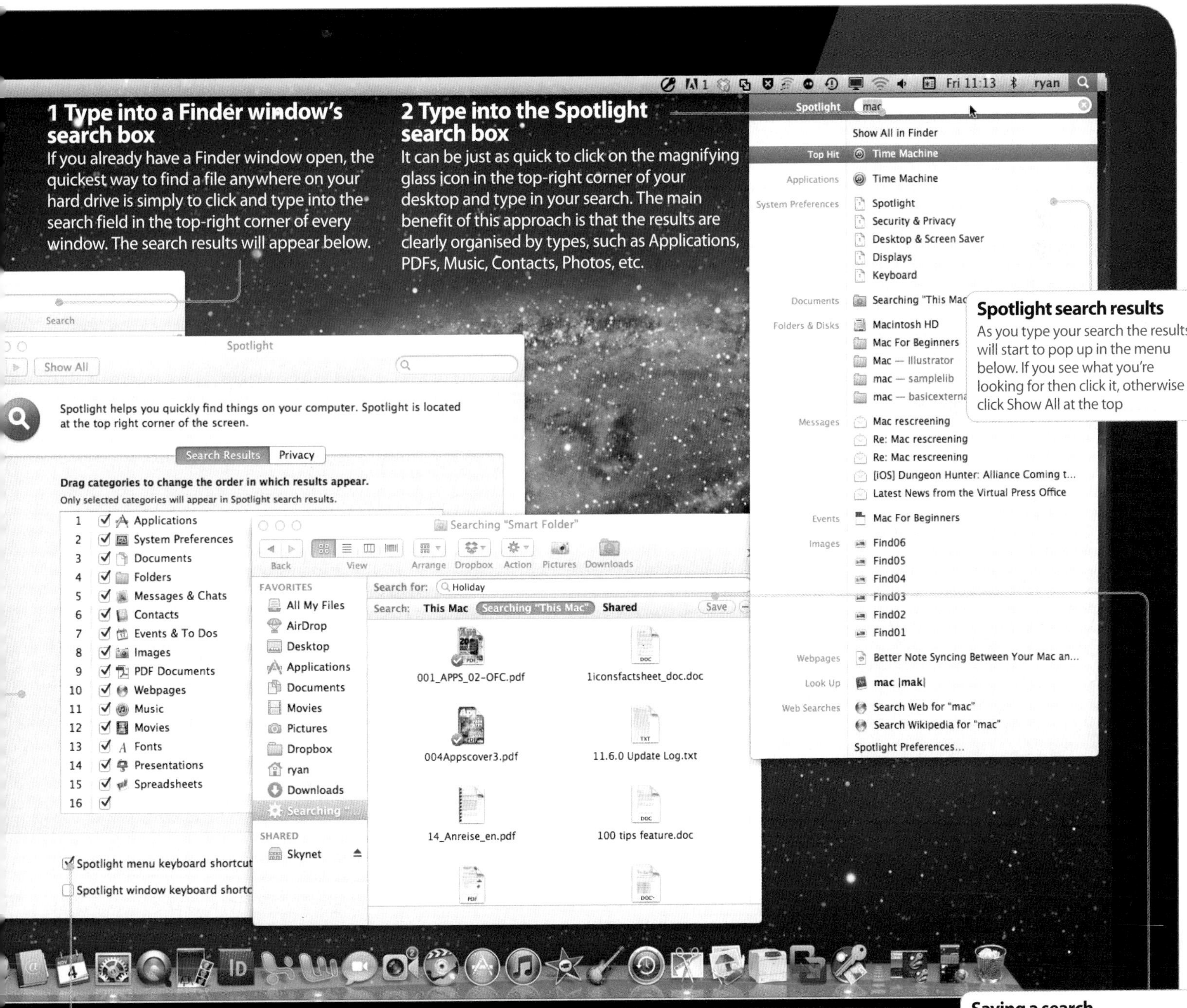

1 Type into a Finder window's search box
If you already have a Finder window open, the quickest way to find a file anywhere on your hard drive is simply to click and type into the search field in the top-right corner of every window. The search results will appear below.

2 Type into the Spotlight search box
It can be just as quick to click on the magnifying glass icon in the top-right corner of your desktop and type in your search. The main benefit of this approach is that the results are clearly organised by types, such as Applications, PDFs, Music, Contacts, Photos, etc.

Spotlight search results
As you type your search the results will start to pop up in the menu below. If you see what you're looking for then click it, otherwise click Show All at the top

Shortcuts to Spotlight
Want an even quicker way to search your Mac? Using a keyboard shortcut to bring up Spotlight makes searching for your files incredibly quick and works from any application

Saving a search
Do you find yourself doing the same search again and again? Click the Save button to save it as a Smart Search in the Search For section of the sidebar in your Finder windows

Use the Put Back function in Finder

Everyone puts files in the Trash by mistake, but by using the Put Back feature you can instantly restore those files to their old position

 **App used:**
Finder

 **Time needed:**
5 minutes

It really does seem as though hard drive space is always at a premium, and as a result it's no surprise when we put things in the Trash by mistake. The trouble with this predicament is that, should we have the foresight to remember before emptying the trash, we have to remember where the file belonged and restore it to the right place. This can be more than tedious and can get pretty frustrating if it happens quite a lot. Luckily, Lion has the answer. Yet again Apple has anticipated our frustrations and built in a very handy feature to solve the problem. The Put Back function will instantly restore the files you have trashed to their original positions. Please do remember though that this will only work for items you can see in the trash folder – anything you have deleted by emptying the trash will require a trip into Time Machine or recovery software.

> "Instantly restore the files to their original positions"

Finder Restore accidentally deleted files with Put Back

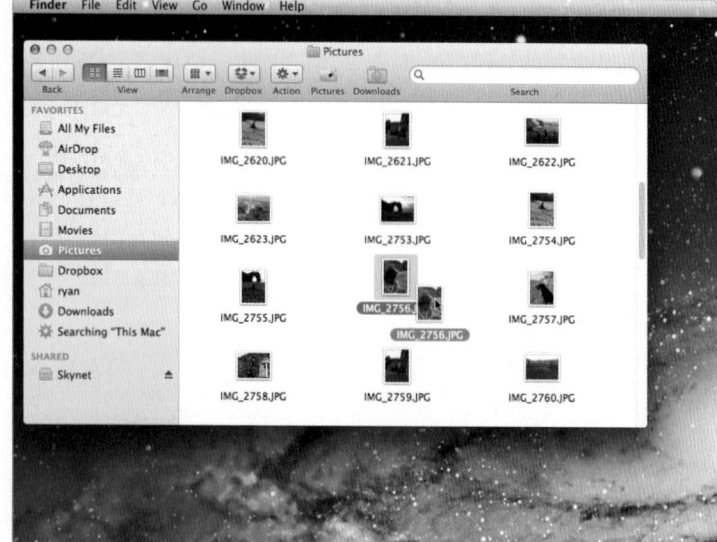

01: Drag and drop

The drag and drop function is so easy that sometimes we can send the wrong file to the Trash by mistake. When this happens just open the Trash by clicking the bin.

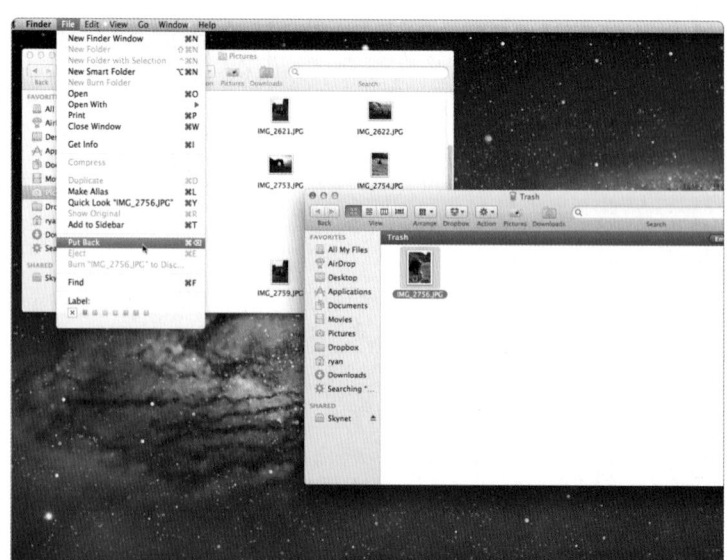

02: File menu

Once the Trash is open select the file that you wish restore to its original position. Now go to the File menu and select Put Back. There you will also see the keyboard shortcut.

Save items from the Trash
Undo your mistakes and save files you accidentally dumped

Plenty of choice
The option to use the contextual menu, file menu or keyboard shortcut means you can complete the manoeuvre in whichever way suits you best

Packed bin
You will also be surprised how often you get the 'did I really want to delete all these files' feeling!

Empty space
You'll be surprised how often you get that 'I'm sure there should be more files in here' feeling. That's when you need this cool trick

Multiples
You can restore as many files as you like by selecting them all and using the Put Back function

TIME MACHINE
Always make sure you back up your files as the Put Back solution only works for those files in the Trash folder. Once you've emptied that folder you'll have to delve into Time Machine. But the cool thing is that you can use a similar process to get back what you lost from there too. Apple really does think of absolutely everything…

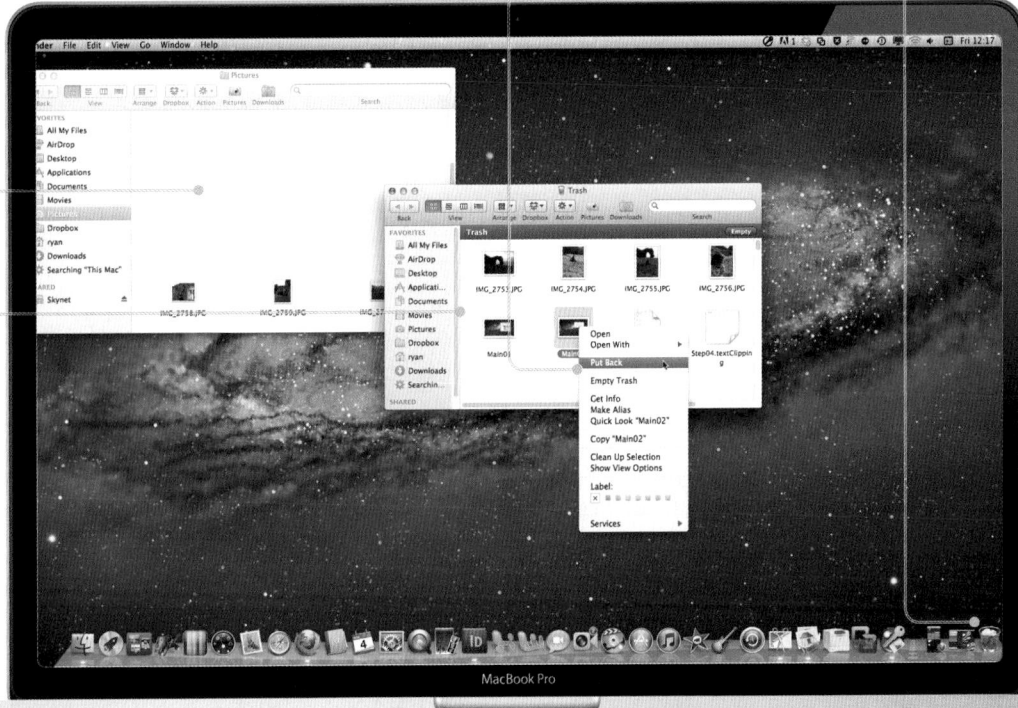

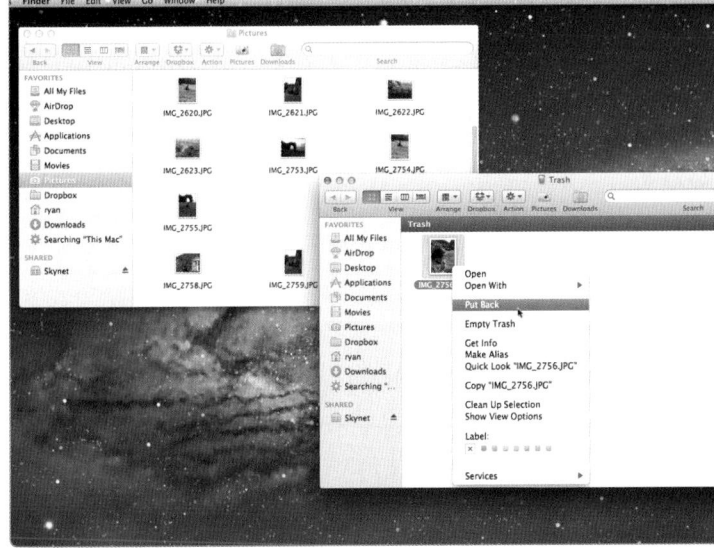

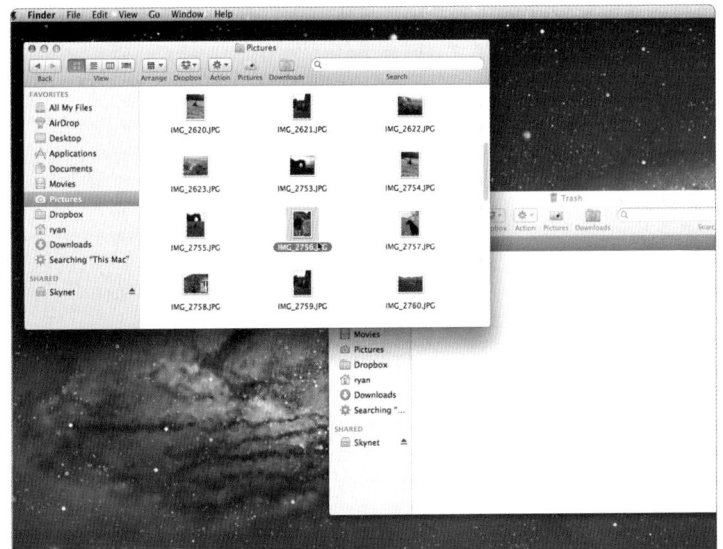

03: Contextual too
For those of you who are right clickers you can also bring up a contextual menu on the selected file and select the Put Back option. To set up the right click on your mouse go to System Preferences>Mouse.

04: It's like magic
Once done the file you trashed is instantly restored to its original home, saving you the need to drag and drop it somewhere and possibly misplace it again.

Delete files securely from your Mac

Safeguard your privacy, enhance the performance
of your Mac and recover valuable disk space

 **App used:** Trash

 **Time needed:** 5 minutes

 In this day and age, ID theft is more than just an idle threat. Overloading your Mac with irrelevant or no longer needed documents means that there is always a possibility that, if your machine was stolen, the information could be put to illegal use. Therefore, removing data from your system and keeping as much available disk space as possible should be part of your daily routine.

Privacy is not only a personal matter, it is also a highly relevant topic when considering client information, whether this belongs to former or currently employed staff and/or confidential company data. Furthermore, having a system cluttered with irrelevant files, either downloaded from the internet or copied onto your system, can vastly hinder your Mac's performance, making it

> "Removing data should be part of your daily routine"

run a lot slower, and limit your ability to use very valuable disk space.

Removing files from your computer can just be a case of dragging the file over to the trash icon, but we will show you how you can delete these files and ensure that they are irretrievable and therefore won't get into the wrong hands.

Follow these simple steps and we will show you how to delete unwanted files safely and securely, so you know you are always protected. It's a very simple process, but one that you need to get into the habit of doing regularly.

Gone for good

Permanently delete files from
your Mac to keep them safe

Finder Preferences
Activate the Finder by clicking on its Dock icon. From the Finder menu, select the Preferences menu item and click on the Advanced tab; the third and fourth options are the Trash preferences

The Empty Trash Securely button
Once the Empty Trash Securely option is selected in the Finder Preferences Advanced tab, the Trash window's Empty button changes to Empty Securely and this option becomes the default file-erasing method

Finder menu items
You can empty the Trash from the Finder menu by selecting the Empty Trash or the Secure Empty Trash menu item; do so while holding the Option key for a prompt-free procedure

The Trash window
The Trash window aspect does not vary greatly from a standard Finder window. It differentiates itself with a Trash banner below the toolbar and a button to the right-hand side of the banner

WHY SECURELY EMPTY THE TRASH?

When using the 'regular' method for deleting items, your system makes them invisible and the disk space occupied by their content is, if needed, marked as rewritable. In addition, the Securely Empty Trash writes a random series of ones and zeros (up to 35 times) on that same disk space, making the content of the file impossible to retrieve.

OS X Permanently remove files/folders from your Mac

01: Select an item to delete

To delete a file/folder, click on it and, without releasing your click, move it on top of the Trash icon. Release the click to put it in the Trash.

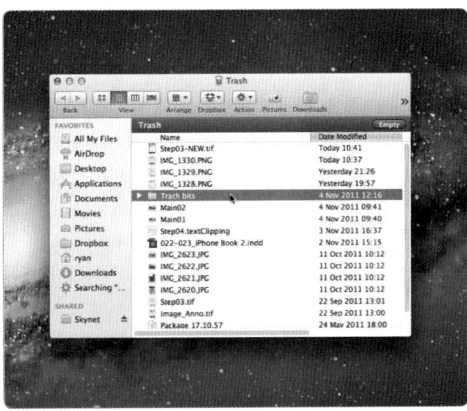

02: Check what you delete

Check that the intended item is in the Trash. Click on the Dock's Trash icon and, in the window, your file/folder should be in the contents of your Trash.

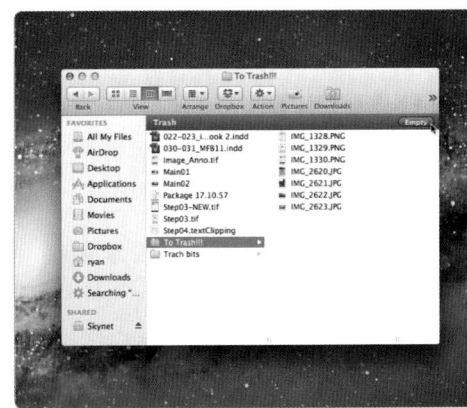

03: Empty the trash

At the top-right of the Trash banner in the Finder window, click on the Empty button to empty the Trash and effectively delete the trashed items.

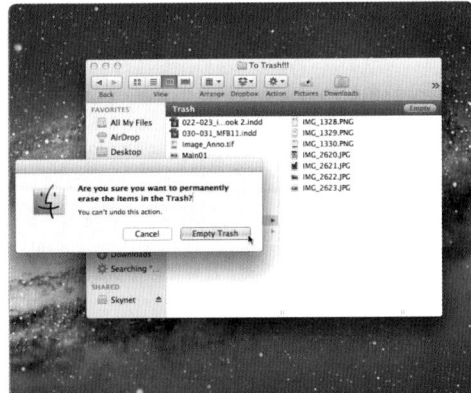

04: Are you sure?

Upon clicking on the Empty button, a dialog box will ask you to confirm the operation. Click Empty Trash to delete, or Cancel to abort the operation.

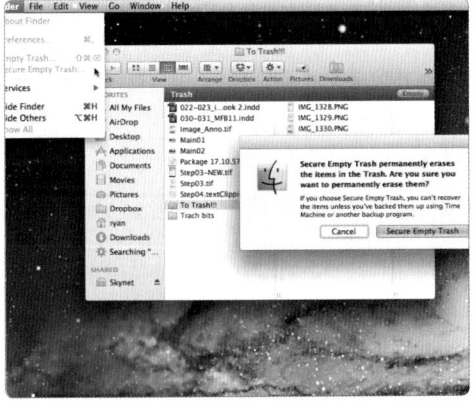

05: Empty the Trash securely

To make a trashed item irretrievable, select the Secure Empty Trash menu item in the Finder menu. Click Empty Trash to delete the file.

06: Bypass warning message

To erase without verification, press the Option key when using the Empty button or the Empty Trash/Secure Empty Trash Finder's menu items.

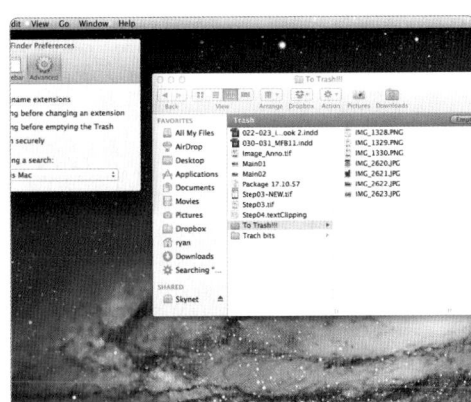

07: Warning messages

From the Finder menu, select Preferences and Advanced. To disable the confirmation dialog, untick 'Show warning before emptying the Trash'.

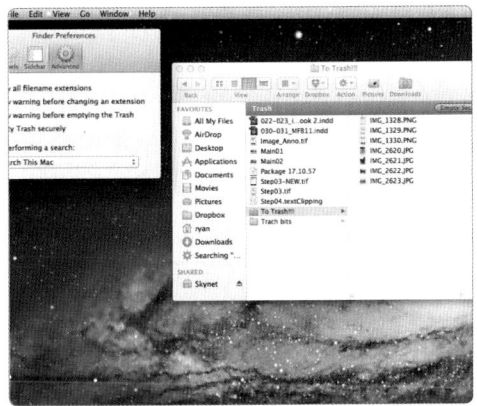

08: Security as standard

From the menu, select Preferences and click the Advanced tab. Tick the Empty Trash Securely option to enable this method of erasing items.

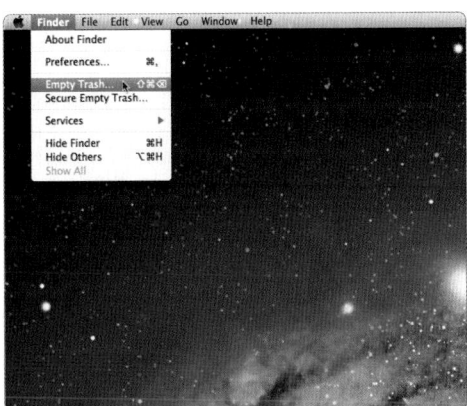

09: Know your shortcuts

Use Cmd+Delete to move an item to the Trash. Add Shift to empty the Trash, or Shift+Option to empty without a confirmation dialog box.

Inside System Preferences: Personal

Learn how to tinker and tune the inner workings of your Mac by following this simple, four-part guide to the System Preferences. First part: the Personal settings…

 Many Mac users are happy to leave their Mac set up the same way it was the day they opened the box. That's fair enough – after all, why fix what isn't broken? But, if you're prepared to take a few minutes to delve into the wealth of settings at your fingertips you may just find a few that could change the way you work, make your Mac a safer place, or just spruce the ol' gall up a little. In the first of a four-part guide, we're going to take you, icon by icon, through the top row of the System Preferences window: the Personal settings…

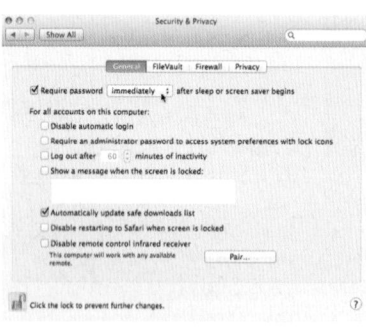

Security

General

By setting your Mac to require a password when you wake it from sleep or the screen saver, your Mac will automatically lock itself while you're away. You can also set it to only respond to a certain remote control.

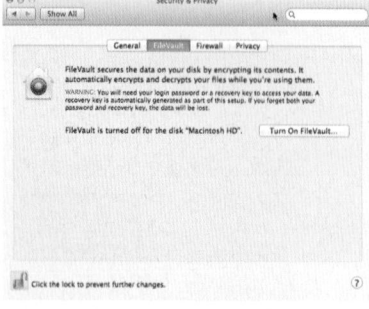

FileVault

By using FileVault you can automatically encrypt every file on your Mac – great for security-conscious laptop users worried about losing their computer, and the sensitive data it contains.

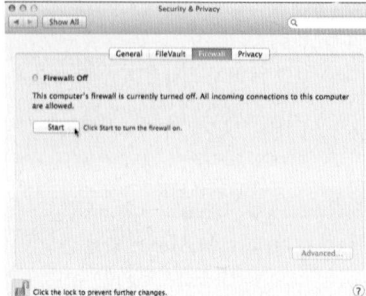

Firewall

It's no myth that Macs are safer on the internet than Windows-based computers, but if you'd rather be safe than sorry you can turn on the Firewall to monitor and block potentially dangerous connections from the net.

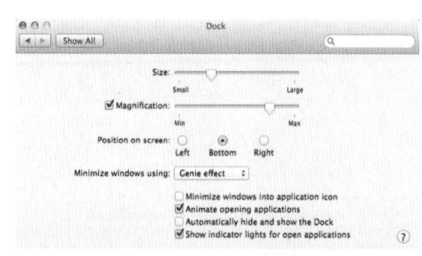

Dock

With these settings, you can easily control how the Dock (the bar of icons along the bottom of your screen) looks and behaves.

Desktop & Screen Saver

Desktop

Set the background picture on your desktop to one of the Apple-supplied images, one of your own photos from iPhoto or one you've downloaded from the internet.

Screen Saver

Set an animation that automatically starts when your Mac hasn't been used for a while. Choose from one of Apple's, or automatically create a slideshow from your iPhoto albums.

Mission Control

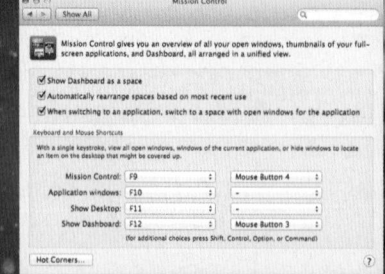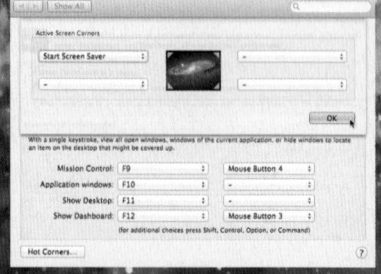

General

Sometimes you can't find the window you need among the many you have open. Mission Control provides a handy overview of all your open windows and applications all arranged in a unified view. You can tailor the views and shortcuts here.

Hot Corners

Accessible from the Mission Control pane is the 'Hot Corners' settings. You can move your cursor into a corner of your screen to trigger certain actions, such as screensavers and sleep mode. You can determine what corner performs which action here.

Scroll bar controls

With a scrolling mouse, you may never have used the scroll bars on the edge of every window, but there may still be settings here that you'll find extremely useful – such as the Jumping options

Text smoothing options

Without smoothing the words on your screen can appear harsh and jagged, but you might find text too fuzzy to read comfortably at smaller sizes. You can fine-tune the effect here

Search System Preferences

If you know there's an option you'd like to change but can't remember where it is, try entering its name into this search box to see matching icons dynamically highlighted

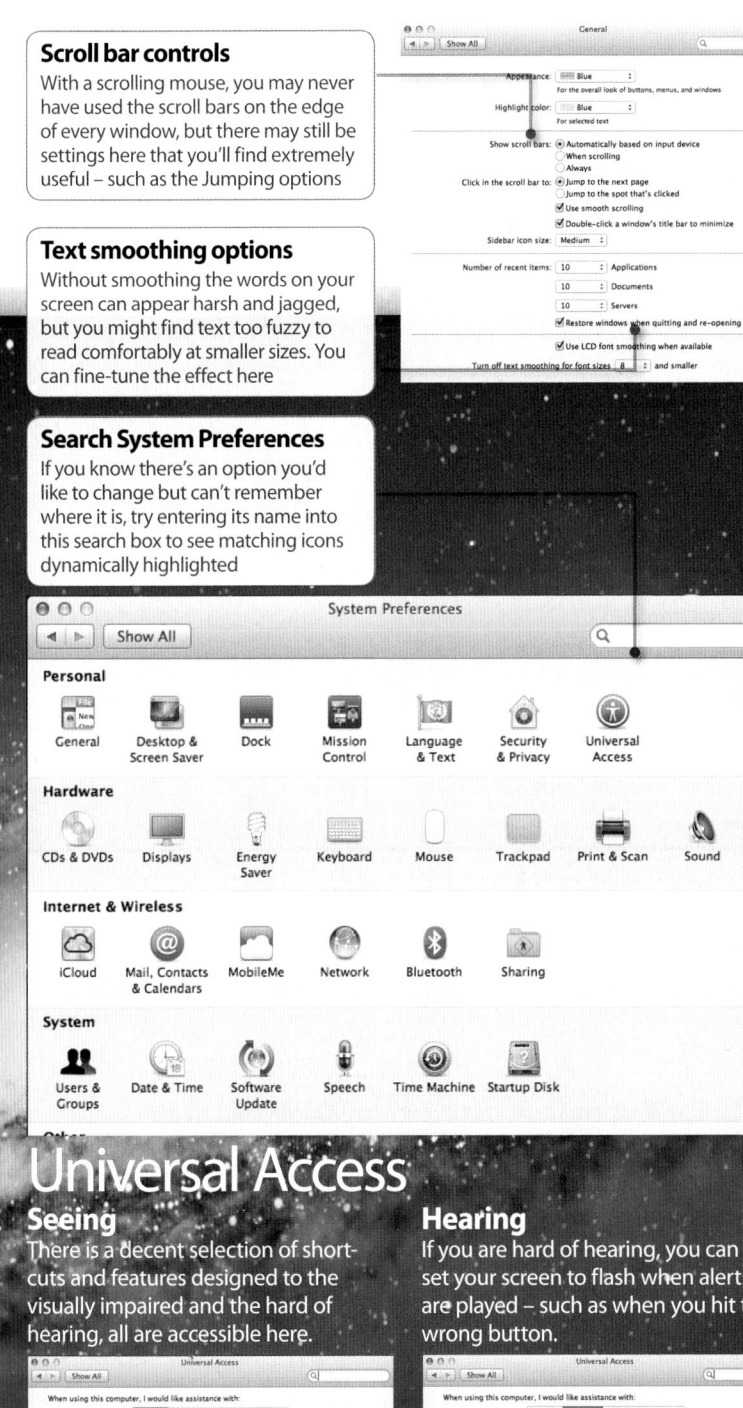

General

In this pane you'll find the settings that affect how your windows and menus appear. You have the choice between the usual Blue theme, with shiny blue controls and red amber and green window widgets, or – if you find all the colour distracting – you can switch to the Graphite theme where all the controls are grey.

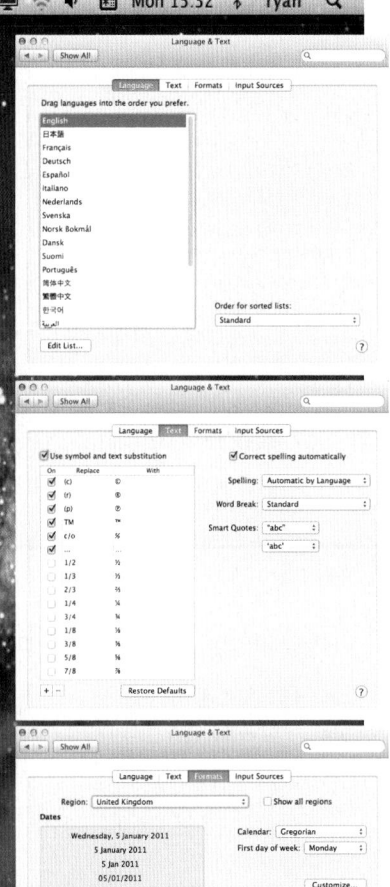

Language & Text

Language

For most users this will come preset, but you can quickly change the language of menus and controls in the Languages tab.

Text

Not only can you set your Spell Checking options here, but you can also set your Mac to automatically replace certain typed shortcuts with special symbols, like automatically swapping (c) for ©. This can be extremely useful, but it only works in supported applications.

Formats

Dates, prices or times not displaying the way that you would like? You can change how your Mac automatically formats numbers using this Control Panel. Presets for most regional variations are already included

Input Sources

The thing most users will find useful in this section of System Preferences is turning on the Keyboard and Character Viewer, which gives you a map of those hard-to-find symbols on your keyboard, like the é, ü or °.

Universal Access

Seeing

There is a decent selection of short-cuts and features designed to the visually impaired and the hard of hearing, all are accessible here.

Hearing

If you are hard of hearing, you can set your screen to flash when alerts are played – such as when you hit the wrong button.

Inside System Preferences: Hardware

Get to grips with the technology inside your Mac by following this simple four-part guide to the System Preferences. Part two: get your hands dirty with the Hardware settings…

 The simplicity of Mac OS X means that you don't have to become an expert on computer hardware to enjoy using your Mac. For most peripherals you can just plug in and play; at the worst you may have to install the occasional driver. But with improvements made with Mac OS X Snow Leopard, even these installs are becoming fewer and farther between. This ease of use doesn't mean there aren't any settings to fiddle with though – System Preferences has a whole row of icons dedicated to fine-tuning the hardware settings of your Mac, and a few well-chosen tweaks could vastly improve the way you work…

Schedule

Want your Mac to be on when you wake up or get home from work? Use the Energy Saver schedule to set when your Mac turns on, turns off, goes to sleep or wakes up

Displays

Make sure you're using the optimum viewing settings to get the most from your monitor

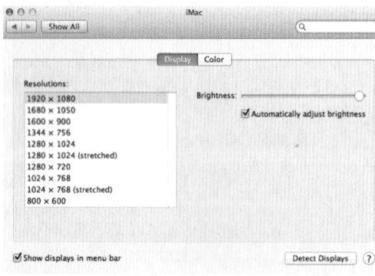

Display

Everything seem a little small on screen? The higher up the list you set the resolution, the bigger everything will get (but you'll fit less on, and it won't look as sharp).

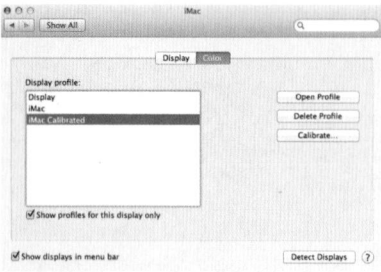

Arrangement

If you're sporting more than one monitor for your Mac, this panel let's you tell your computer how they are positioned and which one you want the Menu bar to appear on.

Colour

Ensure you're seeing the correct colours by either selecting the correct Display profile or, even better, by clicking the Calibrate button to create a bespoke setting.

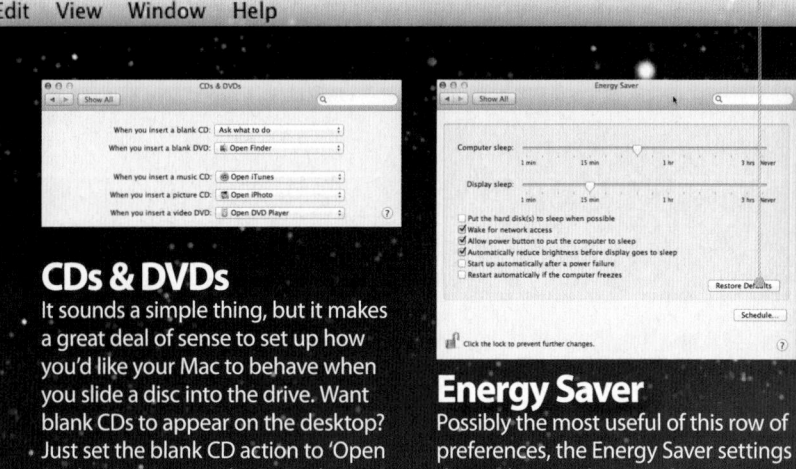

CDs & DVDs

It sounds a simple thing, but it makes a great deal of sense to set up how you'd like your Mac to behave when you slide a disc into the drive. Want blank CDs to appear on the desktop? Just set the blank CD action to 'Open Finder'. Don't want the DVD player to open when you pop in a movie disc? Just choose 'Ignore' from the video DVD menu, or set it to open in Front Row if that's how you prefer to watch your films.

Energy Saver

Possibly the most useful of this row of preferences, the Energy Saver settings do much more than cut down your electricity bill. The Computer Sleep slider sets how long you'd like your Mac to stay on when you're not using it, while a second slider lets you set the same for just the Display.

Keyboard

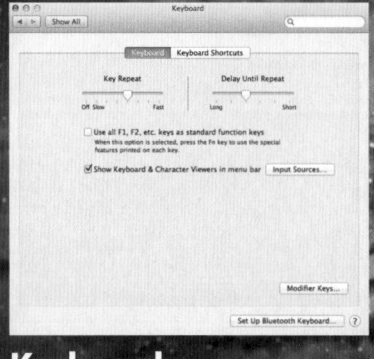

Keyboard

Considering how much of the time you spend sitting in front of your Mac, you also spend time tapping away at your keyboard, so it's good to make sure you've got it set up perfectly. If you're a slow typist then increasing the 'Delay Until Repeat' setting is an especially good idea if you often find yourself typing repeating letters.

Keyboard Shortcuts

Mac OS X comes crammed with many keyboard shortcuts that can speed up how you work, saving your hand a trip to the mouse or trackpad. Not only can you discover what they all are from this pane, you can also tweak and change them to better suit your fingertips – a great way to personalise your Mac for the way you work.

Share your printer

Although Wi-Fi printers are surprisingly cheap these days, if you have a non-networked model you can still share it across multiple Macs (and PCs) by ticking this checkbox

Print & Fax

With every new version of Mac OS X, Apple has significantly improved the printer installation experience. So much so that many users will never need to visit the Print & Fax preference pane – simply plug in your printer and most times it will just work. That said, it's still useful to set your default paper size or check the amount of ink in your printer by clicking the Options & Supplies button.

"If you're the arty type and use a graphics tablet, you might want to have a play with the handwriting recognition built into Mac OS X"

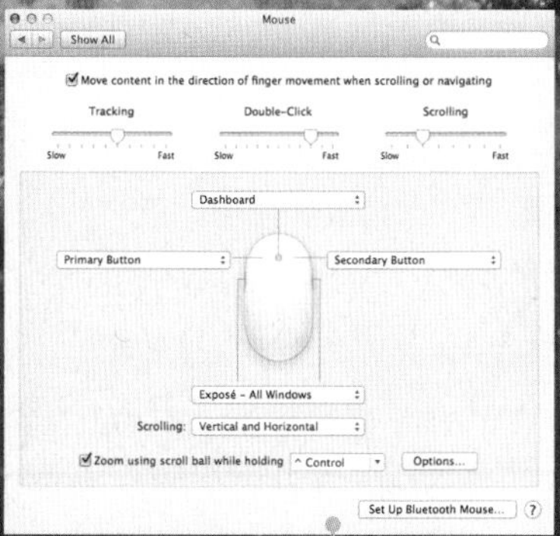

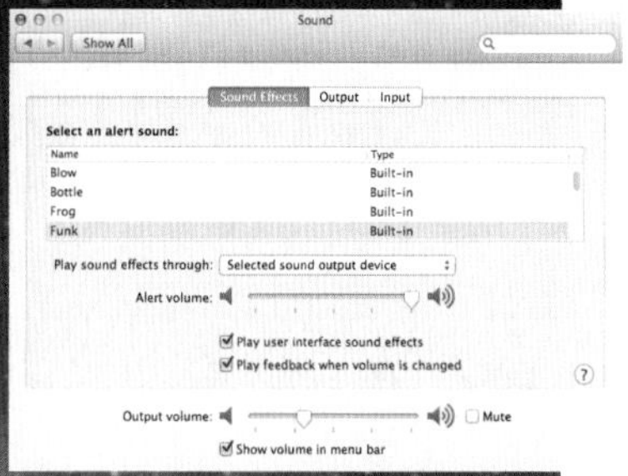

Sound

Sound Effects

Your Mac makes a number of small noises to give you feedback on certain events. Choose which ones you'd like to hear, and how loud you'd like them to be.

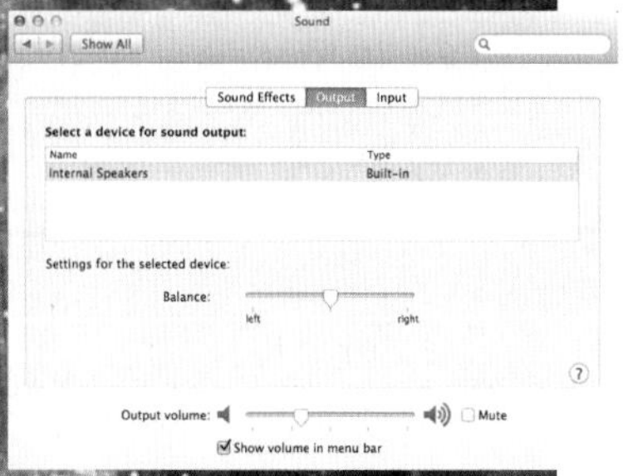

Output

On most Macs there are a number of ways to pipe the audio out – through headphones, the built-in speakers or through a digital optical cable, for example. You can choose which one to use from this pane.

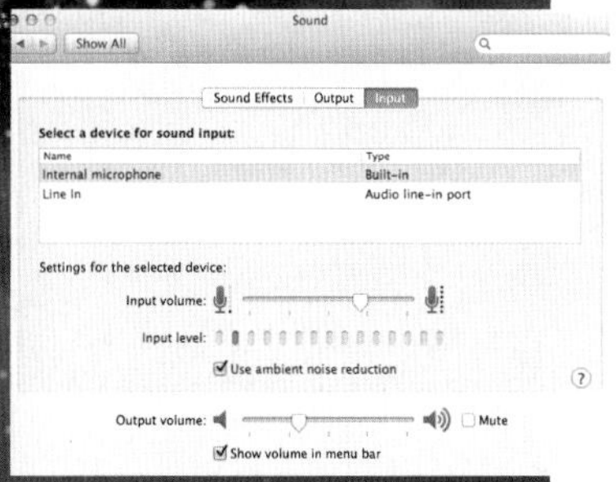

Input

The audio input options are less useful to most users, until you decide to try Skype, record a movie voiceover or experiment with GarageBand. Choosing the right input device will depend on the equipment you use, but it is vital for a great result.

Mouse/Trackpad

The pane that you see here will depend on whether you use a laptop with a trackpad, a Magic Mouse, Mighty Mouse or a third-party mouse. As with the keyboard settings, considering how much time you spend controlling a cursor, it's important to get these settings perfect – especially the tracking and double-click speeds.

Learn your gestures

As multi-touch devices, like the Magic Mouse or the trackpad on your laptop, improve the way you get around your Mac, you'll find yourself faced with more and more gestures and actions. Luckily these example videos make them easy to learn

Ink

If you're the arty type and use a graphics tablet, then you might want to have a play with the handwriting recognition that's built into Mac OS X. Ink allows you to enter text using your pen and tablet instead of the keyboard, and it can be great for taking notes. You can also set up gestures to control your Mac with the pen.

Inside System Preferences: Sharing

Get to grips with the technology inside your Mac by following this simple, four-part guide to the System Preferences. Part three: get generous – share and share alike…

There's one aspect that sets the computers of today far apart from those we were using just ten years ago: **networks.** Back in 2000 the internet was only just starting to become commonplace, and if you did have it you probably only had it on one computer in the house (which wasn't really a problem, as most houses only had one computer). Now, with the advent of easy Wi-Fi and cheaper computers (plus iPods and iPhones), many houses have a handful of connected devices sharing the airwaves and, with a little setup, sharing their connections, files and data too. The Internet & Wireless row of icons in System Preferences is all about your Networks – local and worldwide – how you interact with them and how you choose to share across them; be it sharing your files, screen, printer or even disc drive.

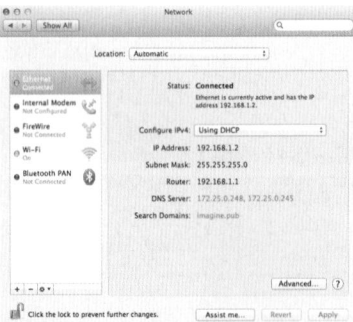

Network

For most users this should hopefully be one of those 'set it and forget it' preference panes, if you ever need to set it at all. With most modern networks you should find your Mac just connects and configures itself. Bliss.

Bluetooth

Check out the status of the Bluetooth peripherals you have connected to your Mac. To add a new Bluetooth device, like a mouse, keyboard or phone, click the '+' button.

"With most modern networks you should find your Mac just connects and configures itself"

Sharing
DVD or CD Sharing

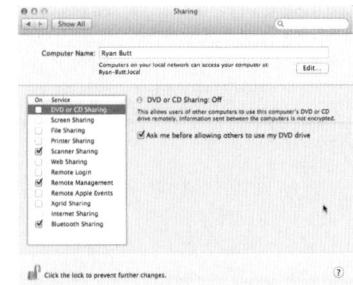

Share your DVD drive with a Mac that either has a broken drive or doesn't have one at all, like the MacBook Air or new Mac mini server.

Screen Sharing

Allow another computer (or iPhone) on your network to see your screen, and even control your Mac remotely.

File Sharing

Make files in certain folders available to other computers on your network. You can control who sees what.

Printer Sharing

With a tick of a box you can share any printer connected to your Mac with any other local computer.

Scanner Sharing

Save the hassle of unplugging and swapping one scanner between Macs by sharing it over the network.

Web Sharing

Mac OS X has its own pretty serious web server built right in, which can be enabled by ticking this box.

Remote Login

For those users happy typing commands in Terminal, this setting allows remote login to the Mac.

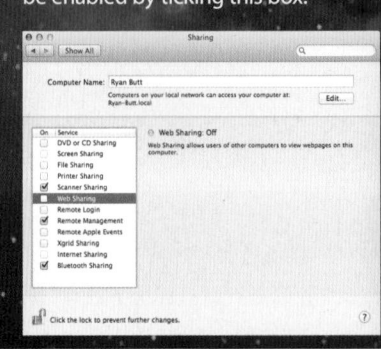

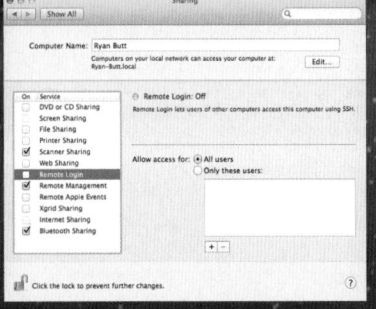

iCloud
Account Details

Sign in with your iCloud details to be able to sync details, files music and movies across all of your devices.

Sync

Syncing across iCloud allows multiple Macs and iPhones, even those in different locations, to share the same bookmarks, address books, calendars and more.

Manage

The iCloud is your virtual hard drive on the internet. You can use it to store photos, movies and files. This preference pane lets you check your space – you are provided with 5GB as standard but can purchase more if you need it.

Manage Account

You can use this option to check that your existing account details or correct or edit them to reflect any changes in your address or credit card information. You can also upgrade your iCloud account with more storage.

Remote Management

A step-up from Screen Sharing, Remote Management allows system-level control of your Mac from afar.

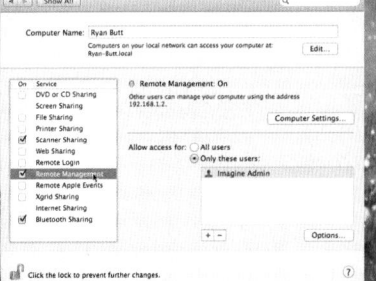

Remote Apple Events

For the real power users, Remote Apple Events allows your Mac to be automated by other computers.

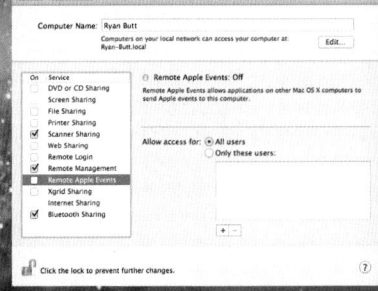

> **Purchase more space**
> Your iCloud account comes with 5GB of free space as standard, but if you come to realise that you require more, then click on 'Manage Account' and then click 'Change' next to the Storage option and purchase anything up to 50GB in storage space

> **Stay safe**
> You don't want to let just anyone send your files over Bluetooth, especially if you use a laptop in crowded areas like airports. To be safe, tick both 'Require pairing' boxes and leave the 'When' options as 'Ask What to Do'

Xgrid Sharing

Share extremely intensive tasks, like video rendering, across multiple Macs using Xgrid – for power users only!

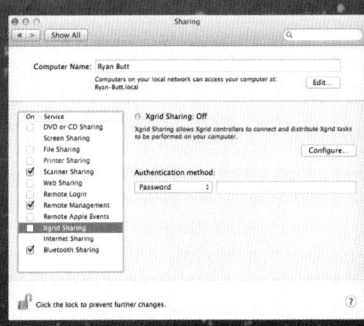

Internet Sharing

Share your internet connection with another computer by ticking the box and selecting the correct ports.

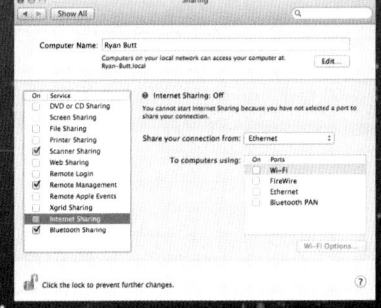

Bluetooth Sharing

Share photos, ringtones and more with a mobile phone using Bluetooth Sharing to create a short-range network to pass files across.

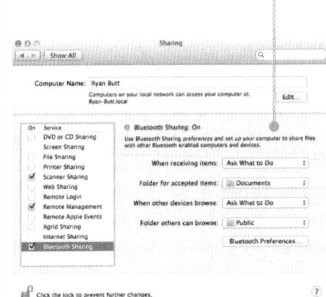

Inside System Preferences: System

Get to grips with the technology inside your Mac by following this final part of our guide to System Preferences. In this section: delve into the final row – the System settings

 The System settings, like the Network row above them, get deep down and dirty into the depths of Mac OS X. Many of the changes affect all users of the Mac, and it's here where you'll discover the tools you need to control which users can do what. It's also where you'll find Universal Access, the first place you should go if you have physical difficulties that make it hard for you to enjoy using your Mac.

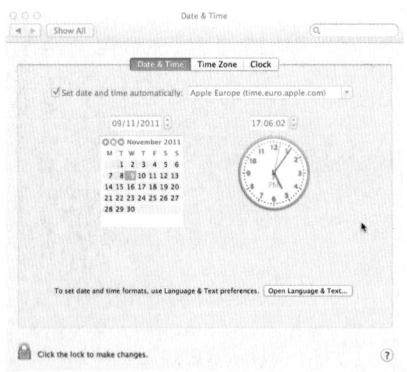

Date & Time

Always be sure that your Mac's clock is bang on time by setting it to automatically stay synchronised with Apple's time servers over the internet.

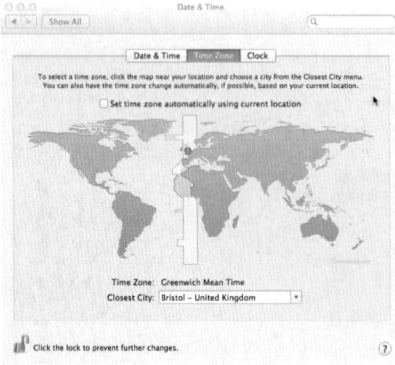

Time Zone

Let your Mac know where you are in the world by clicking the map near where you are, then choosing the closest city to you from the pop-up menu at the bottom of the screen.

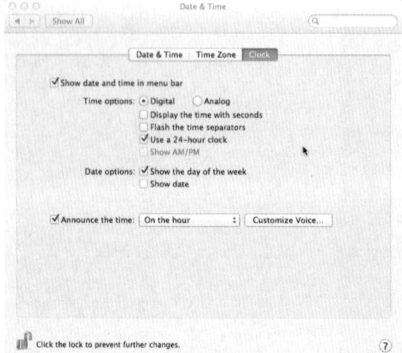

Clock

Set how your Menu bar displays the date and time. If Menu bar space is at a premium you can choose to see a tiny analog clock, or even get rid of it completely and have your Mac announce the time on the hour, every hour.

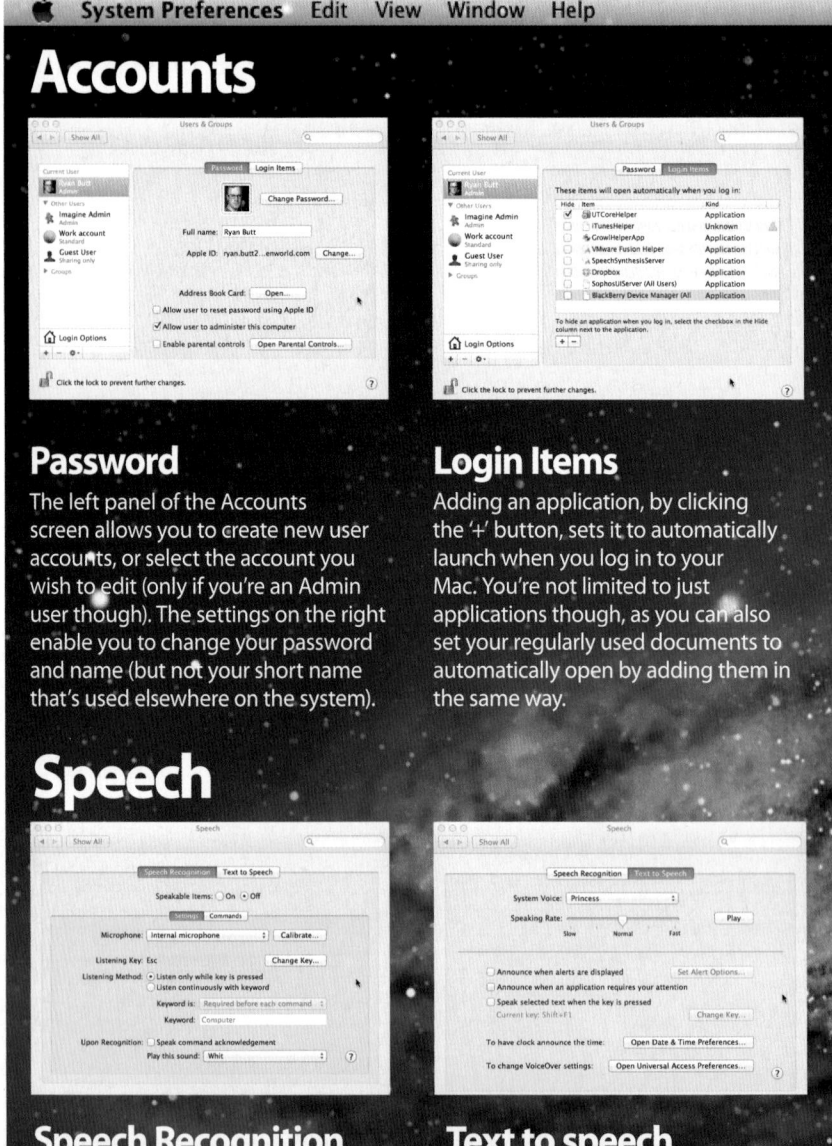

Accounts

Password

The left panel of the Accounts screen allows you to create new user accounts, or select the account you wish to edit (only if you're an Admin user though). The settings on the right enable you to change your password and name (but not your short name that's used elsewhere on the system).

Login Items

Adding an application, by clicking the '+' button, sets it to automatically launch when you log in to your Mac. You're not limited to just applications though, as you can also set your regularly used documents to automatically open by adding them in the same way.

Speech

Speech Recognition

Chances are you may not have realised that it's possible to control your Mac using your voice. Okay, so it's not perfect – in fact, it's likely to turn into one of the most frustrating experiences you've had on a Mac, but it's still cool. And for the rare few that have it working perfectly, invaluable.

Text to speech

Not only can you talk to your Mac, it can talk straight back at you. Text to Speech can give you valuable audio feedback when your Mac requires your attention, speaking alert boxes and more. You can also choose your Mac's voice from a wide range of styles and speeds.

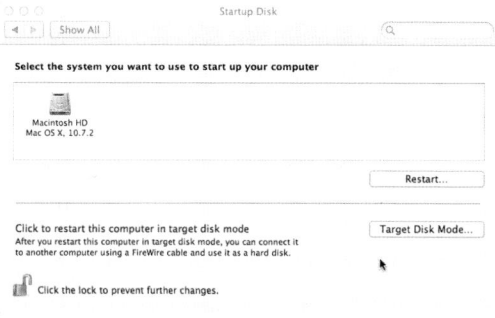

Startup Disk

For power users, with different versions of Mac OS X installed across multiple hard drives, this pane enables you to pick the drive you'd like to start from.

Time Machine

Mac OS X comes with what is arguably the best 'set it and forget it' back-up utility: Time Machine. Turn it on, select a disk and rest assured that your data is safe.

"You can choose how often you would like it to check for updates or run a manual check yourself"

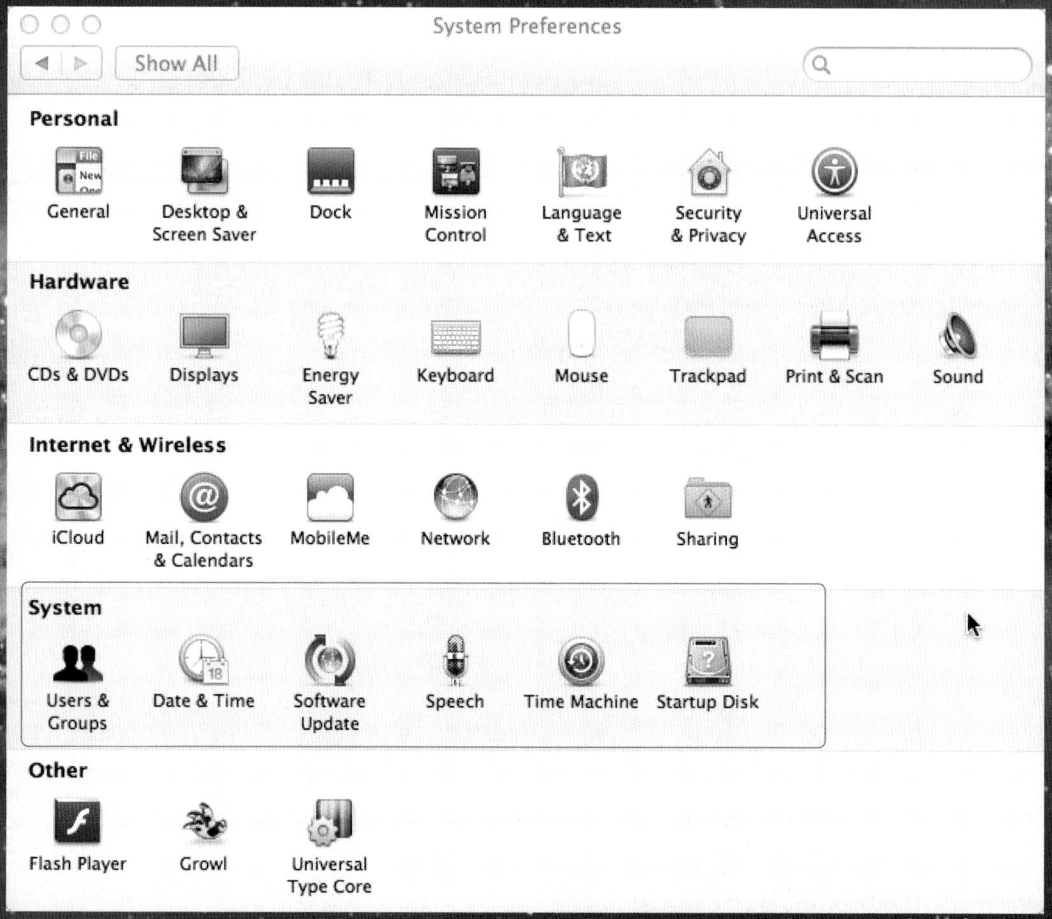

Software Update

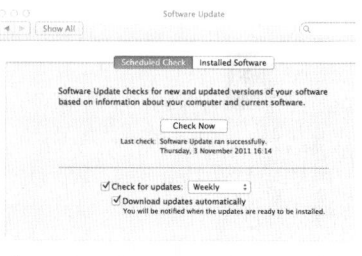

Scheduled Check

Software Update runs automatically to ensure your Mac is always running the most up-to-date version of any Apple software you have installed, including Mac OS X, iLife and the Apple Pro applications. You can choose how often you'd like it to check for updates or run a manual check yourself.

Installed Software

By using this pane you can quickly check the version numbers of any Apple software you have installed and when it was last updated. This can come in handy if you're trying to troubleshoot a problem and think it might be down to a recent update or software install.

Adjust Date & Time settings

For the truly international Mac user there are a wealth of options hidden in the Date & Time section of System Preferences…

 **App used:**
System Preferences

 **Time needed:**
10 minutes

 We admit that this probably isn't the most thrilling topic in the world, but there's no doubt that when you travel abroad, having the right time and date on your Mac can be a life saver. So, you need to be able to get in there and make changes very easily. This is the kind of stuff OS X is great at doing. With a couple of clicks you can change your time zone, calendar type, the view that you get on your Mac, as well as a host of other options. And don't worry, none of the changes are permanent – just go back in and change them again whenever you need to.

Once you get used to the system, even if you're as frequent a flier as Steve Jobs, you will always

"With just a mere couple of clicks you can change your time zone"

know whether you're in time to get a drink at the bar or if the hotel you're staying in is still serving breakfast. And you certainly don't want to be late for that meeting you've flown out for!

Of course, this isn't the only use of this essential feature. We trust our Macs to tell us the correct time and date, and not even changing to British Summer Time should confuse your computer. But if you ever find that the time is slightly out, or even the date, it's useful to know how to change these setting manually. It shouldn't happen very often but the option is always there.

Customise Date & Time
The options on your Mac are plentiful and will keep you up to date

Drops and buttons
The combination of drop-down menus and buttons means that making changes isn't an overwhelming mess of screens. It always feels as though you're on the same page

Changeable
Everything in System Preferences can be easily switched back to the way it was, so if you are travelling you can simply switch everything back when you return

Lockable
Prevent other users from changing settings by clicking the lock shut every time you finish making a change

SAFETY FIRST
System Preferences are password protected to make sure that only a Mac's administrator is able to make changes. The lock is retained even for single users in order to prevent any kind of malicious or would-be-funny changes being made by a guest in your account.

Easy examples
Lion gives you examples of the way dates can be displayed, so you can choose the one you like best or take elements from it before you make the changes

OS X Time it right, make it a date

01: Preferences

Load System Preferences from either your Dock, Applications folder or from the Apple menu. Now head down to and click on Date & Time.

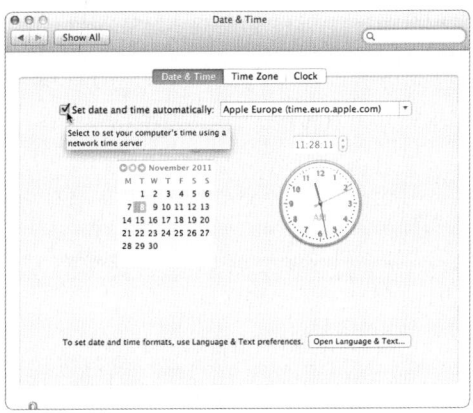

02: Automatic and easy

If you are connected to the internet, your Mac can quickly and easily set the time and date from a network server. Just tick the box.

03: Pick a zone

You will, however, have to make sure that your Mac has the right time zone, so use the drop-down menu and pick the one that applies to you.

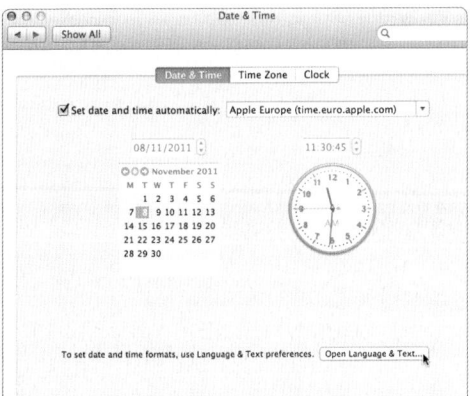

04: Get international

If you want to make further changes to time and date formats then just click the 'Open Language & Text' button under the clock.

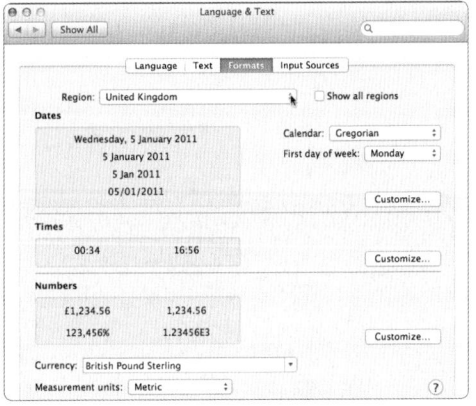

05: Right in the middle

Now that you're on the Language & Text page, click the Formats tab. Here you can begin by selecting your region from the drop-down menu.

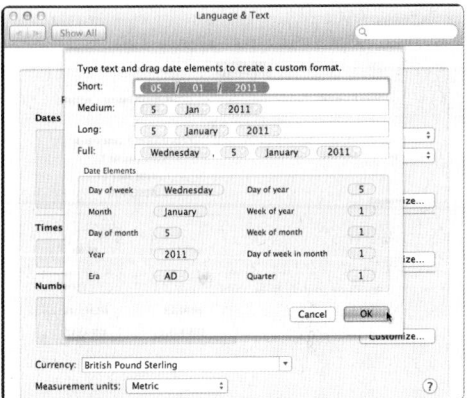

06: Drag and drop

If you click the first Customize button you'll see this drop-down window. Here you can drag-and-drop different elements into the format bar.

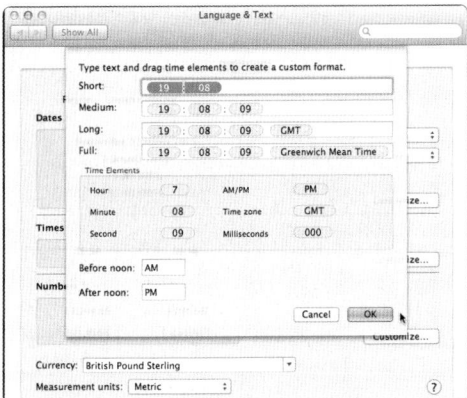

07: Time to get detailed

When done with that one click OK and then hit the second Customize button to do the same thing with the time settings.

08: Calendar

Again, click OK to save the changes and return to the Formats screen. You can now use the drop-down menu to select the calendar to use.

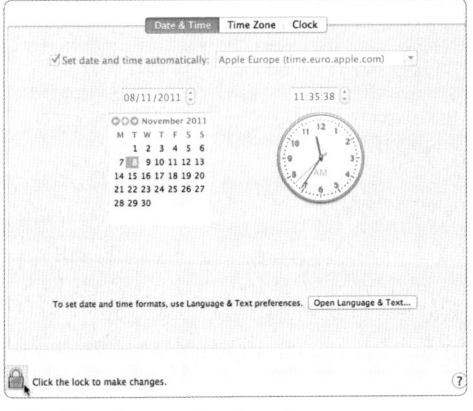

09: Back to the lock

When you are happy with the changes, use the back button to return to the Date & Time page. Now click the lock to prevent further changes.

Set up security on your Mac

If there's more than one person who uses your Mac, protect yourself against unwanted system changes by setting up some security

 **App used:**
System Preferences

 **Time needed:**
5 minutes

 When you first buy a Mac it's very easy to get caught up in the bells and whistles of the iLife suite and the great creative projects that you can complete by using it. So this usually means that OS X, and especially security, can accidentally be overlooked.

Your Mac, just like anything else that you own, needs to be properly cared for. And in most cases your Mac will be used by more than one person, so changes to the system can easily be made without you even being aware of it. These changes could affect the way you use your computer and

cause you a lot of unwanted grief. It could also use up a lot of your time having to constantly go back and return the settings to the way you want

"Changes to your system can be made without you being aware of it"

them every time someone has fiddled with things. But protecting your Mac against these accidental – or indeed intentional – changes is extremely easy and will mean that anyone wishing to make system changes will require a password to do so. Sometimes it's the only way you can stop your kids from putting that Mickey Mouse screen saver on every time they use the computer! It will only take a few minutes of your time, and it will ensure that you remain in control at all times, even when someone else is using your machine. Read on to see our simple steps for adding security.

Make your Mac secure

Remain in control of your settings and stop others from fiddling!

Log out time limit
Use this setting to action a time out for inactivity. The system will require you to log in if the computer is inactive for a certain time period, which you can specify

Enable disable
You can quickly toggle automatic login on and off from here. It means you can be sure that unwanted visitors can't access your Mac when you're away from home or the office

Padlock
The Preferences padlock is Apple's simple way of allowing you to make changes. You can only make changes when the lock is open. Just click on the padlock to open or close it and be ready with your password

HELP AND SUPPORT
If you're ever in a situation where you can't seem to fathom your System Preferences then you can always turn to Apple for help. At the website www.apple.com is a Support section where you can type in a query. Not only will you get stock responses from Apple, but you'll also have the option to access posts made by others about a certain function or problem.

Don't get stuck
If you're new to the system you can get some help by clicking on the question mark button, located in the bottom-right corner

Finder Keeping you safe and secure

01: It's all about Preferences

Open up System Preferences. Do this either from your Dock or by clicking the Apple in the top-left of your screen and selecting System Preferences from the drop-down menu. Now click the Security icon.

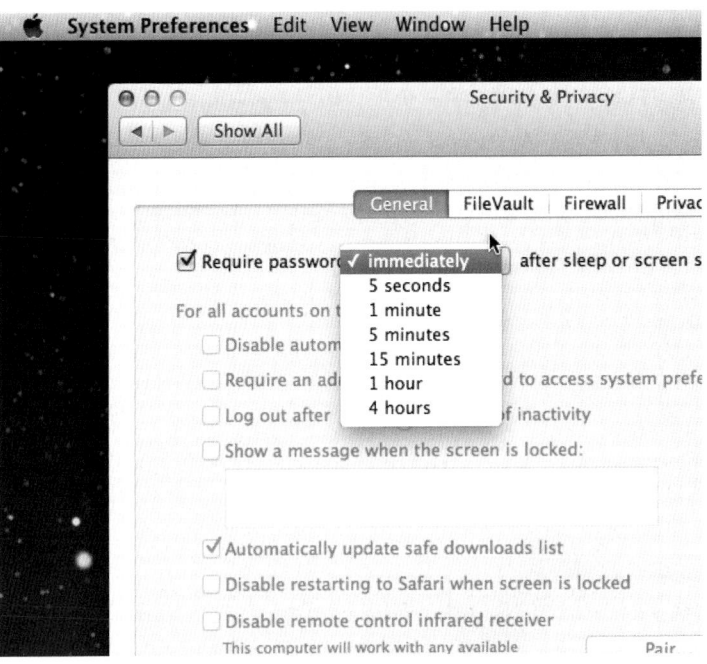

02: Tick the boxes

Tick the top box to set the system up to require a password when waking, either from sleep or from the screen saver. This will then prompt you to decide whether to disable automatic login. Click Yes or No.

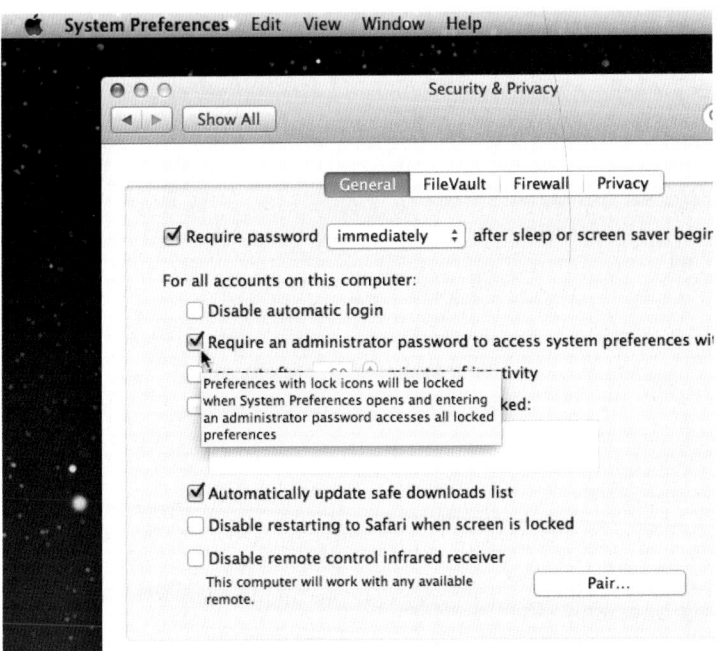

03: Preference panes

On the same window, click the 'Require password to unlock each System Preferences pane' box. This will ensure that none of your settings can be altered without a password.

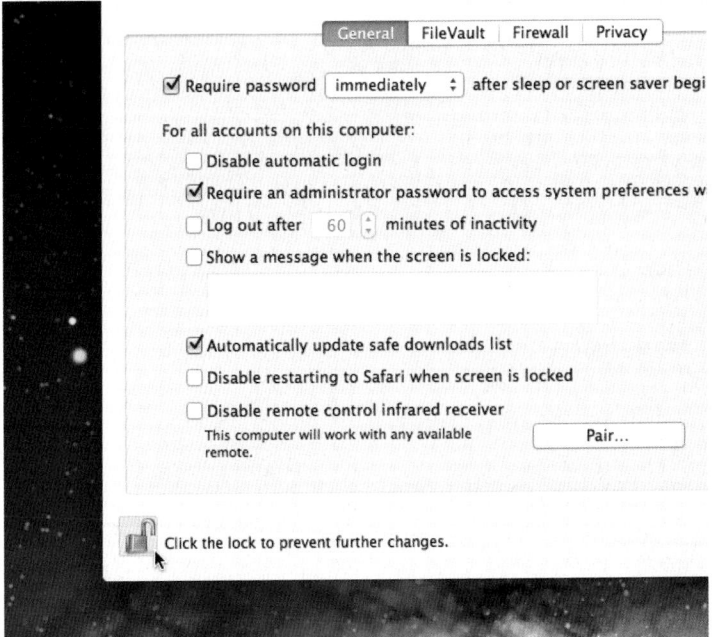

04: Lock it up

Click the lock to prevent any immediate changes and to get the new commands running. You'll now have to type a password to make changes, which should prevent any tampering from unwanted users in future.

Never lose your work with Auto Save

If you have ever lost work, you'll love Lion's Auto Save feature

X When you use apps on your iPad or iPhone, you don't think about saving; you just quit or switch to another one, and when you return you carry on where you left off. Lion brings such a feature to OS X, and you never need to think about saving your document, image or whatever you are working on again, because

Auto Save does it for you. When using TextEdit or Preview, for example, there is no need to save, because every five minutes Auto Save stores your work on the Mac's disk without being tasked to or prompted by yourself. If you quit, then Auto Save writes any changes to disk automatically. It's brilliantly simple and fabulously reassuring. Files can

be locked to prevent accidental changes being saved, and they can be duplicated so that they can easily be used as templates for new documents. Auto Save uses 'Versions' to save your work. You can browse the changes, and go back to an earlier version if you need to. Here we explore how Auto Save works…

PREVIOUS VERSION
The previously Auto Saved version is displayed on the right. Click to select it and zoom in. You may be able to interact with it, too

WINDOW STACK
This stack of windows represent versions of Auto Saved files going back into the past. Click the title bars to select one and view the previous versions

THE TIMELINE
The timeline on the right shows the dates the versions were created. Move the mouse over it, and click a date or time to select a document version

RESTORE A VERSION
After you have found a previous version that you would like to return to, select it and click the 'Restore' button. It will replace the current document

Back up your work

Apply an extra level of security by activating Time Machine

As we have discovered, it is almost impossible to lose your work when you are using Lion's Auto Save feature. But, if like us, you still aren't entirely convinced about your machine's ability to handle your precious files with the greatest of care, then you can also activate your Mac's Time Machine app to automatically back-up your work.

To start using your Time Machine, open your System Preferences from the Dock, look for 'Time Machine' under the 'System' section, and then click on the icon to launch the app. Once it has loaded, select a disk to use as your backup destination, and then relax, safe in the knowledge that all of your important work will be saved and safely stored on an

external device every few minutes without you having to lift a finger. It's a great feature that can ensure you never lose a precious file or folder ever again.

To read up on more information on Time Machine, and a more detailed explanation of how to set it up and configure it, turn to page 82 now.

Key features

Get to know how Auto Save works

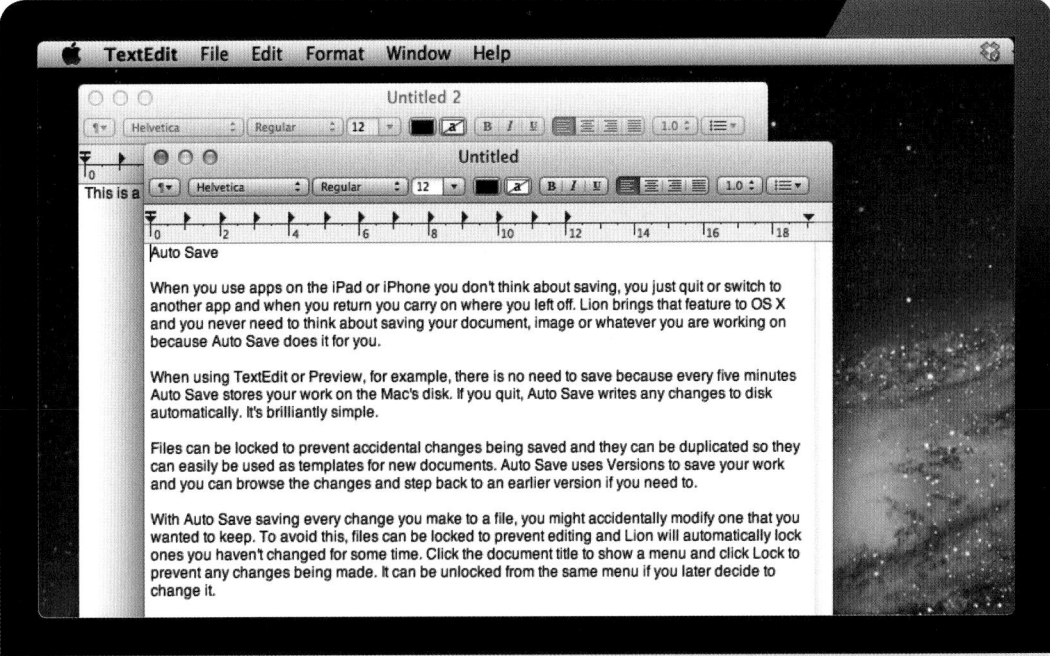

Locking and unlocking

With Auto Save saving every change you make to a file, you might accidentally modify one that you wanted to keep. To avoid this, files can be locked to prevent editing, and Lion will automatically lock ones you haven't changed for some time. Click the document title to show a menu, and click 'Lock' to prevent any changes being made. It can be unlocked from the same menu if you later decide to change it.

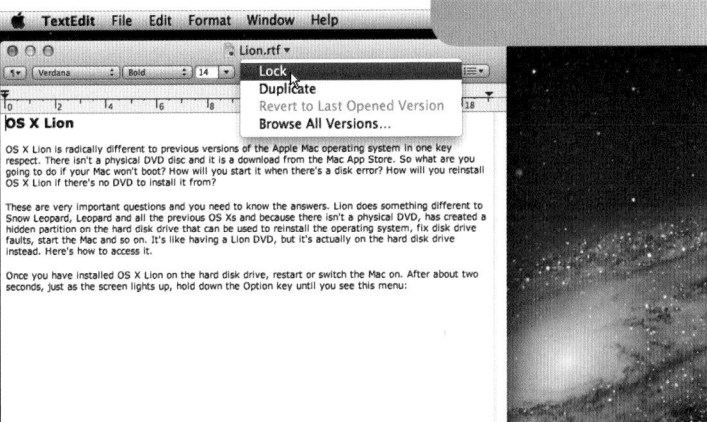

How do I Save As?

The File menu has changed with Lion apps, so there is no longer a 'Save As' option. In fact, after saving a document, there isn't even a Save option, and everything is automatic. There are several options available to you; one is to select 'Duplicate' from the 'File' menu or from the title bar menu. An identical window opens with the document. Choose 'File', and then 'Save' to save it using a new name.

Open files you didn't save

Imagine this scenario, you are working on a document, image or other file, and you remember that you have a meeting or appointment. You look at the clock, see the time, hit Cmd+Q to quit, and whoops! Where is your file? Don't panic, as when you restart an app, such as TextEdit for example, any unsaved documents will be reopened automatically, as Auto Save has saved them in a temporary folder for you.

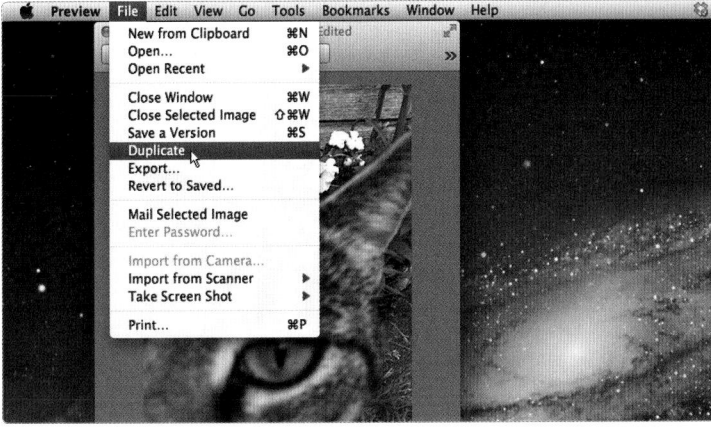

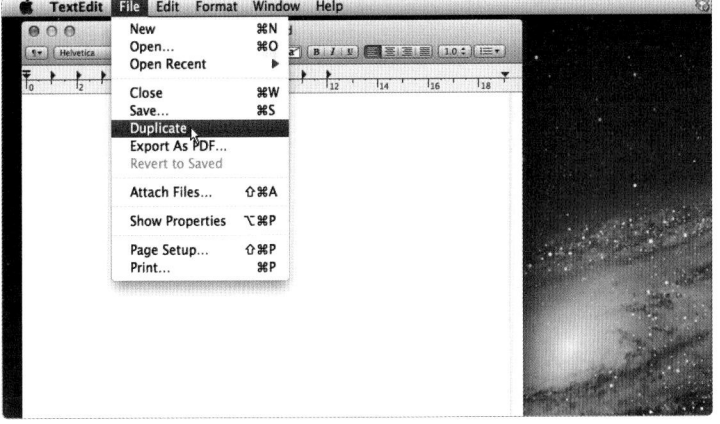

Which apps use Auto Save?

Auto Save is a new feature in OS X, and applications are being designed to take advantage it. Any software released before Lion will not use it. Apple apps like TextEdit, Preview and the latest versions of iWork (Pages, Numbers, Keynote) all use it right now, and soon third-party software will begin including it in the apps. To see if an app uses Auto Save, look for 'Save a version' and 'Duplicate' in the File menu.

Pair a Bluetooth device with your Mac

App used:
Bluetooth

Time needed:
5 minutes

A life without cables: here's how to get set up with Bluetooth devices

X Once you've experienced the joys of linking appliances to your Mac wirelessly, it's hard to imagine there's any other way to do it. Nowadays it is possible to connect a variety of peripherals wirelessly, from keyboards and mice to headphones, printers, speakers, smartphones and much more besides.

The most widely-used method of connecting your Mac to other appliances is through Bluetooth technology, which is built into Macs and many wireless peripherals.

To use Bluetooth devices with your Mac they have to be first paired – or linked – with your Mac. This involves ensuring that the Bluetooth-equipped peripheral is discoverable – which allows it to

"A paired device will be recognised automatically"

be recognised by your Mac, and then pairing it, often by typing in a passcode on your Mac, and sometimes on the device being paired. Typing in a passcode ensures that the device can only transfer information with your Mac, and that a nearby computer won't be able to intercept the communication.

Once paired, recognition is automatic, so when a device that has already been paired is brought into range of your Mac, it should be automatically recognised without user intervention.

Take control, wirelessly
All you need to know to use a Bluetooth device with your Mac

Make it discoverable
Bluetooth devices can't talk to each other until they have been introduced, so make sure your Mac can be seen by remote devices by turning Bluetooth on and making your Mac discoverable

More info
It's not something that you'll use often, but selecting the More Info menu option allows you to find out more information about your device, which is often useful if you're trying to diagnose connection problems

Show in menu bar
For quick access to your Bluetooth settings in the future, you can add it to the Mac's menu bar. Check the 'Show Bluetooth Status in menu bar' option here

Unpairing a device
Once paired, devices remain linked to your Mac. But what if you want to use it with another Mac? You'll need to 'unpair' it from the current Mac by disconnecting it

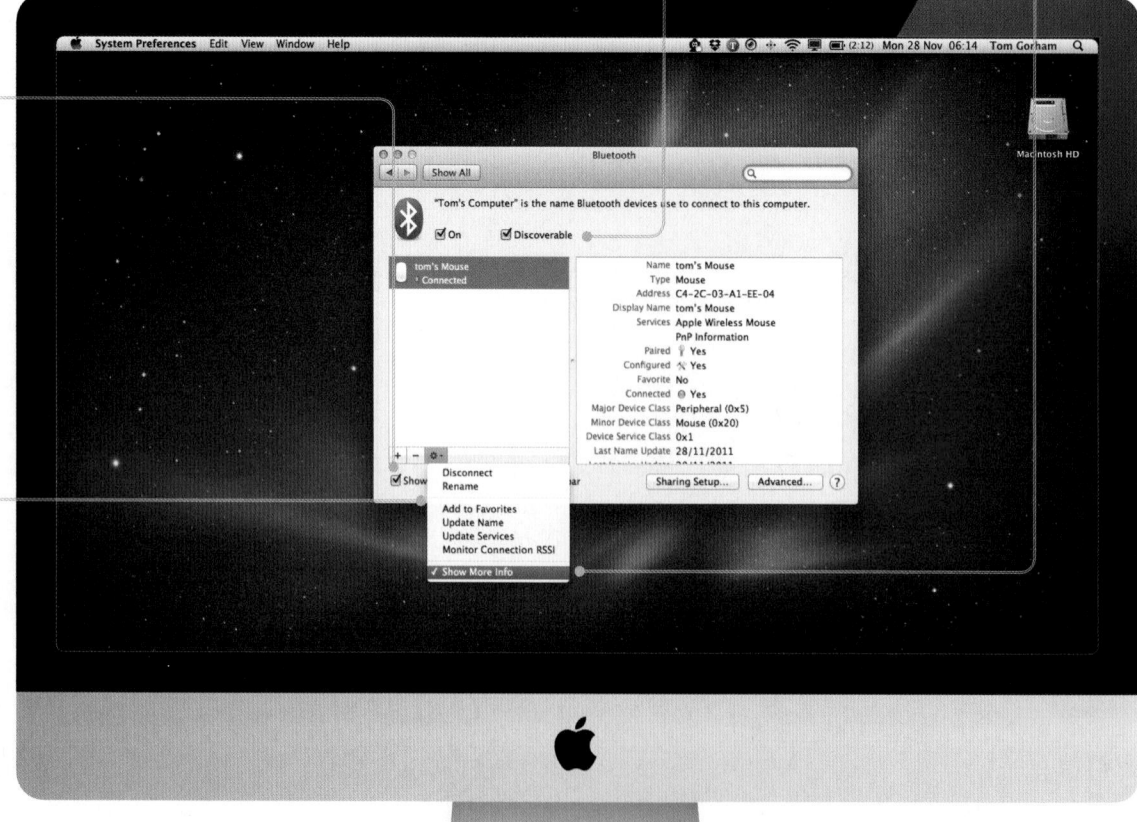

WHAT'S IN A PASSCODE?
Bluetooth devices have a variety of pairing methods. Some, such as headphones, may only require you to click a button before it connects to your Mac. But in most cases, you'll need to enter a passcode. Sometimes, for example, with smartphones, you may need to enter an automatically generated passcode on both devices before they will recognise each other.

Bluetooth Pair a Bluetooth device

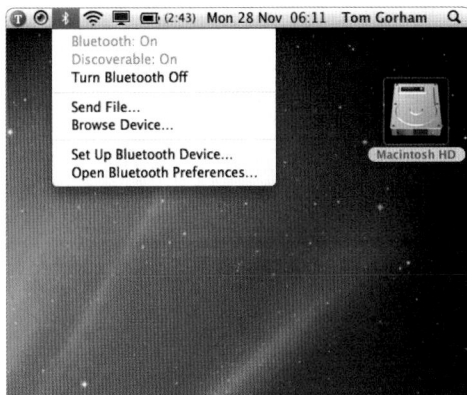

01: Open Bluetooth

Click the Bluetooth icon on the Mac's menu bar and select 'Set up Bluetooth Device'. If there's no icon, you'll need to go to System Preferences.

02: Open Bluetooth

Click on the Apple logo in the menu bar then click on System Preferences, and click the Bluetooth icon to open Bluetooth's preferences.

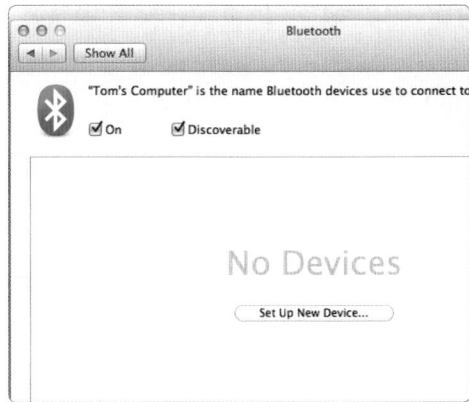

03: Turn Bluetooth on

Check the boxes to ensure that Bluetooth is both on and discoverable, so Bluetooth devices will be able to recognise your Mac and connect to it.

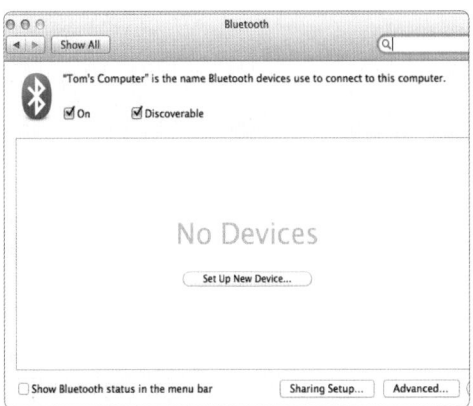

04: Add your device

Click 'Set up New Device' to open Bluetooth Setup Assistant. If you have set a device up before, click the '+' button at the bottom.

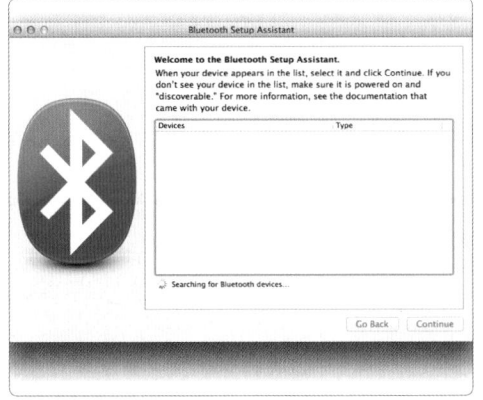

05: Setup assistant

The Setup Assistant will try to connect to any Bluetooth devices nearby. If your device isn't listed, make sure it is turned on and discoverable.

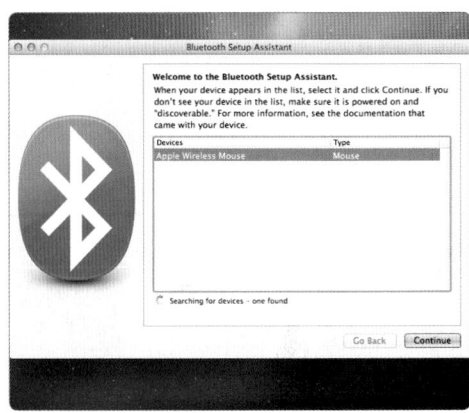

06: Setting up

When your device appears in the list, select it. You now need to pair the device. The first step is to click the Continue button.

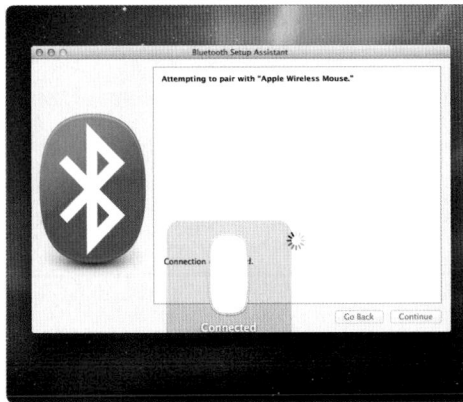

07: Pairing the device

Your Mac will attempt to pair with the device so they can communicate with each other. Some pair automatically, but others require a passcode.

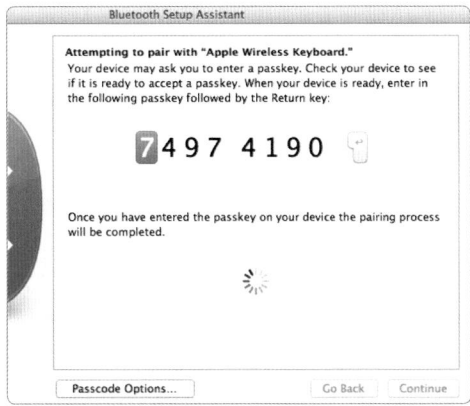

08: Add the code

If given, enter the number here. On some devices, such as an iPhone, you'll also need to enter a passcode on your device.

09: Advanced settings

Once paired, your device should appear in the list. You can click the 'Advanced' button to examine its settings in more detail.

Tweak your trackpad settings in System Preferences

Learn how to change the settings in System Preferences to master multi-touch gestures

 **App used:** System Preferences  **Time needed:** 5 minutes

 If multi-touch gestures are the cornerstone of the OS X Lion experience, then the trackpad can certainly be seen as the bricks and mortar that holds it all together. Without the built-in multi-touch trackpad on the MacBook Pro or MacBook Air, or the amazing wireless Magic Trackpad, Lion and its myriad of new features wouldn't run half as smoothly.

The trackpad settings pane in System Preferences helps to make that experience even better by allowing you to decide which gestures perform what action, as well as playing you a handy video of exactly how to perform them. It means you can make the trackpad work exactly how you want it to and tailor it to your needs. In this tutorial, we'll show you how to get the best out of this little-known feature in order to make the most of your Lion experience. It's an easy process that will soon have you finding your way around your Mac with smooth moves that suit you.

Using the preferences
Make the trackpad settings suit your needs with this window

MASTERING GESTURES
In order to get the most out of Lion, it's a good idea to get used to the gestures that will save you time. For example, pinching with your thumb and three fingers with a claw-like movement will bring up Launchpad, while pushing three fingers upwards will bring up Mission Control. Both gestures allow you to speed up things like organising your desktop and launching apps.

Tabs
Different trackpad settings are grouped under three different tabs – this makes finding exactly what you want to adjust a lot easier and quicker. It also helps to declutter what can often be confusing preference panes

Making settings simple
Lion has vastly improved the UI of its trackpad settings by spacing out different settings and making it clear which ones relate to which gesture with the use of highlights, arrows and videos

Tracking problems?
If your Magic Trackpad is slow or unresponsive, your first port of call should be the tracking speed slider in the trackpad settings. If that doesn't make any difference, try replacing the batteries in your trackpad and reconnecting

Video previews
Even if you don't want to change any of your trackpad settings, the video previews in System Preferences can really help you master some of the more tricky multi-touch gestures. They're time-savers and worth learning

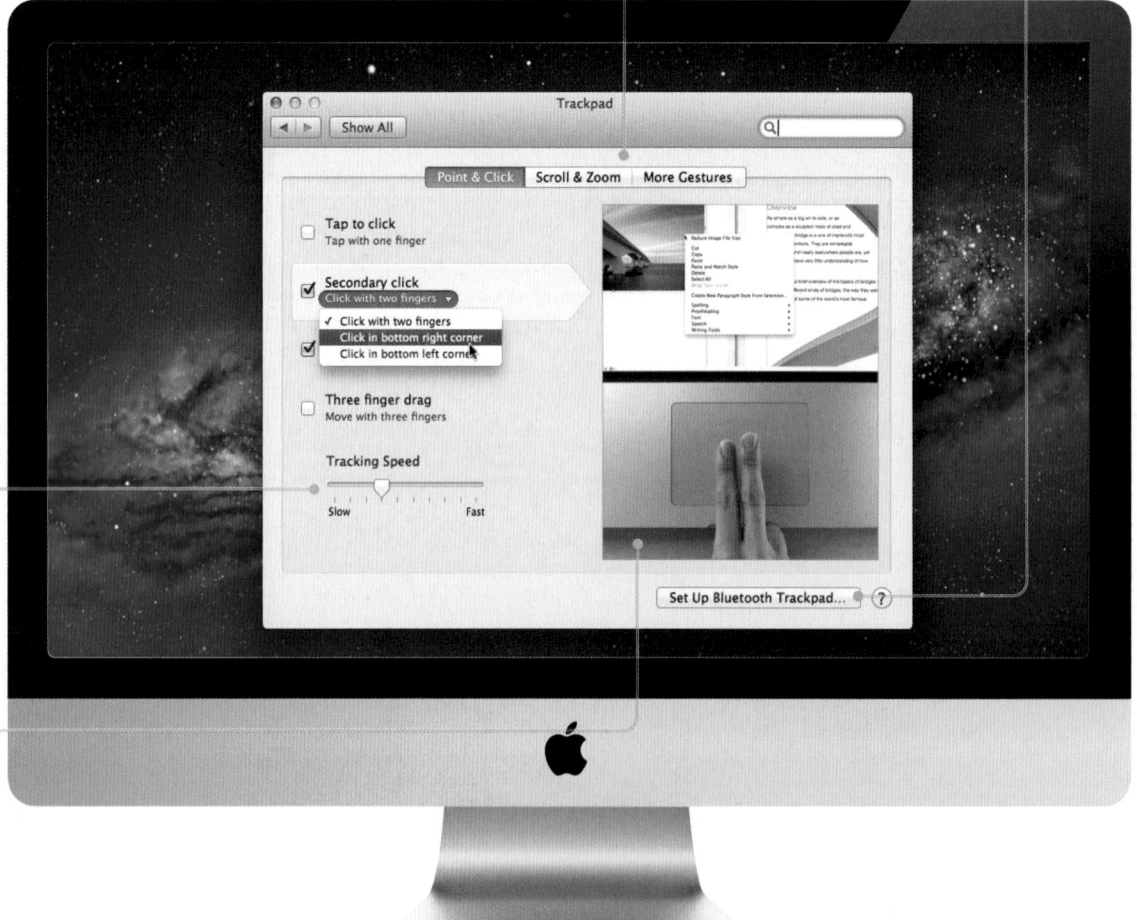

System Preferences Tweak your trackpad settings

01: System Preferences

Click on the Apple logo in the menubar, then click on System Preferences. Here you'll find all the settings for your Mac, apps and OS X Lion.

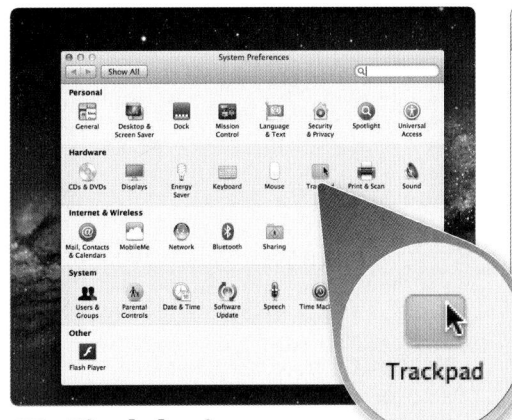

02: Find the icon

Click on the Trackpad icon in System Preferences – this is known as a preferences pane. When you install apps, they'll create preference panes here.

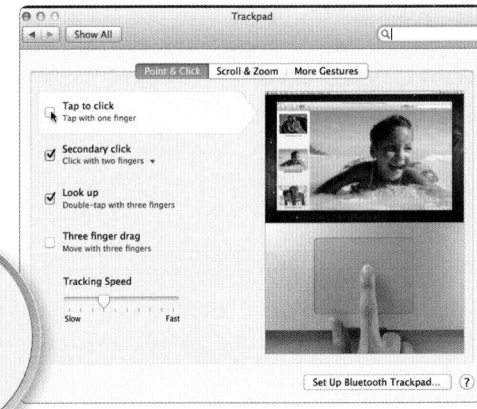

03: Check them

Trackpad settings are displayed as checkboxes; check or uncheck them to activate or deactivate. A video description is included to help you.

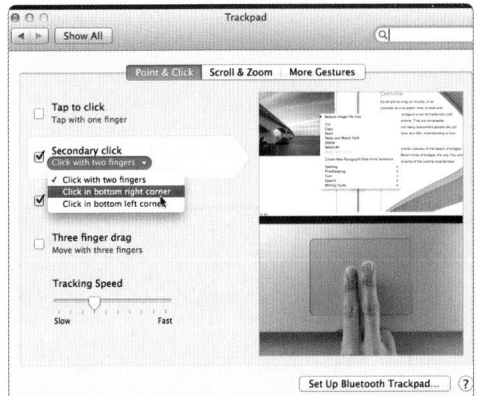

04: Change the gesture

Under some settings you can change the gesture that controls them. Click on the drop-down menu and choose the gesture that best suits you.

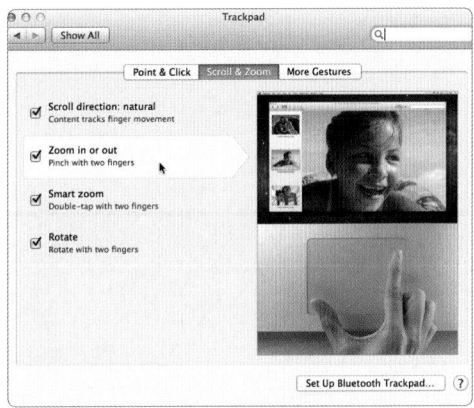

05: Hover and preview

Lion displays a short video animation to help you understand how to perform different gestures. Simply hover over the gesture's name to preview.

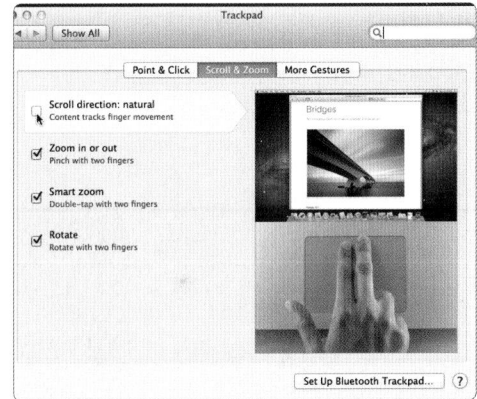

06: Different directions

Uncheck 'Scroll direction: natural' to revert two-finger scrolling to pre-Lion behaviour. In Lion, content follows your finger movement.

07: More Gestures

Under the More Gestures tab you'll find some of the more complex gestures. Make use of the videos to master these new features.

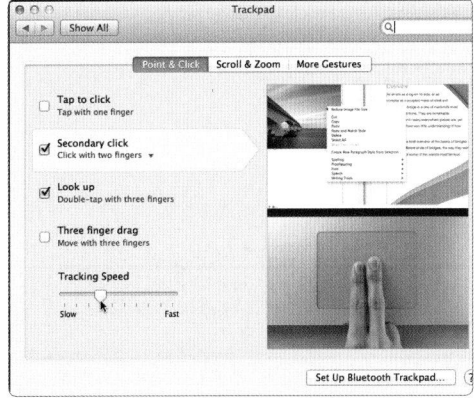

08: Tracking Speed

Drag the Tracking Speed slider to adjust the sensitivity to your finger movement. The faster on the slider, the more responsive it will be.

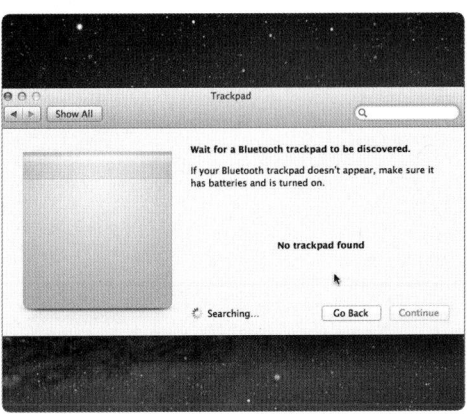

09: Magic Trackpads

If you own a Magic Trackpad, set it up by clicking 'Set Up Bluetooth Trackpad' in the bottom corner of the Trackpad settings window.

Modify your Magic Mouse settings

Your Magic Mouse can do a lot more than point and click
– here's how to add multi-touch gestures

App used:
System Preferences

Time needed:
5 minutes

Thanks to its smooth, buttonless, surface, Apple's Magic Mouse is a thing of beauty. But it's not a case of form before function.

For a start, it's the world's first multi-touch mouse. Its entire surface is made up of a single sensor, so you can click – or double-click – anywhere at all on its surface.

This sensitivity means that the Magic Mouse has advantages over conventional mice. You can scroll left or right in a document by moving your finger horizontally across the surface, or by adding another

finger and moving left or right across the surface you can browse music in iTunes, scroll through web pages in Safari or pictures in iPhoto. Run your finger up or down the mouse to scroll through a web page or document.

Best of all, the Magic Mouse is customisable, which comes in handy when configuring the mouse's secondary button. On most mice you have to click the right-hand button to right-click. On the Magic Mouse, left-handed users can quickly adjust the settings to make the left-hand side act as the secondary button.

> "With a Magic Mouse you can click – or double-click – anywhere at all on its surface"

Customise your Mouse
Change the settings on your
Magic Mouse to suit you

Unnatural scrolling
OS Lion reverses the typical scroll direction used in previous operating systems. If you're uncomfortable with this, you can revert to the standard way used before Lion by unchecking 'Scroll direction: natural'

Battery level
Wireless mice use batteries rather than USB power, but at least the Magic Mouse's should last for a month or more. You can keep a check on the remaining battery life here

Video Previews
Video previews illustrate how to perform a gesture when you hover the mouse over that option. They come in quite handy when it comes to getting the hang of some of the more complicated gestures

Speed up tracking
The default speed at which the Magic Mouse moves across the screen is fairly slow, but it's easy to make it track faster by dragging this slider over to the right-hand side

INERTIAL SCROLLING
A clever feature of the Magic Mouse is support for inertial scrolling. Traditionally scrolling stops as soon as your fingers stop moving on the mouse. But, mimicking the scrolling approach of the iPhone and iPad, scrolling on the Magic Mouse can have momentum, so depending on how quickly you flick your finger you'll continue to scroll after your fingers have left the surface of the mouse.

System Preferences Customise the Magic Mouse

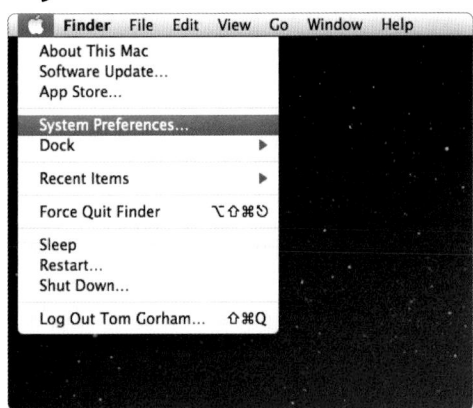

01: System Preferences

Click on the Apple logo in the menu bar then click on System Preferences, which contains many of your basic settings for OS X Lion.

02: Find the icon

Click on the Mouse icon in System Preferences. This pane is where all your settings relating to your mouse are kept.

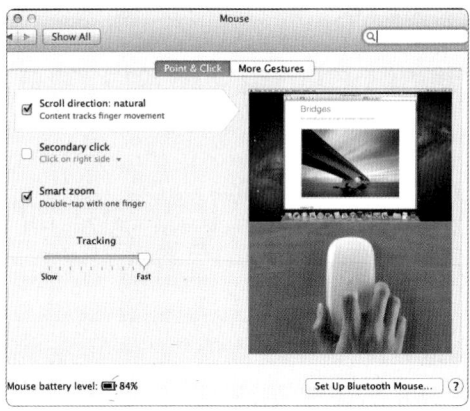

03: Check your settings

Under the Point & Click tab you'll find basic settings for your mouse which you can activate by checking the boxes.

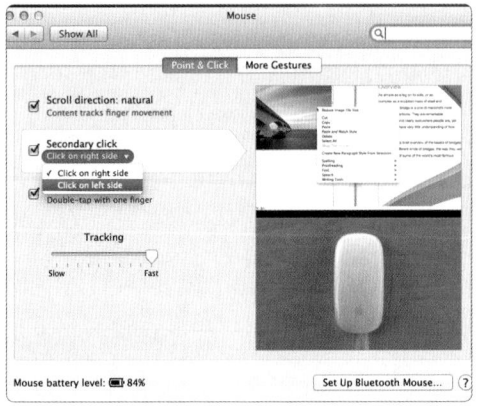

04: Right to left click

Left-handed? Switch the sides of the mouse. Click on Secondary click and from the drop-down menu, select 'Click on left side'.

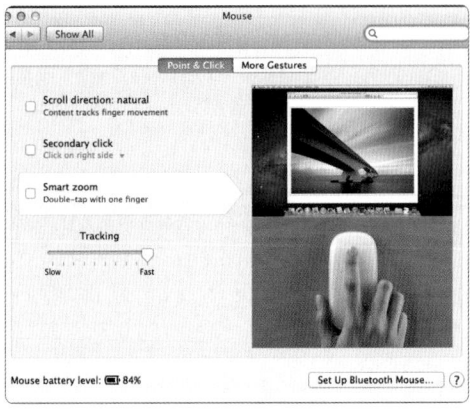

05: No multi-touch

You don't have to have all the bells and whistles. If you prefer your mouse as a standard single-button device, deselect all the checkboxes.

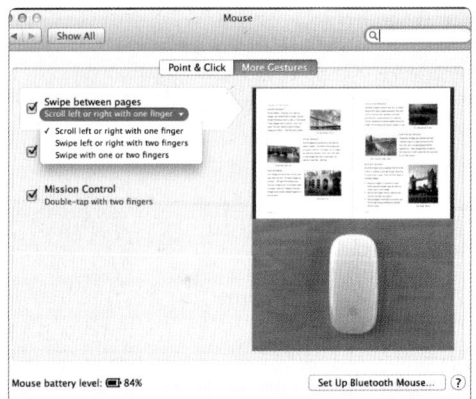

06: More gestures

Under the More Gestures tab you can configure more gestures, such as whether to use one or two fingers to swipe between pages.

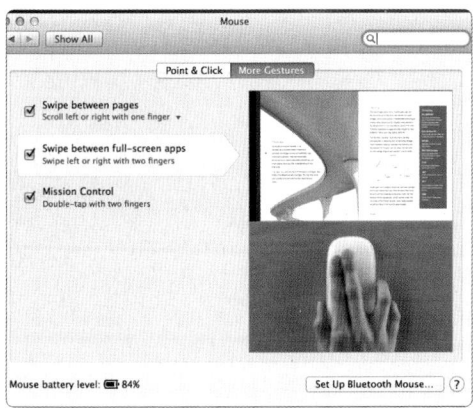

07: Video previews

A short animation on the right illustrates many of settings in action. To view it, hover the mouse over the settings.

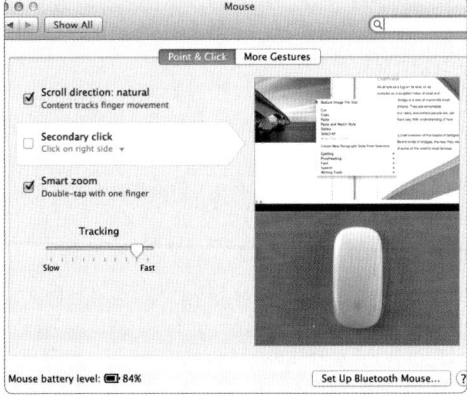

08: Tracking speed

Drag the slider to adjust the sensitivity of your mouse movement. The faster the slider, the more responsive the mouse will be when you move it

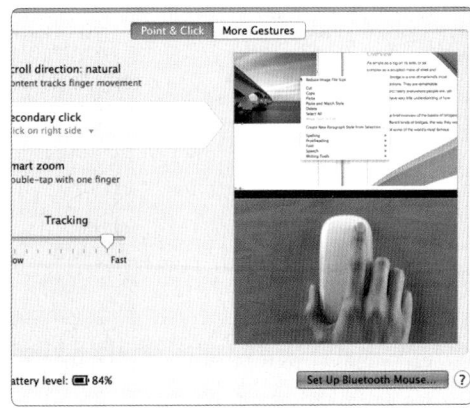

09: Bluetooth settings

The Magic Mouse uses Bluetooth to connect to your Mac. Edit its settings by clicking 'Set up Bluetooth Mouse' in the bottom corner.

Use Disk Utility to check the health of your hard drive and repair it

Checking and improving the health of your hard drive is easier than you think. With a couple of clicks you can set your mind at rest…

 **App used:**
Disk Utility

 **Time needed:**
10 minutes

 It can become pretty scary when your Mac starts to show tell-tale signs of wear and tear. As well built as they are, like everything else on the planet they are susceptible to the pitfalls of ageing. Prolonged use and writing and re-writing of data can cause things to slow down, and in some cases cause errors.

Luckily Apple has made it very easy for you to check on the health of your hard drive. Using an

application called Disk Utility, users can very easily check disks, repair damage and even erase free space to keep the volume healthy and happy. If used on a regular basis you can quite easily keep your hard drive from slowing down and retain that great snappy feeling you had when you first bought your Mac. You will also, with regular use, be able to spot any serious problems before they cause any devastating loss of data.

"Luckily Apple has made it easy to check on the health of your hard drive"

Get a snappier drive with Disk Utility
Clearing free space on your drive can have a marked improvement on performance

Erase options
Here you can choose the level of erasing you wish to use. The 35 step is obviously the best, but it will take an incredibly long time. Pick whichever suits you best

Tab it up
Clicking here will take you to the Erase section. Be extra careful before you click anything here as you could wipe important files

Double check
Make sure you are making changes to the correct disk. Check and double check before starting actions in Disk Utility

Erase Free Space
This will only erase space that isn't being actively used; so if you've done some house keeping and cleared a lot of files out then this is a good way to get some performance back as a result of the change

SERIOUS PROBLEMS
Disk Utility may not be able to repair serious problems, but it will definitely let you know if it spots anything untoward. Any serious problems will be highlighted in red and often there will be advice on the best course of action. In serious cases this will be to contact Apple or a reseller.

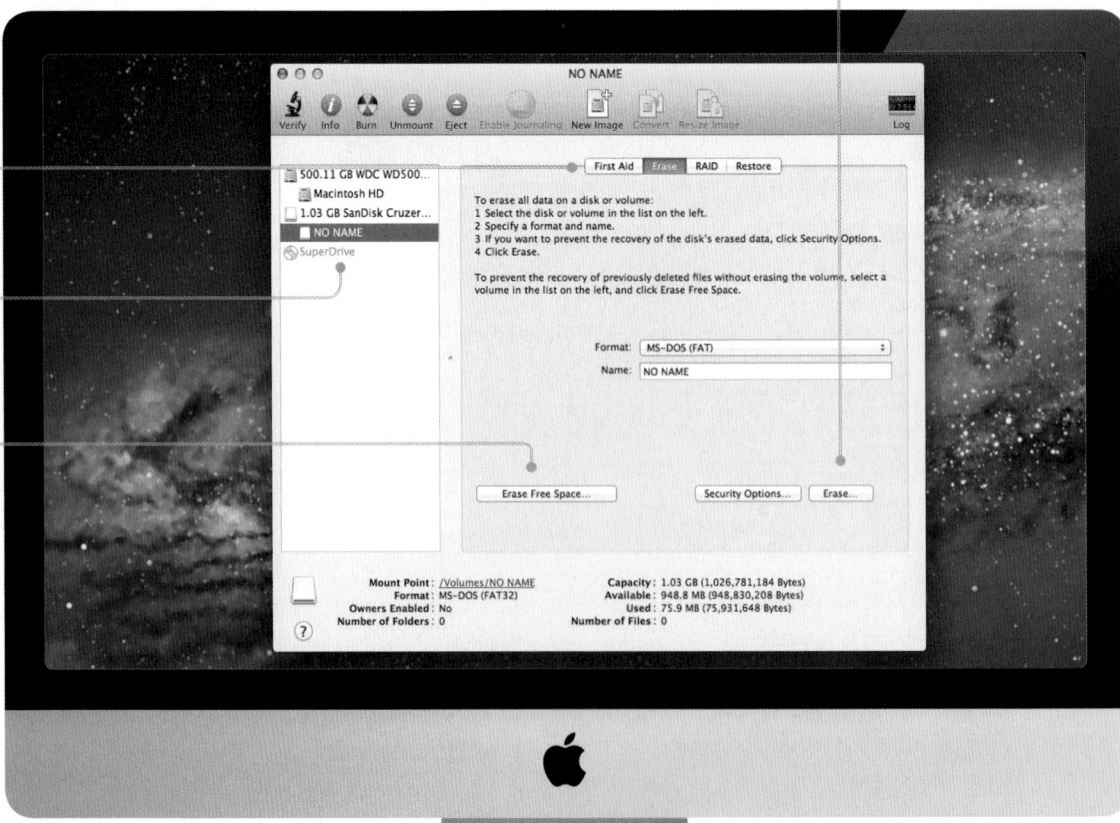

OS X Use Disk Utility to repair your hard drive

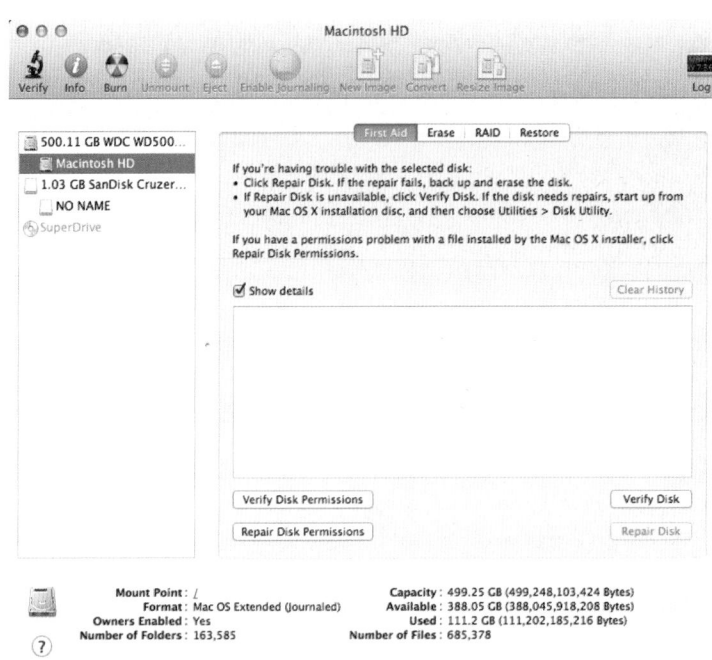

01: Load it

You can find Disk Utility by going to your Applications folder. Once you have navigated here, choose the Utilities folder and double-click on the Disk Utility option as shown in the screenshot above. This will then load the application.

02: Pick a drive

The utility will work on any connected drive, including your startup disk. These will be shown down the left-hand side. You just need to remember to click on the disk that you want to check before you start carrying out any specific actions.

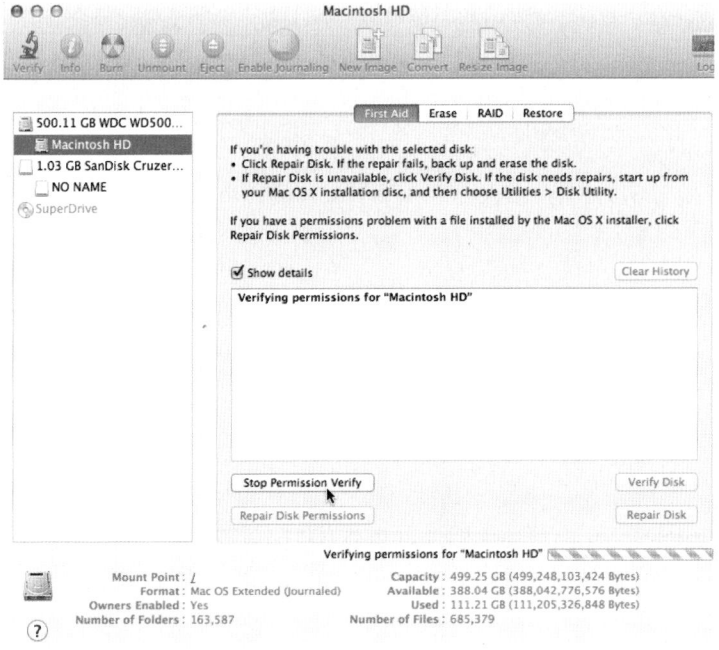

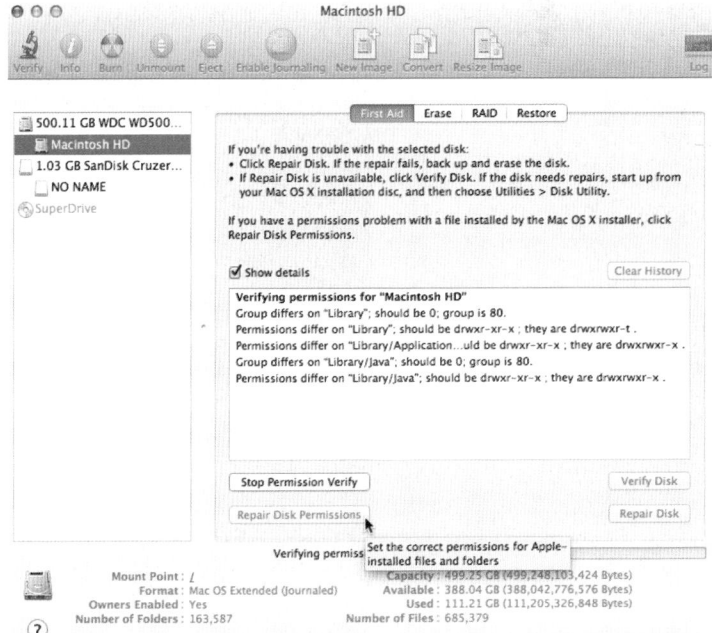

03: Verify Permissions

Click the Verify Permissions button and the utility will begin checking the disk for any errors. Depending on the size of the drive and the speed of your processor, this could take some time so why not go and make yourself a cup of tea while you wait?!

04: Repair Permissions

When the disk has been verified you should get a report detailing what it has found. If there are any warnings in there then you will need to click the Repair Permissions button. Again, this could take a while, so be patient. After that you're all done.

Recover files with Time Machine

Your guide to restoring lost and changed files with Apple's built-in backup app

 **App used:**
Time Machine

 **Time needed:**
10 minutes

 A lot of the files on your Mac will no doubt be quite valuable. There are videos, music, photos, personal and work-related documents, and much more on the disk drive. How would you cope if you lost them? Fortunately, Time Machine aims to solve the problem by making backups – copies – of files, and storing them elsewhere in a safe place. If you lose a file for whatever reason, be it an accidental deletion or a disk fault, then Time Machine lets you recover it.

It is called 'Time Machine' because that's what it is. For all intents and purposes, it effectively allows you to go back in time, and if a folder contained a file last week that you can no longer find, then you simply turn back the clock and retrieve it. It's a brilliant feature, and not just for lost files, you can retrieve earlier versions of files that have changed, too. Time Machine in Lion is the best yet, and you no longer need to have a second disk drive in order to use it.

> "You don't need a second disk drive to use Time Machine"

Work with Time Machine

The key parts of Time Machine you need to know

Browse the disk
Time Machine opens the current Finder window or the desktop. You can then navigate the disk, and change to any folder using the usual Finder features. The Sidebar shows Favourite locations

The timeline
On the right is a timeline that stretches from the present back to the distant past. Dates where backups were made to the Mac's disk are in grey, and purple shows backups to a USB disk drive

LION'S LOCAL BACKUP
Suppose your MacBook at home or work is connected to a USB disk drive to enable Time Machine to back up the whole hard disk drive. When you go out with your MacBook, that Time Machine disk is no longer available. Don't worry, as Time Machine continues to back up files by using spare space on the local internal disk. It's new to Lion.

Restore the file
You can select a single file or a whole folder of files in the Finder window, and click the big 'Restore' button. Right-clicking a file reveals other options, such as 'Get Info' and 'Quick Look'

Back and forth
Guess when your lost file is located by clicking a title bar in the stack, or by clicking on the timeline. Then use the forward and back buttons move one step at a time and find the file

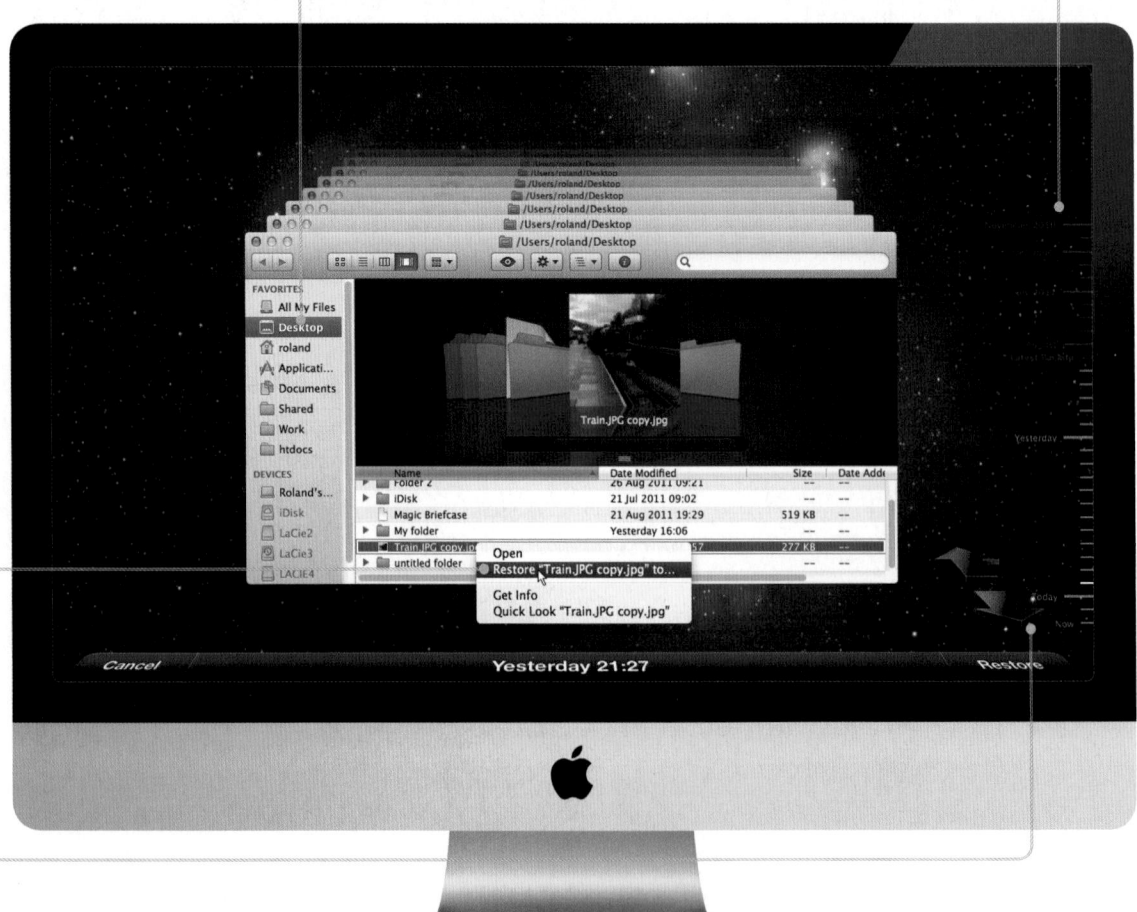

Time Machine Find and restore lost files

01: Turn it on

Go to System Preferences on the Apple menu, and click 'Time Machine'. There is a useful option to show the status in the menu.

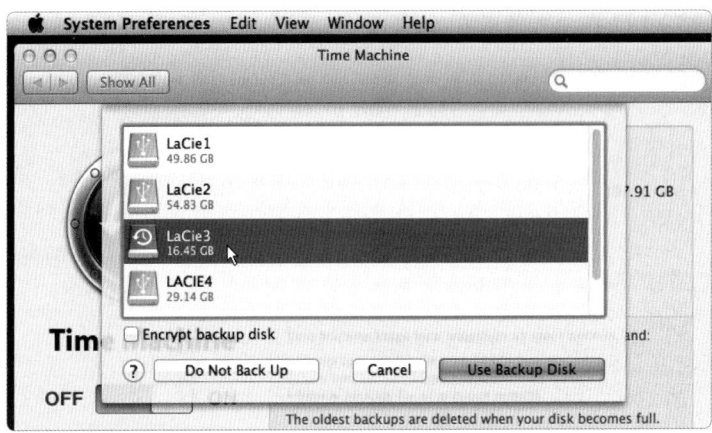

02: Choose a disk

Click the 'Select Disk' button, and the disk drives connected to the Mac are displayed. Time Machine works best if you select a large empty disk.

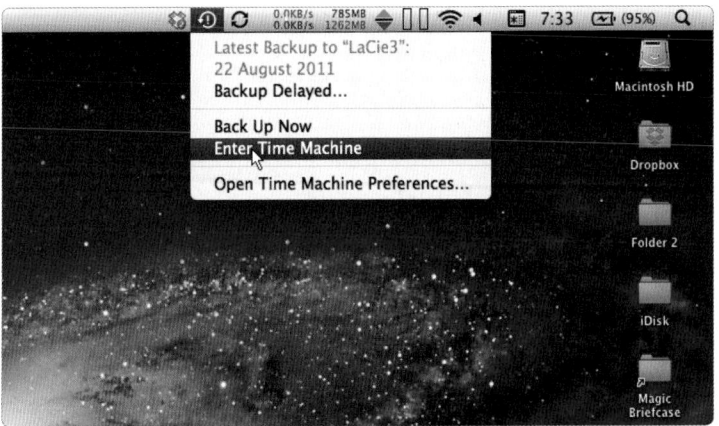

03: Enter Time Machine

Once set up, you won't notice it. Click the menu bar icon, and there are options to start a backup immediately, or enter Time Machine. Let's enter it.

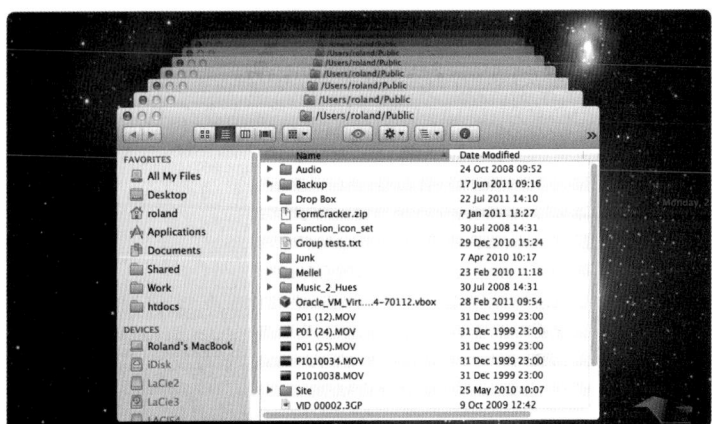

04: Browse the backups

A stack of Finder windows are displayed, and you can navigate the disk to any folder. Move back in time using the arrows or timeline on the right.

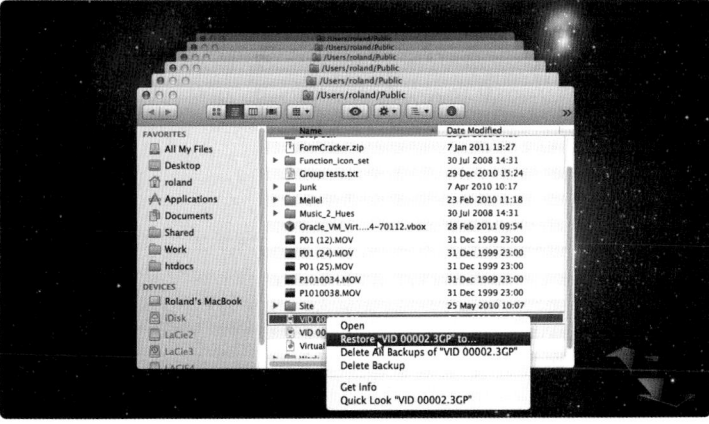

05: Select and restore

A file can be selected in the Finder window, but there are more options available by right-clicking. We will choose 'Restore', though.

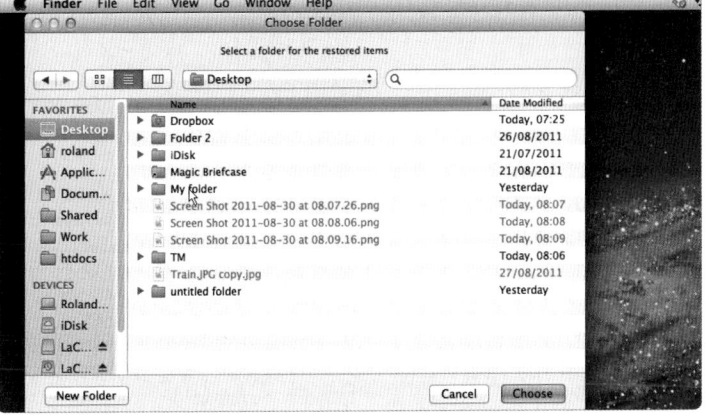

06: Save the file

Time Machine asks you to select a folder in which to put the file. It can be put back in the folder it went missing from, or stored in a different one.

Set up Time Machine for backing up

The Time Machine feature of Mac OS X offers a flexible way to securely back up and restore your files

**App used:**
Time Machine

**Time needed:**
10 minutes

Backing up your important files, although seldom perceived as such, is one of the most important parts of a safe and secure digital life. Fortunately, with the advent of reliable and inexpensive hard disks, the process of backing up and restoring your files has become a lot simpler. One impressive ability of Mac OS X is the built-in feature that allows you to roll back your system to a previous state, or restore an

unsaved version of a specific file through the use of incremental backups. Moreover, with Apple's Time

"Free yourself from physical media and limited software"

Machine, all of these features, and more, are now available to you at the click of a mouse button. Indeed, elegantly complemented by a stunning graphical interface, the Time Machine System Preferences panel and interface facility enables you to set up a powerful backup and restore facility, freeing you of clumsy physical media and limited commercial software. Let's see how it operates as we show you how to set it up.

Get to know Time Machine
Set your preferences and complete your first backup

INTEGRATION WITH TIME CAPSULE
Time Machine is very useful and flexible when used with a regular hard disk; however, this backup software is even more practical when used in conjunction with Apple's own Time Capsule wireless backup device. When pondering the question of the nature and type of backup location, Time Capsule is not to be overlooked without serious consideration.

Time Machine Preferences
The Time Machine Preferences are the central point of call for all your backup configuration and information requirements. The chosen backup setup will take place every hour without any further action

Time Machine backup progress
When performing a backup for the first time, a progress bar is displayed in a dialog. During all subsequent backups, progress is only shown in the Time Machine Preferences or menu bar item

INCREMENTAL BACKUPS
Time Machine uses an incremental backup policy that consists of an initial full copy of all the selected items to backup. Time Machine subsequently creates small individual backups. These only store the version of the items that have changed since the last backup – thus allowing the recovery of a previous version of any item. It is very efficient and highly practical.

Integration in the Finder
During the backup process, the disk image containing your backup is temporarily mounted on the Desktop and in the Devices section of any opened Finder window. The image automatically unmounts at the end of the process

Menu bar item and menu
The Time Machine menu bar item is the simple way to access the Preferences, check the time of the latest backup and perform on-the-spot backups. It is also allows the launch of the Time Machine application

Time Machine Learn about Time Machine features

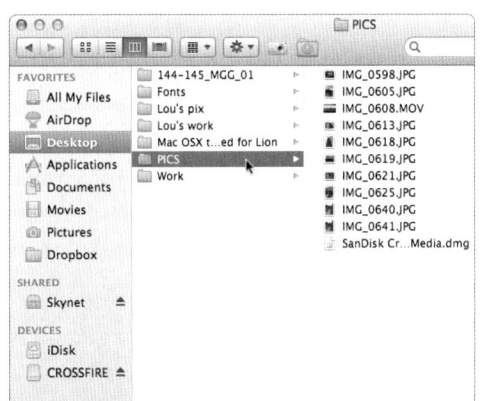

01: What to back up?

The first step is to consider which files to protect: whether to back up your whole system, your home folder or just a part of it.

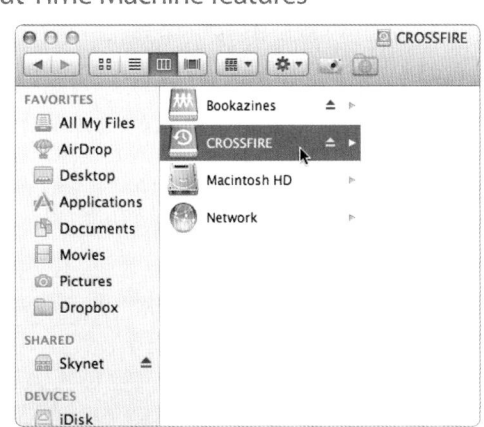

02: Backup location

Next, choose a safe location for the Time Machine. Make sure that there is plenty of free space on the target hard disk, with room to spare.

03: Unlock preferences

In the System section of System Preferences, click on Time Machine. Click the padlock and enter administrative credentials to unlock Preferences.

04: Turn Time Machine on

In the Time Machine Preferences, turn the switch on. Additionally, tick the 'Show Time Machine status…' checkbox to enable the menu bar item.

05: Select a disk

Click 'Select Disk', then select the relevant backup target disk from the list. To start it up, click 'Use for Backup' to initiate a two-minute countdown.

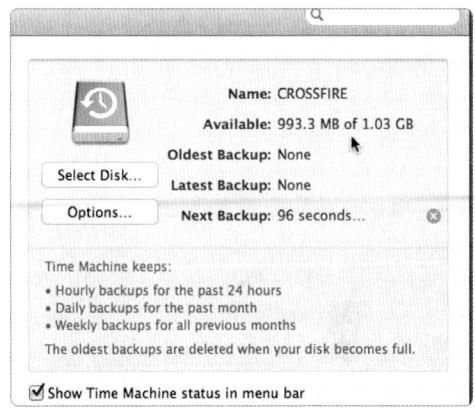

06: Check the information

The information panel shows the countdown, information on the backup location and the time of the last/next and oldest backup operation.

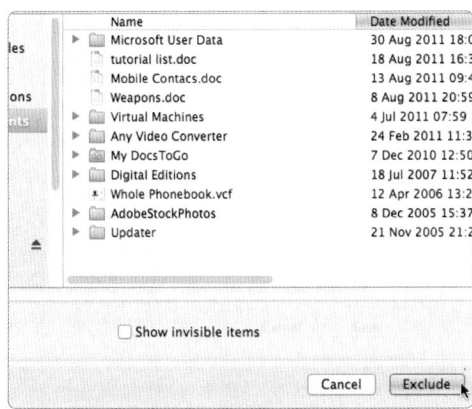

07: Exclude unnecessary files

You can further configure it by excluding entire disks, folders and files. Click on Options and add/remove items to the backup with '+' and '–'.

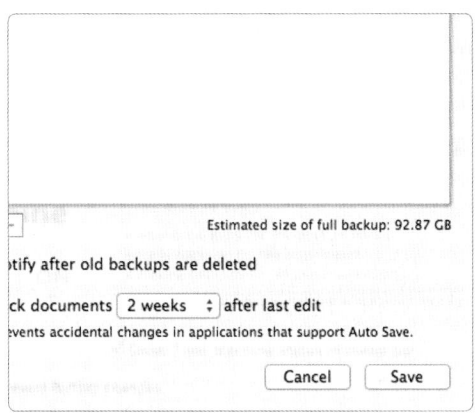

08: Check size of backup

The Options panel also allows you to check, in the list of excluded items, the size of each of them. Below this, the total size of the backup is displayed.

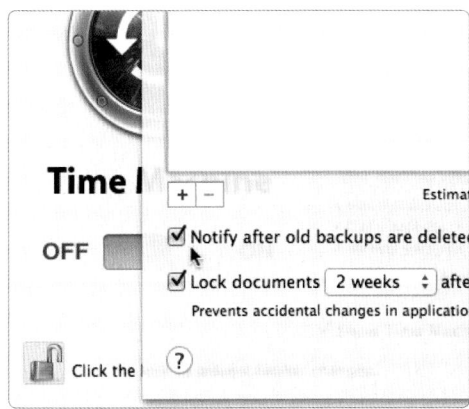

09: Further options

In Options, choose whether to back up while on battery power (on MacBooks) and whether to send a deletion notification for old backups.

Discover the Activity Monitor utility

A lot of your computer functions take place behind the scenes. Activity Monitor helps you check and control these activities

 **App used:** Activity Monitor

 **Time needed:** 15 minutes

Quietly tucked away in your Utilities folder, Activity Monitor is one of those simple yet useful applications that is a crucial part of what makes a Mac great to work with. Firstly, it can give you a great deal of information on what is happening inside your computer and secondly, this very convivial software consists not only of an instructive tool for the beginner but also a troubleshooting powerhouse

for the more experienced user to monitor activity when things are hard to explain.

Activity Monitor principally provides a flexible list of all the system and user processes taking place at any given moment inside your Mac. Additionally, it allows a quick look at your Mac's resource allocation and system performances. Let's see how to use this tool with our step-by-step guide to Activity Monitor's main functions.

"It can give you a great deal of information on what is happening"

Understand processes
The inner workings of your Mac explained

View menu
Activity Monitor's View menu controls many aspects of the information displayed, from the type of Dock icon to the nature and number of columns in the main window, including the update frequency of the readings

WHAT ARE PROCESSES?
Processes are software running in your computer's memory and CPU that take part in the running of applications; some software consists of several processes running together. For instance, Mac OS X is made up of a large number of System processes launched during your computer boot sequence. In contrast, the Finder consists of one single User process initiated at login time.

Terminate a process
When a stalled process or the remains of a crashed piece of software is found, it is possible to terminate it by selecting it in the list and clicking the red hexagonal Quit Process icon in the application toolbar

Application icon
The default Activity Monitor Dock icon can be replaced with a number of alternative ones showing live information about your system. These can display CPU workload, disk activity and network activity as well as memory usage

CPU AND MEMORY MEANINGS
The Central Processing Unit (CPU), also known as the processor, is the brain of your Mac. It works closely with RAM (Random Access Memory) and Virtual memory, also known as swap file. RAM and Virtual memory are kinds of data storage; the latter is located on your hard disk and the former in electronic chips in your computer.

Process sorting or filtering
As column information can be sorted with a click on a header, the list can also be filtered by either typing a keyword in the toolbar search field or choosing a process from the drop-down list

Activity Monitor Inside the Activity Monitor utility

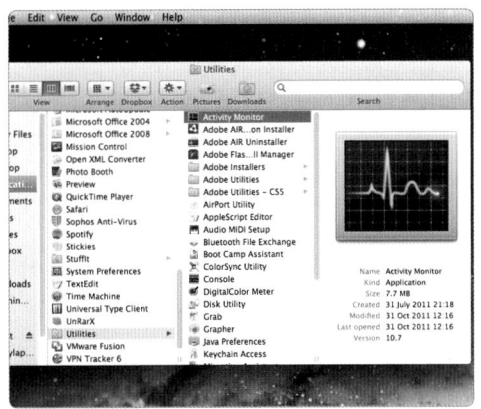

01: Locate and launch

Open a new Finder window in the sidebar, locate system Application, head to the Utilities subfolder and double-click on the Activity Monitor.

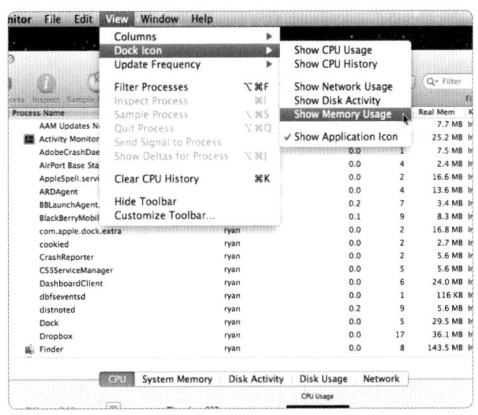

02: Activity Monitor's menus

The Activity Monitor menu has no Preferences menu item – its most relevant functionalities are located in the View and Window menus.

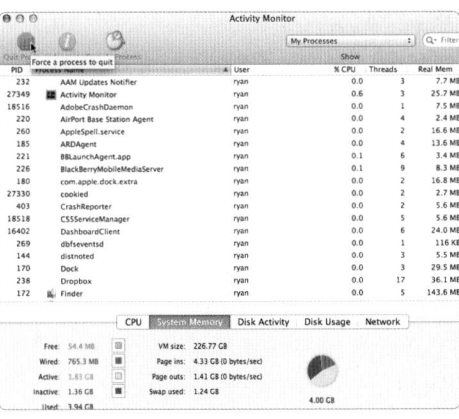

03: Toolbar

Many of AM's functions are accessible from its toolbar: terminating or inspecting processes and allowing the filtering and sorting of process data.

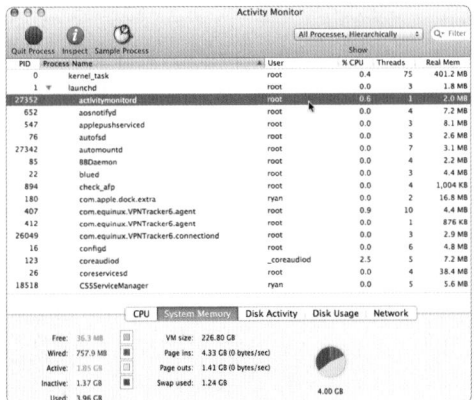

04: Process list

The main window is devoted to listing all the processes taking place on your computer. It's configurable and displays process information.

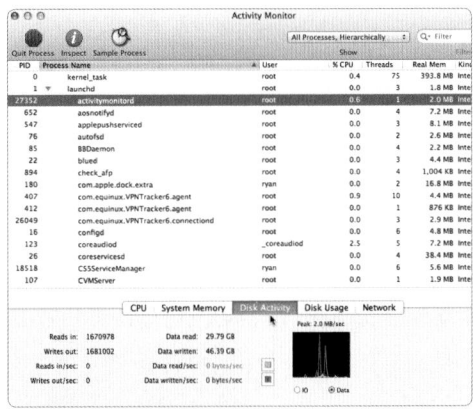

05: Monitor tabs

Below the process list a row of monitoring tabs present info on CPU, System Memory, Disk and Network activity as well as performances.

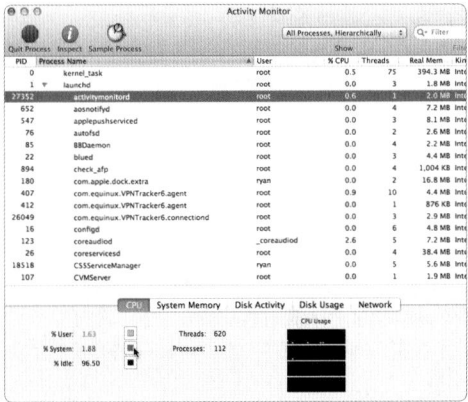

06: Monitor CPU power

Using a live display, this permits the monitoring of processor activity. It shows the amount of power used by User System and idle processes.

07: Monitor System Memory

The System Memory tab interface is very detailed – the colour scheme used to list the amount of memory allocated can also be used in a pie chart.

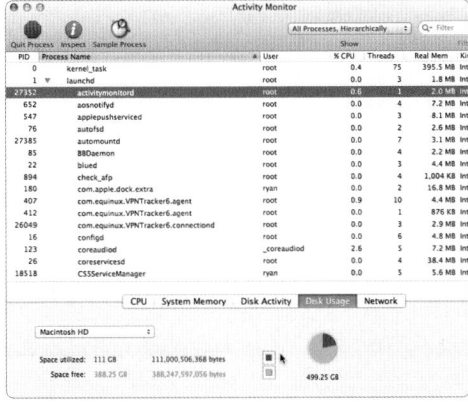

08: Disk Activity & Usage tabs

The Disk Activity and Usage tabs allow you to assess free and used space. They also give control of the amount of read/write operations occurring.

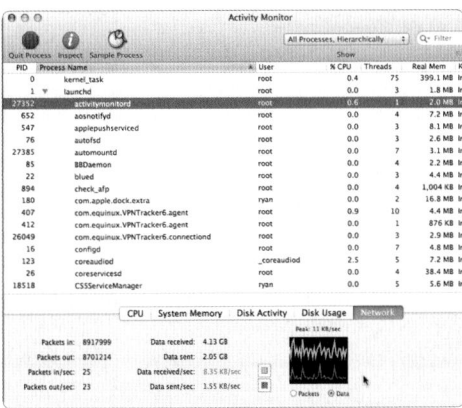

09: Network monitoring tab

The protocol-level, network tab shows the number of sent and received data packets over your connection and a live view of traffic.

Learn about the Audio MIDI settings

Macs are great tools for musicians and can easily be configured as a digital studio with Audio MIDI Setup

 **App used:**
N/A
 **Time needed:**
10 minutes

X Macs are ideal for creative people, especially in the area of audio and musical creation, and at the centre of this particular market dominance lies Apple's Core Audio software suite and its Audio MIDI Setup (AMS) graphical interface.

Indeed, Macs are famous for having all the necessary features to interface with all levels and types of music-making or audio-editing and recording tools. Obviously, the powerful Core Audio set of drivers, which provides an extensively configurable environment for input and output audio and MIDI devices, is essential to this dominance. Not only because the convivial and clever AMS software is able to leverage all the functionalities available from Core Audio; but also because graphic interface greatly contributes to the success of Macs in the world of music making. Let us introduce you to the important points of how to configure your digital studio.

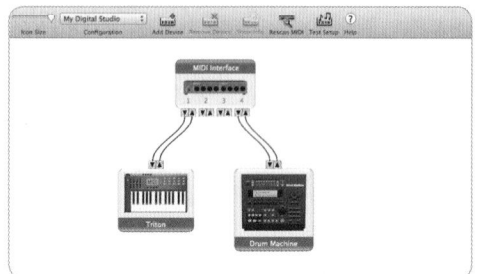

Configure MIDI settings

Allow your Mac to become a digital studio

Core Audio Info
The Core Audio Info pane lists all the built-in audio frameworks and components available on your system. This is very handy for checking all the properties of each part of the Core Audio bundle

Audio Devices window
This window is used to choose and configure input or output audio devices, to add new ones and to create aggregate audio devices from either input or output audio devices by regrouping several existing ones

MIDI device properties
Double-click on any MIDI device in your current configuration to open its Properties window and set its name, model and make and configure its MIDI ports and channels

MIDI Studio window
The MIDI Studio window allows you to set up MIDI configurations, add and extensively configure MIDI devices and reproduce and test the layout of your existing MIDI configuration

WHAT IS MIDI?
Musical Instrument Digital Interface is a communication standard allowing MIDI-compatible instruments, sequencers, special effects pedals or lighting banks to talk to each other in order to play or record a track. A MIDI track is like a music score, but also includes the data to route info through your MIDI environment.

WHAT IS A MIDI CONFIGURATION?
A simple MIDI configuration consists of a USB keyboard plugged in your Mac and a digital studio, such as GarageBand. In more complex setups you will need to have MIDI cables, a MIDI interface with enough MIDI ports for all your synthesisers, sequencers, etc… and to set up a matching MIDI configuration in AMS.

OS X Learn the Audio MIDI settings

01: Locate and launch

Open a Finder window and in your Applications folder, find the Utilities folder. Locate the Audio MIDI Setup software. Double-click to launch it.

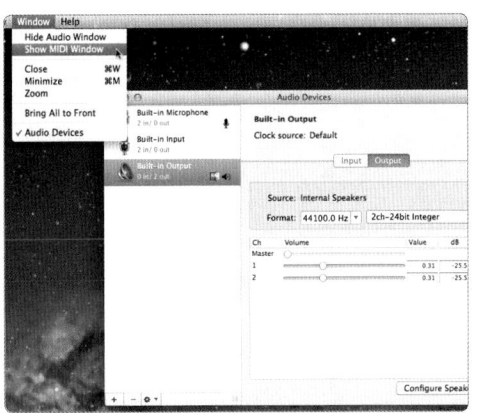

02: AMS menus

The menu presented by AMS is the standard set for any application. The most relevant ones are the Audio MIDI Setup and Windows menus.

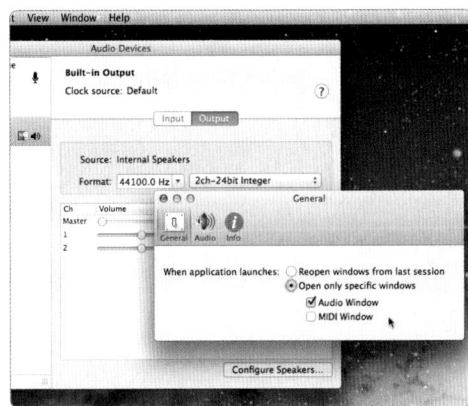

03: Preferences

The Audio MIDI Setup Preferences only offer three categories: General, Audio and Info. These settings and have little impact on operation.

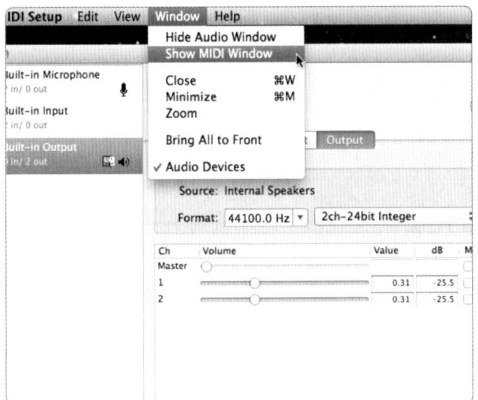

04: Window menu

The Window menu is used solely for the opening and closing of the two main application windows; namely, the Audio Devices and MIDI Studio.

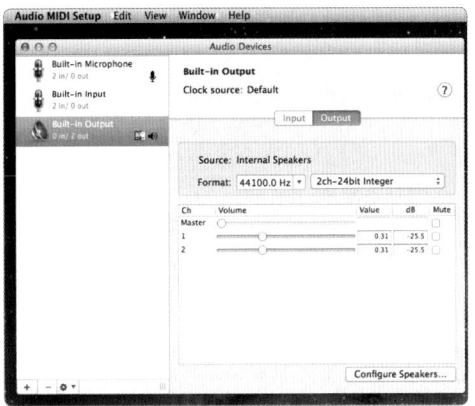

05: Audio Devices window

On the left is a list of connected and powered-up audio devices and on the right, detailed info for the selected device.

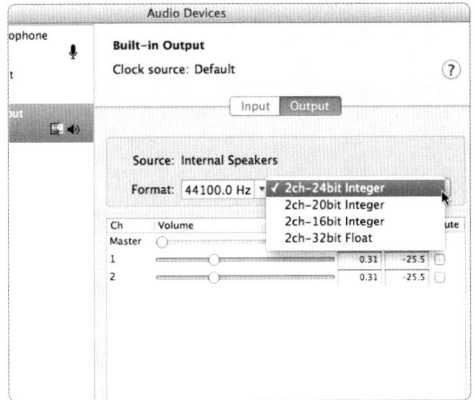

06: Audio Device list

The microphone and speaker pictograms indicate the default input and output devices. The face indicates the default output for sound effects.

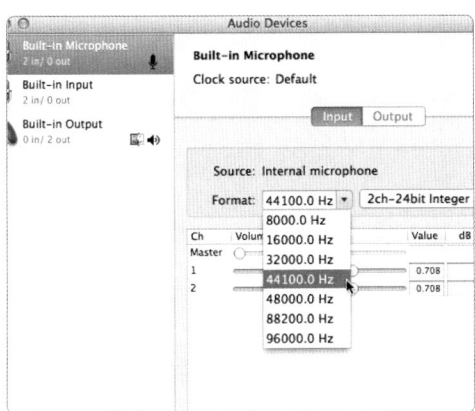

07: Audio Devices options

The Audio Device options panel displays info on the selected device, including if it is an input or output device and its hardware source.

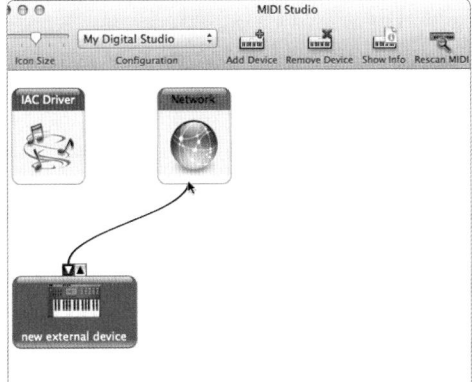

08: MIDI Studio window

This window displays MIDI devices that are powered-uap, installed and connected to your Mac. It is useful to publish your configuration.

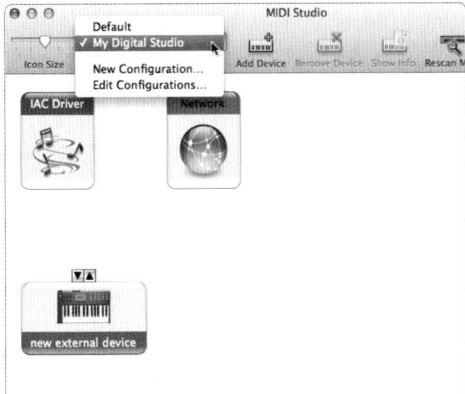

09: MIDI Studio toolbar

The MIDI Studio toolbar provides the basic tools to create MIDI configurations – from adding and configuring MIDI devices to testing.

Use AirDrop to share files

Get to know AirDrop, one of Lion's most useful new features for transferring files fast

App used:
AirDrop

Time needed:
10 minutes

Xtransferring files has, for a long time, been an incredibly tedious process. Before Wi-Fi was as commonplace as it is today, users were forced to save their files to floppy discs and USB Flash drives, unplug them, plug into another device, and drag the files onto their desktops. Even now, for many users the process involves creating an email and sending it to themselves, a process that not only takes time, but takes up inbox space.

In Lion, there is a much simpler solution to this problem, and it's called AirDrop. When you open up the finder, you'll notice that there are a number of icons in the sidebar on the left-hand side. One of these is the AirDrop icon, which is in the shape of

a parcel being borne by a parachute. Clicking this icon will start AirDrop, and any other Lion users who have also opened the AirDrop section will appear in the finder window. From here, you can drag and drop documents, images, movies and more onto the icon and send it through the air quickly and simply in seconds.

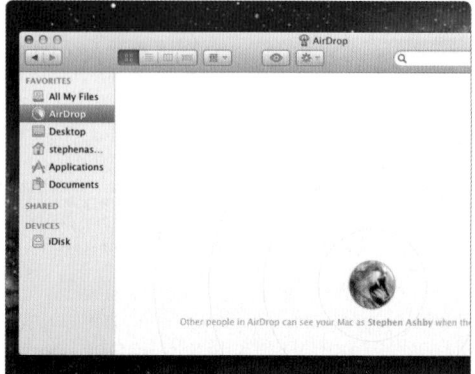

"Drag and drop files and send them through the air"

The AirDrop interface

Find your way around the key parts of this sharing service

Scanning

The spinning radar icon shows that AirDrop is constantly scanning for other users while this window is open. They will need to open the AirDrop tab as well if you want to find them locally

WIRELESS NETWORK

Unlike applications like Dropbox and DropCopy, you don't actually need to be connected to a network to use AirDrop and share your files. When you open AirDrop, your computer will start sending out a wireless signal, and when other users do the same, the machines can detect each other. Even if there is no wireless network around you, you can still send files, as your Mac will create a temporary, secure network specifically for the transfer.

Limited options

Again, because AirDrop is a system-level application, you are severely limited by the view options. For most folders you could change almost everything, but this is strictly limited

Multi-user

If there are a number of computers in the area with Lion installed, you will be able to view them all at once in the same window, and drop your files into any one of them instantly

Get Info

If you right-click and select 'Get Info', this window will open. For most applications there is a lot of information, but for AirDrop, all you can really do is copy the icon from the top left corner

AirDrop Transfer your files wirelessly

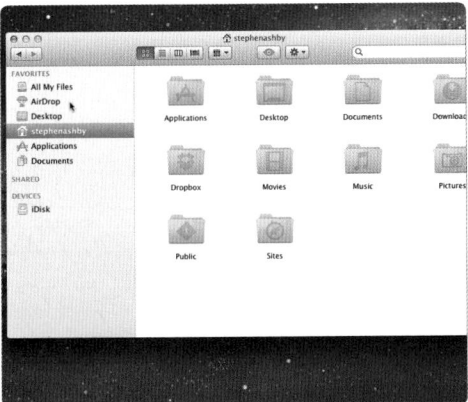

01: Find AirDrop

All you need to do to activate the system is open a Finder window and look in the sidebar. AirDrop is the icon with the parachute carrying a box.

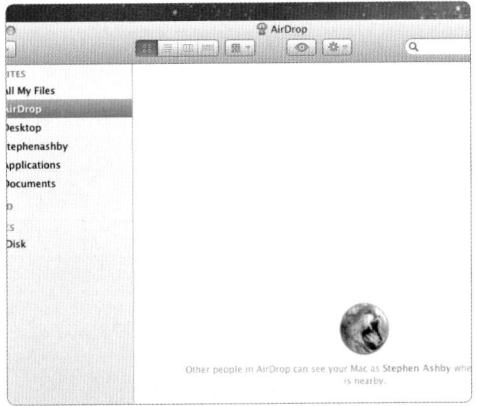

02: Radar on

When you click the AirDrop icon, it will change from this parachute symbol to this one – a radar-style display with a line rotating around the circle.

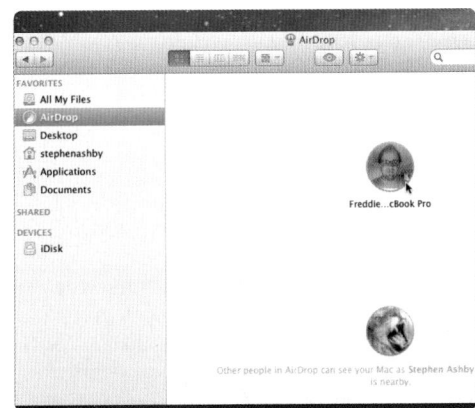

03: View other users

When another Lion user clicks on AirDrop, they will become visible in your AirDrop window. You can have more than two people at once.

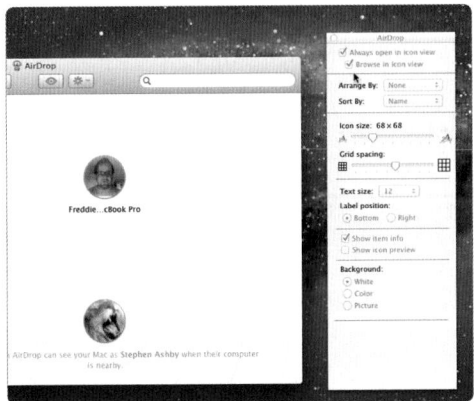

04: View options

If you Ctrl-click in AirDrop and choose 'Show View Options', you'll see a grey Menu. AirDrop is a system app, so you can't change view options.

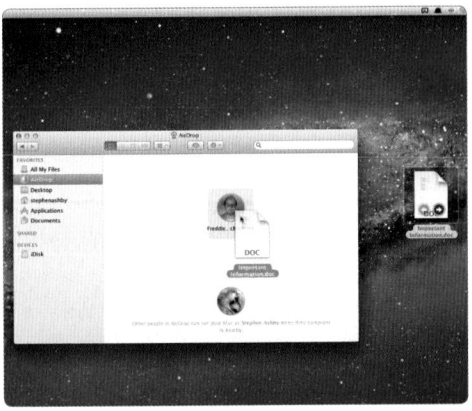

05: AirDrop

When you have found the file you want to transfer, simply drag and drop it onto the icon of the person who has connected to you.

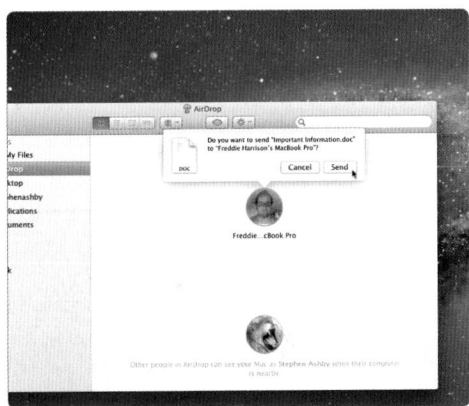

06: Prompted

Before it is sent, you'll be prompted to ensure this is the file you want to send. It will give you the full rundown of what you are transferring, and where.

07: Receiving the file

On the other machine, a prompt will let you know someone is transferring a file. You have to choose an option before the transfer can begin.

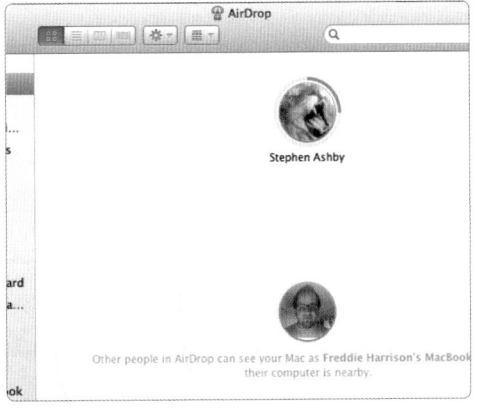

08: Awaiting transfer

As the file is transferring, you will see a progress bar that circles the icon of the sender. It will meet itself at the top when the transfer is complete.

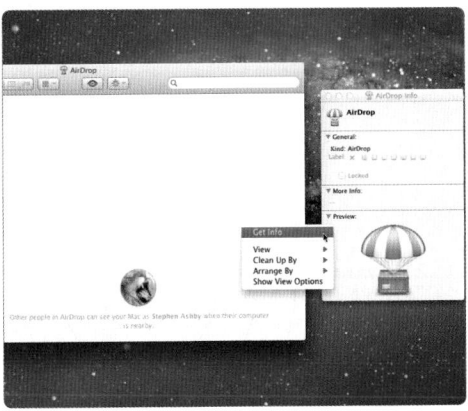

09: Find out more

If you want the AirDrop icon, click in the window and choose 'Get Info' to see this menu. Nothing can be changed about the file, as it's locked.

Create custom keyboard shortcuts

Is there a process in your favourite app that you use over and over?
Creating a custom keyboard command for it is easier than you think

 **App used:**
System Preferences

 **Time needed:**
5 minutes

 Keyboard shortcuts can be a real life saver if you use certain applications often for specific tasks and can speed up your workflow immensely. There is little point in using a computer if it's going to frustrate, annoy or cost you time compared with a manual task. So, we fully understand how annoying it is when certain tasks that need to be done in any piece of software don't have a keyboard shortcut.

We also understand that software makers can't shortcut everything, but sometimes what they omit is frustrating to users who really need to use that

shortcut a lot. Nevertheless, there is a way you can add your own, and in Lion the process has become much more organised and a hell of a lot easier.

> "There is little point in using a computer if it's going to annoy or cost you time"

It means that you can create specific keyboard shortcuts for any task that you repeat so you can save yourself some valuable time.

This is the beauty of owning a Mac, if you feel there is something missing that would enhance your user experience, you can add it yourself. The ability to speed up your workflow is invaluable, so learning how to master keyboard shortcuts is likely to pay dividends, and certainly save you from any occurrence of repetitive strain injury! Read on and we will show you step by step how to create your own bespoke shortcuts.

Save yourself time with keyboard shortcuts

Adding shortcuts is simpler than you might think

Edit
You can edit the existing shortcuts by selecting the application and editing what is already there. Use the Restore Defaults button to revert back to the old commands

Make them easy
Try to make the shortcuts you use as easy to remember and action as possible. It may even be worth noting them down until you learn them

Menu Title
If you are not sure what the exact command is, simply load the app in question and check the menu you use to complete the task/operation

Add and subtract
Use the plus and minus keys to add or remove more shortcuts. If you only need them for a limited time you can use the Restore Defaults button to go back

UNIFORMITY IS THE KEY
Like the shortcut for Copy and Paste, which works across all apps, try to keep any new commands as universal as possible so that you don't accidentally complete the wrong command when you switch between apps.

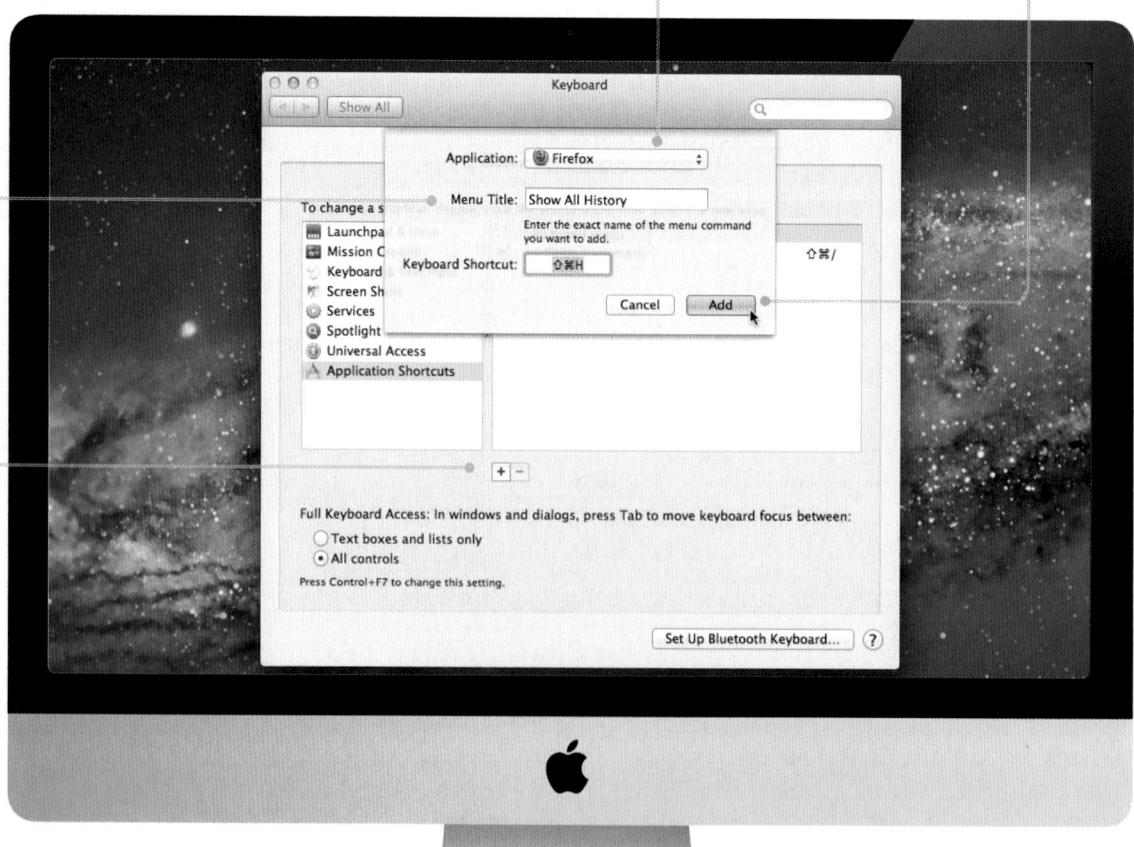

OS X Customise your keyboard commands

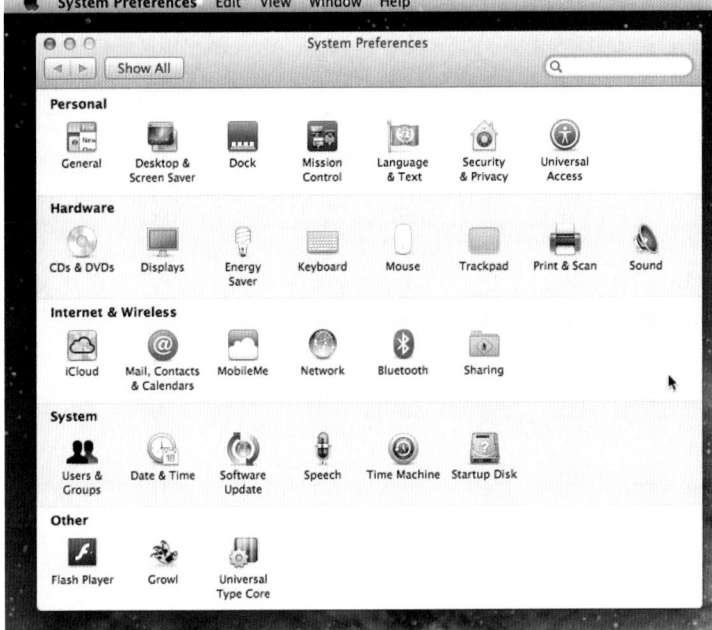

01: Open it up

Open System Preferences either from your Dock, Apple menu or Applications folder, and then simply click on the Keyboard option in the Hardware section.

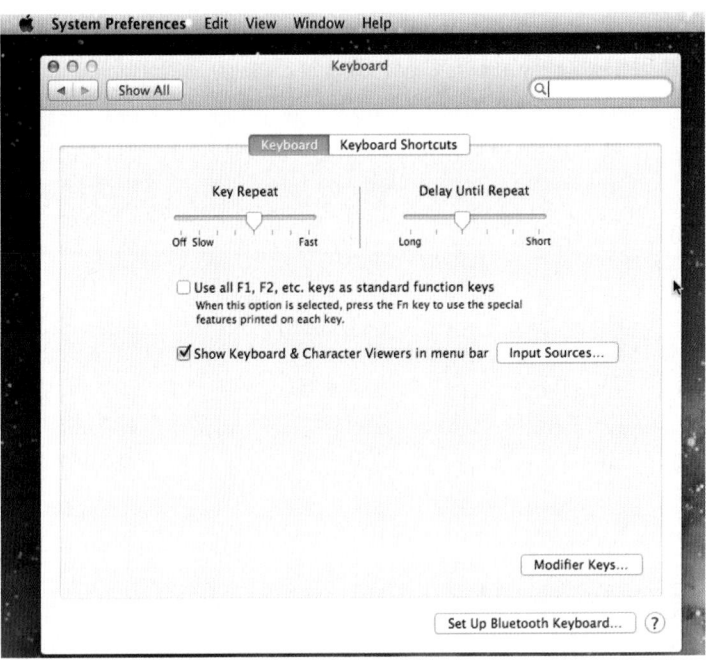

02: Quick click

Click on the Keyboard shortcuts tab at the top of the newly loaded Keyboard Preference pane. This takes you to the screen with all the time-saving power.

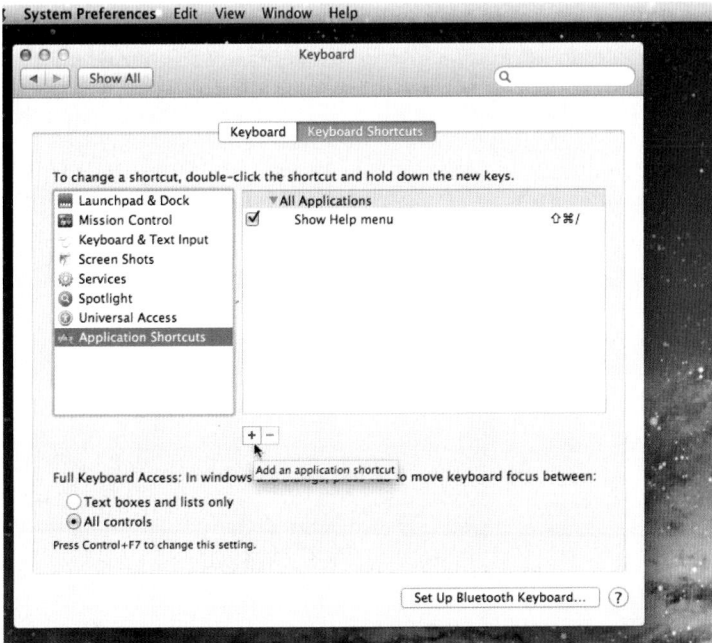

03: Double check, edit, add new

You can now see all of the shortcuts by application. Click on Application shortcuts and then use the plus button at the bottom of the window to add a new shortcut.

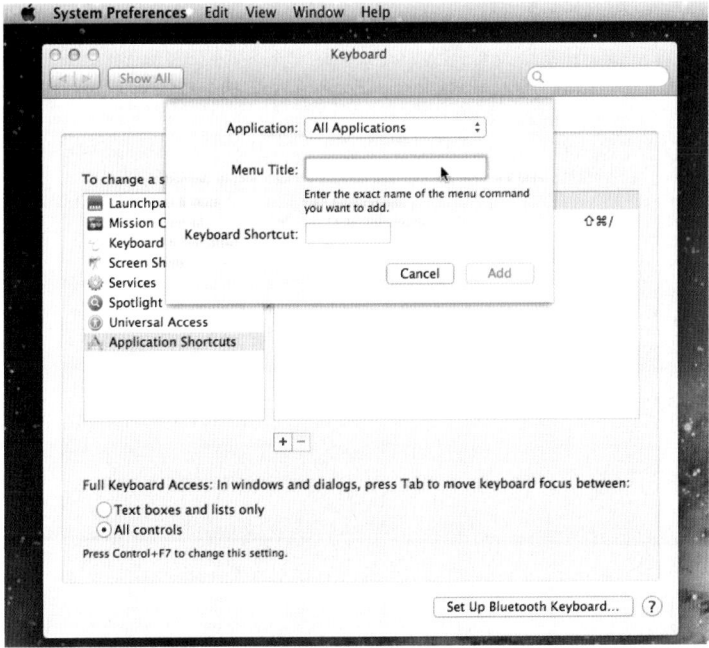

04: Drop down, type in

Use the drop-down menu to select the application you wish to make the shortcut for and then type the command you wish to shorten. Enter the shortcut you'd like to use and click Add.

Learning Apple Apps

From Mail and iCal to Safari and Photo Booth, discover how to use these essential Apple applications

"Apple offers a wonderful variety of built-in apps that will help with your activities"

96
Set up
Mail

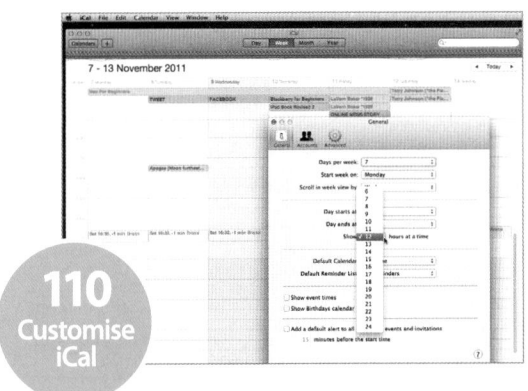

110
Customise iCal

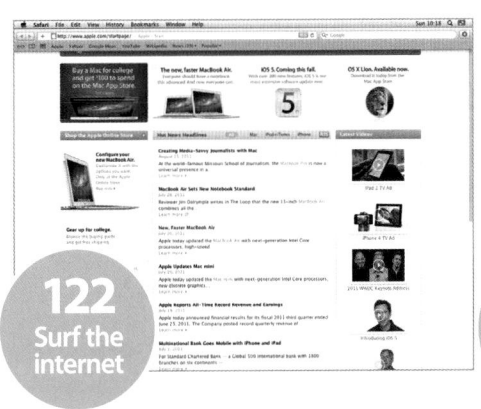

122
Surf the internet

144
Master Preview

Set up Mail on your Mac

Mail on the Mac is as painless as an application can get. Follow these steps to get started and send and receive your emails with ease

 **App used:**
Mail

 **Time needed:**
15 minutes

 It's easy to overlook Mail on the Mac when we're accustomed to browsing emails on the web. And with social networking becoming ever-more popular, many people will communicate solely through the likes of Facebook and Twitter. But if we're lucky enough to own an iMac or MacBook, we really should make use of our sophisticated machines and allow them to do what they do best: make life a whole lot easier! Mail on the Mac is a smart way to manage your emails in Apple's safe hands.

Now, the beauty of your Mac is of course its simplicity. But when that simplicity is a new application staring at you expectantly, it can feel a little intimidating. Pushing buttons at random in the hope you will eventually work it out is never going to be the best approach, so with this helpful little guide to setting up Mail on the Mac, we'll have you sending and receiving emails to and from your favourite people in no time. We'll also show you how to customise your messages to give them that personal feel, and explain how to attach documents

and keep the Mail interface clean and tidy so you know where all your messages are.

> "Mail on the Mac is a smart way to manage your emails as you work and play"

Mail Get your mail up and running

01: Run Mail

Click on the Mail icon in your dock to kick it into motion. After a quick bounce you should be prompted by a Welcome to Mail pop up window.

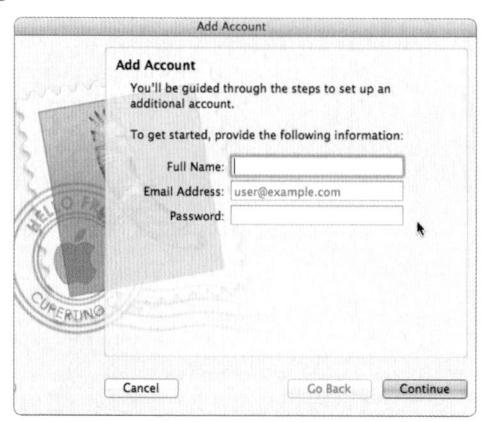

02: Mail's Setup Assistant

This wizard can configure accounts that use the most popular email services, including Gmail and Yahoo. Choose your favourite.

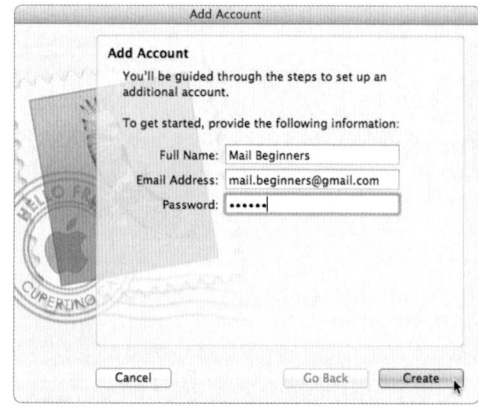

03: Enter your details

Enter the full name, email address and password for your existing email account the same as you would in the browser of your service provider.

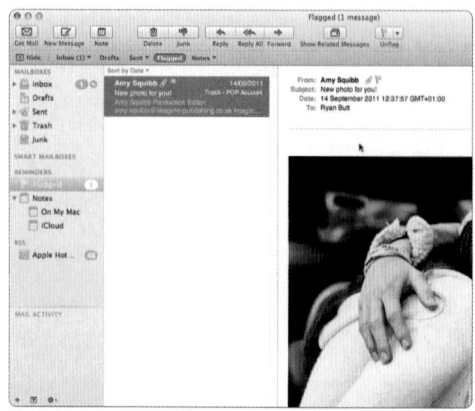

04: Create and enjoy

Click on Create in the Mail Setup Assistant and be taken to your new Mail Inbox. You'll have the same mailboxes as in your web-browsing version.

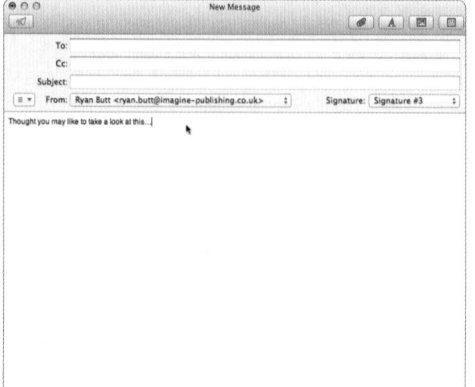

05: Compose a message

Hit New Message to summon an email draft. Enter the address of your recipient in the To field and fill in your Subject and message accordingly.

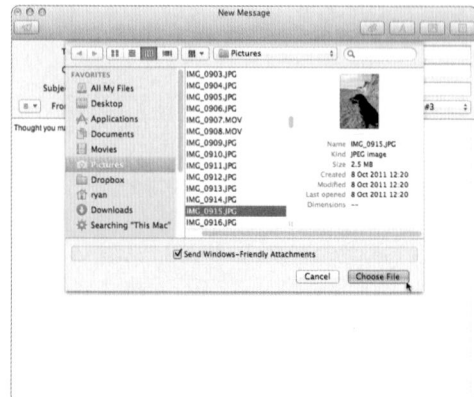

06: Attach a file

To send your recipient a file, click on Attach and choose the file from its location. Be mindful of what you're sending to avoid large email sizes.

Master Mail on your Mac

Everything you need to send
and receive emails

The Mail toolbar
You'll find handy buttons for all the most-used functions right at the top of your Mail interface. Delete, send mail to the Junk folder, Reply, Forward and create New Messages till your heart is content

Happiness is shortcuts
As Mac users, we love our shortcuts. Ctrl and click on the emails in your Inbox to bring up various time-saving options: Reply, Forward, Mark As Unread, Delete, Move To folders of your choice etc

Sort and search
It's there but it's hiding. Sort by From, Subject or Date Received, and use the Search field in the top right to track messages with specific words in the Entire Message, From, To or Subject

Keep it tidy
Creating folders to store your emails for quick reference is a great way to prevent oversized Inboxes. Go to Mailbox>New Mailbox and set the Location and enter a Name for your new folder

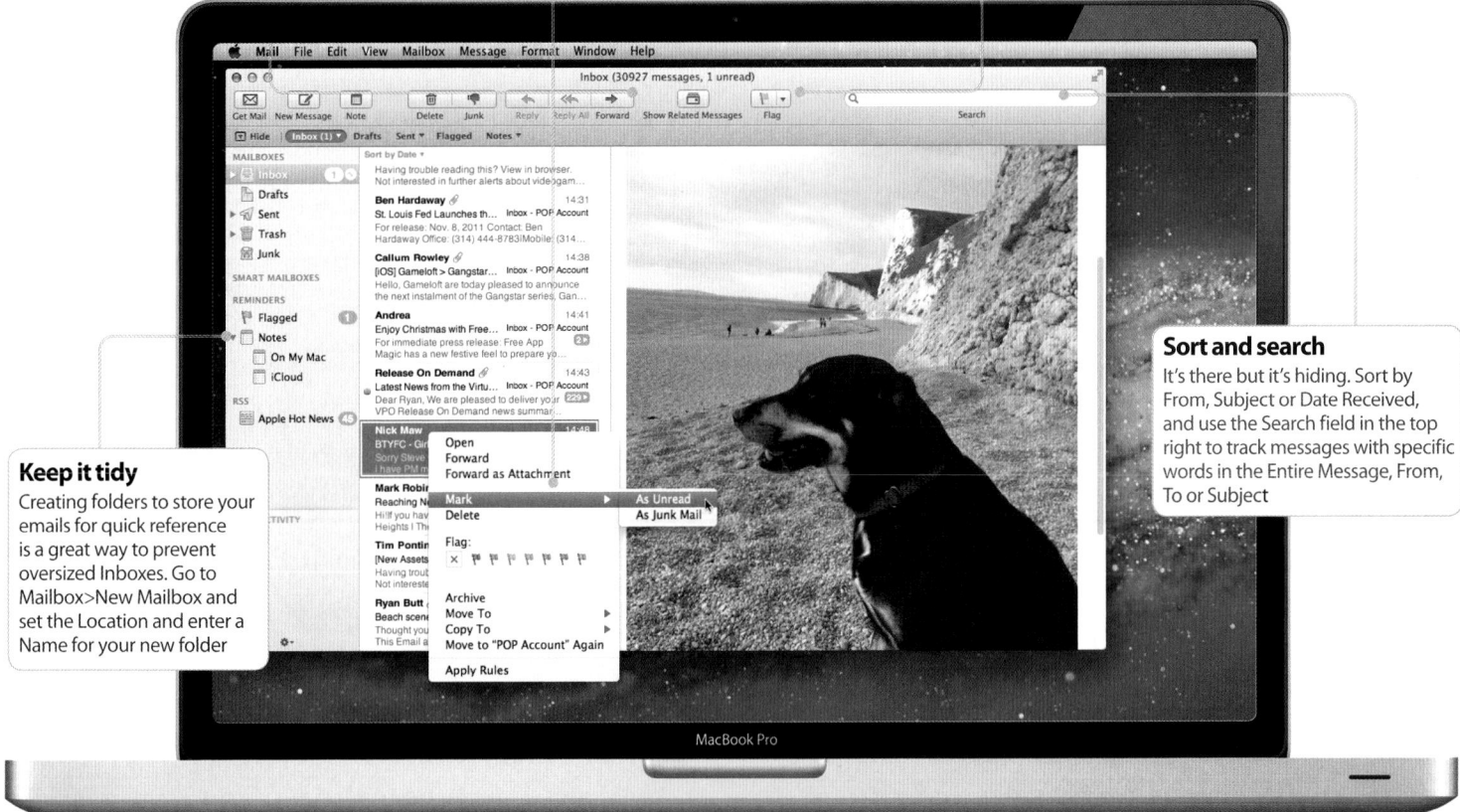

07: Add some style
If you're feeling adventurous, you can change your fonts and add colour by clicking on the appropriate Fonts and Colors buttons.

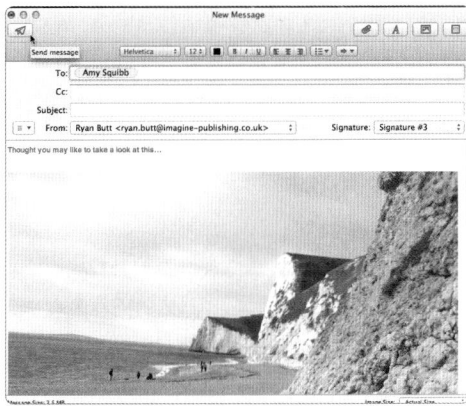

08: Save or send
If you're not yet ready to send, click Save As Draft and it'll wait in your Drafts folder. When happy, hit Send to start your message on its journey.

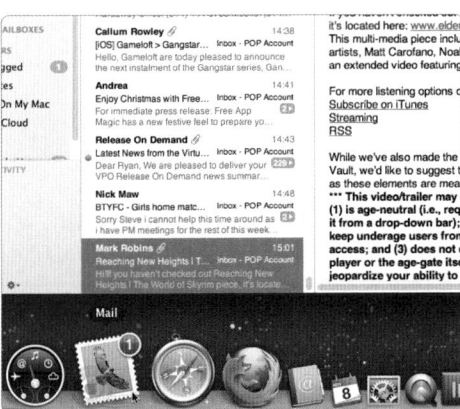

09: You've got mail
Click Get Mail in the top left to download emails. Unread messages are highlighted by blue dots – the icon in your dock also shows new messages.

Send an email

Find out how to send digital correspondence in Apple's intuitive Mail app

 **App used:**
Mail

 **Time needed:**
5 minutes

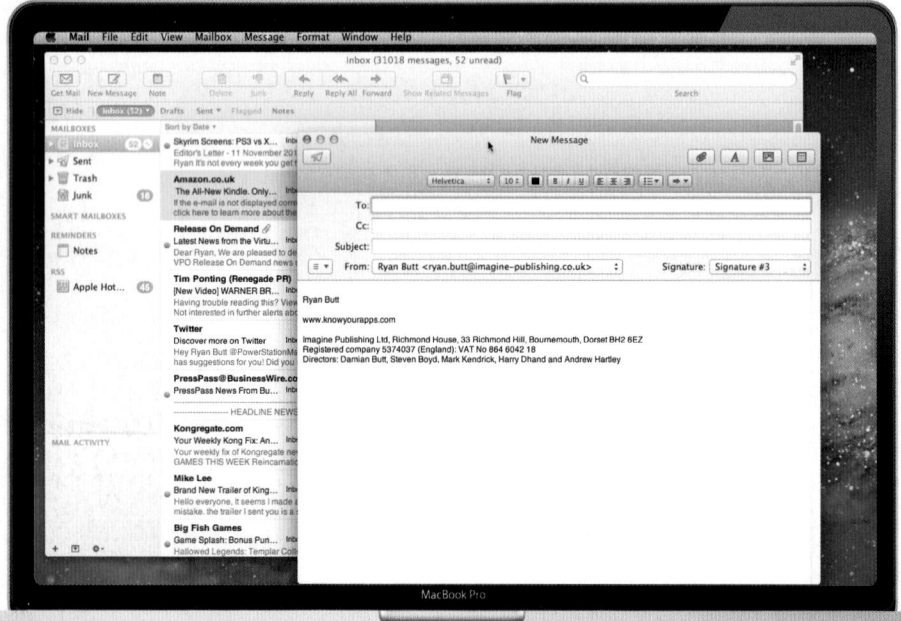

Sending emails has always been quick and easy through the Apple interface. The default Mail app is perfect for all of your message viewing and composing needs and there are plenty of new features with OS X Lion that make it even more essential.

In this tutorial we will guide you through the process of composing and sending emails, but also explore some of the other handy features that Mail affords you, such as experimenting with the style and look of your emails. If you like to send digital files, such as Word documents or images as attachments there are multiple ways to do this in Mail. By clicking on the paperclip icon at the top of your message window you can browse your machine at will and find the files you wish to attach. Alternatively, if you know that you will be attaching pictures from your photo gallery, then there is a picture icon that you can click on to be taken straight to iPhoto, whereby you can quickly choose the images you want to include without having to search through your folders. What's more, you can transform your emails into digital cards! Click on the card icon in the message window (next to the picture icon) and you'll be able to turn your messages into birthday cards or cards to suit any occasion. Read on to find out more about this versatile app.

Mail Sending emails

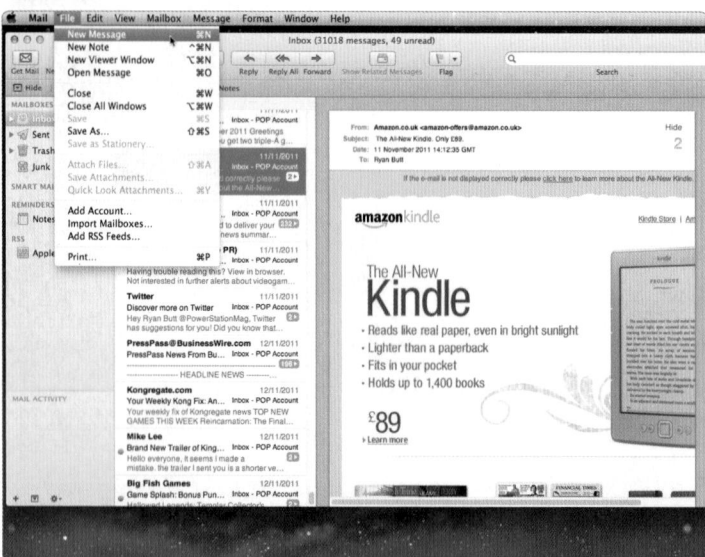

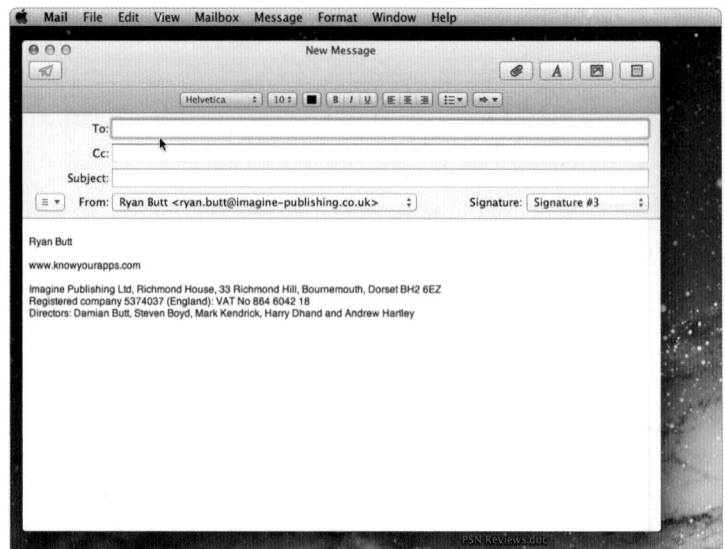

01: Choose New Message

There are three ways to start composing a new email in the Mail app. You can click on the 'File' drop down menu and choose 'New Message', click on the 'New Message' button in the top-left corner of your Mail window or use the shortcut, which is Cmd + N.

02: Add details

You will need to enter the email address of the person you wish to receive the email in the 'To' field, plus a subject header and then your message in the main window. Click on a field to add the details or cycle through them in sequence by pressing the tab key.

Sending emails

How to send and personalise
your electronic messages

Style options
You can change the font, colour,
style and alignment of your text by
clicking on the 'A' icon at the top of
your message window and clicking
the various options that appear

Signatures
Assign you own signatures
to be automatically added to
the bottom of your emails. To
create new ones, click on the
'Mail' dropdown menu, then
choose 'Preferences' followed
by 'Signatures'

Add attachments
If you want to add attachments to
your emails, click on the paperclip
icon at the top of your message
window and you'll be invited to
search for a file to attach

Message window
In order to send an email you have
to know the email address of the
person that you are sending it to.
Type this into the 'To' window and
then click on the other text fields to
enter a subject header and message

SEND PICTURES OR CARDS

Clicking on the paperclip icon is fine for
attaching most files, but if you wish to attach
a particular image then you can click on the
picture icon to make the process quick and
jump straight to iPhoto. You can also click the
card icon to transform your emails into digital
cards for any occasion.

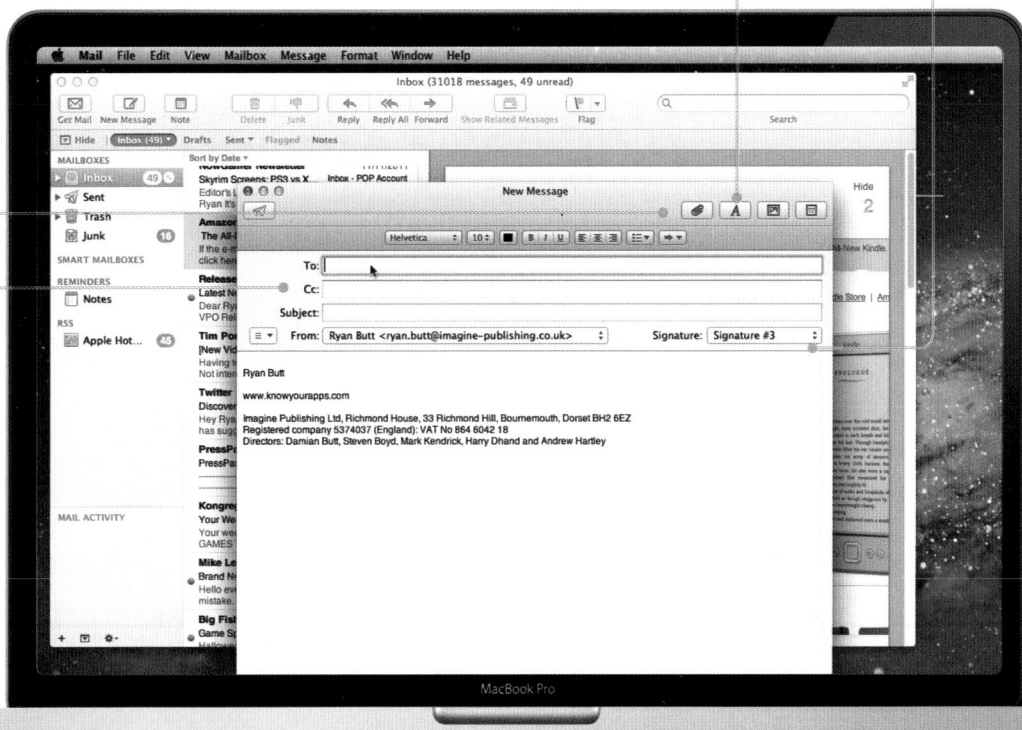

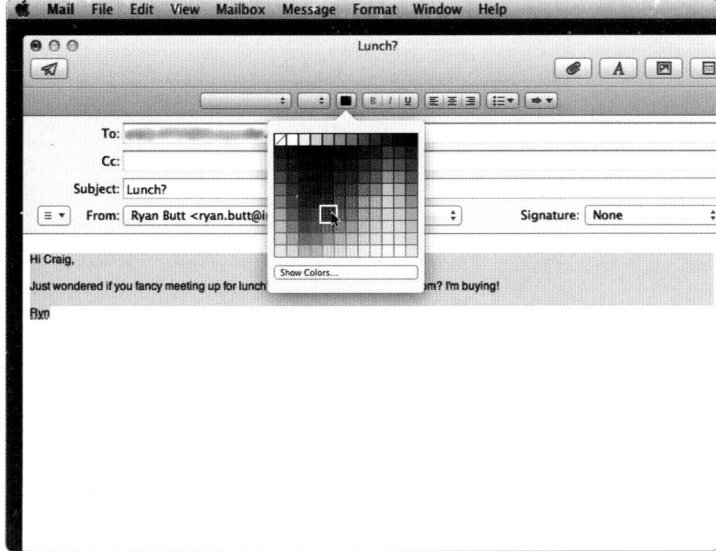

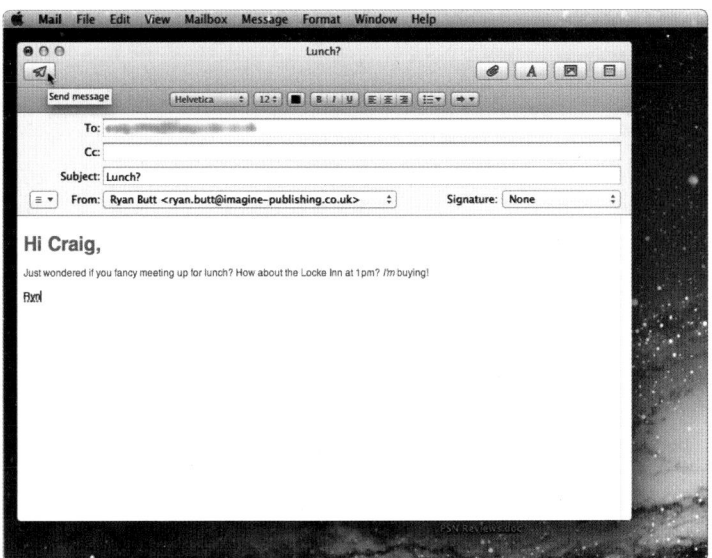

03: Add some style

You can change the font, style and colour of your text by clicking on the 'A'
icon at the top of your message window. Have fun experimenting with the
various text formats and options available and make your message look as
eye-catching as possible.

04: Send it off

When you have finished styling your message and checked that all the
necessary fields are filled you are ready to send it. This is incredibly easy to
do – just click on the paper aeroplane icon in the top-left corner of your
message window to send it on its merry way.

Change the fonts of the Mail interface

App used: Mail

Time needed: 5 minutes

Using Mail's Fonts & Colors preference pane, it is possible to change the default typeface and adjust the colour scheme

Whether you have a preferred font type or a compulsion to customise every single item you possibly can, Mail offers a comprehensive set of options to add a personal touch to its interface. Maybe you want to use a smaller font size in order to see more items or, conversely, you have an aversion to a cramped-looking application interface and prefer to give a lighter feel to its various elements. The Fonts & Colors preference pane is the place to go. The

options presented there also give you the opportunity to alter the colour scheme of quoted text in your replies to messages.

> ## "Mail offers a great set of options to add a personal touch"

In some cases, the choice of a specific typeface can lead to confusion. Fixed-width or mono-spaced fonts, like Courier, or varying width fonts, like Helvetica, can lead to uncertainty with characters like upper-case 'i', '1' or lower-case 'L'. This step-by-step tutorial guides you through the font settings for the Mail viewer window so you can customise your fonts and spruce up your emails in no time at all. It's extremely easy and can improve your emails no end.

Customising Mail fonts

Choose a typeface that will improve the look of your messages

Message list font
Most of the lists displayed in the Mail interface are affected by typeface adjustments made in this text box; this applies to Messages, RSS news, To Do and all types of lists available in Mail

Notes fonts
Unlike the settings for messages, Notes' font setting is the same for the list and content. However, the font size of items in the Notes list is identical to the Message list size setting

Mailbox font
The font type and size adjustment selected here will be applied to all mailboxes, reminder items, folders, RSS feeds listed in the sidebar and section headers. This also applies to the item counters

Message font
In the Fonts & Colors preference pane, the selected font and size settings for the Message font also apply to the content of the RSS items; thus, it is not possible to change the text colour for any of these items

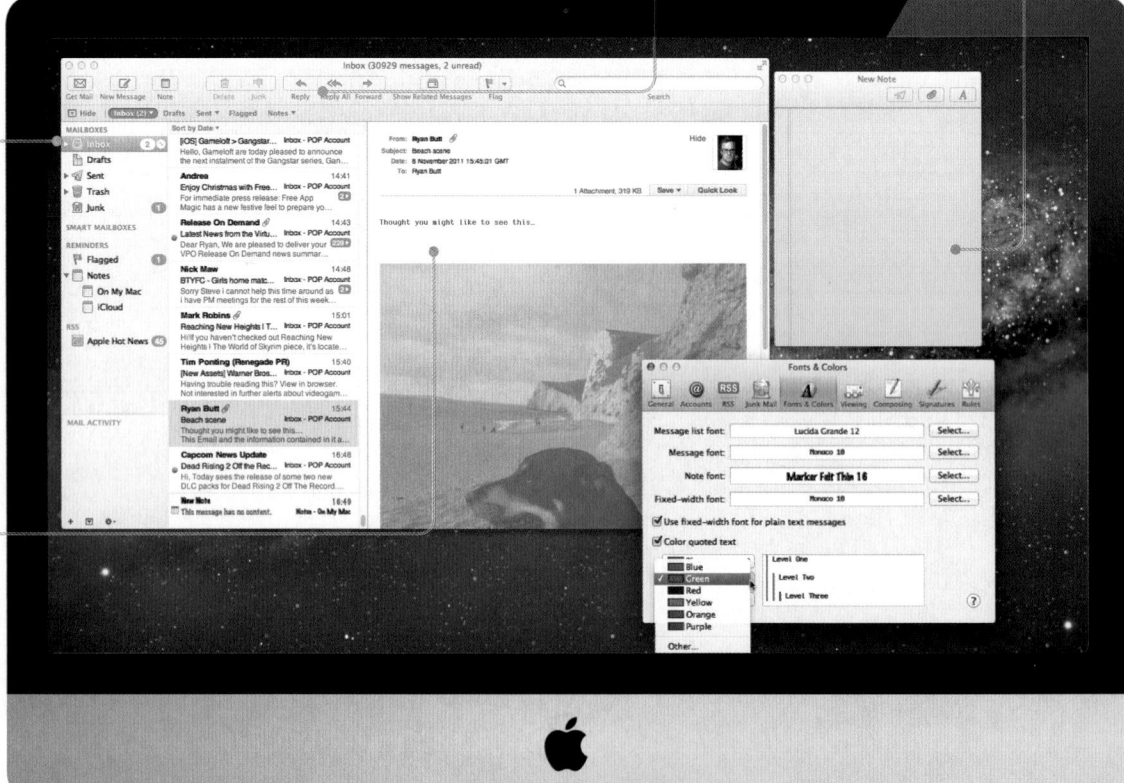

PLAIN TEXT MESSAGES
The plain text message format is the simplest and oldest format used to send emails. Its ease of use, simplicity and light weight are only a few of its unique qualities. It can be read by all email applications; supports attachments; can be scanned easily by antivirus software; and does not allow something dangerous to be concealed within the message.

Mail New fonts for the Mail interface

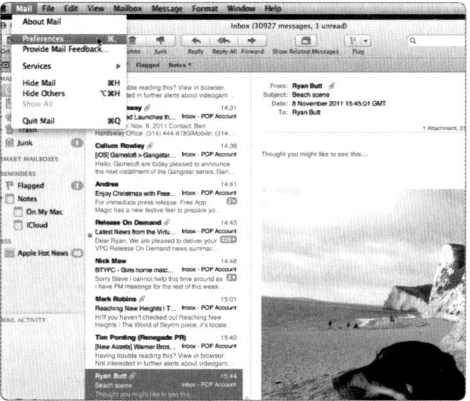

01: Locate Fonts & Colors

Open Mail's Apple menu and select Preferences; the Fonts & Colors section you are after is fifth on the toolbar.

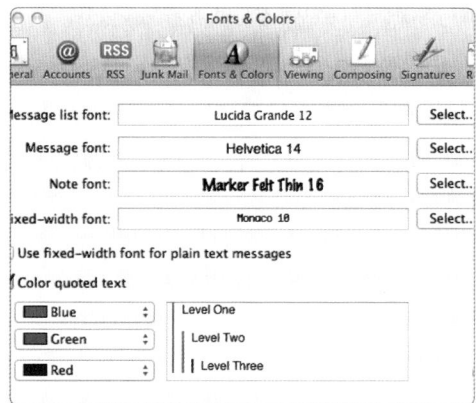

02: Preference pane layout

Fonts & Colors preferences are in two sections. The first lets you change the font displayed; the second caters for quoted text options.

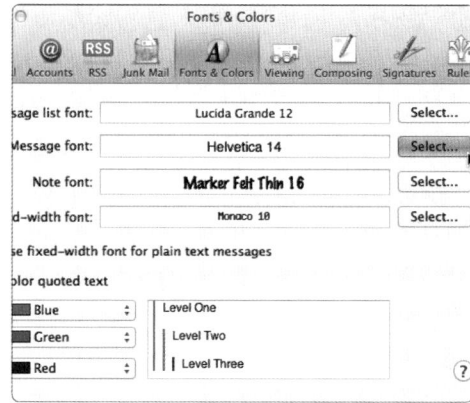

03: Change the font settings

To change the font type for all the Mail interface panes, click on the Select button next to each of the five text boxes in the first (upper) section.

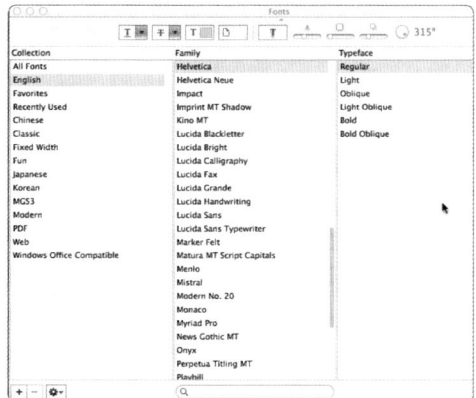

04: The Fonts panel

This shows all the collections, families, typefaces and font sizes available; a single click on one immediately applies it to the selected element.

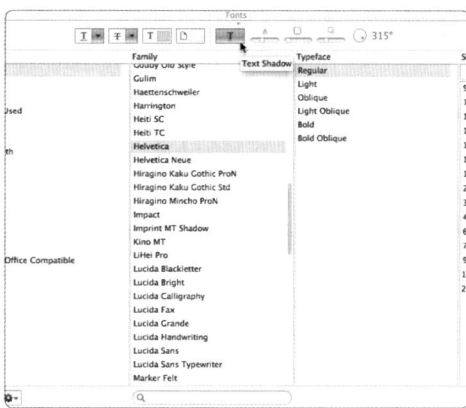

05: The Fonts panel cont.

In the present context, most options in the toolbar are not applicable. You can only modify Mail's typeface and size through the Fonts panel.

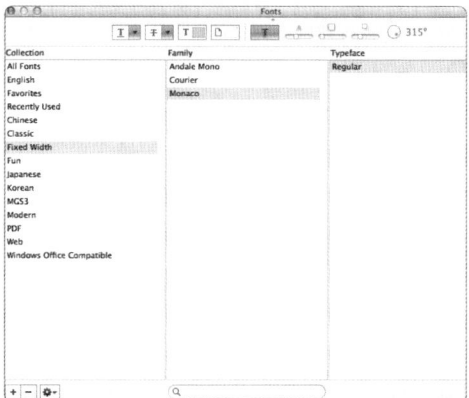

06: Fixed-width fonts

For these, choose from the fixed-width category. This allows the use of an alternate font when receiving a message in an unknown typeface.

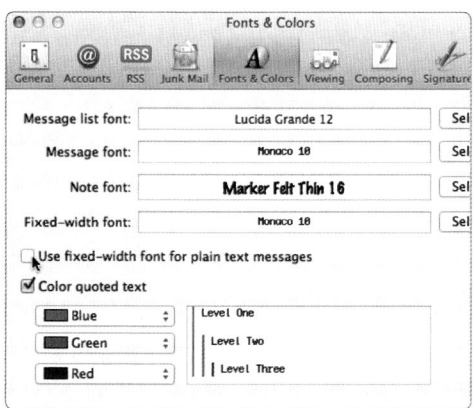

07: The fixed-width fallback

Tick the 'Use fixed-width font' checkbox to apply it to plain text messages. Then Mail has a fallback solution for messages in an unknown font.

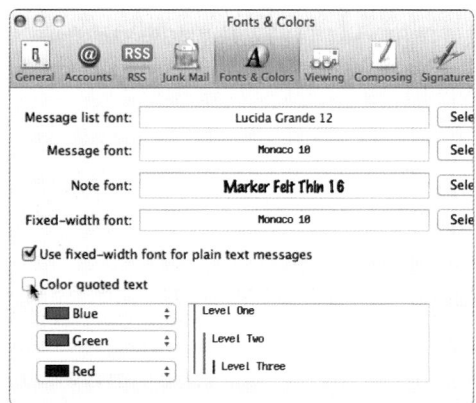

08: The quoted text options

It is possible to modify the colours of the quote-level markers up to the third level. Click the drop-down list and select one to change the setting.

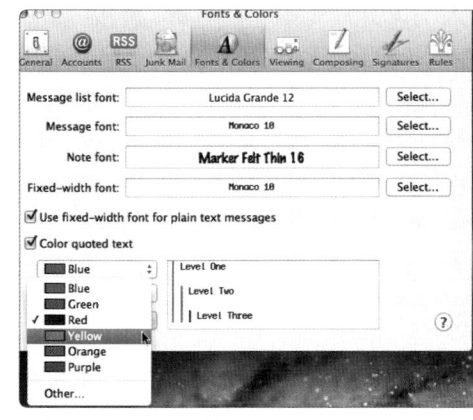

09: Other colours

For a more appropriate standard colour or to help distinguish quoted text, select Other in the drop-down list and pick a colour in the Colors window.

Use Notes in Mail

Understanding Notes in Mail

**App used:**
Mail

**Time needed:**
10 minutes

Sometimes when you're working in Mail, you may find that you need to jot down ideas and snippets of information that don't necessarily need to be put into an email or sent straight away. You could use TextEdit for this, but those files exist in the Finder, outside of Mail. So wouldn't it be better if you could keep these snippets inside the Mail application? The good news is that with Notes, you can. Not only that, but in OS X 10.7, Notes are more powerful than ever, and can not only have their appearance customised, but can have documents and files attached to them, and be converted directly into a new email

message. You can create and store as many Notes as you like, and view them in a separate list to keep track of them. Deleting them is as easy as selecting one and hitting backspace. Simple but useful, Notes can be a great time-saver.

> "Simple but useful, Notes can be a great time-saver"

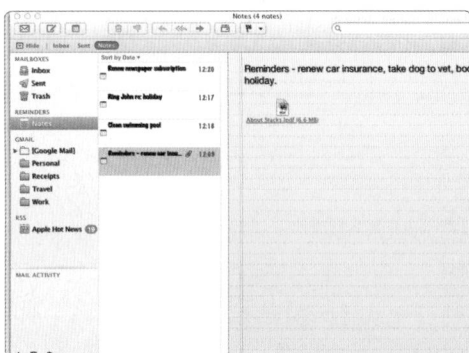

Key parts of Notes in Mail

Filter, flag and add attachments
to your notes found in Mail

Flagging Notes
Like email, Notes can be flagged to show that they have a high priority

Attachments in Notes
Attached files can be stored with Notes, and these can be included if the note is converted to an email

Notes in Mail
Filter the view to show only Notes, and not email

Notes list
Manage your Notes from this view. Right-click to perform actions on them

PHOTO BROWSER
Notes in Mail now have the ability to give you direct access to your photo library thanks to a new button. This is handy, for example, if you want to include a picture of a person or a picture of a holiday along with a note.

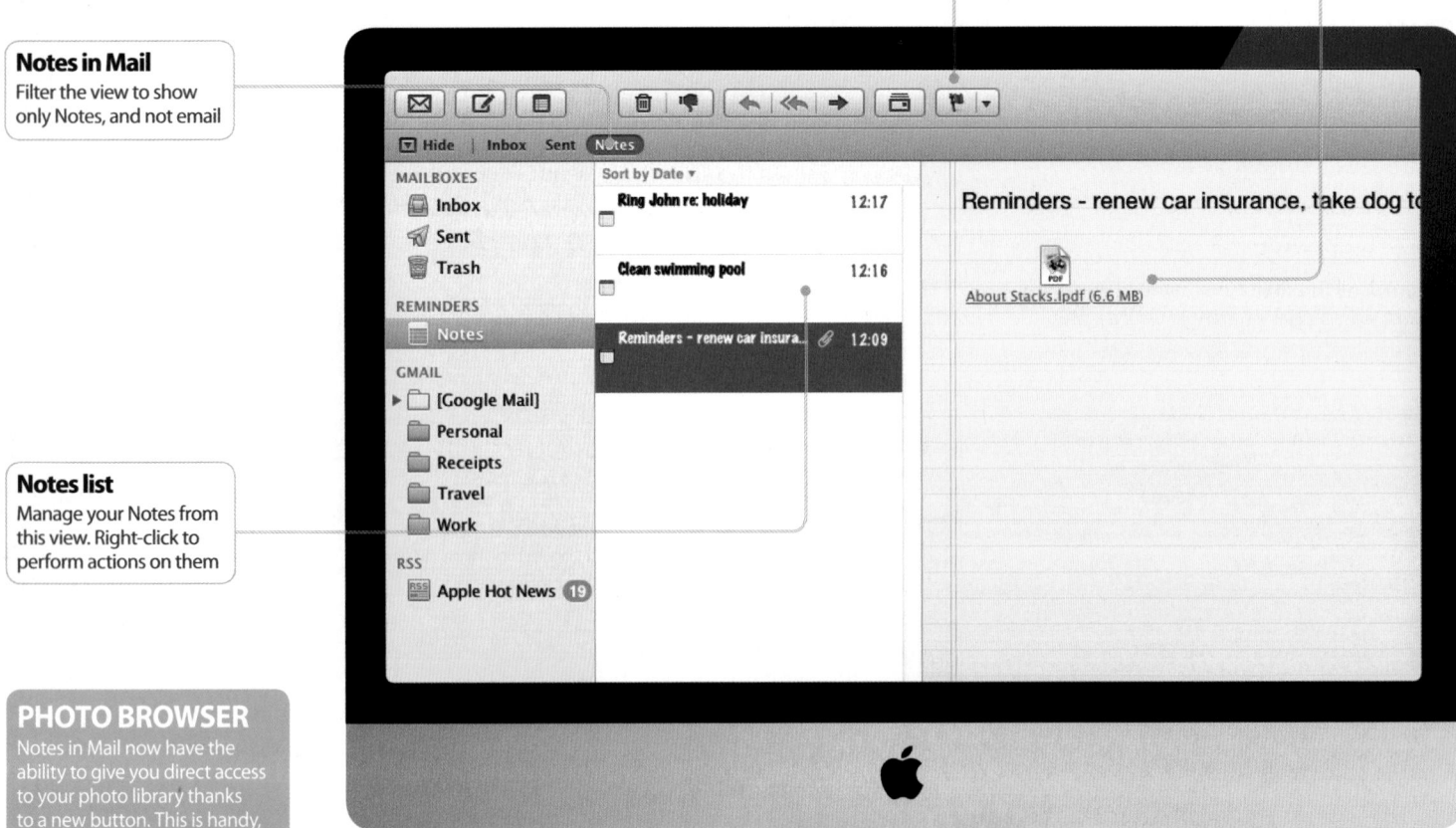

Mail Using Notes in Mail

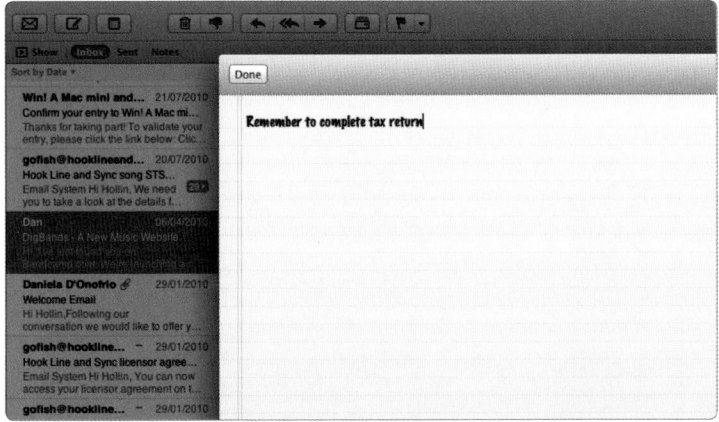

01: Create a Note

In Mail, click on the New Note icon in the top-left corner, and a new note will appear. Type anything you like and it will automatically save as you go.

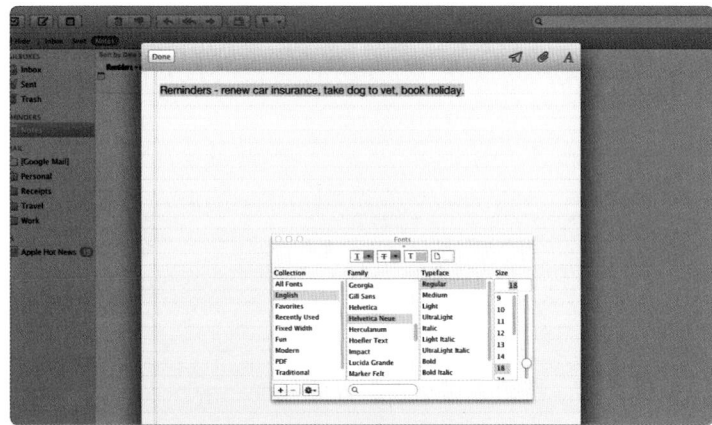

02: Change appearance

Click on the 'A' icon, which reveals the font formatting palette. You can select any font, as well as a size, to customise the appearance of your notes.

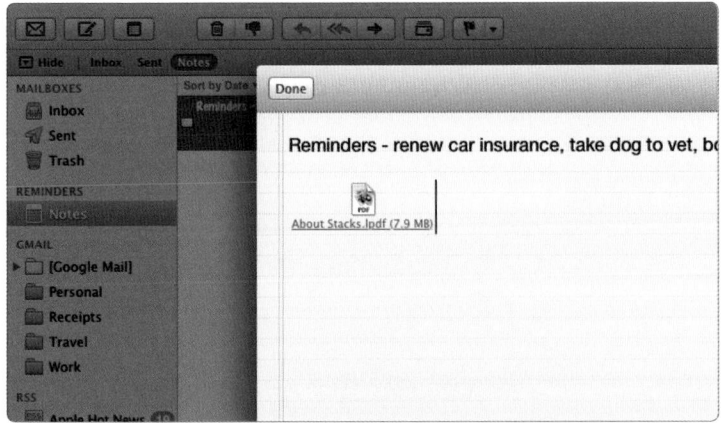

03: Attach a file

Click on the paper clip icon and you can add a file from anywhere on your Mac. It appears in the body of the note, just like in an email.

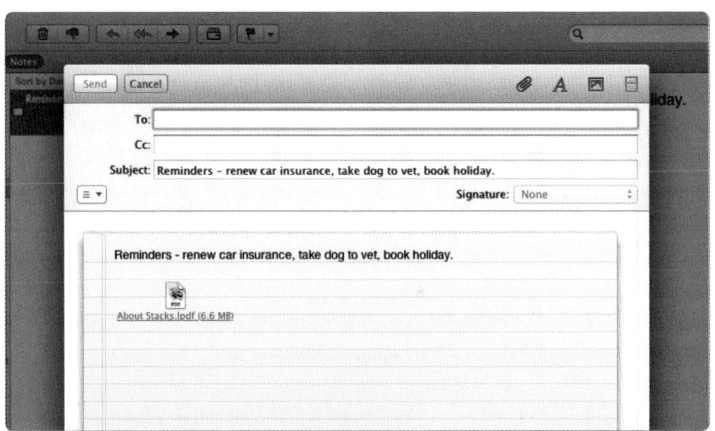

04: Send Note

Click on the paper aeroplane icon to convert the note into an email. The first line of the note becomes the subject and any files become attachments.

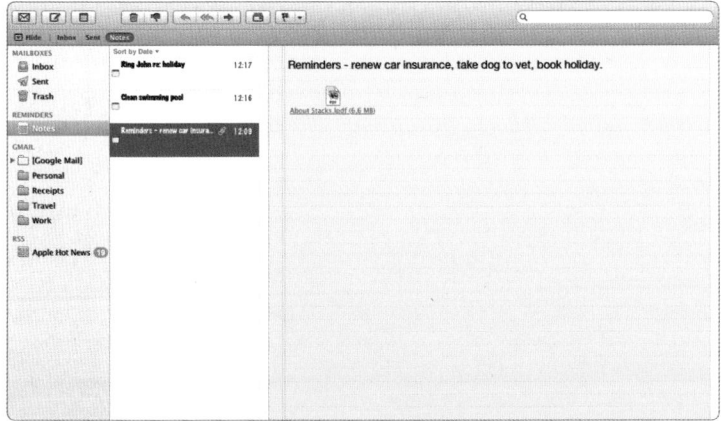

05: Create more notes

In the view bar at the top of Mail's window, select 'Notes' to show only notes, and not your mailbox. All the notes you've created will be visible here.

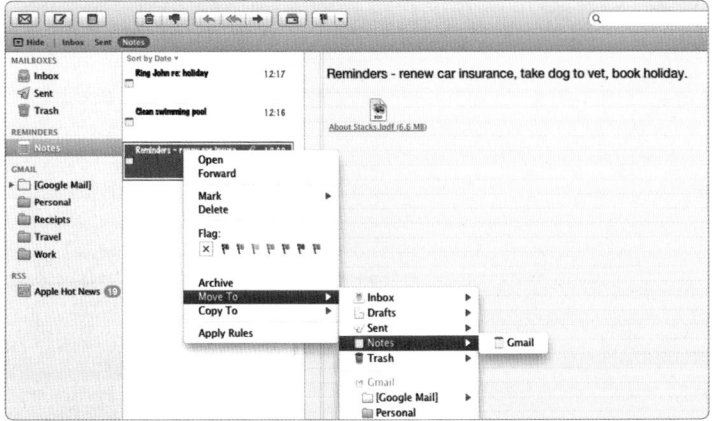

06: Move Notes

Right-click on a note in the list view and you can choose to move it to any folder in Mail on your Mac, or to a Notes folder on the server.

Set up the Junk Mail filter in Mail

Nobody likes spam emails cluttering up their email account, so get organised and filter them out of your Mac life for good

 **App used:** Mail

 **Time needed:** 5 minutes

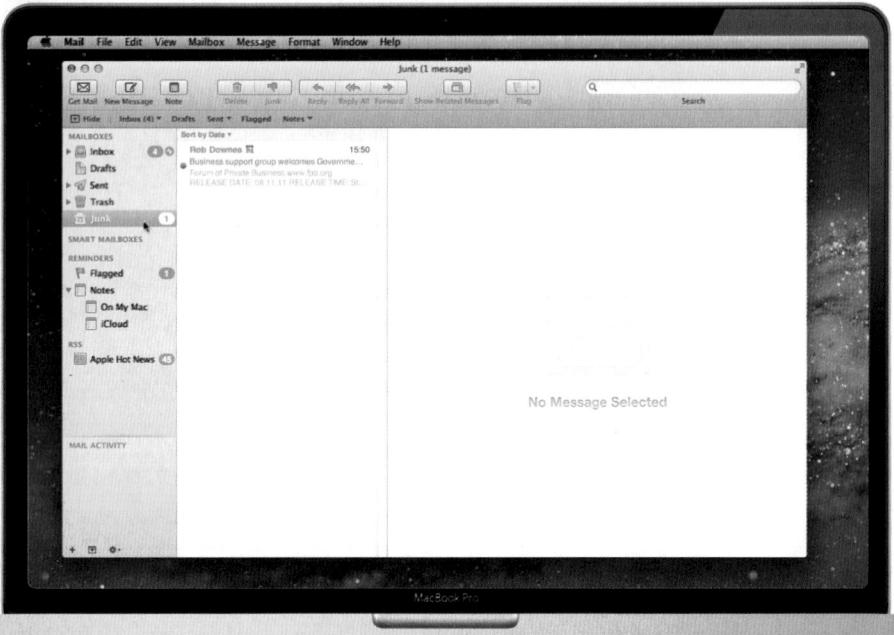

Spam is seen by many people as the bane of the emailing world, and for good reason. It seems that no matter how careful you are not to give your details away when you don't have to, you still end up getting unsolicited messages dropped into your inbox at a rate that is hard to fathom.

Spam can quickly turn a mail account into a cesspit of scams, unlicensed drugs and terrible products. At that point it takes all the fun out of getting emails – who wants to have to delete a ream of rubbish before you can settle in and read a message from a friend?

Luckily, as Mac users we have Mail – and it's possible to customise it to help filter out all the rubbish and keep your inbox full of the emails you want. The process is simple and will mean that as emails pour into your inbox, spam will be immediately filtered out. You may have to tell Mail where to put a few rogue spam messages, but it will then learn from that and the amount of spam you receive will reduce dramatically. You will then be able to enjoy the feeling of receiving a new message, safe in the knowledge that it will be something worth reading and not asking you to enter your bank details because you've won the Nigerian lottery…

Mail Filter out your junk emails

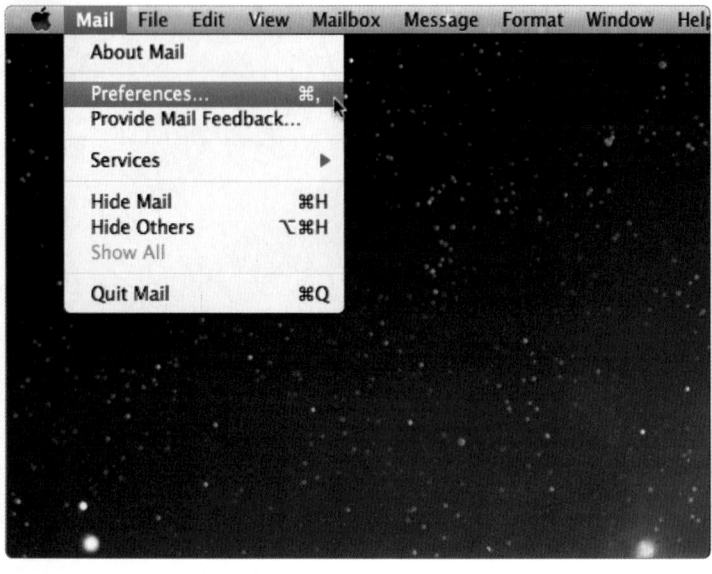

01: Go to Preferences

Once you have opened up Mail go to the top menu, click Mail and then click Preferences. This will bring up the Preferences window. From here you can customise a number of elements in Mail, personalising it and making it work how you want it to.

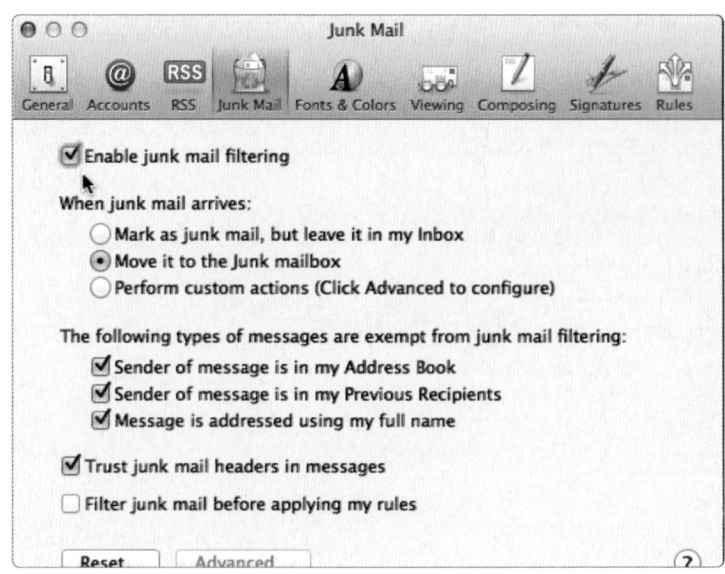

02: Junk tab

In the window that appears, simply click on the Junk Mail tab at the top of the window as shown above and click the 'Enable junk mail' filtering tick box. There are a number of other options presented here, but we'll walk you through them in the next step.

Employ the Junk Mail filter in Mail

Send that spam out of your life for good

One-button vetting
You can also mark or unmark your emails by using the button at the top of the interface

New folder
Once you've created a Junk Mail filter you will see a new Junk Mailbox appear in the left-hand panel of the Mail screen

JUNK IN THE CLOUD
When you set up iCloud, all of your Mail settings will be synced to all of your devices. So if you set up a Junk Mail filter in Mail on your Mac, the same filter will be applied to Mail on your iPad or your iPhone. Just another example of how iCloud works to make your life easier.

It gets smart
Mail will, over time, come to recognise junk mail and will get more proficient at filtering it out

Marked messages
You can mark mail as junk from within the email itself. You will be prompted at the top of an email as to whether you wish to mark or unmark it as junk

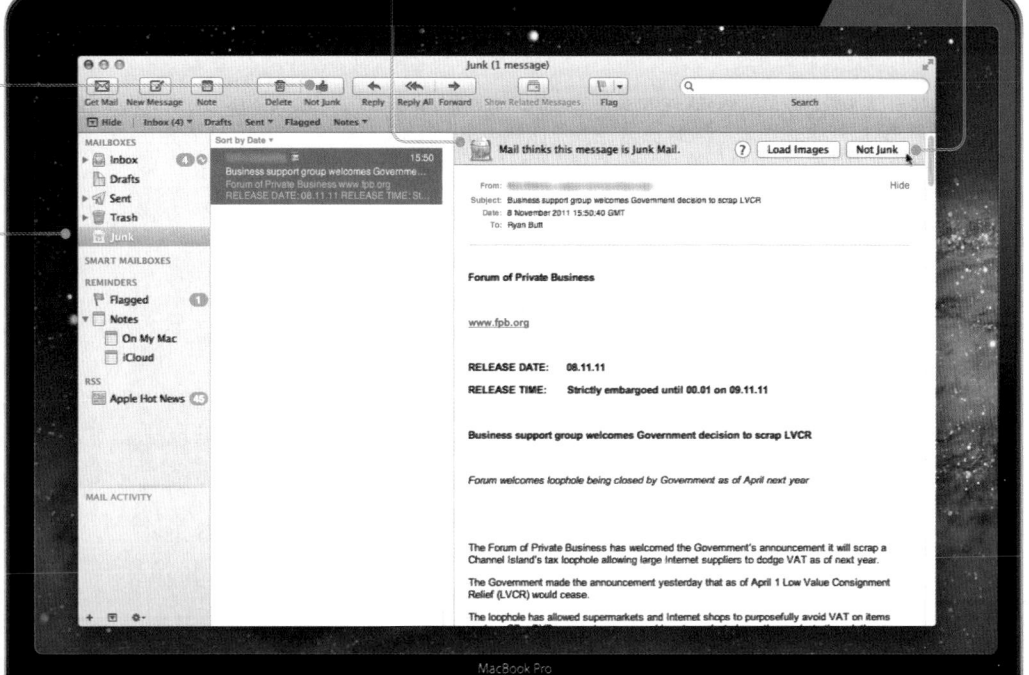

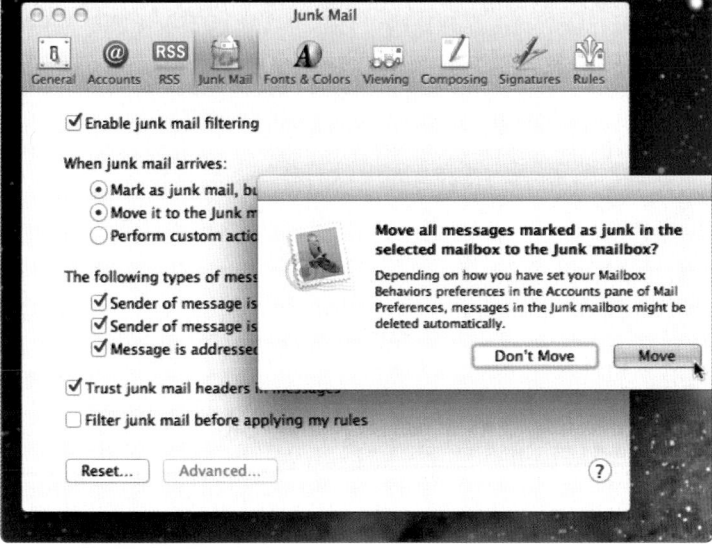

03: When it arrives

In the 'When junk mail arrives' section, tick the 'Move it to the Junk mailbox' box. You will now be prompted about moving mail, so hit the Move button. By selecting this option, when Mail determines something is junk, it will move it to a separate folder instead of cluttering your inbox.

04: Further customise

You can now alter the behaviour of the Junk Mail filter by ticking the boxes you want to apply to your Mail. Your changes will be saved automatically and you can return to this window and alter the settings as and when you wish if you find they're not working for you.

Get to know iCal

iCal is an incredibly important app that can help get you organised

 **App used:**
iCal

 **Time needed:**
15 minutes

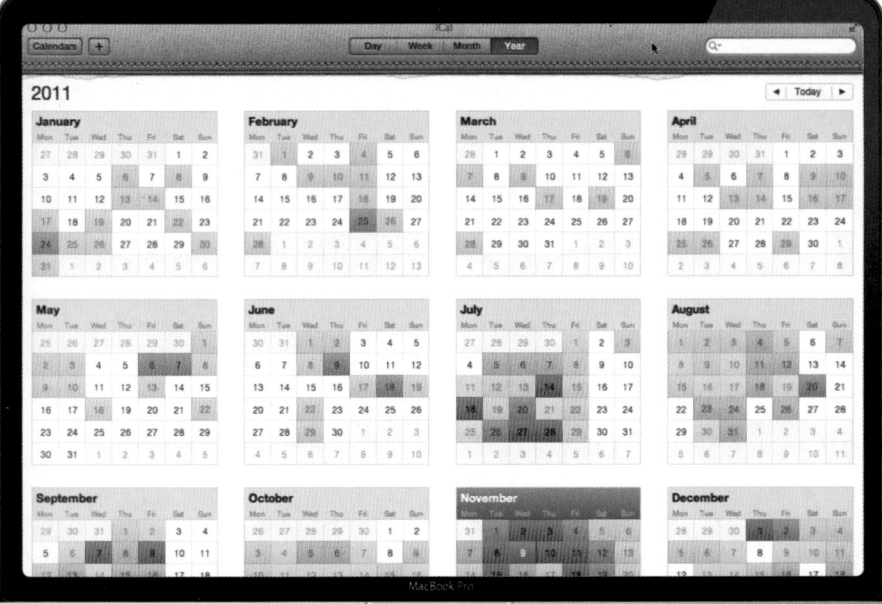

iCal is one of the unsung heroes of OS X and iOS. It is the Mac-based predecessor to Calendar on your iPhone, iPad or iPod touch. This application has the ability to help you organise your life and – with the ability to share your calendars – the lives of others.

As you would expect, Apple has made the app simple yet effective, with an incredibly user-friendly interface. You can colour code certain calendars, so you can set up different ones for work, social events, sport matches and more. You can set the event to a certain time or to 'all-day' and there are plenty of other options that will suit your needs.

In this introduction to the application we'll show you how to add a new calendar and add an event, as well as how best to view your busy schedule. Armed with this information, you can keep track of important meetings, birthdays, social events and much more with ease.

"This app can really help you to organise your life"

iCal Get started with iCal

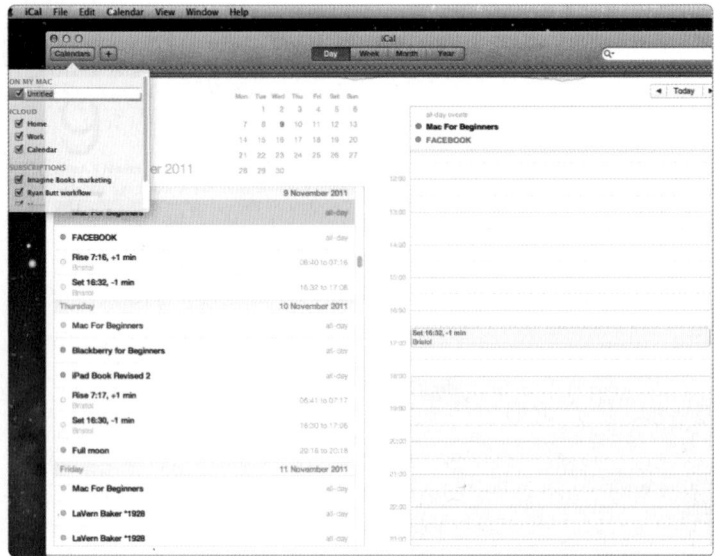

01: Add a calendar

The very first step will be to open up iCal on your Mac. Use the + button in the top-left corner of the iCal interface to add a new quick event. Alternatively you can click on the File menu and click 'New Calendar' to create a new calendar.

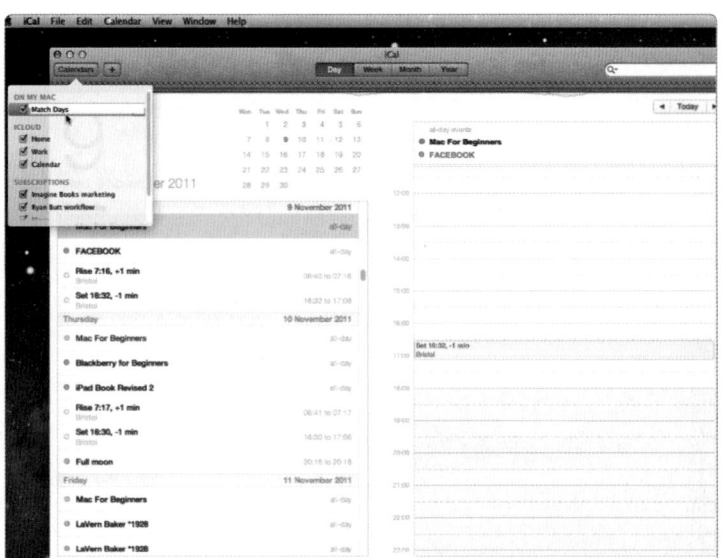

02: Name it

Naming your calendar is important, as it will specify the kind of events you add and help you divide the kinds of tasks you complete in your everyday life. You can, once your calendar is made, tick and untick it to reveal and hide those events.

Grasp the iCal interface

iCal lets you view your calendar
how you want to

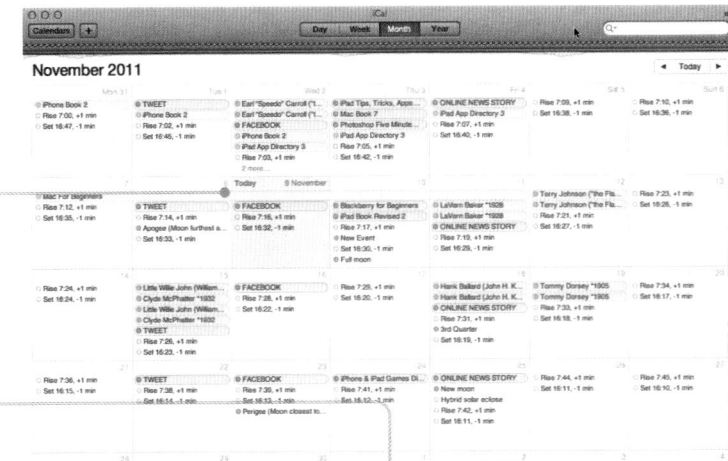

Month view

This is the best way to view the year and to get a feel for how busy you are. You can easily skim through months at a time, which makes it the best place to plan holidays and larger projects

Day view

If you're a really busy bee, this is where you'll need to be to organise every moment of your life. A great way to keep yourself abreast of each minute of the day

Week view

This is our favourite view as it offers enough detail to see entire days well-planned-out, but it also offers an overview of the entire week. We live in this view

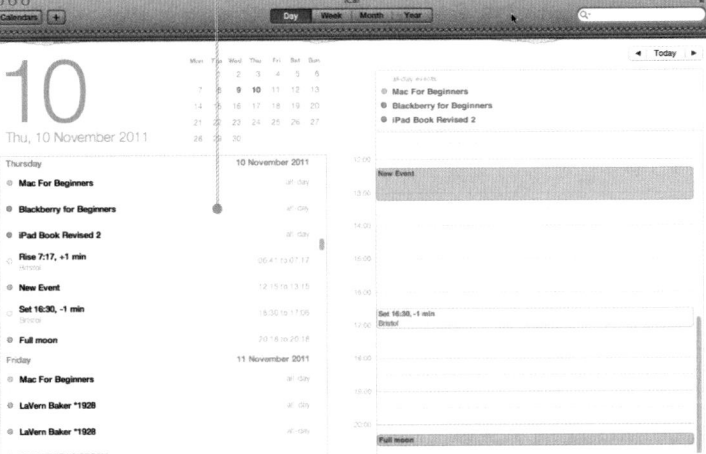

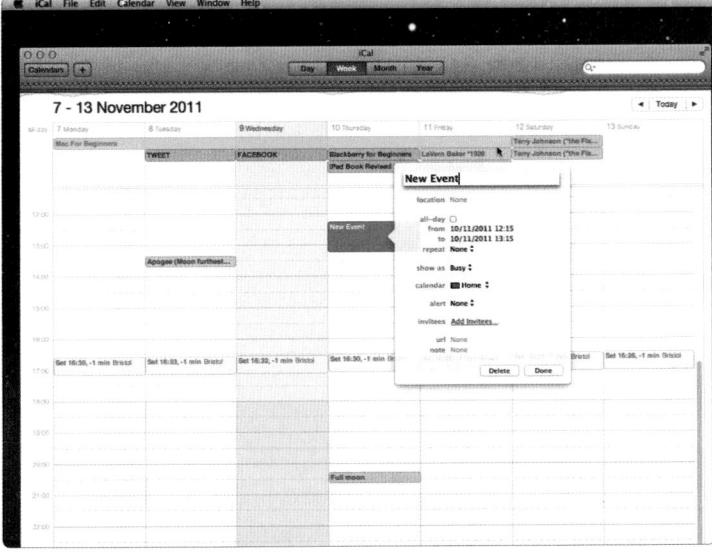

03: Double-click

Double-click on a day and time to add a new event. A pop-up window will appear, allowing you to add all the pertinent information you want to the new event. Be as detailed as you can, as this will help you recall the event when the time comes.

04: Assign to a calendar

If you've changed your mind about the calendar you want this to apply to, click on the drop-down arrow next to 'calendar' and select a different one. As these are colour-coded you can easily distinguish between them. Once finished, click Done.

Add a note to your iCal event

Apply more detail to your iCal events by adding notes

 **App used:**
iCal

 **Time needed:**
5 minutes

 Apple's iCal app is great for keeping track of your hectic schedule, adding events and inviting other people to attend. When creating events that other users will be able to see, it is obviously a good idea to include as much detail as possible – but you don't want to pepper the main event window with too many words, so what can you do? Easy, add a note. Once you have added an event you can double-click on it

to bring up a floating window of information, including the all-important start and finish times, and by clicking the 'Edit' button you can then start adding invitees, alerts and notes. Simply click on 'note' and you'll be able to write as much text as you want into a dialogue box and once you click 'done', this information will be viewable to others clicking on your event. Here's how to start adding in your own event notes.

"Add a note to an event to give as much detail as possible"

iCal Add more information to your entry

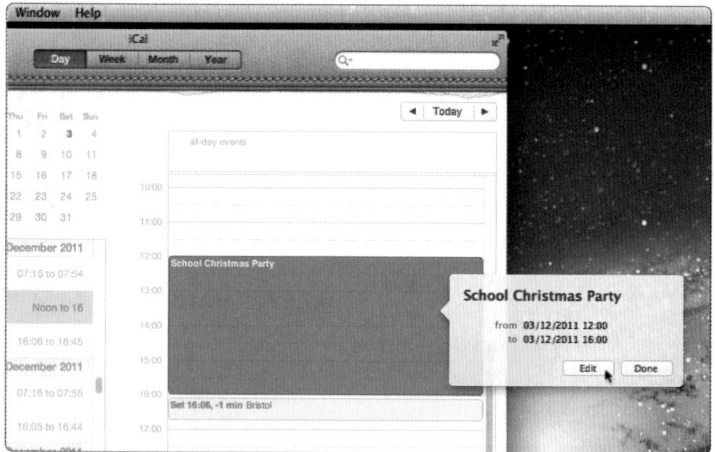

01: Double-click event

Locate the iCal event that you wish to apply a note to and then double-click on it to bring up an overview box of the event. Click on the 'Edit' button.

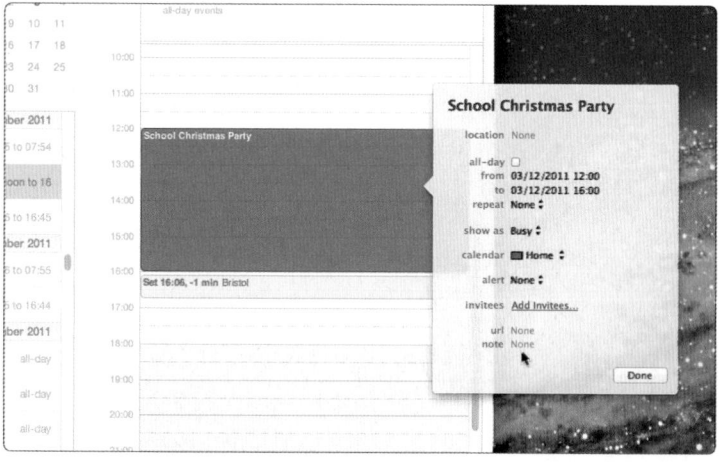

02: Click on 'note'

The overview box will be expanded to show various details and functions. At the bottom of the box will be a 'note' entry that is set to 'None'.

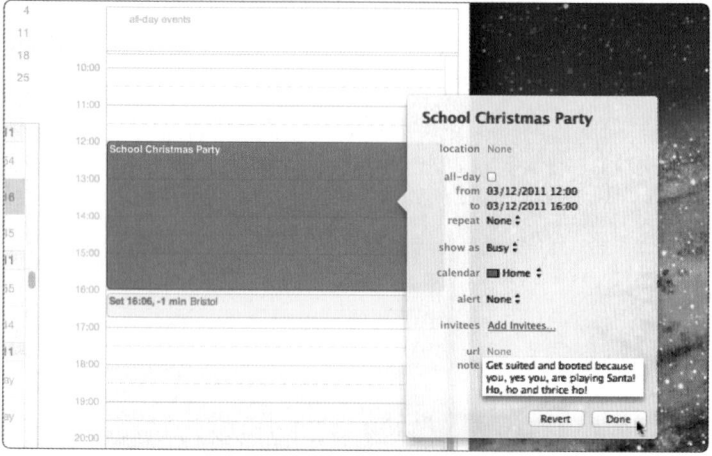

03: Enter text

Click 'None' to bring up a text entry box and then enter what you like. You can enter as few or as many words as you like.

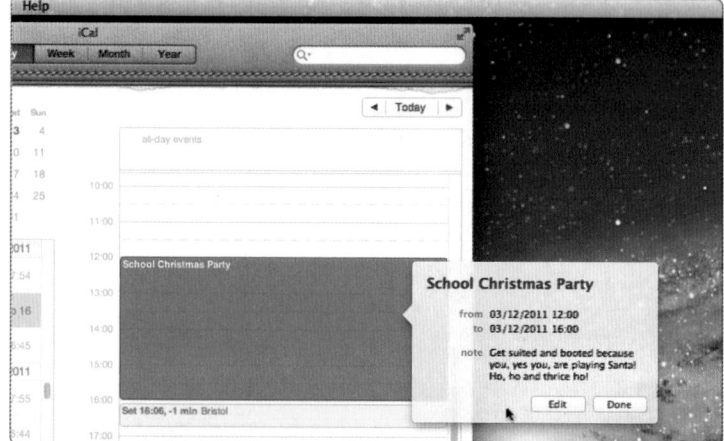

04: Click 'Done'

Click the 'Done' button when you have finished writing and the note will be applied to the event. Anyone linked into your calendar will be able to read it.

Add an alert to your iCal event

Set alerts to ensure you never miss an important iCal event

 App used:
iCal

 Time needed:
5 minutes

For all your good intentions of adding events to your iCal calendars, they don't mean a thing if you fail to take notice and forget about them. Thankfully, to avoid this happening you can set yourself handy alerts so that the app will inform you on the day, hours or minutes before or at a precise time and date that you determine. These alerts can consist of a message, a message with a sound, an email sent to yourself, the automatic opening of an application or, if you use AppleScript then you can set up a specific script, or action, that your Mac will perform when it needs to alert you to your event at the specified time. You have full freedom to determine the time and date of the alert and you can even set up a sequence of alerts if you're worried about missing your event. Simply use the drop-down menus next to 'alert' in the event edit box.

> "Alerts can inform you of an event minutes, hours or days beforehand"

iCal How to apply alerts to events

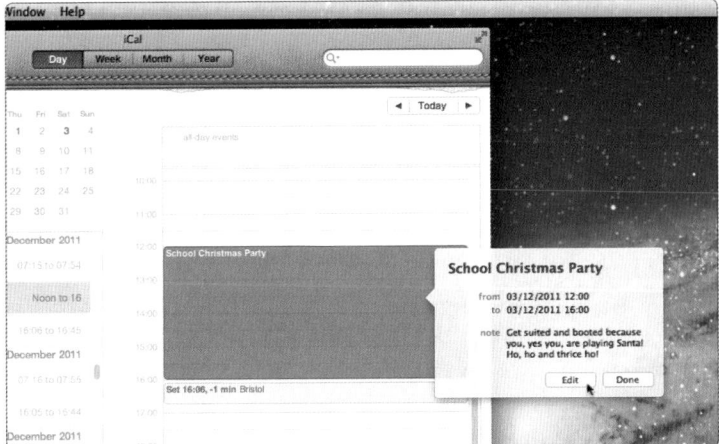

01: Double-click the event

Locate the iCal event that you wish to apply an alert to and double-click on it to bring up an overview box of the event. Click on the 'Edit' button.

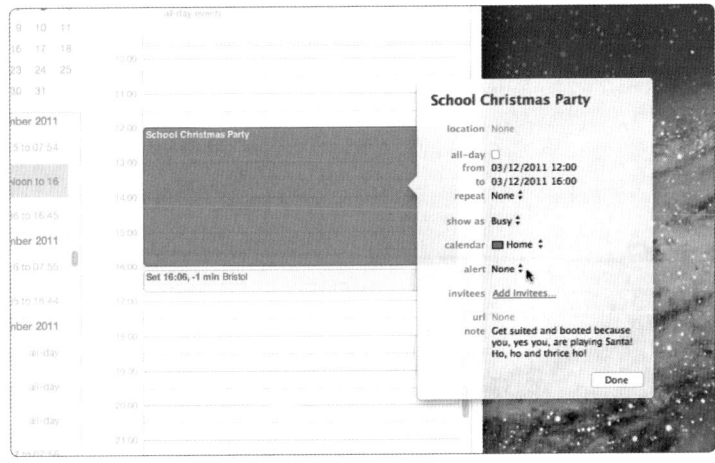

02: Click on 'alert'

The overview box will be expanded to show various details and functions. Near the bottom of the box will be an 'alert' entry that is set to 'None'.

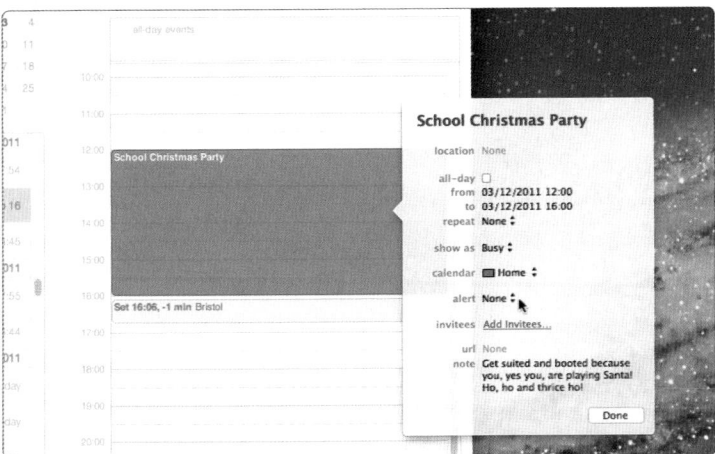

03: Set alert

Click 'None' to bring up a box of options. Now you can set the type of alert you want, including a message, email, open iCal or run a script.

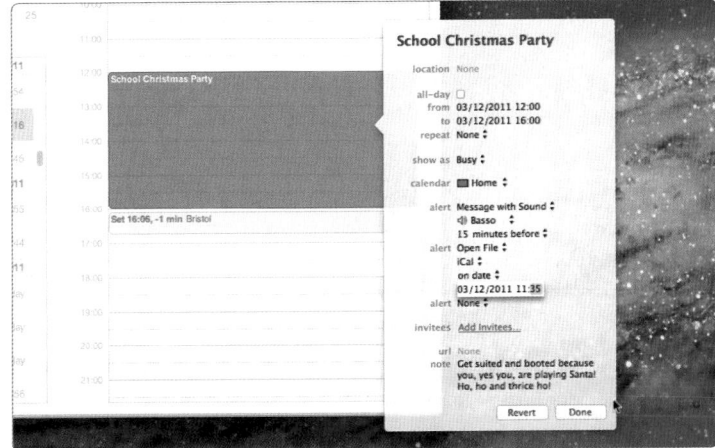

04: Click 'Done'

Click the 'Done' button when you have finished and the alert will be applied to the event and take place at the time you determine.

Change the days per week in iCal

iCal has the flexibility to keep things relevant to the way you live your life. If you only want to see weekdays, it's just a couple of clicks away

 **App used:** iCal

 **Time needed:** 5 minutes

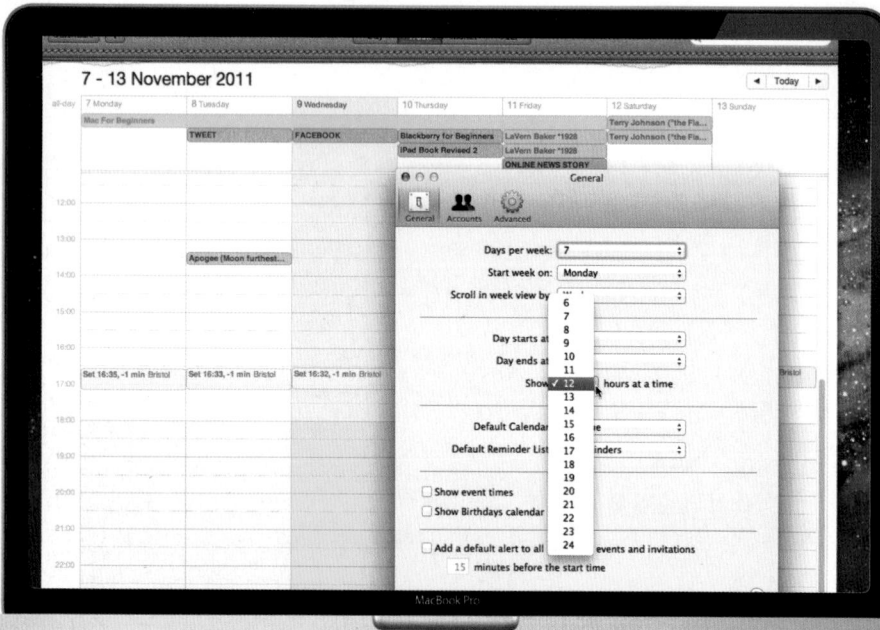

Having iCal on your Mac can be an absolute godsend. Not only can it sync with your iPhone or iPod touch, but it works seamlessly with Mail and your Address Book so you need only do the bare minimum in order to organise your life. This is all pretty common knowledge and often touted on the Apple website, but what a lot of people don't know is that iCal can be easily customised to suit your life. If you use it primarily for work, for instance, you can shorten the number of days shown in the week view to five. You can also, if you work irregular hours, increase the amount of time you can see and edit in the week view. These tweaks may seem like cosmetic fiddling to some, but for those who want to use iCal as a serious organisational tool it can make an impressive difference. In this tutorial we'll take you through the basics of making those changes.

> "iCal can be easily customised to suit your life"

iCal Customise the week view

01: Go to the top

Open iCal from your Dock or from your Applications folder, wherever is easier for you. Now go to the top menu and click iCal>Preferences, as shown in the screenshot above. The Preferences pane will now pop up in the middle of your screen.

02: All happening here

The General section will now appear with lots of options on offer. Here you can make changes to the way you view and use iCal. If you make a change here and then you decide it's not working for you, you can return to this screen and change it back.

Change the week view in iCal
Customise the amount of days and hours shown

Hit it
Click this button to see the week view. This is where all your changes will have taken shape

Hard work
You will now just see the days of the working week on the week view. This is a much more efficient way to view your life if you use iCal for work only

All the hours
The number of hours you set as being viewable in the Preference window will now be available to edit and add events to

Syncing
If you use Apple's free iCloud service then the calendars on your Mac can be synced wirelessly to your iPhone, iPad or iPod touch

SYNC THE IPHONE AND IPOD TOUCH
The iPhone and iPod touch don't have a week view, so when you make the changes to iCal from this tutorial you won't see an immediate difference. But if you go into the day view on the iPhone and iPod touch, however, you will see that the new number of hours viewable in a day has been synced to your device.

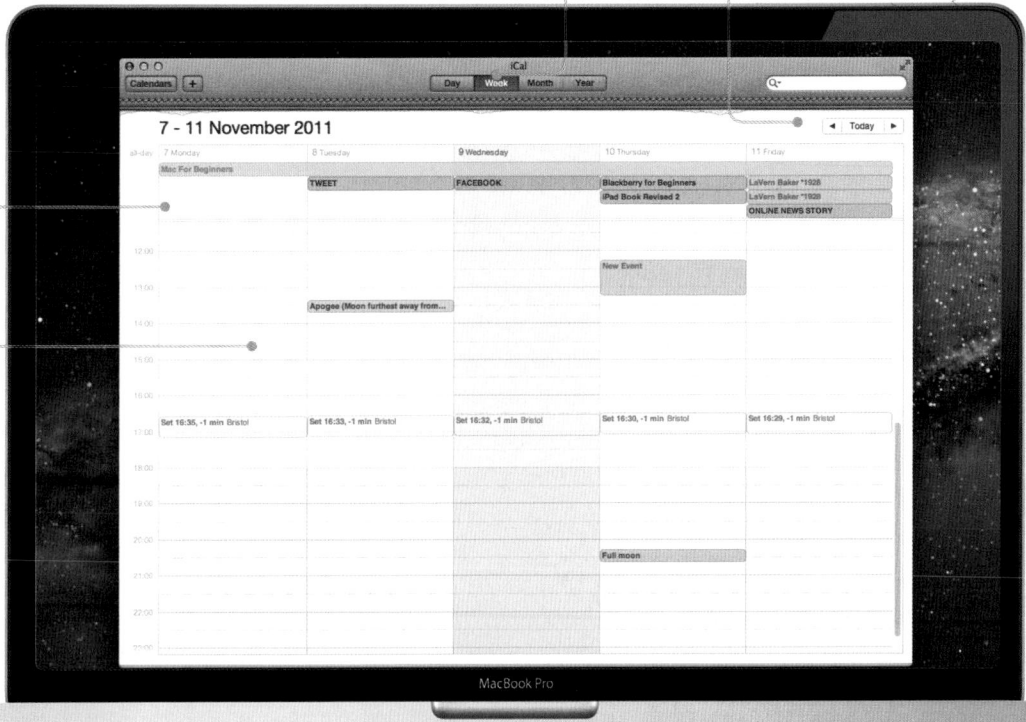

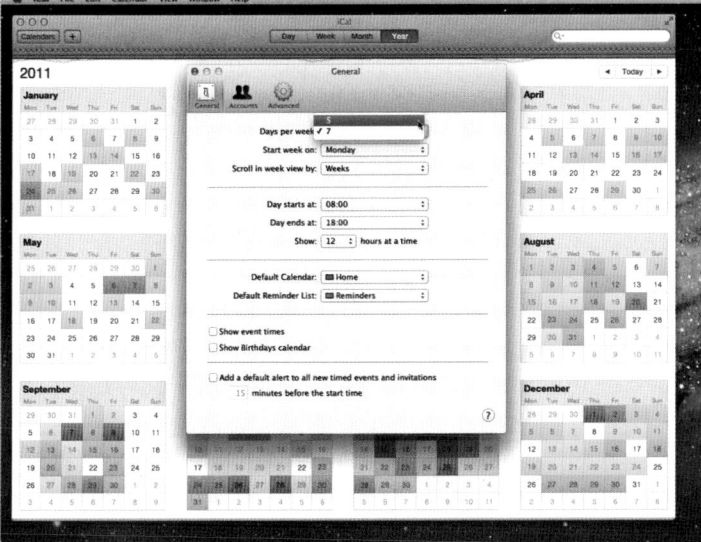

03: Let there be five
You can change the number of days in the week shown in iCal by using the drop-down menu and clicking '5'. A tick will then appear next to it and it will return to the default view with five days in the field instead of the usual seven days.

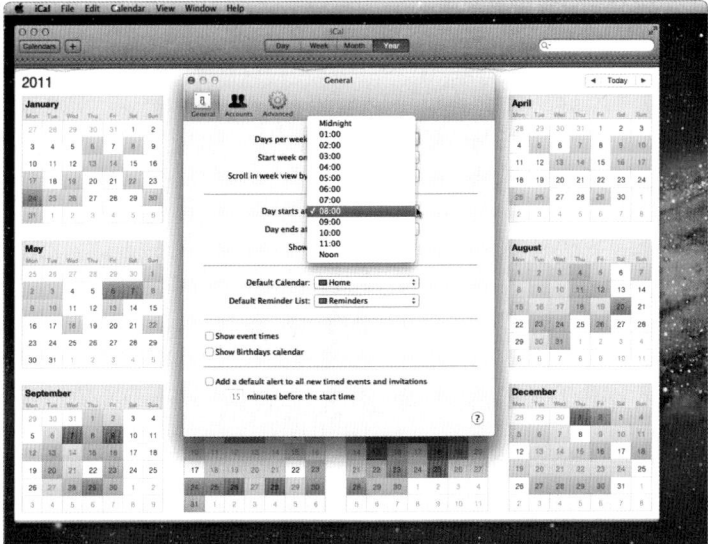

04: Time it right
You can also change the number of hours of the day viewed in the same way. Just use the drop-down menus and click on the value you want to be shown in iCal. This can be handy if you do shift work, or don't want to show the hours you'll be tucked up in bed!

Add iCal events using Automator

Tired of opening iCal and manually adding Events?
Use Automator to simplify and speed up the process

 **App used:** iCal  **Time needed:** 10 minutes

 iCal is a fantastic app for managing your events, birthdays and to-do lists, and in general keeping track of where you are and where you should be. With only a few clicks of your mouse you can add a custom event to any date, with location details, from-and-to dates, repeats, attendees, attachments and alarms.

But what if you're busy working in an application and quickly want to add an event to iCal without actually having to close the current window and switching programs? Don't worry, all is not lost. There's an easy solution using Automator – Apple's

clever scripting program that takes time-consuming processes and simplifies them into one click. Follow us over the next two pages as we explain how to create an Automator script that enables you to add an event to iCal with a minimal amount of fuss.

"Automator simplifies time-consuming processes"

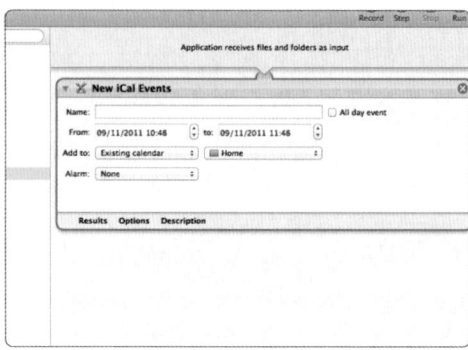

The Automator iCal Events action

Discover how easy it is to use Automator

The results field
After you've created and run your new iCal Events action, click the Results button to see a visual log of it

All day event
If an Event is to last all day, simply tick this button in the upper-right corner to tell iCal to create a 24-hour long Event

Other iCal actions
The column to the left enables you to create other Automator actions that simplify using iCal. If you ever need to quickly delete an iCal Event, you can easily create an Automator application to do this

Add to options
If you wish to add Events to new Calendars, click the 'Add to' drop-down menu and select 'New calendar'. Calendars that already exist in iCal can be chosen from this same menu

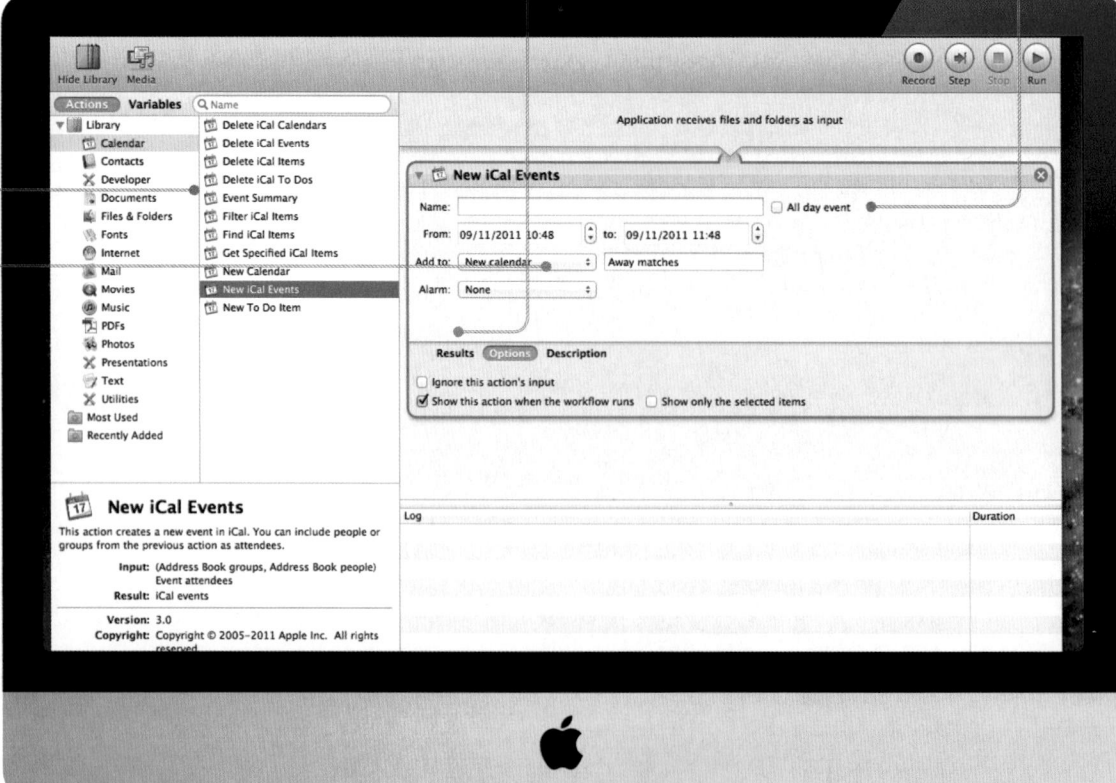

THE VERSATILITY OF AUTOMATOR
Automator can be used to simplify hundreds of tasks, so it's worth exploring its options to see what's possible. A few of our favourite actions include the ability to rename files, take a picture and export QuickTime movies with one click. If that's not enough, you'll find more than 130 new Automators at Apple's Downloads page.

Automator Quickly update iCal with new events via Automator

01: Launch Automator

Open Automator from your applications folder and choose Application from the drop-down list that greets you upon startup.

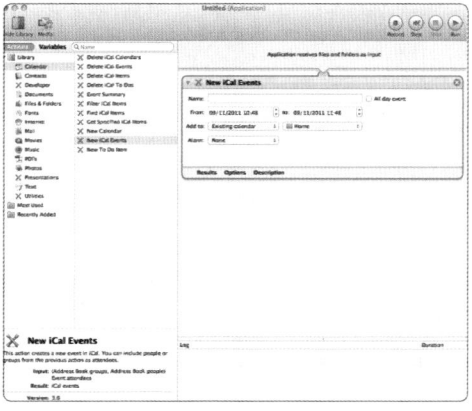

02: New iCal Events

Click on the Calendar listing in the left-hand column, and double-click New iCal Events. The details will appear in the main window.

03: Detailed options

Click the Options button at the bottom of the action window, and enable the button that says 'Show this action when the workflow runs'.

04: Customising details

By clicking this button you're telling Automator to make this action interactive, enabling you to customise the details of each new iCal Event.

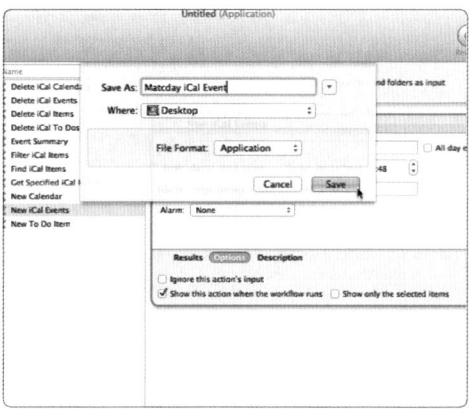

05: No need to name

Don't worry about adding a name right now, as it's likely each new iCal Event will be unique. This is how our new iCal Events box looks.

06: Saving…

Click the File button in the Finder and choose Save. Give your new action a name. Under File Format, choose Application.

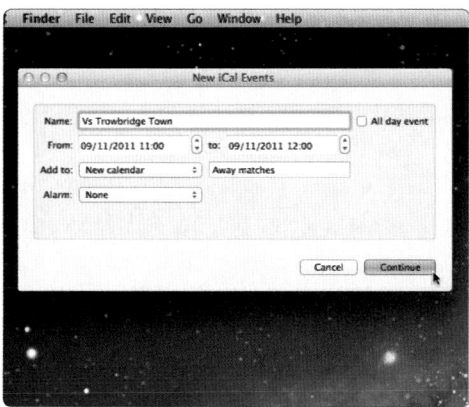

07: Testing

You've now created your own custom application that adds new Events to iCal. Test it by closing both iCal and Automator, and running the app.

08: Event added!

Once you've entered the details into the application window, click the Continue button and the Event will be added to iCal.

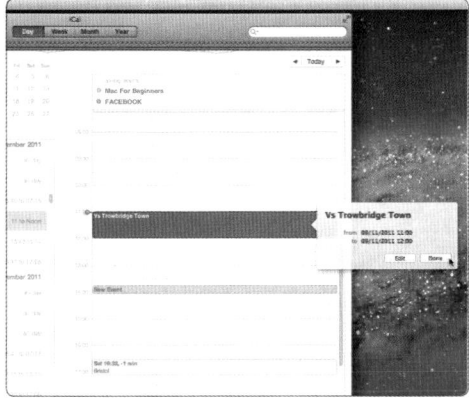

09: Finer details

It's not possible to add attendees, URLs or attachments via this method, but it's still a great way to add simple Events without opening iCal.

Send invites using iCal

Introducing iCal's ability to invite people to your events

 **App used:**
iCal

 **Time needed:**
5 minutes

With iCal, you have the ability to invite other people to events on your calendar. And when they accept, decline or reply with a 'maybe', you will be able to see right away how many people are due to attend.

When you right-click or create any event, you have the opportunity to Add invitees. Clicking on the link lets you type in email addresses or view your Address Book for contacts. You can also open the Address Panel and drag invitees or entire groups over. Either way, your invitees are notified and are prompted to respond.

If your contacts are stored on the same server and share the same CalDAV or Exchange calender

service, you can instantly see when people are available. In the Availability panel you will see the times when they are unavailable (the hours will be greyed out). Meetings can dragged forward or backward accordingly.

Using the invitee facility makes iCal so much more useful and lets you keep a proper check on your calendar using real-time information. Follow our tutorial to find out how it works.

"Instantly see when people are available"

Where to add invitees

The section of the interface
you need to add invitees

AUTOMATIC ICAL INVITES
You can integrate iCal with Mail easily. Go to Mail>Preferences> General and select Automatically in the drop-down field next to Add Invitations to iCal. Now make sure that you check the box which allows invitations to be automatically retrieved from Mail (Mail>Preferences> Advanced). Now if someone invites you, you will receive the invitation in iCal without any effort.

Multiple invites
You are not restricted to one invitee. You can drag in as many as you wish from the Address Panel (Window>Address Panel) or by typing email addresses separated by commas or a return

Your invitees
Once you have invited somebody and pressed send, they will then be notified and can decide whether to accept or not. Their status shows up when you right-click an event

The event
The events are the crucial element. Identify an event in your calendar, right-click and select edit and you will be given an option to Add an invitee. Pull from your Address Book or type an email address

Editing invitees
You can open up the edit box and delete invitees – just right-click on a name and select Remove. Other invitees can be added at any time and you can also select to send them emails

iCal Add an invitee to an iCal calendar

01: Select an event

If you have created an event and you wish to invite some people along, double-click on the event and, in the pop-up box, select Edit.

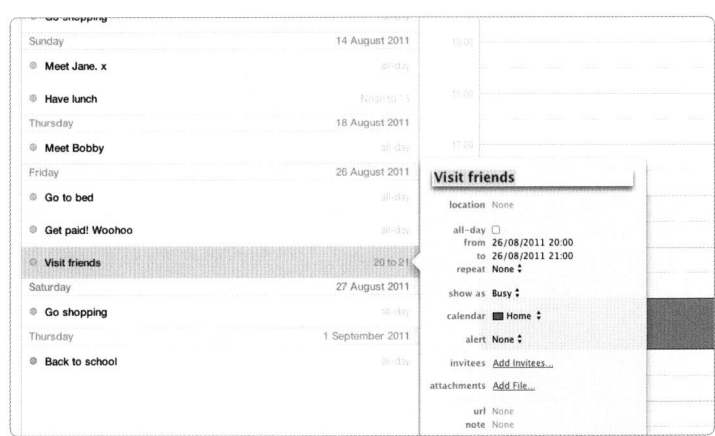

02: Add an invitee

You will see the event editing box which allows you to alter various aspects of your entry and add an invitee. Click on the link which says Add invitees.

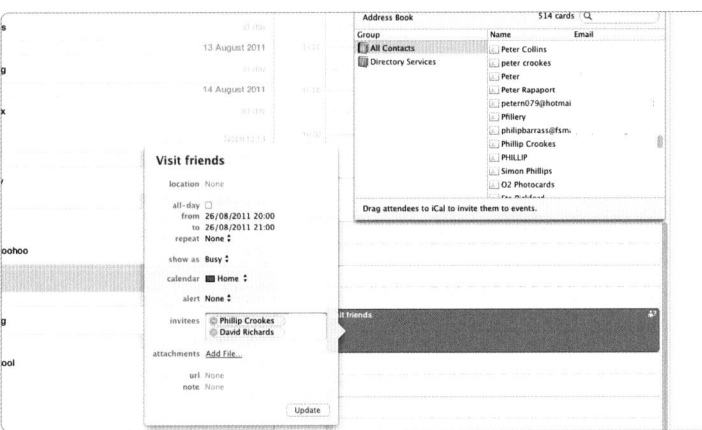

03: Inviting people

Type and iCal checks your Address Book. Select the contact you want. If you go to Window>Address Panel, you can drag contacts' details to your event.

04: Email is sent

More than one person can be invited. When you create an invitee they are notified and they will be asked to accept or decline in their iCal.

05: Accepting or declining

In your list a decline will show as a red circle, green highlights they have accepted and orange denotes a maybe.

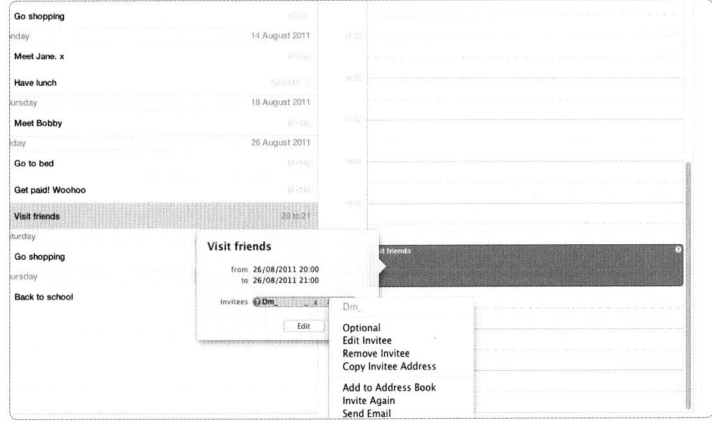

06: Invite options

If you right-click on a name in your invitee list, you can edit or remove it, copy the address, add it to your address book, send an email or invite again.

Share your calendar with others

Use iCal to share events and calendars –
even with non-iCal users

App used:
iCal

Time needed:
10 minutes

In sharing your calendar with others you are able to sync events and information. Single events and reminders can be shared as can entire calendars. And it is also possible to share your calendar, events and reminders with other apps such as Google Calendar. That's because iCal allows for them to be saved as .ics files which can be easily imported not only into other iCal programs but non-iCal apps too.

When you publish your calendar, that too allows for sharing and collaboration and we go into more depth on how you publish on page 118. Sharing has many practical uses – you may be in a work environment in which you need to send a group of people an invitation to a meeting. It is also social – why not send a calendar file with a birthday invite so that those with compatible apps can import it and be reminded later down the line. The bottom line is that a calendar needn't only be for yourself and by sharing it, you can become even more organised than ever before.

"You can sync events with ease"

Share events and calendars

Subscribe, import and email
events with ease

Subscribe
Entire calendars can also be subscribed to by going to Calendar>Subscribe. The URL which is given when you Publish a calendar is inserted in here

Importing an event
When an iCal user goes to iCal>Import>Import, they can import an event, reminder or entire calendar. All they have to do is search for the right .ics file

Emailing events
When the Mail app opens following a request to mail a reminder or event, the .ics file is attached allowing the recipient to import it, either by double-clicking or manually

Mail Reminder and Events
Right-click on an event or a reminder and you can select a menu option to email it. Simply select this option and your Mail app will open, ready for sending

FIND CALENDARS
You can subscribe to a range of calendars that have been posted online via the Apple website. Go to Calendar>Find Subscriptions in iCal and it will bring up a host of calendars that can be downloaded from a Bulgarian Orthodox Calendar through to those associated with specific sports such as F1. They are an easy way of adding handy dates.

iCal Allow others to see your calendar

01: Email your calendar
When you publish your calendar, you are given a URL that can be emailed to people. See page 118 for more on publishing your calendar.

02: Subscribe to a calendar
The URL can be inserted into the subscribe window. Anyone can go to Calendar>Subscribe, insert your URL and subscribe to your calendar.

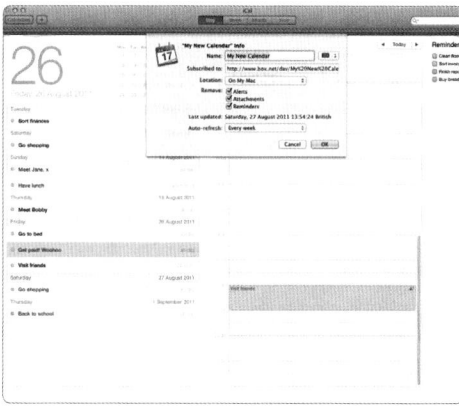

03: Details of calendar
Users can manipulate how they want the calendar to appear. They can remove alerts, attachments, reminders and set the auto-refresh.

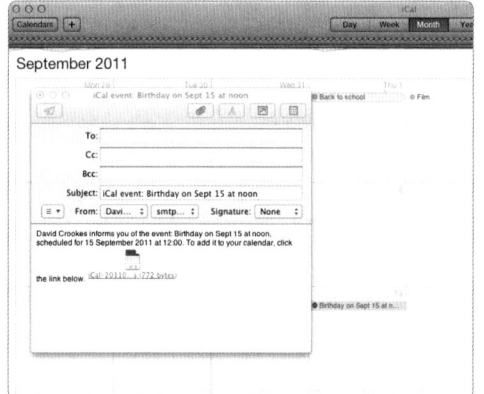

04: Share an event
Right-click on any event or reminder and you can send it via email using the Mail app. The crucial .ics file is automatically attached to the email.

05: Importing an event
The event created in Step 4 will be received by another user as an email. They can import it into iCal by going to iCal>Import>Import.

06: Google calendar
You can also integrate your iCal calendar with a Google account. First-time Mac users of Google Calendar will be prompted to integrate accounts.

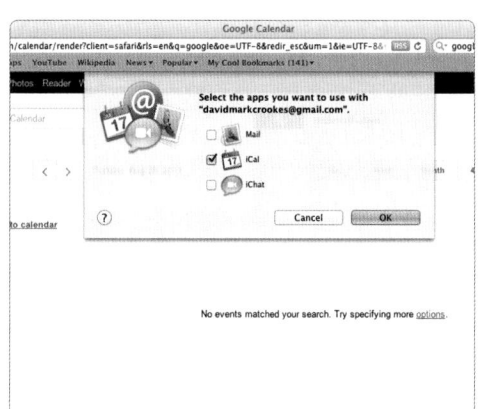

07: Choosing accounts
People can use Mail, iCal and iChat with Google Calendar. Choose the one you wish to integrate and press 'OK'. Relevant settings will port over.

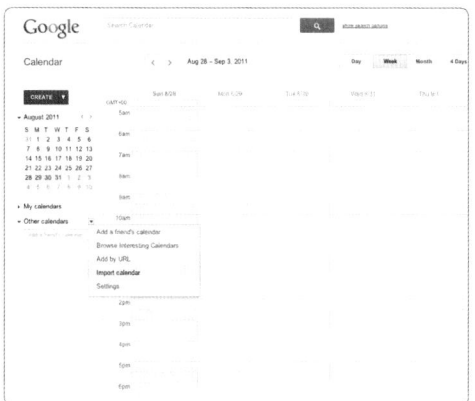

08: Import a calendar
Google Calendar users can import an entire calendar or event. Click the down arrow next to Other Calendars, then browse your hard drive.

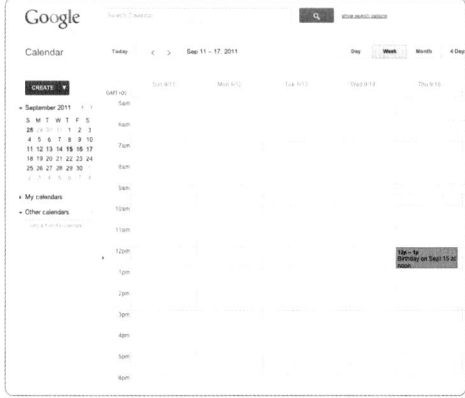

09: Automatic placing
Here we see your iCal event in a Google calendar. You are not restricted to sharing with other iCal users, making iCal more versatile and compatible.

Publish your iCal calendar

Allow people to view your calendar by publishing it

App used:
iCal

Time needed:
10 minutes

Publishing your calendar is a really great way to enable other people to easily see your key events and dates. The in-built Publish function lets you send your iCal calendar straight to a private webspace where it can be viewed by anyone going online and using a specified URL.

You are able to share any or all of your calendars. The process lets you manipulate exactly what can be displayed to others and there are options for users to subscribe to your calendar if they wish to integrate it into their own iCal app. In doing so, you can ensure that people are aware of your events

and day-to-day activity and it's a great way to keep people in the loop.

In this tutorial, we show you how to set yourself up with some free webspace that does the job well but is also very quick and easy too. So read on to learn how to quickly and easily publish your calendar for others to see.

"Ensure people are aware of your events"

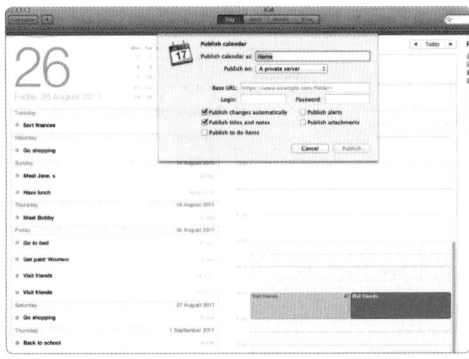

iCal Publishing an iCal calendar

01: Publish your calendar

Go to Calendar and click Publish from the drop-down menu to start the process of allowing other people to view and subscribe to your calendar.

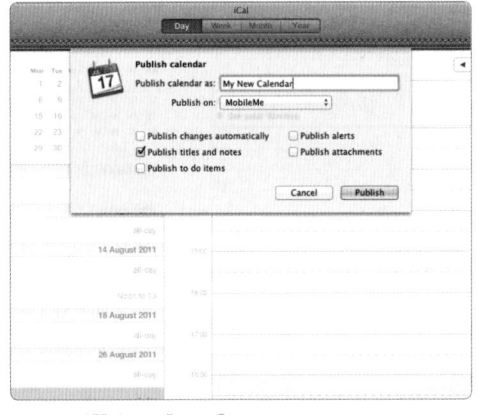

02: Fill in the form

A window will appear with various options. The first is the name of your calendar. Input the name and it will be published under that moniker.

03: Choose a method

In this case, we want to chose to publish on private server. Simply select this option from the drop-down list next to 'Publish on'.

04: Tick some boxes

Now decide which items you wish to publish. You just need to tick or untick the boxes next to each item in order to tailor your calendar.

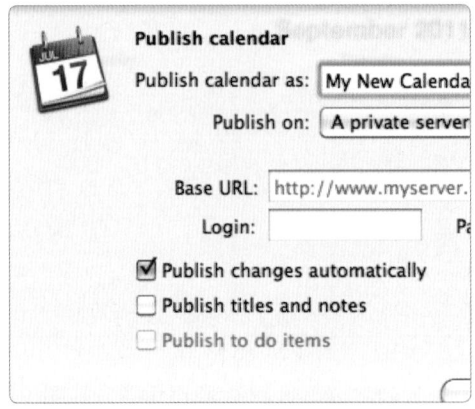

05: Automatically update

It is a good idea to tick the 'Publish changes automatically' box, so that your calendar is kept up to date with any changes you make to it.

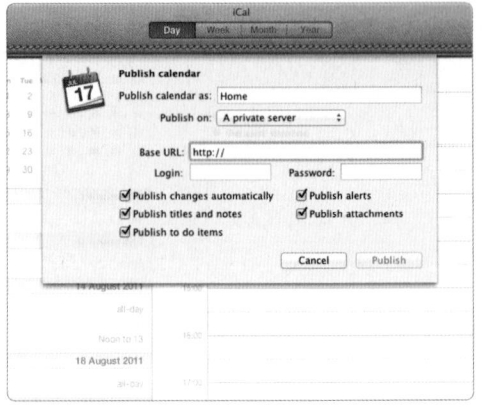

06: Going private

Now you need to enter the Base URL, login and password. It must be a WebDAV-enabled server so check with your provider. Press Publish.

Make your calendar public
The important factors of publishing explained

Publish box
No matter which way you wish to publish you'll need your log in details in order to access your server space. You input them in the Publish calendar box that appears when you go to Calendar>Publish

UNDERSTAND WEBDAV
WebDAV stands for Web-based Distributed Authoring and Versioning. Put simply, it allows documents that are stored on web servers to be edited and managed collaboratively. WebDAV is used by iCal as well as some other calendar services such as Google Calendar. For those who don't want to get too technical, in simple terms it is a great way of keeping your calendars in sync.

Give the calendar a name
You can give your calendar a specific name and when you click publish, you will be shown a URL. This lets you visit the page or send an email to people who you would like to see your calendar

Making choices
The among of information you publish is entirely up to you. There are five options: Publish changes automatically, publish titles and notes, publish To Do items, publish alarms and publish attachments

Calendars
Choose which calendar you wish to publish by clicking the Calendars button and making your choice. So you could publish a work-only or a home-only calendar. The choice is yours

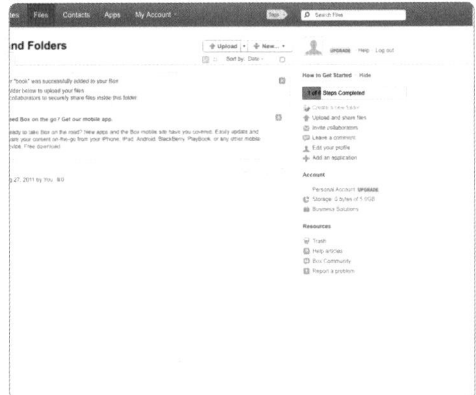

07: Using Box.net
If you don't have any private server space, then consider using box.net. It is very easy to set up and it is free. You get 5GB of server space.

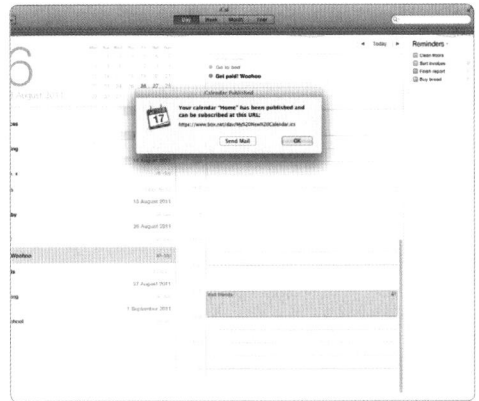

08: Calendar is published
Once you have pressed Publish (Step 6) you will be shown a window that displays the calendar's location. People can use the URL to subscribe.

09: Unpublish a calendar
You can remove your calendar with ease. Go to Calendar and click 'Unpublish'. This will remove your calendar so that it can't be viewed any more.

Sync iCal events to iCloud

How to ensure that any updates you make in iCal are reflected on your mobile calendars too

 **App used:** iCal

 **Time needed:** 15 minutes

 If you lead a busy lifestyle then Macs are perfectly equipped to take all the stress out of your situation and help you manage your hectic schedules. There are a host of ways in which your apps work together, syncing information and data, but the process can be summed up in one word – iCloud. If you have updated your operating system to OS X Lion 10.7.2 then you will be able to start enjoying the same free iCloud service that iPhone and iPad users have been sampling thanks to iOS 5. You can create and log

into your personal iCloud using your Apple ID (the same email address and password that you use to buy media from iTunes) and then give permission for certain apps to sync data.

> "If the app is synced to iCloud, changes will be reflected"

Perhaps the most efficient example of this is displayed in iCal. If you wish to create a new event for your Mac iCal app then, as long as this app is synced to your iCloud then any changes you make will be instantly reflected in the Calendar app on your iPhone or iPad.

The transition is seamless and, more importantly, wireless, so you don't have to worry about manually transferring anything. In this tutorial we will help you get set up and guide you through the process of syncing iCal events and alerts to iCloud.

iCal Syncing iCal reminders to iCloud

01: Add an event
Launch your iCal app and then, in 'Day' view, click on the time at which you wish your event to start to place a new event box within that time frame.

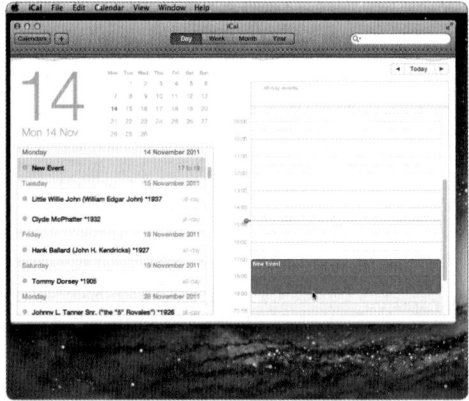

02: Set the time frame
Move your cursor to the top or bottom of the window and you'll be able to drag it up or down to increase or decrease the duration of the event.

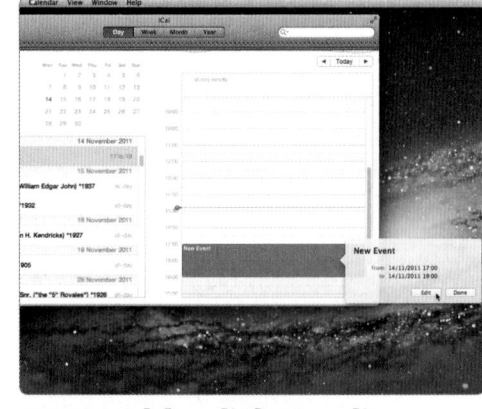

03: Double-click to edit
Double-click your event window to get a basic overview and then click on 'Edit' to fine tune the details of your new event.

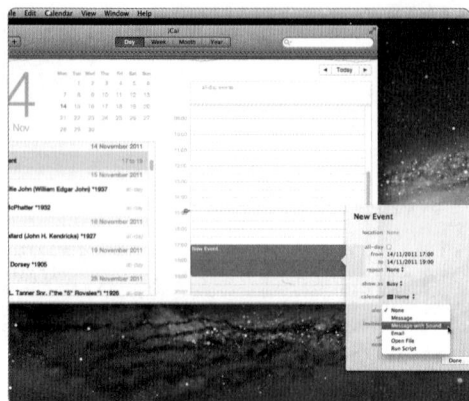

04: Add an alert
Check the time frame of your event and then click on the 'Alert' menu. You can now set yourself a reminder in the run up to the event.

05: Open System Preferences
Now open your System Preferences app from your Applications folder or Dock and once it opens, choose the 'iCloud' option.

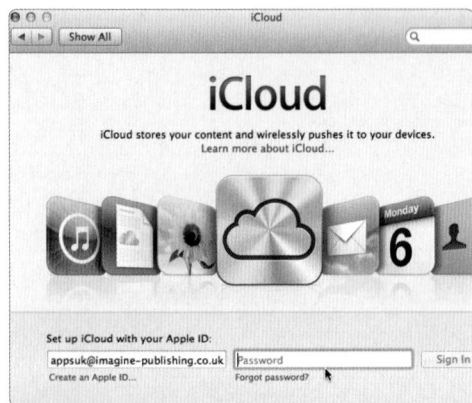

06: Sign in to iCloud
In your iCloud pane, enter your Apple ID and password and then click on the 'Sign In' button to log into your personal iCloud.

iCal and iCloud

With iCloud ensure that your event appears in every calendar

Syncing your Calendars
As long as the Calendars box is ticked in your Mac iCloud window then any updates you make to your Mac calendar will be reflected in those on your mobile devices too

Your iCloud
If you ensure that you are logged into the same iCloud account on all of your devices then data and updates you make will be bandied around freely without the need for wires!

Your Calendars
The iCal app on your Mac is completely universal across all devices, so any changes you make, when synced to your iCloud, will be reflected in the Calendar app on your iPhone or iPad

Your events
Creating a new event in iCal is easy, you just click on a specific time and you'll be able to start adding details, including alerts and sending out invites via your Contacts app

07: Sync your Calendars

You will be asked if you want to use iCloud for contacts, calendars and bookmarks. Tick this option to enable auto syncing between devices.

08: Sync your apps

If you didn't set up your iCloud account prior to reading this tutorial, ensure that the Calendars box is ticked in the main iCloud window.

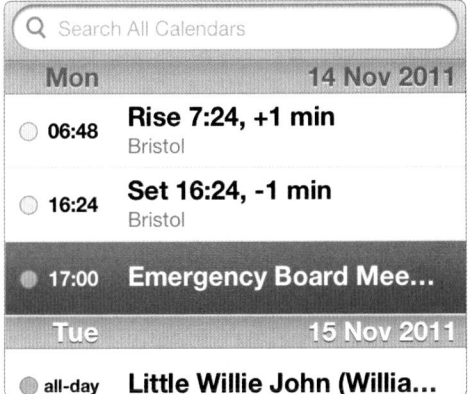

09: Wireless syncing

Now, any events or alterations you make on your Mac iCal app will be instantly reflected in your iPhone or iPad Calendar app, and vice versa.

Go online with Safari

Apple's web browser is even more powerful in Lion…

Safari is Apple's own web browser and it's tightly integrated into the operating system. Although for much of its previous life it was much more stripped-down than other browsers, largely for the sake of speed, it has more recently taken on more features such as Extensions that will enable you to customise it, in addition to a range of things you can change in its preferences.

Perhaps unsurprisingly it is the most Mac-like of any browser – it's sleek and polished and easy to use. Most of its options are accessed through the Preferences section and it is here that you can, for example, change the default search engine and the location for downloaded files.

There are also some great security applications, such as the ability to block those annoying popup windows and warnings when you are visiting a website that might be fraudulent. All in all, you'll discover it's a great way to safely browse the web.

> ## "Safari is sleek and easy to use"

MANAGE SETTINGS
The Preferences toolbar, from where you manage Safari's settings

HANDY PLACEMENT
The full-screen and download manager buttons are both located at the top right-hand corner of the window

HOMEPAGE
Set the default page that Safari will display when you open a new page or tab

SORT EXTENSIONS
The Extensions tab lets you switch Extensions on and off as well as changing their behaviour

---

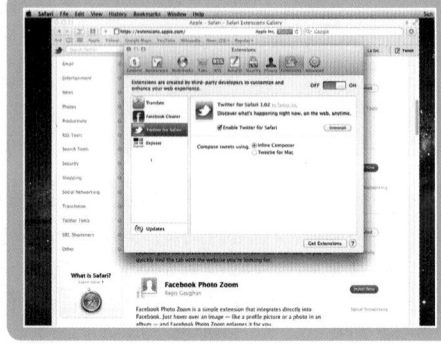

Extensions Add to Safari's functionality with Extensions…

Extensions are small snippets of code that use HTML5, CSS3 and JavaScript technologies to incorporate quick links to other web services or tools (such as ad blocking) into the browser. The idea is that you only download and install the ones you want and that suit your needs. There are none installed by default. Best

of all, Extensions are digital signed, which means you can't accidentally install malicious ones that might do your Mac harm. They are also sandboxed, which means that even if one crashes it won't take Safari or the Mac OS down with it. They even install easily without the need for a restart.

If you head to **http://extensions. apple.com** you will find a list of all the Extensions available. Some of the most popular include Twitter and eBay, the ability to add items to an Amazon wishlist and the all important ad blocker that automatically gets rid of embedded ads. There are some really useful ones here.

Key features

What does Safari do that's new?

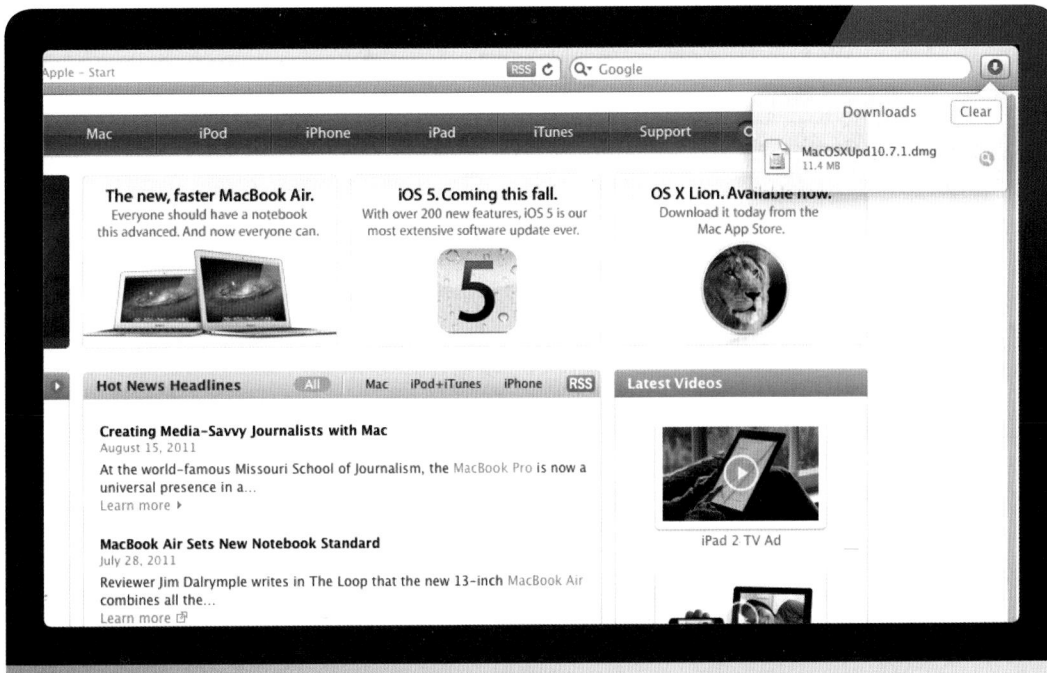

Full-screen toolbar access

Lion supports full-screen applications for the first time and when you enter full-screen mode, everything else on your monitor is hidden. It's a good way to focus only on the task at hand. In Safari, move the mouse to the very top right-hand corner of the window and click on the dual arrows icon. When in full-screen, move the mouse to the same location to reveal the reverse icon, which will return you to windowed mode.

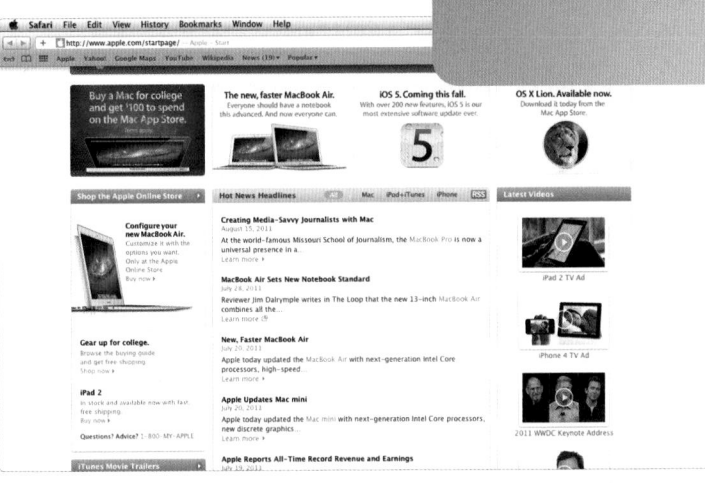

The download section

In Safari on OS X 10.7, the old Downloads window has gone and been replaced by a smaller, integrated window. At the top-right of the window you will see a small icon with a downward pointing arrow and when you download a file, clicking on this will reveal the progress of the download. Even after it has completed you can click on the same icon to reveal recent downloads, and click the magnifying glass icon to reveal them in the Finder.

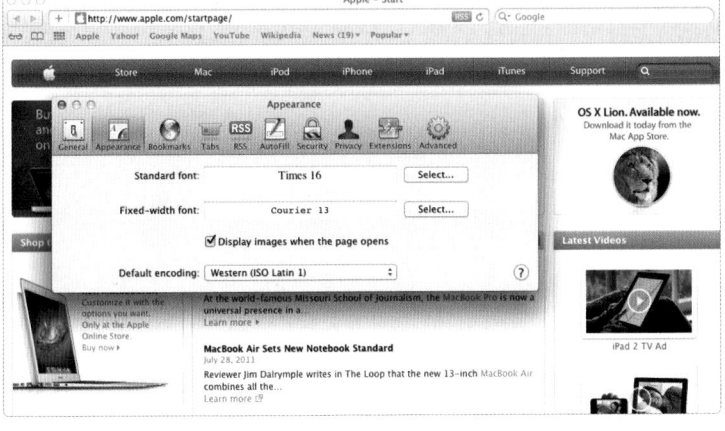

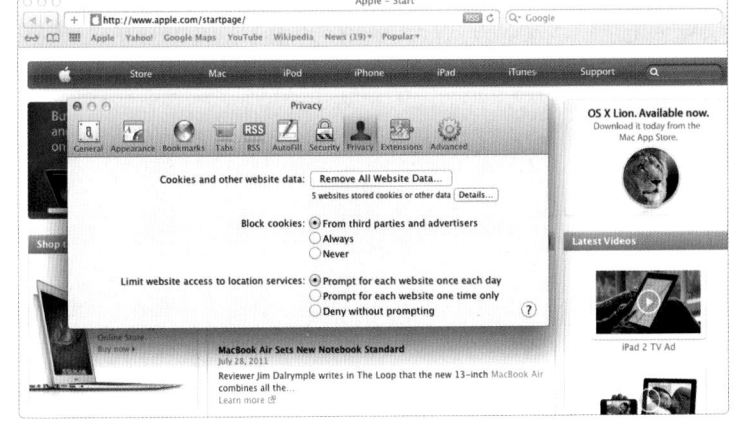

Changing Safari's appearance

In Safari's preferences, go to the Appearance tab and you will see the option to change the standard and fixed width fonts that it uses. While many websites try to define the fonts that they use, you can set Safari up to always display a larger font than that specified, which is helpful if you have trouble with your eyesight. In the Advanced menu there's also the option to prevent the use of small fonts automatically.

Privacy settings

Online security is very important and in Safari's Privacy tab there are some handy options available. The 'Remove All' button lets you delete all stored data from websites plus view this data prior to deletion, and you can choose to block cookies from certain types of site so that advertisers can't track your browsing habits. There's also the option to control whether websites can use information about your location or not.

Add a bookmark to Safari

Discover how you can save and store your
favourite Safari pages to access easily later

 **App used:**
Safari

 **Time needed:**
5 minutes

Surfing around the internet is easy with the browser Safari. A clear, open space for page viewing is complemented with a host of cool options and features to allow you to save and store the sites that you regularly visit, organise them into neat folders and access what you want, when you want it.

Bookmarking has always been an integral part of web browsing and Safari allows you to store your favourite websites in a host of different ways.

You can add bookmarks so that they appear in a dropdown menu or, if you access them frequently, then you can even place bookmarks along the top

> "Safari allows you to store your favourite websites"

bar of your Safari window, ensuring that they are never more than a single click away.

It is also possible to arrange your bookmarks into folders or add them to your own personal Reading List, which will be sync wirelessly via iCloud and updated on all of your devices – meaning you can start reading a page on your Mac and then finish reading it later on your iPhone. In this tutorial we guide you through the many different ways of bookmarking your pages.

Safari and bookmarks

Different ways to save your
favourite websites

Your Collections
The column to the left will display all of your bookmarks. Here you can access your Bookmarks Menu, Bookmarks Bar and all of your bookmark folders. To add bookmarks to your folders, simply drag them from the main History window

Your Bookmarks Bar
You can add bookmarks to the bar that runs along the top of your main Safari window for easy access. Simply click on the name of the bookmark on the top bar and you will be taken to that particular site

Your history
By choosing 'Show All Bookmarks' from the Bookmarks menu, you are taken to your Safari history to see what sites you have accessed in the past 14 days. This is handy if you wish to find a site you visited before but didn't bookmark

Bookmarks menu
All of your bookmark activity can be controlled from this dropdown menu. Here you can add bookmarks, create new folders and add pages to your Reading List to read on other devices later on

READING LIST
You can add pages to your Reading List to read later – even if it's on a different device. If you haven't time to finish a story, choose 'Add To Reading List' from the Bookmarks menu or click on the glasses icon in the top bar to view your Reading List and click 'Add Page'. Your Reading List syncs to all of your devices via iCloud to read anywhere.

Safari How to bookmark your favourite sites

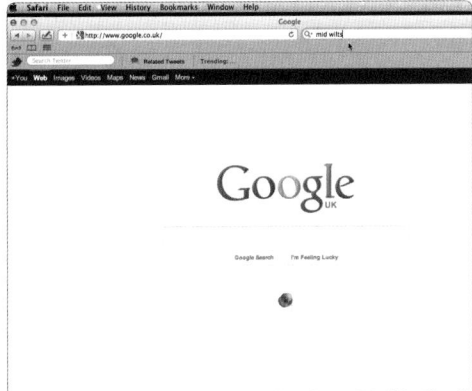

01: Launch Safari

To start surfing the web, launch Safari from the Applications folder or Dock. Once launched, go to a site or type a search into the Google field.

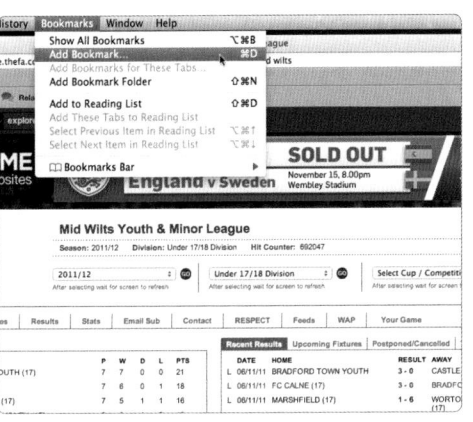

02: Add a bookmark

To add a basic bookmark, click the 'Bookmarks' menu while the site you wish to bookmark is displayed and then choose 'Add Bookmark'.

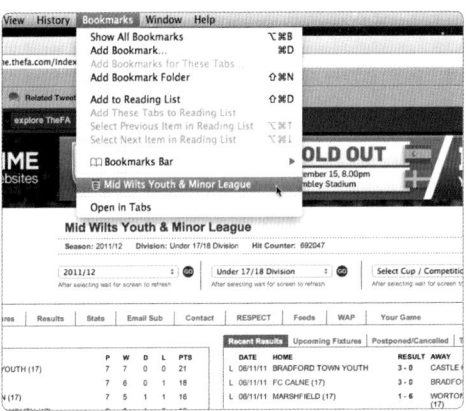

03: Take a shortcut

Instead of going through the menu, you can also store a bookmark by pressing Cmd + D while Safari is displaying a page you wish to bookmark.

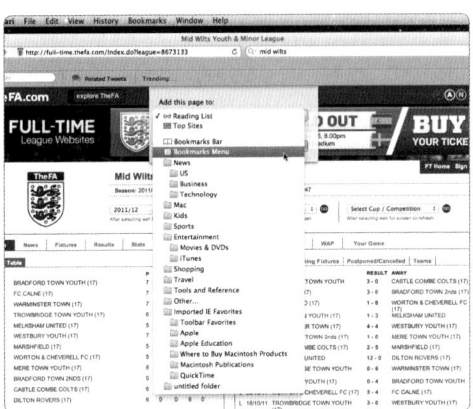

04: Add to…

When you choose to 'Add Bookmark' you will be asked where you would like to add the bookmark to. Choose 'Bookmark Menu'.

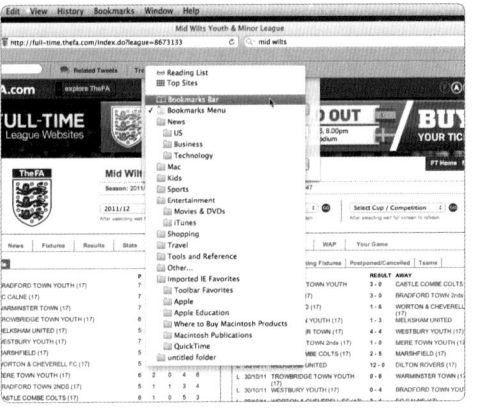

05: Add to Bookmarks Bar

If you choose 'Bookmarks Bar' in the 'Add this page to:' menu, it will appear on the top bar of your browser window for easy access.

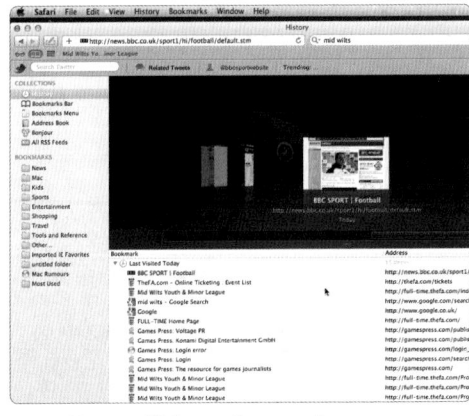

06: See all bookmarks

To view bookmarks, choose 'Show All Bookmarks' from the Bookmarks menu. All bookmarks will be displayed down the left-hand column.

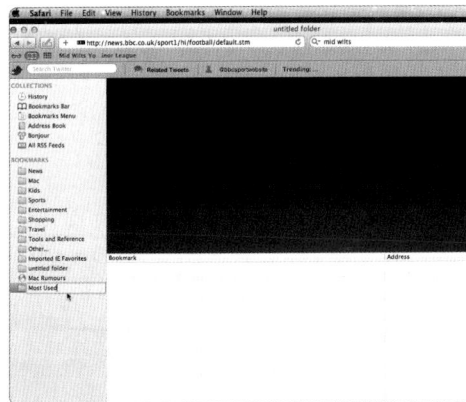

07: Create a new folder

You can categorise your bookmarks into folders. To create a new folder, choose 'Add Bookmark Folder' from the Bookmarks menu.

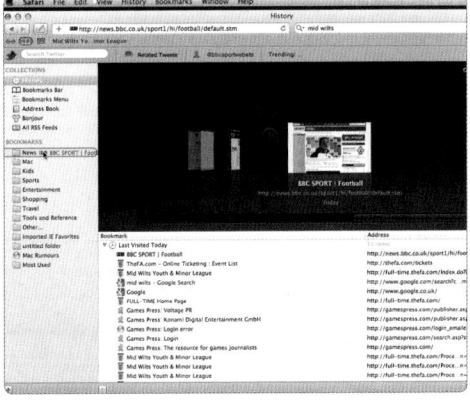

08: Move Bookmarks

To move bookmarks into specific folders, choose 'Show All Bookmarks' and then drag bookmarks from the main window into the folders.

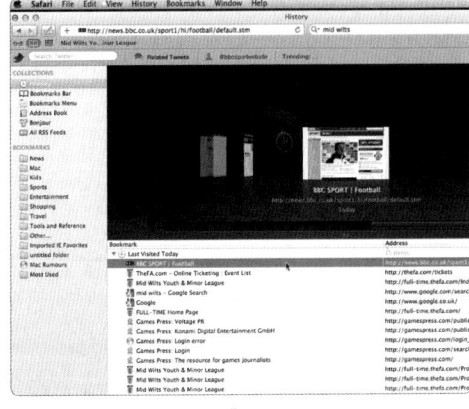

09: View your history

To bookmark a page retrospectively, choose 'Show All History' from the menu and your recent history will be displayed in the window.

View your Safari history

Keep track of all your web history and
learn how to cover your tracks

 **App used:** Safari  **Time needed:** 5 minutes

For those times when your mind gets foggy and misplaces essential facts, figures and data, your Mac keeps track of everything, filing it and storing it safely away for future reference. One area in which this is particularly evident is in your web history. We spend hours surfing the web, trawling hundreds of sites and bookmarking ones that we intend to visit again. But what if you forget to bookmark a site during a particularly sprawling web session and have no idea how to find it again? No problem, just refer to your own personal Safari history (accessible via the 'History' drop-down menu) and all of the sites you have visited in the past seven days (or 14 days if you choose the 'Show All History' option) will be stored in time dated folders.

Of course, there are some disadvantages of having your web history plastered across your menus like the front pages of the gutter press as well. Say, for example, that you are planning an intimate getaway or birthday surprise and don't want the lucky recipient to know anything about it, then you can instantly clear your history and keep your secret safe. In this tutorial we will guide you through the process of managing your own web-based footprint step by step.

"Recently visited websites will be stored in your Safari history"

Navigating Safari history
Discover where you've been, and how often you went there

Your Reading List
Any pages that you have added to your Reading List (see the boxout below) can be accessed easily by clicking on the glasses icon. From this menu you can manage your Reading List, add new pages and delete old ones once you have no further need for them

Show All History
From the drop-down menu, or by clicking the open book icon, you can opt to 'Show All History' and see sites that you accessed in the previous 14 days, as well as your bookmarked pages and folders

Show Top Sites
If you click on the grid icon, which represents 'Show Top Sites', you will be taken to a page of the sites that you access most frequently. The chances are that you may have these bookmarked already, but if not then it is just another way to fast-track to the sites that matter the most to you

History menu
From the History drop-down menu you can view all of your web history from the past seven days, reopen all windows from your last Safari session and clear your entire history to prevent people from seeing which sites you've accessed

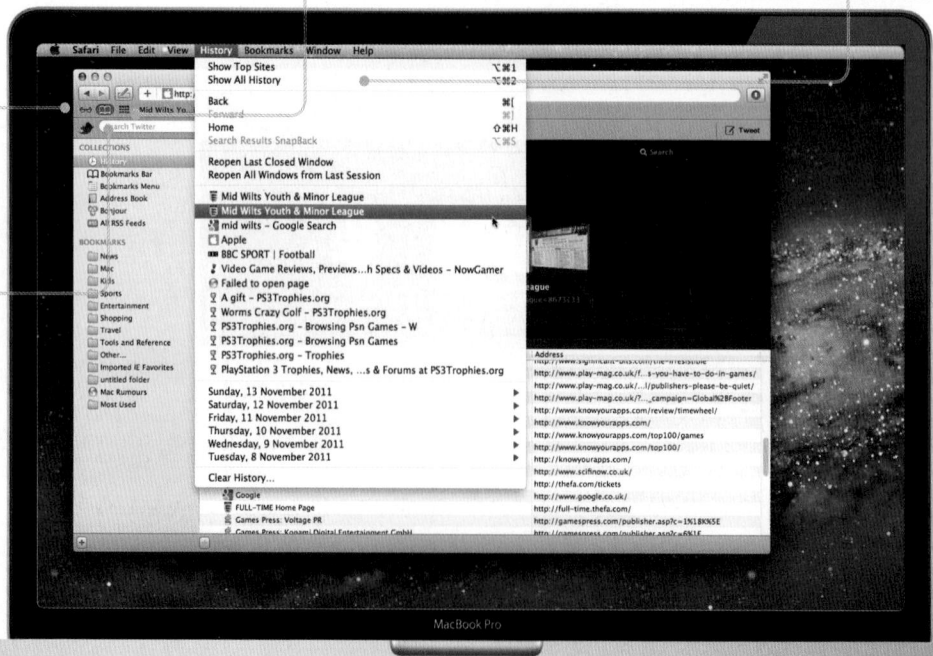

YOUR READING LIST
Instead of bookmarking every page you read, just in case you don't have time to finish reading it, and clogging up your Bookmarks menu with hundreds of random sites, you can add the page to your Reading List where it will be stored for you to access and read later. Your Reading List will also sync to your iCloud, so pages you start reading on your Mac can be finished on your iPhone later.

Safari Browse your web history

01: Click on menu

If you cast an eye across the menu titles that run along the top of the screen in Safari, you'll see one called 'History'. Click on this to get a summary of your web activity over the past seven days. The present day will be loose and the sites visited in all previous days will be arranged in time dated folders.

02: Show All History

Click on the 'Show All History' option at the top of the History dropdown menu (alternatively press Alt + Cmd + 2 or click the open book icon) to get an overview of your history. You can view the complete history for the past 14 days, as opposed to the seven viewed via the drop-down menu.

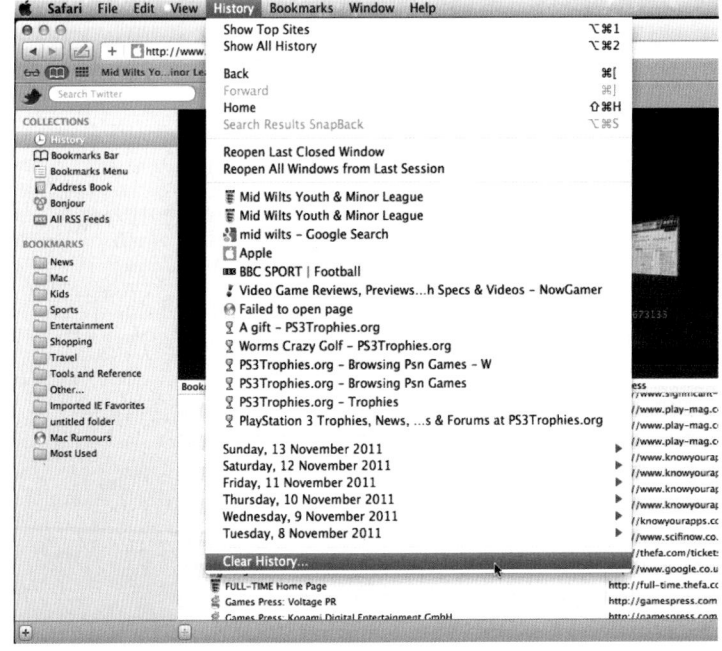

03: Create bookmarks

While in the main History page you can create bookmarks by dragging web addresses from your main History window to the various bookmark folders in the left-hand column. This is useful for retrospectively adding pages as bookmarks that you forgot to earlier so that you can access them later on.

04: Clearing your history

By default, your Safari history will keep continuously updating itself but you can clear your history instantly by clicking on the 'History' drop-down menu and choosing the 'Clear History' option at the bottom of the menu. It really is as quick and simple as that.

Using gestures in Safari

With your fingers and a trackpad, you
can navigate Safari with ease

App used:
Safari

Time needed:
5 minutes

Although gestures have been around for
a while on the Mac, they've really been
pushed to the forefront with Lion. They
work in the same way as on the iPod touch, iPhone
and iPad with various finger presses and swipes
making different things happen effortlessly on
screen using a trackpad.

The aim is to make navigating your machine
much easier and they are very easy to learn. We
have run through Safari gestures here but there
are many more for the operating system in general

with support for Launchpad and Mission Control
for instance. Lion has made things simpler. Whereas
once zooming in and out needed a press of the
control key and two fingers to swipe up and down,
now you just need to pinch with two fingers. After
a while the gestures become intuitive and you may
soon be ignoring the mouse. Small things such as
looking up words with a couple of taps begin to
come naturally and even those that feel alien at first
are so similar to using a mouse that you will soon
work them into your computing life.

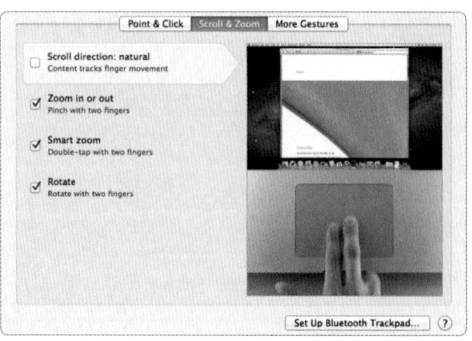

Tweak the trackpad
Set up your gestures to suit you
in System Preferences

The tabs
The gestures are placed into three
different categories: Point & Click, Scroll
& Zoom and More Gestures. This lets you
quickly identify any types of feature which
may be causing issues (for example you
keep accidentally brushing the touchpad)

Trackpad preferences
You can call up the trackpad options
by going to Apple>System Preferences
and selecting Trackpad. This allows you
to toggle various features so that only
the gestures you want work when you
use the trackpad

Turn gestures on and off
If you don't like a particular gesture
and want to turn it off, simply check
the box next to the relevant option
and when you have finished, press
the red 'X' button in the top left-
hand corner to save your choices

Explanations
Each option describes the various
functions and gives an explanation
of what you have to do to achieve a
certain gesture. An image is shown
to hammer home the point

MOUSE OR TRACKPAD
If you want to use gestures but you
don't have a Mac with one built-in,
you can buy a separate Trackpad.
You can also use gestures with a
Magic Mouse. The Multi-Touch area
covers the top surface of the mouse
so you can use your fingers to scroll
or swipe and it is so intelligent it
even knows when you are just
holding it.

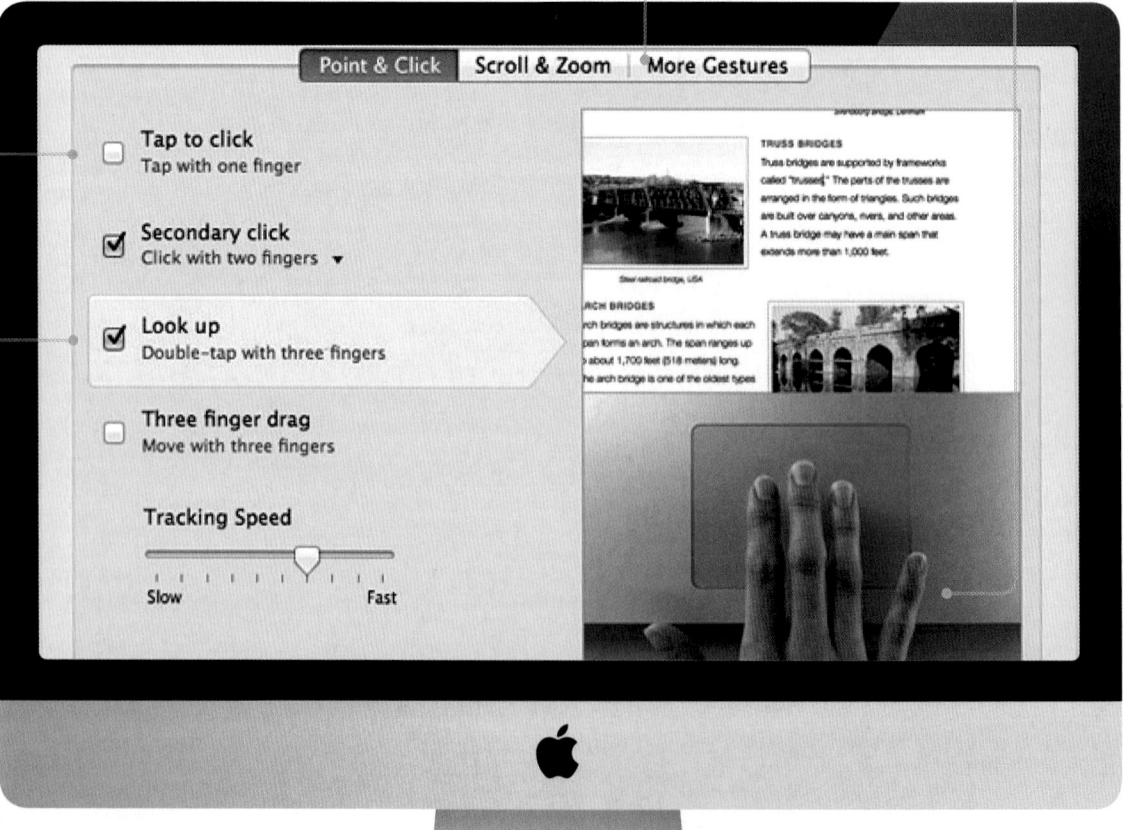

Safari Looking at Safari's gestures

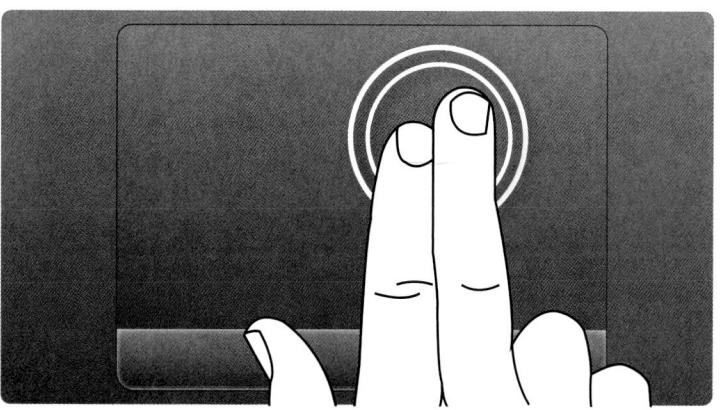

01: Tap to zoom
Take two fingers and double-tap the trackpad while you're in Safari. The webpage will zoom in. To go back to the original size, just tap again.

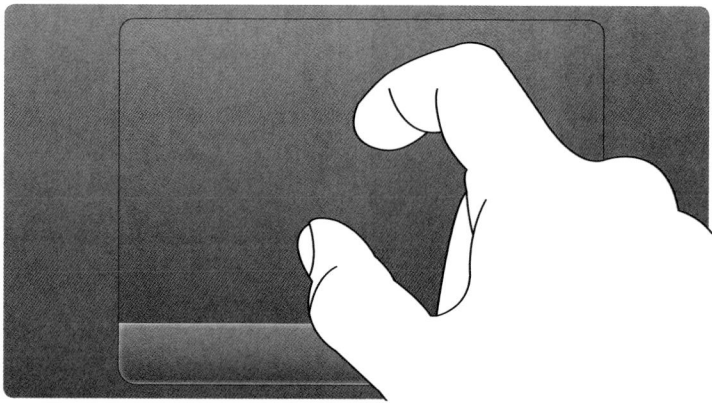

02: Pinch to zoom
Using your thumb and index finger on the trackpad, move them away from each other to zoom in and bring them closer together to zoom out.

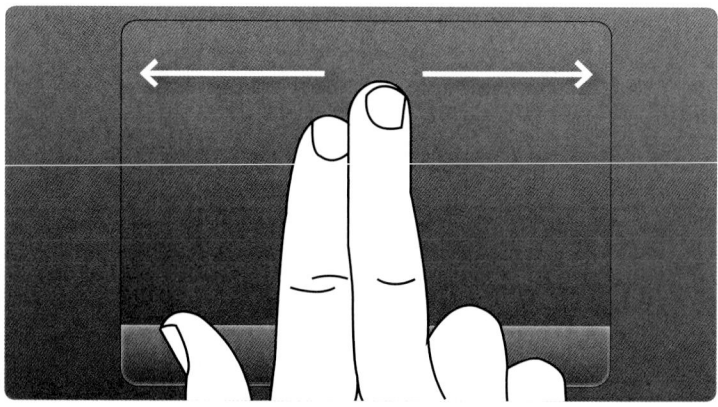

03: Navigate through history
Slide two fingers from right to left and you will go back in your browsing history in Safari. Doing it the other way – left to right – takes you forward.

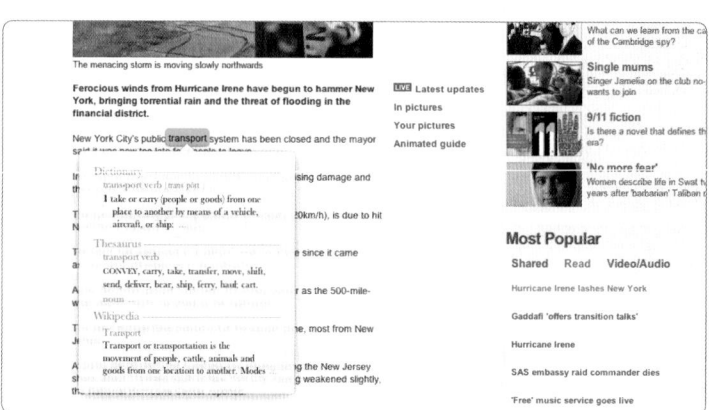

04: Look up words
Hover the cursor over any word on a webpage in Safari and, when you use three fingers to double-tap the trackpad, it will find its dictionary definition.

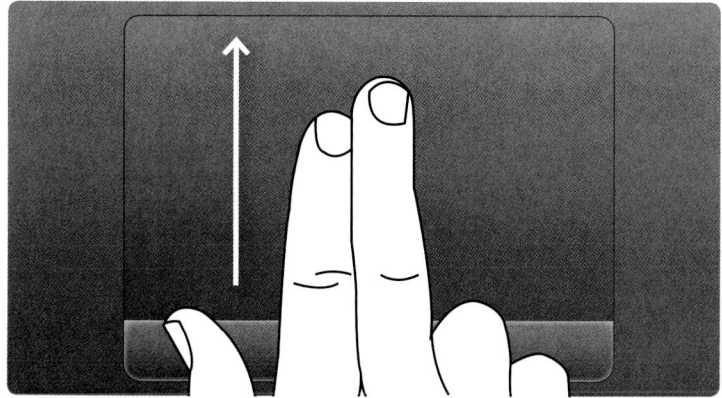

05: Swiping up
When many saw the new scrolling direction in Lion, it was perplexing. But now it feels right. Use two fingers to swipe up and the page moves up.

06: Smart zoom
If you double-tap using two fingers on the column of a webpage, Safari will zoom in on that specific column. By double tapping again, it will zoom out.

Block unwanted adverts on websites

Discover how to configure Safari preferences to block unwanted adverts on your favourite websites

 **App used:** Safari

 **Time needed:** 15 minutes

 Modern websites have marketing policies that throw all sorts of adverts at you. This is the way a lot of sites make money, and no matter how annoying you find them, they won't be going anywhere… or will they? Fortunately, many of these are implemented by using CSS (Cascading Style Sheet) techniques that can be blocked by Safari. Even if advert-blocker CSS files are widely available on the internet, finding the right one is a question of trial and error.

A simple Google search for CSS and adverts returns numerous hits, from userContent.css (from floppymoose.com) to AdSubtract.css (from code.

"Pop-up windows can be very easily blocked by Safari"

google.com/p/adsubtract). Once the chosen file is safely downloaded onto your Mac, Safari is then able to use it to hide the advertisements from view. Other types of advertisement that are encountered on many websites consist in the opening of a new browser window. These 'pop-up windows' can also be very easily blocked by Safari. Following these nine simple steps will free you from all those flashing banners and having to close endless window after window.

Safari adverts

Enhance your browsing experience and banish any distractions

Block Pop-Up Windows
In the Safari menu, the activation of this option is indicated by a tick-mark to the left of the menu item. When activated, it will prevent window-based advertisements from opening automatically when navigating to a new website

Safari Advanced Preferences
In Safari's Preferences you'll find the Style Sheet area of the Advanced section. This allows for the selection of a CSS advert-blocker file. The effect of the CSS advert-blocker is immediate upon selection in the drop-down menu

The CSS advert-blocker
In this example, the CSS advert-blocker is stored in a specially created Safari folder in the Application Support of the User's Library folder. Any other convenient location is acceptable

A blocked advertisement
Once the CSS advert-blocker, downloaded from www.fanboy.co.nz, is selected, notice how the Google results page is devoid of all the sponsored links at the top and the advertisement banner to the right

WHAT ARE CASCAD-ING STYLE SHEETS?
A CSS file, or Cascading Style Sheet, is a text file that contains instructions to enable your browser or newsreader to apply styles and formatting (fonts, colours, spacing, etc) to any web documents. It is an essential part of any website design and allows the implementation of extensive styling policies. For more information, check out www.w3.org/Style/CSS.

Safari Block adverts on webpages

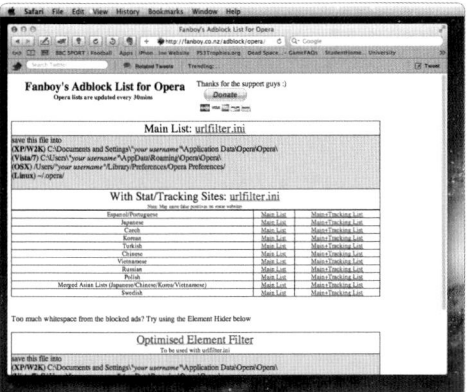

01: Select an advert blocker

Open Safari and choose one of the online resources mentioned before. Navigate to the website and locate the link for the CSS document.

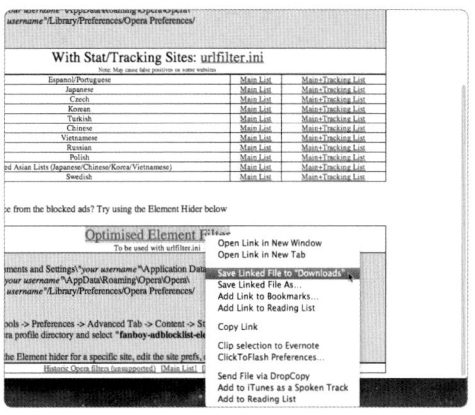

02: Download the CSS file

Locate the link for the CSS advert-blocker file, right-click on it and select the relevant download option. The Downloads window will appear.

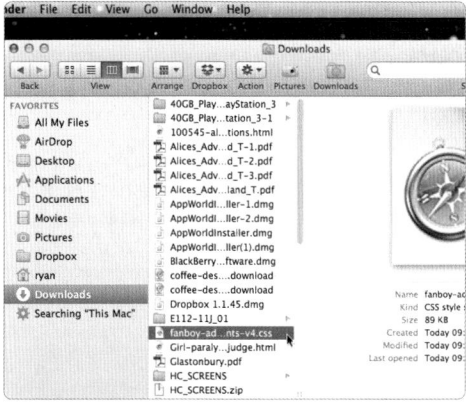

03: Locate CSS advert-blocker

Once the operation is complete, open a Finder window to access your Downloads folder or click on the Dock's download stack. Locate the file.

04: Create a folder

With a Finder window showing your Downloads folder and another showing your location to store the file, create a new folder for the CSS file.

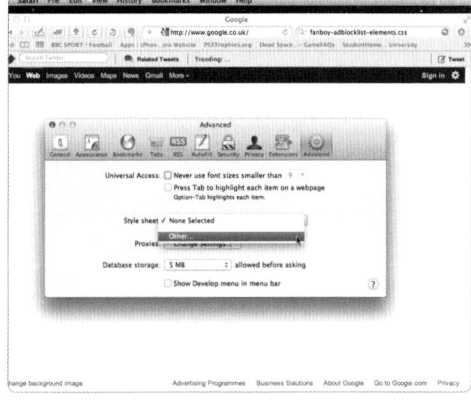

05: Advanced preferences

Activate Safari and select Preferences from the Safari menu. Select the Advanced section and locate the 'Style sheet' drop-down menu.

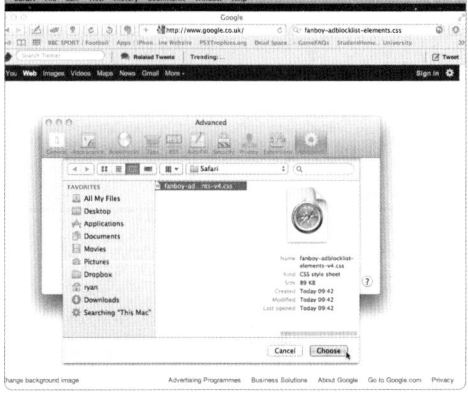

06: Select CSS advert-blocker

Select Other from the menu. In the Finder window, navigate to the new folder storing the CSS file. Select the file and click Choose.

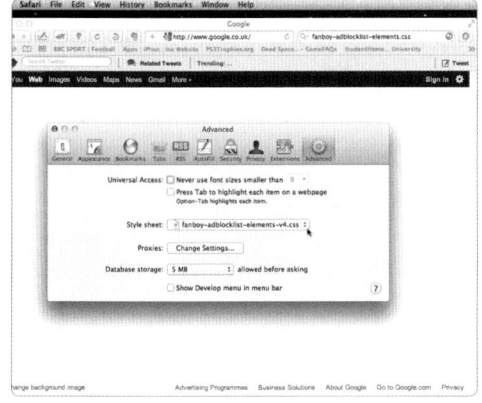

07: Block advertisements

Check that the webpage now displays only the relevant information. Otherwise, restart from Step 1 with a different online resource.

08: Block Pop-Up Windows

With Safari active, click on the Safari menu and locate the Block Pop-Up Windows option. If the option has a tick to its left, it is already activated.

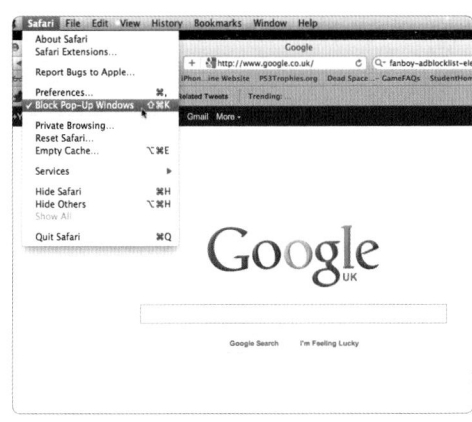

09: Activate the blocking

In order to turn on the Block Pop-Up Windows option, simply click once on the text of the option. A tick-mark will now appear to its left.

Add extensions to Safari

Extend the capabilities and features of Safari and customise your web browser so it suits your individual wants and needs

App used: Safari

Time needed: 15 minutes

One of the reasons people have chosen other web browsers such as Mozilla Firefox in the past is because of the large number of clever plug-ins and extensions that are available for it. Well, finally there's no need to look elsewhere for third-party browsers because with the introduction of Safari 5 there is a very easy way to install extensions for Apple's very own web browser.

Safari extensions are a fantastic way of extending the capabilities of the browser and adding new features that were previously not available. Now you

can block irritating adverts on the web, translate foreign pages with a single mouse click, tweet and access Facebook from any webpage, and a whole lot more. Extensions are fantastic, fun, and can be really useful in a number of different situations. They are also very easy to find and install. Like Widgets before them, as popularity grows and functionality increases the range of extensions will grow. For the moment, there are more than enough options to keep you very busy, so let's explore how you can customise Safari and add your own extensions.

> "Extensions are fantastic, fun, and can be really useful in a number of different situations"

Safari Add and use handy extensions

01: Enable extensions

Make sure that extensions are enabled in Safari. Go to the Safari menu and click Preferences>Extensions. Turn on the feature.

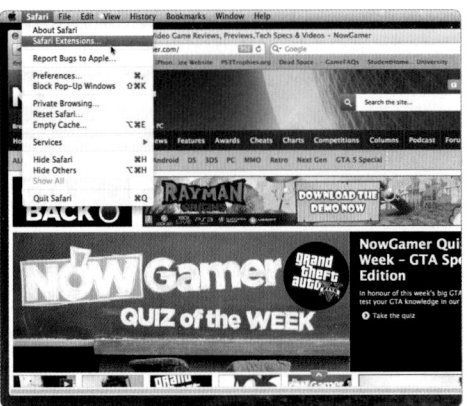

02: Go to the gallery

There are several ways to open the Extensions Gallery and with Preferences open click Get Extensions. You'll also find it on the Safari menu.

03: Browse the extensions

All the extensions are on one page, so scroll down and read the info. As the number grows the gallery may be redesigned.

04: Install an extension

When you've found an extension you like, click the Install Now button. We are going to add the official Twitter for Safari extension to our browser.

05: Use Twitter for Safari

Extensions can add anything to Safari and each is different. With Twitter there's a toolbar at the top of the page. Click Tweet to post a message.

06: Bing search and translate

With Bing you select some text on a page and a magnifying glass appears next to it. Mouse over it and you'll see translations and more.

Time for extensions

Increase Safari's usability by adding extensions

Toolbars and buttons

Some extensions are invisible and work in the background, so you see nothing on the screen, but others add extra items to the right-click menu. Some add toolbars and buttons to the browser window

Enable and disable extensions

Enable tick box so you can choose whether it is operational or not. There's also a global extensions On/Off button at the top, and also buttons to uninstall extensions

Check for updates

If updates are available for any of the extensions you'll see a number just to the right. Here there's one update. If you click Updates you can choose to have Safari automatically install them

Configure your extensions

Some extensions are just plug and play, but others have an extensive array of configuration options that you can use to customise the way that they work. Check each extension carefully

07: Update your extensions

Extensions are sometimes updated. Go to Safari>Preferences>Extensions and click Updates. Click the ones you want or Install All Updates.

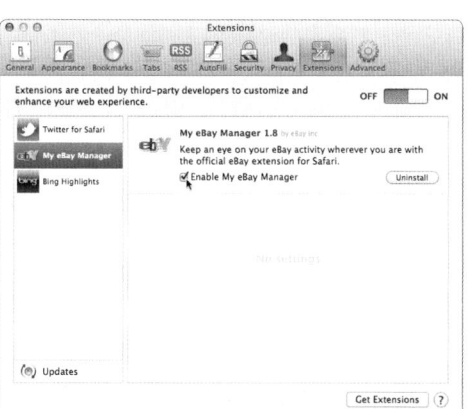

08: Disable an extension

You may not want every extension running all the time. In Preferences choose the ones you need. Select extensions and tick or clear the Enable box.

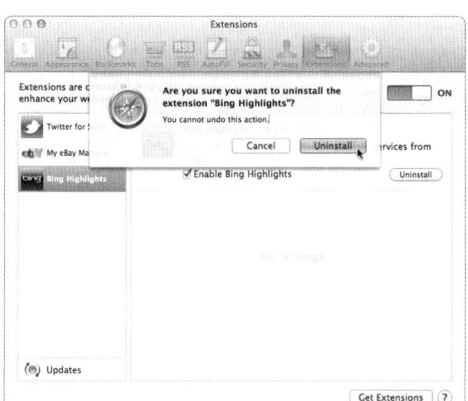

09: Remove an extension

After trying an extension you may find it's not for you. Go to Safari>Preferences>Extensions, select the extension and click the Uninstall button.

Learn about ClickToFlash

Discover ClickToFlash, a Safari extension that gives you control over Adobe Flash elements to make browsing faster and free of Flash-based adverts

 **App used:** Safari

 **Time needed:** 10 minutes

 Like all modern browsers, Apple's Safari allows for the development of third-party software in order to extend its abilities. Among these so-called plug-ins, ClickToFlash is an interesting addition that relates to both the browsing experience and the blocking of adverts, and allows you to improve the efficiency and productivity of your browser.

Indeed, with the release of Safari and the official support for third-party extensions, surfing the web with this excellent browser has reached a whole new level. Although the modern media that is the web is cool, it has also brought about the nasty trend of websites becoming cluttered with adverts and irrelevant content that simply gets in the way

> "ClickToFlash improves the productivity of your browser"

of you accessing the information you're after. Earlier in this book we had a simple tutorial showing you how to block some of these adverts, but one of the main vectors for this nonsense is the ubiquitous Adobe Flash component. For the regular web surfer, it can become vital to regain control over the irritating and omnipresent features of many websites. Enter ClickToFlash, a Safari extension that improves productivity and browser stability, reduces processor temperature, and extends laptop battery life, and is so simple anyone can use it. Read on to find out how to make it work.

Improve Safari browsing

Stop Flash ruining your browsing experience

Uninstall the ClickToFlash extension
Should the need to uninstall ClickToFlash arise, the launch of the uninstallation process can be initiated at the click of a button in ClickToFlash preferences. One further click in a confirmation dialogue and it's done

A blocked advert
When the ClickToFlash extension detects any Flash advert or content from a source or on a location not in the 'Whitelist', it fills the Flash content embedded in the webpage with a grey backdrop and label

Safari's Extensions Preference pane
From 'Safari Preferences', the 'Extensions' pane is easy to access and offers a handy management facility for your installed Safari extensions. It lets you turn off 'Extensions' – either completely or individually – and control how these are kept up

Preferences
The ClickToFlash preferences are extensive, from 'Video Settings' through 'Contextual Menu Items' to a 'Whitelist' facility. The extension is powerful and simple to configure. It even caters for 'Scalable Inman Flash Replacement' (sIFR) text

WHAT ARE EXTENSIONS?
Extensions, plug-ins, add-ons… all different names for the same utility software that can expand or enhance your use of a given application. They can help you turn Safari into a personalised browser. Extensions can become a toolbar item, a contextual menu item or a behind-the-scenes addition to Safari functionalities that interact with a webpage.

Safari Download and install ClickToFlash

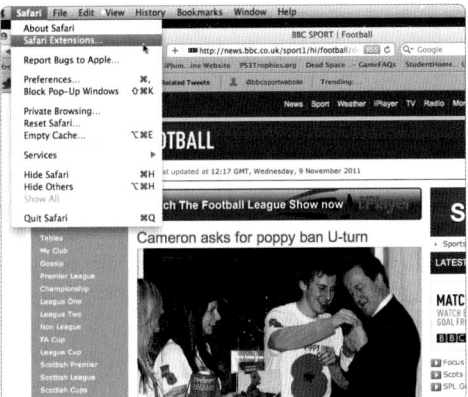

01: Locate the extension

In the Safari menu, select Safari Extensions Gallery. From Apple's selection of plug-ins, scroll down to Productivity to find ClickToFlash.

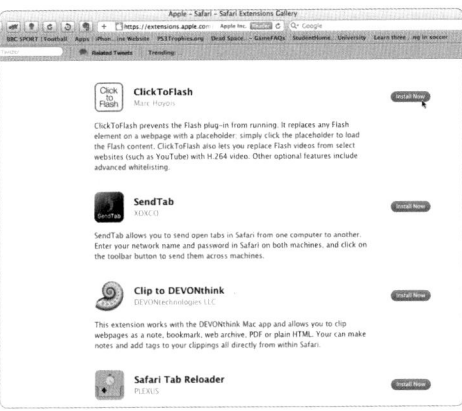

02: Download ClickToFlash

In the ClickToFlash section, click 'Install Now'. Once completed, a green tick box with 'Installed' will appear at the bottom of the section.

03: Enable ClickToFlash

Select the Safari menu and choose 'Preferences'. Click the Extensions tab, find ClickToFlash, tick/untick the Enable ClickToFlash checkbox.

04: How does it work?

Once ClickToFlash is activated, no Flash advert or content is displayed. It's replaced by a grey area in the page on which the word Flash is embossed.

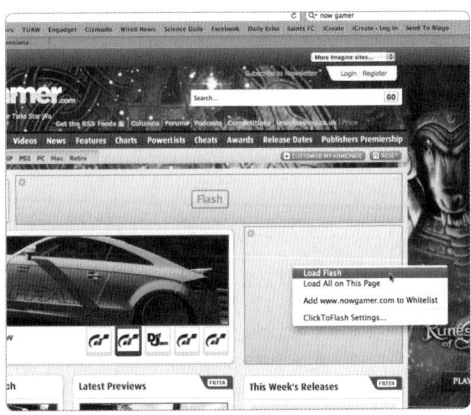

05: Unblock Flash content

To unblock Flash content, click anywhere in the grey backdrop replacing the ad or video. The page element will load, allowing you to watch it.

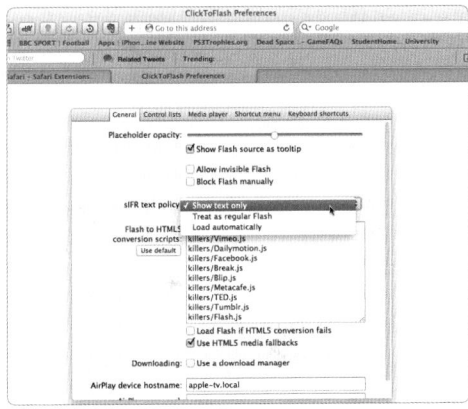

06: ClickToFlash preferences

The preferences for ClickToFlash are, strangely, displayed in a separate Safari tab when you install the plugin…

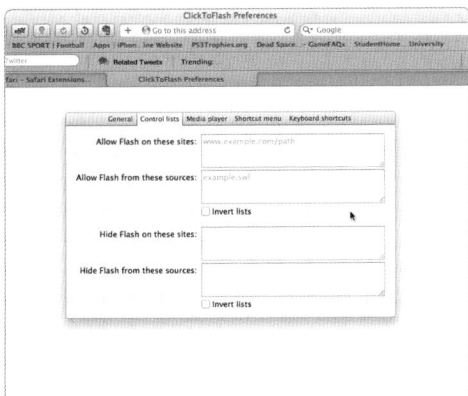

07: Create Whitelists

From the Control Lists section of Preferences, add entries to a list of sources and locations you wish to allow/disallow Flash content to play.

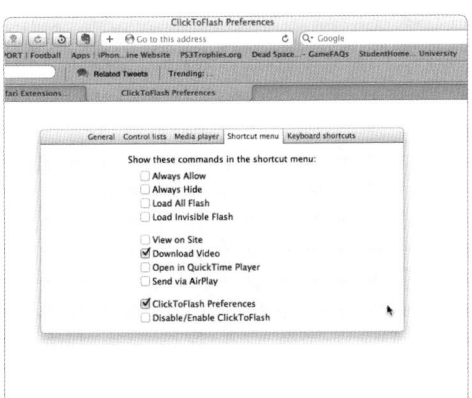

08: Use the contextual menu

In Preferences, the Shortcut Menu Items section allows you to access shortcuts to the extensions via a right-click on the Flash content.

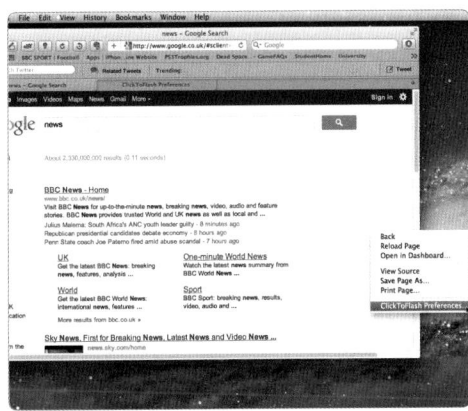

09: Easy access

Make sure you tick the 'ClickToFlash' Preferences box in the Shortcut Menu section and then right-click on a Safari screen to access them easily.

Set up and use AutoFill

Save yourself time online by using AutoFill. It's easy to set up and edit so you always have the right information at your fingertips

 **App used:**
Safari

 **Time needed:**
5 minutes

We've all been in that situation: you need a product or service from the internet and yet cannot face the repetitive nature of filling out form after form in order to get the best deal. Thankfully Safari has a thing called AutoFill to keep you from this monotony.

AutoFill works very cleverly with Address Book; it takes the information you feed it and can summon it at will when you need to fill in a form. For the sake of a couple of minutes' work it can save you an untold amount of annoyance when you find yourself repeatedly tapping details into the web. It's important in the first instance to add as many details as you think you will need to your Address Book card so that Safari can do as much of the form as possible, therefore lessening your need to go in and fill in any blanks. This is such a cool feature that once you've set it up you'll be wondering how you ever lived without it.

"Once you've set AutoFill up you'll be wondering how you ever lived without it"

Use AutoFill in Safari

This tiny little feature can be a great time saver

Menu
You can use the menu to access AutoFill. It's in the Edit section but will cost you a couple of mouse clicks

A breeze
With AutoFill set up you can very quickly negotiate online forms and get exactly what you're after in no time

In action
When you activate AutoFill, Safari will populate the fields it thinks are right. Occasionally it will repeat data, so be warned and be vigilant

USERS
Remember that AutoFill will only work for each individual user on their account so you have to log in to your user account or change which Address Book card represents you should you not be using your own user account.

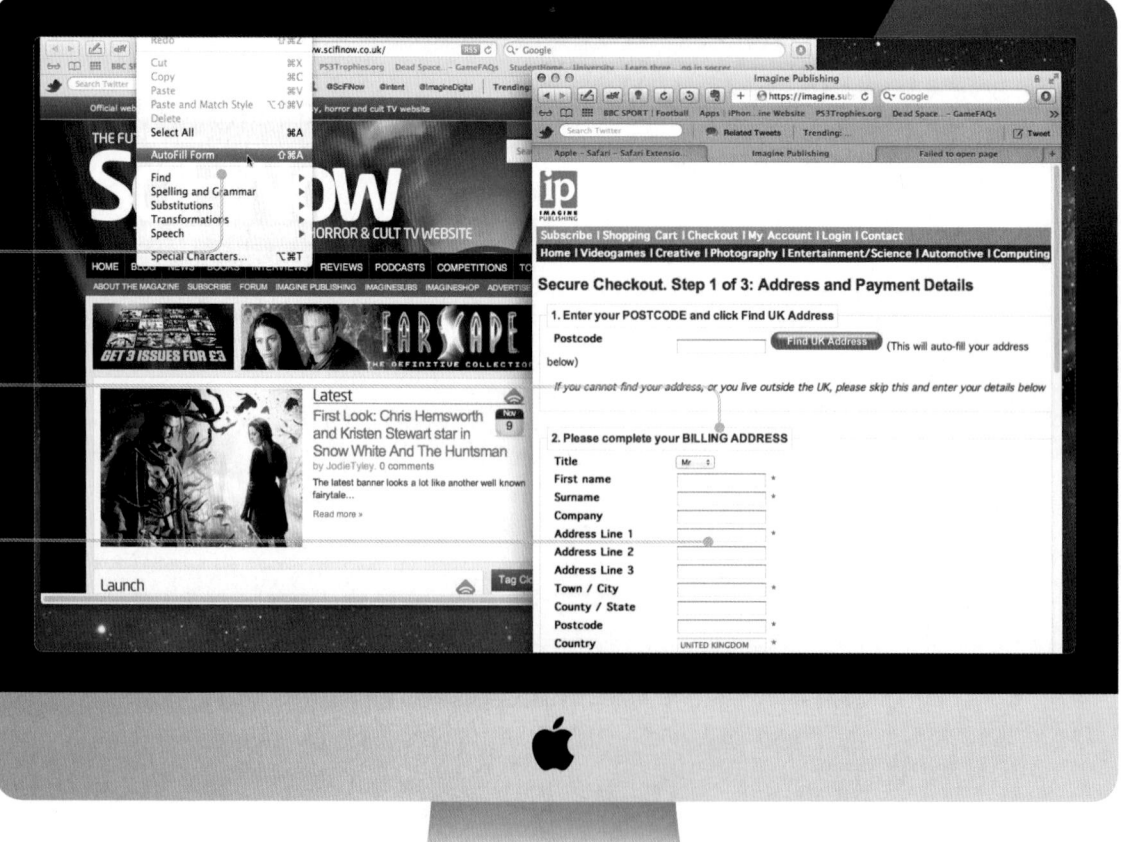

Safari Set up AutoFill from your Address Book

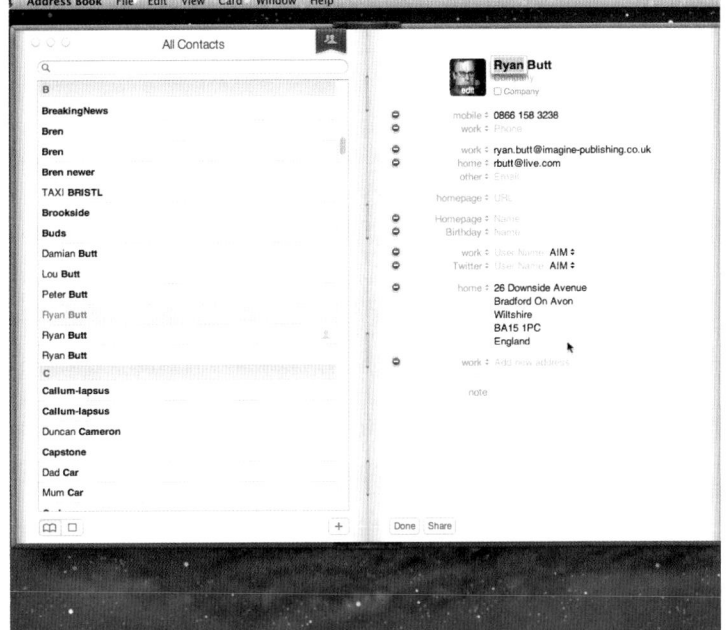

01: From A to B

To kick things off you will need to open up the Address Book and find your details. If you don't have any, click the plus button to add a new contact and fill out as many of the details as possible. This will come in handy later on and save you time filling in extra fields.

02: My card

Double-click on the finished contact card so it opens in a brand-new window. With this window actively selected, go to Card from the top toolbar and select Make This My Card from the drop-down menu. A new icon should appear next to the name.

03: Safari

Now open Safari and head to the top menu. Click on the Safari menu and select the Preferences option (the keyboard shortcut for this is Cmd+,). The Preference window will now pop up allowing you to continue with the next step of the tutorial.

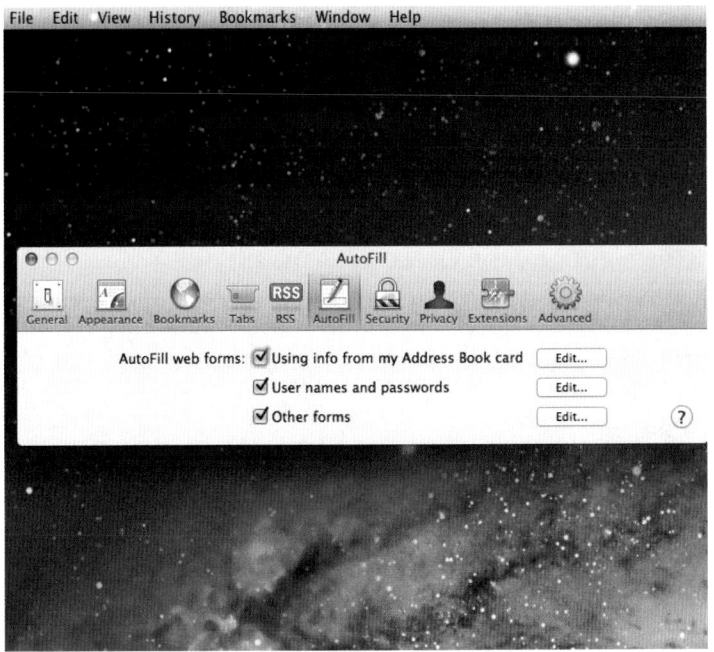

04: AutoFill

Click on the AutoFill tab and then tick the 'Using info from my Address Book card' box. This will then allow you to populate forms using the information you added earlier, saving you an endless amount of time when the next form you need to fill out appears.

Keep your contacts in Address Book

Get to grips with Lion's Address Book and master the iOS-like layout

 **App used:**
Address Book

 **Time needed:**
15 minutes

 Often overlooked, Address Book is a hugely important element of OS X. While it might not be the first thing you open in your dock, it's the hub for all your contacts and makes sure that apps like Mail run a lot more smoothly. It seems only fair then, that Address Book was given the OS X Lion treatment, too. It now sports a leather-bound book effect and a cleaner, simpler interface. There are a couple of new features too, such as a sharing button and social media integration, and the interface itself does require a little more thought to get around. So fire up Address Book and let us take you through some of its newest features. We'll help you master the interface making address keeping slicker than ever.

"An overlooked but important element"

Address Book Explore the contacts directory

01: A whole new look

The first thing you'll notice about the all-new Address Book is that its view is very similar that of its counterpart in iOS. It's a lot cleaner.

02: Find a friend

Searching is as simple as typing a name straight into the search box. Results are displayed in real-time and Address Book will highlight matches.

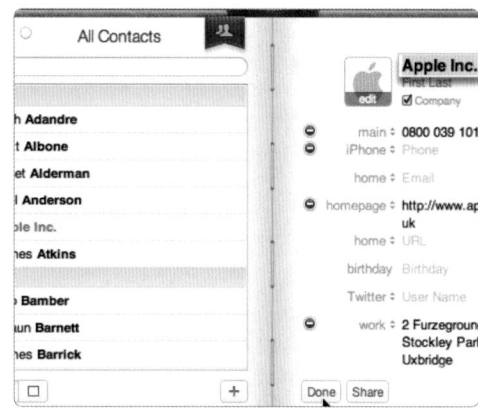

03: Add an entry

Click on the plus icon under your contacts to add a new one. You can change what the default template includes in Address Book's preferences.

04: Business and pleasure

Contact details can be categorised by type such as work or home. Click on the type next to the detail and select one from the list to change it.

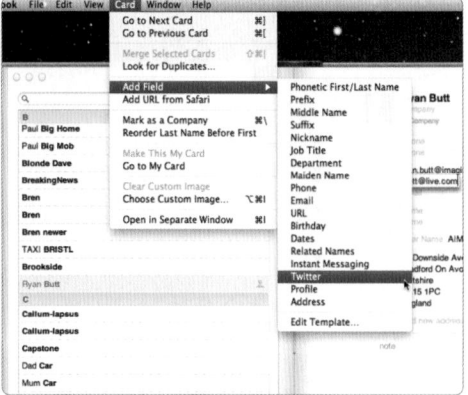

05: All a Twitter

You can add new fields such as Twitter username to this version of Address Book. Clicking on a Twitter username will take you to the Twitter app.

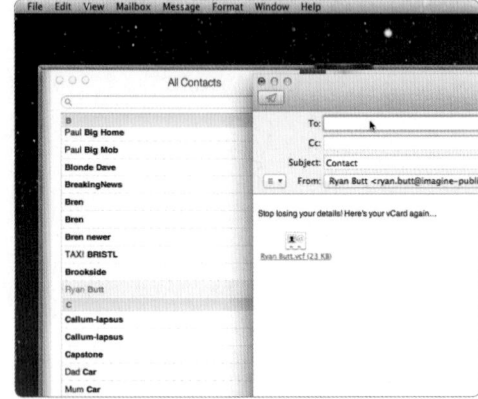

06: Share the details

Click on the Share button underneath a contact card to email that contact to somebody else. Contact cards will attach in vCard format.

Navigate Address Book

Find your way around the
Address Book interface

iOS-like interface

In-keeping with Lion's move to be more like iOS, Address Book sports a new interface that's very similar to that of the one on the iPad or iPhone. Like iOS, it's clean, simple and textured

Getting social

Lion's Address Book includes contact detail fields such as Twitter, Facebook username and Skype username, allowing you to easily integrate social media details into your contacts. They're even compatible with native Mac apps

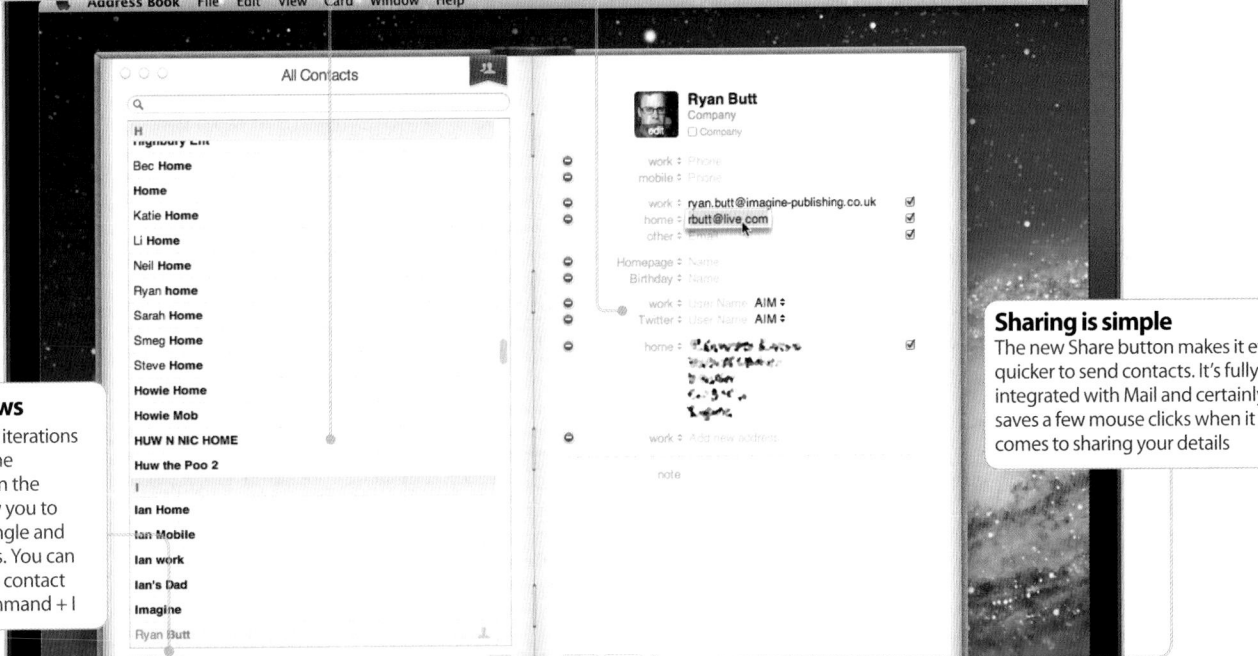

A choice of views

Much like previous iterations of Address Book, the two view buttons in the bottom-right allow you to toggle between single and double-pane views. You can also open separate contact windows with Command + I

Sharing is simple

The new Share button makes it even quicker to send contacts. It's fully integrated with Mail and certainly saves a few mouse clicks when it comes to sharing your details

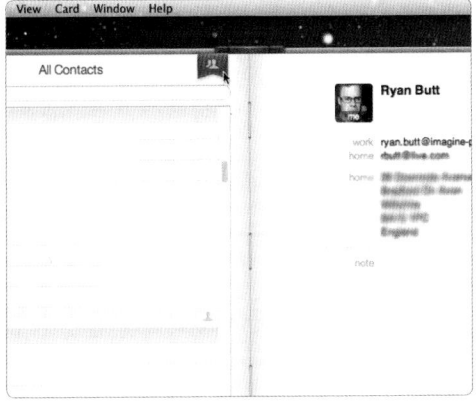

07: Get a group

Clicking on the red bookmark at the top will bring up the contact groups view. It's a lot cleaner than the columned view of the old address book.

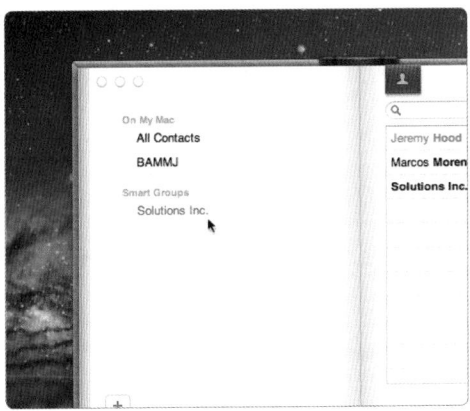

08: Smarter grouping

Smart Groups allow automatic grouping of contacts by certain details. Click 'New Smart Group…' from the File menu to set one up.

09: A single pane

Lion's Address Book still supports the single pane contact view; click on the single pane button in the bottom-left of Address Book to activate it.

Introducing Preview

Use Preview to view and edit files in minutes

 Preview is a multifunction utility that at first sight appears to be a just simple viewer for your photos and PDF files, however it is actually more useful than most people might think. It has editing capabilities, it can print, it can convert files from one format to another, it can display slideshows, it can be used to annotate images and PDFs, and more besides.

A typical scenario is that you have a PDF file that you've been sent via email and you want to view

it. Double-clicking on it opens up the Preview application and displays the document on the screen. It is then possible to highlight and copy text from the rendered page, print it, write your own notes in the margin, highlight important sections, navigate it using a table of contents, draw on it, add speech bubbles and so on. Double-click an image and you have simple editing tools such as resize, saturation, sharpness and other editing controls. It is really quite a powerful app.

> "Preview can print or convert files, it can display slideshows and more besides"

SMALL VIEW
This panel at the side shows the thumbnails of the images loaded or PDF pages

POINT OF VIEW
The buttons in the toolbar on the right select different views. Try each one

ADD TEXT
Annotate the image or PDF either for fun or for work and research purposes

ADJUSTMENTS
Enhance your photographs using this panel to adjust the colour, exposure, contrast and other effects

ZOOM IN
With images you can display a magnifying glass to zoom in on part of a photo

Customise the toolbar

Like Apple's MobileMe service before it, iCloud isn't reserved entirely for Macs

After using Preview for some time you may find that you rarely use some of the icons in the toolbar, but frequently access other features. Now you can swap the ones you don't need with those that are more useful. Like many Lion apps, the toolbar in Preview can easily be customised by simply right-clicking on an empty

part of the bar and select Customize Toolbar from the menu.

A palette of buttons is displayed and some of them will already be on the toolbar. To remove buttons drag them off and drop them anywhere. They disappear in a cloud of smoke. Now drag the tools you want to the toolbar and drop them in one of the

empty spaces. If you want to change the order then just drag them left or right and others scoot along to make room. If you can't remember what each button is for, there is a Show menu at the bottom and you can add text labels. When the toolbar is exactly how you want it, click the 'Done' button.

Key features

Use Preview for viewing, editing and annotating PDFs and images

Best for PDFs

Double-click a PDF or drag one from a Finder window and drop it on Preview in the Dock to launch the app. On the View menu you can choose between a single page view or two side by side. You may need to zoom in and out to make it comfortable to read. Also on the View menu is Table of Contents which is great for navigating a document – click the section you want to go to. The Text Tool allows you to select text and copy it into another app.

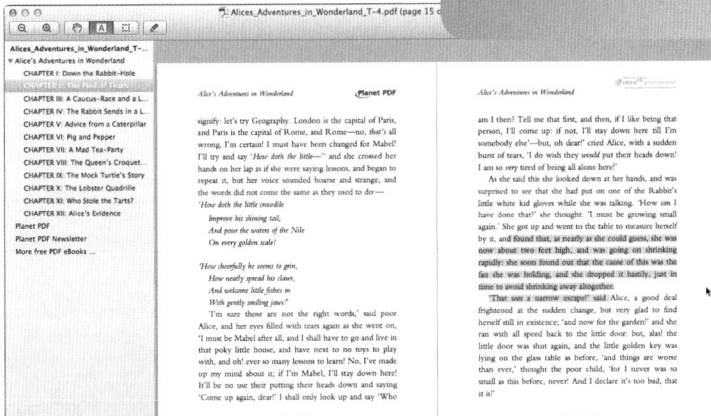

Best for batches of photos

Select several photos in a Finder window and double-click them. Preview opens and displays the first image. The others are displayed as thumbnails on the left, but you can select the view you want using the icons in the toolbar or the View menu. Also on the View menu is Slideshow – a great way of viewing multiple photos full screen. Preview also has tools that you can use to batch edit, such as rotating and resizing multiple images.

Best for annotations

Both images and PDFs can be annotated and you can add notes, speech and thought bubbles, text in boxes, lines, ovals, rectangles and arrows. Click the pencil button in the toolbar or select View, Show Annotations Toolbar. The tools are different for PDFs and images and the former has extra features for working with text, for example, there is a highlighter to mark text. You can also create links within the text that jump to other sections.

Best for single photos

Load a single image into Preview and you can make edits to it and there are lots of useful tools at your disposal. For example, you can resize a photo and choose new dimensions in pixels or print sizes measured in inches or centimetres. If an image contains areas that aren't wanted, you can click and drag to select part of the image and crop them out. Images can be flipped vertically or horizontally and you can copy and paste parts of the image.

Import photos from your iDevice

Preview can make it easy to import photos from your iDevice directly onto your Mac

 **App used:**
Preview

 **Time needed:**
10 minutes

From the early days of Mac OS 9 to the present OS X Lion, Preview has constantly evolved. In fact, with the advent of portable devices, such as smartphones, digital cameras and tablets, Preview is doing more than just keeping up with these modern tools; it allows you to simplify and improve their use in ways you may not be aware of.

Indeed, Preview now offers the unique ability to retrieve photos and pictures from iPhone, iPad or iPod touch and, through a set of smart features, ensures that your time spent downloading photos from your portable device is not wasted. The extended information – displayed for each of the documents – and handy editing tools allow Preview to go further than just matching your adoption of new technology with a few appropriate functionalities. Since some of the more relevant features of Mac OS X's built-in photo download utilities have been integrated to Preview, there are now new ways to retrieve and edit the pictures coming from your iPhone/iPad.

Read on for our step-by-step tutorial on the easiest way to transfer photos from your iPhone, iPad of iPod touch onto your Mac, before you begin to edit and organise them just they way you want to. It really couldn't be any simpler.

Preview Import photos with Preview

01: Get set

Ensure that your iPhone, iPad or iPod touch is plugged in correctly and that it is turned on. Launch Preview from your Applications folder. In the File menu, select 'Import from' and the name of your portable device which should be visible in the menu.

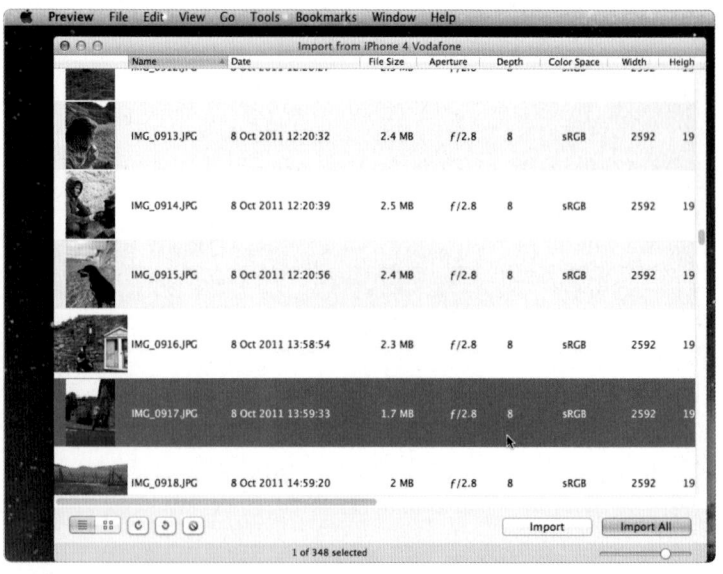

02: View your pictures

A window showing you a list of all the pictures on your iPhone/iPad will now open. Information, such as thumbnail view, name, size, creation date and extensive photographic parameters, will be displayed for you to peruse in the main area.

Navigate the import window
Get to grips with the photo import procedure

Import location
The 'Import All' option allows you to import every image to a chosen destination. You can choose a destination to import to from your favourites or make a new folder

The list of pictures
Once imported, pictures listed in the 'Import from' window will display a green tick. Double-click any of these to switch to the Preview window to see the results of your import

Imported photos
When the import begins, Preview will open a window in the background to show the imported files. You can then navigate through these using Preview's sidebar

The toolbar
All the tools displayed in the toolbar help make this utility flexible. Below the Import buttons, a sliding cursor even enables to you to change the size of the thumbnails

NETWORKED DEVICES
In the File menu, below the first 'Import from' item, another item (labelled 'Import from Scanner') is available. Select 'Include Networked Devices' to be able to use the 'Import from' facility with more devices like scanners and cameras.

03: Get organised
Below the picture list, a set of buttons in the toolbar allows you to toggle between list and icon view, rotate and delete pictures, change the location to which the documents are to be imported and also change the thumbnail size if you wish.

04: Import
To the right-hand side of the toolbar, the Import and Import All buttons enable you to choose a single retrieval or a complete download of all the photos available. Click the relevant button to start the Import. If you're importing a lot of images, this make take a little while.

Master preferences in Preview

The Preview preferences are useful, and understanding how to utilise them can streamline the way you use this handy application

 **App used:**
Preview

 **Time needed:**
15 minutes

 In its introduction to Mac OS X Applications and Utilities, Apple describes Preview as a smart, straightforward, image and PDF viewing application with limited searching and editing functionalities… This is not entirely true as there is more to Preview than meets the eye – and all the more so when properly configured. Although Preview is indeed simple to use, a closer inspection of its Preferences cannot fail to expose its resourcefulness. Preview has four groups of settings: general operations, PDF editing and viewing, image editing and viewing, and PDF bookmarks.

Undeniably, Preview's claimed simplicity of use is genuine, but with just one or two judiciously set Preferences, your usage of this fantastic application can be greatly changed for the better. Let us take a look at how configuring its Preferences can leverage these functionalities.

"There's much more to Preview than meets the eye"

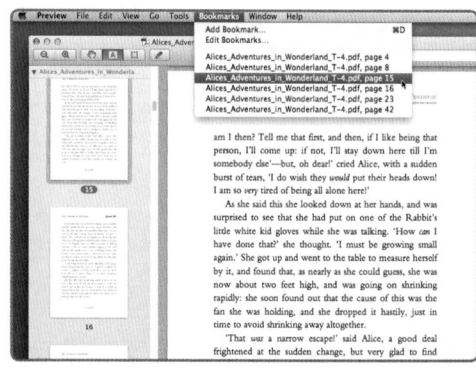

The preferences window
Work your way around the Preview preferences

Bookmark editing
The Bookmarks menu presents you with a list of bookmarks and the ability to edit and remove them. Selecting one bookmark at a time, click the Remove button to delete it

Preferences toolbar
The top section of the Preview Preferences window lets you access four different areas dedicated to the configuration of the software. Click on any of the icons to display the specific settings related to this area

WHAT PDF MEANS
PDF stands for Portable Document Format, also known as open standard ISO/IEC 32000-1:2008, and was originally created by Adobe as a multi-platform and multipurpose file format. Thus, PDFs can be shared across all sorts of different computers and can contain any kind of information, from simple text and graphics to metadata like annotations, table of contents etc. Find out more at http://en.wikipedia.org/wiki/ISO_32000.

Bookmarks tab
One of the four areas accessible from the Preferences toolbar is Bookmarks. This acts as a central repository for all the bookmarks created in all the PDF you have read

WHAT IS ANTI-ALIASING?
Anti-aliasing is a technique that diminishes the jagged contours of graphics and fonts by replacing the pixels at the edge of these with pixels in lighter shades of the same colour. Thus the aliasing, the jagged contours of graphic elements caused by the low resolution of printers or screens, or simply the intrinsic design of the graphic, appears blurred and smoother.

Saved bookmarks
The list of bookmarks saved in Preview is the same as the one displayed in the application's Bookmark menu; in the Preferences, this list is enhanced with extra information, such as the location of the PDF bookmarked

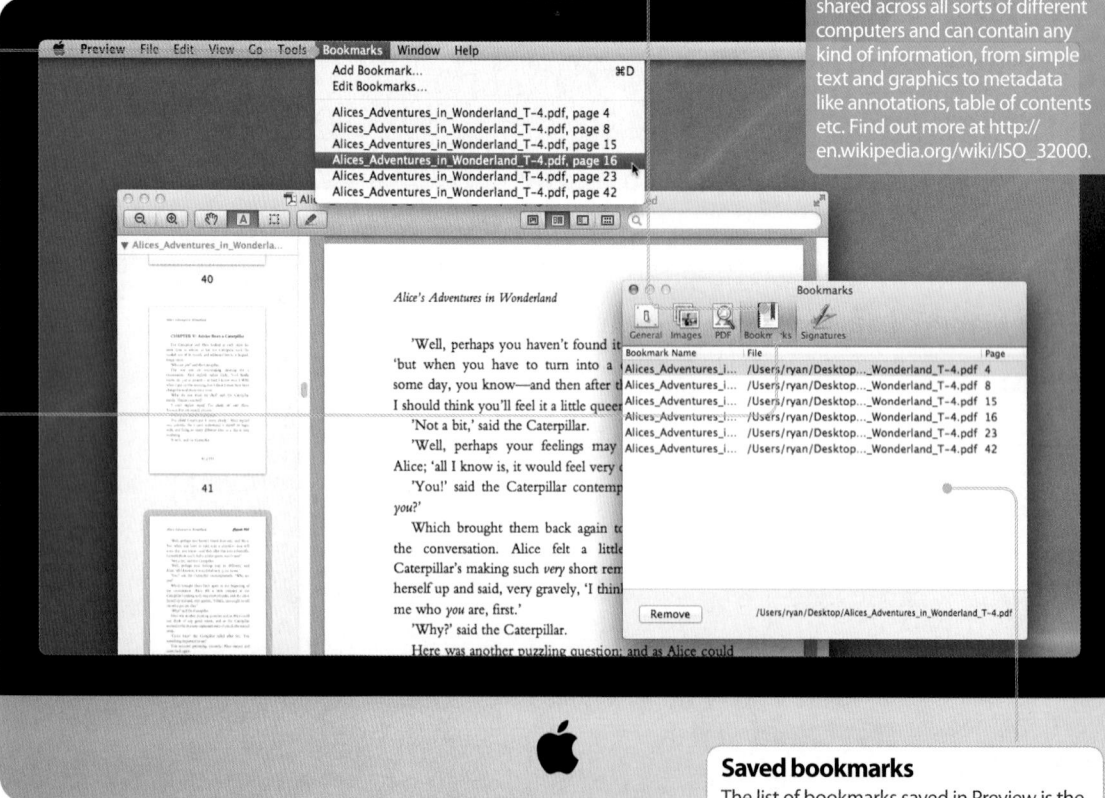

Preview Learn about Preview Preferences settings

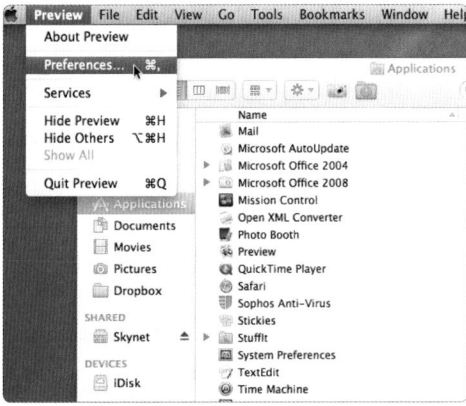

01: Preview Preferences

You can launch Preview from your Applications folder or Dock. Access to the Preferences is via the Preview drop-down menu.

02: Opening files

The 'When opening files' option configures whether groups of files are opened in a single window or each one in its own window.

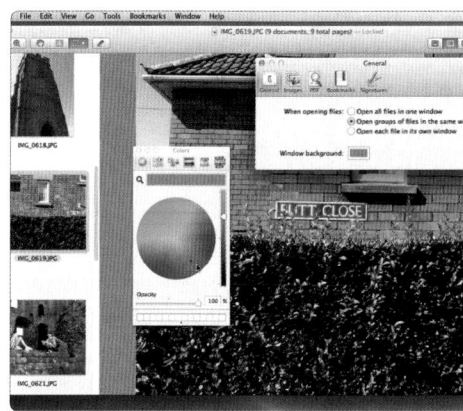

03: Background colour

'Window background' lets you to alter the colour of the empty space which surrounds documents. Click the colour selector and choose a shade.

04: Image-to-screen ratio

'Images' contains options specific to pictures. 'Define 100% scale as' sets the relationship between image size, screen size and resolution.

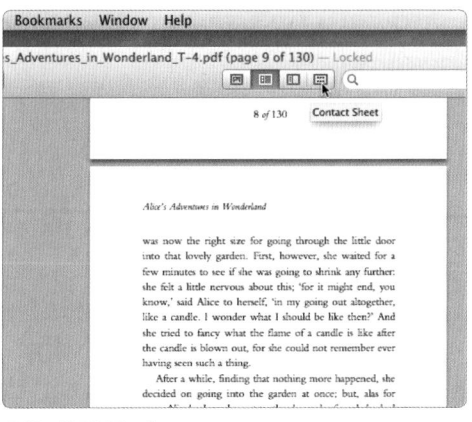

05: PDF size

To alter the way you view PDFs you can swap between four different styles from the top of the window. Adjust the size by clicking '–' or '+' icons.

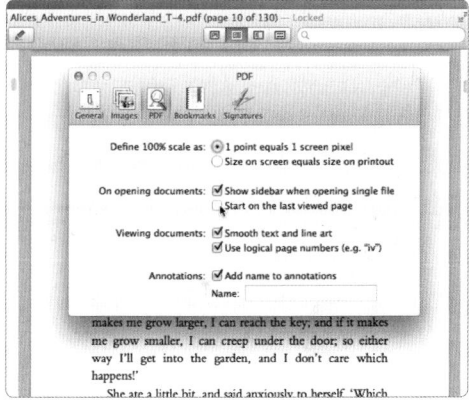

06: PDF-to-screen ratio

'Define 100% scale as' sets the relationship between document size and size on screen, eliminating the impact of screen res.

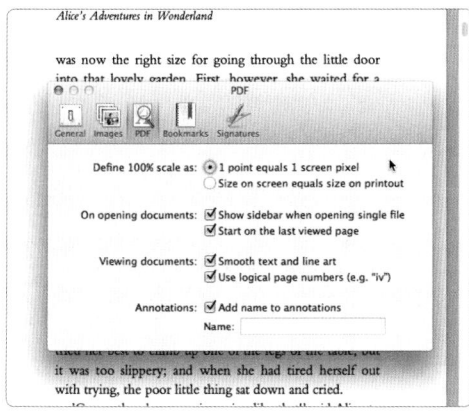

07: Opening PDF files

'On opening…' allows auto-opening of the table of contents and permits automatic return to the last page read prior to closing the document.

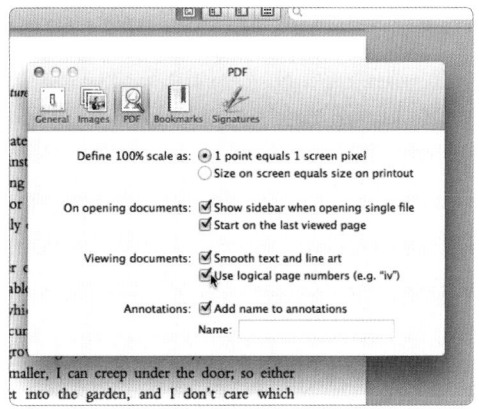

08: PDF rendering quality

'Viewing documents' options enable anti-aliasing for graphics and text, and aid searching using both Roman and Arabic page numbers.

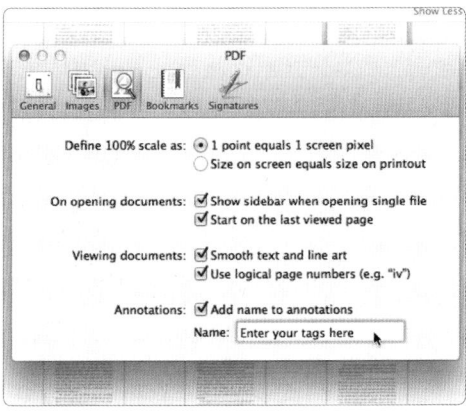

09: PDF annotations

The last option in the PDF Preferences pane permits you to enter the name of your choice to be added to any annotations made to a PDF.

Share your Photo Booth snaps

Photo Booth is a very practical tool, able to make videos or take snapshots with your Mac and share them in a few simple steps

 **App used:**
Photo Booth

 **Time needed:**
10 minutes

 Have you ever wanted to possess your own photo booth or simply make a fun auto portrait? No need to go looking for an expensive solution, as you can do all of this and more with an ingenious little application called Photo Booth and the help of the built-in iSight camera on your Mac. Although the pictures created here may not be ones to fill up a family photo album, they're good fun and a little bit more entertaining and interesting than having the same straight-laced pictures all the time. They can also be great if you want to make a funny birthday card for a friend or family member, or just experiment to see what you would look like if you suddenly put on a lot of weight!

Whether you need a single photo, a 4-up snapshot or a video recording, Apple's Photo

> "With Photo Booth you can make a funny birthday card"

Booth is here to provide all your needs. It allows you to take a picture or make a video and apply various effects – some arty and inspiring, some funny and slightly ridiculous. Then, from a number of integrated options, it lets you choose how to publish and share the result of your work. This fun application is gifted with all the capabilities offered by digital age technology, and you can then compare your photos with your friends.

Read on to find out how to get the most out of Photo Booth and create some fun pictures of you and your friends.

Get more from Photo Booth

Find out where the key parts are to let you create instant fun photos and effects

1, 2, 3 and action!
The camera button is your digital shutter. It is used to start/stop your recording or to take pictures and 4-up snapshots – clicking it will trigger a three-second countdown

Apply an effect
Choose to apply an effect to your work by clicking on the effects button. Browse the library with the right and left arrows. To cancel your choice, select the centre effect

Photo or video
Click on any of the three pictograms located in the left-hand corner below the live feed window to choose between the different types of picture taking: single shot, 4-up snapshot or movie clip

FILE TYPES AND NAMES
In the Photo Booth folder of your Pictures folder, single photos are saved as a single JPEG image while 4-up snapshots are saved as four distinct files. Video recordings are saved as one Apple QuickTime MOV file. All file names reflect the date and time of creation; 4-up snapshots are further numbered from one to four.

Thumbnail view
The result is displayed below the live feed window. Each thumbnail can be deleted by clicking the cross. Browse through the collection with the left and right arrows

Photo Booth Understand how Photo Booth works

01: Get ready

From the Applications folder, locate and launch Photo Booth. When using an external camera, make sure it is properly connected.

02: Choose photos or video

At the bottom-left corner, three icons allow you to choose single photo, 4-up snapshots or video recording. The red camera button is your shutter.

03: Apply an effect

You can choose an effect for your photo or movie with the Effects button. If they aren't suitable, return to the Normal display.

04: Strike a pose

When ready, click the shutter. After a countdown, Photo Booth will take its shots or begin the video. Click the stop button to terminate the recording.

05: Check the results

Your photo or video recording will appear as a thumbnail in the window. Click the camera button to initiate a new picture acquisition.

06: Locate your work

Your work is saved in a Photo Booth folder in your Pictures folder. Click on the 'Pictures' folder in your Favourites side bar to find them quickly.

07: Transfer to iPhoto

To share your work on Facebook, Flickr or MobileMe, export it to iPhoto. Select a thumbnail, and then click on the 'Add to iPhoto' option.

08: Custom account picture

Select a photo thumbnail and then either click on the iChat or Account Picture icon to use it as your application custom account picture.

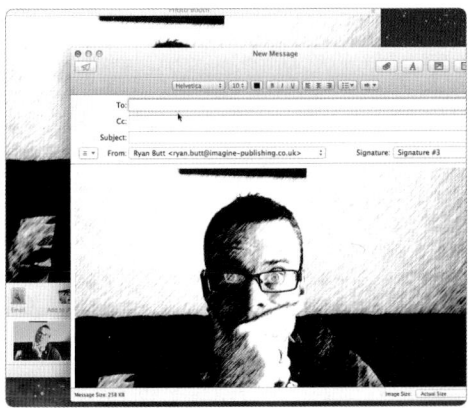

09: Send it away

To attach your work to an email, select the thumbnail and click on the Mail icon. Mail will open and insert your work into a new message.

Create a buddy pic in Photo Booth

The integration in OS X means creating a new buddy picture for iChat in Photo Booth is simple

 **App used:**
Photo Booth

 **Time needed:**
5 minutes

When it comes to software integration, Apple pretty much thinks of everything. The lengths the company goes to in order to make our lives easier is obvious throughout its hardware and software, and there are very few times when you're left wondering "Why doesn't this work like this, it would be much easier".

The point is that Apple constantly improves its software so that actions can be completed with the minimum amount of fuss. It's the reason why people who make the move to Apple fall in love with the OS and can't fathom why other people aren't following suit. It makes all those years struggling with your Windows PC seem like a huge waste of time. Adding an iChat buddy picture directly from Photo Booth is a great example; it requires just a couple of clicks. In this tutorial, we will show you how to do this and create a unique iChat buddy picture in not time at all.

> "Create a unique iChat buddy pic in no time at all"

Photo Booth   Change your buddy picture for iChat in Photo Booth

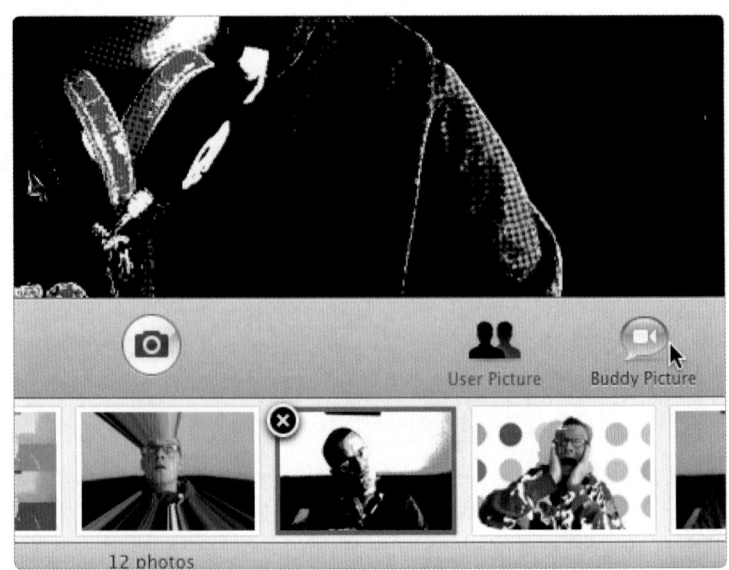

01: Load and snap

Load Photo Booth from the dock or from your Applications folder and simply click the camera button to take a new picture. Use whatever effect you like the look of. The new picture will drop into the reel at the bottom of the window.

02: One-click wonder

With the newest picture selected on the bottom panel simply click the Buddy Picture button that's found on the right-hand side of the interface. This will launch iChat and the preference pane, which allows you to change the pictures.

Take a new buddy picture in Photo Booth

Use OS X's integration to create a new iChat buddy picture

Get it spot on
iChat is also very easy to use and the Buddy Picture window is the perfect example: resize it with a slider and just grab the image to move it around

Easy booth
Having iSight and Photo Booth on your Mac makes creating profile pictures incredibly simple. Add to that the number of cool effects you can use and it's also a great deal of fun

MAC MINI USERS
Obviously Mac mini users don't have a built-in webcam so they will need to buy their own in order to use Photo Booth. Most third-party webcams will work with OS X. Photo Booth still comes loaded on Mac minis, so once the webcam is up and running Photo Booth will detect and use it.

Updates
The updated picture will populate all the necessary windows, replacing the previous or default picture

One-button fun
Photo Booth has a number of integrated buttons that allow you to easily use pictures in other apps. Just select a picture and then click the button

03: Slide and grab

Use the slider in the newly opened Buddy Picture window in iChat to resize your image. You can play around with this until you decide that the dimensions are just right. You can also click on the image and drag it into the correct position.

04: All set

When you are happy that the image has been moved and scaled to perfection, click the Set button. The new buddy picture will then populate your open iChat windows. If you change your mind at any point though and want to select a different picture to use, click Cancel.

Discover FaceTime for Mac

With FaceTime for Mac, video calls are now only a few
clicks away. Learn how to install and configure this great tool

 **App used:**
FaceTime

 **Time needed:**
5 minutes

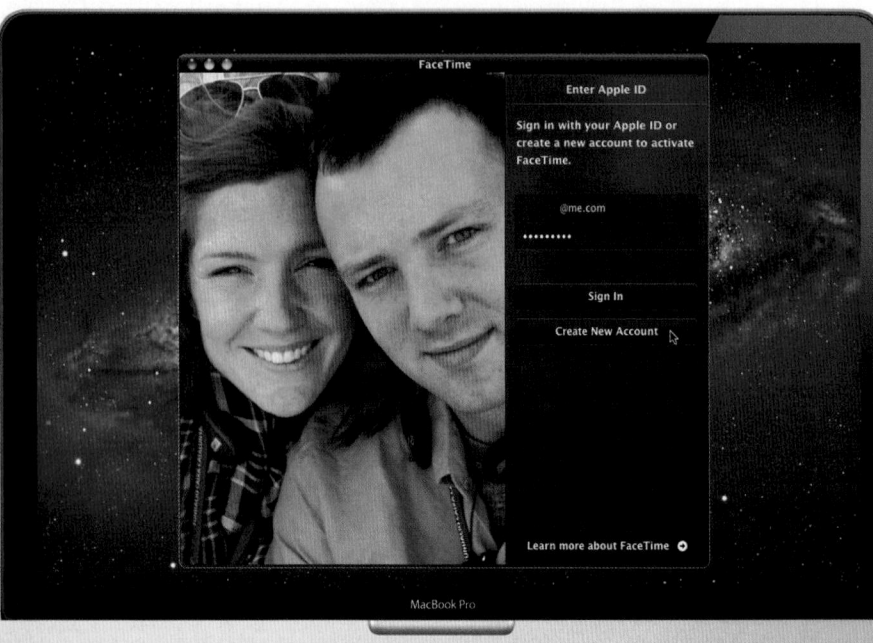

One of the most acclaimed features of the
iPhone 4, iPad 2 and iPod touch is now available
on your Mac. Indeed, if your Apple computer runs
Mac OS X Lion version 10.7.2 or later with FaceTime for Mac,
video calls are now only a few clicks away. From the comfort
of your laptop or desktop Mac, FaceTime for Mac now makes
it possible for you to have a chat or share a smile with your
friends and family who also possess an iPhone 4, iPad 2, iPod
touch or Mac. It is even possible to engage in video calls over
your local network.

With the simple, further requirements of an email address
and an Apple ID, a world of enhanced communication
is now easily accessible. The sleek, simple and powerful
interface of the FaceTime for Mac application is fully
integrated in your Mac OS X environment. This two-page
tutorial takes you through the few simple steps needed to
install and configure it. Let's see how this is done.

"With OS X Lion, video calls are just a few clicks away"

FaceTime Set up and use FaceTime

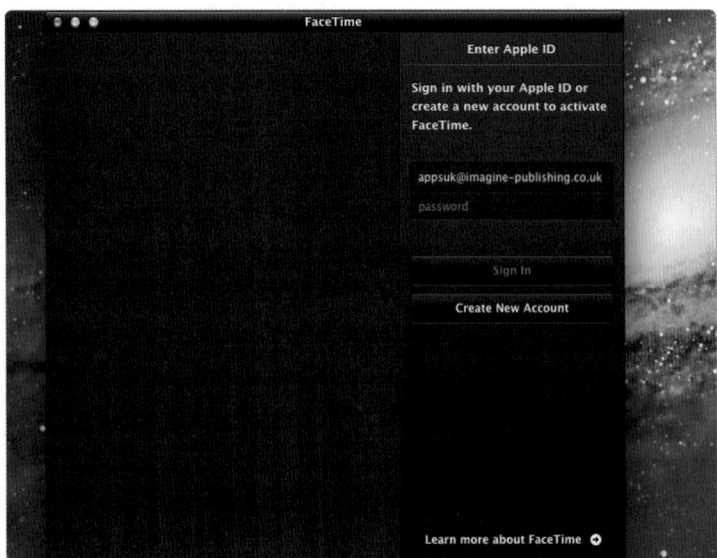

01: Launch the app

You can launch the FaceTime app by locating and double-clicking on the
app icon in your Applications folder. To save time later, drag and drop the
app icon into your Dock to create a shortcut that you can click on to launch
the app instantly without trawling through folders.

02: Sign in

When the FaceTime app has been launched, you will have to sign in with
your Apple ID to start using the app or create a new account, which you can
do by following the prompts within this app. When you have entered your
account details, you will be able to start conducting FaceTime chats.

Find your way around FaceTime

Make video calls to your friends and family with ease

Your Favorites list
It is possible to create a list of preferred contacts in the Favourite list. Click the Favorites button, then select the '+' sign and select the relevant name from the contact list

The video call window
During a call, the video call window shows a picture-in-picture display of your contact which you can drag to any corner of the video call window. Use the Video menu to enter full-screen display

WHAT IS AN APPLE ID?
An Apple ID is a username and password used to identify you on every Apple service. Whether you want to buy software or a device on the Apple Online Store, music or movies on the iTunes Store or log in to iChat, an Apple ID provides you with a single set of login credentials.

The Recents call list
In the Recents call list, all the incoming or outgoing calls are listed. It is possible to filter the list to show only missed calls. Click Clear to empty the list of all calls

The Contacts list
Upon installation, FaceTime will automatically add all your Address Book contacts to its contact list. Changes to any Address Book entry will be immediately reflected in the FaceTime contacts list

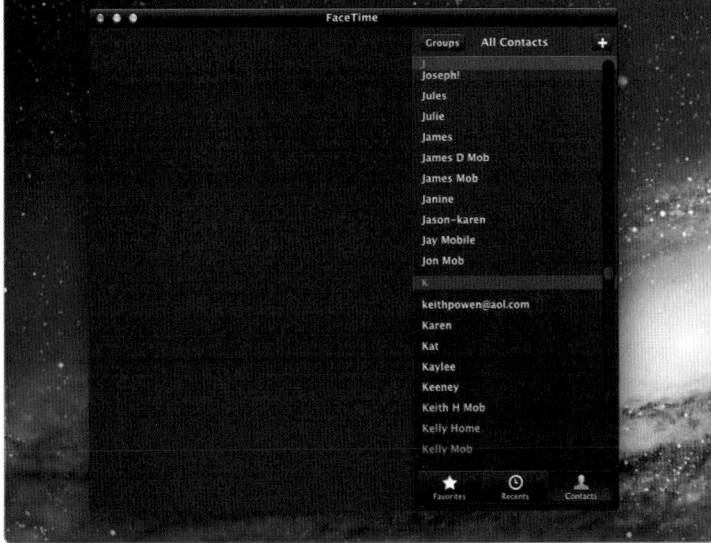

03: Search your contacts
All of the contacts from your Address Book app will be automatically imported into FaceTime, allowing you to search your database for fiends or colleagues with whom to converse with over FaceTime. Click on a contact, followed by their phone number or email address to send an invite.

04: Make a Call
When you friend has been notified of your FaceTime invitation and accepts the call, they will appear in the main window of the app and you will be visible in a stamp-sized screen in the corner. You can change your feed to Portrait or Landscape orientation from the 'View' menu.

Use the built-in Dictionary

Find out how the built-in Dictionary application can become an essential part of your working day

 **App used:**
Dictionary

 **Time needed:**
3 minutes

Ever read an email or a webpage and hit a word whose meaning you didn't quite recognise? Or maybe you keep using the same word over and over and wish you could expand your vocabulary? We have all been there. However, this could all be a thing of the past, because when reading a webpage or eBook on your Mac, the invaluable Dictionary application comes rushing to your aid. With its integration inside the Apple OS, Dictionary's contribution knows no bounds.

Indeed, Dictionary is accessible through a contextual menu item in the Apple suite of utilities and applications – like TextEdit, Safari, and Mail – making checking definitions simple. The addition of a Dashboard widget Dictionary, which also operates as a thesaurus, makes for a highly accessible reference tool. Furthermore, it is not only based on the New Oxford American Dictionary and Oxford American Writer's Thesaurus, but also uses such online resources as Wikipedia and can be extended with the addition of other dictionaries. Follow this tutorial to see how it all works.

"The Dashboard widget, which also operates as a thesaurus, makes for an accessible reference tool"

Using the Dictionary
Discover the options at your fingertips

Select your reference source
Below the Dictionary toolbar, a banner shows the names of all the enabled inline and online reference sources. The first item on the banner allows the results from all sources to be displayed

The results panel
The rest of Dictionary's application window is dedicated to showing the entries found in the selected reference sources for your search term. If several sources are selected, the entries are shown in the preferred order set in the preferences

Dictionary application toolbar
From left to right, the toolbar contains two arrows to browse through the history of search terms; two buttons, which control the font size of the entries found; and the search field where you can type the word being searched

The Dictionary panel
Once the Dictionary panel option is activated, the panel appears whenever you select the 'Look up in Dictionary' item on the contextual menu. It permits changing from word definition to thesaurus and launches the Dictionary application

NEED MORE DICTIONARIES?
If your mother tongue is not English, or if you are looking to enlarge your vocabulary, it is possible to expand Dictionary reference sources to include jargon and professional terms, or even some foreign-language dictionaries. Check your favourite search engine for free Dictionary plug-ins and the Apple Home & Learning Download section at http://www.apple.com/downloads/macosx/home_learning for a few more.

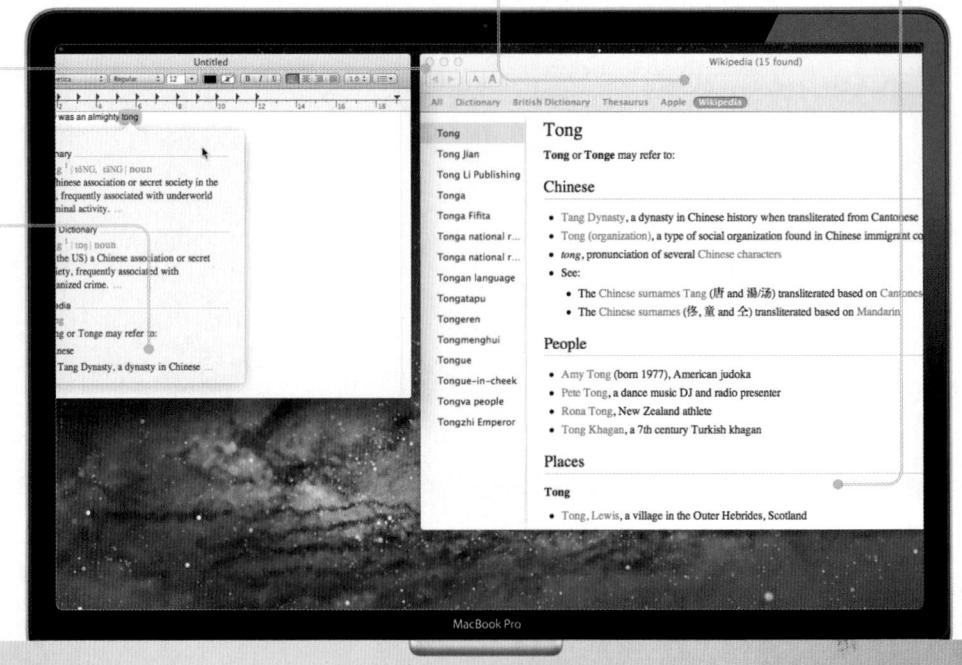

Dictionary Learn about the built-in Dictionary

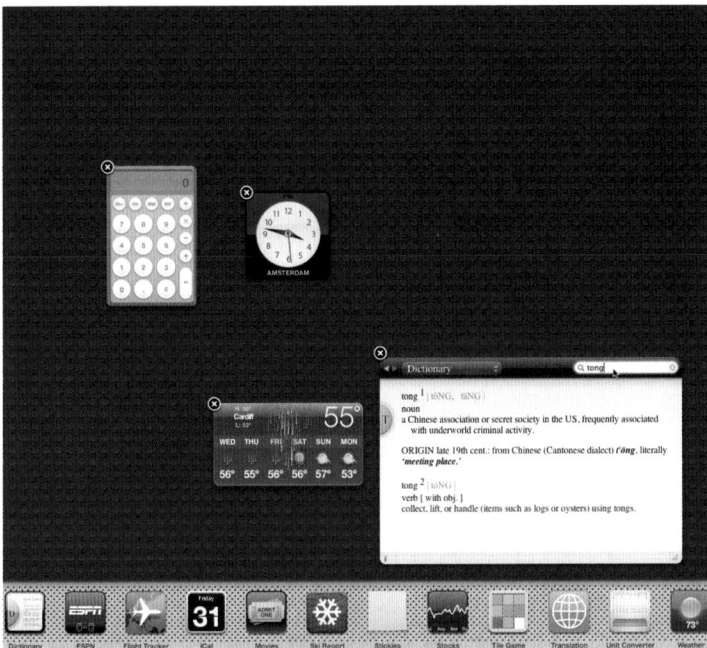

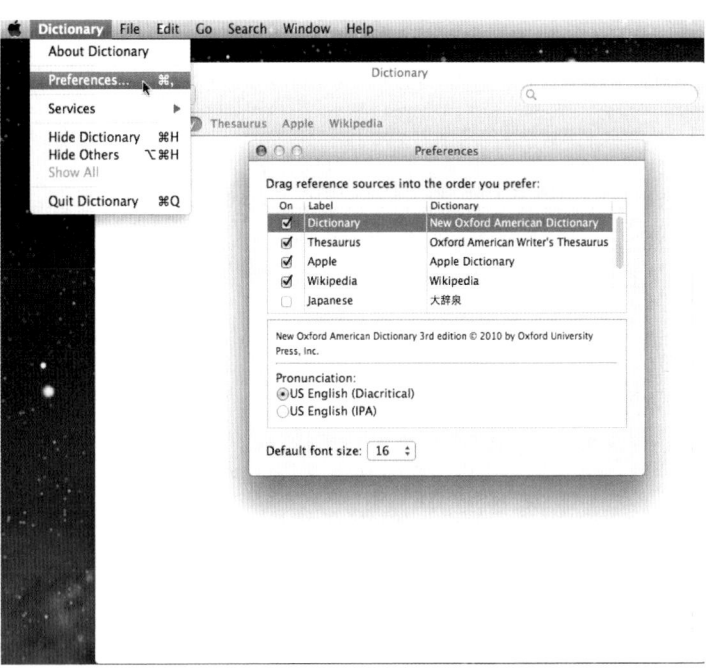

01: Where is Dictionary located?

Dictionary is located in the Applications folder but can also be accessed via the contextual menu item 'Look up in Dictionary'. Adding the widget to the Dashboard is part of the default set of widgets that are installed with Mac OS X.

02: Dictionary Preferences

Preferences are accessed through the Dictionary menu. The pane consists of two sections: the top one shows the list of available reference sources, the other configures how Dictionary reacts to your actions. Set the Preferences to suit your needs and how you work.

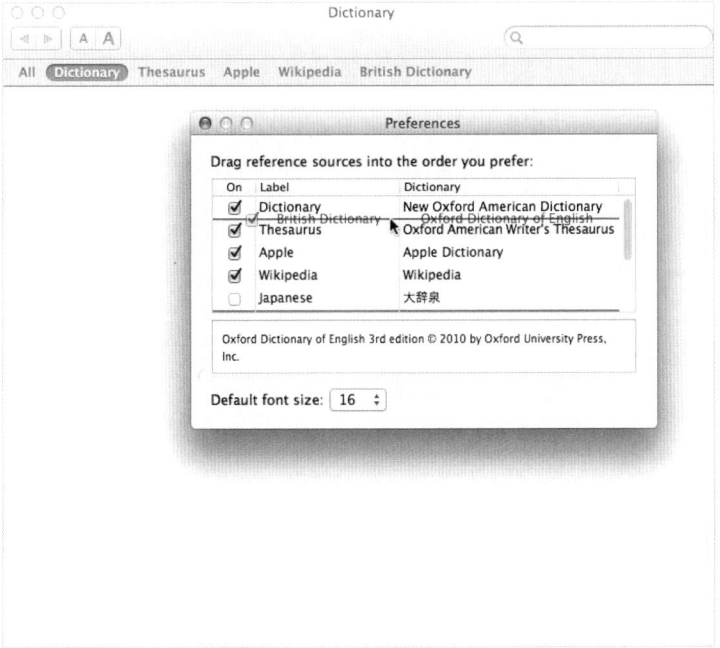

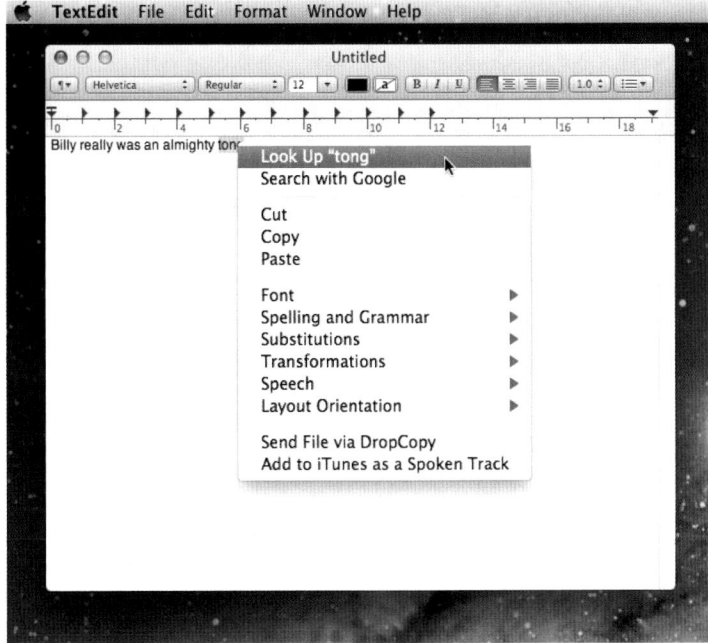

03: Configure additional reference sources

Each reference source on your system can be enabled/disabled. Rearrange the list by dragging items in the order preferred. Further configuration parameters are displayed for each source, if applicable. Here you can also change the font size and pronunciation.

04: Easy access

When typing an apps such as TextEdit, you can now double-click on a word to highlight it and then right-click with your mouse to bring up a menu. Choose 'Look Up' from this menu to get an instant Dictionary definition for your word.

Create a Mac App Store account

Follow our tutorial to create an Apple ID and start downloading apps from the Mac App Store

 **App used:**
Mac App Store

 **Time needed:**
10 minutes

An Apple ID lets you personalise your Apple experience. Once you've created one, you can use it to access Apple resources that require you to identify yourself and make purchases from the Apple Online Store, the iTunes Store and the App Store. If you have held a MobileMe account, or use an iPhone, iPad or iPod Touch to access the iTunes store, you will already have an Apple ID, and this can be used to sign in to the App Store.

But what if you don't have an Apple ID? Well, you can still browse the Mac App Store, but you cannot download either free or paid apps. Creating an Apple ID is a very straightforward process, and although the majority of people use iTunes to set up their account, you'll be pleased to learn that you can also create an Apple ID via the Mac App Store. Read on, and we'll guide you through the process of creating a new Apple ID for either yourself or a member of your family.

> "An Apple ID lets you personalise your Apple experience and access Apple's resources"

Access the App Store

How to use your Apple ID to browse the Mac App Store

Password
Your email address will be your new Apple ID. Type this, and choose a mixed case password of at least eight characters when prompted during the setup process. Use this information to sign in

Sign in
There are two ways to sign in with your new Apple ID. The quickest is to click 'Sign in' under the Quick Links tab. Alternatively, select Store > Sign In from the main App Store menu

Create Apple ID
Enter an Apple ID and password, and you can download and purchase apps. If you haven't got an Apple ID, click the 'Create Apple ID' button to create a new account and personalise your Apple experience

Browse apps
There is a diverse range of apps available for download and purchase from the Mac App Store, but unless you sign in using an Apple ID, all you can do is browse

REDEEM A CODE
Create an Apple ID via the App Store, and you are required to either enter a payment method or redeem a voucher. If you are creating an Apple ID for a younger member of the family, then you may redeem a voucher code. This way, you won't be surprised by unexpected credit card bills!

Mac App Store Create an Apple ID

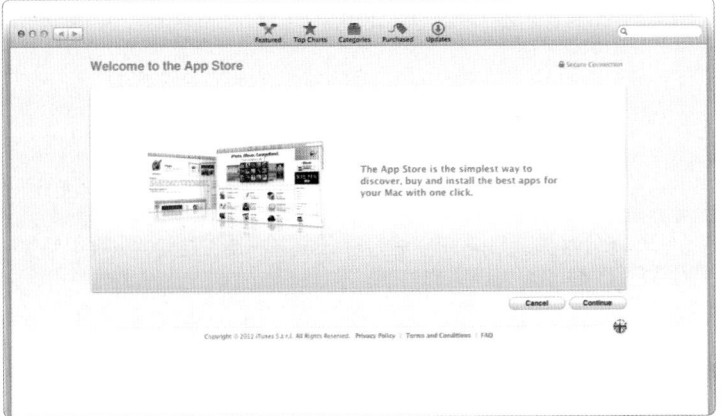

01: Create Account

Launch the App Store. From the main Mac App Store menu, choose Store > Create Account. You will now see the 'Welcome to the App Store' window.

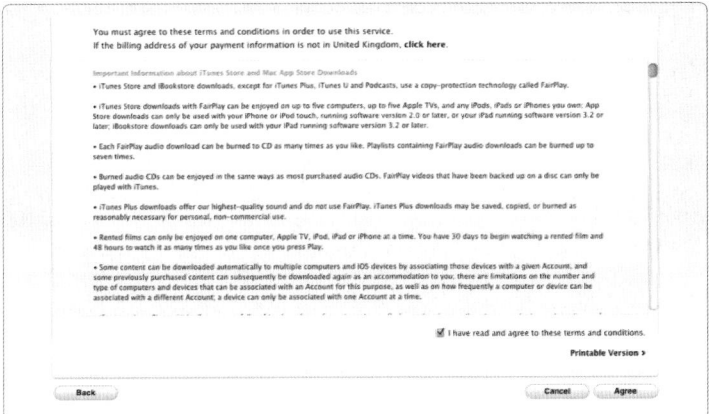

02: Terms and conditions

Click 'Continue', and read the terms and conditions. Confirm that you have read and agree to them, and click the 'Agree' button.

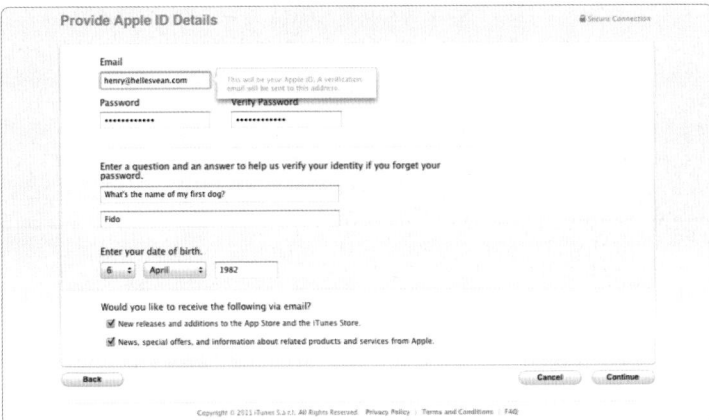

03: Apple ID details

Enter your Apple ID details. Type your email address, a mixed case password of at least eight characters, and the other details requested.

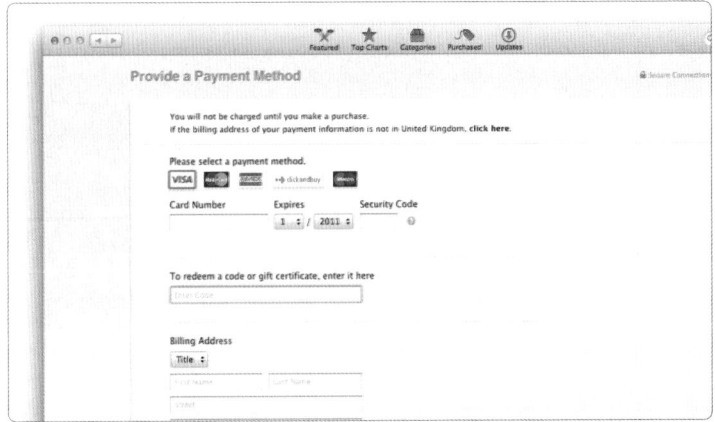

04: Payment method

Click 'Continue', and provide a payment method on the window that appears, or opt to redeem a gift certificate or prepaid iTunes Gift Card.

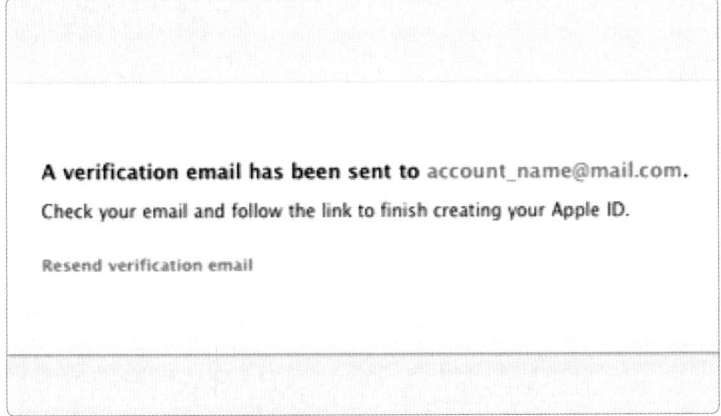

05: Create Apple ID

Enter your name, address and telephone number, then click 'Create Apple ID'. A verification email will now be sent to the email address you provided.

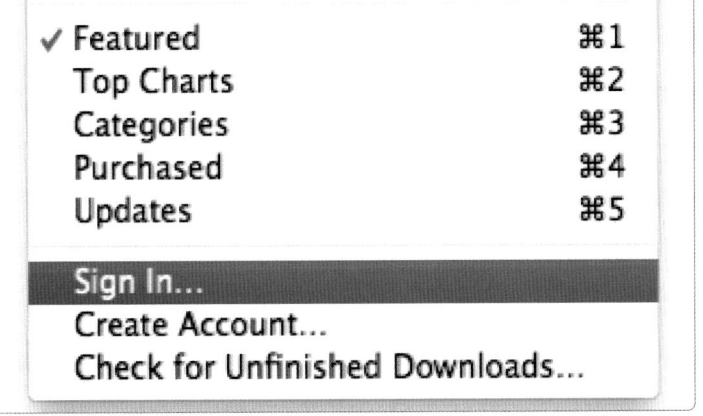

06: Verify email address

Check your inbox, and click the link to verify your email address. You can now use your new Apple ID and password to sign in to the App Store.

Get to know the Mac App Store

The Mac App Store guarantees easy access to a wide range of free and paid apps. Find out what it's all about right here…

The Mac App Store first appeared in Mac OS X v10.6.6, and is home to a diverse range of apps aimed at enhancing the functionality of a Mac computer. As a bonus, the majority of apps are either reasonably priced or free.

As we have come to expect from Apple, the interface is intuitive, and finding and acquiring apps is a breeze. This is largely because the store has adopted a very similar look, feel and process to shopping to that used by the iTunes App Store. When you want to buy an app, simply enter your iTunes ID and password, and it's purchased. It really is as simple as that. The app is automatically downloaded and installed in the Applications folder, and can be accessed via Launchpad when required. You can even search for apps by title, developer/publisher, category or description. All apps are organised into convenient categories and this makes the process of navigating the store an effortless experience. Here we show you how to explore the virtual aisles…

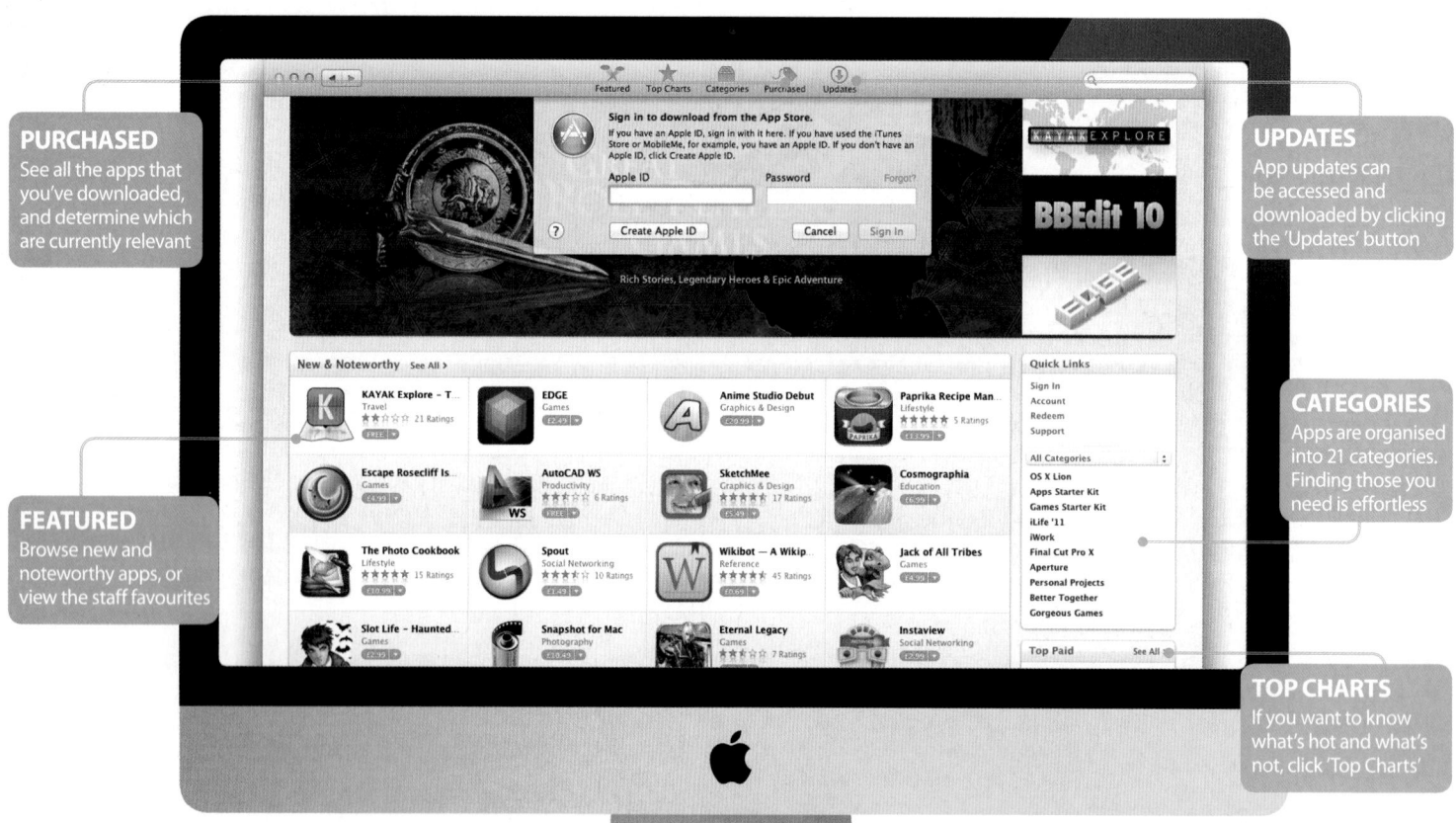

PURCHASED
See all the apps that you've downloaded, and determine which are currently relevant

FEATURED
Browse new and noteworthy apps, or view the staff favourites

UPDATES
App updates can be accessed and downloaded by clicking the 'Updates' button

CATEGORIES
Apps are organised into 21 categories. Finding those you need is effortless

TOP CHARTS
If you want to know what's hot and what's not, click 'Top Charts'

Log in to the Mac App Store

Start downloading apps immediately

If you're new to the Mac App Store, there are two ways to launch the service; either click the App Store icon in the Dock, or click the Apple menu and select 'App Store'. Do this, and you are free to browse the store using the 'Featured', 'Categories' or 'Top Charts' windows.

If you've ever used the iTunes App Store then you'll already have an Apple ID so click 'Sign In' from the 'Quick Links' tab to the right of the window, or Store>Sign In from the Mac App Store menu. When the 'Sign In' screen appears, all you have to do is enter your Apple ID and password, and click 'Sign In'.

If you don't have an Apple ID, click the 'Create Apple ID' button on the 'Sign In' screen, and you'll see a window welcoming you to the App Store. Click 'Continue', agree to the terms and conditions and follow the online instructions to create an Apple ID. Once you've completed the process, you can start downloading apps immediately.

Key features

How to navigate the Mac App Store

Featured

Take a look at the Mac App Store's main storefront window. It's well organised, and you'll see five buttons at the top. Select the 'Featured' view, and you can browse apps that Apple has deemed 'New & Noteworthy', which is handy if you want to see the latest apps Apple deems worthy of your time. If you're more interested in apps with favourable user reviews, however, then scroll to the 'What's Hot' section to see all of the top rated apps.

Top Charts

If you're interested in the most popular apps that people has purchased, click the 'Top Charts' button at the top of the main window, and get instant access to the top apps. Here, you can download OS X Lion, and apps that include Pages, Numbers and Keynote. To the right of the window are links to the categories. Click one, and you'll see a range of popular apps. Each device will have a similar menu available.

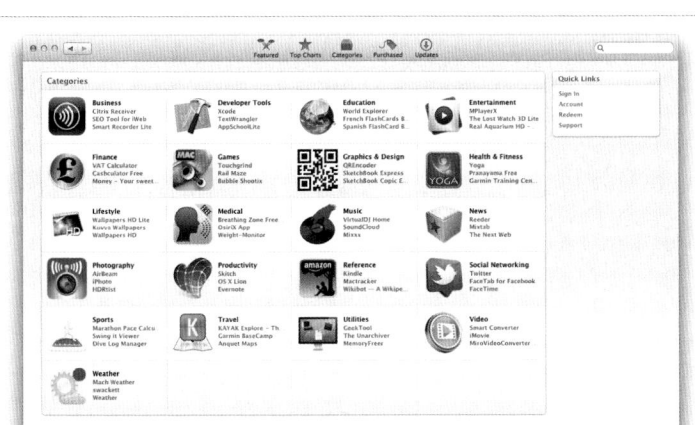

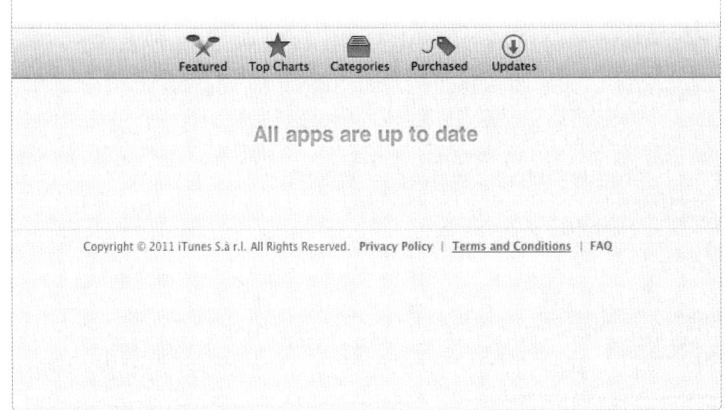

Categories

If you know the type of app that you are looking for, then try using the 'Categories' view. All apps in the Mac App Store are organised into one of 21 categories, ranging from 'Business' and 'Weather', to 'Developer Tools' and 'Video'. Click the category title to see all the apps in that specific category. You can now browse the apps. If you see one you'd like to know more about, then click the thumbnail image.

Updates

The Mac App Store offers similar functionality to the iTunes App Store. If you use an iPhone, you'll know that you are notified of app updates as and when they become available. It's no different with the Mac App Store; click the 'Updates' button, and you'll see all available updates for apps you've downloaded. You are then given the option to install them. These updates may iron out any glitches or add extra features to your apps.

Download and install an app

Use the Mac App Store to add functionality to your Mac

 **App used:** Mac App Store  **Time needed:** 10 minutes

The Mac App Store makes downloading and installing apps a fun and effortless experience. This is partly because the interface is very user friendly, but also because the process is largely automated. One of the many benefits of an online marketplace such as the Mac App Store is that it drives prices down to a reasonable level. Consequently, the majority of apps offer good value for your hard-earned cash. As a bonus, a large number of free apps are also available, many of which are polished, well developed and extremely functional.

If you're new to the App Store, then read on, and we'll guide you through the process of downloading and installing your very first app.

"The interface is very user friendly"

Mac App Store Download and install an app

01: Sign in
Open up the Mac App Store, click the 'Sign In' link in the 'Quick Links' tab, enter your Apple ID and password, and click 'Sign In'.

02: Browse the apps
Browse the App Store until you find an app that you like the look of. Try the Top Charts section first, as this is home to a range of popular apps.

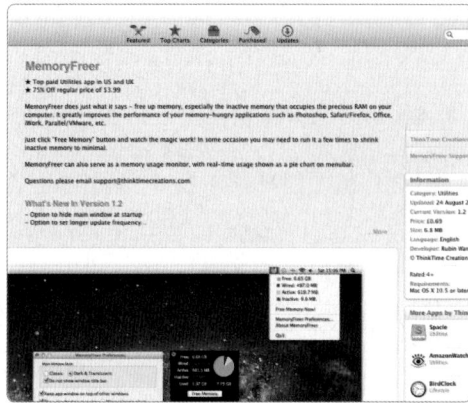

03: Read the description
When you've identified an app, click the icon. Click 'More' to see the full description, and the thumbnails to view sample screenshots.

04: Reviews and ratings
Scroll down and view the customer rating. Read the reviews and check the comments, as these provide useful information about functionality.

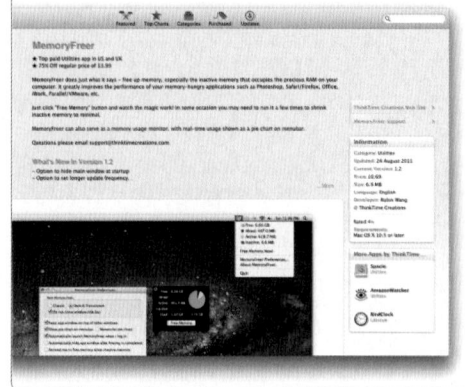

05: Make your decision
When you want to download the app, click the link under the icon with the price. The link will turn green; you can now make the purchase.

06: Track download progress
Click 'Buy App', and the link will turn blue and inform you the app is installing. Track its progress under the Launchpad icon.

Visit the Mac App Store

Where you'll find the key parts needed to purchase an app

Download and install

Downloading an app is a breeze. Find one you like, click on the price, and then click again if you wish to go ahead with the purchase. The app will automatically be downloaded and installed

Top Charts

If you're new to downloading apps, start by browsing the 'Top Charts' view in the App Store, as here you'll find a selection of some of the most popular apps, games and utilities available

Paid or Free?

You don't even have to spend your hard-earned cash, as there is a diverse range of free apps available. For example, Twitter is an extremely polished app that won't set you back a penny

Installed apps

Rather cleverly, the App Store identifies exactly which apps you have installed. This saves a whole lot of confusion if you regularly use the store to download and install apps

---

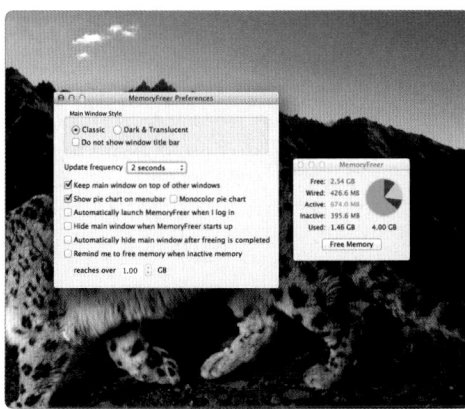

07: Automated process

The beauty of the App Store lies in its simplicity. The process is automated, so just launch the app when it has finished downloading.

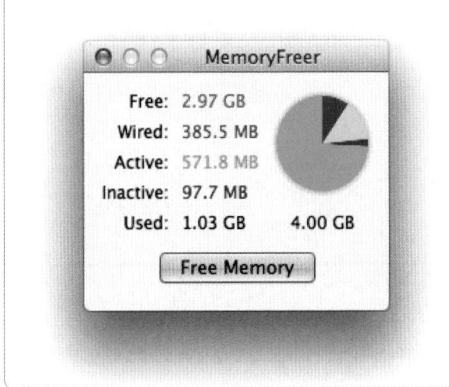

08: Try the app

As you can see, we purchased MemoryFreer. If you're new to the App Store, try downloading some free apps first.

09: Purchased items

Return to the App Store, and click the 'Purchased' button. Your app will now appear in this view, and you can reinstall it from here at any time.

Delete and reinstall apps on your Mac

 **App used:**
Mac App Store

 **Time needed:**
10 minutes

Deleting apps downloaded from the Mac App Store is a breeze

 Uninstalling apps has always been a whole lot easier on a Mac than on a Windows PC, and you'll be pleased to learn that Mac OS X Lion makes the process even easier. Don't go looking for an 'Uninstall Programs' setting, as you won't find one! The latest OS has adopted the automated click-and-hold method used by devices such as the iPhone and iPad. This means that deleting apps downloaded from the Mac App Store (free or paid) is an absolute breeze. In fact, if you've ever used an iOS device such as an

iPhone to remove apps downloaded from the iTunes App Store, then you'll instantly feel familiar with the process.

Read on and we'll show you how to use Launchpad to delete an app that has been downloaded from the Mac App Store. We'll then show you how to reinstall the app should you ever require it again in the future. As a bonus, you don't even need to empty the Trash, as Launchpad handles everything for you. It's an extremely simple process and we show you how to do it.

Delete with ease
A quick look at the app deleting process

Reinstall apps
You can reinstall apps downloaded from the Mac App Store using the Purchased view. Click 'Install', and the app will be reinstalled, and appear in the first available space on the Launchpad screen

Navigate Launchpad
All apps (paid and free) that you download from the Mac App Store can be viewed on Launchpad. If there is more than one page of shortcut icons, use your mouse to swipe through the screens

Confirm deletion
Removing an app that is no longer required is a breeze; simply click the black 'X' badge, and then 'Delete' when asked to confirm that you want to delete the app. The whole process is automated

Click and hold
Click and hold on an app that you wish to delete, and all the app icons will start wiggling. Apps that can be deleted (that is, those downloaded from the Mac App Store) will sport a circular black 'X' badge

DELETE FROM FINDER
Experienced Mac OS X Lion users may have noted that apps downloaded from the Mac App Store cannot be moved to Trash from the Applications folder. Although the easiest way to delete apps is via Launchpad, there is an alternative method. Open Finder, click Go > Applications, and select an app. Press Cmd + delete, enter your password when prompted, and the app will be moved to the Trash.

Mac App Store Uninstall and reinstall apps

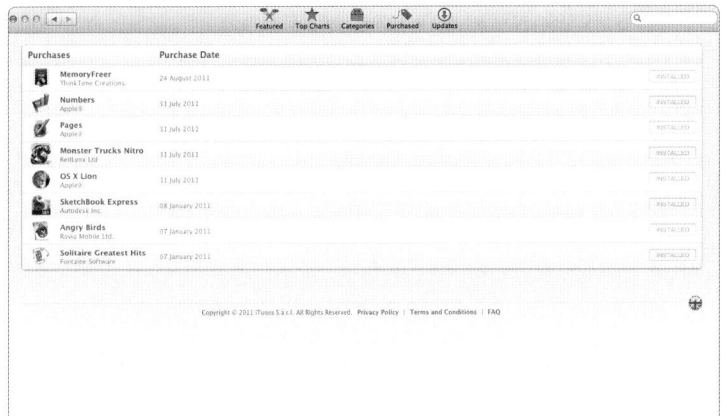

01: Purchased apps

The first step is to check which apps you have downloaded. To do this, launch the App Store, and click the 'Purchased' button at the top.

02: Click and hold

Browse the apps installed, find one you no longer need, and click the Launchpad icon. Click and hold on the app's icon until it starts wiggling.

03: Confirm deletion

All downloaded apps will now sport an 'X' icon. Click the relevant 'X' icon, and when asked to confirm that you want to delete the app, click 'Delete'.

04: Familiar process

The app will now be removed. The process will be familiar to anyone who has used an iDevice, as the tap and hold method is used by all iOS devices.

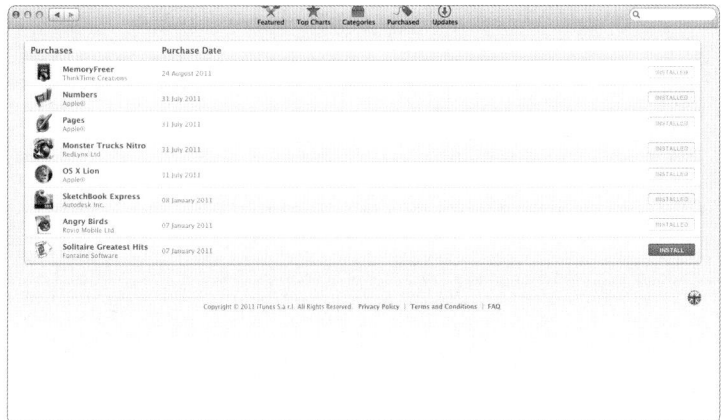

05: Reinstall the app

If you want to reinstall the app, launch the App Store, and navigate to the 'Purchased' view. When the store recalls your purchases, click 'Install'.

06: Track progress

Launchpad will appear. You can track the progress of the app download and reinstallation. The process is automated, with no user input required.

Get to know iTunes

Learn the basics of iTunes and get connected to the Apple Music Store

**App used:**
iTunes

**Time needed:**
10 minutes

iTunes has been around for some years now, starting simply as a music playing app that was available on Apple's various computers, and over the years it has since evolved to become an incredibly diverse and powerful tool. Now it's not only a great way to store and listen to all your tunes from your music

library, it's also place where you can purchase music, books, apps and movies, as well as a way to network with other users. While these features are all great additions to the software, iTunes can be a little daunting when using it for the first time.

If you've not see it before, when you first open it you'll see information bars on either side of the

screen, plus all kinds of buttons in the display; there is a lot to take in. Don't be put off, it's not that complex to get to grips with. While some controls are incredibly simple and intuitive, if you can master the basics of iTunes you will be well on the way to getting the most out of the software. Read on to find out exactly how...

VOLUME CONTROL
The volume slider and basic play/pause controls sit in the top-left corner of the screen

ALBUM ART
Cover Flow is a really great way to flick through your music by seeing each piece of Album Artwork

CLEVER PLAYLISTS
Pick a song and click the Genius button – iTunes will create a playlist for you using similar tunes in your library

VIEW IT AND SEE
These are the view options for your media – try each one and decide which suits you best

SHARE
This small arrow will show or hide the Ping sidebar to allow you to connect with friends

Share your media

Allow other computers to play music and movies from your iTunes Library

When you've downloaded a selection of apps, music and movies, they will be saved to your Mac's iTunes library, and your account with iTunes. Content is now free from Digital Rights Management, allowing you to copy tracks over, but you will need to authorise other computers to allow another iTunes library to access the

content you have bought. If you have a number of computers, this is vital if you want to keep all your tracks up to date on every machine, but you are limited in the number of registrations you are allowed.

To authorise a second computer open iTunes and select 'Store'. In the dropdown menu select 'Authorise

This Computer'. All you need to do now is input your Apple ID and password and wait a few seconds. When the process is finished you will see a small box that tells you how many computers you have authorised and how many you have left, and all your media will be playable on your second machine.

Key features

Get to grips with iTunes' famous Store

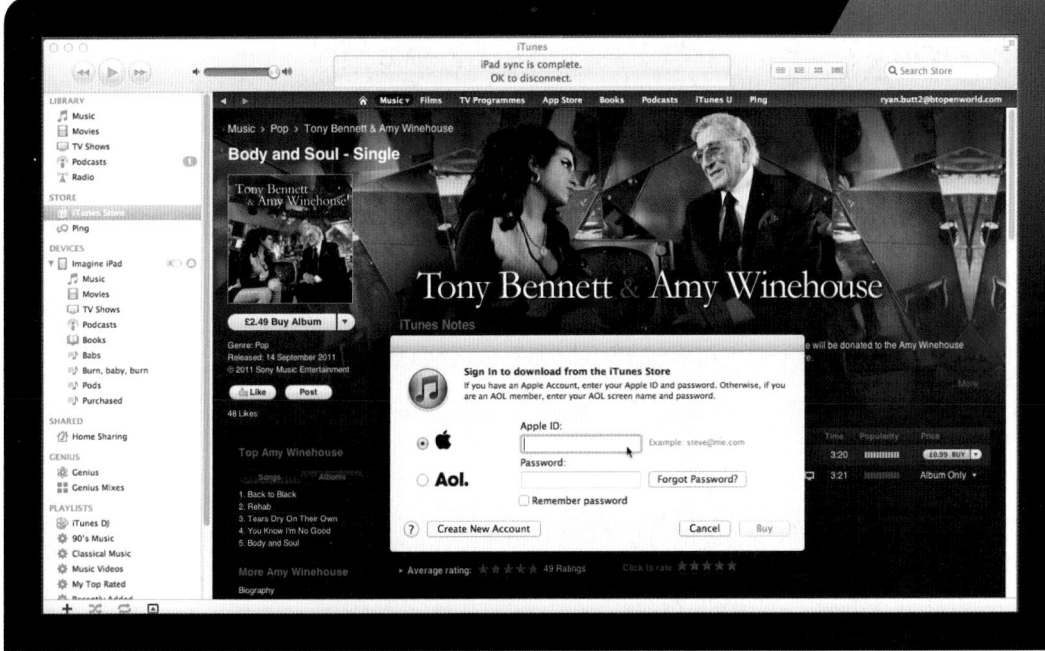

Download Media

When you've found a song, movie or app you want to buy, downloading is simple. Click the 'Buy Now' button and you will be prompted to authenticate the purchase by inputting your Apple ID and password. Once you've done so, the item will be added to the sidebar on the left-hand side of the window as it downloads. When it's done, it will show immediately in your library, and can be played by double-clicking on it.

Use the App Store

The App Store is a huge part of the ecosystem on the iPhone and iPad, and you can download apps to these devices on the move without iTunes. You can also access the App Store through iTunes to download apps to add to your portable devices next time you connect them. You can click the Apps tab at the top of the iTunes Store window and browse the App Store just like any other. Each device will have a similar, contextual menu available.

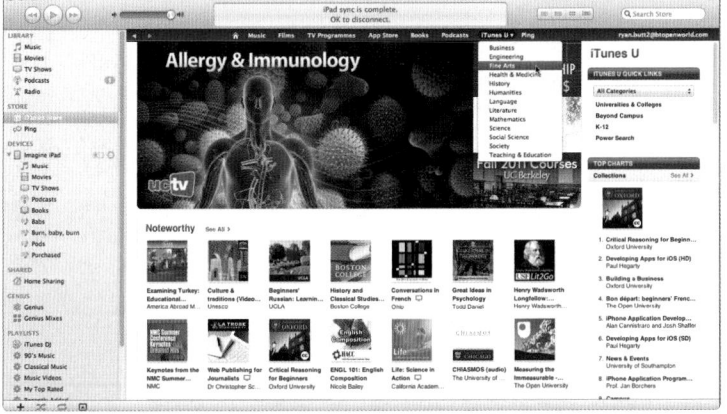

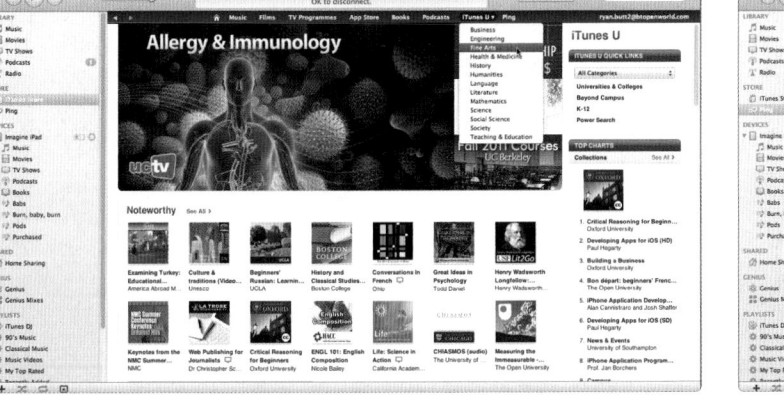

Learn with iTunes U

The iTunes Store's iTunes U section is the place to go if you study at, or work in, an Educational establishment. Packed with useful tools for learning, the store contains items such as audiobooks, lecture videos, podcasts and textbooks. Whether you're a lecturer, teacher or student, this should be your first port of call for all your learning needs, and if you're looking for a new way to distribute your notes this is a great, and simple, option.

Connect through Ping

Ping is Apple's social networking service that allows people to connect through iTunes, share favourite tracks and publicise their own talent all in one place. If you know others who use iTunes to organise their music libraries, Ping will give you the opportunity to share your tastes with them, suggest songs they might like, and even follow some of your favourite artists to keep up to date with their newest releases.

Organise your iTunes library

Doing a bit of iTunes housekeeping to tidy
up your library is easier than you think…

 **App used:**
iTunes

 **Time needed:**
15 minutes

 When iTunes was first launched the
iTunes Store didn't exist, and all the
application could really do was contain
and play your music. Over the years, the
functionality of the app has expanded massively,
and while it still holds your music collection, you can
also store videos, podcasts, books, iPhone apps, TV
shows and more in your library.

With all the content that you could theoretically
hold on your machine, getting yourself organised is
an incredibly important job. It's great to have 60,000

songs in your Music library, but if none of them
have the correct track names it will be hard to find
what you're looking for. iTunes also allows you to
add cover art to all of your albums and movies by
signing into your account through the Store. With a
click you can add the correct artwork to your music
collection, making the prospect of sorting through
your tracks a lot more appealing.

This tutorial will get you started on sorting
through the various media you have on your
machine, so read on and get tidying!

> "With all the content
> on your machine,
> getting yourself
> organised is an
> important job"

Organise iTunes
Spend some time getting your
library clean and tidy

Open in New Window
If you want to view more than one
type of file at once, you can open
a different type of media in a new
window. You can use different views
in each window too

View Options
If you select View Options you can
see and choose which sections will be
displayed in the main window. If you
add more than can fit in the space,
you will need to scroll to see them

Cover Flow
Cover Flow allows you to see several
albums at once and flick through
them with a swipe of your Magic
Mouse or Trackpad. Along the
bottom is a song view with each
track's full information

Song Information
Downloaded songs will
already contain all the relevant
information necessary for sorting,
or you can add your own by
choosing the 'Get Info' panel and
adding it to the sorting options

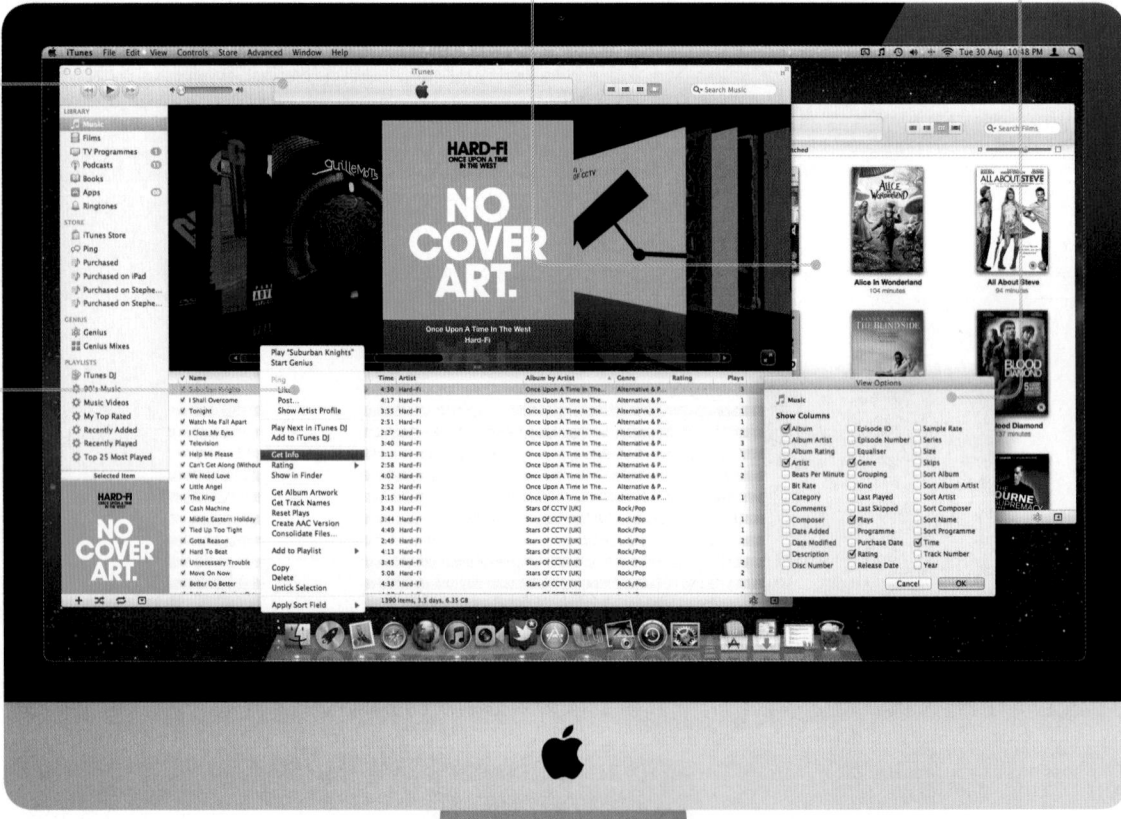

SORTING OPTIONS
You can list your songs in a number
of orders; clicking on the various
options along the top of the track
listing will allow you to order your
songs differently. If, for example,
you want to view your songs in
alphabetical order, you can click on
the Name tab at the top and your
songs will instantly be reordered.

iTunes Navigate and organise your Media

01: Viewing Options

The buttons at the top control how you see your music. Select them to display titles and artwork in Cover Flow mode, or something in between.

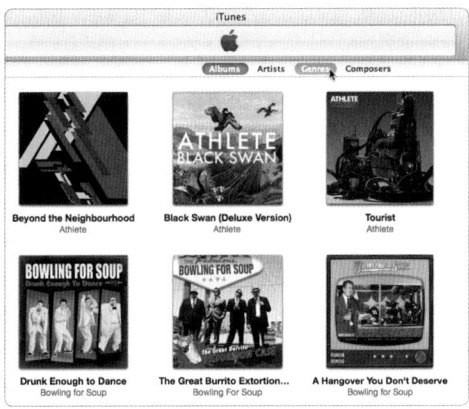

02: Grid View

In Grid View sort your music into Albums, Artists, Genres and Composers by clicking these buttons at the top and narrow down your selection.

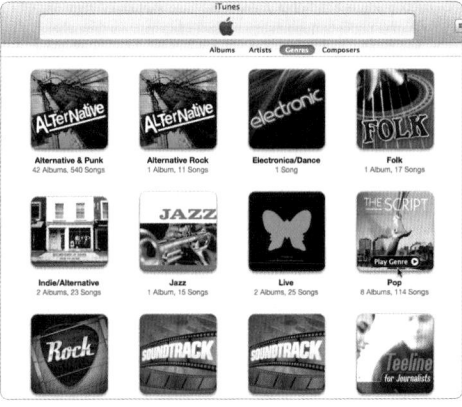

03: Album Browser

If you're using something like Genre to browse in Grid view, you can roll your cursor over each grid entry to scroll through each album in that genre.

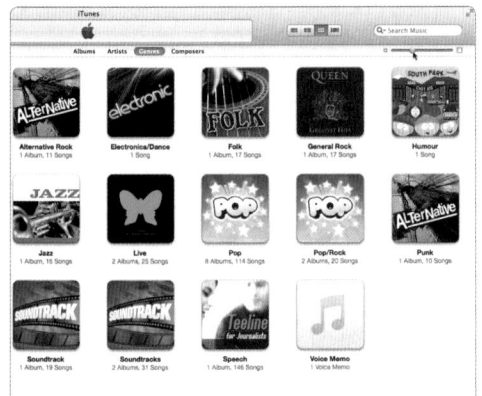

04: Size Slider

This slider in the top right-hand corner allows you to alter the size of each album in the grid. This will give you a better view of album art.

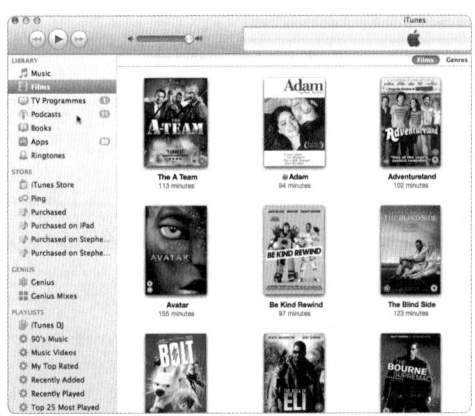

05: Media Type

The Sidebar on the left allows you to flick through your media. The numbers mean there are items in you haven't viewed or listened to.

06: Store Searcher

The next section down in the sidebar shows the Store section, allowing you to also search through and view the purchased media.

07: Genius

Genius allows you to create a playlist based on one song. Genius Mixes contains pre-mixed playlists based on a single genre or album.

08: Playlists

You can create playlists with any songs, but there are playlists that are created automatically, like recently added and most played.

09: New Playlists

Click the bottom-left plus button to create a new playlist, and add songs to create a selection. The other buttons here allow you to shuffle or repeat.

Delete duplicate tracks from iTunes

Is your Library beginning to clutter with duplicates?
Learn how to easily manage and delete them

**App used:**
iTunes

**Time needed:**
10 minutes

Maintaining an organised iTunes Library isn't an easy task. Imported CDs, downloaded albums and random music tracks all find their way into your music collection, no matter how hard you try to prevent it. Before long you can end up with duplicate tracks scattered all over your library, resulting in errant albums with missing artwork and disjointed playback. The situation can become even worse if other members of the family have access to your Mac.

But fear not! Apple has included a number of features within iTunes to make tidying your music collection a simple affair, and in typical Apple fashion it's incredibly easy to access to you can have a spring clean any time you like.

Follow us through this nine-step tutorial to discover how to delete those troublesome duplicate tracks from your iTunes Music Library, consolidate your entire Music Library into a single folder and even more besides.

"Apple has included features to make tidying your music collection a very simple affair"

Get rid of repeats
Learn how to delete duplicate tracks in no time at all

Find those duplicates
To see every duplicate track, simply click on the File menu and select Show Duplicates

Right-click options
When you've selected the duplicate files, right-click on them (using either the right mouse button or two fingers on your trackpad) to bring up a context-sensitive menu, packed with options

Delete multiple tracks
To select more than one track at a time, hold down the Cmd key and click on multiple tracks. This time saver will enable you to delete many tracks with only one press of the Delete key

Return to your Music Library
Once you're ready to return to the regular Music Library, click the Show All button at the bottom of the screen

MANAGE YOUR COLLECTION
If you want every music file on your Mac to be contained within your Music Library, open iTunes, click on the File menu and choose Library>Organize Library. A window will appear giving you the option to consolidate your files. Consolidating every music file to your library will make managing your collection much easier.

iTunes Delete duplicate music tracks from iTunes

01: Find those duplicates

Open iTunes, go to your Music Library and select Display Duplicates from the File menu. iTunes will then display every duplicate file.

02: Time to organise

You can now begin to organise your music. It's easier to sort the files by name. Click on the Name column at the top of the search results.

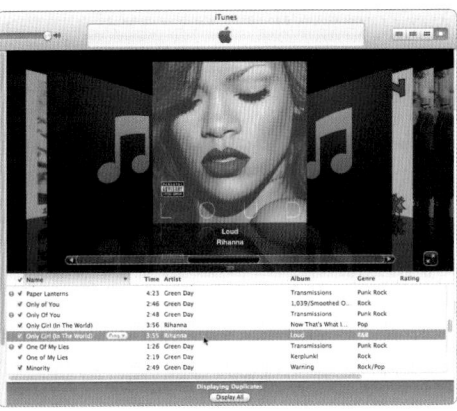

03: Look for clones

Look for songs that have identical names, artists and albums. This is important – you don't want to accidentally delete a live version or remix!

04: Track lengths

In the unlikely event that duplicate songs have the same artist and album, you can also look out for track length differences.

05: How's the sound?

To be totally sure that you're deleting the right track, listen to both duplicates; one may have a higher bit rate, therefore a better sound quality.

06: Move to the Trash

To delete a track, highlight it once by clicking on it, then press the Delete key. iTunes will ask if you would like to move the file to the Trash.

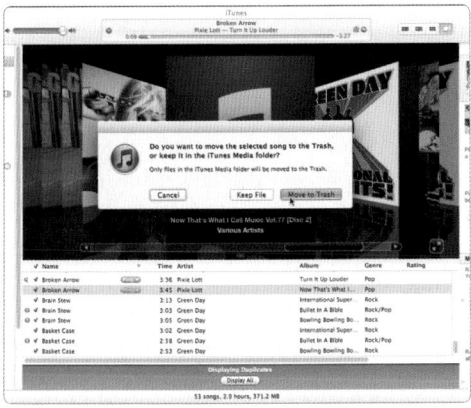

07: Save space

Select Move To Trash to save hard disk space, or Keep File to keep the music track in your Music Library for later reference.

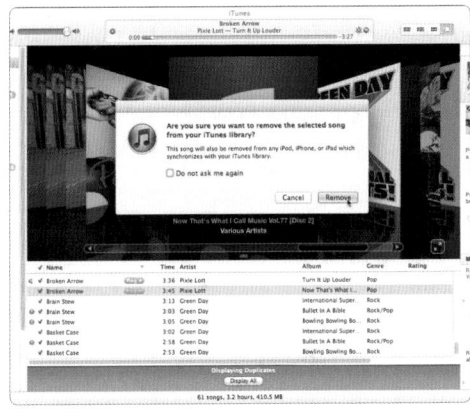

08: Delete multiple files

Hold down the Apple key and click on multiple tracks to delete more than one at a time. This can be a time saver if you have dozens of duplicates.

09: Done and dusted

Finally, make sure to empty your Trash to delete those duplicate files for good. You'll now have a tidier iTunes Music Library and more disk space.

Introducing iLife

Get creative with these in-depth guides to iPhoto, iMovie and GarageBand

174
Quick fixes in iPhoto

180
Sync with iCloud

182
Produce videos

"With iMovie you can turn chaotic clips into smooth video sequences"

"iPhoto can help you make the most of your photos with a variety of edits"

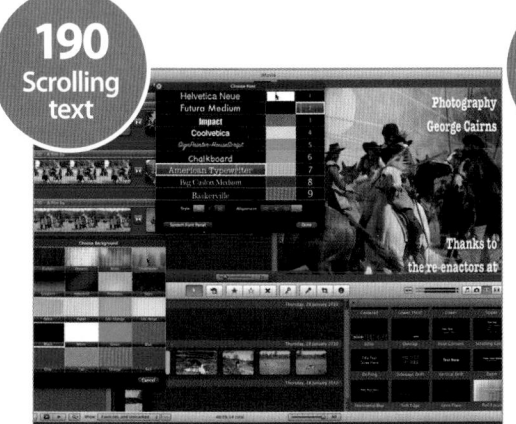

190
Scrolling text

194
Write a song using loops

202
Export audio

Import and erase photos from your camera

Thanks to digital we can click, click and click away! But what do you do when your memory card is full? It's time to import your files…

App used:
iPhoto

Time needed:
10 minutes

Photography can be so wildly creative, but when it comes to the organisation it's a case of 'have to' rather than 'want to'. Thankfully, Apple's iPhoto makes importing and cataloguing all of your images faster and easier than ever before.

Simply connect your camera or iPhone to the Mac via the kit's USB cable, turn the device on and wait for your images to load into the app's Import screen. Make a selection of your top pics, or all of them if you are feeling less brave, and hit the relevant import controls. It's as easy as that!

However, there are a few additional tricks and tips you can employ at the import stage that will save you bundles of time later on. Check out our four-step procedure to find out how to import your images and remove those that you've imported into iPhoto from your camera's memory card so you're free to head back out and snap without any fear of running out of space.

"Simply connect your camera or iPhone to the Mac via USB"

Use iPhoto's Import options to upload snaps

Whether it's a camera or an iPhone, you'll need to know how to import

Import all/selected
These are the two Import buttons that are mentioned in step 2. Pick the button that suits you best

Remove photos already imported
Once you have imported all of the images from your camera, you can opt to remove the originals from your device so as to free up space. Rest assured, they are safe

Autosplit events after importing
Be sure to check this helpful tick box; by doing so iPhoto will organise your photos better by date. If you'd rather they were kept together, leave the box blank

Device
Your device, whether it be iPhone or camera, will be logged here while the importing process is in session

MAKE KEY PHOTO
Now that your set of images forms an Event in its own right you can scan over the thumbnails to run through your pictures. If you find an image which sums up the Event well or will act as the best reminder for the contents, simply Control-click and select Make Key Photo from the menu.

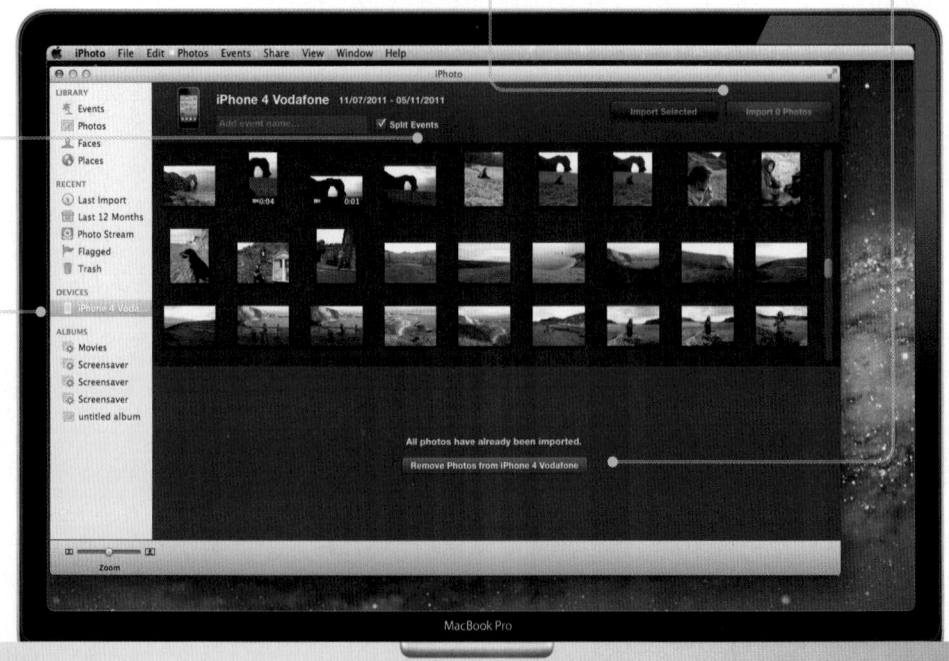

iPhoto Use the Import options to upload your photos

01: Import

Open iPhoto and connect the camera's USB cable to the Mac. Turn the camera on and follow any on-screen instructions. iPhoto will detect the device and log it in the Source pane. Once the preview frames appear, head to Event Name and Description where you can enter details to save time.

02: All or selected?

The great thing about iPhoto's Import function is that it allows you to decide whether to import all of the files on your camera or just selected ones. To make a selection hold down Command and opt for the frames you want to import. Hit the Import Selected button when you're ready.

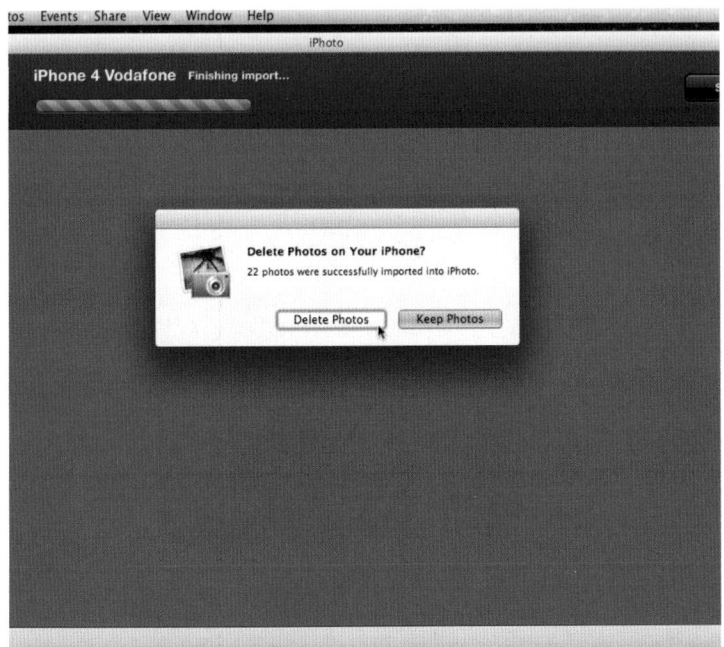

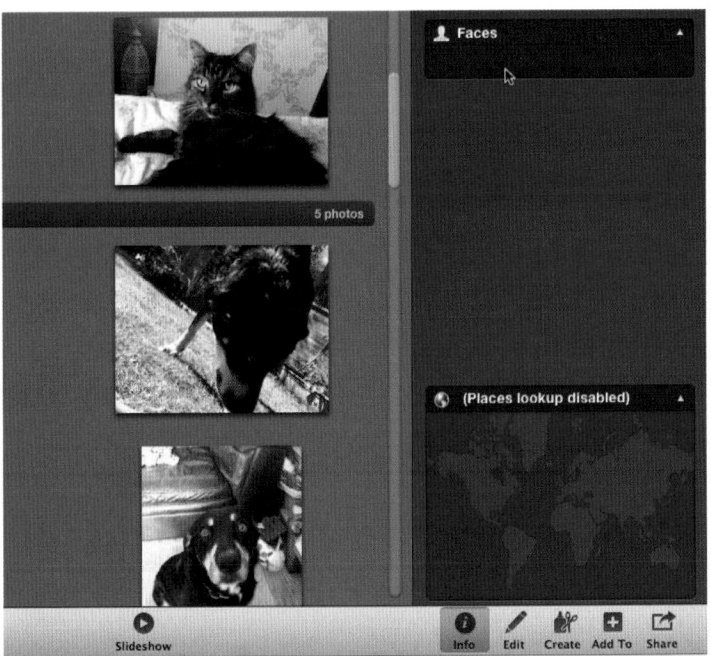

03: Delete or keep?

Once you've selected Import All/Selected, iPhoto will start uploading and storing your files. You can watch as each one is processed. When the process is complete the app will ask you whether you want it to delete or keep the files on your camera or iPhone.

04: Finishing touch

iPhoto will turn this latest import into its own Event. To save time later why not add some additional details right away? Use the Info button to bring up a new window where you can add info about the people in the picture. You can also share the picture or create a slideshow, album, card or photobook.

Organise iPhoto in minutes

Give your photo collection a good old clean-up with these two simple but very effective techniques

App used:
iPhoto

Time needed:
15 minutes

With the sheer simplicity of iPhoto you can get carried away when importing pictures and much sooner than you think, your library can be stuffed to bursting point with your images. This is a great way to collect memories, but you may not want to see every shot you've taken, all of the time. On the other hand, you don't want to delete any pictures either. Luckily iPhoto has a really simple way for you to hide photos and clean up your library without having to get rid of a single picture.

At the other end of this scale it would be nice to have a way to see all the very best pictures in your collection, so you don't have to wade through the ones that you're not as pleased with. iPhoto has

> "iPhoto has a really simple way for you to hide photos"

a nifty way of dealing with this too, which is also so simple you'll wonder how you ever managed without it. All you have to do is apply a star rating to your shots and they will then be grouped automatically by their rating.

In this step-by-step tutorial we show you how you can go about rating and hiding pictures with ease. Another great tip is do this just after every import so you don't end up having to do a massive clearing up operations every couple of months. It's a really simple and quick process then.

iPhoto Show off the best, hide the rest

01: Hover time
Hover your mouse over the bottom portion of a photo and an arrow icon will appear. Click on the arrow to reveal a contextual menu.

02: Rating is a drag
Click and drag your mouse over the dark stars to light them. This rating is stored in the photo's info so that you can view the pic by rating later on.

03: Same but different
Use the same technique to hide an image. Just click the orange Hide icon in the contextual menu. The picture will then disappear from view.

04: Give us a clue
You can check on the progress of your spring-clean here at the top of the interface. The number of hidden images will be displayed here.

05: Rinse and repeat
Use the two techniques detailed to clean and rate an event, or your entire library if you have time. You should be left with a much tidier interface.

06: Check them out
At any time you can see the photos you have hidden by going to the View option in the top iPhoto menu and then clicking on Hidden Photos.

Hide and rate photos
Where you need to go in the interface to
view hidden and rated photos

Indicator
This shows what's going on with
the library. Here it's telling us how
many hidden images are being
shown – an easy way to keep tabs
on the numbers involved in your
spring-clean

Simple system
You can see all the rated images and
all the hidden ones when you like. So
you can opt to have a concise library
for others to view and the full-fat
version when you need it too

Get creative
With your newly organised library
it should be even easier to create
cool slideshows, emails, books and
calendars. Just hit the Create button

Zoom it
Use the zoom slider to get a
view of a whole event. Slide
the slider to the left to reveal
more and more pictures in
the viewer

07: Back for a bit
The photos will reappear in your library with a
marker to show that they've been hidden. To hide
them again, just go back to the View option.

08: See the stars
Use the same View option in the iPhoto menu
to see the ratings on your pictures. Once you've
ticked the option, you'll see the ratings appear.

09: Rate the unrated
Using this view, not only can you see the ratings
you've given but you can easily rate more
pictures using the same technique from step 2.

Use the Quick Fix tools in iPhoto

You don't need to be an expert to get great results –
sometimes a few quick fixes are all that's needed

 **App used:**
iPhoto

 **Time needed:**
10 minutes

 The majority of problems with the photos most people take are not that serious or difficult to fix, and you don't need anything as heavyweight as Photoshop to do it. Even if you're working with images more professionally, a lot of the editing you do is the kind of stuff that iPhoto can do. The idea with iPhoto is to make it as simple as possible while offering the best results, and not blinding you with science. And so it is that you get the ability to crop, rotate and straighten images to fix their orientation. To deal with the dreaded red-eye there's a special tool, and

blemishes can be removed with the Retouch tool. Finally there's a simple one-click 'Enhance' tool which adds definition, brightness and contrast to liven up images that might be lacking something. Read on to find out more…

"The problems with photos most people take are easy to fix"

The Quick Fixes pane
Find out where all the best
photo tweaks can be found

Quick Fixes menu
Enter Edit mode for any picture and click Edit. The first section that appears is the Quick Fixes tools, which let you perform commonly used edit operations

Undo
If you decide you don't like the changes you have made, you can always undo them or indeed revert back to the original. iPhoto always keeps an unedited, original copy of each image

The tools
Crop, rotate and straighten your image or correct red-eye, enhance and get rid of blemishes. Thanks to iPhoto's smart tools, these are all easy to achieve

Settings
Some tools have settings, such as the Retouch tool's size setting. Use this to set the size of the area you want to 'heal' using the blemish removal tool

COMPARE AND CONTRAST
If you have made edits, holding down the Shift key will show you the unedited image, for as long as you hold the key down. This is a good way to see how far you have come from the original, and if you maybe need to stop editing. iPhoto keeps copies of all original images, so you can always try this trick.

iPhoto Use Quick Fix tools

01: Choose an image
Double click on an image, then click on the Edit button at the bottom-right to open the Edit tools. From the menu at the top, choose Quick Fixes.

02: Rotate the image
Click the Rotate button and you can flip images 90 or 180 degrees. iPhoto is good at guessing the orientation of your pictures, however.

03: Enhance your image
Click the Enhance button and iPhoto will add sharpness, contrast and definition. If you don't like the results, you can hit the Undo button.

04: Fix red-eye
Red-eye occurs when a camera's flash reflects in people's eyes. Click on Fix Red Eye, then use the Size slider to match that of the affected area.

05: Zoom in
If needed, use the zoom slider to zoom in to fix red-eye. The auto-fix option will fix problems after recognising that a photo contains a face.

06: Straighten a picture
The Straighten tool can help you to fix wonky images without changing the overall shape of the picture, which it does by zooming in slightly.

07: Crop a picture
Cropping can help you focus on the main interest. Drag to set the area, or choose a preset size value from the drop-down menu under the tool.

08: Retouch a picture
The subject may have a blemish or there may be dirt on the lens, but these things can be removed easily from a shot with the Retouch tool.

09: Make the edit
Set the size of the tool to match the blemish. Click on it and iPhoto takes a sample of the area around it and paints it over the blemish.

Easily edit info for multiple photos

With iPhoto's really easy to use batch editing features you can rename and organise multiple shots in no time at all

App used:
iPhoto

Time needed:
5 minutes

 Importing photos from your camera to your Mac is one thing, keeping them organised with correct titles and descriptions as well as making use of iPhoto's Places feature is another. Fortunately, iPhoto '11 provides two easy ways to batch edit your photo info, leaving you with a perfectly organised iPhoto library without hours of work.

Firstly, the intuitive info pane allows you select a group of photos or a new event and edit details with just a few clicks. The info pane only shows

you the details that affect all photos, leaving off individual info elements such as star ratings. Secondly, the Batch Change item in the menu bar allows for more detailed editing of info such as numbering of your snaps. Here we'll show you how to master both methods of batch info editing.

"Edit details in just a few clicks"

iPhoto Batch edit your photo information

01: Pick it out

Select the event or photos you want to batch edit the info of. Events that haven't had their details edited will show up as 'Untitled event'.

02: Bring up the info

Click on the Info icon in the bottom-right of the window to bring up your event or photo's info pane. Here you can batch edit certain details.

03: Give it a name

Click on the 'Untitled event' title to rename the event; each photo will show up with this title. You can drag new photos into events at a later date.

04: Say what you see

Add a description to give more detail to photos and their events; it's an opportunity to include smaller details such as what an event was like.

05: Locate it

At the bottom of the info pane, enter a location for the photos or event. Type a location and select a more exact match from the list.

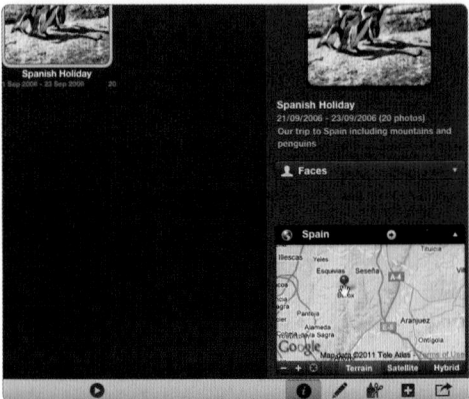

06: An exact match

The pin on the map represents the location where your photos were taken; drag this pin wherever you like to change the geotags.

Batch edit info
Change the details of multiple shots with ease

New events
New events will appear in the Events view titled with either the date the photos were originally imported or the name 'Untitled Event', so it's easy to see which events and photos need their info editing

The info pane
The info pane will display common info elements when you select a group of photos or new event

ADVANCED BATCH EDITING FUNCTIONS
If you're looking to use more advanced batch editing functions, such as adjusting the contrast or exposure for a set of photos, there are a few iPhoto add-ons available online. Alternatively, you could look into creating an Applescript that edits your photos for you.

Last import
If you have a large collection of photos, it might be quicker and easier to click on the 'Last Import' tab in the sidebar to view the photos you most recently imported

Geotags
Some modern cameras will automatically add a geotag to photos to say exactly where they were taken, but you can do this manually from within iPhoto to see your photos on a map

07: Batch change
With your event/photos highlighted, click Photos in the menu bar then click 'Batch Change…' to batch change details such as file name and date.

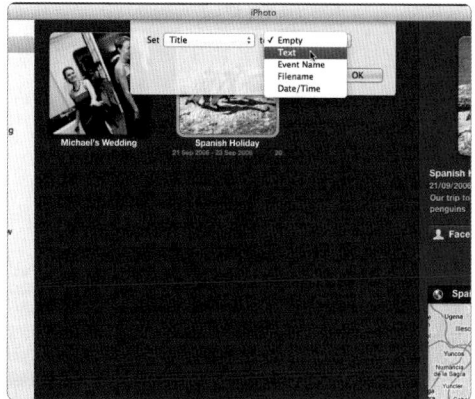

08: Change a title
In the Batch Change panel, select Title and Text from the drop-down menus. Using custom texts for titles make the most sense.

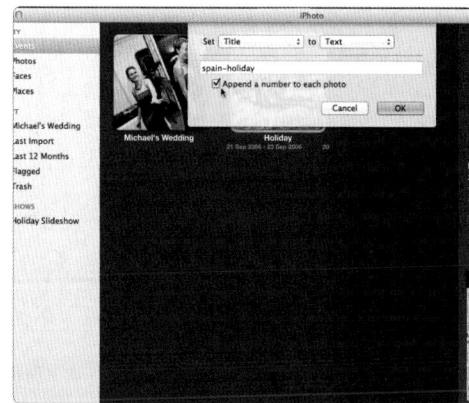

09: Name and number
Enter a title then select 'Append a number to each photo'. This will number each photo making similar snaps easy to distinguish and identify.

Using the Find Faces feature in iPhoto '11

As photo collections grow larger it becomes hard to find pictures of people that are not already tagged. Luckily, Faces is on hand to help

 **App used:** iPhoto

 **Time needed:** 5 minutes

 It's tempting to think that the Faces technology in iPhoto '11 might have originally been developed for some kind of hi-tech security scanning system or something similar. Here, of course, it has far more benign uses, helping you to tag photos of people and make searching easier inside libraries that can run to thousands of photos. Pictures in iPhoto include metadata and you can organise them by date, location and event, but until now there has not been a way to search the actual content of a picture.

> "Faces is a great way to search and group pictures"

Faces changes all that, letting you identify a person then automatically matching other pictures of them, even if they are not looking directly at the camera. It's a great way to search and group pictures. In this tutorial we take you through the simple steps needed to use this amazing feature of iPhoto, so you can quickly organise your photos by tagging people. It's a process that can help keep your photos much more organised.

Find your way around Faces

Organising photos by Faces is really easy. Here's where to go…

A Faces stack
In this view, all pictures of a person that have been identified, after naming by you, are displayed on the corkboard

The Info tab
Press to reveal the Info tab and you can see if there are any unconfirmed matches for that person – pictures that iPhoto thinks might be of them but isn't sure. You can confirm or reject these. The more pictures you correctly tag, the better it gets at guessing

Faces tab
As well as Events, Photos and Places, you can now search and group images using Faces as well. iPhoto automatically scans your library, picks out faces and matches them

The wall
Double-click the name of any person you have identified to change it. This will be updated in the rest of the images tagged of that person

USE FACES WITH FACEBOOK
You can use the Faces feature with Facebook. When you tag people's faces in iPhoto then upload those pictures to Facebook, the tags are carried across. If people's accounts are set up to allow it, they will be notified that a picture of them has been uploaded. When your friends add more tags they appear in your iPhoto library.

iPhoto Set up Faces in iPhoto '11

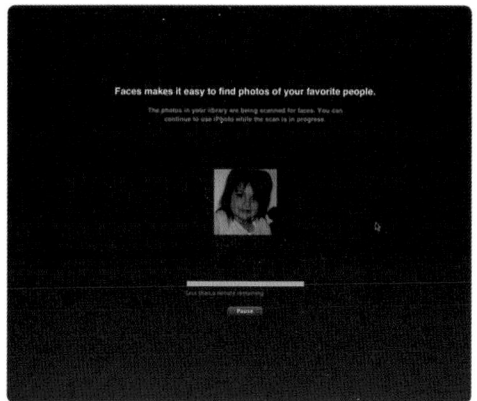

01: Open iPhoto

The first time you open iPhoto '11 it will automatically scan your library for faces. The bigger the library the longer this will take.

02: Click on Faces

Click on the Faces tab on the left to be taken to a corkboard where you can see identified faces. Click in the name fields to add a name them.

03: Continue to Faces

Click Continue to Faces to go to the main wall. Click any person, looking at the bottom-left to see other possible photos of that person.

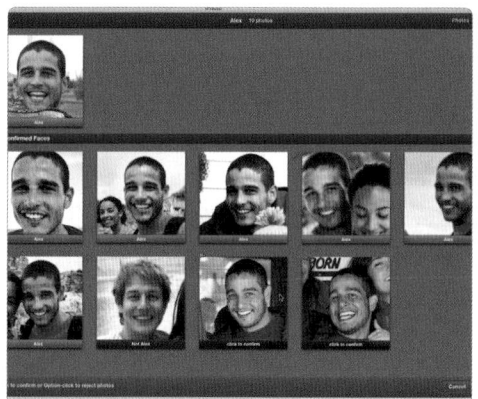

04: Confirm faces

Click Confirm Additional Faces to review any faces and select those that are correct, or click again to reject incorrect matches. Then click Done.

05: Add more faces

From the toolbar at the bottom-right of iPhoto, click on Find Faces and any new or untagged pictures will be shown. Reject, or add names.

06: Quickly preview faces

From the main wall, move the mouse over any Face to see all photos of that person in sequence. Hit space bar on any image to make it topmost.

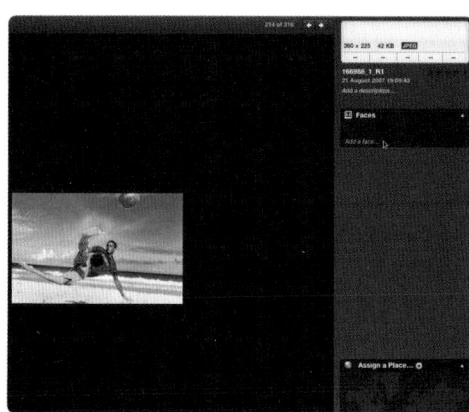

07: Manually add a face

If iPhoto has failed to identify a face, you can double-click the picture and hit the Info button. From the Faces tab on the right click Add A Face.

08: Tag the person

Drag the box over the person's face. Click to add their name in the name field. Hit return to tag. Click the arrow to see all pictures of that person.

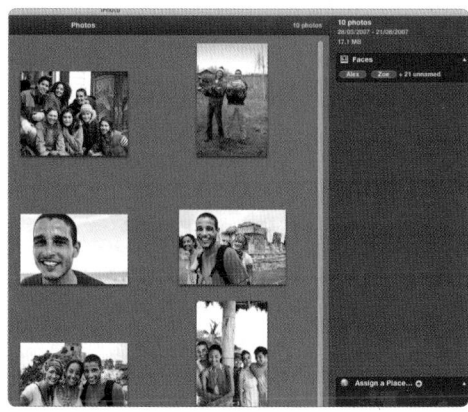

09: Search for faces

When you run a search, you can use a name to see all photos of that person, even if their name is not in the name of the image.

Sync photos between your Mac and iDevice

How to transfer your photos wirelessly and automatically between devices, as soon as you take them

 **App used:** iPhoto

 **Time needed:** 10 minutes

 Apple's new iCloud service, which comes free with the OS X Lion 10.7.2 update, is designed to make your life easier and Photo Stream is a prime example of how it goes about it. With iCloud, when you take a photo on one device – like your iPhone – it will automatically appear on your other devices, including your Mac via Photo Stream. There is no manual syncing to

worry about, no sending, your photos just appear, as if by magic, on all of your devices, so you will always have them close at hand. It's a wondrous

"Your photos will appear magically"

system and easy to set up, all you have to do is ensure that all of your devices are logged into your iCloud account and then activate the Photo Stream feature – after which the only thing you have to worry about is taking great pictures! In this tutorial we guide you through the process of activating your Photo Stream and showcase some of the other great features it offers you.

iPhoto Syncing your images with Photo Stream

01: Open System Preferences

Start by opening your System Preferences app from your Applications folder or Dock and choose the 'iCloud' option under Internet & Wireless.

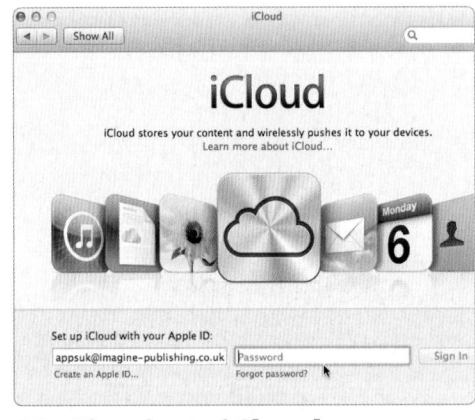

02: Sign in to iCloud

In your iCloud pane, enter your Apple ID and password (or create a new ID) and click on the 'Sign In' button to log into your personal iCloud.

03: Enable Photo Stream

Once you've logged in and set up your personal iCloud, ensure that the 'Photo Stream' option is ticked in the main list of compatible apps.

04: Launch iPhoto

Now launch iPhoto from your Applications and, by default, any photos that are currently on your Mac will be displayed in the main window.

05: Turn on Photo Stream

Click on the 'Photo Stream' option under the 'Recent' section in the left-hand column and then click on the option to 'Turn on Photo Stream'.

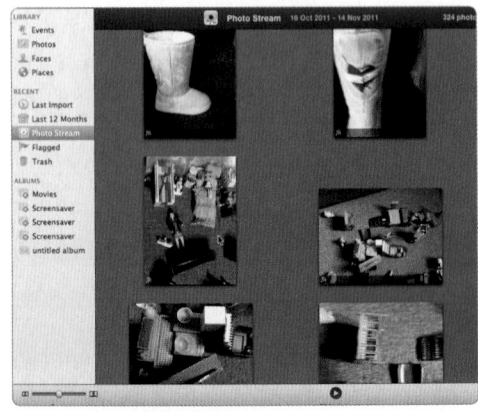

06: Auto upload

Any images taken on devices that are connected to your iCloud, such as your iPhone or iPad 2 will be automatically uploaded to your Photo Stream.

Transfer photos
With iCloud you can instantly transfer photos

Your Photo Stream
Images uploaded to your iCloud Photo Stream will be automatically downloaded to the iPhoto app on your Mac and will be viewable in the 'Photo Stream' section in the left-hand column

Syncing your photos
As long as the Photo Stream box is ticked in your Mac iCloud window then all of you photos will be synced to your personal iCloud without the need to manually transfer

Your iCloud
If you are logged into the same iCloud account on all of your devices, then images you take on one device will be pushed to your other devices wirelessly without prompting

07: Clear out
Once photos appear in your Photo Stream you can delete them from the original source to free up space to continue taking more.

08: Your photo library
Copies of images synced via Photo Stream will be added to your iPhoto library, meaning you can instantly edit and share them with the world.

09: Multi-formats
If you connect a digital camera to your Mac, photos on that device will be added to your Photo Stream and pushed to other devices.

Produce great holiday season videos

 **App used:** iMovie

 **Time needed:** 25 minutes

Turn chaos into order and produce smooth-flowing video sequences

During holiday seasons, the combination of free time and a house full of partying family and friends often leads to the camcorder being whipped out to record the chaos. This can mean lots of raw footage to plough through once the party season is over.

With a little thought you can capture party footage that will edit together in iMovie as a slick sequence that you can share with friends and family to relive the highlights of the holiday season.

We've supplied party footage on your disc for you to work with, but you can apply our shooting and editing tricks and techniques to your own holiday footage. Read on and you'll transform your rough footage into an entertaining video in no time.

"Transform footage into a slick movie"

iMovie Shoot and edit great holiday videos

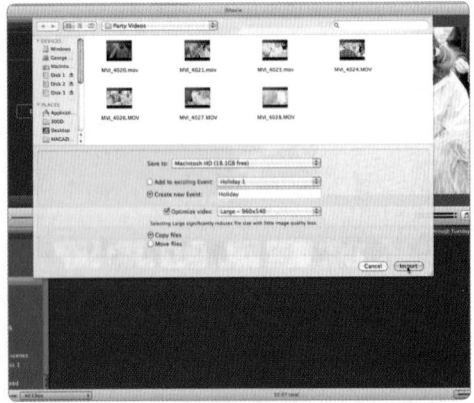

01: Import Movies
Go to File>Import>Movies. Import Party Videos' clips to an Event called Holiday. Copy Files. Tick Import. Tick Optimize Video Large – 960x540.

02: Create new project
Go to File>Create New Project. Call it Holiday Video. As the clips are HD, choose a 16:9 Aspect Ratio. Set Theme to None. Click Create.

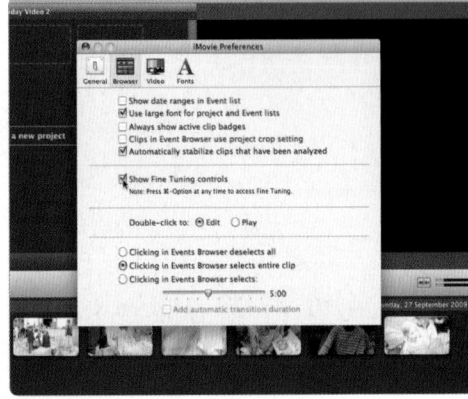

03: Set preferences
Go to iMovie Preferences. Click on the Browser tab. Select 'Clicking in Events Browser selects entire clip'. Tick 'Show Fine Tuning controls'.

04: Chronological order
The clips in the Event Browser are displayed chronologically. We'll refer to them as Clip 1 for the first shot, Clip 2 for the second and so on.

05: Establishing shot
Click on Clip 2 and drag it to the Project window. Click on the clip to activate the yellow editing box. Expand the box to select the first seconds.

06: Quick Trim
Right-click inside the yellow box and choose Trim to selection from the list of options. We now have a wide shot of the location that sets the scene.

Set the mood

Your choice of font, colour and styling
can affect the mood of your video

Audio inserts

If a particular piece of footage
is out of focus, you can still
salvage its soundtrack and use
it to enhance your programme.
Here we've inserted dialogue
from one clip over another
clip's picture

HD happy

iMovie will happily combine HD
quality footage with high-resolution
stills from your digital camera to
produce a holiday video with high
production values

Name in lights

The animated titles in the Titles
browser are like the icing on the
cake. The sparkling stars in the
Boogie Lights title are perfect
for introducing your holiday-
themed video

Video Inspector

When dealing with a chaotic
holiday shoot you may not
have time to tinker with
camera settings. You can use
the Video Inspector to tweak
exposure and colour to help
problem shots fit in with
correctly exposed clips

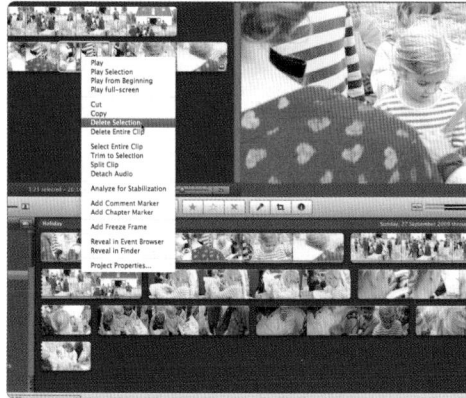

07: Delete duff moves

Add Clip 4 to the project. Select the shaky zoom
from a mid-shot to a close-up of the birthday girl.
Right-click and choose Delete Selection.

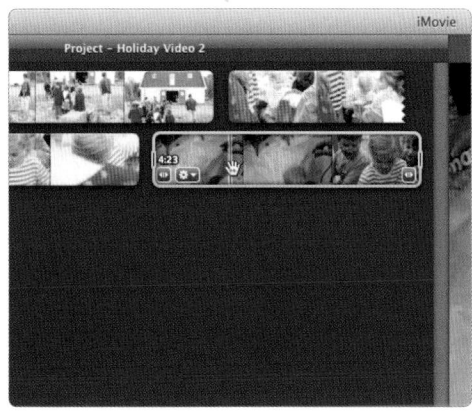

08: Visual variety

Add Clip 6. This starts with a shot of the gift, then
tilts up to the child. This variety of subject matter
avoids lots of jarring jump cuts of the same child.

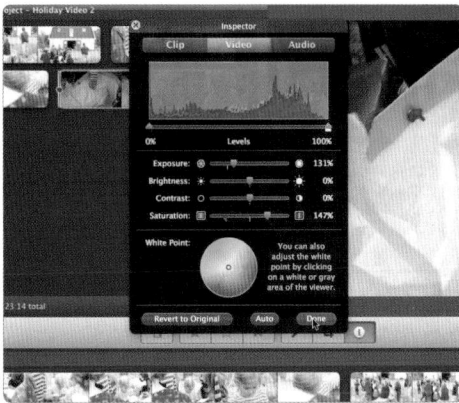

09: Adjust Exposure

Clip 6 is under-exposed. Press V to open the
Video Inspector. Drag Exposure to 131% and
saturation to 147%, helping shots look consistent.

iMovie Shoot and edit great holiday videos (continued)

10: Fine-tune
Click the Fine-tune icon at the end of the last clip and drag it back 11 frames so it ends when the boy says "whoa!" This avoids clipping words.

11: Change angle
Add Clip 5. This cuts from a low to a high angle, as if we had two cameras running simultaneously. Tilting to the dad allows us to cut back to the girl.

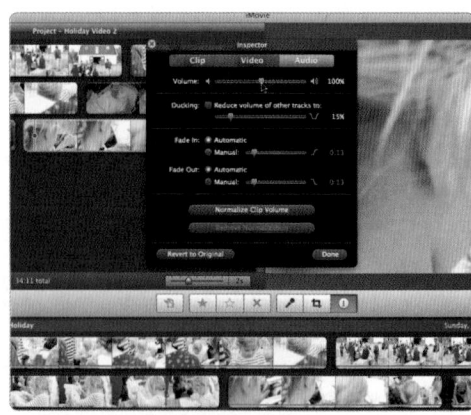

12: Moving camera
Keep the camera moving. Add Clip 4, in which we start low and stand up to create a no-budget crane shot. Press A to open Audio Inspector.

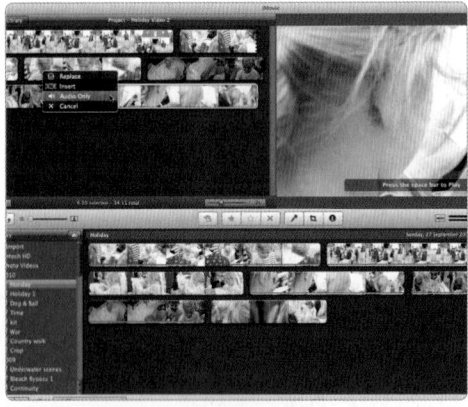

13: Replace sound
The cameraman is talking, so fade the Volume. Click Done. Drag Clip 3 onto the last clip and choose Audio Only.

14: Overlap sound
To avoid gaps in audio drag the green sound bar so that it overlaps the previous clip. Fine-tune the end of the clip so it finishes when the sound does.

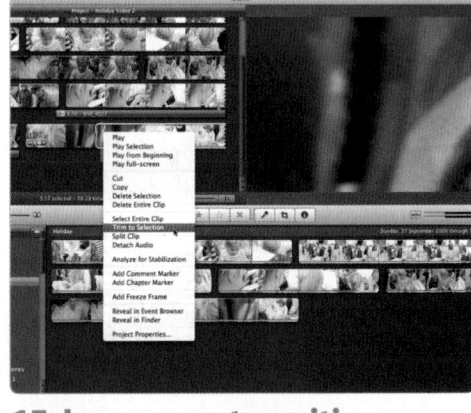

15: In-camera transition
Add Clip 2. Select and trim the clip so that it starts with the balloon obscuring the girl. The balloon floats away to reveal her, like a wipe transition.

16: Import stills
Drag the folder of party stills onto iPhoto's icon. Then in iMovie click the Show Photos Browser. Go to Last Import to see the party stills.

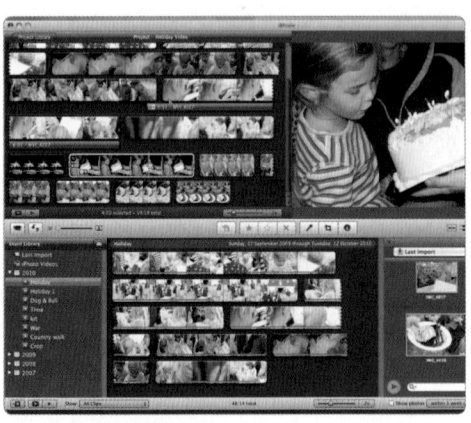

17: Add stills
Add the stills from the Photos Browser. By default they'll run for four seconds, with a random animated Ken Burns effect adding movement.

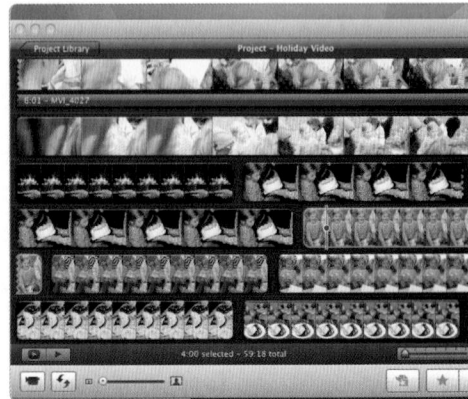

18: Edit movement
Ken Burns effects won't suit every photo. Click the Gear icon and choose Cropping, Ken Burns & Rotation. Set a suitable start and end point.

Adding effects
Get creative with your home movies

SHORTCUTS
After clicking on a clip you can open the Inspector by pressing I. This gives you access to the Inspector's Clip, Video or Audio tabs so that you can tweak the clip's speed, adjust its exposure or boost its sound levels for example. For a faster work flow, jump straight to the Video inspector by pressing V. Summon the Audio Inspector by pressing A.

Marvellous music
Drop a music track onto the background of the Project window to apply it to the whole movie. The music helps knit all the individual photos and video clips together into a seamless, smooth-flowing sequence

Following
Tap the Following button to see a list of everyone you currently follow. If you want to unfollow, tap the person's name and then tap the Unfollow button

Duration
For a short and snappy photomontage keep the transitions short and consistent. Click on a transition's gear icon, choose Transition Adjustments and type in a value like 1:00 second. Tick the Applies to all transitions box

19: Add transitions
Click Show Transitions icon. Drag a Page Curl Left transition between the last video clip and the first still. Click the Gear and set Duration to 1:00 sec.

20: Add title
Click the Show Titles icon and drag the Boogie Nights Title onto the first shot. Edit the text then hit the spacebar to preview the animated title.

21: Incidental music
Add a suitable soundtrack from the Music Browser. Use the Inspector to reduce Volume to 16%. Manually fade the music out over 1:00 sec.

Create a better soundtrack

The key to a good movie is getting the sound as well as the visuals right. iMovie '11 now has all the tools you need

 **App used:** iMovie

 **Time needed:** 10 minutes

 While visuals for movies are obviously very important, poor sound can make a project seem less professional. The biggest culprit is uneven sound – sound that jumps wildly from one scene to another. In one it might be really quiet and in the next really loud, creating a jarring crossover that is unpleasant for the viewer. In one scene you might have a lot of deep rumble in the sound from an air conditioner or road noise but in the next, no background noise at all.

Of course, it would be unnatural to mess with the sound too much, but there's a happy medium where you edit just enough to give a smooth and polished feel to the overall sound. We'll show you how it works…

> "Uneven sound creates a jarring crossover that is unpleasant to hear"

Get to grips with audio
Use the iMovie inspector to tweak your noises

Level meters
Keep an eye on the level meters to see how the overall sound levels are looking. These give you a better representation than simply believing your speakers, because they may be turned up or down too far and so give you an inaccurate reading

Equalisation
EQ is really handy as it lets you cut or boost ten bands, in this case, of frequencies. If a clip is too bassy, knock off some of the bottom end. To enhance voices, try pulling up the mid-range. To get rid of hiss, knock down the very top end

Volume slider
The most fundamental control you have to work with audio, this controls the overall volume of the clip. Match volume relative to other clips

Enhance
You can choose to reduce the background noise in a clip using a variable amount slider. This is good for getting rid of road noise or hiss, but be careful not to knock out sounds you wanted to keep

VOICE-OVER
By clicking on the microphone button in iMovie's toolbar you can access the voice-over tool. This allows you to use your Mac's built-in mic or an external mic to record voice-over directly into a project and associate it with a clip if you like. It's great for narrating holiday or even corporate videos.

iMovie Editing sound for better results

01: Select a clip

Find a clip with 'problem' sound, eg one louder than those next to it. Double-click it to open the floating Inspector window. Click on the Audio tab.

02: Change the volume

Here you can change the overall volume of the video's audio. This is the quickest way to deal with a clip being too loud or too short.

03: Normalise the volume

If a clip is too quiet, use the Normalize button to have it analysed and raise its volume so it doesn't clip. This action can be undone if it's not right.

04: Reduce background noise

If a clip has too much background noise, hit Enhance and use the slider to determine how much noise is removed.

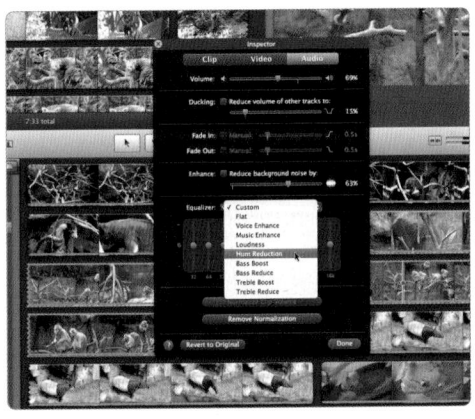

05: Use EQ

Equalisation is useful. Activate it then choose a preset like Hum Reduction or Treble Reduce. Play back to see if they fix the sound to your liking.

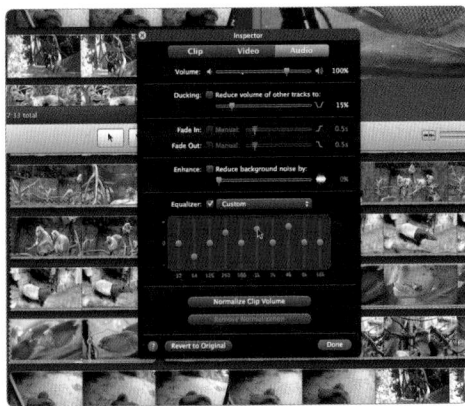

06: Set EQ manually

To tweak an EQ preset, move the sliders. Lowest frequency is on the left and highest on the right. Raise or lower one to boost or cut the level.

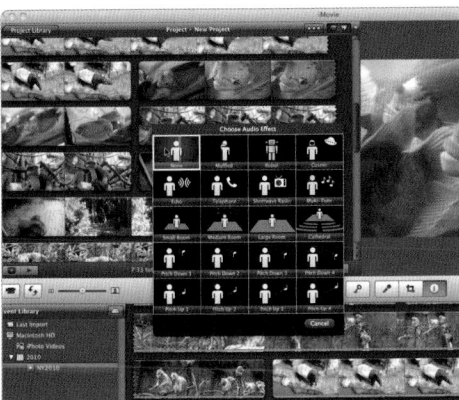

07: Use effects

In the Clip menu and you can add an audio effect to the clip. Choose from the presets and hover over one to hear the sound played through it.

08: Use fades

In the Audio menu, you can add manual fade-ins/outs, independent of transitions – handy at the start and end or when you need some silence.

09: Cut and paste settings

Select a clip you've edited and Edit>Copy. Choose other clips and Edit>Paste Adjustments >Audio to apply the same settings to those clips.

Add slo-mo special effects in iMovie '11

Use iMovie '11 to add interest and character to your projects by using slow motion and other speed effects

App used: iMovie

Time needed: 5 minutes

Manipulating speed is made much easier by the technology behind digital video. When working with analogue tape, slowing the speed of playback could cause unwanted side effects like wobble and jitter. With digital source material, however, the computer can easily alter the number of frames per second. Slow motion in movies is often used in action scenes to show things that happen very quickly in more detail, which enhances the dramatic tension. For home movies it can also be useful for changing the pace

"Enhance your film's drama and tension"

of a scene, or simply to make a short clip last a bit longer than its original duration for the purposes of filling out some time.

iMovie makes adding slo-mo effects extremely simple, enabling you to add a sense of drama to your video footage and create something really professional. Follow this step-by-step tutorial to find out how it's done.

iMovie   Add a slo-mo effect

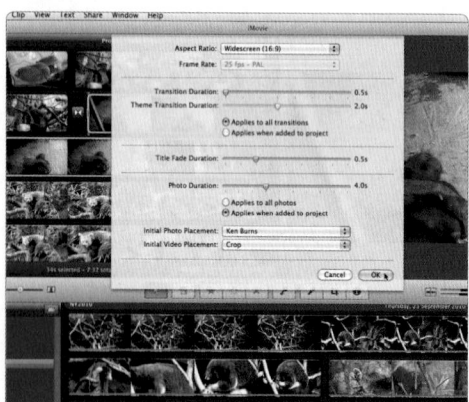

01: Import your footage

Import footage from your camera. It's likely to be a high frame rate (25 or 30fps). To check the project frame rate, go to File>Project Properties.

02: Select the clip

Select a clip in the project, but not in the source bin. Only when a clip exists in a project can you modify its speed.

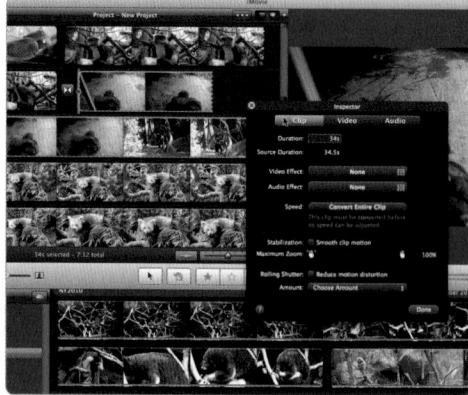

03: Open the Inspector

Click the 'I' button in the toolbar or choose Window>Clip Adjustments. This is contextual and will show properties for whichever clip you select.

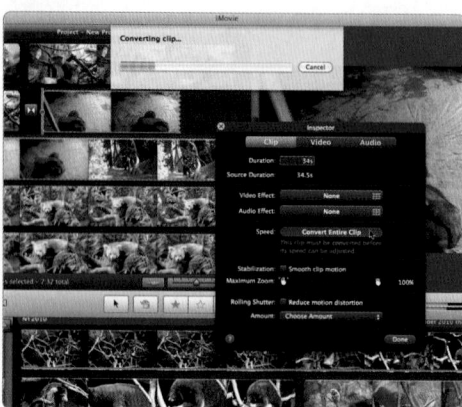

04: Convert the clip

Before clip speed can be changed, the clip must be analysed by iMovie. Click the button marked "Convert Entire Clip" in the Speed section.

05: Change the speed

Use the Speed slider to change the speed, or, enter a numerical value for a percentage of the original speed or a new value in seconds.

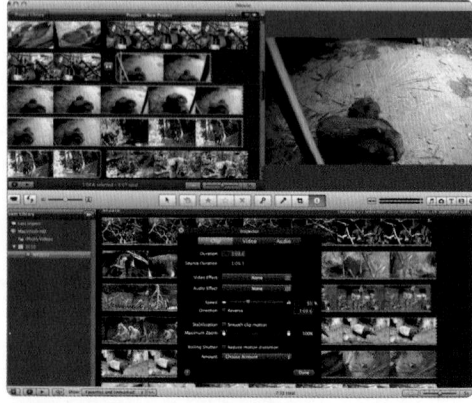

06: See the results

You should see the clip extend itself on the timeline. Try playing it back. It may look a more jerky but it should be slower.

Find your way around the Inspector panel

Discover the flexibility of editing your clips in iMovie '11

Speed slider
Change a clip's speed by using this slider. Left for slower and right for faster. Use the Reverse button to play it backwards

Duration
The duration of your clip and also the source duration. Use this to see if a clip has been altered, and by how much

SLOW SOUND
If you want to slow a clip's sound down independently of the video, right click on a clip then select Detach Audio. Then use the Inspector panel to independently change the speed of the audio using controls similar to those for video. Once audio is separated like this, you can move it around a project independently, for greater flexibility.

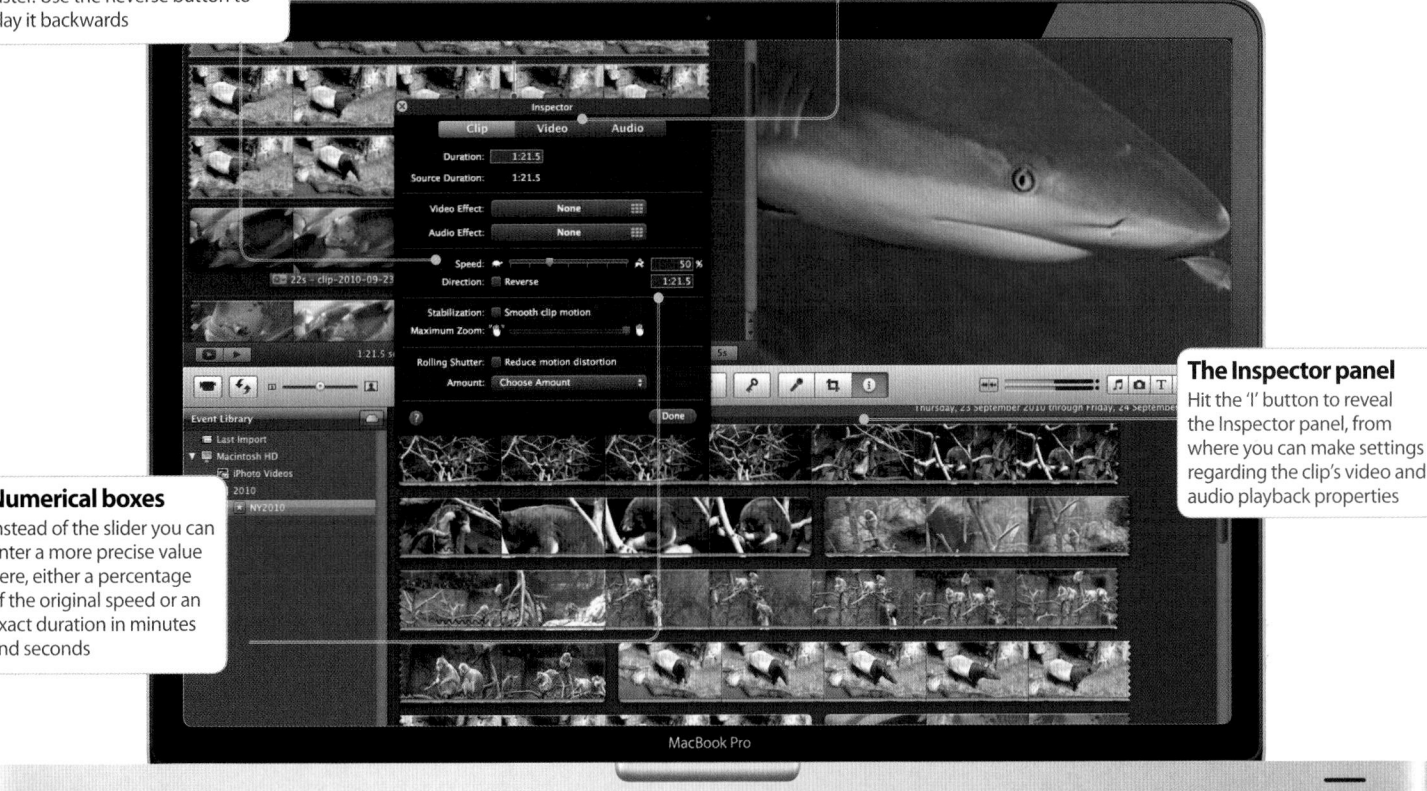

Numerical boxes
Instead of the slider you can enter a more precise value here, either a percentage of the original speed or an exact duration in minutes and seconds

The Inspector panel
Hit the 'I' button to reveal the Inspector panel, from where you can make settings regarding the clip's video and audio playback properties

07: Try a new value

For extreme slowness, choose a low value. You can also go to the Clip menu and choose Clip>Slow Motion and then use a preset value.

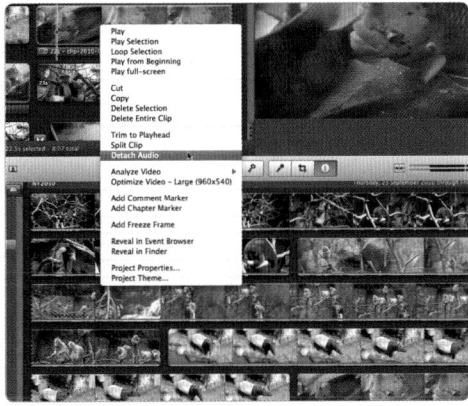

08: Save the sound

You may notice the sound has slowed. To avoid this, before you slow the clip, right-click on it and choose Detach Audio. Then perform the slo-mo.

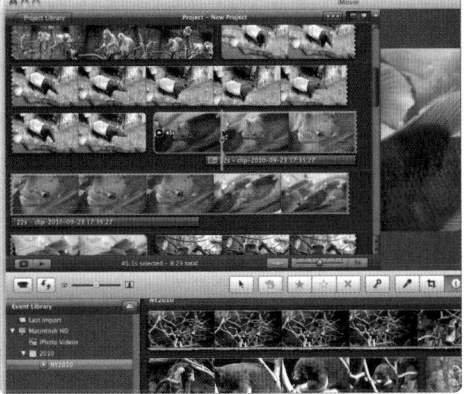

09: Move the sound

The video may be slower but the sound is the same speed and no longer covers the length of the clip. Add sound to fill the gaps.

Add a scrolling text effect

A video is incomplete without being top and tailed by a title and credits sequence. Here's how to make those credits roll!

 **App used:** iMovie

 **Time needed:** 5 minutes

 Veterans of tape-to-tape video editing suites will remember the hassle of adding captions and titles to their films. You had to print your title or credits on a sheet of paper, use a vision mixer to invert the clip and turn black lettering to white, then key the text over the footage. To get the text to actually scroll involved splashing out cash on an expensive caption generator. Thanks to iMovie, however, we can add slick-looking text with ease (and customise font, colour and alignment to suit our footage too). We can also make those credits scroll in a smooth and professional looking way. Read our tutorial to find out how you can easily add scrolling text to your video footage.

> "Thanks to iMovie we can easily add slick looking text"

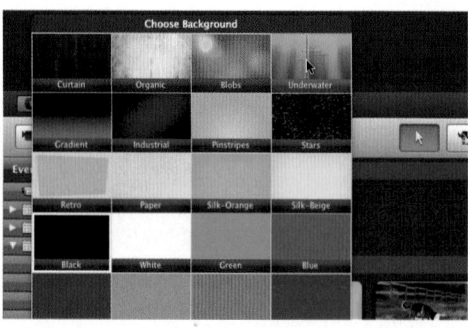

iMovie Create a rolling credits sequence

01: Import photos
To begin your titles, you need to drag your own photos into iPhoto. You can then easily import them into iMovie.

02: Open iMovie
In iMovie create a new project. Click the Show Photo browser icon and click on Last Import. Drag the stills into the Project window.

03: Change duration
By default each still runs for four seconds. To speed the sequence up select a clip and press 'i'. Type a Duration of 3:00. Tick 'Applies to all stills'.

04: Add transitions
Each still is given a random camera move to make it more interesting. To blend the stills together, drag a Cross Dissolve transition between each image.

05: Scrolling text
Click on the Show Titles browser icon. Drag Scrolling Credits onto the first still. Drag the blue bar to extend the credits through the whole sequence.

06: Edit the text
Replace the placeholder text with something more relevant. Tap the Return key a few times to put some space between each credit.

Create a credits sequence in iMovie

Use iMovie's Titles browser to add rolling text to your footage

Flattering font
When choosing a font, make sure that it's legible – especially if you're rendering a small video for iPod viewing

Neutral colour
Although it is tempting to add colour to your text (see step 7), you'll find that a nice neutral white suits any footage and is a lot easier to read

MAY THE FORCE BE WITH YOU...
One of the most famous scrolling text sequences in a movie is the long intro at the beginning of the Star Wars films. This epic scrolling text slowly recedes into the distance over a star field backdrop. You can pay homage to this sequence by adding the Far Far Away title to your project. There's even a starscape backdrop in the Choose Background panel.

Alignment
By aligning your font to the right (instead of the default central position) you can stop it from obscuring any of your on-screen footage

Animated backgrounds
Instead of scrolling text over footage or stills you can choose one of several animated backdrops, like this cool underwater caustic lighting effect

07: Modify fonts

Click Show Fonts and choose a font to suit your footage. We picked a red to match the tunics of our riders and aligned the text to the right.

08: Quality control

You can add more credits at any time. iMovie will underline possible spelling mistakes to help your production look more professional.

09: Add music

Rolling credits look more professional with an accompanying score, so drag a suitable jingle (like Pursuit) into the Project window.

Change the available fonts in iMovie

Customise your titles with any of the fonts on your Mac

App used:
iMovie

Time needed:
10 minutes

iMovie can be a confusing application, not because it's hard to use, but because some of the more advanced functions can be tucked away in unlikely places. Changing the fonts often requires using the font panel and then locating a desired font each and every time you create text for titles. It is possible to save yourself some vital time and change the stock fonts that appear in the list of nine every time you hit the Fonts button on the titles screen.

Luckily we're here to tell you that this can be done very simply indeed, but you'll need to load the fonts you want in the iMovie preferences first. Then, when you come to add your titles you can use the perfect font each and every time without having to search and select. You are still limited to the nine available in the dialogue box but it can be any nine that you have selected in the Preferences. So, spice up your work with cool fonts today.

"Save yourself some vital time searching for fonts"

iMovie Add fonts to iMovie

01: Load it, font it

Load the Preferences by clicking on iMovie in the menu and then selecting Preferences. Now click on the Fonts tab at the top of the dialogue window.

02: Drop down, choose

Click on the drop-down arrow next to the font you wish to change. Then pick the font you wish to add to the list in place of the one you selected.

Create stills for your projects

Turn the best frames from your video footage into stunning stills, which you can then use to add texture and variety to your iMovie projects

 **App used:** iMovie

 **Time needed:** 10 minutes

 When you shoot a photograph with your digital camera, it can sometimes be tricky to trigger the shutter at the perfect moment. This means you might miss capturing spontaneous events. By shooting a scene on video you have hundreds of potential still images to play with. Take this tutorial's source footage for example – you'll find it on the disc. In the clip a little girl runs around on a beach, then brings a seashell to her parents. The moment she hands the shell to her mother creates a perfect composition. This special moment would be easy to miss if we were just shooting photos with a digital camera.

Luckily iMovie enables us to turn this frame into a still image of any duration. You can use the techniques described in our walkthrough to generate several stills, then mix between them using transitions to create a montage sequence that adds texture and a sense of variety to your video projects.

"Add texture and variety to you video projects"

iMovie Turn video footage into stills

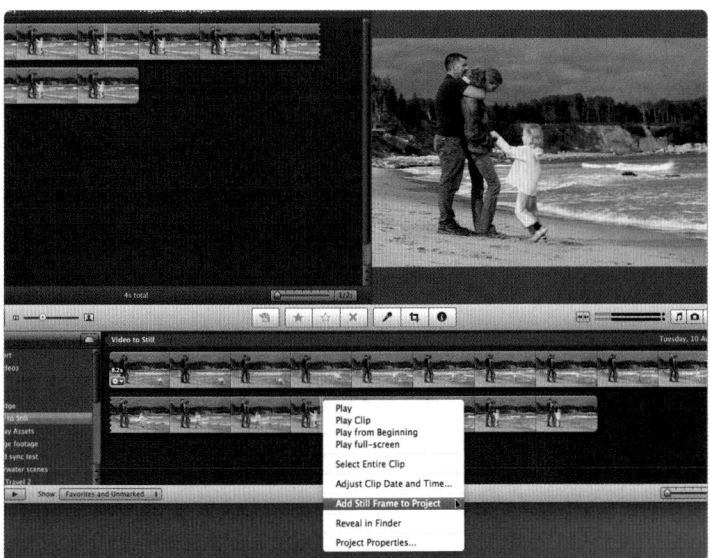

01: Import footage
Choose File>Import>Movies. Browse to Beach.mov on your disc. Set Optimize Video to Full – Original Size. Create a new event and click OK.

02: Create still frame
Scrub the cursor over the clip until the girl hands over the shell. Control click then choose Add Still Frame to Project to make a four second still.

Write a song in GarageBand

GarageBand's Apple Loop library contains more than a thousand potential seeds to kick-start your next project

 **App used:**
GarageBand

 **Time needed:**
50 minutes

There are no hard and fast rules when it comes to writing a song. Some people start off with a melody or lyric idea, others come up with a chord progression on piano or guitar, while many use a drum beat for their initial inspiration. Each and every time though, however you start, the essential building blocks of chords, melody and rhythm remain constant, so just that little extra push to get started is often all that's required.

GarageBand ships with a library of over 1,000 Apple Loops that can be great catalysts to get those creative juices flowing. We're going to examine how to use these to help your musical ideas take shape, with the aim of having a finished song at the end of the process. Obviously, everybody writes songs in their own way, so the order of the steps below is subject to some individual interpretation!

> "GarageBand ships with a library of over 1,000 Apple Loops to get those creative juices flowing"

Get a song started with GarageBand

Let Apple Loops be your muse

Special arrangement
The beauty of using the Arrangement track when songwriting is that entire sections of your project can be swapped around, copied or deleted just by dragging the Arrangement track regions

Loop families
Some Apple Loops form part of a series of similar loops known as a family. These are identified by small arrows near the loop's name which, when clicked, reveal other similar loops that can be selected

RECORDING GUITAR
If you prefer to write on guitar, you can plug your guitar into your Mac using an adapter such as IK Multimedia's iRig, then create a new electric guitar track by clicking the + button in the lower-left of the screen and choosing the electric guitar option. This will give you access to GarageBand's collection of software guitar amps and pedals.

Switch input source
Switching your Mac's input source between its built-in line and mic inputs is done by changing the Audio Input setting in the Audio/MIDI pane of GarageBand's preferences menu

Count in
When recording new parts, you can enable or disable the one-bar count-in and metronome features by clicking on them in the Control menu

GarageBand Songwriting from scratch in GarageBand

01: Create new project

From the intro screen, select a new Songwriting project by clicking the icon and then Choose. Set a save location, tempo & key and click Create.

02: Prepare project

The project contains some preloaded tracks and a drum loop. You can delete this by clicking it and choosing Delete from the Edit menu.

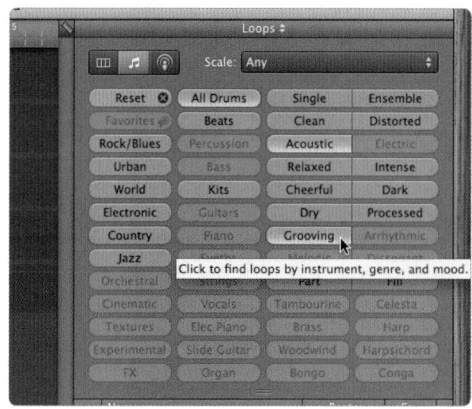

03: Browse loops

Click the eye icon in the lower-right corner to reveal the Loop browser. Click the filter buttons to narrow your search to the type of loops you want.

04: Drag and drop

Click the name of a loop to listen to it. Find one you like, drag it into the arrange window, then drag the upper-right corner to the right length.

05: Add bass and keyboards

Click the track and record a part with a MIDI keyboard. Click the + button to add new tracks and keep adding until you've built a section.

06: Record melody

If you have a melody idea, select the voice track and click the Record button. Record your melody over your tracks, then hit the space bar to stop.

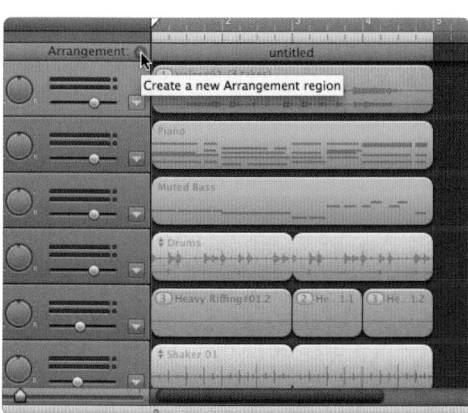

07: Show Arrangement Track

Choose Show Arrangement Track from the Track menu. Click the + button to create a new arrange region. If it's too long, drag the right edge back.

08: Rename and copy

Double-click where it says Untitled and name the section Verse or Chorus. Click-hold the name, hold the Alt key and drag to the right to copy.

09: Change parts

To replace regions in your copied section, select them and choose a new take or hit the Backspace key and record in new parts.

Import and edit MIDI files in GarageBand

App used: GarageBand

Time needed: 30 minutes

Download MIDI file versions of your favourite tunes from the web and import them into GarageBand for editing

MIDI files contain musical performance data – sequences of recorded notes programmed to use the standard set of 128 general MIDI sounds found on most PC soundcards. By importing the data into GarageBand, you can reproduce a performance by assigning your own choice of GarageBand's built-in software instrument sounds to the individual MIDI parts. The beauty of this system is that you can dissect MIDI parts and assign better sounds to

them, creating something that sounds closer to or even better than the original. This means you have the freedom to rework your favourite tunes into something really special. We show you how to do it – let's get searching!

"Rework tunes into something special"

Use MIDI files in GarageBand
Produce your own versions of your favourite songs

Add your own
Once you've got all your parts playing back correctly, why not add your own? GarageBand makes it easy to record in additional MIDI parts or add Apple Loops to further embellish your version of the tune

Muted melody
As these are instrumental versions, there will usually be a part playing the main vocal melody. You can mute this out with this button if you don't need to hear it

Note events
These blocks represent notes like the notches in a paper piano roll. The higher up the screen they are, the higher in pitch the note they represent. Drag notes up and down to change their pitch

VELOCITY
Velocity sensitivity differs from sound to sound, so once you've assigned a new sound to a part, it's likely that you'll need to tweak the velocity response. The harder you hit a key when you play it, the higher that note's velocity value will be. Higher velocities therefore equal louder parts.

Push the tempo
To adjust the tempo of your project once your MIDI file has been imported, select the Project option from the LCD display mode pop-up menu, then drag the slider to set the new tempo

GarageBand Importing MIDI files

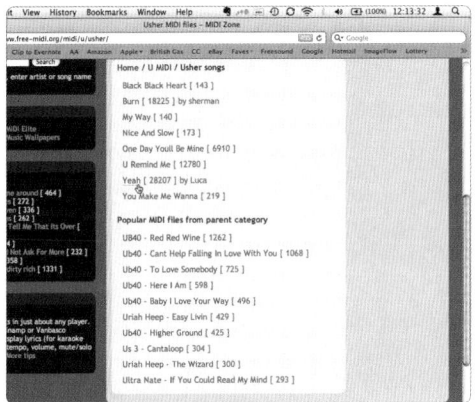

01: Search for MIDI files
Search online for MIDI files and several MIDI file sites will appear, many of them offering free downloads. Browse the site and choose a song.

02: Download file
Ctrl-click the desired file and select Download Linked File As. Now save it to your hard drive in an easy-to-find location, such as the desktop.

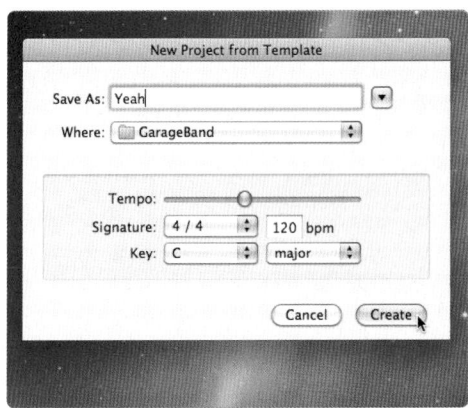

03: Create new project
Launch GarageBand and choose the Piano option. In the Save As window, type the name of the track you're about to import.

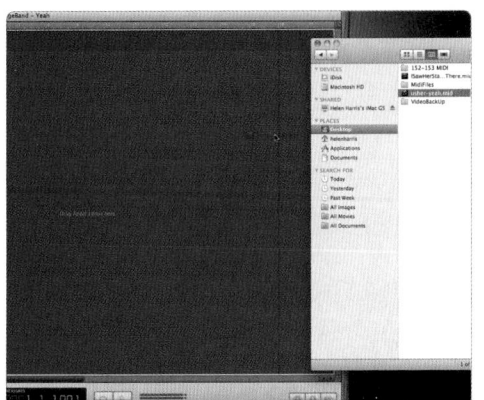

04: Drag and drop
Drag the downloaded file from the Finder into the Arrange window, and watch as the tracks split out. Hit play and have a listen to what you've got.

05: Change instrument
If a part is being played by the wrong instrument, highlight the track header and click the 'i' button to open the Track Info pane.

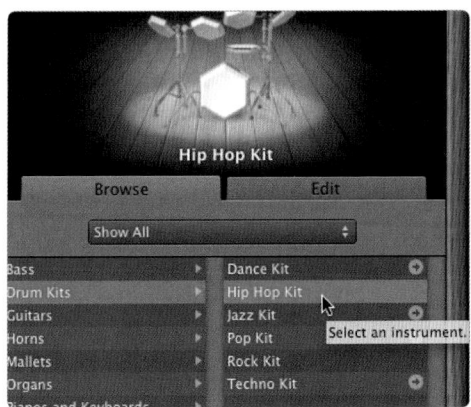

06: Select new sound
Select a new instrument and sound preset from the list. You can do this while the track is playing back to audition sounds quicker.

07: Edit instrument
Click the Edit tab at the top of the Track Info pane to access the Effects panel. Here you can insert effect plug-ins to change the instrument's sound.

08: Edit part
To edit the notes within a part, double-click it in the Arrange window, or select the part and click the scissors button in the bottom toolbar.

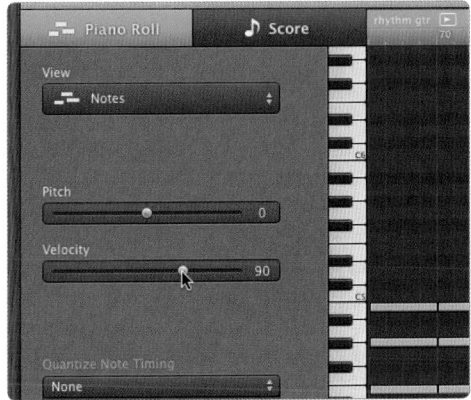

09: Adjust note velocity
To make your parts dig in a bit more, alter the overall velocity of a part by selecting all the notes with Cmd+A and using the Velocity slider.

Introducing iLife

Use the Master Track in GarageBand

Learn how to insert automation and effects on the Master Track

 **App used:** GarageBand  **Time needed:** 10 minutes

 As a multitrack audio and MIDI workstation, GarageBand is capable of handling projects containing large numbers of tracks. In addition to all the regular tracks, however, each project also contains a Master Track through which the audio from the entire project passes before it reaches your audio outputs. This is normally hidden, but with the exception of pan, solo and mute controls, it actually behaves just like a regular track. Any effects you insert on the Master Track will be placed across the whole song, so

you can use it to compress and EQ your mix and use automation to fade your track in and out.

Which brings us neatly to the subject of this tutorial. It's unusual for commercial tracks to have a structured, abrupt ending, the norm being to fade the track out over a repeated section at the end of the song. This follows a tradition going back many years, so if you want your song to have the classic 20-second fadeout, here is how you do it. It's not as hard as you might think, so follow our steps and you will have a more professional track in not time at all.

The Master Track panel
Where you need to go to fade your music out

Track Info
Reveal the Master Track info pane by double-clicking the Master Track's header. Alternatively, you can also do it by clicking the 'i' button in the lower right toolbar and clicking the Master Track tab

Fade away
You can place automation nodes anywhere you like along the volume curve to vary the overall volume of your song. Fadeouts are standard, but why not fade it in as well?

Automation menu
As well as volume, you can choose to automate the master pitch or tempo settings by selecting the desired parameter from this menu and placing nodes on the curve in the same way

NODES JOB
Nodes are control points used to set particular parameter values at particular points in time. Clicking anywhere on an automation curve will create a node that can then be dragged up or down to set a level change. To delete an unwanted node, simply select it (currently selected nodes are displayed white and larger than normal) and press the Backspace key

Automate effects
If you enable one of the Master Effects, all its parameters should become available in the automation menu in the Master Track's track header

GarageBand Automate the Master Track

01: Show Master Track
Load your project and choose 'Show Master Track' from the Track menu. The Master Track should appear at the bottom of the Arrangement window.

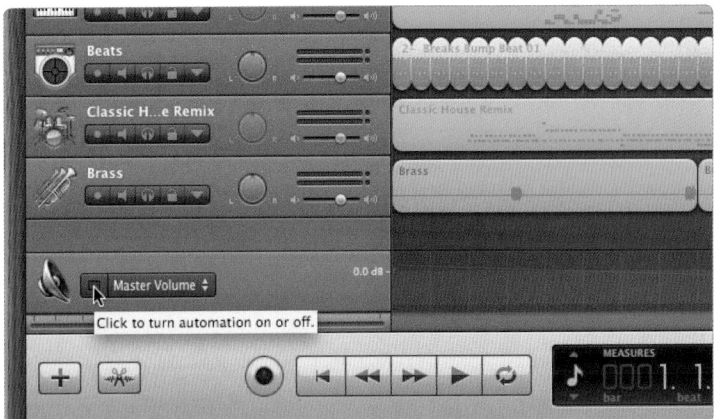

02: Enable automation
By default, the Master Volume automation lane is showing when the Master Track appears. Click on the purple button to turn the automation feature on.

03: Set fadeout start point
If you want your song to fade out naturally, you need to click to place a control node on the curve at the point where you want the fade to begin.

04: Set fadeout end point
Click to place another node on the curve at the point that you want the fadeout to end. This will be the point at which the volume reaches zero.

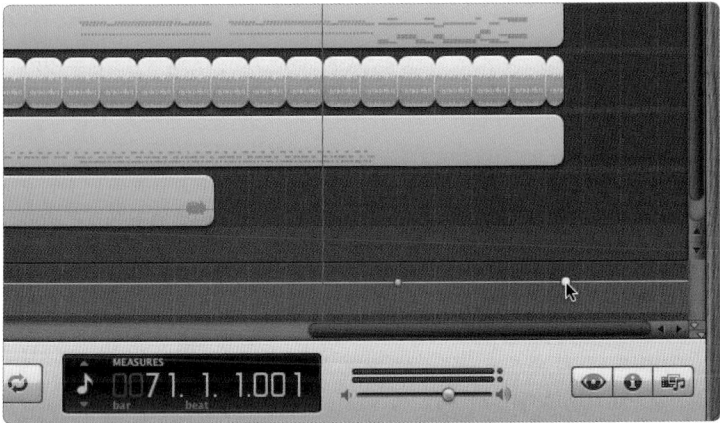

05: Fade down
Drag the second node to the bottom until the value reads -144.0dB. This will create a linear fadeout between your start and end points.

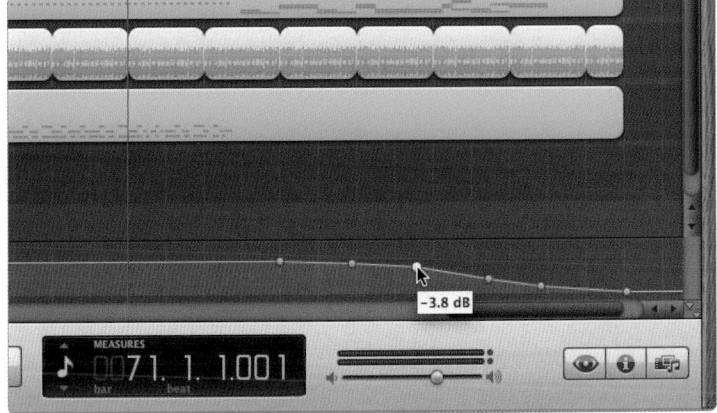

06: Add more nodes
Click as many times as you like between the original start and end points to create extra nodes with which to fine-tune the shape of your fadeout curve.

Introducing iLife

Record and edit Magic GarageBand tracks

Play along with Magic GarageBand and edit too

 **App used:** GarageBand  **Time needed:** 10 minutes

If you are any kind of musician then you'll know that practice makes perfect. It's a universal rule and one that, if kept to, can improve your skills dramatically – even over a short period of time. As a Mac user you have a fantastic practice tool at your disposal in the form of GarageBand. The free music suite that comes pre-loaded on all new Macs is a total powerhouse, and one of the many unsung features is Magic GarageBand. Often regarded as a bit of a gimmick, Magic GarageBand actually has the power to be incredibly useful for musicians wishing to practice in a live situation without inviting the band or orchestra round to rehearse. It comes pre-loaded with nine styles for you to play along with and, as an added bonus, you can delve into any of these and edit them so they are tailored to suit your needs. As you would expect, the process is simplicity itself. Users of older Macs may find that Magic GarageBand takes a few minutes to load, but just be patient as the system is a little heavy on the processors.

"The Magic GarageBand process is simplicity itself"

GarageBand Edit Magic tracks

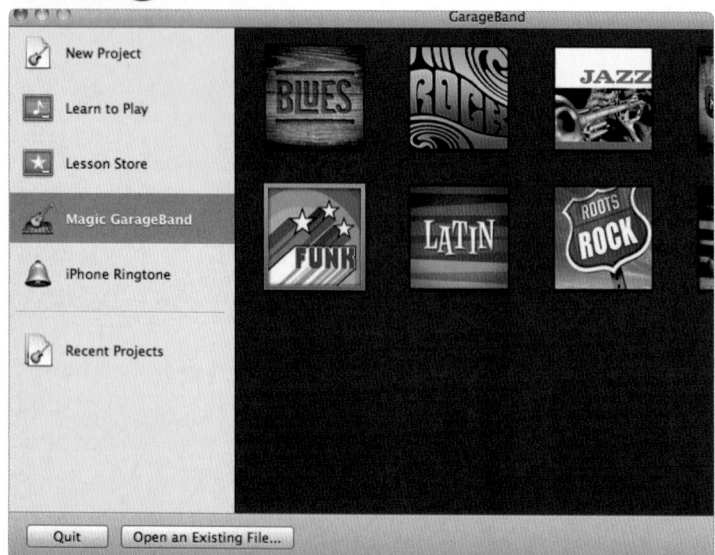

01: Lock and load

Launch GarageBand and a window of options will appear. Click Magic GarageBand then pick the genre you want to play and hit Choose.

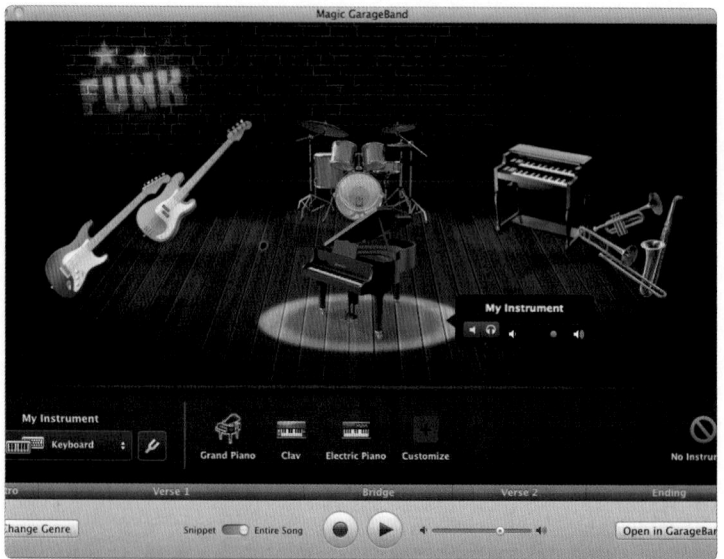

02: Visualiser

Magic GarageBand uses a visual system to show you the song. Edit all the instruments from here; just click on an instrument to edit it.

Edit a Magic GarageBand jam

Add the professional touches to a great rehearsal

Record it all
With GarageBand you can keep on recording over and over again, and then choose the best take and use it in the final mix

Share it, learn it
From here you can Share your song to disk and load it onto your iPod or iPhone so you get to know the song and can mentally practice when away from your instrument

Tweak the backing
If your lead solo was drowned out by the rest of the band, you can easily automate a ducking of their sound so your super shredding or quick keys stand out the right amount

Your part
Once you've recorded your part, you can edit all the facets of its sound – including the panning and automation – from here

REPLACE LOOPS
You don't have to stick with the Magic GarageBand templates if you don't want to. You can easily drop other loops in and out in all of the other parts so that the song has the features you need to rehearse properly. Just remember to save the project…

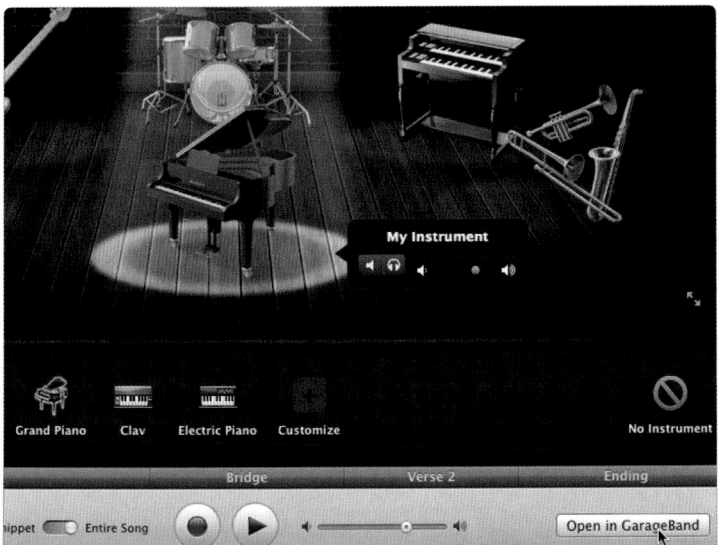

03: Ready to edit
Once you've played with the settings and are ready to edit, click the 'Open in GarageBand' button in the bottom right-hand corner of the screen.

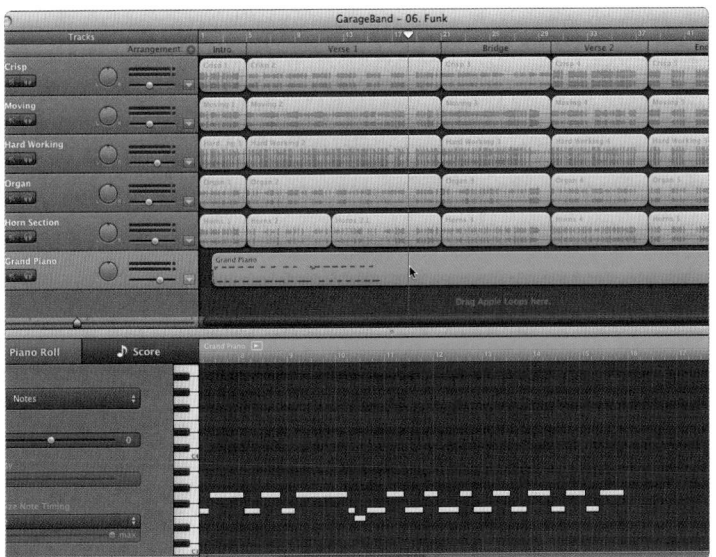

04: Familiar interface
The song will now be loaded and you can edit the elements. You can also record your own part, adding effects and automation as you see fit.

Export high-quality audio from GarageBand

App used:
GarageBand

Time needed:
10 minutes

How can you ensure the export quality is as high as it can be?

Due largely to its being a main component of the iLife suite, the audio export options in GarageBand tend to be geared towards sending finished tracks in .mp3 format to your iTunes library. In the majority of cases this makes complete sense, as it means that the audio files you export of your own GarageBand projects line up neatly quality-wise with all the other .mp3 files in your library, despite the trade-off degradation in sound quality that this involves. The audio will still be of acceptable quality to most

listeners, but every so often you will want to make sure that the audio file you are producing is of the highest possible quality, with no data compression whatsoever, for example if you are producing a mix for commercial mastering.

It's a matter of just a few simple steps to make sure that your project is rendered at the highest possible resolution and bit depth to ensure a great-sounding result. So if you want to maximise the quality of your audio output, read on to find out how it's done.

Maximise your audio quality

The audio quality controls explained

Mix compression
Use mix compression to raise the overall level of your track. To do so, open the Track Info pane, click Master Track, click Edit, then click the LED button to turn on the compressor

Auto Normalize
Preserving the integrity of your exported audio means nothing if you don't exploit the full dynamic range available to begin with. Select the Auto Normalize checkbox to maximise loudness when exporting

Audio Resolution
Set the Audio Resolution setting to Best, as this ensures that GarageBand will both record and export audio at 24-bit, the industry-standard bit-depth for professional audio recordings

COMPRESSED AUDIO FILES
MP3 is a form of data compression, meaning that an algorithm removes data from the file during the export process to reduce the amount of space it takes up on a hard drive, making it easier to send via email or fit onto an iPod. Mix compression, however, refers to reducing the difference between the loudest and quietest parts of a mix.

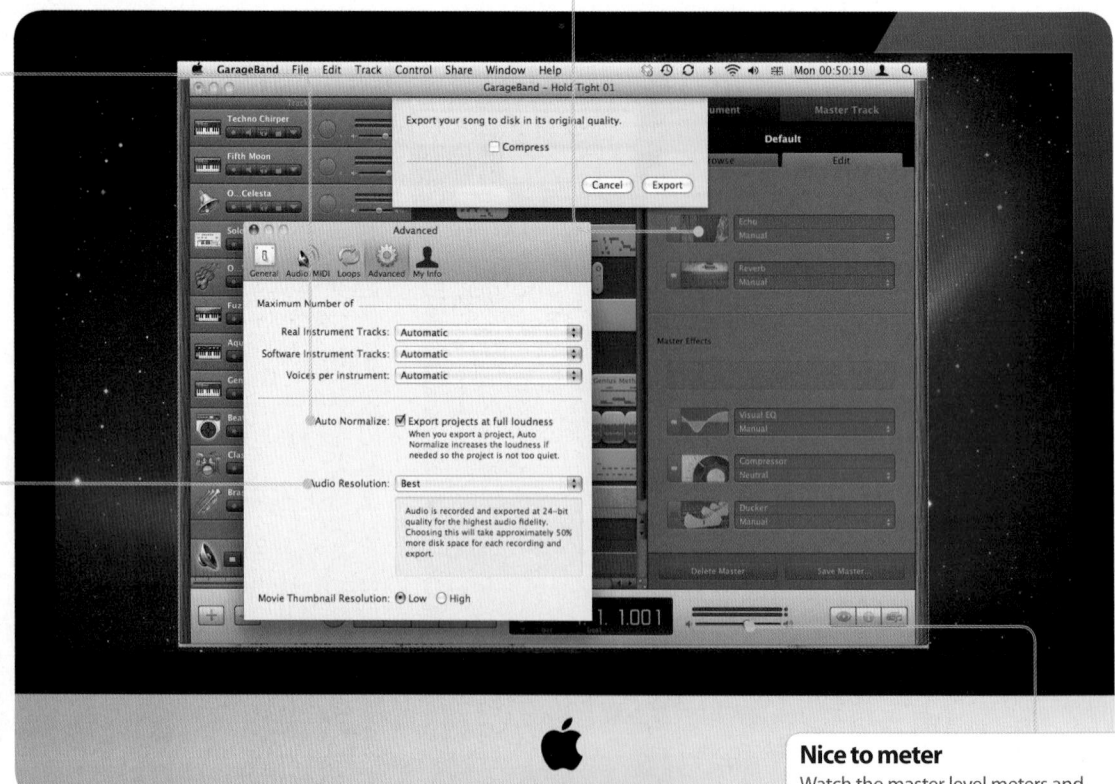

Nice to meter
Watch the master level meters and adjust the master volume level slider as you play the track. When you export the project, the slider should be as far to the right as possible without the clipping indicators lighting

GarageBand Turn up the quality control

01: On the menu

Open the GarageBand project from which you want to export the audio. From the Share menu, select 'Export Song to Disk…'.

02: Empty the box

You will be presented with a window containing various export options. Ignore them all and just uncheck the 'Compress' checkbox.

03: Push the button

The window will now ask if you want to export the file at its original quality setting. Click 'Export' to continue.

04: Select destination

Browse to the location on your hard drive that your want to export the file to and type a name for it in the box provided. Then click 'Save'.

Introducing iWork

From spreadsheets to word processors, iWork is a vital tool for any Mac user

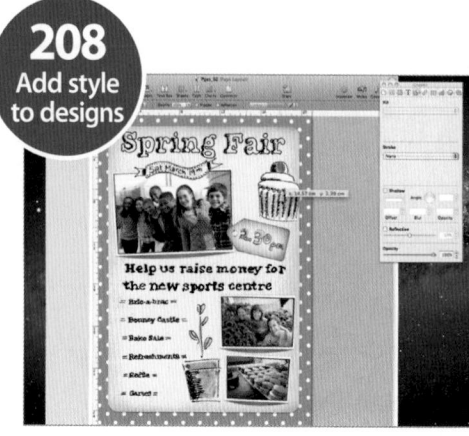

208 Add style to designs

210 Tweak your fonts

"You can use Pages to design impressive-looking leaflets and even small magazines"

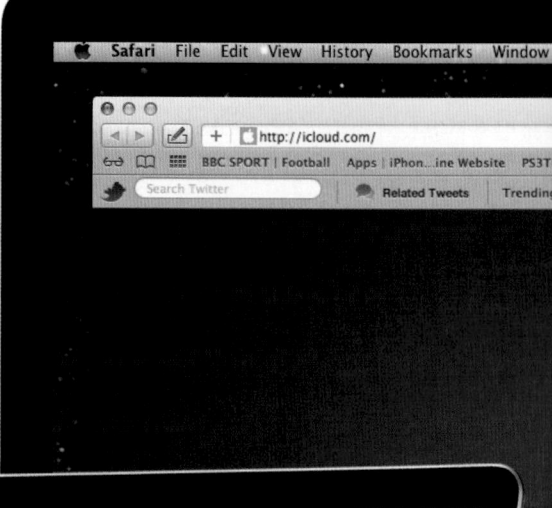

Getting to know Pages

Why creating professional-looking documents is quick
and easy with Apple's intuitive desktop publishing app

 **App used:** Pages

 **Time needed:** 20 minutes

 Seeing is very much believing with Apple's Pages app. Available for Mac, iPhone and iPad, Pages is both a streamlined word processor and an easy-to-use page layout tool that allows you to get creative and produce professional-looking documents in next to no time. You can get started easily by choosing one of 180 pre-designed templates and apply your own

text or images to an existing layout. Or you can create something from scratch, which is made easy by an intuitive interface that stokes your imagination and enables you to transfer your ideas to the digital page effortlessly.

What's more, Pages is universal across all platforms and compatible with iCloud, so you can start a project at the office and then continue it later

on your iPad without having to manually transfer any files – or even save them! You'll be amazed at what you can create using this versatile app.

"Create professional-looking documents"

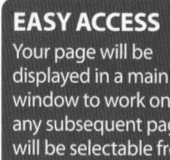

EASY ACCESS
Your page will be displayed in a main window to work on and any subsequent pages will be selectable from the list to the left

STYLE ICON
You can quickly experiment with different fonts, styles and sizes by choosing 'Show Fonts' from the 'Format' menu option

TEMPLATES
You can choose from 180 Apple-developed templates or choose a blank template to create something from scratch

INSPECTOR
The Inspector tool lets you easily apply style to text, images, charts and anything else that you want to include in your document

IMPORT MEDIA
You can easily import any of your own media, including pictures, movies and audio, to include in your document by clicking on the 'Media' option

Turn your documents into eBooks

View your documents in style and even publish them as eBooks

Any documents you create in Pages can be stored and read in the iBooks app on your iPhone, iPad or iPod touch. Any documents or reports containing lots of text can be exported in the ePub format, which is an open eBook standard that works with just about any e-reader you'd care to mention. You can send your ePub document to iBooks via iTunes, self-publish it on the iBookstore

or send it in an email to friends or colleagues. Once your document has been transferred to iBooks you can select a font and size that are easy to read and peruse it in comfort, on your mobile device, away from your desk – and the text will then automatically reflow to fit the size and orientation of your device's screen.

If you have produced graphics-heavy documents with more

advanced layouts, such as newsletters and brochures, you can opt to export your document as a PDF file, which will keep your document looking exactly like the original – no matter what device you're viewing it on, or PDF-compatible app you're viewing it through – and PDFs can also be imported into iBooks to sit proudly on the virtual shelves ready for selection and easy reading.

Key features

Why Pages is great for desktop publishing

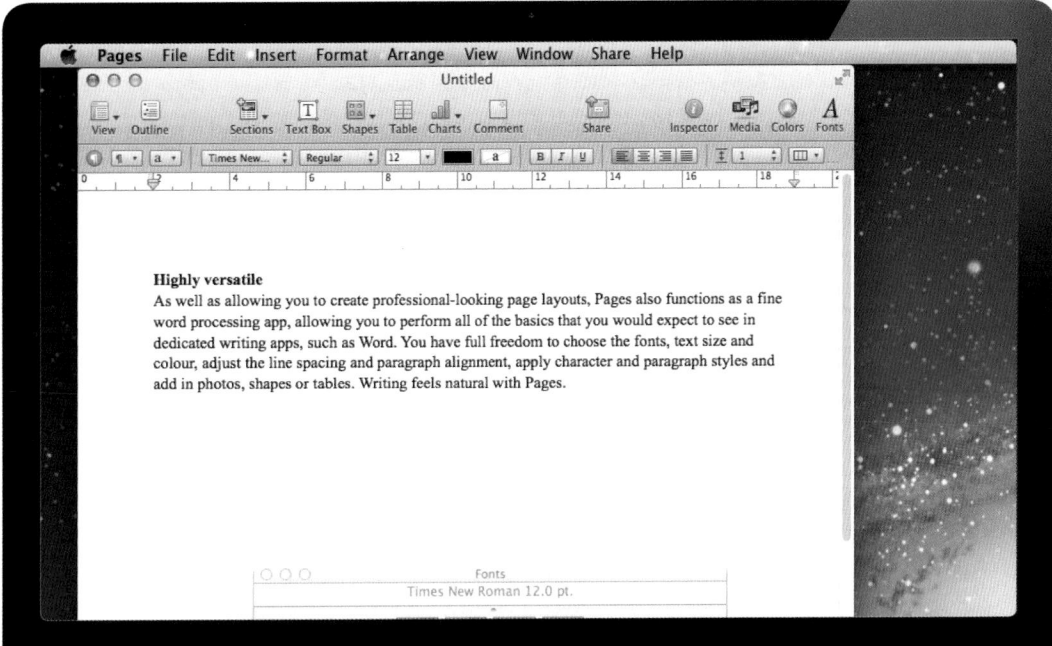

Easy to grasp

With over 180 Apple-designed templates to choose from, it is easy to drop in your own elements, replace the existing text and create professional-looking brochures, fliers, reports, invitations, or pretty much anything else in minutes. Using the app is so intuitive that you can even cut and paste elements, such as charts, from Numbers into your document and the data will be linked – so if changes are made in Numbers, they will be reflected in Pages.

Highly versatile

As well as allowing you to create professional-looking page layouts, Pages also functions as a fine word processing app, allowing you to perform all of the basics that you would expect to see in dedicated writing apps, such as Word. You have full freedom to choose the fonts, text size and colour, adjust the line spacing and paragraph alignment, apply character and paragraph styles and add in photos, shapes or tables. Writing feels natural with Pages.

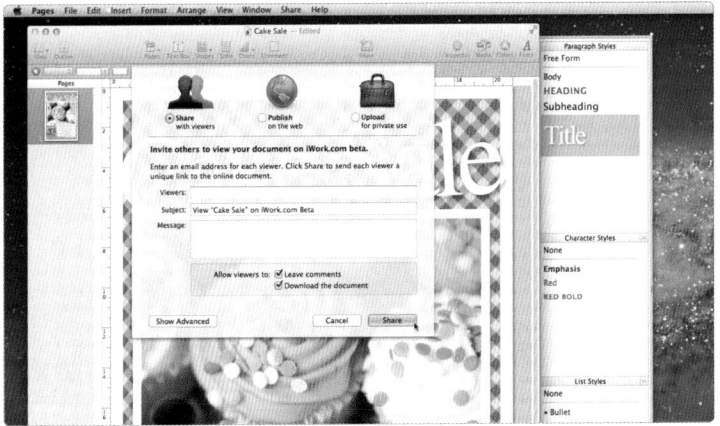

Powerful page layout

Pages makes it easy to create your own designs from a blank canvas. You can select fonts and import whatever images, graphics, tables and 3D charts you wish and a powerful graphics tool lets you resize and rotate photos, apply reflections and shadows, add pictures frames and even erase backgrounds from images with a simple point and click. You can also control how the text looks, flows and wraps around images.

Easy transferral and sharing

Pages will accommodate all Microsoft Word files, allowing you to read, edit and save them within the interface – making it a great app for remote working. You can also upload your documents to iWork.com and invite friends or colleagues to download them and add comments. Pages also utilises iCloud, so your work will be synced automatically and wirelessly and you'll be able to pick up where you left off on another device.

Add your own style to designs in Pages

 **App used:** Pages    **Price:** £13.99/$19.99    **Time needed:** 10 minutes

Import your own assets into Pages to create a completely bespoke document…

If you don't like the pre-installed templates in Pages, or if you prefer to make your own mark, an alternative is to import your own design elements. It's easy to do, and a great way to add your own touch to your designs. Following the recent revival for hand-rendered type and illustration, we've created our own elements by sketching them out then scanning them into a computer and saving them. Don't panic if you can't even draw a stick-man though; there is a wealth of resources available online, such as clip art and textures. All you need to do is check the copyright if you intend to publish your project commercially. Here is everything you need to add your own creative flair to your projects.

> "There's a wealth of resources available online, such as clip art and textures, much of which is free"

Online resources

Here are the most useful sites

01: www.sxc.hu

Stock.xchng is a free stock photo site. It takes seconds to set up an account and you have access to thousands of images.

02: www.istockphoto.com

iStock isn't free, but it is cheap. Anyone can set up an account, all you need to do is purchase credits to download images.

03: www.dafont.com

Add graphic elements to your projects using fonts or download a selection of free fonts from dafont.com.

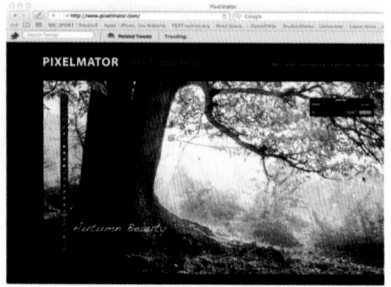

04: www.pixelmator.com

Create assets in software such as Pixelmator. It's available to download on the Mac App Store for £20.99/$29.99.

Drop shadows
Use the Inspector pallette to add drop shadows to your design elements to give your project a more three-dimensional look

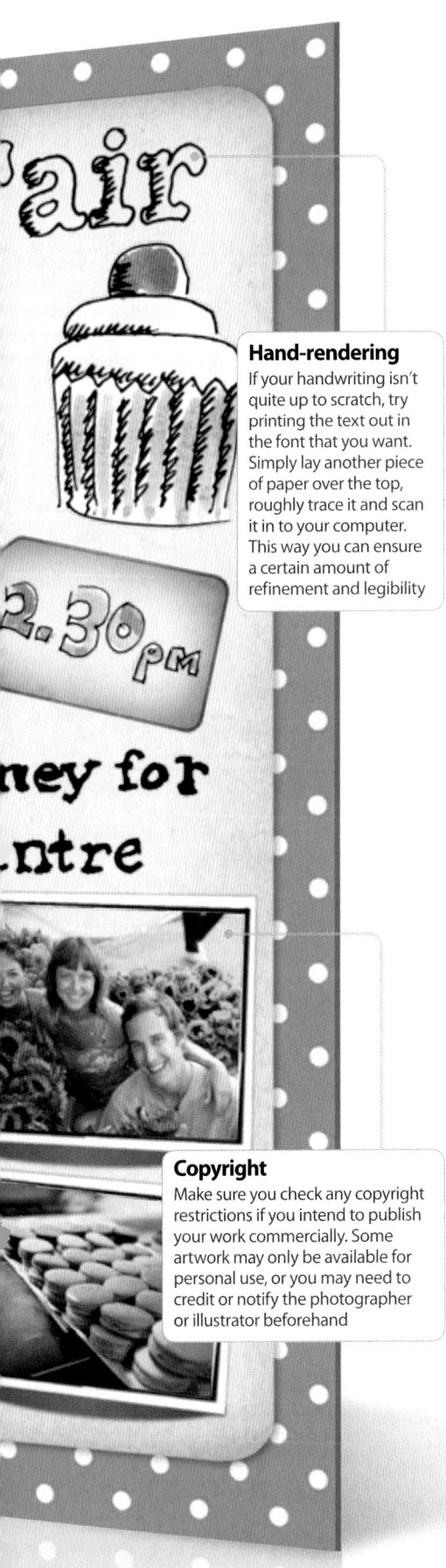

Hand-rendering
If your handwriting isn't quite up to scratch, try printing the text out in the font that you want. Simply lay another piece of paper over the top, roughly trace it and scan it in to your computer. This way you can ensure a certain amount of refinement and legibility

Copyright
Make sure you check any copyright restrictions if you intend to publish your work commercially. Some artwork may only be available for personal use, or you may need to credit or notify the photographer or illustrator beforehand

Pages Import your own assets

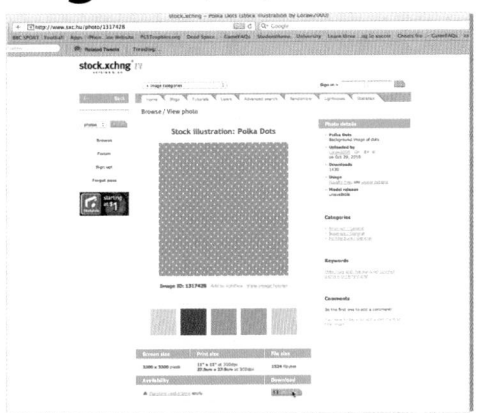

01: Collect assets
Collect the assets you think you may want to use and save them into a folder on your desktop. We downloaded this background from www.sxc.hu.

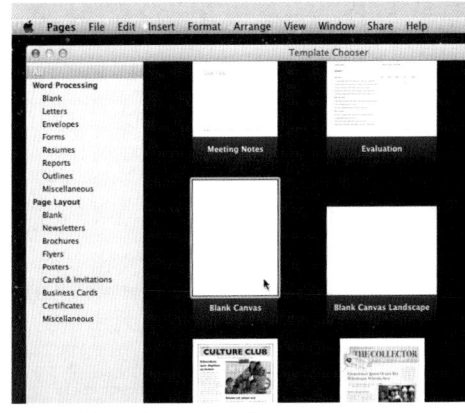

02: Blank template
Open Pages and select a blank template. Alternatively, select a template you like the look of and delete the elements you don't like.

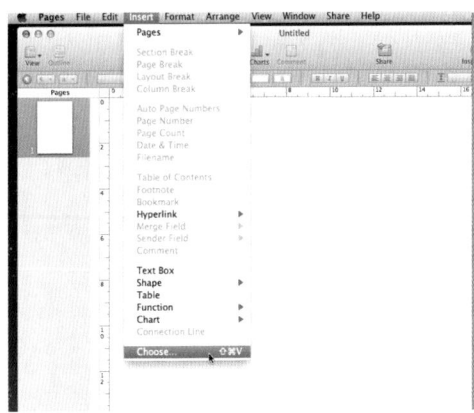

03: Add assets
There are two ways to import assets. The first is to go to the Insert drop-down menu at the top of the interface and select the option Choose.

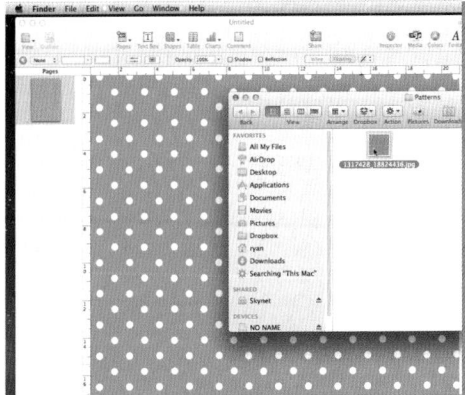

04: Alternatively
Another way to add your own elements is to select it on your desktop and drag it onto the Pages template.

05: Sketching
If you have a scanner, try scanning in hand-drawn illustrations. If not, try creating them on your Mac using software such as Pixelmator.

06: Keep on adding
Keep adding your own elements until you're satisfied with your design. Experiment with how they sit on the page, so that you create a balance.

Use Styles Drawer to format work

Use the full range of style themes in every template by activating the Styles Drawer

 **App used:** Pages

 **Price:** £13.99/$19.99

 **Time needed:** 10 minutes

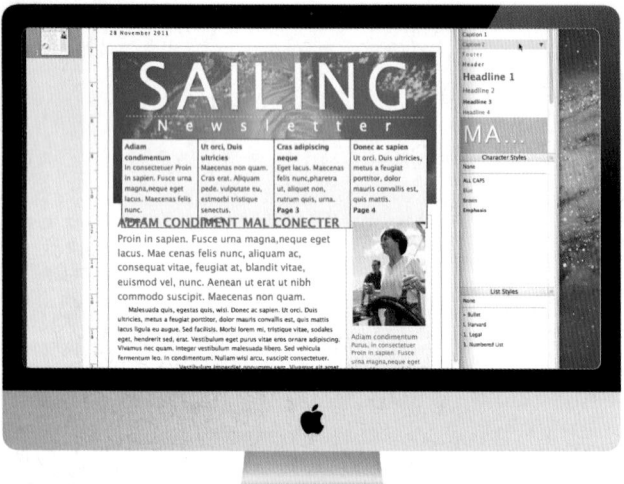

Pages is a fantastic, easy-to-use application that can have you laying out cool pages in a matter of minutes. Each and every one of the templates that is available has its own unique style, and has been included because each one has a specific use. This style has its own fonts, which have been picked by the design team at Apple, to complement each other and make the page work as a whole unit.

The trouble is that you may not like all of the fonts used, or you may wish to use them in different places. Luckily the font styles of your template can be accessed using a tool called the Styles When activated, this is a virtual drawer that springs out of the left-hand side of your document allowing you to easily change the style of a text box you are working on. It's so simple it requires just a single click of your mouse, and before you know it you'll be tweaking the Pages styles to suit your own needs.

The Styles Drawer is a fantastic way of making sure your pages have a complementary set of fonts, so your work always looks good and you have the typography style you desire. So if you want to personalise one of the styles in Pages, simply follow this four-step tutorial and in no time at all you'll have your very own styles to work from.

> "The Styles Drawer makes sure your pages have complementary fonts"

What's in your drawer?

A closer look at this essential Pages tool

Formatting
You can still make changes using the formatting palette, as you would normally. The Styles Drawer is just there to make life a little easier

Headlines
There is an array of headline styles to keep your work consistent. Use these to title your sections and draw the reader in

Hot keys
Each style can be given a hot key so you can quickly change styles using your keyboard. Use the arrow to bring up a menu and select a hot key for that particular style

Same for colour
You may find that you want to use a completely different set of colours than those on the template. You can still use the Styles Drawer font selections but change the colour using the formatting palette and colour palette

MAKE YOUR OWN
It is possible to rename each style so it makes more sense to your own workflow needs. Use the menu arrow to the side of the style and then select Rename Style. You can then input the name you wish to use for this style so it becomes easier to use in your own working methodology.

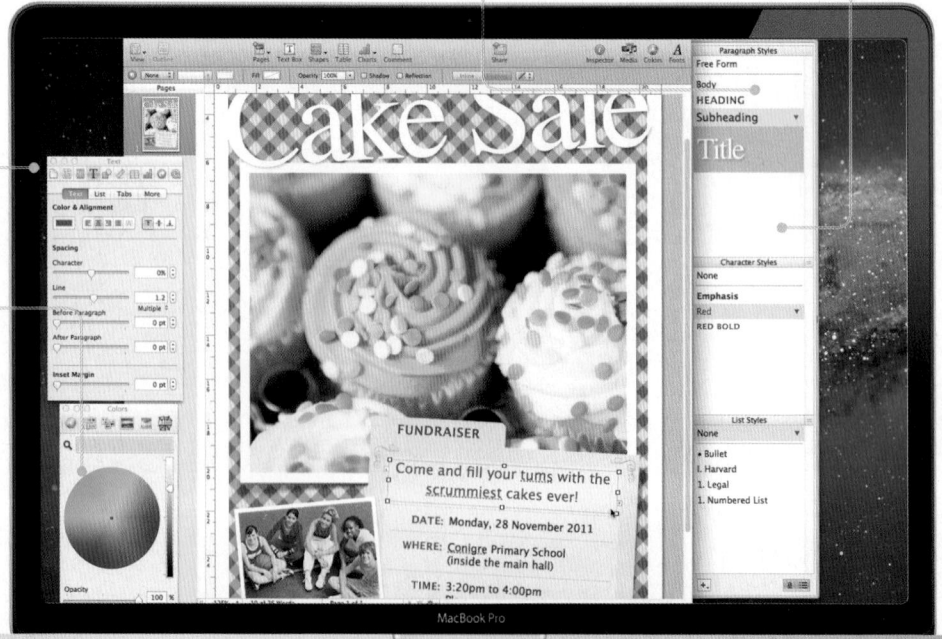

Pages Activate and use the Styles Drawer

01: Load it, change it

Load a Pages document from the templates chooser and fill in all of the text with your new copy. If you want to mess around with styles first, you can do so with the dummy text that is pre-loaded in the template. By doing this, you don't have to worry if you accidentally delete any of your copy!

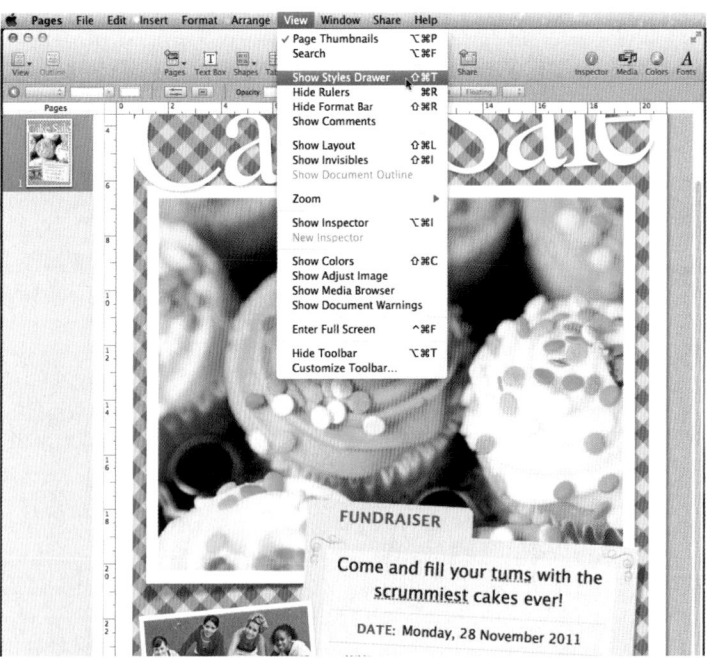

02: Menu, or shortcut

Go to the View section of the menu and select Show Styles Drawer. Alternatively, you can use the keyboard shortcut Shift+Apple+T. The drawer will now spring to life on the left of your document, bringing with it a whole new raft of options for you to explore.

03: Click away

You will see all of the fonts and font styles that are currently used in your document. You can now select a text box and then select a font style on the left and click on it to activate it. The text in the text box will change instantly to what you selected.

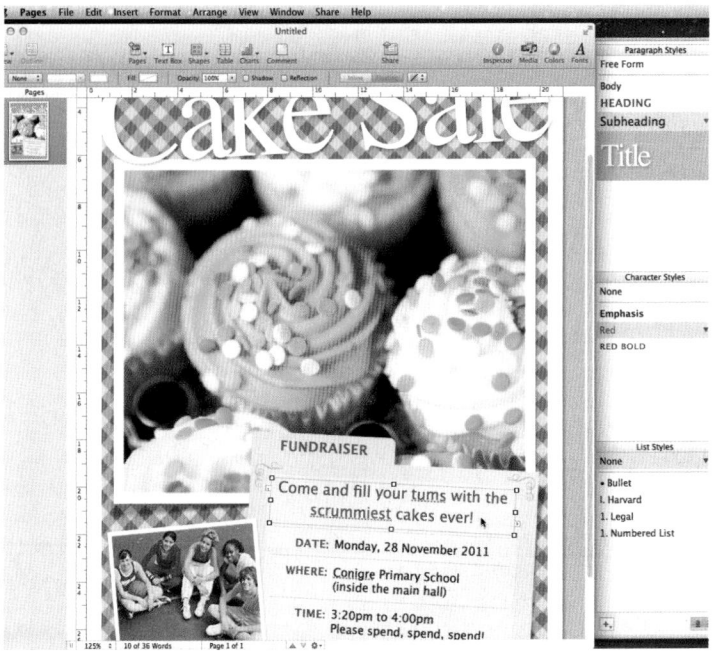

04: Experimentation

The best way to find out what works best and which styles compliment each other is to experiment with different styles. A lot will depend on the content you are adding to the page and how you want it to work with other elements on your page.

Create a certificate in Pages

There's more to Pages than just a word processor. Learn how to use its arsenal of templates and tools to create your very own certificate

 **App used:** Pages

 **Price:** £13.99/$19.99

 **Time needed:** 15 minutes

 The times when a word processor was essentially just a digital equivalent to the venerable typewriter are long gone. These days any respectable program of this type can handle photos and graphics with ease, allowing you to extend the functionality of the software and often leave little need to look elsewhere to create visually impressive documents. But some go even further than this, like Pages, which is actually a desktop publishing program masquerading as a consumer word processing application. There is so much you can do with this fantastic software.

For instance, you can use Pages to design impressive-looking leaflets or even small magazines, and it comes with a vast array of templates that you can use to base your work on. One such template is the Certificate, which provides a great starting point

> "It comes with a vast array of templates that you can use"

for a brilliant, customisable award you can print for friends and family. It's also a great aid for teachers who want to reward their students. In a time when gold stars don't quite cut the mustard any more, giving a child a certificate to acknowledge good work or behaviour can be a great incentive for the younger generation.

This tutorial will familiarise you with the Page Layout section by helping you design a new certificate from scratch rather than copy Apple's default option. It's a simple process that produces clever results.

Use Pages to design a certificate

Discover how Pages is much more than just a simple word processor

Fill me in
If you wanted to, you could choose more than two colours to create a gradient, such is the flexibility that this versatile app offers to create pretty much whatever you want

The colour palette
These little squares help you preserve a specific colour. To set one, drag the desired colour from the big rectangle at the top of this window onto it

The Graphic inspector
The Inspector's Graphic tab is the perfect place to go when you wish to customise your shape. You can set a gradient, fill it with a photo, add a frame, a shadow, or even alter its opacity

Group items
You can group items together to make changing their location a breeze: select them all (click on the first then Command-click on all the others) and go to Arrange>Group

CUSTOMISE A SHAPE
When adding a shape you aren't bound by its default look. For instance, you can modify the star shape to have up to 20 points instead of the default five. Look closely on its inner circle and you'll find a small blue dot. Drag it to increase or decrease the spikes' size. Have a look at the other shapes to see how versatile some of them can be.

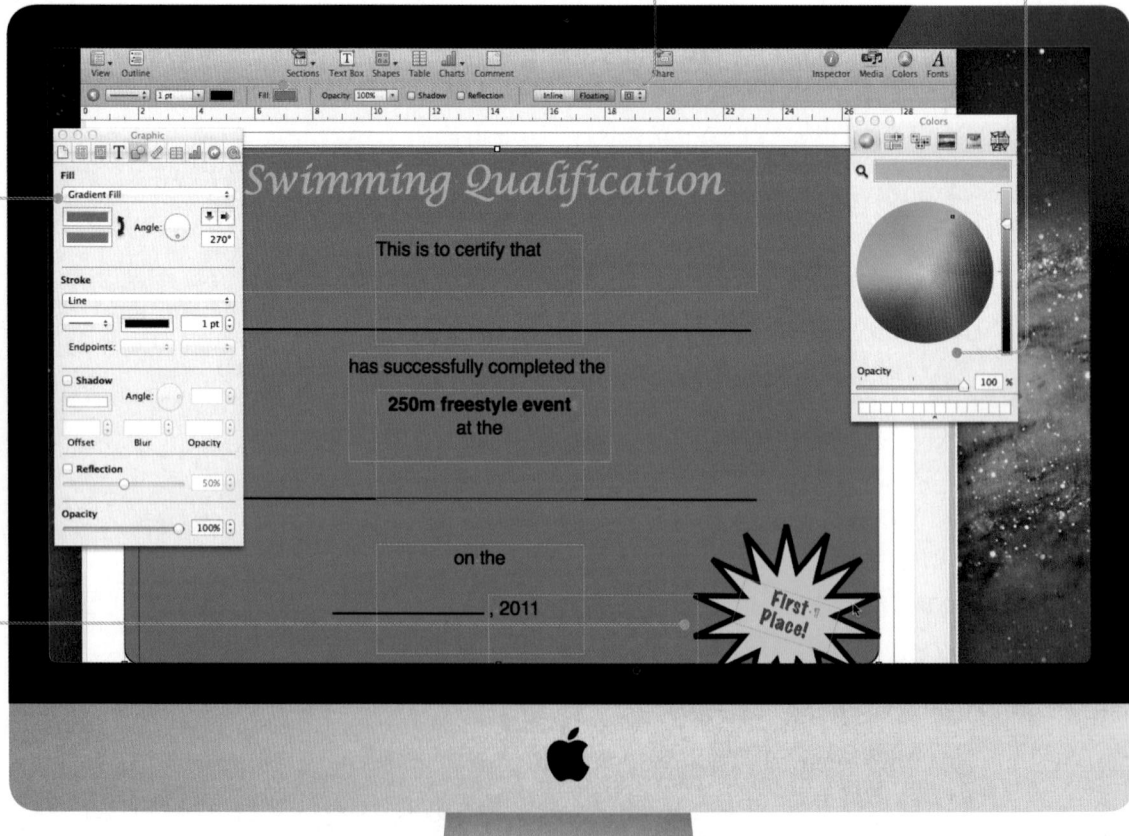

Pages Use the Page Layout section to design a certificate

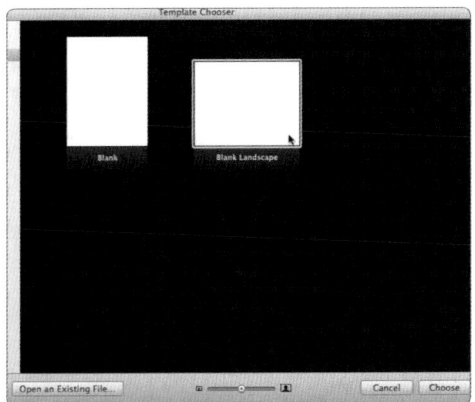

01: Get started
Create a new document. Go to File>New From Template Chooser. Click the Page Layout section's Blank option and select Blank Canvas Landscape.

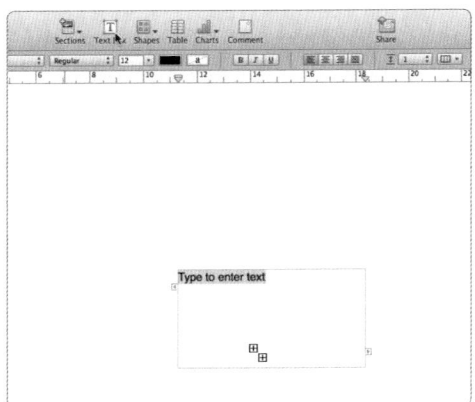

02: Add a Text Box
Unlike a word processor, you can't start typing right away – you need to add a text area first. Click on the toolbar's Text Box button.

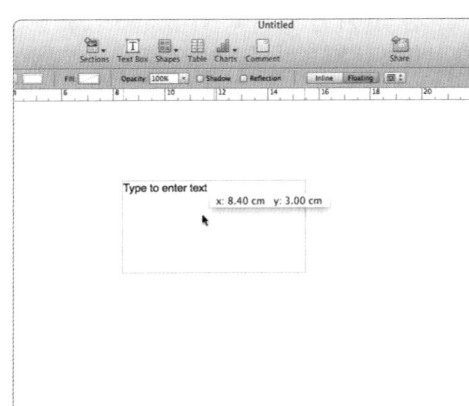

03: Moving and resizing
To move the box, click outside it to deselect it. Click on it again to reveal resize handles. You can now move it using alignment guides.

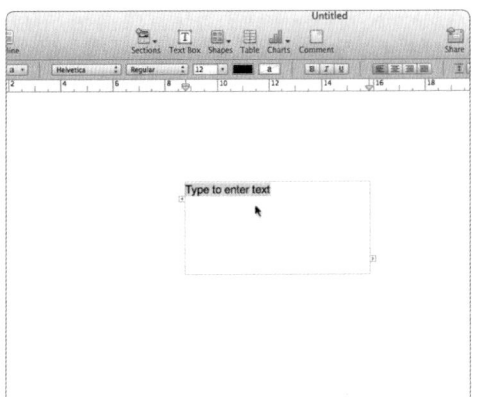

04: Edit text
To select the text itself, click on it again. If the text box isn't already selected, double-click on it to jump straight to the text editing mode.

05: Customise its look
You can alter the font, size and colour just like you can in the word processing section; via the Format Bar (directly beneath the toolbar).

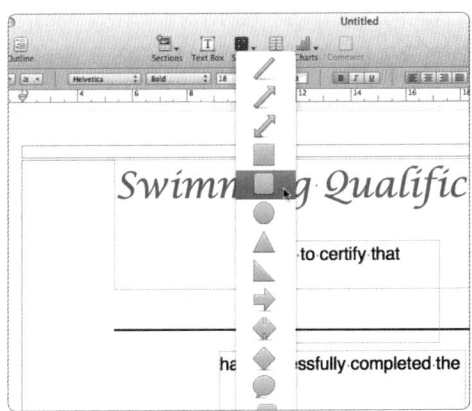

06: Add shapes
A certificate needs fancy graphics. Click the Shapes button and choose a curved rectangle. Move it near the top-left of your document.

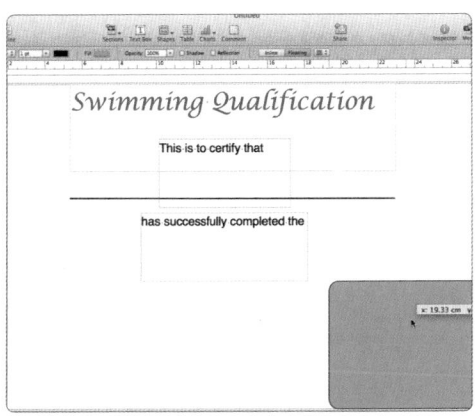

07: Shape customisation
Resize it towards the bottom-right. Notice an alignment guide appears once both sides are equal from the edge of the page.

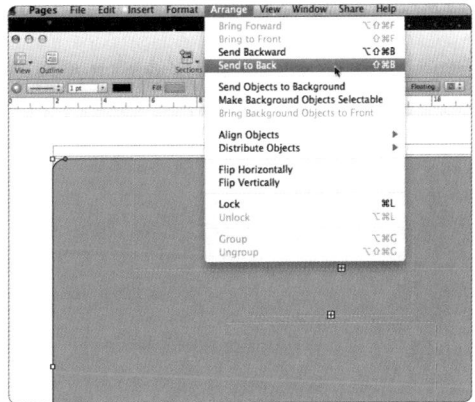

08: Re-order objects
This square obstructs your text. To alter its position, go to Arrange>Send To Back (or use the keyboard shortcut Shift+Cmd+B).

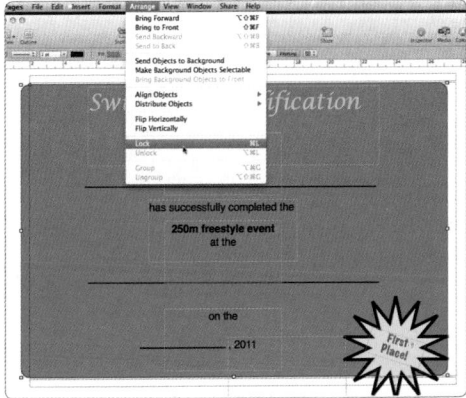

09: Lock into place
If you're happy with it, you can even lock it into position by going to Arrange>Lock (note that the Unlock option is just beneath it).

Introducing iWork

Working with Numbers

With Apple's spreadsheet app you can create detailed charts to share with others in minutes

Whether you're keeping a budget or tracking your workloads, spreadsheets can help you organise and plan all aspects of your life and Numbers, part of Apple's iWork package (that also includes Keynote and Pages), is the perfect app for creating them. Using a friendly and intuitive interface, Numbers guides you through the process of transferring your data to charts and cells that can be linked together with the click of a mouse to convey your data in easy-to-follow and eye-catching sheets. You can create

"Convey data in eye-catching sheets"

stacks of sheets in minutes, either by working from one of many pre-installed templates or by creating one from scratch and the accessible and user-friendly toolset makes the process quicker and easier than you may be accustomed to with other spreadsheet apps. Once you have compiled your information you can share your sheets easily with others, making it a great app for working remotely.

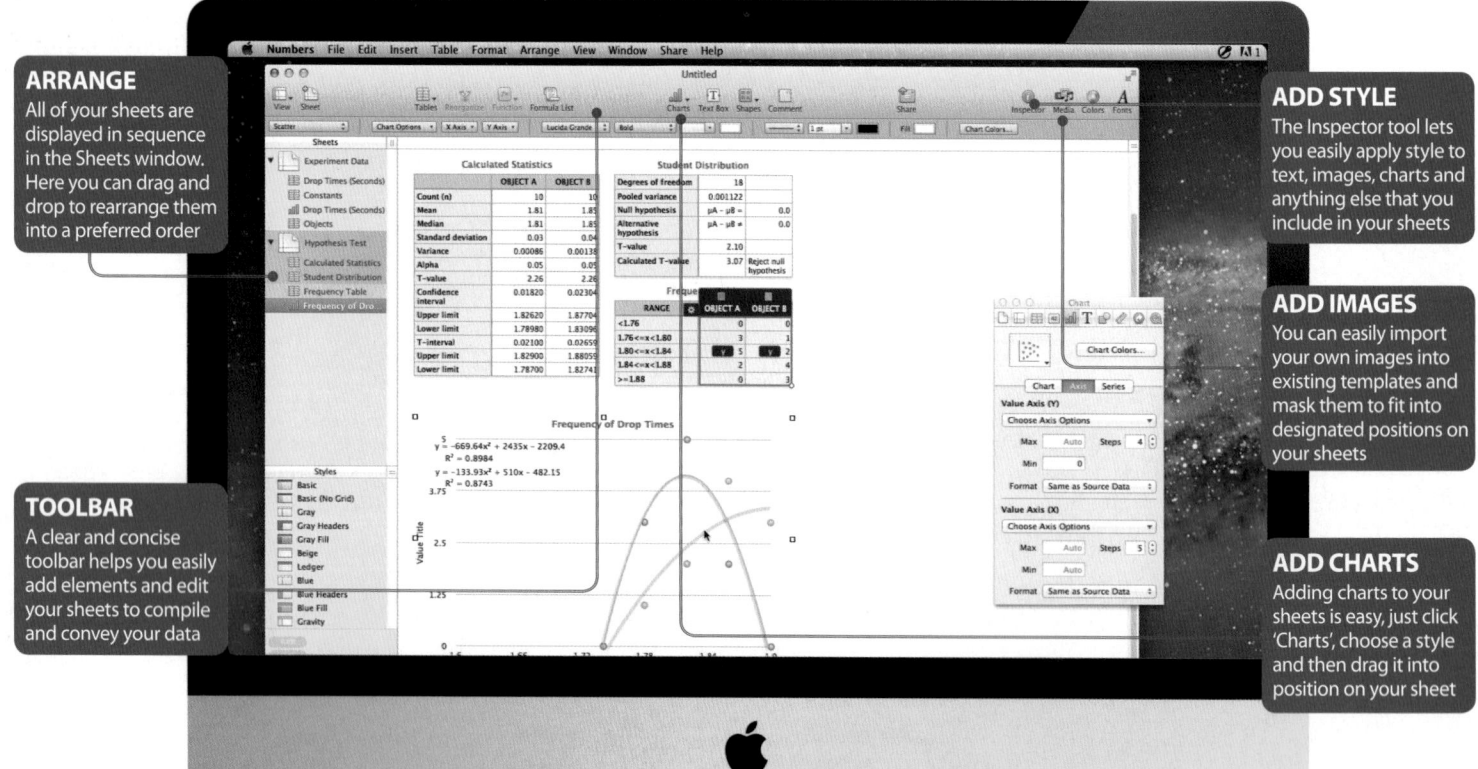

ARRANGE
All of your sheets are displayed in sequence in the Sheets window. Here you can drag and drop to rearrange them into a preferred order

TOOLBAR
A clear and concise toolbar helps you easily add elements and edit your sheets to compile and convey your data

ADD STYLE
The Inspector tool lets you easily apply style to text, images, charts and anything else that you include in your sheets

ADD IMAGES
You can easily import your own images into existing templates and mask them to fit into designated positions on your sheets

ADD CHARTS
Adding charts to your sheets is easy, just click 'Charts', choose a style and then drag it into position on your sheet

Adding textures

Ditch the old-look, two-dimensional charts in favour of something far more engaging

Each Numbers template has coordinated chart textures to complement table styles and texture fills. However, it is easy to change and enhance chart textures to make them look more eye-catching. To add a new chart, click on the 'Charts' menu on the main toolbar and choose the style of chart to suit the information you are trying to convey. Once you have dragged your new chart into place you can then start manipulating the appearance. For example, if you have added a 3D chart, highlight it by clicking on the chart and then use the 3D Chart widget to adjust the angle. When you are happy with the basic positioning and slant of your chart, select the 'Inspector' tool from the main toolbar, then click on the Chart tab and then click on 'Chart Colours'. From here you can choose a variety of schemes and effects to apply to your chart. When you find the desired scheme, click 'Apply All' and the changes will be made instantly – making your charts look instantly more engaging and attractive than the default versions.

Key features

A condensed summary of how Numbers can work for you

No experience necessary

It is very easy to get started using Numbers; the app handily provides over 30 templates that come in a wide range of styles with ready-made formulas in place and fonts assigned – all you have to do then is drop in your own data. All spreadsheets are built on a flexible, free-form canvas, so you can move what you want where you want and resize and adjust items to fit in with your own personal requirements.

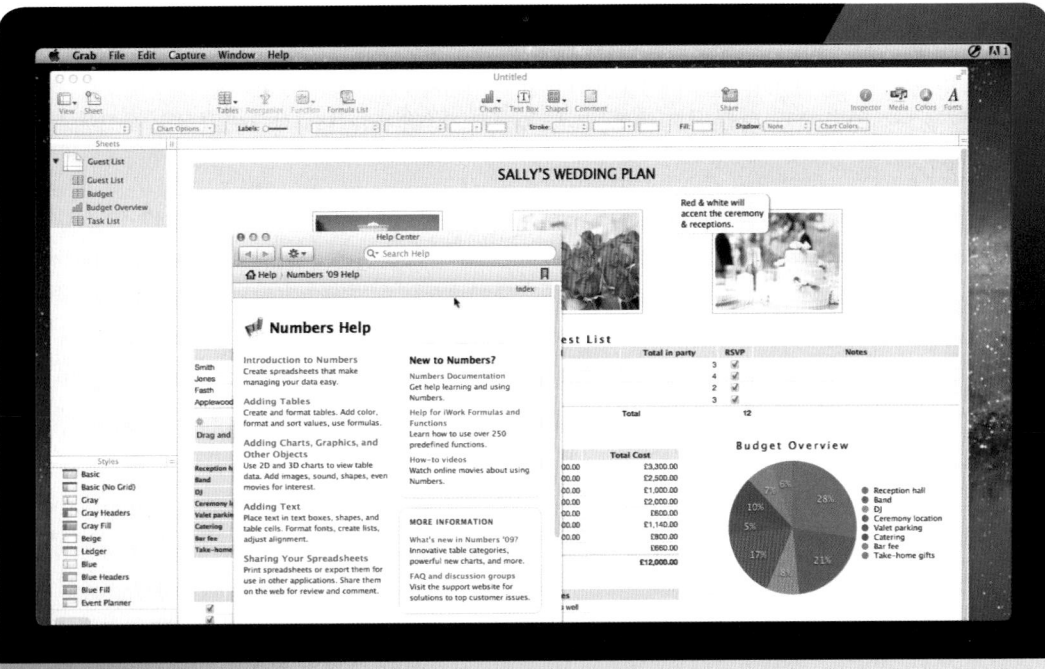

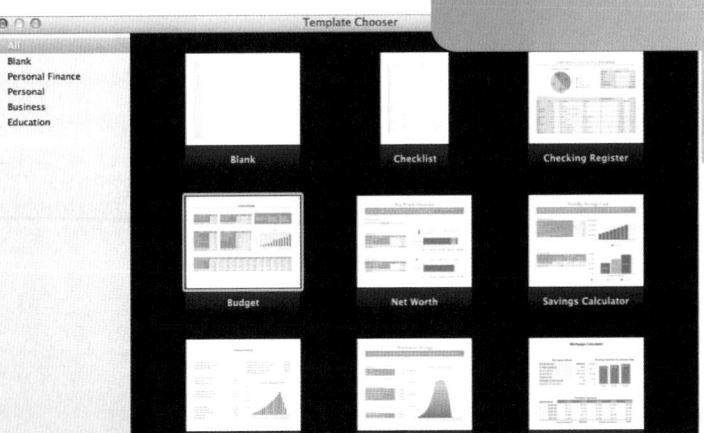

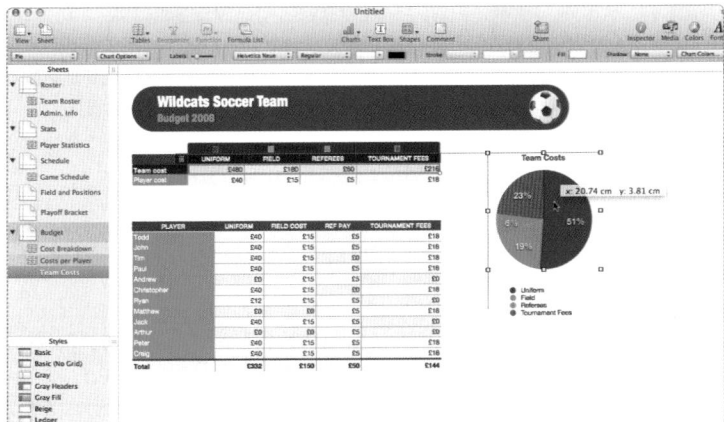

Formulas for everything

Numbers makes creating formulas refreshingly uncomplicated. Using the intuitive interface you can choose from over 250 functions and a built-in help engine provides clear and concise explanations of each variable. The Formula List view displays every calculation on your spreadsheet at once, and with a few clicks on the toolbar you can create tables and charts and add in your own images and graphics.

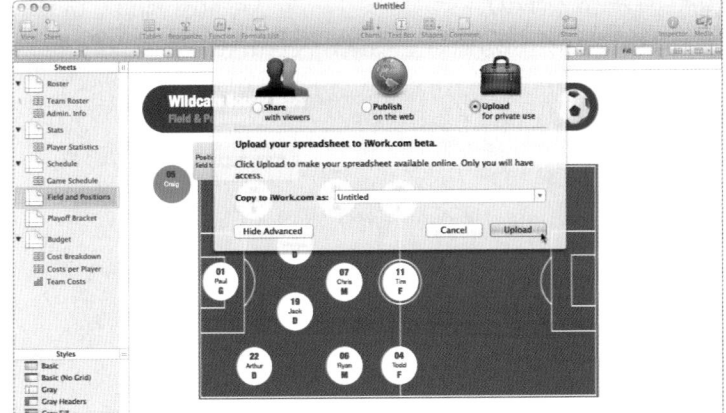

Top tables and charts

You can create as many tables and charts as you want in Numbers – 2D and 3D – and resize them as needed. The layout of each table is independent, so whatever you do to one won't affect the others. You can move tables anywhere, even to a different sheet, and the calculations will remain intact. You can even share content between tables and an easy-to-use toolset lets you analyse data, change values, use sliders and pop-up lists.

Easy access

Numbers will accommodate all Microsoft Excel spreadsheets, allowing you to read, edit and save them within the interface. You can also upload your sheets to iWork.com and invite colleagues to view them, download them and add comments. Numbers utilises Apple's Documents in iCloud, meaning any work will be synced automatically and wirelessly to your iCloud and you'll be able to pick up where you left off on another device.

Learn how to use formulas in Numbers

Manage your finances with simple, bespoke formulas

 **App used:** Numbers
 **Price:** £13.99/$19.99
 **Time needed:** 30 minutes

 Unless you're lucky enough to be a mathematical genius, anything regarding the word formula can initially be intimidating and confusing. Luckily, you don't need to be a genius to use Numbers as it does all the hard work for you. A formula in a spreadsheet basically refers to how the value of a cell is calculated. So if C represents a column and 1, 2 and 3 refer to rows, C3 = C1 + C2 would be a basic formula. In this tutorial, we'll show you how anyone can use this simple function to make organising your finances simple and effective. In this case, we'll show you how to plan your budget for a birthday party so you don't end up overspending.

"Numbers does the hard work for you"

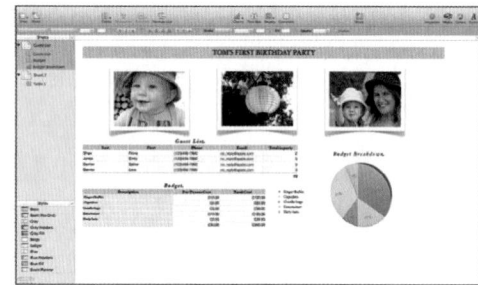

Numbers Create a formula in Numbers

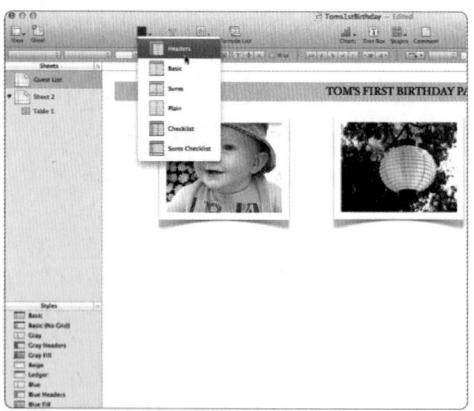

01: Add a table

Open a template and add a title, images or both. When you're ready to start adding data, go to the Tables menu and select the Headers option.

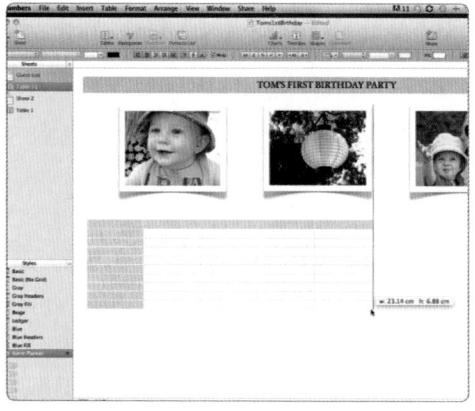

02: Resize

Resize the table by dragging the handle bars. Delete the rows and columns you don't need by right-clicking while holding down the Control key.

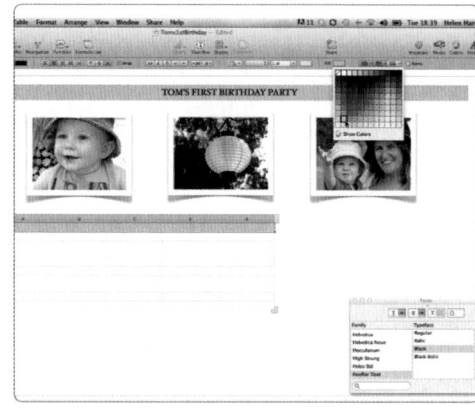

03: Adding colour

Colour will make your chart more appealing. Highlight headers by selecting the top row and tapping the Fill option on the Format bar.

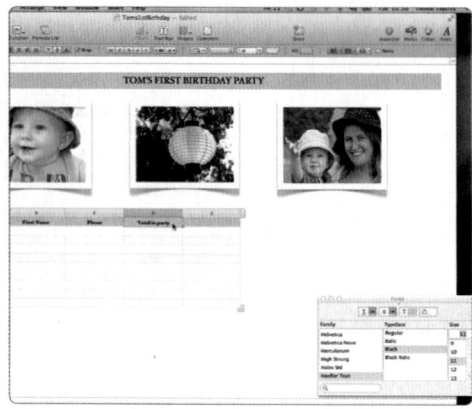

04: Adding text

Add text by clicking in each cell and typing. This table is going to be your guest list. Include names, contact details and the number per family.

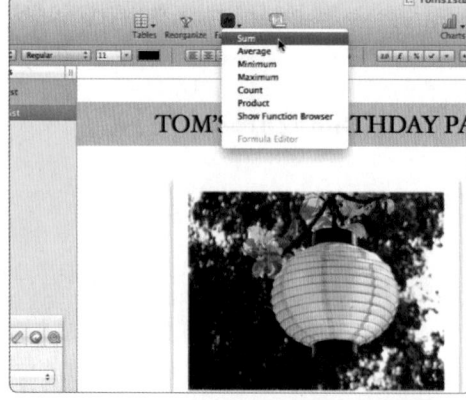

05: Sum

First of all add up the number of guests. Select the last column and select Sum from the Function menu. The value will appear in the cell below.

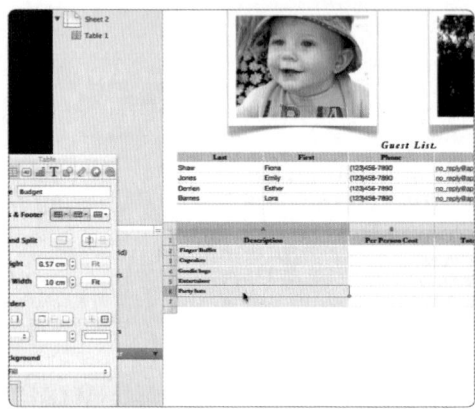

06: Budget

Add a three columned table below for a budget. Include a description in the first column and Per Person Cost in the next. The last is for Total Cost.

Get to grips with formulas

Create a budget for a birthday party

Formula

The formula will appear here as you create it or whenever you click in a cell that contains one. Clicking the Formula list option above will open a box at the bottom of the page with a list of all formulas contained within the document

FORMULAS

If you're new to Numbers, formulas can seem very confusing. However, once you get the hang of them, they really are easy and very effective to use. When you see data such as C1 or E6, all it is referring to is the cell reference. For example, C1 will be the first cell in the third column.

Functions

This drop-down menu will enable you to add functions such as sums of averages to your formulas. You can also open the Formula editor from here

Budget pie chart

Use a pie chart to break down your budget in a more visually engaging way. To make this chart, just select the Total Cost cells in the budget table (excluding the overall total) and select a chart from the Format bar

Table inspector

Use the Table inspector to format your table and make it more visually interesting. Try adding colours to alternative rows to make the data more digestable

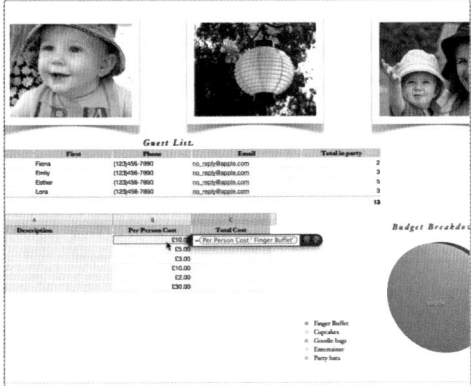

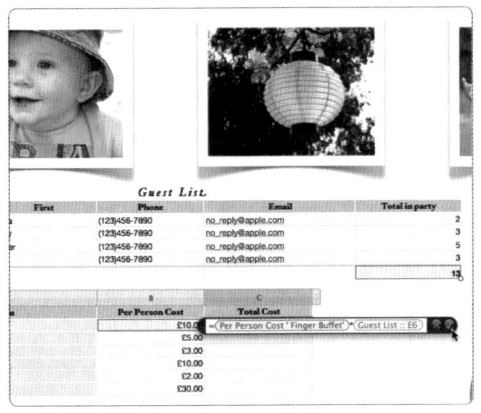

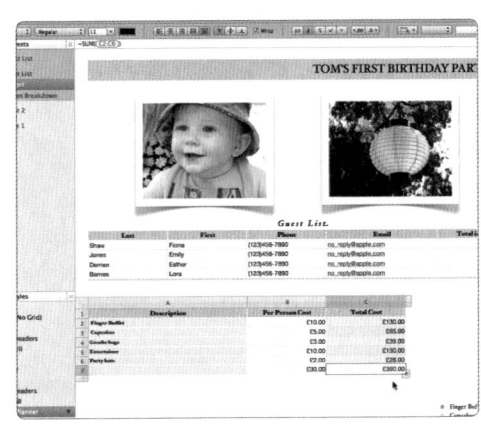

07: Doing the maths

Click the first Total Cost cell and tap '='. Click inside the cell to the immediate left (Per Person Cost) – this will add it to the formula.

08: Multiplication

Add an asterisk (*) to indicate a multiplication and click in the Total in party cell. It will automatically multiply 10 x 13. Hit the tick to accept.

09: Totals

The formula will now have calculated the Total Cost for that item. Repeat this for each item then repeat Step five to get an overall Total Cost.

Create an incentive chart for your children

App used:
Numbers

Price:
£13.99/$19.99

Time needed:
10 minutes

Make tasks more fun for your kids by creating an incentive chart in Numbers

If, like most parents, you find it difficult to get your children motivated, why not use your computer skills to give them a little inspiration? This fun and easy-to-make incentive chart simply comprises of a list of tasks to be done for each day of the week. Tick the box for each day that the child has completed the task, and if they complete that task for five days or more (everyone deserves a day off!) then reward them with a gold star at the end of the week. A set number of stars will be rewarded by a treat – the perfect way to get them to make their bed.

Of course, you don't have to make your chart exactly the same as the one shown here; you can make it as simple or as complicated as you like. All you need to do is create a basic table in Numbers, add a title and a name box, and then use the Inspector panel to add some professional-looking touches – such as a bright background, some bold text and lots of fun shapes to attract attention. It's as easy as ABC, so let's show you how it's done.

> "Use the Inspector panel to add professional touches"

Numbers Make an incentive chart

01: Bright and bold

Launch Numbers and choose a Blank template. Use Inspector to add some bright shapes and colours and don't forget to add a name box.

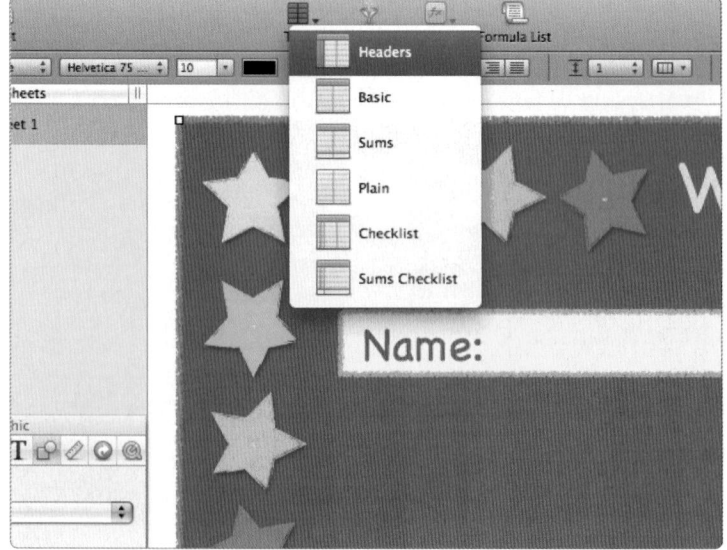

02: Add a table

When you're happy with the design, head to the Tables icon (top-left). Choose the table you want and use the outside corners to resize it.

Design in Numbers

Create a reward chart to keep your kids in check

Tweak the text
Use these little icons to align the text in your table. Drag the cursor over the text and click the icon to align it left, right, top, bottom or centre. The same icons can be found in the Text Inspector

Shapes
To add shapes around the chart, use the Shapes icon at the top of the interface. Rotate them by heading to the Metrics Inspector and using the Rotate bubble at the bottom

DISTRIBUTE EVENLY
To make your columns even widths, select all of them and choose 'Distribute columns evenly' from the Table menu. To make one bigger, hover the cursor over the dividing line at the top, click and drag. Apply the same method to rows.

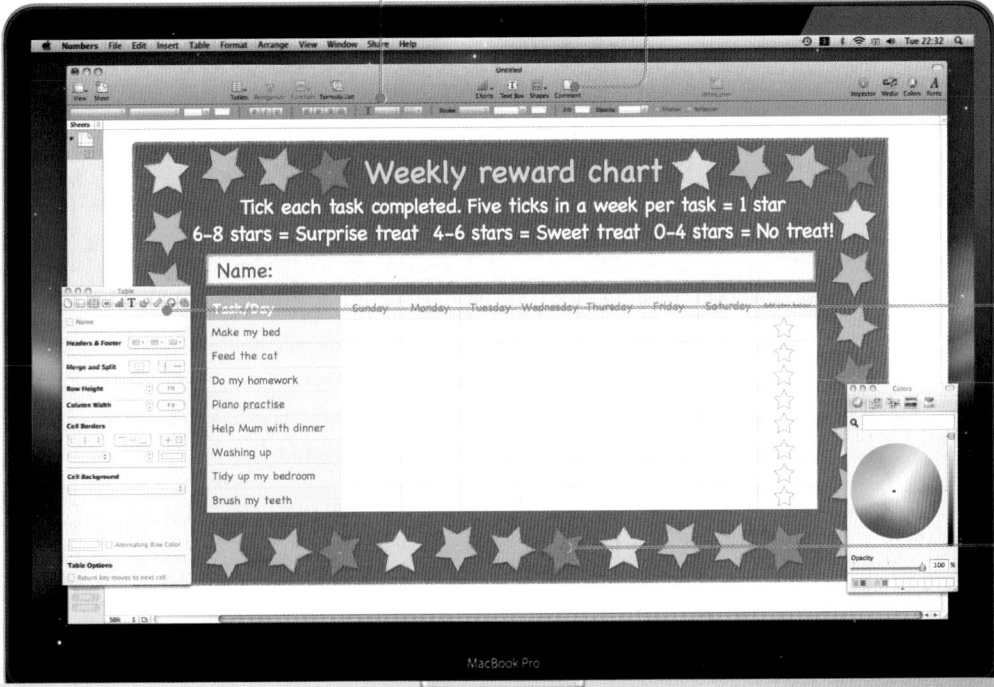

Graphic Inspector
Use the Graphic Inspector to add professional touches to your chart, like adding shadows to your shapes to make them more three-dimensional

Cell block
To change the background colour of a cell or the outline, select it and use the 'Cell background' option in the Table Inspector

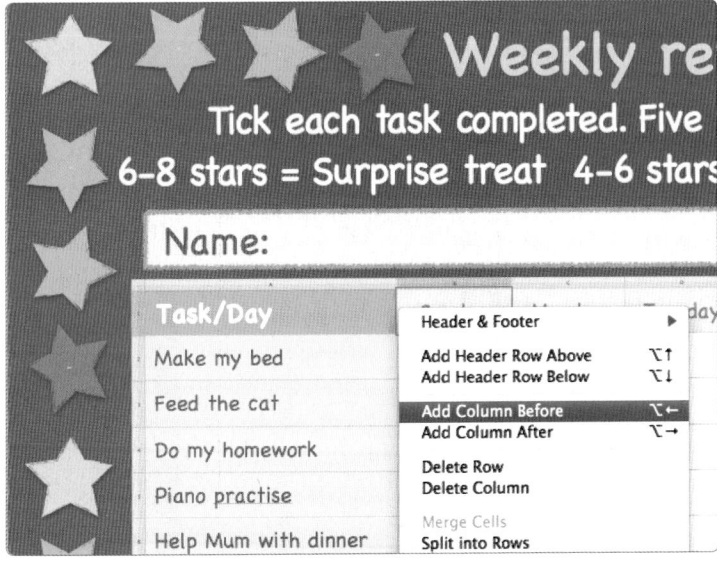

03: Add columns and rows

Add columns and rows by Ctrl-clicking on the table and selecting Add Column. Add your text by clicking inside each cell.

04: Print

Now save it and go to File>Print. You need to print bigger than standard A4 to use it effectively, so use the Print menu to make it A3 or bigger.

Share spreadsheets with iWork.com

When collaborating with others on a document, not being in the same office can be a pain. iWork.com is here to help

 **App used:** iWork

 **Time needed:** 10 minutes

 iWork.com is Apple's answer to collaborating on a document remotely. The idea is simple: post your work online for others to see, comment on and even communicate during the process. This can be a great tool if you're working as part of a team, or simply if you're uncertain that the work you've done is the best it could be and you would like the input of others to provide feedback on where you're going wrong and what you can do to improve. This service is compatible with any program of the suite, be it Pages, Keynote or Numbers, but for the

purpose of this tutorial we'll be illustrating how this works with the help of a Numbers spreadsheet.

Be aware though that this service is still in beta, which means it isn't perfected yet and is currently a work-in-progress. Some features may change over

> ## "This service is compatible with any program of the suite"

time and you may encounter the occasional strange glitch, but it won't damage your original file that's stored safely on your own Mac.

After you have discovered just how simple it is to use this excellent feature, you'll find yourself using it all the time, and there's still the distinct possibility that Apple will add even more features over time to extend the abilities of iWork.com.

This tutorial takes you through the process step by step so you can see exactly how easy it is to do. So let's get cracking and share those all important iWork files!

Share your spreadsheets
Send your spreadsheets to iWork.com

The toolbar
The toolbar has very few buttons. From left to right they are; Add Comment, Show/Hide Comments, Print (turns the file into a PDF for printing) and Download

Exporting options
The Download button offers you three format options depending on your needs: Numbers, PDF and Excel. Only the Numbers format appears to preserve your iWork.com comments

Linked comments
When a comment is linked to a cell in your spreadsheet, a line connects the two. You can drag the comment anywhere and that line will keep it tethered to the correct cell

Floating comments
If nothing is selected when you add a comment, it'll remain as a floating window and not connected to anything. To delete a comment, click on its 'x' button

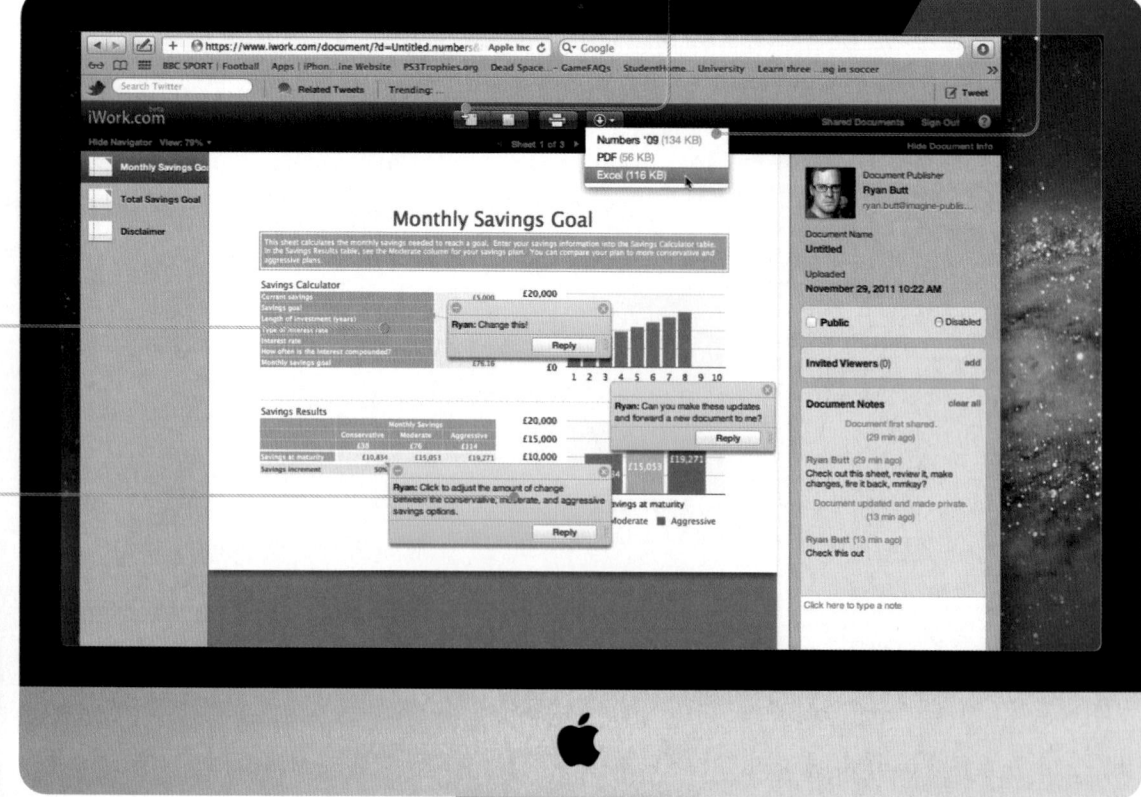

SEMI-LIVE COMMENTS AND NOTES
You can reply to any comment by using its Reply button. Once you hit Post the information will take a little while to be seen on your colleague's computer (it's not like iChat, so you have to be a little patient). The same applies for the Document Notes, although it's not immediately obvious since the field doesn't scroll down to reveal them – you have to do this manually. Using Comments is currently the better option.

Numbers Share, view and comment on a spreadsheet using iWork.com

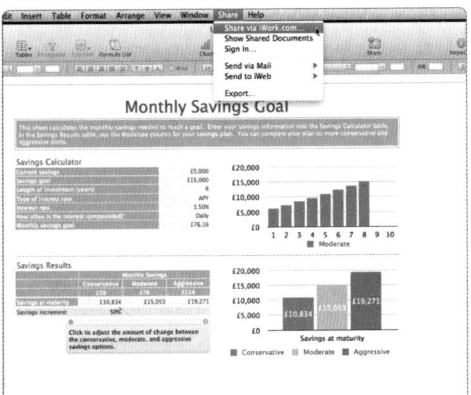

01: The Share menu

Open one of your spreadsheets and modify it if you need to. When you're ready to upload it, go to Share>Share via iWork.com.

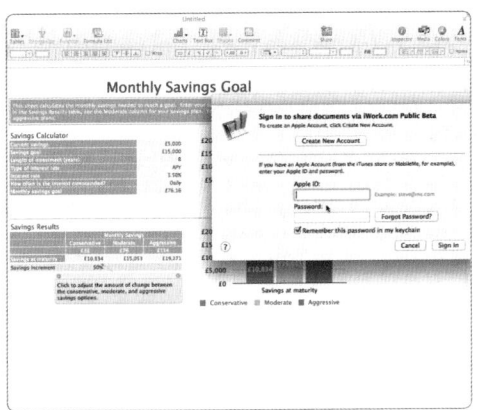

02: Signing in

You'll be requested to sign in. Your iTunes or account will work for this, so there's no need to create a unique one for iWork.com.

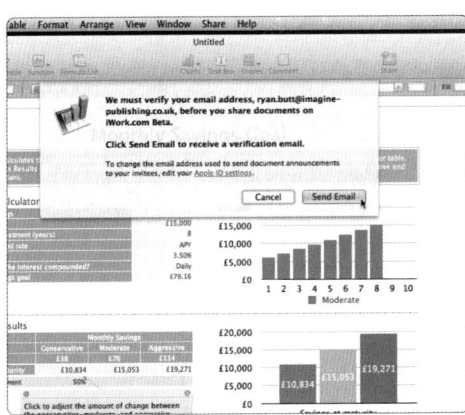

03: Email verification

You need to have your account verified if this is your first time. Click 'Send email' then follow the link in the email you receive.

04: Advanced options

Go back to Share>Share via iWork.com. A drop-down sheet will now appear offering you options. Click on Show Advanced to reveal more choices.

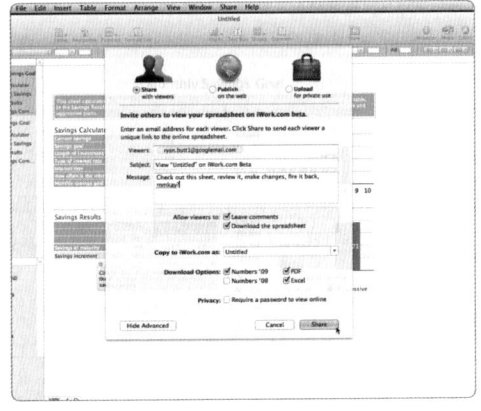

05: Send a message

In the 'To' field write the email address of the person(s) you wish to share your document with. You can also add a message. Now click Share.

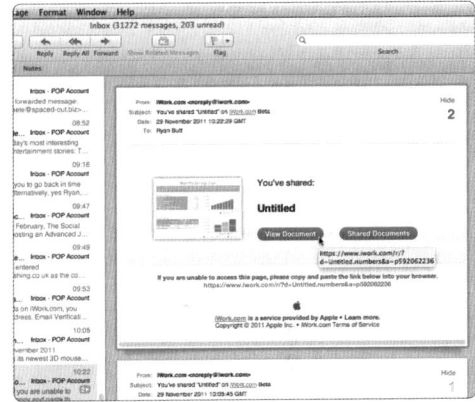

06: The colleague's view

The recipient will receive an email with a link directing them to iWork.com. Clicking on it will reveal the spreadsheet online.

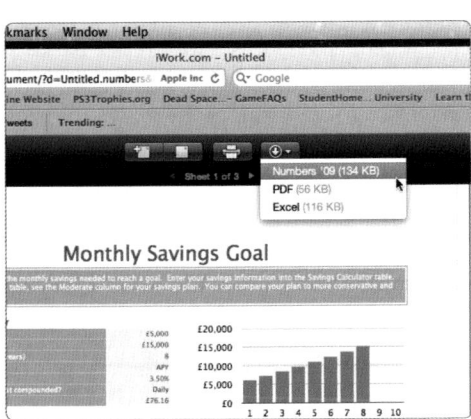

07: Download a copy

You can peruse the document but cannot modify it online. But you can download a copy by clicking on the fourth button in the toolbar.

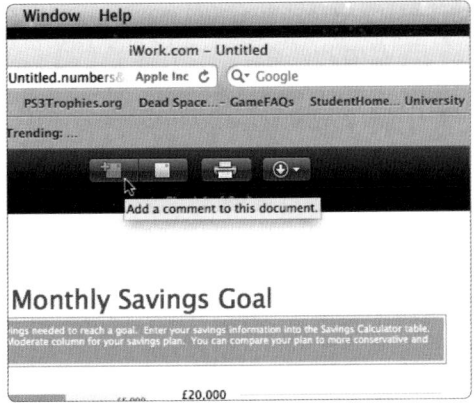

08: Post a comment

You can also post comments by selecting a cell and clicking on the yellow button in the toolbar. Click on Post in the yellow box to set it.

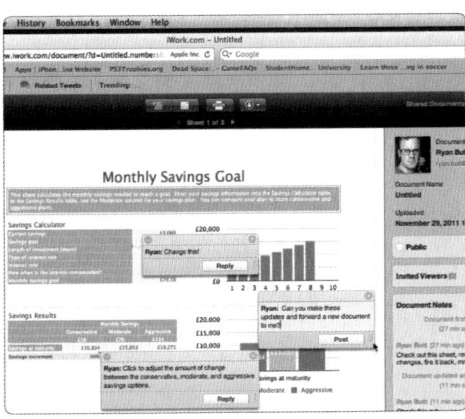

09: Document Notes

The Document Notes is for general information about the spreadsheet. The notes won't be saved when downloading the file, unlike the comments.

Create presentations in Keynote

Making attention-grabbing presentations with Apple's intuitive iWork app couldn't be simpler

 **App used:** Keynote

 **Time needed:** 15 minutes

If you need to present ideas and projects then Keynote, part of Apple's iWork package (that also includes Numbers and Pages), is the perfect app for you. Using the slick and intuitive interface you can create captivating slides from scratch or quickly put them together based on a selection of 44 pre-installed templates, replacing images with your own and changing the text in an existing layout to suit your own presentation. You can create entire selections of slides in minutes and add a wide range of attention-grabbing transitional effects for maximum impact and, once you have finished creating, the Presenter Display feature is on hand to ensure that you deliver your presentation in a smooth and professional manner. Everything you need to get your point across is present within the app, including the flexibility to add you own notes to read out as each slide is displayed, apply audio narration if you can't be present in person and a handy timer to make sure that you don't ramble on over the allotted time and risk losing your audience. As you will discover, the only limitations you'll encounter are your own imagination.

THUMBNAIL
All of your slides are displayed in sequence in the Slides window. Here you can drag and drop to rearrange them into a certain order

TOOLBAR
A clear and concise toolbar helps you easily add elements and edit your slides for maximum impact

ADD STYLE
The Inspector tool lets you easily apply style to text, images, charts and anything else that you include in your slides

PROFESSIONAL
With the Magic Move tool you can make the transitions between slides truly captivating

INTUITIVE
You can import your own images into existing templates and mask them to fit into designated positions on your slides

Other ways to present

How Keynote embraces all technology to help you get your point across to others

With the Presenter display feature you can keep the pace of your presentations flowing smoothly. While your presentation appears on the main display for your intended audience, you can see the current and subsequent slides, all of your slide notes and a clock and timer to ensure that you keep to tight time limits on a second display. Even if you aren't there to present in person the show can go on. Using a built-in narration tool, Keynote captures your audio voiceover and timing as you step through builds or move from one slide to the next.

If you like to pace around and be animated during your presentations for a more professional approach then you can also download and install the Keynote Remote app on your iPhone, iPad or iPod touch.

Using Wi-Fi, Keynote Remote turns your device into a wireless controller to keep your presentation rolling when you aren't stood over your computer to move it along manually. In landscape view you can see the current and next slides and in portrait see the current slide with all of your notes intact – tap to play and swipe to advance, wherever you are in the room.

Key features

Use Keynote to style slides to enthral and captivate your colleagues

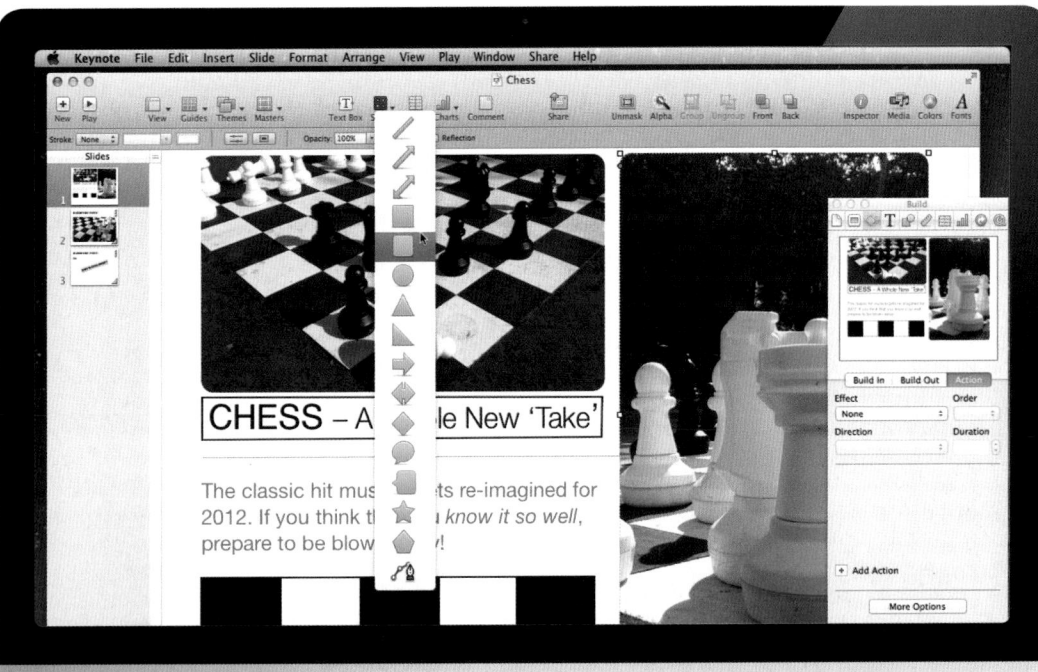

Ease of use

With over 40 Apple-designed templates to choose from, it is easy to drop in your own elements, replace the existing text and create professional-looking slides within minutes of first launching the app. Easy-to-use tools let you add additional elements, such as tables, charts, media and shapes to your slides and thanks to the Slide Navigator, the progress of your presentation and how it is organised is always in view.

Tools for the trade

With Keynote you can create captivating presentations using a powerful set of built-in graphics tools. With the Instant Alpha tool you can quickly remove the background of an image or mask it within a pre-drawn shape. With alignment and spacing guides you can find the centre of the slide and see if objects are spaced evenly – so anything you add to your slides, such as graphics, images or text boxes, are placed precisely where you want them.

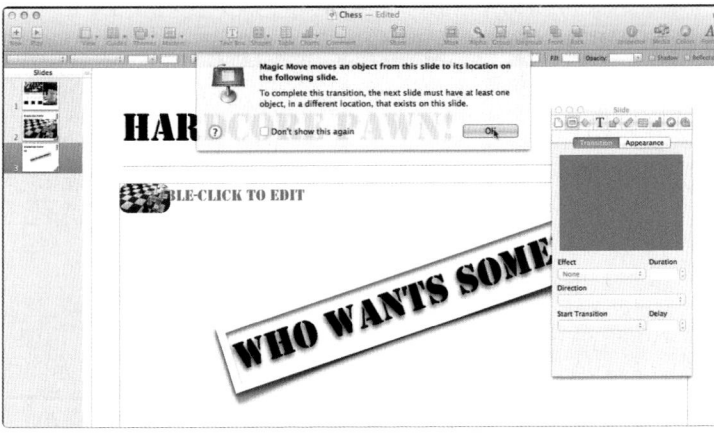

Animations and effects

With a choice of over 25 transitions you are sure to keep all eyes riveted on your awe-inspiring presentation as you move from one slide to the next. With the Magic Move transitional tool, you can duplicate slides, making changes to the secondary slide so that it looks like the objects become animated on the slide as it moves seamlessly to the next. The app provides freedom to add creative elements to help get your point across.

Compatibility and sharing

Keynote accommodates all Microsoft PowerPoint presentations, allowing you to read, edit and save them within the interface. You can upload your documents to iWork.com and invite others to view them, download them and add comments. Keynote utilises Apple's Documents in the Cloud feature, meaning any work will be synced automatically to your iCloud and you'll be able to pick up where you left off on another device.

Rehearse your Keynote slideshow

If you want a slick presentation you'll have to practise. Luckily Keynote has a great tool to help you do just that

**App used:** Keynote

**Price:** £13.99/$19.99

**Time needed:** 15 minutes

If you want to give professional and entertaining presentations in Keynote, **you will need to rehearse.** A lot. First of all you'll need to build a slick, interesting and engaging presentation, which is easy to accomplish using Keynote's broad range of tools and easy-to-access functions.

Once you've done this you'll need to practise what you want to say as each slide appears. You'll also want to check that all the animations, effects and other elements are working as strongly as they should be. Keynote has a great full-screen tool to help you do this. The full-screen nature is incredibly important as it gives you the 'Keynote Feel'. There are timers on the bottom of the screen as you practise so you can make sure that you are adhering to any time limits, whether they are imposed by yourself or others. Not only that, but you can customise the display so it is working as hard as possible to help you hone and perfect your speech.

Follow this tutorial as we take you through the key processes step by step that you need to take to rehearse your slideshow. Do this right and you will be fully prepared for the big presentation and set to impress.

"You'll need to practise what you want to say as each slide appears"

Rehearsal is key
Give presentations that entertain and enthrall

Slides
Position these wherever you like. We have ours arranged so slides move from right to left but you can go the other way or even up and down too

Make it big
You can drag and resize any of the windows you like. Here we've made the time remaining window as big as possible, so it's easy to see as we practise the presentation

Tick them
Use the tick boxes to select elements you want to see on screen. Experimentation will help you find the right combination. When you are finished click the Done button

Slide indicator
At the bottom of your current slide is an indicator to show you how far through the presentation you are

EXPORT
Once you have got your presentation as polished as possible, you can export it for all kinds of uses. Use the File menu and then select Export. There, in the new window that has appeared, you can select the way you would like to export your presentation.

Keynote Use the Rehearse Slideshow tool in Keynote

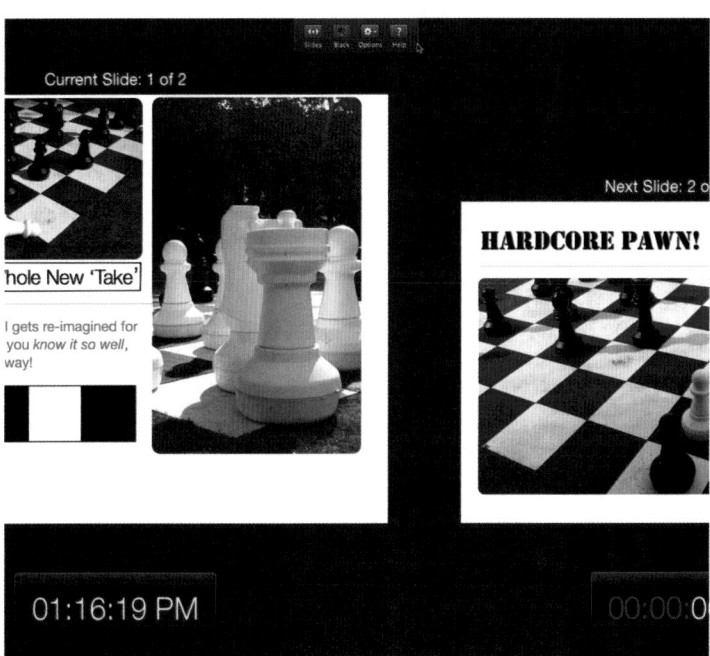

01: Make it, rehearse it

Once you have built your scintillating presentation, go to the Play section of the top menu and then click on the Rehearse Slideshow option. Everything will then fade into full-screen mode and you can begin your presentation once ready.

02: Mouse to the top

Flick through the slides to rehearse your presentation and the timers will then begin. If you wish to make any changes to the display at this point, direct your mouse to the top of the display and a hidden menu will magically appear.

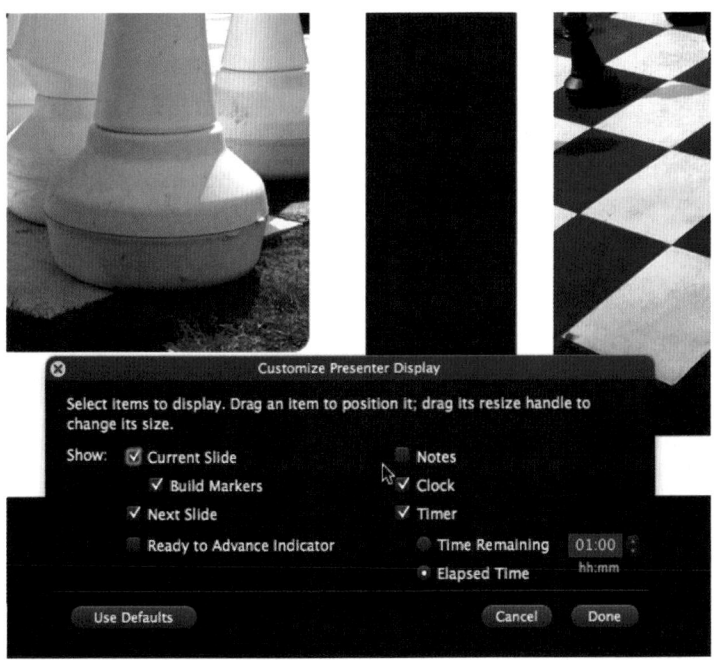

03: Options

Click on Options in the menu and then select Customize Presenter Display. This will freeze the presentation at the current point and allow you to rearrange the elements that are present on screen. You will just need to click and drag them around.

04: Floating window

A floating options window will also appear that will let you pick the elements that appear on screen. Tick boxes are used so you can simply click to add or remove elements from your display. Once you're happy you can then continue to practise your presentation.

A grand finalé for your presentation

Use animations in Keynote to give your presentation a much more climatic ending

 **App used:** Keynote
 **Price:** £13.99/$19.99
 **Time needed:** 10 minutes

Some people might say that a climatic ending is what makes a good movie. Whether that's true or not, it's definitely the part that everybody remembers most. Be it a movie, book, piece of music, videogame or – as in our case – a simple presentation, suspense, pace and drama are crucial to keeping the audience captivated and hanging off your every word. You also want the viewer or reader to feel that everything that went before it was worth it, and you want to leave them satisfied with the ending that you leave them with.

This common technique of slowly building suspense to culminate in a grand finalé is especially useful when creating presentations, particularly if you are building up to a big announcement that's going to really appeal to your captivated

> "Pace and drama are crucial to keep the audience captivated"

audience. The example that we are using here is the annual financial report for a small business. The big announcement at the end is the net profit – which for many people is what the presentation is all going to be about – so we are going to use a combination of animation techniques in order to give it extra importance and to emphasise that this is the highlight of the presentation.

Follow these easy steps to learn how and discover ways in which you can blow your audience away with an explosive finalé. It really is simple and definitely worth it.

Finish presentations on a high
Make sure you go out with a bang while presenting

Suspense
Keep your audience captivated by teasing them. Create suspense by adding a cliff-hanger at the end of the penultimate slide

Magic Move
Make an image move from slide to slide using Magic Move. It only works with identical images and works best if the image is resized

HOW IT WORKS
From the first to the second slide, the cupcake will decrease in size and move bottom-left. At the same time, the images will align themselves to the right. The big figure will appear one number at a time with a sparkly effect over the duration of eight seconds. Once this has finished, the figure will spin around.

Duration
Edit the duration of your animation by using the arrows in the Duration box. From the Start Transition menu, you can opt whether to start the animation yourself with a click or start automatically

Play
Tap in the image to view each animation. From within this palette you can also choose your Builds and Actions, from the duration and order to colour and direction

Keynote Use animation to emphasise your presentation

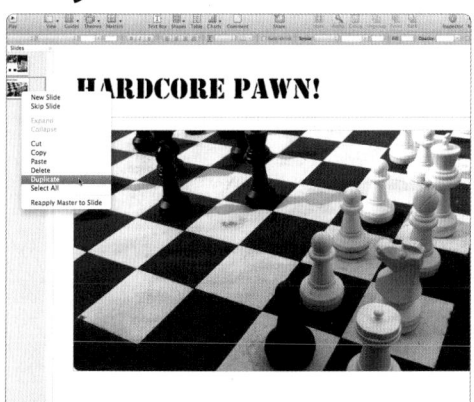

01: Duplicate slide

Try using Magic Move to create impact. Begin by duplicating what will be the penultimate slide. Control-click and select Duplicate.

02: Resize

Magic Move works best if you resize and rearrange your images. On the duplicated slide, click the image and drag the corner points.

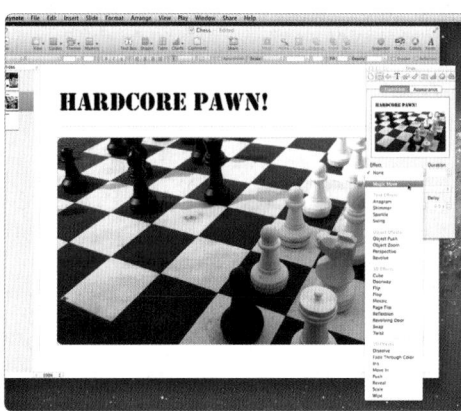

03: Magic Move

Go back to the previous slide. Open the Slide Inspector and select Transition. From the Effect drop-down menu, select Magic Move.

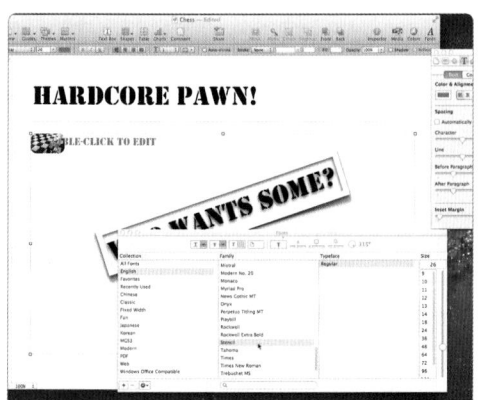

04: Format text

Type the data onto the last slide and open the Font palette. Make the text as big and bold as you can for maximum impact.

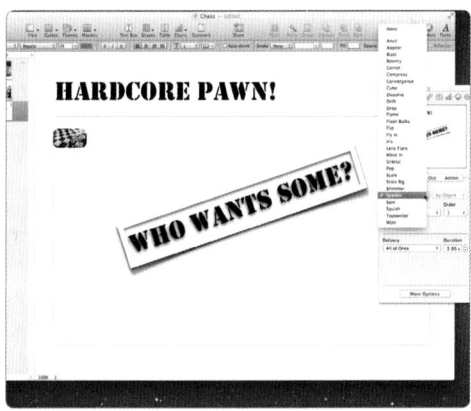

05: Build

With the box selected, go to the Build Inspector and choose an effect. We've chosen Sparkle. Edit the effect by direction, order and duration.

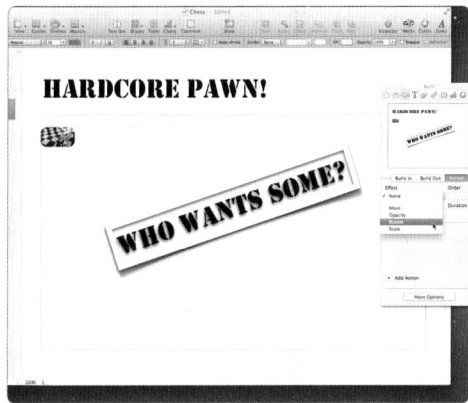

06: Rotation

The data will appear onto the slide with the effect. Once completed, add a rotation for extra emphasis. Click on Action and choose an effect.

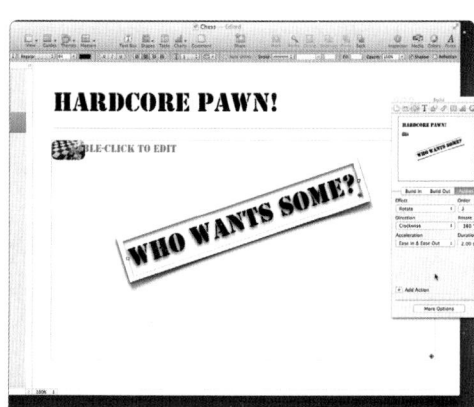

07: Full circle

Edit the rotation by the direction and degrees. The Order refers to its position within the sequence. For more on this, tap on More Options.

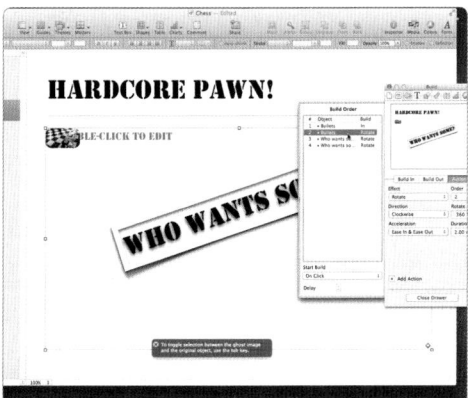

08: Build Order

This menu shows a list of your animations. Drag them around to change the order. You can determine how they start and the delay.

09: Play

Play each animation from within the Inspector palette by clicking on the image, or to view the entire presentation full-screen click Play.

Create an iMovie title in Keynote

Set the tone of your iMovie project by creating a beautiful title sequence using Keynote themes and a little creative flair

 **App used:** Keynote

 **Price:** £13.99/$19.99

 **Time needed:** 20 minutes

Keynote isn't just for presentations, as it can help you create other things, such as the topic of this tutorial – a title for your iMovie project. Choosing the right theme, font and colours for your opening title sequence can really help to set the tone of your movie – just look to the big screen for inspiration. For example, you won't often see the opening credits of a horror film designed using a beautiful script font in a muted cream or pink, or a romantic love story using a distressed-looking typeface with a combination of black and blood red.

In this instance, we're going to create a title sequence to accompany a movie of an elegant birthday tea party. In keeping with the theme of the movie, we want to use a sequence that has something of a vintage feel to it. Although iMovie

> ## "We're turning to Keynote for some inspiration"

has some great themes, none are really suitable for this project, so we're turning to Keynote for some inspiration. This application is a great piece of kit that many will overlook, but we find an essential part of the iWork suite. The options on offer give you more choice than being confined to what iMovie brings to the table. Just a few simple steps will make all the difference to your iMovie project.

Follow this tutorial to find out how to create and export a fantastic title screen for your movie that will spruce up your work and make it look much more professional overall.

Movie titles in Keynote

Use the iWork application to catch your viewer's eye

Hierarchy
Don't forget to make your headline bigger than your subtitle – this helps the audience navigate the page. Using two different fonts can also help differentiate between lines, as can using different weights such as Bold and Italic

Animating
If you're going to use animation between slides or for text, choose a build that is in keeping with your theme. Typewriter works well in this instance. To add animation to the text, make sure that it is highlighted first

Master slides
The master slides will appear by dragging this icon in a downwards direction. To change the template of a slide, select it and then select the one you want to use from Masters

Sensitive colour use
Be sensitive when choosing colour for your text. Bright colours won't evoke the feeling of a bygone age. Muted colours, such as cream and gold, are much more appropriate

ADDING MEDIA
To add audio or graphics to your sequence, head to the Media panel (top right of the interface) and choose the Audio or Photo tab. If you do import audio, make sure that the 'Include audio' option is selected when exporting to iMovie.

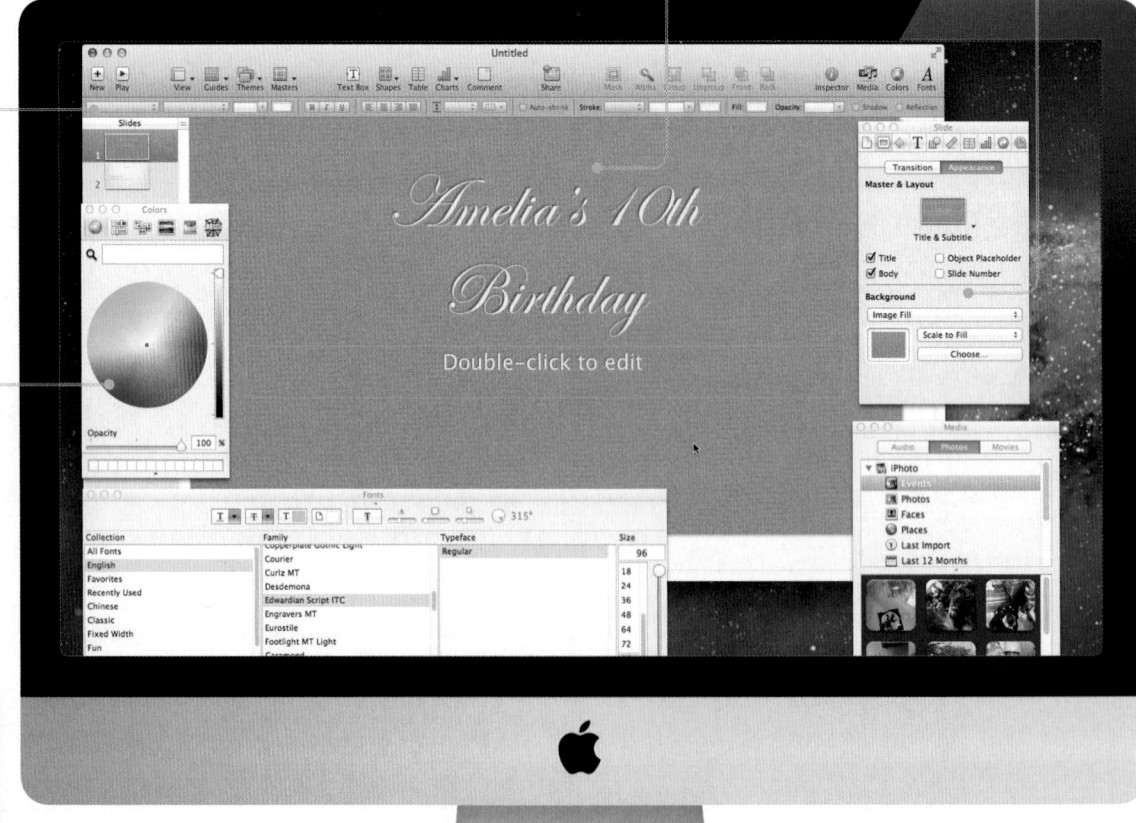

Keynote Create a vintage-style title sequence for iMovie

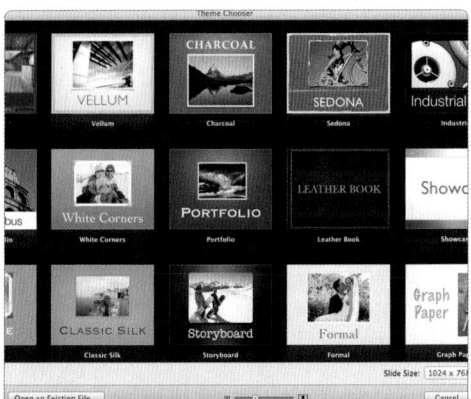

01: Choose a template

Select a template, then click on the 'Inspector'. Select the 'Document Inspector' tab and select 'Custom slide size' from the Slide Size menu.

02: Check the size

Make sure your slide is set to a dimension that is consistent with your iMovie project's size. If it's a widescreen project, it should be 960x540 pixels.

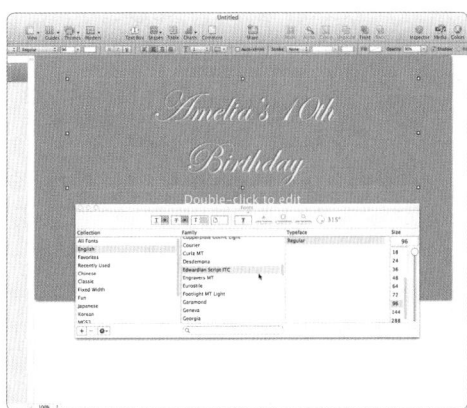

03: Editing text

Click in the box to start typing and drag the cursor over the text to edit. In the Fonts panel, select a font that evokes the feel of your movie.

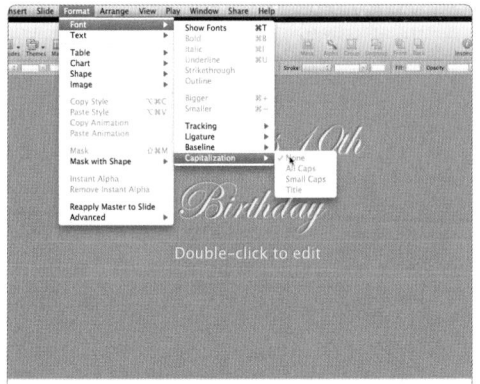

04: Lower case

You can change the text from upper to lower case by going to the Format menu and selecting Font>Capitalization>None.

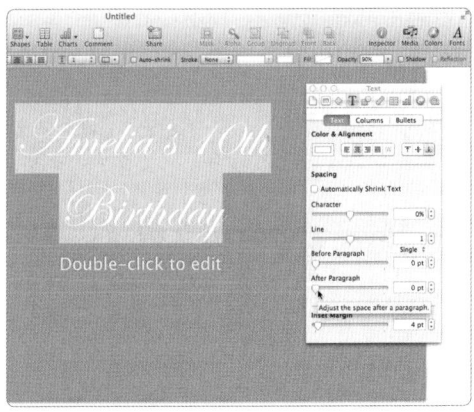

05: Tweaking

Go to the 'T' tab within the Inspector panel to make text adjustments. You can change the alignment and colour, or change the spacing.

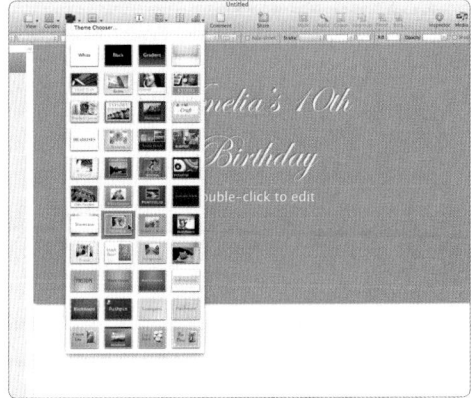

06: Change of heart

If you decide that you don't like the selected theme, it's not too late to change. Simply go to Theme Chooser and choose another.

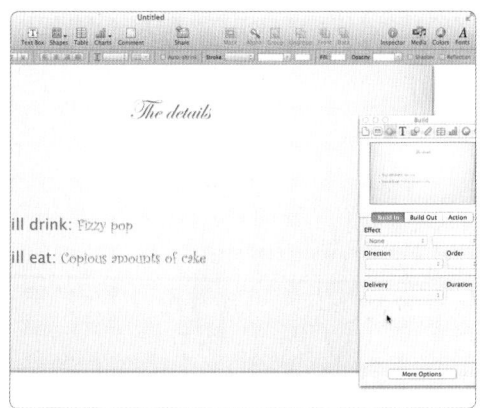

07: Builds

Click Shift+Cmd+N simultaneously to add a new slide and select a new design from Masters. Add animations by going to the Build Inspector.

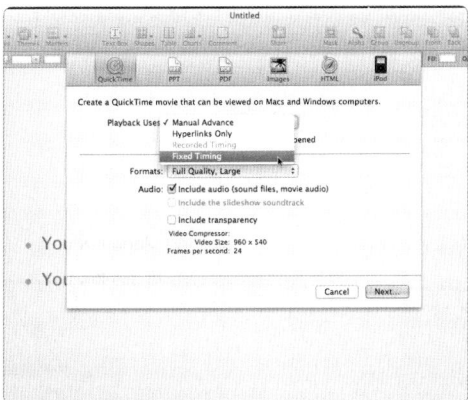

08: Fixed timing

When you're finished, go to Share>Export and choose the QuickTime option. Under the Playback Uses pop-up menu, select Fixed Timing.

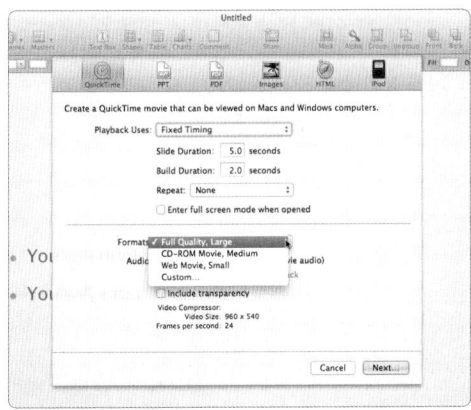

09: Exporting

Using the Formats pop-up menu, select 'Full Quality, Large'. When you're done, click Next to name and save. Now you're ready for iMovie.

Move iWork documents to your iOS device with iCloud

How to use documents in the Cloud to continue working on your iWork documents on your iOS device

 **App used:** iCloud

 **Time needed:** 10 minutes

iCloud is a great free service from Apple that enables all of your contacts, calendars, Safari bookmarks, photos and music to be synced across your Mac and your iOS devices wirelessly over Wi-Fi. You are provided with 5GB of virtual cloud storage for free (additional space can be purchased) and it is integrated into you apps so that updates, data transfers and syncs occur automatically without you having to do anything.

One of the best features of this service being able to sync documents to the Cloud. If you have the same iCloud-enabled apps on more than one device, iCloud will automatically keep your documents up to date across all of your devices, meaning you don't have to email documents form your Mac to your iOS devices, and vice versa, or use third-party apps such as Dropbox. You don't even have to save because all changes and edits you carry out in a compatible document on your Mac will be updated and reflected in the same document on your iPhone, iPad or iPod touch. Naturally, all of Apple's iWork apps (Pages, Keynote and Numbers) support iCloud, so you can work on a Pages document, Keynote presentation or Numbers spreadsheet on your Mac at work and, without you having to lift a finger, carry on working on the same document on your iOS device during your commute home or in the comfort of your lounge later on. Here's how to set up this revolutionary process.

iCloud Transferring iWork docs with iCloud

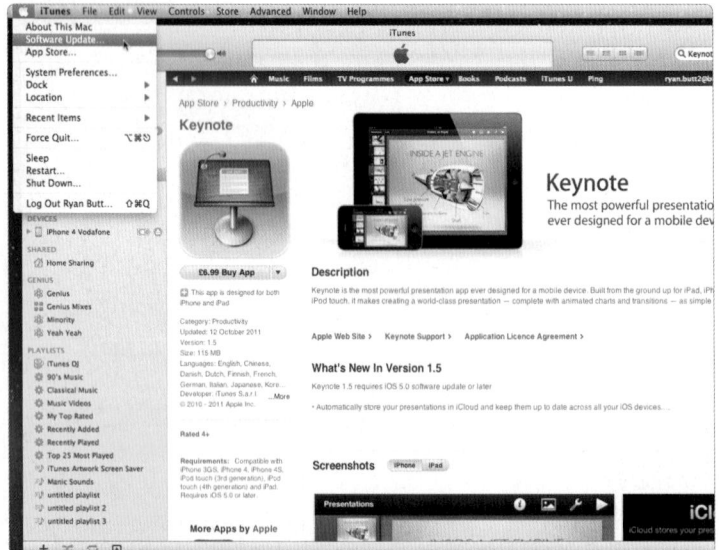

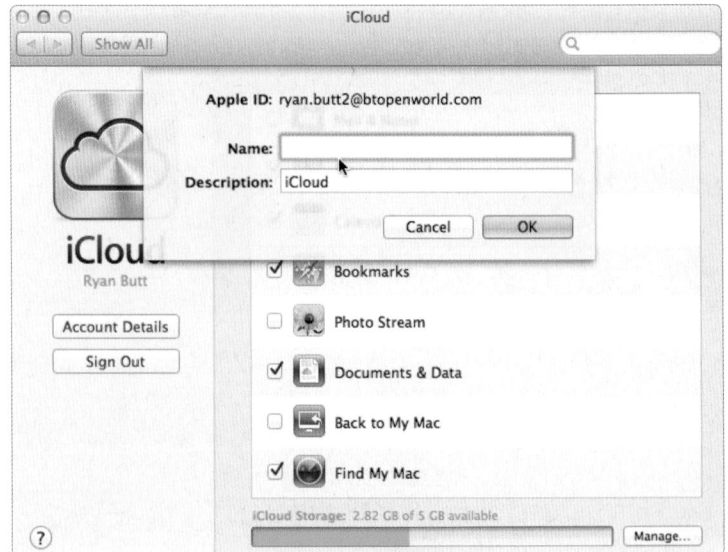

01: Install iCloud

To enjoy the benefits of iCloud's Documents you must have the latest version of OS X Lion (10.7.2) on your Mac and iOS 5 installed on your device, along with the latest versions of the iWork apps. Click on the Apple menu and then choose 'Software Update…' to get the latest software.

02: Open System Preferences

Click on System Preferences in your dock and then click on the iCloud option, which will be listed under Internet & Wireless in OS X 10.7.2. Log into your iCloud account using your Apple ID and ensure that the same account is enabled on your iOS device.

A new way to work
iCloud means that you can work wherever you want

Documents in the Cloud
When you have set-up your iCloud account, ensure that the 'Documents & Data' tickbox is checked to have all iWork documents transferred wirelessly between your Mac and your iOS device without hassle

Your documents
The beauty of iCloud is that you can work on any iWork documents in Pages, Keynote or Numbers and any changes or edits you make will be automatically reflected in the same documents on your iOS device

Your iCloud
iCloud is a free service that comes as part of the OS X 10.7.2 and iOS 5 updates. Log into your account using your Apple ID and wirelessly sync and transfer data over Wi-Fi without having to lift a finger

UNIVERSAL ICLOUD ACCESS
The iCloud service isn't just restricted to Macs and iOS devices, you can access your synced files on PC too, and, indeed, any computer in the world – not just your own. All you have to do is access any web browser and then go to **www.icloud.com**. Then enter your Apple ID and password and you will be able to access your iWork documents, as well as calendars, emails and contacts.

03: Enable documents in the Cloud
Ensure that the 'Documents & Data' tickbox is checked in the list of iCloud enabled apps and do likewise on your iOS device. Now launch an iWork app (Pages, Keynote or Numbers) and start working. That's really all there is to the set-up process. Simple, eh?

04: Continue working
When you stop working on an iWork app on your Mac, there is no need to save. Just pick up your iOS device, launch the same app (if you have recently updated you may be prompted to 'Use iCloud') and carry on exactly where you left off. Quick, easy and convenient.

100 Essential Mac Apps

The ultimate guide to the Mac apps you simply have to have

Finding and installing Mac apps is now easier than ever, thanks to the arrival of the Mac App Store. It works by letting you install apps with just a click, and you can be assured that they will be safe for the Mac device you are using. You can still download and install apps from anywhere on the web, but the App Store is by far the most efficient and safe way to add new software to your computing setup. The apps extend the functionality of any Mac greatly, and without them your choices are limited as to what you can do. There are thousands available, and they cover near enough every conceivable subject or task that you need to complete. This feature will highlight the essential apps from every app category, and hopefully narrow down your search for the best of the best. Your choice of apps is genuinely unlimited.

5 essential apps

01: Desktop Task Timer
Price: £2.99/$4.99 Developer: Eric Asmussen

Time is money, and many people need to bill that time to customers and contractors. This kind of billing needs to be precise and accurate at all times, and most importantly unobtrusive. You don't want your timings to get in the way of the work you are doing, and this app ensures that everything you do is monitored automatically. You can add notes to each task, and switch between tasks with just one click; and all you need to do is calculate what your customer owes. This is perfect for anyone whose time really is money.

02: SharePlus
Price: £10.49/$14.99 Developer: Daniel Gomez

Collaborating with colleagues is a huge time-saver in the world of business, and SharePlus is the platform of choice for many. With this app, you can share all types of media, and also deal with calendars, reports and internal and external lists. The presentation is clean and simple, as you would expect from a Mac, and it truly is a great tool for any collaborator who needs to share information with others.

03: friedEgg Touch
Price: £10.49/$14.99 Developer: friedEgg Limited

Creating and analysing complex charts is not an easy task, and often requires specialists to complete the job. This is not the case any longer, however, because this app will let you build impressive 3D charts whenever you need to, and also lets you manipulate them in real-time. It looks as good as it works, and allows anyone to create complex charts relating to any subject. A truly impressive business tool.

04: Splashtop Remote Desktop
Price: £1.99/$2.99 Developer: Splashtop Inc

Imagine being able to remotely access your PC or Mac from the computer that is in front of you. You can now do this thanks to this app which works cross-platform at high speed. You will never be away from the office again, wherever you are at any given time.

05: OfficeHaven Pro
Price: £34.99/$49.99 Developer: Holy Cox

OfficeHaven Pro is an ideal app for anyone who is self-employed, or who works freelance on various projects. It includes the most needed tools, all of which work in tandem in order to successfully create a one-stop solution that will ensure that you always get the job done on time and in a quality fashion.

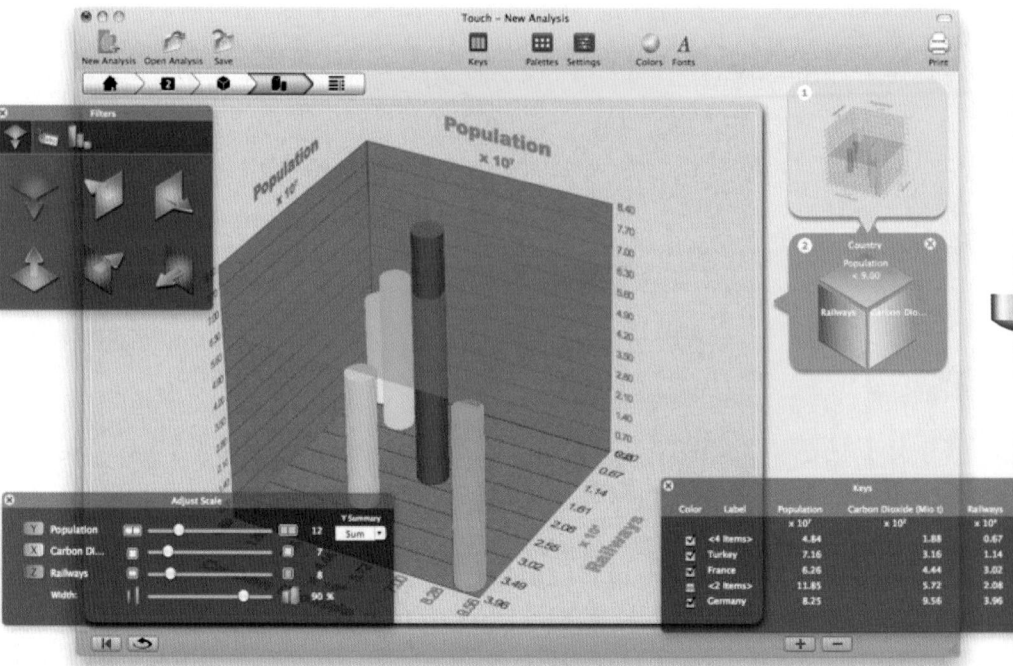
■ friedEgg Touch's visuals are stylish, clear and impressive.

Business
Tailor to your work-related needs

Business apps can take a variety of forms, and cover everything from general communication to solutions for specialist industries. Despite the fact that many companies have bespoke software for their tasks, it is often possible to improve

productivity by using third-party applications. Computers can be remotely monitored and used from miles away, employees can collaborate on projects using a single app, and there are solutions available for every conceivable task. With some planning and the careful selection of the right apps, anybody's Mac can be greatly extended to become perfectly functional for whatever task you need to do. Often, it isn't just the well-known or expensive apps that do the best job, because there are a variety of solutions available for every single business need. Business is a wide-ranging topic, and fortunately there is a wide range of Mac apps available to support your needs.

"Business apps take a variety of forms"

■ Splashtop lets you view videos on another computer.

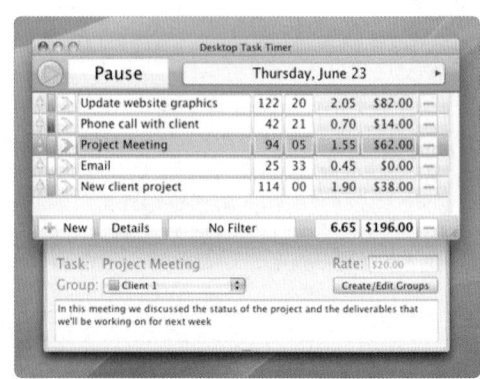
■ Desktop Task Timer makes tasks accessible all of the time.

■ Lots of information is displayed within World Explorer's clean interface.

■ AlphaBaby's vibrant colours and shapes will keep young children happy.

■ Statistics about your learning are available in Mental Case.

Education

Get well and truly schooled with this collection of apps

Education is something that stays with us for all of our lives, from the day we are born to the moment we die. It doesn't matter how old you are or how clever you are; there will always be software solutions that can help you. Children can benefit from colourful and imaginative visual games, and adults can benefit from learning about the complexities of advanced topics. Education works best when it is fun, and the imagination put into many educational software solutions makes the Mac platform ideal for learning. No matter what is the topic or the individual needs, Mac apps will help you and your family learn whenever is convenient for you. This is one of the most important areas of computing today, and one that can be potentially beneficial to all Mac users, because the platform is perfectly suited to all areas of education.

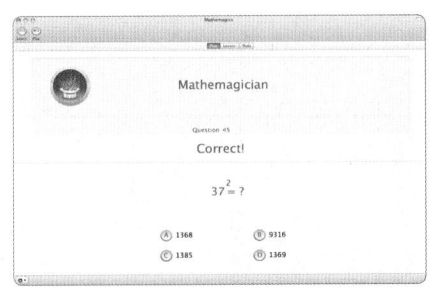

■ The Mathemagics interface is sparse but effective.

5 essential apps

01: Mental Case - The Study App
Price: £20.49/$29.99
Developer: The Mental Faculty

 Flashcards are recognised as one of the very best ways to revise. Mental Case lets you create your own flashcards, use existing sets and even integrate with an iPad or iPhone. You can quiz yourself, view statistics to check the likelihood of passing a test, or simply read the cards over and over again until you are sure of your competence.

02: World Explorer PREMIUM
Price: £2.99/$4.99
Developer: Regis ANDRE

 If you're going to learn about the world, you may as well do it in style, and World Explorer contains everything you need. With more than 600,000 points of interest, photos and descriptions of each location, the world is at your fingertips. It supports multiple languages, and also includes slideshows, so we can think of few better places to start exploring.

03: Mathemagics
Price: £1.99/$2.99
Developer: Blue Lightning Labs

 Mathemagics feels like a game, but there is a serious motive behind the design. You can learn tricks to impress your friends, or help yourself if you are struggling with maths. It teaches you some methods to quickly multiply, divide or find the square root, and in our tests it proved to be extremely effective. This is a map for everyone, no matter what your level of expertise.

04: AlphaBaby
Price: £0.69/$0.99
Developer: Laura Dickey

 AlphaBaby not only works in an environment which makes it impossible for a child to play with, or be distracted by other applications, but it also serves as an excellent learning tool for children. It is probably best suited for the very young, and allows them to understand letters and shapes at a steady pace. Overall, it works brilliantly, and we wouldn't hesitate to recommend it.

05: Smartr
Price: £1.99/$2.99
Developer: Barefoot Hackers AB

 Smartr is a map-based app that is designed to utilise flashcards in order to help you learn, but it has a trick up its sleeve. It analyses your past performance while using this app, and then asks you questions based on your lowest performances in particular subject areas, which should ensure that you cover all of the areas of any subject you are learning.

Entertainment
Have a whole lot of fun on your Mac

The word 'entertainment' can cover a multitude of things. From listening to internet radio to watching movie clips and enjoying clever screensavers, you can entertain yourself in almost any way you like. It is a broad category, and is hard to define completely, but it is also a category with a wealth of apps that will help you pass your spare time. You can learn magic tricks, watch Earth from space, or simply sit back and watch a realistic fireplace fill your Mac screen. The days of computers being used purely for business are over; now, you can use them for any activity you like. Entertainment is one activity that everyone should spend some time enjoying on their Mac – the only dilemma is choosing from the huge range of apps that are designed to make everyday life a little more fun.

■ The presentation of The Lost Watch 3D is stunning.

■ DinoSingers will keep children amused for hours.

> "There are a wealth of apps to help you pass your spare time"

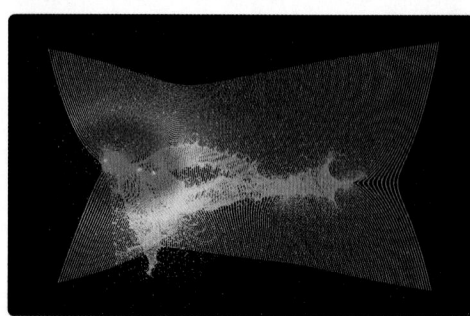
■ Gravilux becomes more engrossing the more you use it.

■ Media is recreated perfectly in MPlayerX.

5 essential apps

01: iBank

Price £39.99/$59.99
Developer IGG Software LLC

Personal finance is often overlooked, which is a shame, as many apps bring a simple solution to what should be a complex problem. iBank turns this on its head, by offering the ability to monitor every aspect of your money. You can track your spending, plan for the future and even deal with digital receipts, foreign exchange rates and schedules of events. The presentation maintains a personal approach, despite masking some complex calculations, and it all comes together to create an app that is perfect for anyone who wants to keep a close eye on their personal finances.

02: StockSpy

Price £13.99/$19.99 **Developer** Calcin Schut

StockSpy is not designed to provide you with the latest market prices, but instead offers a wealth of information to help you decide where to invest next. It allows you to track significant changes in the market, and automatically view the news that may have led to this change. Despite not being a full solution for traders, it most certainly is a useful addition, but for anyone dealing in stocks it works perfectly.

03: Investoscope

Price £39.99/$59.99 **Developer** Morten Fjord-Larsen

The interface is unusual in that it just uses one screen. However, you can monitor multiple areas of your portfolio without having to continually click to find the information you need. Charts are included alongside real-time trends to ensure you are always up-to-date, and it should provide enough information to ensure you don't lose that important trend. It is likely to become a one-stop shop for many investors.

04: Pay It Down

Price £7.49/$11.99 **Developer** Snowmint Creative Solutions LLC

Paying off debt sounds easy, but that is far from the truth. This app offers you multiple methods of paying down debt, and lets you easily visualise the best method to use. It is quite simple, but that is all you need, and it could change your life.

05: XTick Extreme

Price Free **Developer** Arthur Roshchin

It is rare that an app involved in charting stock markets is free, but this is the case here. It is basic in its aims, but is presented nicely, and will serve anyone who needs to keep an eye on the markets very well indeed.

■ XTick Extreme has a busy interface for busy people.

Finance
Keep track of the money side of things

From dealing with your bank account to monitoring complex share dealing, the world of finance is often a complex area. It doesn't have to be, however, because there are thousands of apps available that have been designed to make money-management that little bit easier. Accountants can deal with complex databases, a housewife can manage household bills, and even a teenager can keep track of their pocket money. If there is a need to deal with finance in any way, then the chances are there will be an app that supports the task at hand. You may also find that using a Mac to manage your money will, in the long run, save you lots more money. You can now have control over every aspect of your finances, be they for work or home. You just need to spend some time getting used to the solutions available.

> "Apps make money-management easier"

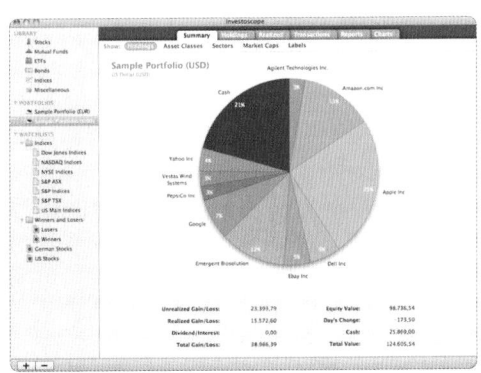

■ Judge investment performance visually with Investoscope.

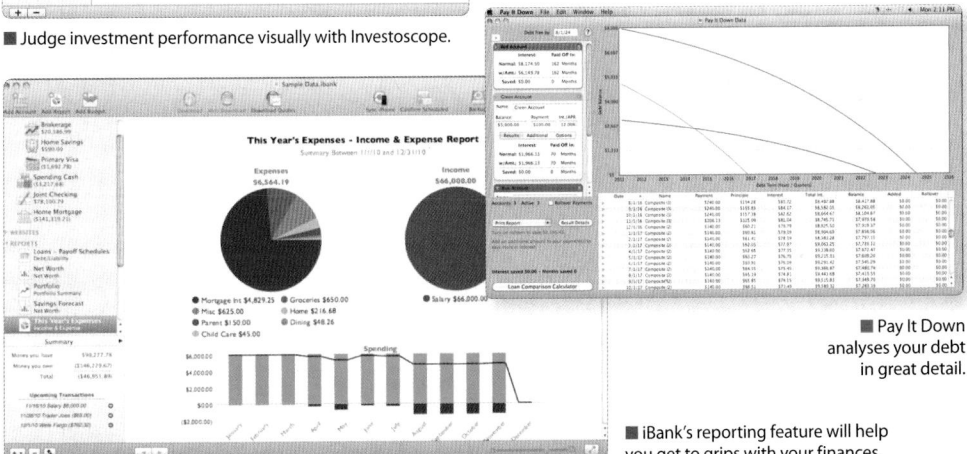

■ Pay It Down analyses your debt in great detail.

■ iBank's reporting feature will help you get to grips with your finances.

■ The physics in International Snooker HD have been recreated accurately.

■ The depth of gameplay in LEGO Harry Potter is matched by the visuals.

Games
Have fun and keep your brain engaged

Gaming has historically been somewhat lacklustre on the Mac platform, but the huge growth of iOS gaming has transferred to its bigger brother. Popular titles in the puzzle and strategy categories have long been standard, but there are now many hundreds more options available, most of which are at very cheap prices. To complement these simple titles, there is now a variety of high-end arcade titles available, some of which actually rival games consoles in terms of quality, longevity and addictiveness. You can choose almost any game type you like, depending on your preferences and the budget available, and can be sure that the games you like to play are available. Every possible genre is covered, and once you start you may find that you play games on your Mac more than anything else. Everyone needs some fun from time to time, and a Mac is the perfect tool to help you relax and enjoy yourself.

■ The simplicity of Rail Maze's visuals hides an immersive gameplay experience.

5 essential apps

01: Jelly Defense
Price £2.99/$4.99
Developer Infinite Dreams

 Jelly Defense contains visuals, a soundtrack and gameplay like we have rarely seen before. Despite falling into the tower defence category (you defend the jelly nation from invaders), it has many unique aspects, and will keep you coming back time and time again. It's addictive enough to make you pull your hair out, but it is sensational to play, and you will keep playing for hours at a time.

02: Osmos
Price £2.99/$4.99
Developer Hemisphere Games Inc

 This is a difficult game to describe, because it is unique in almost every way. Your goal is to become the biggest orb on the screen, which you do by devouring other orbs. It sounds bizarre, but the music and visuals drag you in like few other games can. Once you start playing, you will find it hard to stop, and it is the perfect mixture of relaxation and frantic gameplay.

03: LEGO Harry Potter
Price £20.99/$29.99
Developer Feral Interactive

 LEGO Harry Potter combines immersive gameplay with graphics that are suitable for all ages. Using Lego as the basis for each character means violence is kept to a minimum, and adds to the feel of the game. It will get your brain thinking, but most of all you will enjoy the longevity, which never seems to end. You could play this for months, and still enjoy every minute.

04: International Snooker HD
Price £4.99/$6.99
Developer Big Head Games Ltd.

 Snooker is not an easy game to recreate in digital form, but this is nevertheless one of the best examples we have seen to date. The physics have been perfectly recreated, and function to enable players of all levels the chance to enjoy the experience. Indeed, you can probably play this game better than you can in real life.

05: Rail Maze
Price Free
Developer Spooky House Studios UG

 Sometimes, the most simple games are the best ones, and Rail Maze, where you build railroads, is an example where simplicity has been successfully married with superb replay value. The levels get harder as you progress, but that won't stop you stepping up to the challenge as your abilities improve. This game will certainly keep you on the right track.

Graphics and design

Don't neglect your artistic side; discover the best there is to offer on the Mac

The Mac platform has long been preferred by those who like to create, and the options available today are greater than ever before. Whether you want to annotate a simple image or produce a work of art, there will be a solution ready and waiting for you. You can have fun tweaking photos, create photo albums for the family, or spend hours producing a completely original digital painting. No matter what your budget or level of talent, you will be able to find an app that sparks your creative juices, and some of the titles are truly extraordinary. Indeed, it is now possible to create graphics that only a few years ago would have required roomfuls of computers. So it is time to have a look around to see what is available, and spend some time creating like you never have before.

"Whatever you want to do, there's a solution waiting for you"

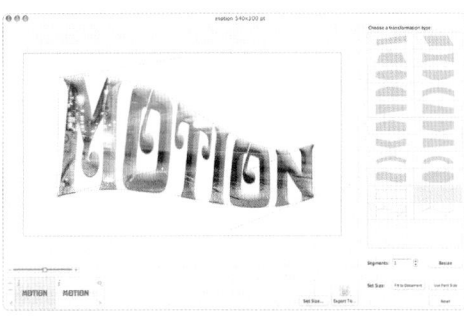
■ With Art Text 2 you can turn text into any design you like.

■ ImageWell is particularly useful for annotating images.

■ VintageScene can produce some stunning effects.

■ Delve as deep as you want into Pixelmator.

5 essential apps

01: Art Text 2

Price £13.99/$19.99 Developer Belight Software Ltd

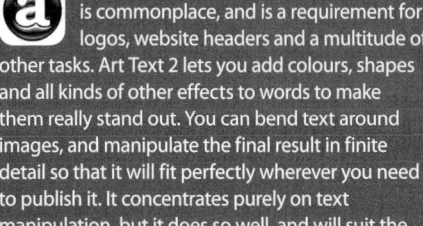 The need to make text look more creative is commonplace, and is a requirement for logos, website headers and a multitude of other tasks. Art Text 2 lets you add colours, shapes and all kinds of other effects to words to make them really stand out. You can bend text around images, and manipulate the final result in finite detail so that it will fit perfectly wherever you need to publish it. It concentrates purely on text manipulation, but it does so well, and will suit the many people who need this kind of solution.

02: Pixelmator

Price £20.99/$29.99 Developer UAB Pixelmator Team

 Pixelmator sits somewhere in between high-end graphics manipulation apps and very simple solutions. It includes almost all of the tools a typical user will need, and lets you create some stunning effects. You can work in layers, prepare images for the web and use myriad correction tools and filters to achieve the exact end-results you desire. It is all achieved within a design that makes every feature easily accessible.

03: ImageWell

Price £2.99/$4.99 Developer XtraLean Corporation

 ImageWell is promoted as a graphics manipulation app, but works best for annotations and specialist functions. You can easily add arrows and text to images, which is particularly useful for presentations or any type of publishing. It is lightweight, easy to use, and best of all, extremely functional, with some features that more expensive apps fail to deliver. If you need to annotate images, this is the first app you should try.

04: VintageScene

Price £5.49/$7.99 Developer JixiPix LLC

 You would think that deliberately making photos look old is a bad thing, but strangely it can add a great deal of personality to your snaps. VintageScene contains a unique algorithm that really does add special effects to any photo, and the end results are marvellous.

05: SplitPrint

Price £3.99/$5.99 Developer Iikka-tuote Oy

 Sometimes, an app comes along that makes you think "Why didn't I think of that?" SplitPrint automatically splits a large image into pieces for printing so that you can make an extra large poster. The uses for this kind of effect are virtually unlimited.

5 essential apps

01: Perfect Diet Tracker

Price £17.49/$24.99 **Developer** Byoni Ltd

If there is one thing you need when trying to diet, it's motivation, and this app is a very good source of this. It can track every aspect of your regime, offer advice, and crucially show you how well you are succeeding. It is designed to take away all of the hard work, and let you concentrate on your goals. Without this much-needed motivation, you are more likely to fail, and so it's exceptional value for money. This is one of the most complete diet trackers we have seen so far on the Mac, and is highly recommended.

02: SmartMeal

Price £5.99/$8.99
Developer Manuel Garcia-Estan Martinez

It is extremely difficult to feed a family healthfully without spending lots of time checking calories and nutritional information, and this is why SmartMeal works so effectively. You will still need to spend some time planning the meals you make, but most of the hard work will now be done for you. This is not an app for everyone, but those who take the time to understand it will benefit the most.

03: rubiTrack

Price £27.49/$38.99 **Developer** Markus Spoettl

If you're serious about exercising, it pays to be serious about analysing what you have achieved. rubiTrack will provide you with all sorts of information, such as how far you have walked or ran, and can also be used with accessories to ensure real-time tracking. The level of detail is astonishingly complex, and should provide you with enough motivation to keep running your way to ultimate fitness. Definitely one for the serious exerciser.

04: Stop Smoking

Price £0.69/$0.99 **Developer** Wicked Bytes UG

There is no easy way to stop smoking, but any help you can get is a good thing. Stop Smoking works by monitoring how much you have smoked each day, and how much money you have saved. It also highlights other benefits, and may be just enough to help you on your quest to be smoke free.

05: Relax Now

Price Free **Developer** Tommy Connolly

Relax Now is designed to help take away the stresses of modern living. It works using therapeutic videos and recordings to let you relax. You can wake up to the sounds or go to sleep to the sounds, but either way it will definitely help you to relax a little.

■ Simplicity is key in the design of Relax Now.

Health & Fitness

Stay fit with the help of your Mac

Sometimes you need a little help to get healthy, and this is particularly true when undertaking a new diet or fitness regime. Being able to monitor your progress is often all the encouragement you need to keep going, and a Mac can help with the serious stuff such as tracking an illness or trying to stop smoking. There are apps available in every health category, and everything from specific illnesses to specialist diets are covered. It may not sound that important, but remember that when you use an app that helps you, it has the potential to greatly improve, or even save, your life. This is a category that serves as an example of the wide range of Mac apps available, as it truly does cover every possible health subject. It is time to improve your life with your Mac and a few apps.

"Your Mac can help with the serious stuff"

■ The Stop Smoking app uses a deliberately simple design.

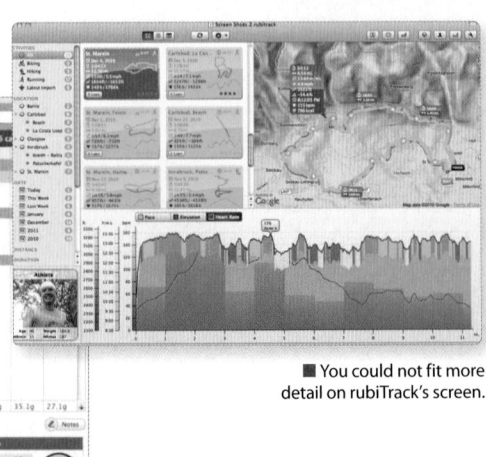

■ You could not fit more detail on rubiTrack's screen.

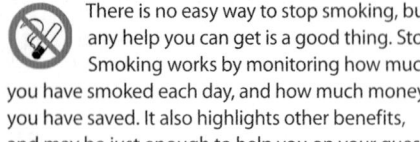

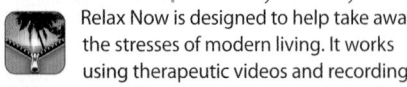

■ You can track what you eat every single day with Perfect Diet Tracker.

5 essential apps

01: Daily Jotter

Price £2.99/$4.99 Developer Rob Allen

 When it comes to taking notes, the simplest solutions often work best. Daily Jotter is indeed simple, but also includes all of the features you'll need. You can add images to notes, export your notes to Dropbox and manage each entry within the simplest of interfaces. The lightweight nature of the app also means that your database should not become too large, which offers more flexibility as to how you will deal with your information in the future.

02: Clox

Price £1.99/$2.99 Developer Vitaliy Golubenko

 Clox is somewhat of a novelty, but is the perfect solution for anyone who is serious about timekeeping. It lets you pin a clock to your desktop, and choose from 26 different styles. You can also export your favourite style and clock settings to another Mac. That is all it does, but the charm included in the presentation is enough to make this a worthwhile app.

03: Vinoteka

Price £34.99/$49.99
Developer Elodie Morin-Rager

 Serious devotees of wine like the thought of having their own wine cellar, and whether you have one or not, you can now experience this feeling through Vinoteka. It will let you monitor every aspect of your wine collection, and is particularly useful for businesses involved in this industry. No matter what your level of expertise or interest, this app is a true example of what can be achieved on a Mac.

04: Yummysoup!

Price £13.99/$19.99
Developer Kenneth Humbard

 Yummysoup! has been created to let you bring all of your favourite recipes to one place. You can import recipes from your favourite sites or add text notes that your friends have given you. The presentation is professional, and really does help to bring the recipes to life.

05: Alarm Pro

Price £1.99/$2.99
Developer smartieAnts Inc

 Alarm Pro takes the humble alarm clock and improves it tenfold. You can wake up to your favourite iTunes music, current and local weather forecasts are included, and you can even slowly dim the screen on your Mac to fall asleep naturally. This is the perfect way to wake up.

■ Vinoteka's presentation is about as good as any app gets.

Lifestyle

Tailor your Mac to fit in with your life

We all have different lifestyles, hobbies and interests, and as such a wide range of apps are required to cater for the majority. This particular category is more wide-ranging than any other because it covers all of our interests. From waking up in the morning to keeping a diary, all of these and more can fit in the Lifestyle category. With the right choice of apps, and used properly, they can be truly beneficial to your day-to-day life, and it is worth checking as many as possible to ensure that you are using the ones that are right for you. It is testament to the creativity of Mac developers that even the most obscure of interests are covered by Mac apps, and it goes to show just how flexible and powerful the platform truly is. Whatever your lifestyle, there will be an app for it.

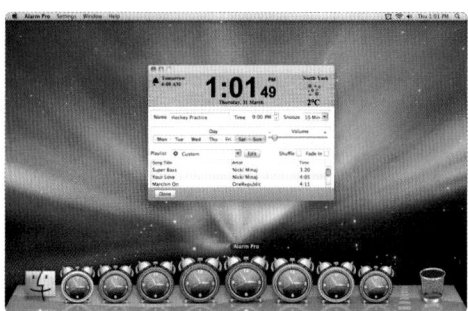

■ Alarm Pro's industrial design contains everything.

■ Recipes comes to life in Yummysoup!

"The right choice of apps can benefit your day-to-day life"

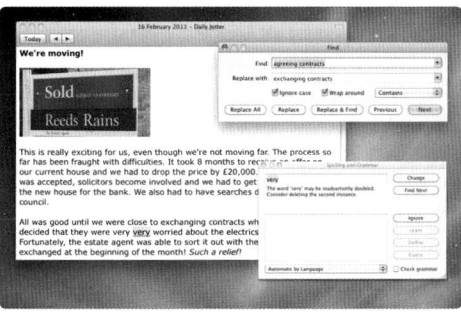

■ For quick notes, Daily Jotter could not be more simple.

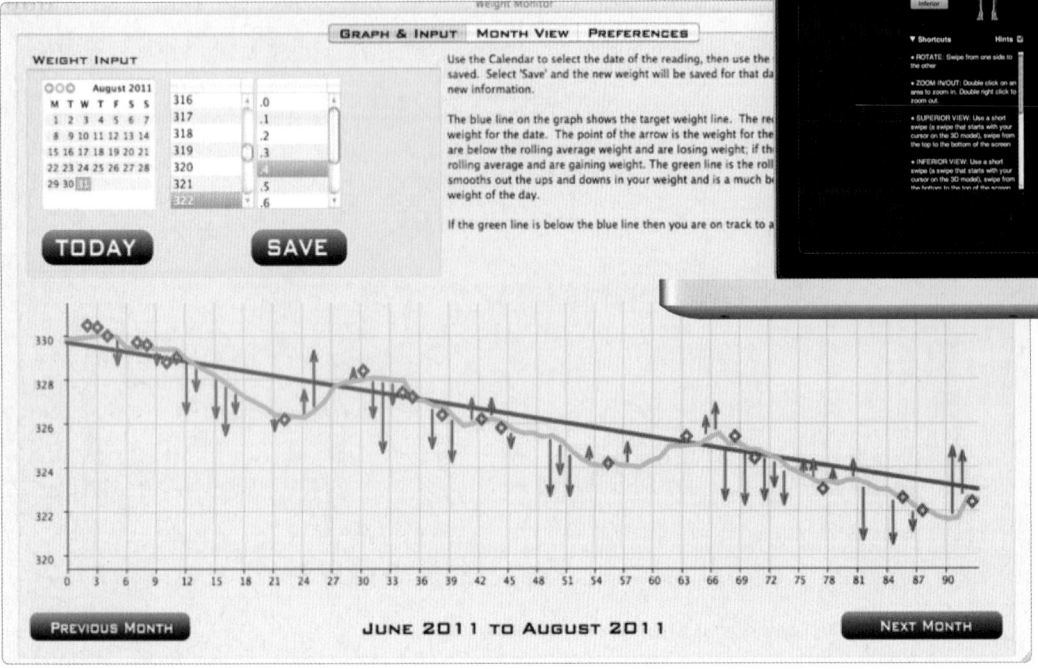

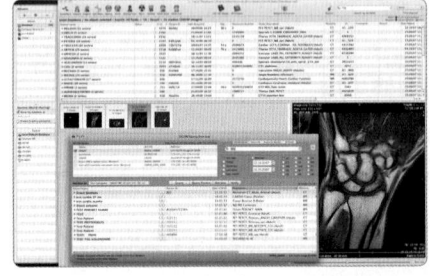

■ More than 5,000 diagrams are included in Muscle System Pro II.

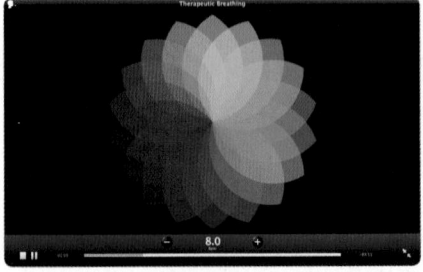

■ The calendar feature in Weight-Monitor will ensure your weight is managed properly.

■ A huge range of images can be catalogued and viewed with OsiriX.

Medical
Never let important matters like your health slide

Medical apps tend to fall into two categories: those that are designed to help the individual, and those designed to aid medical professionals. These apps can be as simple as helping you monitor your weight, or as complex as showing X-rays on a Mac screen. There are serious uses for the individual as well, and people with diabetes and asthma, as well as other ailments that require constant monitoring, will benefit

from specialised apps. The way many of them have been designed makes them accessible to anyone. Doctors can quickly look up patient information, and the individual can easily understand complex medical data that is pertinent to them. It is an area that is very important, and the Mac OS is a platform that is more than capable of helping anyone who has a need for medical help, which is ultimately all of us.

■ The colourful visuals of Breathing Zone help you understand the exercises.

5 essential apps

01: Muscle System Pro II
Price £13.99/$19.99
Developer 3D4Medical.com

 Muscles are not easy to visualise, but with this app you will be able to view every single detail. It allows the labelling of specific areas, and you can zoom, rotate and manage the view in almost every way. If you're using this app in a professional capacity, there is a quiz included to check your own knowledge on the subject matter.

02: Weight-Monitor
Price £1.49/$1.99
Developer Jim Chapple

 When you're trying to lose weight, you always need encouragement. That could come from friends and family, but the best way is to monitor your progress and to try to continue your success. This app lets you input your daily weight, which is then plotted on a graph. Seeing the graph drop over time is the perfect incentive, and also lets you see your average weight and work towards a specific goal.

03: Glucose Tracker
Price £1.49/$1.99
Developer Vimukti Technologies Private Limited

 When you consider the consequences of not managing diabetes properly, the value of this app becomes apparent. You can use it to monitor the glucose levels of your whole family, and the inclusion of historic graphs will help you ensure that your medication is working. It's very much a preventative solution, but one that is incredibly important for anyone who is a sufferer.

04: Breathing Zone
Price £1.99/$2.99
Developer Breathing Zone Limited

 Breathing is not just something that we all do naturally. Done properly, and it can greatly reduce the effects of asthma, alleviate stress-related symptoms, and offer countless other benefits. The exercises themselves are very well presented and easy to follow, and if you take the time to mimic them as closely as possible, then you will surely benefit.

05: OsiriX App
Price Free
Developer Antoine Rosset

 This app is highly specialised, but is one that could ultimately prove to be incredibly useful if in the right hands. The in-built ability to display complex medical images on a standard Mac means that results can be gathered much more conveniently, and that the speed of processing can be greatly enhanced, thus potentially helping out every patient.

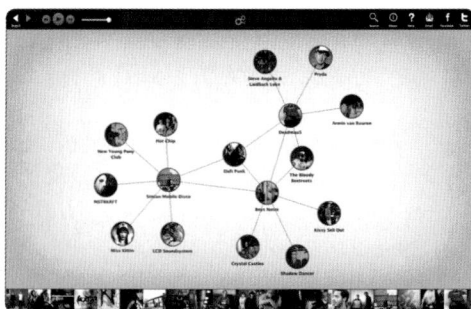
■ Discovr gives you a huge amount of info on each artist.

■ Ecoute's presentation rivals iTunes in clarity.

■ Tunesify can convert a multitude of audio formats.

■ Djay's authentic turntables make you feel like a real DJ.

Music Get down to the sound of the beat

The days of playing instruments and recording the resulting sounds to make music could be numbered. You can now create music in thousands of different ways, and record your output in extremely high quality. People now have the capacity to use instruments that haven't been designed yet, and have fun searching for new music using apps that understand their tastes. No matter what you want to do in the musical field, you can now do it, and some of the solutions also suit professional musicians. Songwriters, guitar players and producers can all use complex apps to create new work. DJs can mix music, and individuals can create completely original ringtones. Music has truly reached the digital age, and the digital age has brought music to anyone, no matter how talented they are. Now, we can all create music, just as we wanted to do when we were children.

5 essential apps

01: Mixtab

Price Free Developer Mixtab Inc

There are many news apps that offer the ability to read news in a tweaked format, but few bring such a quick and easy-to-use interface to the experience. Mixtab includes predefined news channels which collect news from topic-based websites, and lets you build your own topics for your own interests. Full articles are available, and in theory you could do almost all of your browsing within this app and leave the web altogether. This is an exceptional solution, which is as well designed as many expensive alternatives.

02: NewsRack

Price £5.49/$7.99 Developer Ole Zorn

NewsRack takes the middle ground between news readers that attempt to offer lots of clever effects, and the more simple RSS readers. It strikes the balance well, and brings a speedy experience which is particularly useful if you follow many different sources. With integration to third party services like Instapaper, you may find this to be perfect for your news gathering needs.

03: NewsBar

Price £2.99/$4.99 Developer Andras Porffy

Sometimes you want your news to be available, but not dominate everything you are doing. NewsBar sits on the desktop and unobtrusively presents the latest news in a stream. You can also quickly hide news items with a swipe, or read them in full with a tap for ultimate control, and the way it updates the feeds means that you will not be constantly glancing at the latest stories. It's a streamlined way of getting your news delivered to you.

04: Reeder

Price £6.99/$9.99 Developer Silvio Rizzi

With the ability to read news in the simplest possible fashion, and then share articles via a variety of mediums, Reeder is an example for other apps to follow. It is the preferred option for many users, and with good reason, as it does exactly what it needs to.

05: TWiT Live

Price Free Developer David Cann

TWiT provides a succession of news videos, and this incredibly simple app gives you one-click access to all of them. It does little more than stream the shows and present upcoming show times, but it really does do what it needs to perfectly. It's a great way to keep up to date with the latest goings-on.

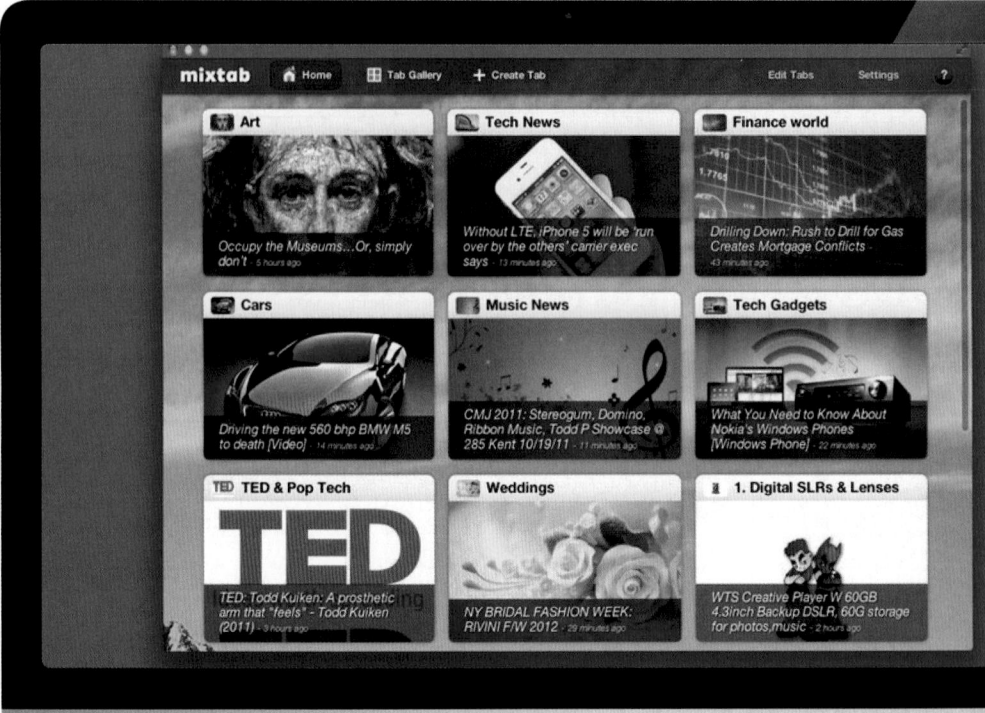

■ Each stream of news is divided into topics in Mixtab.

News

Keep informed on everything in the world today

It used to be that the best way to keep up with the news was to visit websites. Of course this works well for sites like the BBC, but for specialist topics it can involve hunting around for the right places. Some Mac apps are now capable of recreating news provided by websites in a way that is more friendly, logical and easier to read. Other apps will automatically grab the latest news and present it on the desktop, and the options for reading a variety of topics are almost unlimited. No matter what the topic or your visual preference, there will be a solution that suits the way you want to catch up with the world around you. Indeed, some are so good that you may never visit a traditional website for news again.

> "Some Mac apps are capable of recreating news from websites"

■ Whole articles can be read without leaving the NewsRack app.

■ You can check the schedule of upcoming programmes with one click in TWiT Live.

■ A variety of effects are included in Plastic Bullet to choose from.

■ Sharing the results on social networks is easy with Analog.

■ You can create astonishing effects in minutes with Color Splash.

Photography

Store your memories, and create new ones

Photographers will tell you that often a lot of the work required to create a great photograph happens on a computer after the photo has been taken, and this makes the Mac platform ideal for anyone with an interest. It doesn't matter if you are experienced or new to the world of photography, because there will be a solution, and the majority are designed to be as easy to use as possible. From adding speech bubbles to making photos look like they were taken many decades ago, you can do almost anything you want with a Mac and a collection of digital images. You can take this as far as you like, or just play around, but either way, the platform and available apps will offer you everything you need to get started and enjoy the world of photography for professional or personal reasons.

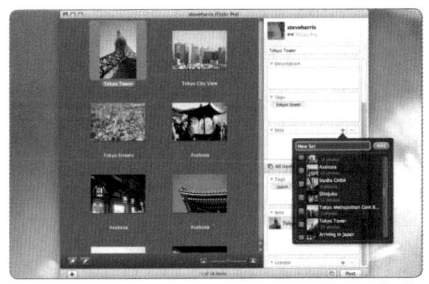

■ Poster's entire interface is built around sharing your images.

5 essential apps

01: Color Splash Studio

Price £1.99/$2.99
Developer macphun.com

The ability to add colour to black and white photos has until recently only been accessible by professionals with expensive equipment. Anyone can now create this effect, and all it takes is a steady hand and a mouse. The end results can be stunning, and the amount of effort required is little, which is testament to how well it is programmed. A clever app.

02: Analog

Price £5.49/$7.99
Developer Realmac Software Limited

Most people want to add effects to their photos without having to learn new processes. Analog takes away the learning process, and lets you choose from a variety of filters. There's some clever technology behind the process, but the user need never see that. The front interface is user-friendly, and you can share the results using a variety of services.

03: Plastic Bullet

Price £2.99/$4.99
Developer Red Giant Software

Plastic Bullet is part novelty, part creative tool. Its main purpose is to make photos look like they were taken with a plastic camera, and while this may sound self-defeating, some of the effects are impressive. It won't appeal to everyone, but there is potential to use the results in a variety of places. It's a one-trick pony, albeit producing clever results.

04: Poster

Price £6.99/$9.99
Developer Steve Harris

The process of sharing images on social networks rarely turns out to be as easy as it should be, but Poster will help if this is a task that you regularly undertake. It uses the facilities of each network, and simplifies them to the point that sharing photos will soon become second nature, as well as a whole lot quicker. As an app-based solution, there are few alternatives around better than this.

05: Photo Album

Price Free
Developer Mediaparts Interactive SA

The digital medium provides great ways to share your photos. With this in mind, Photo Album enables you to create personalised sets of photos, which you can then share with friends and family via a variety of online services, all in a matter of moments. This way, you can share your holiday snaps with anyone who is interested in a couple of minutes.

■ RapidWeaver's simple interface hides its advanced functions.

Productivity
Maximise your output

Productivity takes many forms, and there are solutions that will help you be more productive, no matter what your speciality or need. Everything from creating text documents to building databases can fall into this category,

and it is without doubt one of the more diverse categories, encompassing a wide range of apps. If there is any task that you need to be more productive at, there will likely be a solution available. It may require some careful searching, but a solution will arrive that could potentially speed up every aspect of your work, which can have major benefits for almost everything you do with your desktop or laptop. Sometimes, the smallest solutions offer as many benefits as the larger apps and you should take time to see if a collection of smaller apps will work better than one large app.

"There are many great productivity solutions"

■ The emails stand out in Sparrow's minimalist interface.

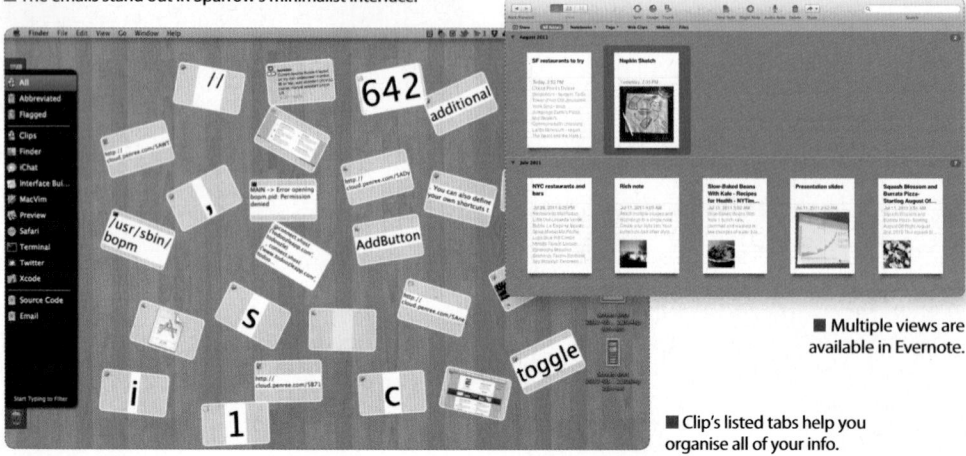

■ Multiple views are available in Evernote.

■ Clip's listed tabs help you organise all of your info.

5 essential apps

01: Sparrow

Price £6.99/$9.99 **Developer** Sparrow SARL

Sparrow takes the idea of complex email management, and breaks it down into bite-sized pieces so that you can manage your emails more efficiently and still have view of other work if you need to multi-task. Setting up is simple, and the presentation ensures that the important data is brought to the front. It follows the Mac design principles, and as such fits in with the entire operating system perfectly. It looks good, works well, and could solve your email problems.

02: RapidWeaver

Price £54.99/$79.99

Developer Realmac Software Limited

Many people want to create websites, but few have the time or knowledge to do so effectively. RapidWeaver offers a multitude of templates, and will also automate many of the site building tasks that trip up many people. It will suit the home user best, but even those who take a more professional approach will find value here.

03: OmmWriter Dana II

Price £2.99/$4.99

Developer Herraiz Soto & Asociados SL

When you need to focus on creative writing, the last thing you need is to have to deal with a crowded interface. OmmWriter offers the cleanest possible presentation, and also includes soothing music and subtle backgrounds to get you in the mood. Great care has been taken to ensure that the environment is ideal for any writer and with some familiarity, it really does help you to clear your mind.

04: Clips

Price £2.99/$4.99

Developer Conceited Software

We all need to keep information handy from time to time, and Clips is the ideal tool. It sits in the background, and will collect everything you copy for accessing later. A highly useful little app that could really help you keep on top of things.

05: Evernote

Price Free **Developer** Evernote

Evernote is a hugely popular online note system and can help you manage many aspects of your life. This free app brings all of your notes and quick synchronisation to any Mac and is designed to offer all of the main features on your desktop all of the time.

Reference
Keep things at the forefront

Reference data is helpful for all sorts of reasons, and can form the backbone of many tasks we need to perform. Without accurate data, we could be working with information that makes a whole project pointless, and of course there are countless times when you will simply want to find information to help you. Whether you are writing a thesis or settling an argument with friends, reference data is required, and there are many ways in which it can be presented. Some apps will make complex data more accessible simply by stripping out the visual interference from certain websites, while others act as a layer over the major reference portals. Whether you are looking for new information or require known data to be presented more clearly, there will be ready-made solutions available which make searching and using information much quicker than ever before.

> ## "There are many ways data can be presented"

■ Keeping track of books looks fantastic with Bookpedia.

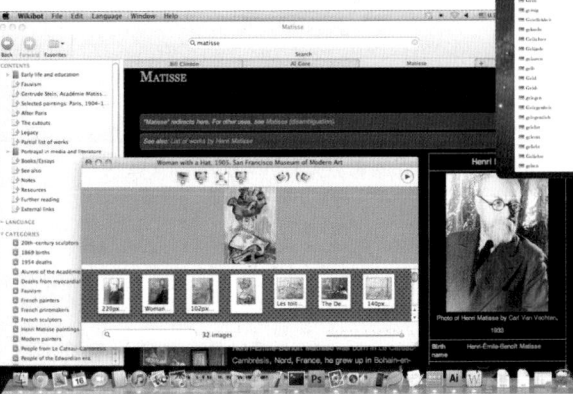

■ Wikipedia looks much better when it is cleaned up using the Wikibot app.

■ You can even hear the translations in One World Dictionary.

■ The detail in Art Authority is high.

Essential Apps

5 essential apps

01: Twitterific for Twitter

Price £2.99/$4.99 Developer The Iconfactory

 Twitter is growing quickly, and continues to dominate social networking for millions of people, but using it in a web browser is not ideal when you're trying to work at the same time. Twitterific is housed in a small panel which you can resize, and also comes with every feature you need. Trends, translations, colour-coding and so much more is included within a beautifully presented solution that will serve you well for all of your Twitter needs. There are few better solutions available on any platform.

02: MarsEdit

Price £27.99/$39.99
Developer Apparent Software

 MarsEdit is designed to replace the often slow interfaces offered by blog hosting services. It lets you create content offline in a setting that is ideal for quick editing or complex article writing. Compatibility with a wide range of services is also available, and once you start using it you will be able to manage multiple blogs from multiple services with ease. It takes some time to learn, but your efforts will be rewarded.

03: Socialite

Price £6.99/$9.99
Developer Apparent Software

 Most people use more than one social network, which can make communicating laborious. Socialite lets you post to multiple blogs and read your incoming messages on the one screen. Even though not every feature from each network is supported, it is still a great solution for multiple account holders. If you spend some time with the smart folders, you will speed up your networking even further.

04: Trillian

Price Free Developer Cerulean Studios

Instant messaging is still incredibly popular, and Trillian brings multiple services together within one app. You can hold multiple conversations at the same time, and won't need to log in to different services every time you want to speak to someone. It's an elegant solution to an old problem.

05: Flicker1

Price £1.49/$1.99 Developer Andrea Prosperi

 When you consider that Flickr is all about the visuals, the overall structure of the site could be more inclusive. Flicker1 attempts to streamline the viewing process, and also makes notations much easier. It is a clever solution that does exactly what it needs to perfectly.

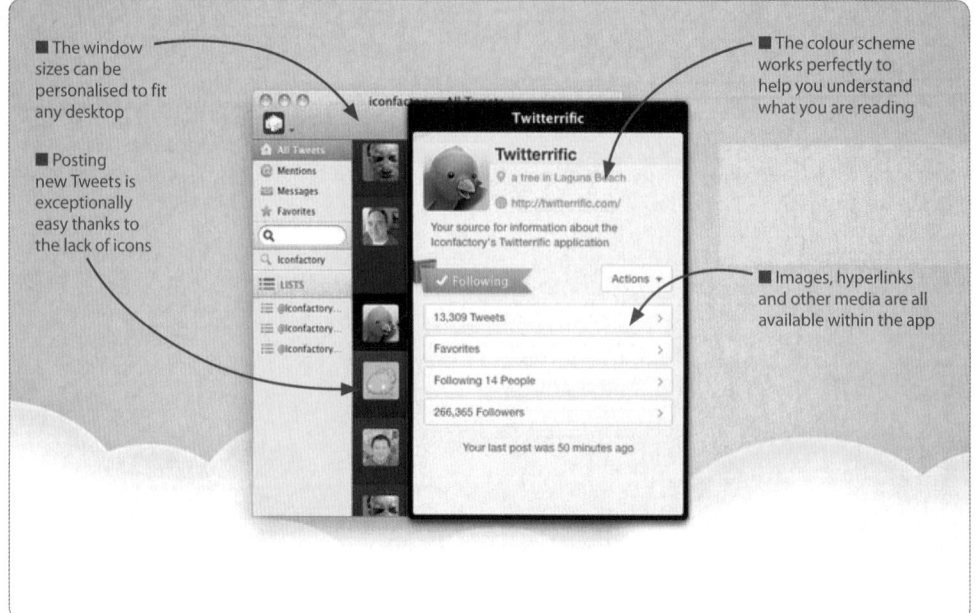

■ The window sizes can be personalised to fit any desktop

■ Posting new Tweets is exceptionally easy thanks to the lack of icons

■ The colour scheme works perfectly to help you understand what you are reading

■ Images, hyperlinks and other media are all available within the app

Social Networking
Stay connected with a variety of fantastic apps

Social networking has grown to be one of the most-used forms of internet communication, and for some people the big services like Twitter and Facebook take up the majority of their online time. Each service has websites associated with them, but rarely is the web experience as good as standalone apps on a desktop or mobile. There are apps available that can sit on the desktop and update you as they work, and others that offer more features than the social networks do officially. Other solutions attempt to bring all of your social networks to one place, and even allow you to update multiple sites at once. If you use any of the social networks, then there are apps available that will completely transform the way you communicate with friends and strangers. It's just a question of finding the ones that work best with the way you like to talk.

"You can update multiple sites at once"

■ Full statistics are available for every image in Flicker1.

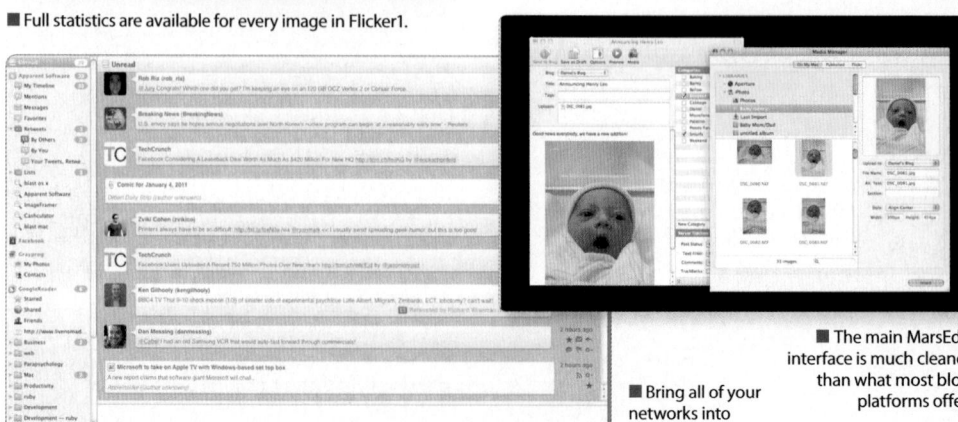

■ Bring all of your networks into one timeline with Socialite.

■ The main MarsEdit interface is much cleaner than what most blog platforms offer.

5 essential apps

01: Swing It Pro
Price £99.99/$149.99
Developer FKE Datakonsult AB

 Golf is all about the swing. Without a good technique, your scores will be higher and your enjoyment less. You can either pay lots of money to get some coaching, or purchase this app and learn at home. It uses videos to help you visualise what you need to do. You can crop the videos, create notes and work in your spare time. It isn't cheap, but compared to professional coaching, it could produce similar results, and ultimately save you money.

02: MotoGP 2011 Official Live Timing - Premium Pass
Price £3.99/$5.99
Developer Soft Pauer Solutions Limited

 For serious fans of MotoGP, this app offers the perfect way to see what is happening in real-time. The level of detail is astonishing, matched by the way the information is presented. It is immersive, fun, and will teach you more about the vagaries of the sport that you may have been unaware of. At the heart is the map view, which you can observe from any angle you like.

03: Coach's clipboard ultimate
Price £6.99/$9.99
Developer J Plus Corporation Limited

Teaching strategies and tactics is never easy, and visual teaching is often the best method. With this app, you can draw your plays for almost any sport, animate them and get the message over as effectively as possible. It has the potential to increase player participation, results and morale. For anyone who coaches sport, this should not be ignored.

04: Dive Log Manager
Price Free Developer Janice McLaughlin

One important aspect of diving is to monitor your previous dives and gauge how quickly you're learning. This app lets you do that, and will also help you monitor your diving equipment. It is incredibly feature-rich, and will cover all your diving needs.

05: Mini Ramp 101
Price £2.99/$4.99
Developer APPDESIGNER.COM INC.

 Skateboarding is more popular than ever before, and the best way to learn is by watching others perform tricks. You can now do so on your Mac, and learn some secrets to improve your tricks in very quick time. If you're a skateboarder, it's time to make the jump.

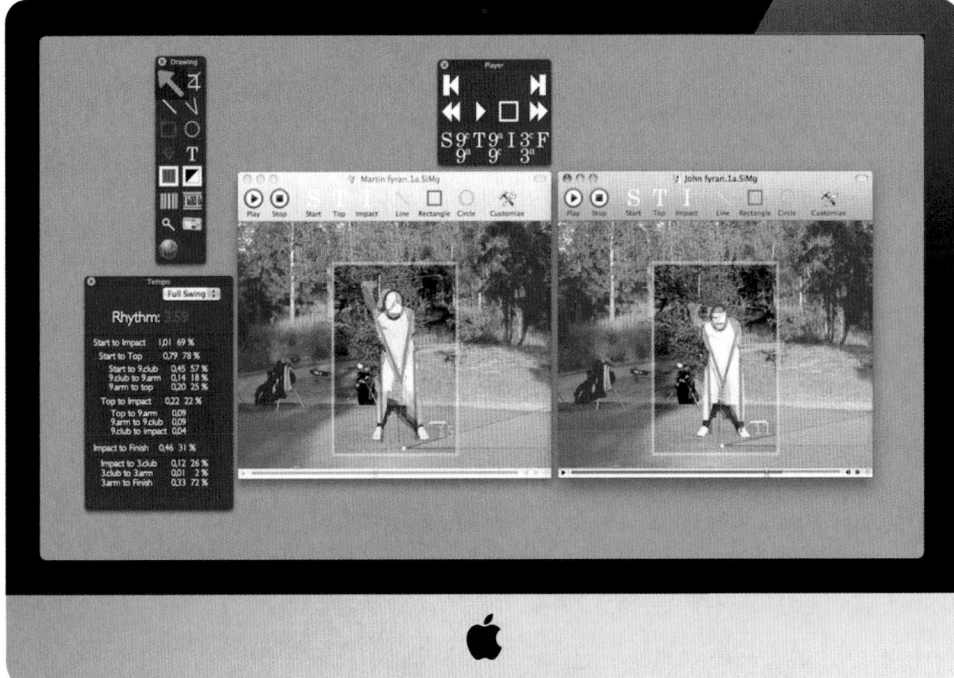

■ With Swing It Pro you can analyse any aspect of the perfect golf swing.

Sports

Make the most of your sporting abilities

Sports is a category that is broad in that it has to cater for a wide range of different activities. Within each sport there are further groups of people; coaches, players, fans and so on. This means that app developers have to build a variety of solutions for every conceivable activity, and this category alone highlights just how popular the Mac platform is for apps. No matter what sport you enjoy, you should be able to find an app that will increase your enjoyment or participation. From getting up-to-the-minute timings on motor racing laps to building strategies and plans for a team you coach, you can do it with a Mac. As a fan, you can also find specialist apps that will present news and gossip for particular sports, and this includes information from official sources, which are presented in a unique way for the desktop.

■ A varied selection of tricks are included in Mini Ramp 101.

■ The amount of data in the MotoGP app is remarkable.

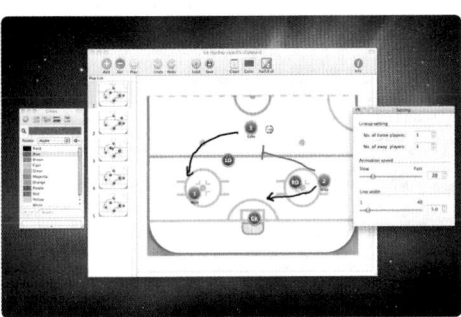

■ You can customise many aspects in Coach's clipboard.

"No matter the sport, you should be able to find an app to help"

Essential Apps

5 essential apps

01: Arrivals & Departures
Price £2.99/$4.99 Developer Krishna Vegesna

One of the major gripes for frequent travellers is having to continually monitor arrival and departure times. This is also true for those working in companies who need to check when people will arrive, and so this app will be a boon for them, or you. It displays real-time flight times for thousands of airports and is very accurate. You can choose favourite airports and even view flight paths if you are interested. The level of information is high and for some people it will be the perfect solution to their flight tracking needs, which they will use every day.

02: myTracks
Price £10.99/$15.99 Developer Dirk Stichling

Walkers and those who like to explore have a need to understand 'exactly' where they have been, and to keep detailed logs of their travels. myTracks is an advanced solution that has built-in compatibility with a number of other apps, and also works with iOS devices, which is ideal for those on the move. It is a little technical in places, but serious walkers will understand the need for this extra functionality.

03: Manage Fear of Flying Now
Price £1.99/$2.99 Developer Tommy Connolly

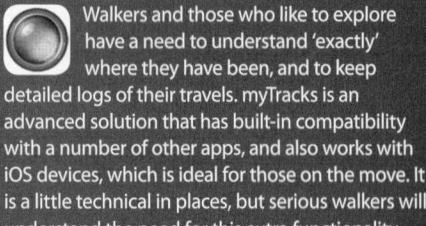

Millions of people are afraid of flying, and most courses designed to help them include a flight at the end of the course, which they worry about too much. This solution is more personal, and can be used anywhere to try to overcome this fear using videos, therapeutic techniques and other methods. It has the potential to completely change the way you feel about travelling, and may make it a lot easier in the future.

04: Time Palette
Price £12.99/$17.99 Developer Xeric Design Ltd

Time Palette offers a wealth of information for thousands of cities around the world. This makes it ideal for many groups of people who need to know the weather and other specific information for particular locations. It is ideal for businesses, but potentially useful for everyone.

05: KAYAK Explore
Price Free Developer Kayak Software Corp

KAYAK Explore is a tool that will help you plan a holiday on a budget, be confident that you are paying for quality services and understand more about what is available for any future trip. It is comprehensive to say the least, and should be the first app you use when planning your next trip.

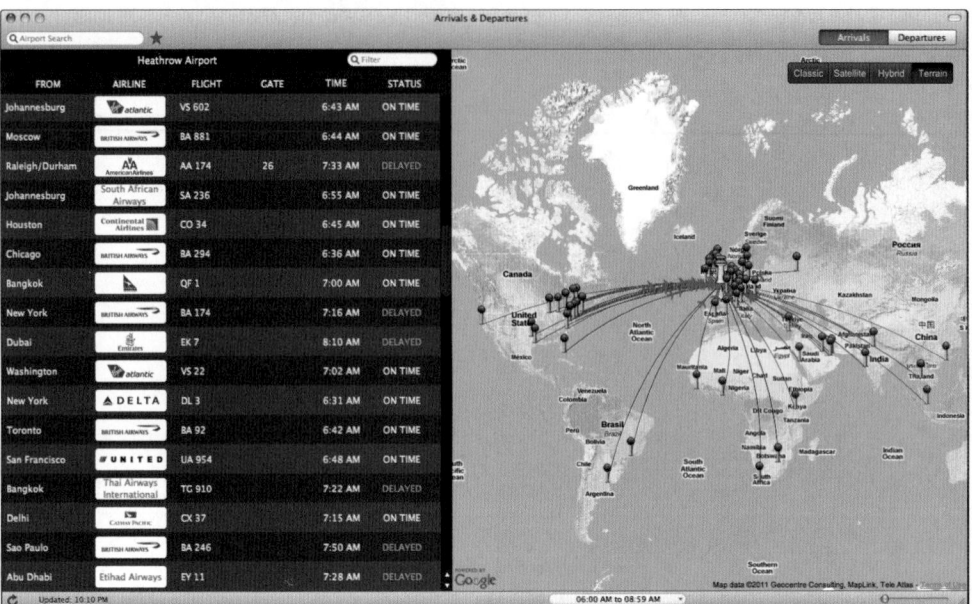

■ Half flight times and half map; the Arrivals & Departures app works very well.

Travel
Around the world with your Mac

Planning a trip beforehand will likely make it a more pleasant experience, and you can do this on a Mac in a variety of ways. You can build a basic itinerary or plan every single minute, which can be particularly useful for business trips where money is of paramount importance. The travel category also covers apps that will help you decide where to stay, who to fly with, and to even use the reviews of other travellers to understand if a service is worth paying for. It doesn't end there; you can use some of these services when abroad using a laptop to check on live flight times, and to see how the weather will be for days out, and as such the benefits quickly become clear. No matter what you want to do that is travel related, you will be able to do it on a Mac with the use of some clever apps.

"Planning a trip will make it more pleasant"

■ A huge variety of places are available through KAYAK.

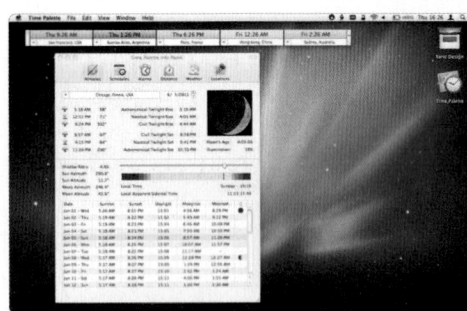

■ Each part of Time Palette contains comprehensive info.

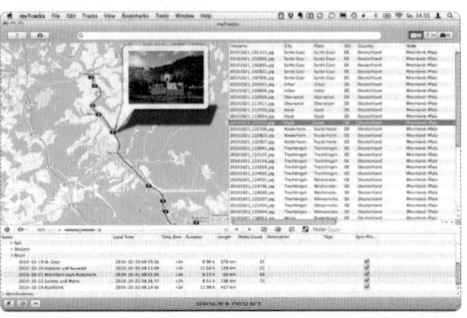

■ You can store as many tracks as you like with myTracks.

■ Manage Fear's videos and sounds are a calming influence.

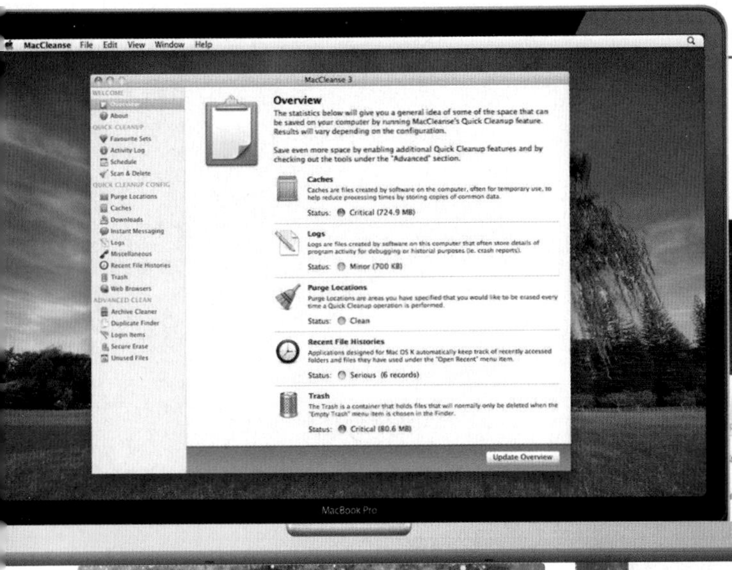

■ The number of tasks MacCleanse takes care of is immense.

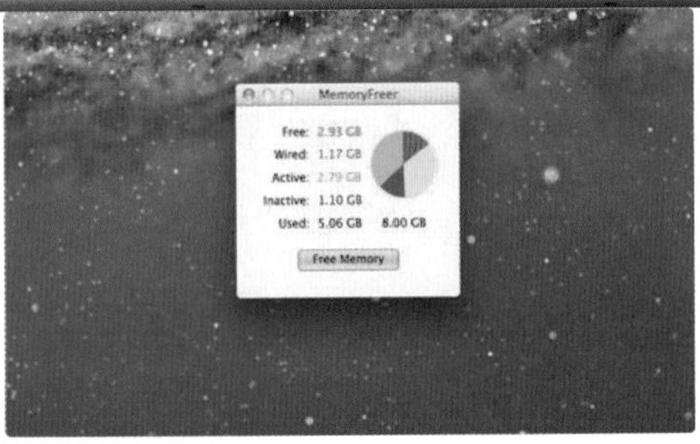

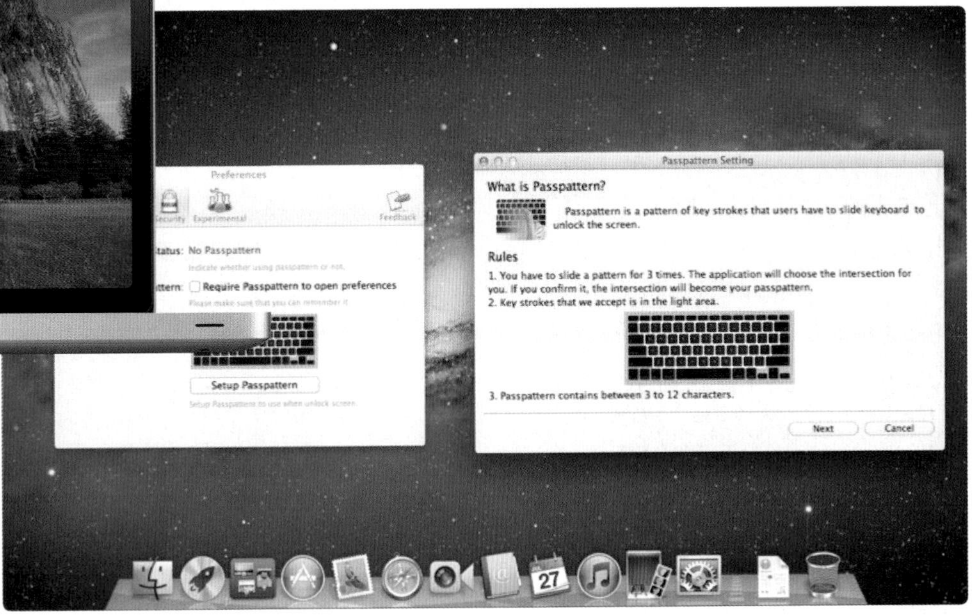

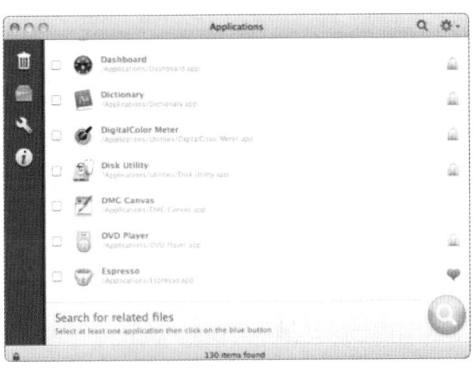
■ With Lock Screen 2 you can choose to unlock your Mac in many different ways.

Utilities

Customise your Mac in a way that suits you best

All computers have a default configuration that is designed to let the user undertake many tasks, but there are sometimes functions you really wish it could do. Whether it is something to make your Mac run smoother or to add another level of ease to your workflow, there are missing elements from your Mac There are, thankfully, utility apps available form the Mac App Store that will not only improve stability, but also enable you to do things with a Mac that you may not have considered before. With the right utility, you can potentially complete a process you need to undertake in half the time, and then repeat this with more utilities. There are hundreds available that can be used for every conceivable task, and once you are used to them, you will able to flexibly deal with any given situation. Utilities can completely change the way you work once you have installed the ones that suit you best.

■ Trash Me's interface could not be any more simple.

---

5 essential apps

01: MemoryFreer
Price £0.69/$0.99
Developer Rubin Wang

For some Macs that have lower specifications, at times the speed may slow down. The standard solution is to power it down and turn it back on, but this can be time-consuming and inconvenient. MemoryFreer can free up memory with one click, and let you carry on working at full speed. It take a second to activate, and is a must-have utility for anyone who has this problem from time to time.

02: MacCleanse
Price £5.49/$7.99
Developer Koingo Software

It's always good practice to keep a Mac running as smoothly as possible, but to do this you often have to follow many processes to ensure every tweak has been completed. MacCleanse automates this process, and will take care of more than 50 tasks without you having to jump through hoops. It is not an app you will even notice, but is well worth scheduling to work every week or so.

03: Lock Screen 2
Price £1.49/$1.99
Developer iDevelop Co Ltd

Just because a Mac may stay in the same place, this does not mean that you shouldn't take precautions to stop people using it. Lock Screen 2 brings the mobile world to your desktop, and lets you secure your Mac in a variety of ways. You can set when the Mac locks itself, and also use the classic slide function to unlock it. It is a bit of fun, but with a potentially crucial use.

04: TrashMe
Price £2.49/$3.99
Developer Jean-Baptiste Zedda

When in the process of deleting apps, it is all too easy on a Mac to just drag them to the trash bin. The problem is that often files are left over that take up space and end up slowing the system down. TrashMe will ensure that every file has been comprehensively deleted without you even having to think about what is happening. Great for an issue that many take for granted.

05: Mobile Mouse Server
Price Free
Developer RPA Tech INC

When combined with an iPhone or iPad, this app will let you use your iOS devices to control your Mac. They can become touchscreen mice, keyboards and even dictation machines. If you use this software in conjunction with an iPhone 4S, then you can read into the phone, and subsequently watch the text appear on your Mac!

Essential Apps

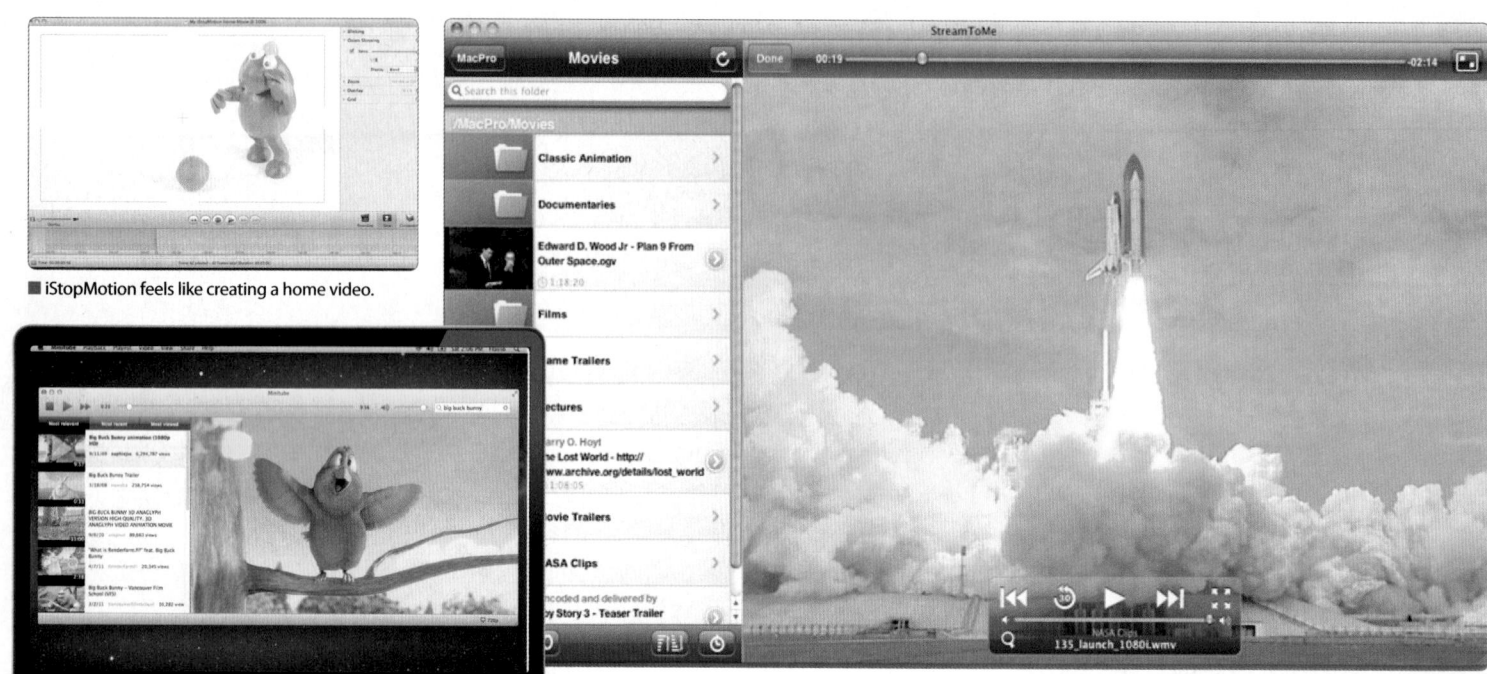

■ iStopMotion feels like creating a home video.

■ The streaming quality makes you feel like you are watching a local file while using StreamToMe.

Video
Watch the latest and best videos in high-quality output

The world of digital video is a curiosity in that most people will have already been exposed to it, but few take the time to enhance their creations. It is very much seen as a static media form; you take a video, and leave it as it is to view at a later date. However, you can do so much with your creations, and there are all sorts of apps to help you manipulate all of your personal and work-related videos. You can add special effects,

funny commentary and even incorporate them into professional presentations. The beauty of the Mac is that even the lower-end systems are able to cope with memory-intensive video production really well. The platform is designed to cope with all types of media, even high-definition video files, and the video apps available on the Mac App Store make it all work together in an even more efficient manner.

■ Adjustments add extra control in Video-Converter.

5 essential apps

01: Video-Converter
Price £13.99/$19.99
Developer Wondershare Software Co Ltd

Varying video and audio formats cause lots of problems for Mac users who own mobile devices, as not all formats work with every device. This app caters for a variety of formats, and should cover almost every file you own. The conversion process is quite straightforward, and once you first use it, you will soon view it as something that comes in handy over and over again.

02: Minitube
Price £6.99/$9.99
Developer Flavio Tordini

YouTube is easy to become engrossed in, but not as easy to use when you watch one video after another. Minitube lets you pick a keyword and then watch a stream of videos that are related to your search without you needing to do anything else. It caters for HD, and uses QuickTime rather than Flash for efficiency. It is a solution that could change the way you view YouTube videos forever.

03: Media Library Lite
Price £1.49/$1.99
Developer Wondershare Software Co Ltd

DVDs get lost, scratched to the point of unplayability, or friends borrow them and forget to return them. This lets you monitor every DVD you own, and gives you the ability to add ratings. The process of adding titles is helped by barcode scanning, and the entire setup lends itself perfectly to the task at hand.

04: iStopMotion Home
Price £34.99/$49.99
Developer Boinx Software Ltd

Stop motion is a video effect that most people have no access to… until iStopMotion came along. With this app, you can spend time creating a stunning stop-motion film which will surprise anyone that you show it to. The time required to become adept at using this is surprisingly low for the potential results.

05: StreamToMe
Price Free
Developer Matthew Gallagher

StreamToMe enables you to stream media from a Mac to mobile devices on the same network using 3G or Wi-Fi, and will even convert the media in real-time if it is incompatible. This could potentially allow you to store most of your media away from the phone, and still gain the same end result. For its stated aim, it works excellently, and is as such recommended.

Weather

Find out the forecast easily with a range of Mac apps

The weather is a subject that we are all quite obsessed with. We talk about it with friends, strangers and anyone else who will listen, but the subject is much bigger than you may realise. Besides just tracking the forecast and current conditions, you can use Mac apps for highly specialised weather-related tasks. You can track everything from local conditions to world tides and climate change, and that is just the start. There are apps for all weather-related subjects, and for most people there are more apps than they will ever need. However, the apps available will cover the needs of everyone who has interest in the subject, and you may even find some of them to be a source of learning that builds your interest even further. This category highlights the breadth of Mac apps available, and is as complete or inconsequential as you need it to be.

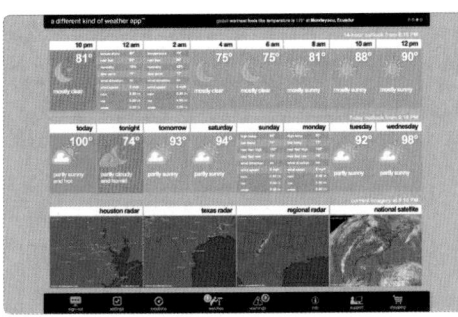
■ A lot of data is collected by swackett.

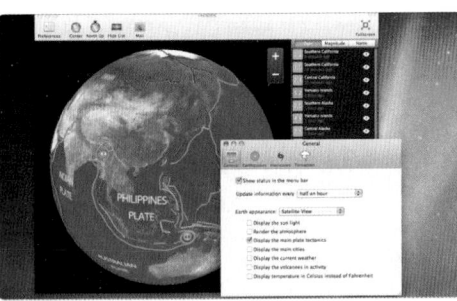
■ Tectonic lets you chose only information pertinent to you.

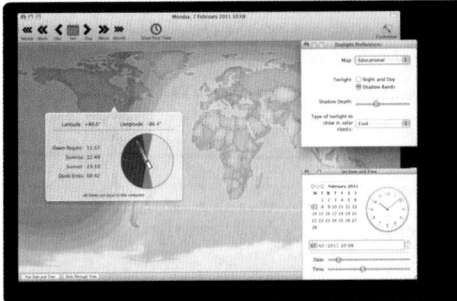
■ The Sun's movements are shown in data form in Daylight.

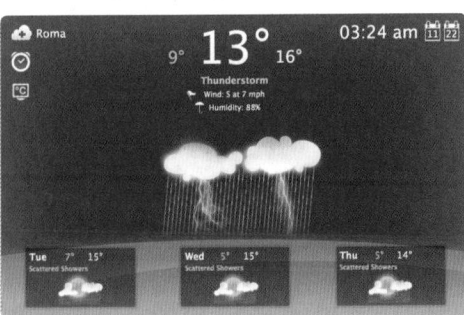
■ The Weather app icons feed the data with a quick glance.

■ 3D Weather Globe's visuals are remarkably detailed for a weather app.

5 essential apps

01: Daylight
Price £2.99/$4.99 **Developer** Andrew Cook

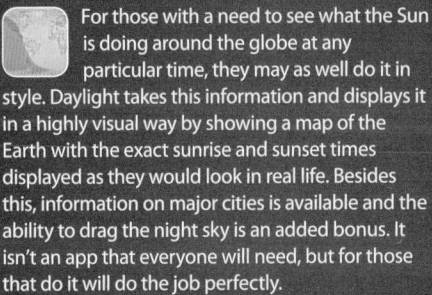

For those with a need to see what the Sun is doing around the globe at any particular time, they may as well do it in style. Daylight takes this information and displays it in a highly visual way by showing a map of the Earth with the exact sunrise and sunset times displayed as they would look in real life. Besides this, information on major cities is available and the ability to drag the night sky is an added bonus. It isn't an app that everyone will need, but for those that do it will do the job perfectly.

02: Weather
Price £0.69/$0.99 **Developer** Presselite

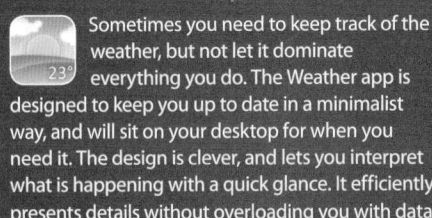

Sometimes you need to keep track of the weather, but not let it dominate everything you do. The Weather app is designed to keep you up to date in a minimalist way, and will sit on your desktop for when you need it. The design is clever, and lets you interpret what is happening with a quick glance. It efficiently presents details without overloading you with data.

03: 3D Weather Globe & Atlas Deluxe
Price £34.99/$49.99
Developer Software MacKiev

For visual appeal, this app really does shine. It feels like you have the whole world on your desktop thanks to the splendidly detailed graphics and real-time weather information. You can tilt the globe to see natural landmarks in detail, and even if you do not need the exact weather information, it is still an enjoyable experience, and the ability to track hurricanes and other weather phenomena takes it even higher up the value league.

04: swackett
Price Free **Developer** AGLogic LLC

For sheer visual clarity, swackett is ahead of the pack. Complex weather data is presented in an environment that makes conditions obvious to anyone who can understand normal images. It's cute, original, accurate, and adds a sense of fun to tracking the weather.

05: Tectonic
Price £2.99/$4.99 **Developer** adnX SARL

The seriousness of the subject that Tectonic covers can't be underestimated, and its ability to show earthquake activity in detail could be a life-saver. It is a specialist app, but one that could be of interest even to those who are unlikely to experience such an event.

Your Mac Glossary

What does it all mean? We guide you through the common features and terms that you're likely to encounter while using Macs

Apple ID
This is the name and password you use to log into the various Mac services, such as iTunes, the App Store and iCloud.

Apple Menu
Located in the top-left corner of the screen, the Apple Menu provides access to items and services that are always available, regardless of which app is running. These items include Software Update, Recent Items, Force Quit and Shut Down.

Apple Menu jargon:

About this Mac
This provides a detailed overview of the specs and operating system of your Mac.

Software Update
This option scans your computer to determine if any system apps have newer versions that you can update to free of charge.

Recent Items
This sub-menu provides at-a-glance convenience to find the most recent files that you have been using.

Force Quit
If an app freezes then you can select this option to automatically quit the problematic app.

Application (app)
An application, or app, is a software program designed to perform one or more functions. Apps are stored in the Applications folder on your Macintosh HD.

Launchpad
Need to launch and app quickly? We have lift-off!

App Store
The Mac App Store is a digital distribution platform for Mac OS X 10.6.6 and above. Similar to the iOS App Store, users are able to browse, purchase and download Mac-compatible apps from the App Store to run on their computer.

Dashboard
Dashboard creates a layer in the Mac OS X operating system for running mini-applications called 'widgets'. You can access these by selecting the 'Dashboard' icon from your Dock or by clicking the scroll button on your mouse.

Desktop
The desktop is the first thing you see after logging in and booting up your Mac. Files and folders can be saved to the desktop and dragged around. You can change the image that appears on your desktop in System Preferences.

Dock
The Dock is a row of icons that can be set to appear at the bottom or sides of your screen. You can click on an icon in the Dock to launch an application and check the Dock to see which apps are currently active. You can add and remove icons from the Dock by dragging and dropping.

Finder
The Finder lets you organise, view and access practically everything on your Mac, including apps, files, folders, discs, SD memory cards and shared drives on a network.

Firewall
A firewall is a barrier that prevents unauthorised access to a computer or network. A firewall may be hardware-based, software-based or a combination of the two.

iChat
This is Apple's easy-to-use instant messaging software that supports video, audio and standard text-based messaging.

iCloud
The iCloud is a free cloud storage and syncing service introduced as part of the OS X Lion 10.7.2 update (and iOS 5 on mobile devices). With iCloud you can share data, files, music and photographs between all of your devices without the need for manual connecting, syncing and transferring.

Safari
Slick, intuitive and a joy to use

iCloud jargon:

iTunes in the Cloud
With iCloud, the music you purchase from iTunes appears automatically on all of your devices. You can also download past purchases where you want, when you want.

Photo Stream
With iCloud, when you take a photo on one device, it automatically appears on all of your devices. Photos transferred from a digital camera connected to your Mac will also be pushed to your mobile devices automatically.

Documents in the Cloud
If you have the same iCloud-enabled apps on more than one device, iCloud automatically keeps your documents up to date across all devices.

iOS
Whereas Macs run on an operating system called Mac OS X, your mobile devices – iPhone, iPad and iPod touch – use iOS. The latest version is iOS 5 and you will need this installed on your mobile devices to enjoy the benefits of iCloud.

iTunes
This is Apple's flagship digital distribution centre that lets users browse, purchase and download a wide range of digital media, including music, books, movies and TV shows. Using an Apple ID, users log into the store and can save payment details to make

> "Browse, purchase and download a wide range of digital media via the iTunes Store"

iTunes
The ultimate digital music and entertainment mega-store

downloading media quick and easy. You can also convert your own CD library to MP3 format and create music playlists through the iTunes interface.

iTunes jargon:

App Store
Browse, purchase and download apps for your iOS device. You can view apps by category or see what's hot and featured in the main window.

Genius
This is a feature that recommends new music, films and shows based on what is currently in your library. Genius can also create playlists for you.

iTunes U
iTunes is also a great source of educational materials and you'll find a wide range of digital books, videos and podcasts by clicking on the 'iTunes U' link.

Redeem
Occasionally you may be gifted a product from iTunes in the form of a code. Click on the 'Redeem' link and input the code to download the product.

Launchpad
If you wish to launch an application that may not be in your Dock and without going to the trouble of finding it in the Applications folder, you can just click on the Launchpad icon in your Dock and view all of your applications arranged in a grid on your desktop.

Lion
Mac OS X Lion is the latest Mac operating system that follows Apple's tradition of naming its main operating platforms after big cats. Lion is the seventh incarnation of the operating system from Apple.

Mail
This is Apple's email app that comes as standard with any OS X. Easy to use, Mail supports Yahoo! Mail, AOL Mail, Gmail and Exchange and can be synced to your iCloud so you can catch up on your mail anywhere.

Mission Control
This feature, which is accessible from your Dock, allows you to instantly find what you want on a cluttered desktop, separating apps and folders for easy access.

Safari
This is Apple's premier web browsing application that comes as standard with all Mac operating systems. Bookmarks can be synced across devices via iCloud.

Spotlight
This is a selection-based search engine that creates a virtual index of every item and file on your Mac and allows you to find items with ease.

System Preferences
Accessible from the Dock or the Apple Menu, the System Preferences is where you can tweak all aspects of the apps and utilities that make your Mac tick and tailor them to your needs.

Time Machine
Time Machine lets you automatically back up your entire system so you never lose your important files and documents.

Wi-Fi
Wi-Fi (Wireless Fidelity) refers to a networking system that allows you to access the internet wirelessly. You will need a wireless router for this to work. A Wi-Fi signal is needed to sync your iCloud to mobile devices.

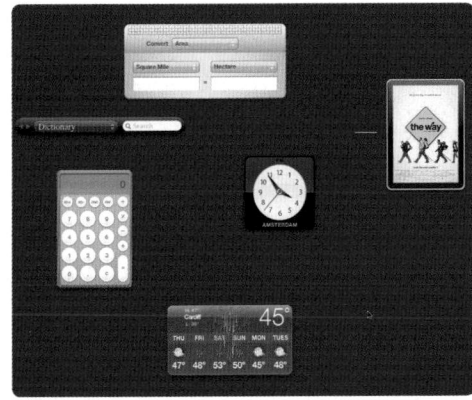

Dashboard
A host of handy utilities at your fingertips

On your free disc

All the resources you need to master everything your Mac has to offer

Attached on the opposite page is your free **Mac for Beginners** disc. Here you'll find all the files you need to complete the tutorials in this book, as well as a wealth of other top resources that will help you to improve your Mac projects. On offer are 11 top fonts, Pages templates, audio files, 10 Mail templates, podcasts, 4 video tutorials and much more! Everything is easy to access and downloads straight from the disc, meaning you can be experimenting with these fantastic tools in no time at all. So if you're raring to let your creative side run wild, pop the disc into your Mac and away you go!

Menu

Tutorial files
Follow the Bookazine

Free Pages template
Worth $29

4 video tutorials
From MacMost

10 Mail templates
From Jumsoft

Free audio files
Worth $49

11 free fonts
Create amazing text

Top 5 Mac apps
Our round-up

Welcome to the cover disc...

A wealth of goodies await you on this disc. Kicking things off is a free Pages template from Inkd, worth $29. An event planning postcard template, it features a dark palette with light background flourishes that give the template a classical feel. Also included is a free branding kit with business card, letterhead and envelope files. While on the subject of templates, we also have 10 Mail stationary templates from Jumsoft. Designed to give your emails a beautiful and unique appearance, they are a great way to catch someone's eye.

From MacMost comes four video tutorials that take a look at GarageBand and iMovie for iPad, compare the iPad 2 and iPhone 4 cameras and explain basic layout in Pages. We have five great Mac app trials for you to enjoy, that include an MS-DOS emulator, photo effects editor, home planner and more.

We also have free audio content from SoundSnap worth $49, all the tutorial files needed to follow the bookazine, podcasts and more.

Mail Templates
Impress your friends and family with these 10 free Mail templates from Jumsoft, each with its own colour theme and design variation.

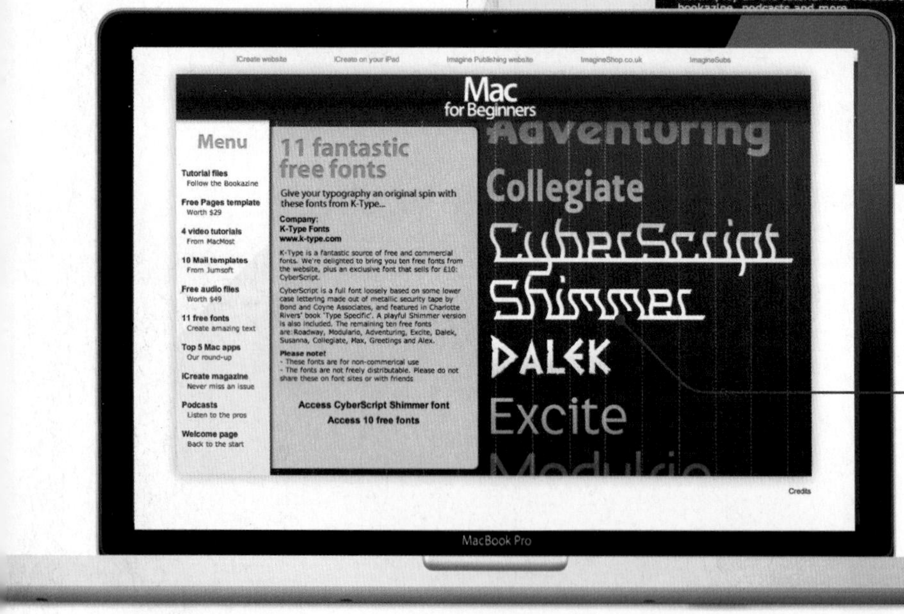

11 fantastic free fonts

Give your typography an original spin with these fonts from K-Type...

Company:
K-Type Fonts
www.k-type.com

K-Type is a fantastic source of free and commercial fonts. We're delighted to bring you ten free fonts from the website, plus an exclusive font that sells for £10: CyberScript.

CyberScript is a full font loosely based on some lower case lettering made out of metallic security tape by Bond and Coyne Associates, and featured in Charlotte Rivers' book 'Type Specific'. A playful Shimmer version is also included. The remaining ten free fonts are: Roadway, Modularia, Adventuring, Excite, Dalek, Susanna, Collegiate, Max, Greetings and Alex.

Please note!
- These fonts are for non-commercial use
- The fonts are not freely distributable. Please do not share these on font sites or with friends

Access CyberScript Shimmer font

Access 10 free fonts

11 free fonts

K-Type Fonts has kindly provided 11 excellent fonts for you to use, including the sci-fi-esque CyberScript. Be aware that these fonts are for non-commercial use

Navigate the disc

Upon start-up, this is the screen you'll be taken to. From here you can navigate your way around the disc, accessing all the free resources and assets for the book

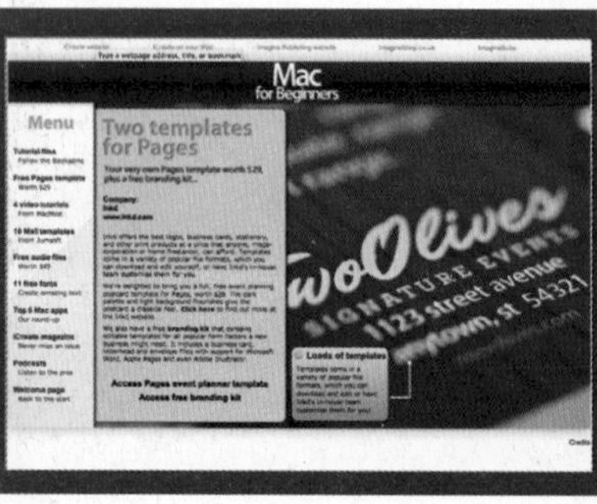

Pages templates

Pages is a great tool for Mac users, and the tutorials in the book will show you how to perform some basic tasks in the application. But we've also included a free Pages event planning postcard template from Inkd on the disc, as well as a free branding kit.

Mail templates

If you wish to spice up your emails, these great resources will do the job. Jumsoft has provided ten free Mail templates for you to apply to your emails, all of which are part of its latest Mail Stationary 3.1 set.